THOMAS HUTCHINSON.
Born in Boston, Sept. 9, 1711. Governor of Massachusetts 1771-4. Died in London
June 3, 1780.

THE
LOYALISTS OF MASSACHUSETTS

AND

THE OTHER SIDE OF THE AMERICAN REVOLUTION

BY

JAMES H. STARK

"*History makes men wise.*"—BACON.

BOSTON
JAMES H. STARK
17 MILK STREET
1910

Notice

In many older books, foxing (or discoloration) occurs and, in some instances, print lightens with wear and age. Reprinted books, such as this, often duplicate these flaws, notwithstanding efforts to reduce or eliminate them. The pages of this reprint have been digitally enhanced and, where possible, the flaws eliminated in order to provide clarity of content and a pleasant reading experience.

Copyright © 1907, James H. Stark

Originally published
Boston, Massachusetts
1910

Reprinted by:

Janaway Publishing, Inc.
732 Kelsey Ct.
Santa Maria, California 93454
(805) 925-1038
www.janawaygenealogy.com

2014

ISBN: 978-1-59641-326-9

To
The Memory of the Loyalists
of
The Massachusetts Bay

WHOSE FAITHFUL SERVICES AND MEMORIES ARE NOW FORGOTTEN
BY THE NATION THEY SO WELL SERVED, THIS
WORK IS DEDICATED BY THE
AUTHOR

TABLE OF CONTENTS.

INTRODUCTION 5

CHAPTER I
THE FIRST CHARTER 7

CHAPTER II
THE SECOND CHARTER 16

CHAPTER III
CAUSES THAT LED TO THE AMERICAN REVOLUTION 27

CHAPTER IV
BOSTON MOBS AND THE COMMENCEMENT OF THE REVOLUTION .. 40

CHAPTER V
THE LOYALISTS OF MASSACHUSETTS 54

CHAPTER VI
THE REVOLUTIONIST 68

CHAPTER VII
INDIANS IN THE REVOLUTION 88

CHAPTER VIII
THE EXPULSION OF THE LOYALISTS AND THE SETTLEMENT OF CANADA 93

CHAPTER IX
THE WAR OF 1812 AND THE ATTEMPTED CONQUEST OF CANADA .. 98

CHAPTER X
THE CIVIL WAR AND THE PART TAKEN BY GREAT BRITAIN IN SAME 107

CHAPTER XI
RECONCILIATION. THE DISMEMBERED EMPIRE REUNITED IN BONDS OF FRIENDSHIP. "BLOOD IS THICKER THAN WATER." 113

CONTENTS

PART II

BIOGRAPHICAL SKETCHES OF THE LOYALISTS OF MASS. 122
THE ADDRESS OF THE MERCHANTS AND OTHERS OF BOSTON TO GOVERNOR HUTCHINSON 123
ADDRESS OF THE BARRISTERS AND ATTORNEYS OF MASSACHUSETTS TO GOVERNOR HUTCHINSON 125
ADDRESS OF THE INHABITANTS OF MARBLEHEAD TO GOVERNOR HUTCHINSON 127
ADDRESS TO GOVERNOR HUTCHINSON FROM HIS FELLOW TOWNSMEN IN THE TOWN OF MILTON 128
ADDRESS PRESENTED TO GOVERNOR GAGE ON HIS ARRIVAL AT SALEM 131
ADDRESS TO GOVERNOR GAGE ON HIS DEPARTURE 132
LIST OF INHABITANTS OF BOSTON WHO REMOVED TO HALIFAX WITH THE ARMY MARCH, 1776 133
MANDAMUS COUNSELLORS 136
THE BANISHMENT ACT OF MASSACHUSETTS 137
THE WORCESTER RESOLUTION RELATING TO THE ABSENTEES AND REFUGEES 141
THE CONFISCATION ACT 141
    CONSPIRACY ACT 141
    ABSENTEES ACT 143

BIOGRAPHIES

THOMAS HUTCHINSON 145
LIST OF GOV. HUTCHINSON'S CONFISCATED ESTATES IN SUFFOLK COUNTY 174
THOMAS HUTCHINSON, SON OF THE GOVERNOR 175
ELISHA HUTCHINSON 177
FOSTER HUTCHINSON 177
ELIAKIM HUTCHINSON 178
LIST OF ELIAKIM HUTCHINSON'S CONFISCATED ESTATES IN SUFFOLK COUNTY 180
ANDREW OLIVER—LIEUT. GOVERNOR 181
THOMAS OLIVER 183
PETER OLIVER—CHIEF JUSTICE 188

CONTENTS

SIR FRANCIS BERNARD 191
SIR WILLIAM PEPPERRELL 205
JOHN SINGLETON COPLEY AND HIS SON LORD LYNDHURST 216
KING HOOPER OF MARBLEHEAD 221
WILLIAM BOWES 224
CONFISCATED ESTATES OF WILLIAM BOWES IN SUFFOLK COUNTY 225
GENERAL TIMOTHY RUGGLES 225
THE FANEUIL FAMILY OF BOSTON 229
THE COFFIN FAMILY OF BOSTON.   ADMIRAL SIR ISAAC COFFIN
    SIR THOMAS ASTON COFFIN   ADMIRAL FROMAN H. COFFIN
    GENERAL JOHN COFFIN 233
CONFISCATED ESTATES OF JOHN COFFIN IN SUFFOLK COUNTY .. 246
JUDGE SAMUEL CURWEN 246
JAMES MURRAY 254
SIR BENJAMIN THOMPSON—COUNT RUMFORD— 261
COL. RICHARD SALTONSTALL 272
REV. MATHER BYLES 275
THE HALLOWELL FAMILY OF BOSTON 281
CONFISCATED ESTATES OF BENJAMIN HALLOWELL IN SUFFOLK
    COUNTY 284
THE VASSALLS 285
CONFISCATED ESTATES OF JOHN VASSALL IN SUFFOLK COUNTY 290
GENERAL ISAAC ROYALL 290
GENERAL WILLIAM BRATTLE 294
CONFISCATED ESTATE OF WILLIAM BRATTLE IN BOSTON 297
JOSEPH THOMPSON 297
COLONEL JOHN ERVING 298
CONFISCATED ESTATES BELONGING TO COL. JOHN ERVING 293
MAJOR GENERAL SIR DAVID OCTHERLONY 299
JUDGE AUCHMUTY'S FAMILY 301
CONFISCATED ESTATES OF ROBERT AUCHMUTY 305
COLONEL ADINO PADDOCK 305
CONFISCATED ESTATES OF ADINO PADDOCK IN SUFFOLK COUNTY 308

CONTENTS

THEOPHILUS LILLIE 308
CONFISCATED ESTATES IN SUFFOLK COUNTY BELONGING TO THEOPHILUS LILLIE. 313
DR. SYLVESTER GARDINER 313
CONFISCATED ESTATES IN SUFFOLK COUNTY BELONGING TO SYLVESTER GARDINER 317
RICHARD KING 317
CHARLES PAXTON 318
JOSEPH HARRISON 319
CAPTAIN MARTIN GAY 321
CONFISCATED ESTATES IN SUFFOLK COUNTY BELONGING TO MARTIN GAY 325
DANIEL LEONARD... 325
JUDGE GEORGE LEONARD 332
COLONEL GEORGE LEONARD 333
HARRISON GRAY—RECEIVER GENERAL OF MASSACHUSETTS 334
CONFISCATED ESTATES IN SUFFOLK COUNTY BELONGING TO HARRISON GRAY 337
REV. WILLIAM WALTER, RECTOR OF TRINITY CHURCH 338
CONFISCATED ESTATES IN SUFFOLK COUNTY BELONGING TO REV. WILLIAM WALTER 342
THOMAS AMORY 343
REV. HENRY CANER 346
CONFISCATED ESTATES IN SUFFOLK COUNTY BELONGING TO REV. HENRY CANER 349
FREDERICK WILLIAM GEYER 350
CONFISCATED ESTATES IN SUFFOLK COUNTY BELONGING TO FREDERICK WILLIAM GEYER 351
THE APTHORP FAMILY OF BOSTON 351
CONFISCATED ESTATES IN SUFFOLK COUNTY BELONGING TO CHARLES WARD APTHORP 354
THE GOLDTHWAITE FAMILY OF BOSTON 355
CONFISCATED ESTATES IN SUFFOLK COUNTY BELONGING TO JOSEPH GOLDTHWAIT 361
JOHN HOWE 361
SAMUEL QUINCY, SOLICITOR GENERAL 364

CONTENTS

COLONEL JOHN MURRAY	376
JUDGE JAMES PUTNAM, ATTORNEY GENERAL OF MASSACHUSETTS BAY	378
JUDGE TIMOTHY PAINE	382
DR. WILLIAM PAINE	385
JOHN CHANDLER	388
JOHN GORE	392
JOHN JEFFRIES	394
THOMAS BRINLEY	395
CONFISCATED ESTATES IN SUFFOLK COUNTY BELONGING TO THOMAS BRINLEY	397
REV. JOHN WISWELL	398
HENRY BARNES	399
THOMAS FLUCKER, SECRETARY OF MASSACHUSETTS BAY	402
MARGARET DRAPER	404
CONFISCATED ESTATES IN SUFFOLK COUNTY BELONGING TO MARGARET DRAPER	405
RICHARD CLARKE	405
PETER JOHONNOT	409
CONFISCATED ESTATES IN SUFFOLK COUNTY BELONGING TO PETER JOHONNOT	411
JOHN JOY	411
RICHARD LECHMERE	413
CONFISCATED ESTATES IN SUFFOLK COUNTY BELONGING TO RICHARD LECHMERE	414
EZEKIEL LEWIS	414
BENJAMIN CLARK	415
LADY AGNES FRANKLAND	417
COLONEL DAVID PHIPS	418
THE DUNBAR FAMILY OF HINGHAM	421
EBENEZER RICHARDSON	422
COMMODORE JOSHUA LORING	423
CONFISCATED ESTATES IN SUFFOLK COUNTY BELONGING TO JOSHUA LORING	426
ROBERT WINTHROP	426

CONTENTS

NATHANIEL HATCH 429
CONFISCATED ESTATES IN SUFFOLK COUNTY BELONGING TO
    NATHANIEL HATCH 430
CHRISTOPHER HATCH 430
WARD CHIPMAN 431
GOVERNOR EDWARD WINSLOW 433
CONFISCATED ESTATES IN SUFFOLK COUNTY BELONGING TO
    ISAAC WINSLOW 439
SIR ROGER HALE SHEAFFE, BARONET 439
JONATHAN SAYWARD 443
DEBLOIS FAMILY 445
CONFISCATED ESTATES IN SUFFOLK COUNTY BELONGING TO
    GILBERT DEBLOIS 446
LYDE FAMILY 447
CONFISCATED ESTATES IN SUFFOLK COUNTY BELONGING TO
    EDWARD LYDE 447
JAMES BOUTINEAU 448
CONFISCATED ESTATES IN SUFFOLK COUNTY BELONGING TO
    JAMES BOUTINEAU 449
COL. WILLIAM BROWNE 449
ARCHIBALD CUNNINGHAM 451
CAPTAIN JOHN MALCOMB 451
THE RUSSELL FAMILY OF CHARLESTOWN 452
EZEKIEL RUSSELL 453
JONATHAN SEWALL 454
CONFISCATED ESTATES IN SUFFOLK COUNTY BELONGING TO
    SAMUEL SEWALL 457
THOMAS ROBIE 457
BENJAMIN MARSTON 459
HON. BENJAMIN LYNDE, CHIEF JUSTICE OF MASSACHUSETTS 462
PAGAN FAMILY 464
THE WYER FAMILY OF CHARLESTOWN 465
JEREMIAH POTE 467
EBENEZER CUTLER 468

CONTENTS

APPENDIX

THE TRUE STORY CONCERNING THE KILLING OF THE TWO SOLDIERS AT CONCORD BRIDGE, APRIL 19, 1775. THE FIRST BRITISH SOLDIER KILLED IN THE REVOLUTIONARY WAR 471
THE ENGAGEMENT AT THE NORTH BRIDGE IN CONCORD WHERE THE TWO SOLDIERS WERE KILLED 476
PAUL REVERE, THE SCOUT OF THE REVOLUTION 477
WILLIAM FRANKLIN, SON OF BENJAMIN FRANKLIN 481
THE ROYAL COAT OF ARMS 482
JUDGE MELLEN CHAMBERLAIN'S OPINION OF COLONEL THOMAS GOLDTHWAITE 482
NOTE ON PELHAM'S MAP OF BOSTON 483
NOTE ON GOV. JOHN WINTHROP 483
LIST OF LOYALISTS WHOSE NAMES OR BIOGRAPHIES ARE NOT FOUND IN THIS WORK 484
PELHAM'S MAP OF BOSTON IN POCKET IN THE BACK COVER.

ACKNOWLEDGMENT.

The author wishes to acknowledge the great assistance he has received from the New England Historic Genealogical Society, of which he has been a member for twenty-eight years,—whose library consisting of biographies and genealogies is the most complete in America. Other authorities consulted, have been the "Royalist" records in the original manuscript preserved in the archives of the State of Massachusetts, the Record Commissioners' Reports of the City of Boston, the Proceedings of the Massachusetts Historical Society, and the numerous town histories, and ancient records published in recent years, to the most important of these I have acknowledged my obligation in the reference given, and also to the Boston Athenæum for the use of their paintings and engravings, in making copies of same.

The author also wishes to acknowledge the assistance rendered him by his daughter, Mildred Manton Stark, in preparing many of the biographies, also the assistance rendered him by Mr. Thomas F. O'Malley, who prepared the very copious index to this work, which will, I think, be appreciated by all historical students who may have occasion to use same.

James H. Stark

ILLUSTRATIONS.

Thomas Hutchinson's Portrait .... Opposite the title page.
James H. Stark, Portrait, ... Opposite page 7.
Landing of the Commissioners at Boston, 1664, ..." " 13.
Randolph threatened ...." " 15.
Proclaiming King William and Queen Mary, ..." " 17.
Killing and scalping Father Rasle at Norridgewock, ..." " 32.
Reading the Stamp Act in King street, opposite the State House .." " 37.
Andrew Oliver, Stamp Collector attacked by the Mob, ..." " 41.
Bostonians paying the Exciseman or Tarring and Feathering, .." " 49.
Colonel Mifflin's Interview with the Caughnawaga Indians, ..." " 89.
Cartoon illustrating Franklin's diabolical Scalp story, ..." " 91
Burning of Newark, Canada, by United States Troops, ..." " 103.
Burning of Jay in Effigy, ..." " 105.
Map, Boundary line between Maine and New Brunswick, ..." " 115.
Governor Hutchinson's House Destroyed by the Mob .... Page 155.
Benjamin Franklin Before the Privy Council, ... Opposite Page 165.
Views from Governor Hutchinson's Field, ... Page 168.
Governor Hutchinson's House on Milton Hill, ..." 170.
Inland View from Governor Hutchinson's House, ..." 171.
Andrew Oliver, portrait, ... Opposite page 181.
Andrew Oliver Mansion, Washington street, Dorchester, ..." " 183.

ILLUSTRATIONS.

Thomas Oliver and John Vassall Mansion, Dorchester, ..." " 185.
Revolutionists Marching to Cambridge, ..." " 187.
Sir Francis Bernard, Portrait, ..." " 191.
Province House, ..." " 195.
Pepperell House, ..." " 210.
Reception of the American Loyalists in England, ...Page 214.
Arrest of William Franklin by order of Congress, ...Opposite page 215.
John Singleton Copley, Portrait, ..." " 218.
Lord Lyndhurst, Lord High Chancellor of England, Portrait, .." " 221.
King Hooper Mansion, Danvers, ..." " 223.
Admiral Sir Isaac Coffin, Portrait,................................" " 239.
Curwin House, Salem, ...Page 247.
Samuel Curwin, Portrait, ...Opposite page 253.
Country Residence of James Smith, Brush Hill, Milton, ...Page 256.
Birthplace of Benjamin Thompson, North Woburn, ..." 261.
Sir Benjamin Thompson, Portrait, ...Opposite page 267.
Rev. Mather Byles, D. D., Portrait, ..." " 277.
The Old Vassall House, Cambridge, ..." " 285.
Colonel John Vassall's Mansion, Cambridge, ..." " 289.
General Isaac Royall's Mansion, Medford, ..." " 293.
Major General Sir David Ochterlony, Portrait, ..." " 299.
British Troops preventing the destruction of New York, ..." " 303.
Landing a Bishop, Cartoon, ..." " 341.
Rev. Henry Caner, Portrait, ..." " 349.
Leonard Vassall and Frederick W. Geyer Mansion, ..." " 351.
Bishop's Palace, Residence of Rev. East Apthorp, ..." " 353.
Samuel Quincy, Portrait, ..." " 369.
Dr. John Jeffries, Portrait, ..." " 395.
Clark-Frankland House, ..." " 417.

ILLUSTRATIONS.

Sir Roger Hale Sheaffe, Baronet, Portrait, ..." " 439.

The Engagement at the North Bridge in Concord, ..." " 471.

Monument to Commemorate the Skirmish at Concord Bridge, .." " 475.

Pursuit and Capture of Paul Revere, ..." " 479.

Pelham Map of Boston, ...In the envelop of the back cover.

INTRODUCTION.

At the dedication of the monument erected on Dorchester Heights to commemorate the evacuation of Boston by the British, the oration was delivered by that Nestor of the United States Senate, Senator Hoar.

In describing the government of the colonies at the outbreak of the Revolution, he made the following statement: "The government of England was, in the main, a gentle government, much as our fathers complained of it. Her yoke was easy and her burden was light; our fathers were a hundred times better off in 1775 than were the men of Kent, the vanguard of liberty in England. There was more happiness in Middlesex on the Concord, than there was in Middlesex on the Thames."* A few years later Hon. Edward B. Callender, a Republican candidate for mayor of Boston, in his campaign speech said: "I know something about how this city started. It was not made by the rich men or the so-called high-toned men of Boston—they were with the other party, with the king; they were Loyalists. Boston was founded by the ordinary man—by Paul Revere, the coppersmith; Sam Adams, the poor collector of the town of Boston, who did not hand over to the town even the sums he collected as taxes; by John Hancock, the smuggler of rum; by John Adams, the attorney, who naively remarked in his book that after the battle of Lexington they never heard anything about the suits against John Hancock. Those were settled." †

These words of our venerable and learned senator and our State Senator Edward B. Callender, seemed strangely unfamiliar to us who had derived our history of the Revolution from the school text-books. These had taught us that the Revolution was due solely to the oppression and tyranny of the British, and that Washington, Franklin, Adams, Hancock, Otis, and the host of other Revolutionary patriots, had in a

* Speech of Senator Hoar at South Boston, March 18, 1901.
† Speech of Hon. Edward B. Callender, at Dorchester, Nov. 10, 1905.

supreme degree all the virtues ever exhibited by men in their respective spheres, and that the Tories or Loyalists, such as Hutchinson, the Olivers, Saltonstalls, Winslows, Quincys and others, were to be detested and their memory execrated for their abominable and unpatriotic actions.

This led me to inquire and to examine whether there might not be two sides to the controversy which led to the Revolutionary War. I soon found that for more than a century our most gifted writers had almost uniformly suppressed or misrepresented all matter bearing upon one side of the question, and that it would seem to be settled by precedent that this nation could not be trusted with all portions of its own history. But it seemed to me that history should know no concealment. The people have a right to the whole truth, and to the full benefit of unbiased historical teachings, and if, in an honest attempt to discharge a duty to my fellow citizens, I relate on unquestionable authority facts that politic men have intentionally concealed, let no man say that I wantonly expose the errors of the fathers.

In these days we are recognizing more fully than ever the dignity of history, we are realizing that patriotism is not the sole and ultimate object of its study, but the search for truth, and abiding by the truth when found, for "the truth shall make you free" is an axiom that applies here as always.

Much of the ill will towards England which until recently existed in great sections of the American people, and which the mischief-making politician could confidently appeal to, sprung from a false view of what the American Revolution was, and the history of England was, in connection with it. The feeling of jealousy and anger, which was born in the throes of the struggle for independence, we indiscriminately perpetuated by false and superficial school text-books. The influence of false history and of crude one-sided history is enormous. It is a natural and logical step that when our children pass from our schoolroom into active life, feelings so born should die hard and at times become a dangerous factor in the national life, and it is not too much to say that the persistent ill will towards England as compared with the universal kindliness of English feeling towards us, is to be explained by the very different spirit in which the history of the American Revolution is taught in the schools of one country and in those of the other.

The Loyalists of Massachusetts

AND THE OTHER SIDE OF THE AMERICAN REVOLUTION

CHAPTER I.

THE FIRST CHARTER.

A nation's own experience should be its best political guide, but it is not certain that as a people we have improved by all the teachings of our own history, for the reason that our "patriot" writers and orators mostly bound their vision in retrospect by the revolutionary era. And yet, all beyond that is not dark, barren, and profitless to explore. It should be known that the most important truths on which our free forms of government now rest are not primarily the discoveries of the revolutionary sages.

Writing of the Revolution, Mr. John Adams, the successor of Washington, declared that it was his opinion that the Revolution "began as early as the first plantation of the country," and that "independence of church and state was the fundamental principle of the first colonization, has been its principle for two hundred years, and now I hope is past dispute. Who was the author, inventor, discoverer of independence? The only true answer must be, the first emigrants." Before this time he had declared that "The claim of the men of 1776 to the honor of first conceiving the idea of American independence or of first inventing the project of it, is ridiculous. I hereby disclaim all pretension to it, because it was much more ancient than my nativity."

It was the inestimable fortune of our ancestors to have been taught the difficulties of government in two distinct schools, under the Colonial and Provincial charters, known as the first and second charters. The Charter government as moulded and modelled by our ancestors, was as perfect as is our own constitution of today. It was as tender of common right, as antagonistic to special privilege to classes or interests, and as sensitive, too, to popular impulses, good or evil. And it is thus in all self-governing communities, that their weal or woe, being supposedly in their own keeping, the freest forms of delegated government written on parchment are in themselves no protection, but will be such instruments of blessing or of destruction as may best gratify the controlling influences or interests for the time being.

In tracing the origin and development of the sentiment and the desires, the fears and the prejudices which culminated in the American Revolution, in the separation of thirteen colonies from Great Britain, it is necessary to notice the early settlement and progress of those New England colonies in which the seeds of that Revolution were first sown and nurtured to maturity. The Colonies of New England were the result of two distinct emigrations of English Puritans, two classes of Puritans, two distinct governments for more than sixty years—one class of these emigrants, now known as the "Pilgrim Fathers," having first fled from England to Holland, thence emigrated to New England in 1620 in "the Mayflower," and named their place of settlement "New Plymouth." Here they elected seven governors in succession, and existed under a self-constituted government for seventy years. The second class was called "Puritan Fathers." The first installment of their immigrants arrived in 1629, under Endicott, the ancestor of Mr. Joseph Chamberlain's wife. They were known as the "Massachusetts Bay Company," and their final capital was Boston, which afterwards became the capital of the Province and of the State.

The characteristics of the separate and independent governments of these two classes of Puritans were widely different. The one was tolerant, non-persecuting, and loyal to the King, during the whole period of its seventy years' existence; the other was an intolerant persecutor of all religionists who did not adopt its worship, and disloyal, from the beginning, to the government from which it held its Charter, and sedulously sowed and cultivated the seeds of disaffection and hostility to the Royal government until they grew and ripened into the harvest of the American Revolution.

English Puritanism, transferred from England to the head of Massachusetts Bay in 1629, presents the same characteristics which it developed in England. In Massachusetts it had no competitor, it developed its principles and spirit without restraint; it was absolute in power from 1629 to 1689. During these sixty years it assumed independence of the government to which it owed its corporate existence; it made it a penal crime for any immigrant to appeal to England against a local decision of courts or of government; it permitted no oath of allegiance to the King, nor the administration of the laws in his name; it allowed no elective franchise to any Episcopalian, Presbyterian, Baptist, Quaker or Papist. Every non-member of the Congregational church was compelled to pay taxes and bear all other Puritan burdens, but was allowed no representation by franchise, nor had he eligibility for any public office.

When the Puritans of the Massachusetts Bay Company emigrated from England, they professed to be members of the Church of England, but Endicott, who had imbibed views of church government and of forms of worship, determined not to perpetuate here the worship of the Established Church, to which he had professed to belong when he left England, but to establish a new church with a new form of worship. He seemed to have brought over some thirty of the immigrants to his new scheme, but a majority either stood aloof from, or were opposed to his extraordinary proceeding. Among the most noted adherents of the old Church of the Reformation were two brothers, John and Samuel Brown, who refused to be parties to this new and locally devised church revolution, and resolved for themselves, their families, and such as thought with them, to continue to worship God according to the custom of their fathers.

It is the fashion of many American historians, as well as their echoes in England, to apply epithets of contumely or scorn to these men. Both the Browns were men of wealth, one a lawyer, the other a private gentleman, and both of them were of a social position in England much superior to that of Endicott. They were among the original patentees and first founders of the colony; they were church reformers, but neither of them a church revolutionist. The brothers were brought before the Governor, who informed them that New England was no place for such as they, and therefore he sent them both back to England, on the return of the ships the same year.

Endicott resolved to admit of no opposition. They who could not be terrified into silence were not commanded to withdraw, but were seized and banished as criminals.*

A year later John Winthrop was appointed to supersede Endicott as Governor. On his departure with a fleet of eleven ships from England an address to their "Fathers and Brethren of the Church of England" was published by Winthrop from his ship, the Arabella, disclaiming the acts of some among them hostile to the Church of England, declaring their obligations and attachment to it. He said: "We desire you would be pleased to take notice of the principles and body of our Company as those who esteem it an honor to call the Church of England, from whence we rise, our dear Mother, and cannot part from our native countrie, where she especially resideth, without much sadness of heart and many tears in our eves." It might be confidently expected that Mr. Winthrop, after this address of loyalty and affection to his Father and Brethren of the Church of England, would, on his arrival at Massachusetts Bay, and assuming its government, have rectified the wrongs of Endicott and his party, and have secured at least freedom of worship to the children of his "dear Mother." But he did nothing of the kind; he seems to have fallen in with the very proceedings of Endicott which had been disclaimed by him in his address.

Thus was the first seed sown, which germinated for one hundred and thirty years, and then ripened in the American Revolution. It was the opening wedge which shivered the transatlantic branches from the parent stock. It was the consciousness of having abused the Royal confidence, and broken faith with their Sovereign, of having acted contrary

* Mass. His. Soc. Vol. lx-3-5.

to the laws and statutes of England, that led the Government of Massachusetts Bay to resist and evade all inquiries into their proceedings; to prevent all evidence from being transmitted to England, and to punish as criminals all who should appeal to England against any of their proceedings; to claim, in short, independence and immunity from all responsibility to the Crown for anything they did or might do. This spirit of tyranny and intolerance, of proscription and persecution, caused all the disputes with the parent Government, and all the bloodshed on account of religion in Massachusetts, which its Government inflicted in subsequent years, in contradistinction to the Governments of Plymouth, Rhode Island, Connecticut and even Maryland.

The church government established by the Puritans at Boston was not a government of free citizens elected by a free citizen suffrage, or even of property qualification, but was the "reign of the church, the members of which constituted but about one-sixth of the population, five-sixths being mere helots bound to do the work and pay the taxes imposed upon them by the reigning church but denied all eligibility to any office in the Commonwealth." It was indeed such a "connection between church and state" as had never existed in any Protestant country; it continued for sixty years, until suppressed by a second Royal Charter, as will appear in the next chapter.

The Puritans were far from being the fathers of American Liberty. They neither understood nor practiced the first principles of civil and religious liberty nor the rights of British subjects as then understood and practiced in the land they had left "for conscience sake."

The first Charter obtained of Charles I. is still in existence, and can be seen in the Secretary's Office at the State House, Boston. A duplicate copy of this Charter was sent over in 1629 to Governor Endicott, at Salem, and is now in the Salem Athenæum.

If the conditions of the Charter had been observed the colonists would have been independent indeed, and would have enjoyed extraordinary privileges for those times. They would have had the freest government in the world. They were allowed to elect their own governor and members of the General Court, and the government of the Colony was but little different from that of the State today, so far as the rights conferred by the charter were concerned. The people were subjects of the Crown in name, but in reality were masters of their own public affairs. The number of the early emigrants to New England who renounced allegiance to the mother church was exceedingly small, for the obvious reason that it was at the same time a renunciation of their allegiance to the Crown. A company of restless spirits had been got rid of, and whether they conformed to all the laws of church and state or not, they were three thousand miles away and could not be easily brought to punishment even if they deserved it, or be made to mend the laws if they broke them. The restriction of subjecting those who wished to emigrate to the oaths of allegiance and supremacy did not last long.

THE FIRST CHARTER

Those who chose "disorderly to leave the Kingdom" did so, and thus what they gained in that kind of liberty is a loss to their descendants who happen to be antiquaries and genealogists.

Under the charter they were allowed to make laws or ordinances for the government of the plantation, which should not be repugnant to the laws of England; all subjects of King Charles were to be allowed to come here; and these emigrants and their posterity were declared "to be natural-born subjects, and entitled to the immunities of Englishmen." The time of the principal emigration was auspicious. The rise of the civil war in England gave its rulers all the work they could do at home. The accession of Oliver Cromwell to the Protectorate was regarded very favorably by the colonists, who belonged to the same political party, and they took advantage of this state of affairs to oppress all others who had opinions different from their own. The Quakers, both men and women, were persecuted, and treated with great severity; many were hung, a number of them were whipped at the cart's tail through the town, and then driven out into the wilderness; others had their ears cut off, and other cruelties were perpetrated of a character too horrible to be here related. It was in vain that these poor Quakers demanded wherein they had broken any laws of England. They were answered with additional stripes for their presumption, and not without good reason did they exclaim against "such monstrous illegality," and that such "great injustice was never heard of before." Magna Charta, they said, was trodden down and the guaranties of the Colonial Charter were utterly disregarded.

The following is a striking example of the very many atrocities committed by the authorities at that time: "Nicholas Upshall, an old man, full of years, seeing their cruelty to the harmless Quakers and that they had condemned some of them to die, bothe he and Elder Wiswell, or otherwise Deacon Wiswell, members of the church in Boston, bore their testimony in publick against their brethren's horrid cruelty to said Quakers. And Upshall declared, *'That he did look at it as a sad forerunner of some heavy judgment to follow upon the country.'*.. Which they took so ill at his hands that they fined him twenty pounds and three pound more at their courts, for not coming to this meeting and would not abate him one grote, but imprisoned him and then banished him on pain of death, which was done in a time of such extreme bitter weather for frost, and snow, and cold, that had not the *Heathen Indians* in the wilderness woods taken compassion on his misery, for the winter season, he in all likelihood had perished, though he had then in Boston a good estate, in houses and land, goods and money, as also wife and children, but not suffered to come unto him, nor he to them."*

After the death of Oliver Cromwell, Charles II. was proclaimed in London the lawful King of England, and the news of it in due time

* "Persecutors Maul'd With Their Own Weapons," p. 41. See also Court Records, 1662.

reached Boston. It was a sad day to many, and they received the intelligence with sorrow and concern, for they saw that a day of retribution would come. But there was no alternative, and the people of Boston made up their minds to submit to a power they could not control. They, however, kept a sort of sullen silence for a time, but fearing this might be construed into contempt, or of opposition to the King, they formally proclaimed him, in August, 1661, more than a year after news of the Restoration had come. Meanwhile the Quakers in England had obtained the King's ear, and their representations against the government at Boston caused the King to issue a letter to the governor, requiring him to desist from any further proceedings against them, and calling upon the government here to answer the complaints made by the Quakers. A ship was chartered, and Samuel Shattock, who had been banished, was appointed to carry the letter, and had the satisfaction of delivering it to the governor with his own hand. After perusing it, Mr. Endicott replied, "We shall obey his Majesty's command," and then issued orders for the discharge of all Quakers then in prison. The requisition of the king for some one to appear to answer the complaints against the government of Boston, caused much agitation in the General Court; and when it was decided to send over agents, it was not an easy matter to procure suitable persons, so sensible was everybody that the complaints to be answered had too much foundation to be easily excused, or by any subterfuge explained away. It is worthy of note that the two persons finally decided upon (Mr. Bradstreet and Mr. Norton) were men who had been the most forward in the persecutions of the Quakers. And had it not been for the influence which Lord Saye and Seale of the king's Council, and Col. Wm. Crowne, had with Charles II., the colony would have felt his early and heavy displeasure. Col. Crowne was in Boston when Whalley and Goffe, the regicides, arrived here, and he could have made statements regarding their reception, and the persecution of the Quakers, which might have caused the king to take an entirely different course from the mild and conciliatory one which, fortunately for Boston, was taken. Having "graciously" received the letter from the hands of the agents, and, although he confirmed the Patent and Charter, objects of great and earnest solicitude in their letter to him, yet "he required that all their laws should be reviewed, and that such as were contrary or derogatory to the king's authority should be annulled; that the oath of allegiance should be administered; that administration of justice should be in the king's name; that liberty should be given to all who desired it, to use the Book of Common Prayer; in short, establishing religious freedom in Boston." This was not all—the elective franchise was extended "to all freeholders of competent estates," if they sustained good moral characters.

The return of the agents to New England, bearing such mandates from the king, was the cause of confusion and dismay to the whole country. Instead of being thankful for such lenity, many were full of resent-

LANDING OF THE COMMISSIONERS AT BOSTON, 1664.
The Royal Commissioners were appointed to hold Court and correct whatever errors and abuses they might discover.

ment and indignation, and most unjustly assailed the agents for failing to accomplish an impossibility.

Meanwhile four ships had sailed from Portsmouth, with about four hundred and fifty soldiers, with orders to proceed against the Dutch in the New Netherlands (New York), and then to land the commissioners at Boston and enforce the king's authority. The Dutch capitulated, and the expedition thus far was completely successful. The commissioners landed in Boston on Feb. 15th, 1664, and held a Court to correct whatever errors and abuses they might discover. The commission was composed of the following gentlemen: Col. Richard Nichols, who commanded the expedition; Sir Robert Carr, Col. Geo. Cartwright and Mr. Samuel Maverick. Maverick had for several years made his home on Noddle Island (now known as East Boston), but, like his friends, Blackstone of Beacon Hill and other of the earliest settlers, had been so harshly and ungenerously treated by the Puritan colonists of Boston that he was compelled to remove from his island domain. An early adventurous visitor to these shores mentions him in his diary as "the only hospitable man in all the country." These gentlemen held a commission from the king constituting them commissioners for visiting the colonies of New England, to hear and determine all matters of complaint, and to settle the peace and security of the country, any three or two of them being a quorum.

The magistrates of Boston having assembled, the commissioners made known their mission, and added that so far was the king from wishing to abridge their liberties, he was ready to enlarge them, but wished them to show, by proper representation of their loyalty, reasons to remove all causes of jealousy from their royal master. But it was of no avail; the word loyalty had been too long expunged from their vocabulary to find a place in it again. At every footstep the commissioners must have seen that whatever they effected, and whatever impressions they made, would prove but little better than footprints in the sand. The government thought best to comply with their requirements, so far, at least, as appearances were concerned. They therefore agreed that their allegiance to the king should be published "by sound of trumpet;" that Mr. Oliver Purchis should proclaim the same on horseback, and that Mr Thomas Bligh, Treasurer, and Mr. Richard Wait, should accompany him; that the reading in every place should end with the words, "God save the King!" Another requirement of the commissioners was that the government should stop coining money; that Episcopalians should not be fined for non-attendance at the religious meetings of the community, as they had hitherto been; that they should let the Quakers alone, and permit them to go about their own affairs. These were only a part of the requirements, but they were the principal ones. Notwithstanding a pretended acquiescence on the part of the government to the requests of the commissioners, it was evident from the first that little could be effected by them from the evasive manner in which all their orders and recommendations were accepted. At length the commissioners found it necessary to put the question to the Governor and Council direct, "Whether they acknowledged his Majesty's Commission?" The Court sent them a message, desiring to be excused from giving a direct answer, inasmuch as their charter was their plea. Being still pressed for a direct answer, they declared that "it was enough for them to give their sense of the powers granted them by charter, and that it was beyond their line to determine the power, intent, or purpose of his Majesty's commission." The authorities then issued a proclamation calling upon the people, in his Majesty's name (!), not to consent unto, or give approbation to the proceedings of the King's Commission, nor to aid or to abet them. This proclamation was published through the town by sound of trumpet, and, oddly enough, added thereto *"God save the King."* The commissioners then sent a threatening protest, saying they thought the king and his council knew what was granted to them in their charter; but that since they would misconstrue everything, they would lose no more of their labor upon them; at the same time assuring them that their denial of the king's authority, as vested in his commission, would be represented to his Majesty only in their own words. The conduct of Col. Nichols, at Boston, is spoken of in terms of high commendation; but Maverick, Carr and Cartwright are represented as totally unfitted for their business. It is, however, difficult to see how any commissioners, upon such an errand, could have given greater satisfaction; for a moment's consideration is sufficient to convince any one that the difficulty was not so much in the commissioners, as in their undertaking.

After the return of the commissioners to England the government continued their persecutions of the Quakers, Baptists, Episcopalians, and all others who held opinions differing from their own. The laws of England regulating trade were entirely disregarded; the reason alleged therefor being, "that the acts of navigation were an invasion of the rights and privileges of the subjects of his Majesty's colony, they not being represented in Parliament."

Again the king wrote to the authorities of Boston, requiring them not to molest the people, in their worship, who were of the Protestant faith, and directing that liberty of conscience should be extended to all. This letter was dated July 24th, 1679. It had some effect on the rulers; but they had become so accustomed to what they called interference from England, and at the same time so successful in evading it, that to stop now seemed, to the majority of the people, as well as the rulers, not only cowardly, but an unworthy relinquishment of privileges which they had always enjoyed, and which they were at all times ready to assert, as guaranteed to them in their charter. However, there was a point beyond which even Bostonians could not go, and which after-experience proved.

Edward Randolph brought the king's letter to Boston, and was required to make a report concerning the state of affairs in the colony, and to see that the laws of England were properly executed; but he did

RANDOLPH THREATENED.

This Royal Commissioner reported that he was in danger of his life, and that the authorities resolved to prosecute him as a subverter of their government.

not fare well in his mission. He wrote home that every one was saying they were not subject to the laws of England, and that those laws were of no force in Massachusetts until confirmed by the Legislature of the colony.

Every day aggravated his disposition more strongly against the people, who used their utmost endeavors to irritate his temper and frustrate his designs. Any one supporting him was accounted an enemy of the country.

His servants were beaten while watching for the landing of contraband goods. Going on board a vessel to seize it, he was threatened to be knocked on the head, and the offending ship was towed away by Boston boats. Randolph returned to England, reporting that he was in danger of his life, and that the authorities were resolved to prosecute him as a subserver of their government. If they could, they would execute him; imprisonment was the least he expected. Well might the historian exclaim, as one actually did, "To what a state of degradation was a king of England reduced!" his commissioners, one after another, being thwarted, insulted and obliged to return home in disgrace, and his authority openly defied. What was the country to expect when this state of affairs should be laid before the king? A fleet of men-of-war to bring it to its duty? Perhaps some expected this; but there came again, instead, the evil genius of the colony, Edward Randolph, bringing from the king the dreaded *quo warranto*. This was Randolph's hour of triumph; he said "he would now make the whole faction tremble," and he gloried in their confusion and the success which had attended his efforts to humble the people of Boston. To give him consequence a frigate brought him, and as she lay before the town the object of her employment could not be mistaken. An attempt was made, however, to prevent judgment being rendered on the return of the writ of *quo warranto*. An attorney was sent to England, with a very humble address, to appease the king, and to answer for the country, but all to no purpose. Judgment was rendered, and thus ended the first charter of Massachusetts, Oct. 23rd, 1684.

CHAPTER II.

THE SECOND CHARTER.

Charles II. died Feb. 6th, 1685, and was succeeded by his brother, James II. News of this was brought to Boston by private letter, but no official notification was made to the governor. In a letter to him, however, he was told that he was not written to as governor, for as much as now he had no government, the charter being vacated. These events threw the people of Boston into great uncertainty and trouble as to what they were in future to expect from England. Orders were received to proclaim the new king, which was done "with sorrowful and affected pomp," at the town house. The ceremony was performed in the presence of eight military companies of the town, and "three volleys of cannon" were discharged. Sir Edmund Andros, the new Royal Governor, arrived in Boston Dec. 20th, 1686, and, as was to be expected, he was not regarded favorably by the people, especially as his first act after landing was a demand for the keys of the Old South Church "that they may say prayers there." Such a demand from the new governor could not be tolerated by the now superseded governing authority of Boston, and defy it they would. The Puritan oligarchy stoutly objected to being deprived of the right to withhold from others than their own sect the privileges of religious liberty. To enjoy religious liberty in full measure they had migrated from the home of their fathers, but in New England had become more intolerant than the church which they had abandoned, and became as arbitrary as the Spanish inquisition. Under direction of the king, Andros had come to proclaim the equality of Christian religion in the new colonies. Too evidently this was not what was wanted here.

At last came the news of the landing of the Prince of Orange in England and the abdication of James the Second. The people of Boston rose against Andros and his government and seized him and fifty of his associates and confined them in the "Castle" until February, 1690, when they were sent to England for trial; but having committed no offence, they were discharged. Andros was received so favorably at home that under the new administration he was appointed governor of Virginia and Maryland. He took over with him the charter of William and Mary college, and later laid the foundation stone of that great institution of learning.

Andros has never received justice from Massachusetts historians. Before his long public career ended he had been governor of every Royal

PROCLAIMING KING WILLIAM AND QUEEN MARY, 1689.
This is said to have been the most joyful news ever before received in Boston.

Province in North America. His services were held in such high esteem that he was honored with office by four successive monarchs.

It is gratifying to notice that at last his character and services are beginning to be better appreciated in the provinces over which he ruled, and we may hope that in time the Andros of partisan history will give place, even in the popular narratives of colonial affairs, to the Andros who really existed, stern, proud and uncompromising it is true, but honest, upright and just; a loyal servant of the crown and a friend to the best interests of the people.

Not only were the governor and all of his adherents arrested and thrown into jail, but Captain George, of the Rose frigate, being found on shore, was seized by a party of ship carpenters and handed over to the guard.

So strong was the feeling against the prisoners that it was found necessary to guard them against the infuriated people, lest they should be torn into pieces by the mob. The insurrection was completely successful, and the result was that the resumption of the charter was once more affirmed. A general court was formed after the old model, and the venerable Bradstreet was made governor. Nothing now seemed wanting to the popular satisfaction but favorable news from England, and that came in a day or two. On the 26th of May, 1689, a ship arrived from the old country with an order to the Massachusetts authorities to proclaim King William and Queen Mary. This was done on the 29th, and grave, Puritanical Boston went wild with joy, and all thanked God that a Protestant sovereign once more ruled in England. This has been said to have been the most joyful news ever before received in Boston.

May 14, 1692, Sir William Phipps, a native of Massachusetts, arrived in Boston from England, bringing with him the new Charter of the province, and a commission constituting him governor of the same. Unfortunately he countenanced and upheld the people in their delusion respecting witchcraft, and confirmed the condemnation and execution of the victims. The delusion spread like flames among dry leaves in autumn, and in a short time the jails in Boston were filled with the accused. During the prevalence of this moral disease, nineteen persons in the colony were hanged, and one pressed to death. At last the delusion came to an end, and the leaders afterwards regretted the part they had taken in it.

The new Charter of Massachusetts gave the Province a governor appointed by the Crown. While preserving its assembly and its town organization, it tended to encourage and develop, even in that fierce democracy, those elements of a conservative party which had been called into existence some years before by the disloyalty and tyranny of the ecclesiastical oligarchy.

Thus, side by side with a group of men who were constantly regretting their lost autonomy, and looking with suspicion and prejudice at every action of the royal authorities, there arose another group of men who constantly dwelt upon the advantages they derived from their connection with the mother country. The Church of England also had at last waked up to a sense of the spiritual needs of its children beyond the seas. Many of the best of the laity forsook their separatist principles and returned to the historic church of the old home. This influence tended inevitably to maintain and strengthen the feeling of national unity in those of the colonists who came under the ministration of the church. In all the Royal Provinces there was an official class gradually growing up, that was naturally imperial rather than local in its sympathy. The war with the French, in which colonists fought side by side with "regulars" in a contest of national significance, tended upon the whole to intensify the sense of imperial unity.

"The people of Massachusetts Bay were never in a more easy and happy situation than at the conclusion of the war with France in 1749. By generous reimbursement of the whole charge of £183,000 incurred by the expedition against Cape Breton, the English government set the Province free from a heavy debt by which it must otherwise have remained involved, and enabled by it to exchange a depreciating paper medium, which had long been the sole instrument of trade, for a stable medium of gold and silver. Soon the advantage of this relief from the heavy burden of debt was apparent in all branches of their commerce, and excited the envy of other colonies, in each of which paper was the principal currency."*

The early part of the eighteenth century was filled with wars: France, England and Spain were beginning to overrun the interior of North America. Spain claimed a zone to the south, and France a vast territory to the north and west of the English colonies. Each of the three countries sought aid from the savage to carry on its enterprises and depredations. While the English colonies were beset on the north by the French, on the south by the Spaniards, on the west by native Indians along the Alleghany Mountains, and were compelled to depend on the "wooden walls of England" for the protection of their coasts, they were then remarkably loyal to the Crown of England. Their representative assemblies passed obsequious resolutions expressing loyalty and gratitude to the King, and the people; and erected his statue in a public place. This feeling of loyalty remained in the minds of a large majority of the people down to the battle of Lexington.

In May, 1756, the English government, goaded by the constantly continued efforts of the French to ignore her treaty obligations in Acadia, and her ever-harrassing, irritating "pin-pricks" on the frontiers of the English colonies, declared war against France. Long before this official declaration the two countries had been, on this continent, in a state of active but covert belligerency. Preparations for an inevitable conflict were being made by both sides. French intrigue and French treachery were met with English determination to defend the rights of the mother

* Hutchinson, History Mass. Bay, Vol. III., page 1.

country and of her children here. Money was pledged to the colonies to aid in equipping militia for active service, and the local governments and the inhabitants of every province became as enthusiastic as the home government in the prosecution of war.

On the northern and western borders of New England and of New York, along the thin fringe of advanced English settlements bordering Pennsylvania and Virginia, Indians had long been encouarged or employed in savage raids, and in Nova Scotia, which, by the treaty of Utrecht had been ceded to England, systematic opposition to English occupation was constantly kept up.

Intriguing agents of the French government, soldiers, priests of the "Holy Catholic" church—all were active in a determined effort to check and finally crush out the menacing influence and prosperity of the growing English colonies.

The ambushing and slaughter of Braddock's force on the Monongahela, the removal of Acadians from Annapolis Valley, the defeat of Dieskau at Crown Point, the siege and occupation of Fort Beausejour, all occurred before the formal declaration of war. Clouds were gathering. Men of fighting age of the English colonies volunteered in thousands; British regiments, seasoned in war, were brought from the old country to the new, and with them and after them came ships innumerable. A fight for life of the English colonies was at hand. The brood of the mistress of the seas must not be driven into the ocean. France must be compelled to give pledges for the performance of her treaty engagements or find herself without a foothold in the country.

With the hour came the man. Under the direction of the greatest war minister England had ever seen, or has since seen, William Pitt, the "Great Commoner," war on France was begun in earnest.

At first a few successes were achieved by the French commanders. Fort William Henry, with its small garrison, surrendered to Montcalm, and Abercrombie's expedition to Fort Ticonderoga was a disastrous failure. But the tide of battle soon turned.

The beginning of the end came in 1758. Louisbourg, the great fortress which France had made "The Gibraltar of the West," became a prize to the army and navy of Britain. New England soldiers formed a part of the investing force on land, and their record in the second capture of Louisbourg was something to be proud of. Fort Frontenac, on Lake Ontario, was taken, together with armed vessels and a great collection of stores and implements of war. Fort Duquesne, a strongly fortified post of the French, whose site is now covered by the great manufacturing city of Pittsburgh, surrendered to a British force. For many years after it was known as Fort Pitt, so called in honor of the great minister under whose compelling influence the war against France had become so mighty a success.

In 1759, General Wolfe, who had been the leading spirit in the siege of Louisbourg, was placed in command of an expedition for the capture of Quebec. Next after Louisbourg, Quebec was by nature and military art the strongest place in North America. The tragic story of the capture of Quebec has been so often told that it is not necessary for us to repeat it here.

Of the long, impatient watch by Wolfe, from the English fleet, for opportunity to disembark his small army, drifting with the tides of the St. Lawrence, passing and repassing the formidable citadel, the stealthy midnight landing at the base of a mighty cliff, the hard climb of armed men up the wooded height, and the assembly, in early morning mist, on the Plains of Abraham, are not for us to write of here. In the glowing pages of Parkman all this is so thrillingly described that we need not say more of the most dramatic and most pathetic story in all American history, than that Quebec fell, and with it, in short time, fell the whole power of France in North America.

In the following year (September 8, 1760), Montreal, the last stronghold of the French in Canada, capitulated to Sir Jeffrey Amherst, who had ascended the St. Lawrence with a force of about 10,000 men, comprising British regiments of the line artillery, rangers and provincial regiments from New York, New Jersey and Connecticut. The provincial contingent numbered above four thousand.

With the fall of Montreal the seven years' fight for supremacy was ended.

Such a defeat to proud France was a bitter experience, and definite settlement of the terms of peace, which Great Britain was able to dictate, was not made until, on the 10th of February, 1763, the treaty of Paris was signed.

By this treaty to Great Britain was ceded all Canada, Nova Scotia, Cape Breton and the West India Islands of Dominica, St. Vincent, Tobago and Grenada. Minorca was restored to Great Britain, and to her also was given the French possession of Senegal in Western Africa. In India, where the French had obtained considerable influence, France was bound by this treaty to raise no fortifications and to keep no military force in Bengal. To remove the annoyance which Florida had long been to the contiguous English colonies, that province of Spain was transferred to the English in exchange for Havana, which had been only recently wrested from the occupation of Spain by the brilliant victory of Pocock and Albamarle.

And so 1763 saw the British flag peacefully waving from the Gulf of Mexico to the northern shores of Hudson's Bay. The coast of the Atlantic was protected by the British navy, and the colonists had no longer foreign enemies to fear.

For this relief the colonists gave warm thanks to the king and to parliament. Massachusetts voted a costly monument in Westminster Abbey in memory of Lord Howe, who had fallen in the campaign against Canada. The assembly of the same colony, in a joyous address to the governor, declared that without the assistance of the parent state the colonies must have fallen a prey to the power of France, and that without money sent from England the burden of the war would have been too great to bear. In an address to the king they made the same acknowledgment, and pledged themselves to demonstrate their gratitude by every possible testimony of duty and loyalty. James Otis expressed the common sentiment of the hour when, upon being chosen moderator of the first town meeting held in Boston after the peace, he declared: "We in America have certainly abundant reason to rejoice. Not only are the heathen driven out, but the Canadians, much more formidable enemies, are conquered and become fellow subjects. The British dominion and power can now be said literally to extend from sea to sea and from the Great River to the ends of the earth." And after praising the wise administration of His Majesty, and lauding the British constitution to the skies, he went on to say: "Those jealousies which some weak and wicked minds endeavored to infuse with regard to these colonies, had their birth in the blackness of darkness, and it is a great pity that they had not remained there forever. The true interests of Great Britain and her plantation are mutual, and what God in his providence has united, let no man dare attempt to pull asunder."

In June, 1763, a confederation, including several Indian tribes, suddenly and unexpectedly swept over the whole western frontier of Pennsylvania and Virginia. They murdered almost all the English settlers who were scattered beyond the mountains, surprised every British fort between the Ohio and Lake Erie, and closely blockaded Forts Detroit and Pitt. In no previous war had the Indians shown such skill, tenacity, and concert, and had there not been British troops in the country the whole of Pennsylvania, Virginia, and Maryland would have been overrun.

The war lasted fourteen months, and most of the hard fighting was done by English troops, assisted by militia from some of the Southern colonies. General Amherst called upon the New England colonies to help their brethren, but his request was almost disregarded. Connecticut sent 250 men, but Massachusetts, being beyond the zone of immediate danger, would give no assistance. After a war of extreme horror, peace was signed September, 1764. In a large degree by the efforts of English soldiers Indian territory was rolled back, and one more great service was rendered by England to her colonies, and also the necessity was shown for a standing army.*

The "French and Indian War," as it was commonly called, waged with so much energy and success, doubled the national debt of England and made taxation oppressive in that country. The war had been waged mainly for the benefit of the colonists, and as it was necessary to maintain a standing army to protect the conquered territory, it was considered but reasonable that part of the expense should be borne by the Americans. This was especially so in view that the conquest of Canada had

* Trumbull's " His. of the U. S.," 445-467. Hildreth, Graham, Hutchinson.

been a prime object of statesmen and leading citizens of the colonies for many years.

It has been said on good authority that Franklin brought about the expedition against Canada that ended with Wolfe's victory on the Plains of Abraham. In all companies and on all occasions he had urged conquest of Canada as an object of the utmost importance. He said it would inflict a blow upon the French power in America from which it would never recover, and would have lasting influence in advancing the prosperity of the British colonies. Franklin was one of the shrewdest statesmen of the age. After egging England on to the capture of Canada from the French, and then removing the most dreaded enemy of the colonies, he won the confidence of the court and people of France, and obtained their aid to deprive England of the best part of a continent. He was genial, thrifty, and adroit, and his jocose wisdom was never more tersely expressed than when he advised the signers of the Declaration of Independence to "hang together or they would hang separately."

At the conclusion of the Peace of Paris in 1763, Great Britain had ceased to be an insular kingdom, and had become a world-wide empire, consisting of three grand divisions: the British Islands, India, and a large part of North America. In Ireland an army of ten or twelve thousand men were maintained by Irish resources, voted by an Irish Parliament and available for the general defence of the empire. In India a similar army was maintained by the despotic government of the East India Company. English statesmen believed that each of these great parts of the empire should contribute to the defence of the whole, and that unless they should do so voluntarily it was their opinion, in which the great lawyers of England agreed, that power to force contributions resided in the Imperial Parliament at Westminster, and should be exercised. It was thought that an army of ten thousand men was necessary to protect the territory won from France and to keep the several tribes of American Indians in subjection, especially as it was believed that the French would endeavor to recapture Canada at the first opportunity.

Americans, it should be remembered, paid no part of the interest on the national debt of England, amounting to one hundred and forty million pounds, one-half of which had been contracted in the French and Indian war. America paid nothing to support the navy that protected its coasts, although the American colonies were the most prosperous and lightly taxed portion of the British Empire. Grenville, Chancellor of the Exchequer, asked the Americans to contribute one hundred thousand pounds a year, about one-third of the expense of maintaining the proposed army, and about one-third of one percent of the sum we now pay each year for pensions. He promised distinctly that the army should never be required to serve except in America and the West India islands, but he could not persuade the colonists to agree among themselves on a practical plan for raising the money, and so it was proposed to resort to taxation by act of Parliament. At the time he made this proposal he assured the Americans that the proceeds of the tax should be expended solely in America, and that if they would raise the money among themselves in their own way he would be satisfied. He gave them a year to consider the proposition. At the end of the year they were as reluctant as ever to tax themselves for their own defence or submit to taxation by act of Parliament. Then the stamp act was passed—it was designed to raise one hundred thousand pounds a year, and then the trouble began that led to the dismemberment of the empire. Several acute observers had already predicted that the triumph of England over France would be soon followed by a revolt of the colonies. Kalm, the Swedish traveller, contended in 1748 that the presence of the French in Canada, by making the English colonists depend for their security on the support of the mother country, was the main cause of the submission of the colonies. A few years later Argenson, who had left some of the most striking political predictions upon record, foretold in his Memoirs that the English colonies in America would one day rise against the mother country, that they would form themselves into a republic and astonish the world by their prosperity. The French ministers consoled themselves for the Peace of Paris by the reflection that the loss of Canada was a sure prelude to the independence of the colonies, and Vergennes, the sagacious French ambassador at Constantinople, predicted to an English traveller, with striking accuracy, the events that would occur. " England," he said, "will soon repent having removed the only check that would keep her colonies in awe. They stand no longer in need of her protection; she will call upon them to contribute towards supporting the burden they have helped to bring on her, and they will answer by striking off all dependence."*

It is not to be supposed that Englishmen were wholly blind to this danger. One of the ablest advocates of the retention of Canada was Lord Bath, who published a pamphlet on the subject, which had a very wide influence and a large circulation.† There were, however, some politicians who maintained that it would be wiser to restore Canada and to retain Guadaloupe, St. Lucia, and Martinique. This view was supported with distinguished talent in an anonymous reply to Lord Bath.

This writer argued "that we had no original right to Canada, and that the acquisition of a vast, barren, and almost uninhabited country lying in an inhospitable climate, and with no commerce except that of furs and skins, was economically far less valuable to England than the acquisition of Guadaloupe, which was one of the most important of the sugar islands. The acquisition of these islands would give England the control of the West Indies, and it was urged that an island colony is more advantageous than a continental one, for it is necessarily more dependent upon the mother country. In the New England provinces there are already colleges and academies where the American youths can receive

* Bancroft's His. of the U. S., Vol. I., 525.
† " Letters to Two Great Men on the Prospect of Peace."

their education. America produces or can easily produce almost everything she wants. Her population and her wealth are rapidly increasing, and as the colonies recede more and more from the sea, the necessity of their connection with England will steadily diminish. They will have nothing to expect, they must live wholly by their own labor, and in process of time will know little, inquire little, and care little, about the mother country. If the people of our colonies find no check from Canada they will extend themselves almost without bounds into inland parts. What the consequences will be to have a numerous, hardy, independent people, possessed of a strong country, communicating little, or not at all, with England, I leave to your own reflections. By eagerly grasping at extensive territory we may run the risk, and that, perhaps, in no distant period, of losing what we now possess. The possession of Canada, far from being necessary to our safety, may in its consequences be even dangerous. A neighbor that keeps us in some awe is not always the worst of neighbors; there is a balance of power in America as well as in Europe."*

These views are said to have been countenanced by Lord Hardwicke, but the tide of opinion ran strongly in the opposite direction; the nations had learned to look with pride and sympathy upon that greater England which was growing up beyond the Atlantic, and there was a desire, which was not ungenerous or ignoble, to remove at any risk the one obstacle to its future happiness. These arguments were supported by Franklin, who in a remarkable pamphlet sketched the great undeveloped capabilities of the colonies, and ridiculed the "visionary fear" that they would ever combine against England. "This jealousy of each other," he said, "is so great that, however necessary a union of the colonies has long been for their common defence and security against their enemies, yet they have never been able to effect such a union among themselves. If they cannot agree to unite for defence against the French and Indians, can it reasonably be supposed there is any danger of their uniting against their own nation, which protects and encourages them, with which they have so many connections and ties of blood, interest, and affection, and which it is well known, they all love *much more than they love one another.*"†

Within a few years after Franklin made this statement he did more than any other man living to carry into effect the "visionary fear" which he had ridiculed.

The denial that independence was the object sought for was constant and general. To obtain concessions and to preserve connection with the empire was affirmed everywhere. John Adams, the successor of Washington to the presidency, years after the peace of 1783 went farther than this, for he said, "There was not a moment during the Revolution when I would not have given everything I possessed for a restoration

---

* Remarks on the Letter Addressed to Two Great Men. Pp. 30-31.
† Canada Pamphlet, Franklin's Works, IV., 41-42.

to the state of things before the contest began, provided we could have had a sufficient security for its continuance."

In the summer of 1774, Franklin assured Chatham that there was no desire among the colonists for independence. He said: "Having more than once travelled almost from one end of the continent to the other, and kept a variety of company, eating and conversing with them freely, I have never heard in any conversation from any person, drunk or sober, the least wish for a separation or a hint that such a thing would be advantageous to America."

Mr. Jay is quite as explicit: "During the course of my life," said he, "and until the second petition of Congress in 1775, I never did hear an American of any class or of any description express a wish for the independence of the colonies."

Mr. Jefferson affirmed: "What eastward of New York might have been the disposition towards England before the commencement of hostilities I know not, but before that I never heard a whisper of a disposition to separate from Great Britain, and after that its possibility was contemplated with affliction by all."

Washington in 1774 fully sustains their declarations, and in the "Fairfax County Resolves" it was complained that "malevolent falsehoods" were propagated by the ministry to prejudice the mind of the king, particularly that there is an intention in the American colonies to set up for independent state.

Mr. Madison says: "It has always been my impression that a re-establishment of the colonial relations to the mother country, as they were previous to the controversy, was the real object of every class of the people till they despaired of obtaining redress for their grievances."

This feeling among the revolutionists is corroborated by DuPortail, a secret agent of the French government. In a letter dated 1778 he says: "There is a hundred times more enthusiasm for the revolution in a coffee-house at Paris than in all the colonies united. This people, though at war with the English, hate the French more than they hate them; we prove this every day, and notwithstanding everything that France has done or can do for them, they will prefer a reconciliation with their ancient brethren. If they must needs be dependent, they had rather be so on England."

Again, as late as March, 1775, only a month before the outbreak of hostilities at Lexington, John Adams wrote: "That there are any that hunt after independence is the greatest slander on the Province."

This feeling must have arisen from gratitude for the protection afforded by the mother country, or at least satisfaction with the relations then existing. It is true, as has been shown in a previous chapter, that for some years before the English Revolution, and for some years after the accession of William and Mary, the relations of the colonies to England had been extremely tense, but in the long period of unbroken Whig rule which followed, most of the elements of discontent had subsided. The wise neglect of Walpole and Newcastle was eminently conducive to colonial interests. The substitution in several colonies of royal for proprietary government was very popular. There were slight differences in the colonial forms of government, but everywhere the colonists paid their governor and their other officials. In nearly every respect they governed themselves, under the shadow of British dominion, with a liberty not equalled in any other portion of the civilized globe; real constitutional liberty was flourishing in the English colonies when all European countries and their colonies were despotically governed. The circumstances and traditions of the colonists had made them extremely impatient of every kind of authority, but there is no reason for doubting that they were animated by a real attachment to England. Their commercial intercourse, under the restructions of the navigation laws, was mainly with her. Their institutions, their culture, their religion, their ideas were derived from English sources. They had a direct interest in the English war against France and Spain. They were proud of their English lineage, of English growth in greatness, and of English liberty. On this point there is a striking answer made by Franklin in his crafty examinations before the House of Commons in February, 1766. In reply to the question, "What was the temper of America towards Great Britain before the year 1763?" he said, "The best in the world. They submitted willingly to the government of the crown, and paid their courts obedience to the Acts of Parliament. Numerous as the people are in the several old provinces, they cost you nothing in forts, citadels, garrisons, or armies to keep them in subjection, they were governed by this country at the expense only of a little pen, ink, and paper; they were led by a thread. They had not only a respect, but an affection for Great Britain, for its laws, its customs, and manners, and even a fondness for its fashions that greatly increased the commerce. Natives of Britain were always treated with particular regard; to be an 'Old England' man was of itself a character of some respect and gave a kind of rank among us." In reply to the question, "What is their temper now?" he said, "Very much altered." It is interesting to inquire what happened during the three years intervening to change the temper of the colonists.

CHAPTER III.
CAUSES THAT LED TO THE AMERICAN REVOLUTION.

One of the principal causes that led to the American Revolution was the question of what was lawful under the constitution of the British empire, and what was expedient under the existing circumstances of the colonies. It was the contention of the American Whigs that the British parliament could not lawfully tax the colonies, because by so doing it would be violating an ancient maxim of the British constitution: "No taxation without representation."

On the contrary, many of the profoundest constitutional lawyers of America as well as of England, both rejected the foregoing contention, and at the same time admitted the soundness and the force of the venerable maxim upon which the contention was alleged to rest, but the most of them denied that the maxim was violated by the acts of parliament laying taxation upon the colonies. Here everything depends on the meaning to be attached to the word "representation"—and that meaning is to be ascertained by examining what was understood by the word in England at the time when this old maxim originated, and in subsequent ages during which it had been quoted and applied. During this whole period the idea was that representation in parliament was constituted not through any uniform distribution among individual persons, but rather through a distribution of such privileges among certain organized communities, as counties, cities, boroughs, and universities. Very few people in England then had votes for members of the house of commons—only one-tenth of the population of the entire realm. Such was the state of the electoral system that entire communities, such as the cities of Leeds, Halifax, Birmingham, Manchester, and Liverpool, communities which were as populous and as rich as entire provinces in America, and yet they had no vote whatever for members of parliament. The people of these several communities in England did not refuse to pay taxes levied by act of parliament, because of that reason. It is still a principle of parliamentary representation that from the moment a member is thus chosen to sit in parliament, he is the representative of the whole empire, and not of his particular constituency. He "is under no obligation, therefore, to follow instructions from the voters or the inhabitants of the district from which he is chosen. They have no legal means of enforcing instructions. They cannot demand his resignation. Moreover, members of the house of lords represent, in principle, the interest of the whole empire and of all classes, as truly as the Commons."* Therefore the historic meaning of

* John W. Burgess, "Political Science and Comparative Constitutional Law," 67-68, also 65-69.

the word "representation," as the word has always been used in English constitutional experience, seemed to justify the Loyalist contention that the several organized British communities in America, as an integral part of the British empire, were to all intents and purposes represented in the British parliament, which sat at the capital as the supreme council of the whole empire and exercised legislative authority coextensive with the boundaries of that empire. The Loyalists admitted that for all communities of British subjects, both in England and America, the existing representation was very imperfect; that it should be reformed and made larger and more uniform, and they were ready and anxious to join in all forms of constitutional agitation under the leadership of such men as Chatham, Camden, Burke, Barre, Fox and Pitt, to secure such reform, and not for a rejection of the authority of the general government, nullification, and disruption of the empire. Accordingly, when certain English commoners in America at last rose up and put forward the claim that merely because they had no votes for members of the house of commons, therefore that house did not represent them, and therefore they could not lawfully be taxed by parliament, this definition of the word "representation" up to that time had never been given to it in England or enjoyed by commoners in England. Nine-tenths of the people of England did not vote. Had not those British subjects in England as good a right as these British subjects in America to deny they were represented in parliament, and that they could not be lawfully taxed by parliament? It was the right and duty of the imperial legislature to determine in what proportion the different parts of the empire should contribute to the defence of the whole, and to see that no one part evaded its obligation and unjustly transferred its part to others. The right of taxation was established by a long series of legal authorities, and there was no real distinction between internal and external taxation. It now suited colonists to describe themselves as apostles of liberty and to denounce England as an oppressor. It was a simple truth that England governed her colonies more liberally than any other country in the world. They were the only existing colonies which enjoyed real political liberty. Their commerical system was more liberal than that of any other colony. They had attained under British rule to a degree of prosperity which was surpassed in no quarter of the globe. England had loaded herself with debt in order to remove one great danger to their future; she cheerfully bore the whole burden of their protection by sea. At the Peace of Paris she had made their interests the very first object of her policy, and she only asked them in return to bear a portion of the cost of their own defence. Less than eight millions of Englishmen were burdened with a national debt of 140,000,000 pounds. The united debt of about three millions of Americans was now less than 800,000 pounds. The annual sum the colonists were asked to contribute was less than 100,000, with an express condition that no part of that sum should be devoted to any other purpose than the defence and protection of the colonies, and the country which refused to bear this small tax was so rich that in the space of three years it had paid off 1,755,000 pounds of its debt. No demand could be more moderate and equitable than that of England. The true motive of the resistance was a desire to pay as little as possible and to throw as much as possible upon the mother country. Nor was the mode of resistance more honorable—the plunder of private houses, and custom-houses, and mob violence, connived at and unpunished. This was the attitude of the colonies within two years after the Peace of Paris, and these were the fruits of the new sense of security which British triumphs in Canada had given to the colonists.

This is a brief statement and a fair one of the principal arguments of the Loyalists. Certainly the position taken by them was a very strong one. A learned American writer upon law, one of the justices of the Supreme Court of the United States, in referring to the decision of Chief Justice Hutchinson sustaining the legality of the writs of assistance, gave this opinion: "A careful examination of the question compels the conclusion that there was at least reasonable ground for holding, as a matter of mere law, that the British parliament had power to bind the colonies."* This view has been sustained by the highest English authorities upon British constitutional law, from the time of Lord Mansfield to the present. "As a matter of abstract right," says Sir Vernon Harcourt, "the mother country has never parted with the claim of ultimate supreme authority for the imperial legislature. If it did so, it would dissolve the imperial tie, and convert the colonies into foreign and independent states." It is now apparent that those Americans who failed in their honest and sacrificial championship of measures that would have given us political reform and political safety, but without civil war, and without an angry disruption of the English-speaking race can justly be regarded as having been, either in doctrine or in purpose, or in act, an unpatriotic party, and yet even at the present time it is by no means easy for Americans, if they be descended from men who fought in behalf of the Revolution, to take a disinterested attitude, that is an historical one towards those Americans who thought and fought against the Revolution.

No candid historian, however, now contends that the government of England had done anything prior to the commencement of the Revolutionary War that justified a Declaration of Independence; for, as previously stated, the amount of taxes required by Parliament was moderate, the money was needed for a proper purpose, and it seemed there was no other way of obtaining it.

Another important factor in the causes of the American Revolution was the so-called "Quebec Act." This act John Adams asserted constituted a "frightful system," and James Bowdoin pronounced it to be "an act for encouraging and establishing Popery." The policy of this legislation may be doubted. Of its justice there can be no doubt. The establishment of the Catholic clergy in Canada and their resultant domi-

* Horace Gray, Quincy's Mass. Reports, 1761-62, Appendix I., page 540.

nation has entailed many disadvantages upon the governing powers of the dominion. But at the time the law was passed it was a simple act of justice. Had Parliament refused to do this it would have been guilty of that tyranny charged against it by the Revolutionists, and today the dominion would not be a part of the British Empire. To the student of American history it at first seems very strange and unaccountable why at the outbreak of the Revolution, the recently conquered French provinces were not the first to fly to arms, especially as their mother country, France, had espoused the cause of the Revolutionists. Instead of this the French Canadians remained loyal to their conqueror and resisted by force of arms all attempts to conquer Canada. The explanation of this curious state of affairs is the "Quebec Act."

By this act the French Canadians were to retain their property, their language, their religion, their laws, and to hold office. In fact, they were allowed greater liberty than they had when subject to France. All this was allowed them by the British Parliament, and this was resented by the English colonists, for they were not allowed to confiscate their lands and drive out the inhabitants as the New Englanders did when they conquered Nova Scotia, New Brunswick, and Prince Edward Island. They also claimed that by the laws of the realm Roman Catholics could not vote, much less hold office. At a meeting of the first Continental Congress, held October 21, 1774, an address to the people of Great Britain was adopted, setting forth the grievances of the colonies, the principal one of which was as follows:

"Nor can we suppress our astonishment that a British Parliament should ever consent to establish in that country a religion that has deluged your island in blood and dispersed impiety, bigotry, persecution, murder and rebellion through every part of the world, and we think the legislature of Great Britain is not authorized to establish a religion fraught with such sanguinary and infamous tenets."

This act also granted the Catholic clergy a full parliamentary title to their old ecclesiastical estates, and to tithes paid by members of their own religion, but no Protestant was obliged to pay tithes. It provided for a provincial governing council in which Catholics were eligible to sit, and it established the Catholic clergy securely in their livings. There were then in the Province of Quebec two hundred and fifty Catholics to one Protestant*. Surely it would have been a monstrous perversion of justice to have placed this vast majority under the domination of this petty minority, it would have degraded the Catholics into a servile caste and reproduced in America, in a greatly aggravated form, the social conditions which existed in Ireland, but those determined sticklers for freedom of conscience and "the right of self-government," those clamorers for the liberty of mankind, the disunion propagandists, were horrified at the bestowal of any "freedom" or "right" upon a people professing a

* In the debates on the Canadian bill in 1779, it was stated that there were but 365 Protestants and 150,000 Catholics within the Province of Quebec.

religion different from their own. "The friends of America" in England, Chatham, Fox, Burke, Barre and others, joined them in their denunciation of the act, the last named especially deprecating the "Popish" measure.

On February 15, 1776, it was resolved that a committee of three, "two of whom should be members of congress," be appointed to pursue such instructions as shall be given them by that body.* Benjamin Franklin, Samuel Chase and Chas. Carroll were chosen for this purpose, and John Carroll, a Jesuit, who afterwards became the first Roman Catholic Archbishop of the United States, accompanied them. The two Carrolls were chosen because they were Catholics, but they were not justified in joining an expedition that might kindle the flame of religious war on the Catholic frontier. The commissioners carried with them an Address to the Inhabitants of the Province of Quebec"† from Congress, which for cool audacity and impertinence can scarcely be paralleled. It commenced with "We are too well acquainted with the liberality of sentiment distinguishing your natures to imagine that difference of religion will prejudice you against a hearty amity with us," etc.

The address from the Continental Congress was translated into French and was very favorably received. They then begged the translator, as he had succeeded so well, to try his hand on that addressed to Great Britain. He had equal success in this, and read his performance to a numerous audience. But when he came to that part which treats of the new modelling of the province, draws a picture of the Catholic religion and Canadian manners, they could not restrain their resentment nor express it except in broken curses. "O the perfidious, double-faced Congress! Let us bless and obey our benevolent prince, whose humanity is consistent and extends to all religions. Let us abhor all who would seduce us from our loyalty by acts that would dishonor a Jesuit, and whose address, like their resolves, is destructive of their own objects."

While the commissioners were applying themselves with the civil authorities, Rev. Mr. Carroll was diligently employed with the clergy, explaining to them that the resistance of the united colonies was caused by the invasion of their charter by England. To this the clergy replied that since the acquisition of Canada by the British government its inhabitants had no aggression to complain of, that on the contrary the government had faithfully complied with all the stipulations of the treaty, and had in fact sanctioned and protected the laws and customs of Canada with a delicacy that demanded their respect and gratitude, and that on the score of religious liberty the British government had left them nothing to complain of.

And therefore that when the well-established principle that allegiance is due to protection, the clergy could not teach that even neutrality was consistent with the allegiance due to such ample protection as Great

---

* Washington's Writings, Vol. III., page 361.
† Debates, etc., page 603.

Britain had shown the Catholics of Canada. The judicious and liberal policy of the British government to the Catholics had succeeded in inspiring them with sentiments of loyalty which the conduct of the people and the public bodies of some of the united colonies had served to strengthen and confirm. Mr. Carroll was also informed that in the colonies whose liberality he was now avouching, the Catholic religion had not been tolerated hitherto. Priests were excluded under severe penalties and Catholic missionaries among the Indians rudely and cruelly treated.

John Adams, who was a member of the congress that sent the commissioners to Canada, in a letter to his wife, did not state the true reason for sending a Jesuit priest there, and also warned her against divulging the fact that a priest had been sent, for fear of offending his constituents*

He wrote as follows:—

"Mr. John Carroll of Maryland, a Roman Catholic priest and a Jesuit, is to go with the committee, the priests of Canada having refused baptism and absolution to our friends there. Your prudence will direct you to communicate the circumstances of the priest, the Jesuit, and the Romish religion, only to such persons as can judge of the measure upon large and generous principles, and will not indiscreetly divulge it."*

John Adams also wrote: "We have a few rascally Jacobites and Roman Catholics in this town (Braintree), but they do not dare to show themselves."†

To any statesman who looked into the question inquiringly and with clear vision, it must have appeared evident that, if the English colonies resolved to sever themselves from the British Empire, it would be impossible to prevent them. Their population was said to have doubled in twenty-five years. They were separated from the mother country by three thousand miles of water, their seaboard extended for more than one thousand miles, their territory was almost boundless in its extent and resources, and the greater part of it no white man had traversed or seen. To conquer such a country would be a task of greatest difficulty and stupendous cost. To hold it in opposition to the general wish of the people would be impossible. The colonists were chiefly small and independent freeholders, hardy backwoodsmen and hunters, well skilled in the use of arms and possessed of all the resources and energies which life in a new country seldom fails to develop. They had representative assemblies to levy taxes and organize resistance. They had militia, which in some colonies included all adult freemen between the ages of sixteen and fifty or sixty, and, in addition to Indian raids, they had the military experience of two great wars. The first capture of Louisburg, in 1745, had been mainly their work. In the latter stages of the war, which ended in 1763, there were more than twenty thousand colonial troops under arms, ten thousand of them from New England alone, and

* Letter of John Adams to his wife, Vol. I., page 86.
† Life and Works of John Adams, Vol. IX., page 335.

KILLING AND SCALPING OF FATHER RASLE AT NORRIDGEWOCK

By Massachusetts scalp hunters. £100 bounty was offered for the scalp of a male Indian, and £50 for that of women or children.

more than four hundred privateers had been fitted out in colonial harbors.*

There were assuredly no other colonies in the world so favorably situated as these were at the close of the Seven Years' War. They had but one grievance, the Navigation Act, and it is a gross and flagrant misrepresentation to describe the commercial policy of England as exceptionally tyrannical. As Adam Smith truly said, "Every European nation had more or less taken to itself the commerce of its colonies, and upon that account had prohibited the ships of foreign nations from trading with them, and had prohibited them from importing European goods from any foreign nation," and "though the policy of Great Britain with regard to the trade of her colonies has been dictated by the same mercantile spirit as that of other nations, it has, upon the whole, been less illiberal and oppressive than any of them."†

There is, no doubt, much to be said in palliation of the conduct of England. If Virginia was prohibited from sending her tobacco to any European country except England, Englishmen were prohibited from purchasing any tobacco except that which came from America or Bermuda. If many of the trades and manufactures in which the colonies were naturally most fitted to excel were restrained or crushed by law, English bounties encouraged the cultivation of indigo and the exportation to England of pitch, tar, hemp, flax and ship timber from America, and several articles of American produce obtained a virtual monopoly of the English market by their exemption from duties which were imposed on similar articles imported from foreign countries.

The revenue laws were habitually violated. Smuggling was very lucrative, and therefore very popular, and any attempt to interfere with it was greatly resented. The attention of the British government was urgently called to it during the war. At a time when Great Britain was straining every nerve to free the English colonies from the incubus of France, and when millions of pounds sterling were being remitted from England to pay colonists for fighting in their own cause, it was found that French fleets, French garrisons, and the French West India Islands were systematically supplied with large quantities of provisions by the New England colonies. Pitt, who still directed affairs, wrote with great indignation that this contraband trade must be stopped, but the whole community of the New England seaports appeared to favor or was partaking in it, and great difficulty was found in putting the law into execution.‡

From a legal point of view, the immense activity of New England was for the most part illicit. In serene ignorance the New England sailor penetrated all harbors, conveying in their holds, from the North, where

* Ramsey, History of the American Revolution, Vol. I, page 40; Hildreth, Vol. II., page 486; Grahame, Vol. IV., page 94.
† Wealth of Nations, Vol. IV., chapter 7; Tucker's Four Tracts, page 133.
‡ Hildreth Vol. II., page 498; McPherson's Annals of Commerce, Vol. III., page 330; Arnold's History of Rhode Island, Vol. II., pages 227-235.

they belonged, various sorts of interdicted merchandise, and bringing home cargoes equally interdicted from all ports they touched. The merchants, who since 1749, through Hutchinson's excellent statesmanship, had been free from the results of a bad currency, greatly throve. The shipyards teemed with fleets, each nook of the coast was the seat of mercantile ventures. It was then that in all the shore towns arose the fine colonial mansions of the traders along the main streets, that are even admired today for their size and comeliness. Within the houses bric-a-brac from every clime came to abound, and the merchants and their wives and children were clothed gaily in rich fabrics from remote regions. Glowing reports of the gaiety and luxury of the colonies reached the mother country.* The merchants and sailors were, to a man, law-breakers. It was this universal law-breaking, after the fall of Quebec, that the English ministry undertook to stop over its extended empire. This caused friction, which gave rise to fire, which increased until the ties with the mother land were quite consumed.

As early as 1762 there were loud complaints in Parliament of the administration of custom houses in the colonies. Grenville found on examination that the whole revenue derived by England from the custom houses in America amounted only to between one and two thousand pounds a year, and that for the purpose of collecting this revenue the English exchequer was paying annually between seven and eight thousand pounds. Nine-tenths, probably, of all the tea, wine, fruit, sugar and molasses consumed in the colonies, were smuggled. Grenville determined to terminate this state of affairs. Several new revenue officers were appointed with more rigid rules for the discharge of their duties. "Writs of assistance" were to be issued, authorizing custom house officers to search any house they pleased for smuggled goods. English ships of war were at the same time stationed off the American coast for the purpose of intercepting smugglers.

Adam Smith, writing in 1776, says:

"Parliament, in attempting to exercise its supposed right, whether well or ill-grounded, of taxing the colonies, *has never hitherto demanded of them anything which even approached to a just proportion to what was paid by their fellow subjects at home.* Great Britain has hitherto suffered her subjects and subordinate provinces to disburden themselves upon her of almost the whole expense."

The colonists had profited by the successful war incomparably more than any other British subjects. Until the destruction of the French power, a hand armed with a rifle or tomahawk and torch seemed constantly near the threshold of every New England home. The threatening hand was now paralyzed and the fringe of plantations by the coast could now extend itself to the illimitable West in safety. No foreign foe could now dictate a boundary line and bar the road beyond it. The colonists were asked only to bear a share in the burden of the empire by

---

* Gordon's History of the American War, Vol. I., page 157.

a contribution to the sum required for maintenance of the ten thousand soldiers and of the armed fleet which was unquestionably necessary for the protection of their long coast line and of their commerce.

James Otis started the Revolution in New England by what Mr. Lecky calls an "incendiary speech" against writs of assistance, and if half of what Hildreth asserts and Bancroft admits in regard to smuggling along the coast of New England is true, there is no reason to wonder that such writs were unpopular in Boston. James Otis, whose father had just been disappointed in his hopes of obtaining a seat upon the bench, was no doubt an eloquent man and all the more dangerous because he often thought he was right. That it is always prudent to distrust the eloquence of a criminal lawyer we have ample proof, in the advice he gave the people on the passage of the Stamp Act. "It is the duty," he said, "of all, humbly and silently to acquiesce in all the decisions of the supreme legislature. Nine hundred and ninety-nine in a thousand of the colonists will never once entertain a thought but of submission to our sovereign and to authority of Parliament, in all possible contingencies. They undoubtedly have the right to levy internal taxes on the colonies."

In private talk he was more vigorous than in his formal utterance. "Hallowell says that Otis told him Parliament had a right to tax the colonies and he was a d—— fool who denied it, and that this people would never be quiet till we had a council from home, till our charter was taken away and till we had regular troops quartered upon us."*

John Adams wrote in his diary, under date of January 16, 1770, concerning Otis, as follows: "In one word Otis will spoil the club. He talks so much and takes up so much of our time and fills it with trash, obsceneness, profaneness, nonsense and distraction that we have none left for rational amusements or inquiries. I fear, I tremble, I mourn for the man and for his country. Many others mourn over him with tears in their eyes."

Again John Adams says, after an attack upon him by Otis: "There is a complication of malice, envy and jealousy in the man, in the present disordered state of his mind, that is quite shocking."† On the 7th of May, 1771, Otis, who at this time had recovered his reason, was elected with John Hancocok to the assembly. They both left their party and went over to the side of the government. John Adams wrote, "Otis' change was indeed startling. John Chandler, Esq., of Petersham gave me an account of Otis' conversion to Toryism, etc." Hutchinson, writing to Governor Bernard, says. "Otis was carried off today in a postchaise, bound hand and foot. He has been as good as his word—set the Province in a flame and perished in the attempt."

In Virginia the revolutionary movement of the poor whites or

* John Adams' Diary, January 16, 1776.

† John Adams' Diary, October 27, 1772; John Adams' Works, Vol. II., page 26; Letters to Bernard December 3, 1771.

"crackers," led by Patrick Henry, was against the planter aristocracy, and Washington was a conspicuous member of the latter class. In tastes, manners, instincts and sympathies he might have been taken as an admirable specimen of the better class of English country gentlemen, and he had a great deal of the strong conservative feeling which is natural to that class. He was in the highest sense a gentleman and a man of honor, and he carried into public life the severest standard of private morals.

It was only slowly and very deliberately that Washington identified himself with the disunionist cause. No man had a deeper admiration for the British constitution, or a more sincere desire to preserve the connection, and to put an end to the disputes between the two countries. From the first promulgation of the Stamp Act, however, he adopted the conviction that a recognition of the sole right of the colonies to tax themselves was essential to their freedom, and as soon as it became evident that Parliament was resolved at all hazards to assert its authority by taxing the Americans, he no longer hesitated. Of all the great men in history he was the most invariably judicious, and there is scarcely a rash word or action of judgment related of him. America had found in Washington a leader who could be induced by no earthly motive to tell a falsehood or to break an engagement or to commit a dishonorable act.

In the despondency of long-continued failure, in the elation of sudden success, at times when his soldiers were deserting by hundreds, and when malignant plots were formed against his reputation; amid the constant quarrels, rivalries and jealousies of his subordinates; in the dark hour of national ingratitude and in the midst of the most universal and intoxicating flattery, he was always the same calm, wise, just and single-minded man, pursuing the course which he believed to be right, without fear, favor or fanaticism.

In civil as in military life he was pre-eminent among his contemporaries for the clearness and soundness of his judgment, for his perfect moderation and self-control, for the quiet dignity and the indomitable firmness with which he pursued every path which he had deliberately chosen.

As previously stated, the heart of the Old Dominion was fired by Patrick Henry, one of the most unreliable men living. Byron called him a forest-born Demosthenes, and Jefferson, wondering over his career, exclaimed: "Where he got that torrent of language is inconceivable. I have frequently closed my eyes while he spoke and, when he was done, asked myself what he had said without being able to recollect a word of it." He had been successively a storekeeper, a farmer and a shopkeeper, but had failed in all these pursuits and became a bankrupt at twenty-three. Then he studied law a few weeks and practiced a few years. The first success he made in this line was in an effort to persuade a jury to render one of the most unjust verdicts ever recorded in

READING THE STAMP ACT IN KING STREET: OPPOSITE THE STATE HOUSE.

court. Finally he embarked on the stormy sea of politics. One day he worked himself into a fine frenzy, and in a most dramatic manner demanded "Liberty or Death," although he had both freely at his disposal. He was a slaveholder nearly all his life. He bequeathed slaves and cattle in his will, and one of his eulogists brags that he would buy or sell a horse or a negro as well as anybody.

John Adams of Braintree, now Quincy, was a graduate of Harvard College, and a lawyer by profession. He ranks next to Washington as being the most prominent of the Revolutionary leaders. He was the son of a poor farmer and shoemaker. He married Abigail Smith, the daughter of the Congregational minister in the adjoining town of Weymouth. Much disapprobation of the match appears to have been manifested, for Mr. Adams, the son of a poor farmer, was thought scarcely good enough to be match with the minister's daughter, descended from many of the shining lights of the colony.*

John Adams was a cousin of Samuel Adams. He joined the disunionists, probably, because he saw that if the Revolution was successful there would be great opportunity for advancement under the new government. This proved to be the case, for he was the first minister to Great Britain, the successor of Washington as second president of the United States. His eldest son became the sixth president, and his grandson, Charles Francis Adams, ably represented his country as minister to Great Britain during the Civil War of 1861.

The Stamp Act received the royal assent on March 22, 1765, and it was to come into operation on the first day of November following. The "Virginia Resolutions," through which Patrick Henry first acquired a continental fame, voted by the House of Burgess in May following, denied very definitely the authority of Parliament to tax the colonies. At first men recoiled. Otis was reported to have publicly condemned them in King street, which was no doubt true, for, as we have seen, he fully admitted the supremacy of Parliament.

The principal objection made by the colonists to the Stamp Act was that it was an internal tax. They denied the right of Parliament to impose internal taxation, claiming that to be a function that could be exercised only by colonial assemblies. They admitted, however, that Parliament had a right to levy duties on exports and imports, and they had submitted to such taxation for many years without complaint.

In order to soften the opposition, and to consult to the utmost of his power the wishes of the colonists, Grenville informed the colonial agents that the distribution of the stamps should be confided not to Englishmen but to Americans. Franklin, then agent for Pennsylvania, accepted the act and, in his canny way, took steps to have a friend appointed stamp distributor for his province. This made him very unpopular and the mob threatened to destroy his house.

The Stamp Act, when its ultimate consequences are considered,

* "Letters of Mrs. Adams." Memoirs, XXIX.

must be deemed one of the most momentous legislative acts in the history of mankind.

A timely concession of a few seats in the upper and lower houses of the Imperial Parliament would have set at rest the whole dispute. Franklin had suggested it ten years before, anticipating even Otis, Grenville was quite ready to favor it, Adam Smith advocated it. Why did the scheme fail? Just at that time in Massachusetts a man was rising into provincial note, who was soon to develop a heat, truly fanatical, in favor of an idea quite inconsistent with Franklin's plan. He from the first claimed that representation of the colonies in Parliament was quite impracticable or, if accepted, would be of no benefit to the colonies, and that there was no fit state for them but independence. His voice at first was but a solitary cry in the midst of a tempest, but it prevailed mightily in the end.

This sole expounder of independence was Samuel Adams, the father of the Revolution. Already his influence was superseding that of Otis, in stealthy ways of which neither Otis nor those who made an idol of him were sensible, putting into the minds of men, in the place of the ideas for which Otis stood, radical conceptions which were to change in due time the whole future of the world. "Samuel Adams at this time was a man of forty-two years of age, but already gray and bent with a physical infirmity which kept his head and hands shaking like those of a paralytic. He was a man of broken fortunes, a ne'er-do-well in his private business, a failure as a tax collector, the only public office he had thus far undertaken to discharge."* He had an hereditary antipathy to the British government, for his father was one of the principal men connected with Land-Bank delusion, and was ruined by the restrictions which Parliament imposed on the circulation of paper money, causing the closing up of the bank by act of Parliament and leaving debts which seventeen years later were still unpaid.

It appears that Governor Hutchinson was a leading person in dissolving the bank, and from that time Adams was the bitter enemy of Hutchinson and the government. Hutchinson in describing him says, "Mr. S. Adams had been one of the directors of the land bank in 1741 which was dissolved by act of Parliament. After his decease his estate was put up for sale by public auction, under authority of an act of the General Assembly. The son first made himself conspicuous on this occasion. He attended the sale, threatened the sheriff to bring action against him and threatened all who should attempt to enter upon the estate under pretence of a purchase, and by intimidating both the sheriff and those persons who intended to purchase, he prevented the sale, kept the estate in his possession and the debts to the land bank remained unsatisfied. He was afterwards a collector of taxes for the town of Boston and made defalcation which caused an additional tax upon the inhabitants. He was for nearly twenty years a writer against government in the public

* Hosmer, Life of Hutchinson, page 82.

newspapers. Long practice caused him to arrive at great perfection and to acquire a talent of artfully and fallaciously insinuating into the minds of readers a prejudice against the characters of all he attacked beyond any other man I ever knew, and he made more converts to his cause by calumniating governors and other servants of the crown than by strength of reasoning. The benefit to the town from his defence of their liberties, he supposed an equivalent to his arrears as their collector, and prevailing principle of the party that the end justified the means probably quieted the remorse he must have felt from robbing men of their characters and injuring them more than if he had robbed them of their estates."*

In a letter written by Hutchinson about this time he thus characterizes his chief adversary:

"I doubt whether there is a greater incendiary in the King's dominion or a man of greater malignity of heart, who has less scruples any measure ever so criminal to accomplish his purposes; and I think I do him no injustice when I suppose he wishes the destruction of every friend to government in America."†

In a letter dated March 13, 1769, Adams petitioned the town, requesting that he be discharged from his indebtedness to the town for the amount that he was in arrears as tax collector. He states that the town treasurer, by order of the town, had put his bond in suit and recovered judgment for the sum due £2009.8.8. He stated that his debts and £1106.11 will fully complete the sum which he owes and requests "that the town would order him a final discharge upon the condition of his paying the aforesaid sum of £1106.11 into the province treasury." This letter of Adams to the town of Boston fully confirms the statement made by Hutchinson that he was a defaulter, for it appears from this letter that during the several years he was collector of taxes for the town, that he did not make a proper return for the taxes which he had collected, and it was only after suit and judgment had been obtained against his bondsmen that restitution was made, his sureties having to pay over $5000 in cash and the balance was made up of uncollected taxes."‡

Adams was poor, simple, ostentatiously austere; the blended influence of Calvinistic theology and republican principles had indurated his whole character. He hated monarchy and the Episcopal church, all privileged classes and all who were invested with dignity and rank, with a fierce hatred. He was the first to foresee and to desire an armed struggle, and he now maintained openly that any British troops which landed should be treated as enemies, attacked and if possible destroyed.

* Hutchinson's History, Vol. III., pages 294-295.
† M. A. History, Vol. XXV., page 437.
‡ This letter was purchased at the E. H. Leffingwell sale of January 6 1891, for $185, by the city of Boston, and can be seen at the city clerk's office. In connection with this see "Life of Samuel Adams," by his great-grandson, William V. Wells, Vol. I., pages 35-38. Here he emphatically denies that bonds or sureties were given by collectors. Evidently he had not consulted Boston Town Records, 1767, page 9, when it was voted that Samuel Adams' bond "shall be put in Suit," and when bonds and sureties were required of his successor, neither could he have known of the existence of this letter.

CHAPTER IV.

BOSTON MOBS AND THE COMMENCEMENT OF THE REVOLUTION.

After the adoption in Massachusetts of Patrick Henry's resolves, the people, brooding over the injuries which Adams made them believe they were receiving under the Stamp Act, became fiercer in temper. Open treason was talked, and many of the addresses to the Governor, composed by Adams, were models of grave and studied insolence. The rough population which abounded about the wharves and shipyards grew riotous, and, with the usual indiscrimnation of mobs, was not slow to lift its hands against even the best friends of the people. "Mob law is a crime, and those who engage in mobs are criminals." This is a fundamental axiom of orderly government that cannot be denied.

The first great riot was in anticipation of the arrival of the stamps. On the morning of August 14, 1765, there appeared, at what is now a corner of Washington and Essex streets, two effigies, hanging on an elm tree, representing Andrew Oliver, the stamp agent, and Lord Bute, the former prime minister. In the evening these images were carried as far as Kilby street, where there was a new unfinished government building, wrongly supposed to have been erected for use as a stamp office. This the mob completely demolished, and, taking portions of its wood-work with them, they proceeded to Fort Hill, where a bonfire was made in front of the house of Mr. Oliver, burning the effigy of Lord Bute there, and committing gross outrages on Oliver's premises, which were plundered and wrecked.

A few nights later riots recommenced with redoubled fury, the rioters turning their attention to the house of Lieutenant-Governor Hutchinson, who was also chief justice, and kinsman of Oliver. Hutchinson was not only the second person in rank in the colony, but was also a man who had personal claims of the highest kind upon his countrymen. He was an American, a member of one of the oldest colonial families, and, in a country where literary enterprise was very uncommon, he had devoted a great part of his life to investigating the history of his native province. His rare abilities, his stainless private character, and his great charm of manner, were universally recognized. He had at one time been one of the most popular men in the colony, and although Hutchinson was opposed to the Stamp Act, the determined impartiality with which, as Chief Justice, he upheld the law, soon made him obnoxious to the mob.

When the mob surrounded his house in Garden Court street, they called for him to appear on his balcony, to give an account of himself as

ANDREW OLIVER, STAMP COLLECTOR ATTACKED BY THE MOB.

His beautiful mansion on Oliver street, Fort Hill, was wrecked and he narrowly escaped with his life.

to the Stamp Act. He barred the doors and windows and remained within. One of his neighbors, alarmed, no doubt, as to the safety of his own property, told the mob that he had seen Hutchinson drive out just at nightfall, and that he had gone to spend the night at his country house at Milton. On hearing this the mob dispersed, having done no other damage than the breaking of windows.

The popular fury had now become so ungovernable and perilous that Governor Bernard took refuge in the Castle, leaving Hutchinson to bear the brunt of this vehement hostility. Shortly after the governor's retreat, on the 26th of August, occurred a riot as disgraceful as any on record on either side of the Atlantic. It commenced at dusk with a bonfire on King street. One of the fire-wards attempted to extinguish it, but he was driven from the ground by a heavy blow from one of the mob which had assembled. The fire was doubtless kindled as a signal for the assembling of a ruffianly body of disguised men, aremd with clubs and staves. They first went to the house of the register of the admiralty court, broke into his office in the lower story, and fed the fire hard by with the public archives in his keeping, and with all his own private papers. Next they went to the house of the comptroller of customs in Hanover street, tore down his fence, broke his windows, demolished his furniture, stole his money, scattered his papers, and availed themselves of the wine in his cellar as a potent stimulant to greater excesses.

They then proceeded to Hutchinson's house, the finest and most costly in Boston. He had barely time to escape with his family, otherwise murder would no doubt have put a climax to the criminal orgies of the night. The rioters hewed down the doors with broad axes, destroyed or stole everything that lecting, and papers which, if preserved to his countrymen, would be worth many times their weight in gold; and still further maddened by the contents of the cellar, the incendiary crowd broke up the roof and commenced tearing down the wood-work of the mansion.

There exists competent evidence that the municipal authorities had timely notice of the pendency of this riot. They held a town meeting next day, denounced the rioters by unanimous vote. in which many who had been foremost in the affair gave assent to their own condemnation, but nothing was done towards punishing the perpetrators of the outrages, and it was evident that the prevailing feeling was with the rioters. Those who were arrested and committed for trial were released by a formidable body of sympathizers, undoubtedly fellow criminals. who went by night to the jail, forced the jailer to deliver up the keys, and released the culprits.

The Custom House was selected for assault and pillage on the following night. The collector somehow gained information of this purpose. He had in his custody about four thousand pounds in specie, which could not be removed so secretly as to elude the espionage of eyes intent on rapine and plunder. The governor, at the urgent demand of the collector, called out the cadets, who constituted his special guard. The mob assembled. The commanding officers addressed them, first with persuasion, then with threats, but in vain. Driven to extremity he ordered his company to prime and load, and then begged the rioters to retire. They remained immovable until the order was given to "aim," when a hurried retreat of the tumultuous rabble ensued.

There were, subsequently, various public demonstrations of a disorderly character; effigies of unpopular members of the home and provincial governments were hanged and burned, and there were frequent displays of violent hostility to the administration; but it was not till June, 1768, that there was another dangerous and destructive riot. In this there cannot be the slightest doubt that the mob had on their side as little moral justification as legal right. The sloop "Liberty," belonging to John Hancock, a leading merchant of the patriot party, arrived at Boston, laden with wine from Madeira, and a custom-house officer went on board to inspect the cargo. He was seized by the crew and detained for several hours, while the cargo was landed, and a few pipes of wine were entered on oath at the Custom House as if they had been the whole. On the liberation of the customs' officers the vessel was seized for a false entry, and in order to prevent the possibility of a rescue it was removed from the wharf to the protection of the guns of a man of war. A mob was speedily collected, and as the rabble could not get possession of the sloop, they attacked the revenue officers for doing their duty in properly seizing the vessel for false entry and smuggling. The collector, his son, and two inspectors, received the most barbarous treatment, were badly bruised and wounded, and hardly escaped with their lives. The mob next went to the house of the inspector-general, and to that of the comptroller of customs, and broke their windows. They then dragged the collector's boat to the Common and burned it there.

When we consider the lawless condition of Boston, there cannot be any question that Governor Bernard was fully authorized to seek the presence of troops. The crown officers were in a rightful possession of their offices, and it would have been cowardly for them to desert their posts and sail for England, and thus to leave anarchy behind them. Meanwhile their lives were in peril, and they had an unquestionable right to demand competent protection. This they could have only by sending out of the province for it. The colonial militia could not be relied upon, for the mob must have been largely represented in its ranks. Nor could dependence be placed on the cadets, for Hancock, in whose behalf the last great riot had been perpetrated, was an officer of that corps. The only recourse was to the importation of royal troops—a measure which legal modes of remonstrance by patriots worthy of the name would never have rendered necessary or justifiable.

Two regiments, the 14th and 29th, of about five hundred men each, arrived on Sept. 28, 1768. These soldiers were, of course, a burden and annoyance. They could not have been otherwise. Individually they were not gentlemen, and they could not have been expected to be so. Yet had their presence been desired or welcome, there is no reason to suppose that there would have been any unpleasant collision with them.

The first token of resentment on the part of the populace occurred eleven days after their arrival. The colonel of one of the regiments had ordered a guard-house to be built on the Neck. The site was visited in the night by a mob, who tore down the frame of the building and cut it in pieces, so that no part of it could be put to further use. From that time on there were perpetual quarrels and brisk interchanges of contumely, abuse, and insult between the soldiers and the inhabitants, in which gangs of ropemakers bore a prominent part. There was undoubtedly no lack of ill-blood on either side, but, after patiently reading the contemporary record of what took place, we are inclined to adopt the statement of Samuel G. Drake, whose intense loyalty as a loving citizen of Boston no one can question, and who writes "That outrages were committed by the soldiers is no doubt true; but these outrages were exaggerated, and they probably, in nine cases out of ten, were the abused party."*

Passing over intervening dissensions and tumults, we now come to the so-called "Boston Massacre," on the 5th of March, 1770, an occasion on which loss of life was inevitable, and the only question was whether it should be among the soldiers or their assailants. The riot was evidently predetermined, as one of the bells was rung about eight o'clock, and immediately afterwards bands of men, with clubs, appeared upon the streets. Early in the evening there had been some interchange of hostilities, chiefly verbal, between the soldiers and town people, but an officer had ordered his men into the barrack-yard, and closed the gate. The "main guard," for that day's duty, was from the 29th regiment.

About nine o'clock a solitary sentinel in front of the custom-house on King street, now known as State street, was assailed by a party of men and boys, who pelted him with lumps of ice and coal, and threatened him with their clubs. Being forbidden by the rules of the service to quit his post, he called upon the "main guard," whose station was within hearing. A corporal and seven soldiers were sent to his relief. They were followed by Captain Preston, who said, "I will go there myself to see that they do no mischief." By that time the crowd had become a large one, intensely angry, and determined on violence. The mob supposed the soldiers were helpless and harmless; that they were not permitted to fire unless ordered by a magistrate. The rioters repeatedly challenged the soldiers to fire if they dared, and the torrent of coarse and profane abuse poured upon the soldiers is astonishing even in its echoes across the century, and would furnish material for an appropriate inscription on the Attucks monument. The soldiers stood on the defensive while their lives were endangered by missiles, and till the crowd closed upon them in a hand-to-hand conflict. The leader of the assault was

* "History of Boston," Samuel T. Drake, page 778.

"Crispus Attucks," a half Indian and half negro, who raised the blood-curdling war-whoop, the only legacy save his Indian surname and his strength and ferocity, that he is known to have received from his savage ancestry. He knocked down one of the soldiers, got possession of his musket, and would, no doubt, have killed him instantly had not the soldiers fired at that moment and killed Attucks and two other men, two more being fatally wounded. There is no evidence that Captain Preston ordered the firing, though if he did he certainly deserved no blame, as the shooting was, for the soldiers, the only means of defence. There is no doubt that the mobs on these occasions were set in movement and directed by some persons of higher rank and larger views of mischief than themselves.

Gordon, the historian of the American Revolution, informs us that the mob was addressed, in the street, before the firing, by a tall, large man, in a red cloak and white wig, and after listening to what he had to offer in the space of three or four minutes, they huzza for the "main guard" and say, "We will do for the soldiers." He also said, "But from the character, principles, and policies of certain persons among the leaders of the opposition, it may be feared that they had no objection to a recounter that by occasioning the death of a few might eventually clear the place of the two regiments."

This avowal, which, coming from such a source, has all the weight of premeditation, chills us with its deliberate candor, and begets reflections on the desperate means resorted to by some of the leaders of the populace in those trying times, which historians generally have shrunk from suggesting.

Hutchinson fulfilled at this time, with complete adequacy, the functions of chief magistrate. He was at once in the street in imminent danger of having his brains dashed out,* expostulating, entreating, that order might be observed. His prompt arrest of Preston and the squad which had done the killing was his full duty, and it is to the credit of the troops that the officer and his men, in the midst of the exasperation, gave themselves quietly into the hands of the law.

In the famous scenes which followed, the next day, Samuel Adams and other leading agitators, as representatives of the people, rushed into the presence of Hutchinson, and rather commanded than asked for the removal of the troops. Hutchinson hesitated. He was not yet governor—Bernard was in England. The embarrassment of the situation for the chief magistrate was really appalling. He knew that their removal would, under the circumstances, be a great humiliation to the government and a great encouragement to the mob. On the other hand, if the soldiers remained it was only too probable that in a few hours the streets of Boston would run with blood. He consulted the council, and found, as usual, an echo of the public voice. He then yielded, and the troops were sent to Fort William, on Castle Island, three miles from the town.

* "Life of Thomas Hutchinson," page 162.

Although, from that day to this, it has been held that the British uniform was driven with ignominy out of the streets of Boston, they deserve no discredit for their submission to the Governor and his council. They were two weak regiments, together amounting to not more than eight hundred effective men, isolated in a populous province which hated them, and were in great peril of life. It does not appear that they showed the white feather at all, but rather that they were law-abiding. Probably few organizations in the British army have a record more honorable. The 14th was with William III. in Flanders; it formed, too, one of the squares of Waterloo, breasting for hours the charges of the French cuirassiers until it had nearly melted away. The 29th was with Marlboro at Ramillies, and with Wellington in the Peninsula; it bore a heavy part, as may be read in Napier, in wresting Spain from the grasp of Napoleon. To fight it out with the mob would no doubt have been far easier and pleasanter than to yield; for brave soldiers to forbear is harder than to fight, and one may be sure that in the long history of those regiments few experiences more trying came to pass than those of the Boston streets.

Few things contributed more to commence the American Revolution than this unfortunate affray. Skillful agitators perceived the advantage it gave them, and the most fantastic exaggerations were dexterously diffused. It, however, had a sequel which is extremely creditable to the citizens of Boston.

It was determined to try the soldiers for their lives, and public feeling ran so fiercely against them that it seemed as if their fate was sealed. The trial, however, was delayed for seven months till the excitement had in some degree subsided. Captain Preston very judiciously appealed to John Adams, who was rapidly rising to the first place among the lawyers and the popular party of Boston, to undertake his defence. Adams knew well how much he was risking by espousing so unpopular a cause, but he knew also his professional duty, and though violently opposed to the British Government, he was an eminently honest, brave, and humane man. In conjunction with Josiah Quincy, a young lawyer who was also of the popular party, he undertook the invidious task, and he discharged it with consummate ability. Three years afterwards he wrote in his diary: "The part I took in defence of Capt. Preston and the soldiers procured me anxiety and obloquy enough. It was, however, one of the most gallant, generous, manly, and disinterested acts of my whole life, and one of the best pieces of service I ever rendered my country. Judgment of death against those soldiers would have been as foul a stain upon this country as the execution of the Quakers or witches, anciently. As the evidence was, the verdict of the jury was exactly right."

These noble words and his actions in this matter are sufficient alone to prove that John Adams was a fit successor to President Washington. He was entirely just in the estimate he put upon his conduct in these frank terms. His defence of the soldiers was one of the most courageous acts that a thoroughly manly man performed, and his summing up of the matter just quoted, is perfectly accurate. If John Adams showed himself here a man of sense and a hero, as much cannot be said of his cousin, Samuel Adams, who undoubtedly was one of the leaders who incited the mob to attack the soldiers, as hinted at by Gordon. And, again, in the vindictive persecution which followed, in the attempt to arouse in England and America indignation against the soldiers, by documents based on evidence hastily collected in advance of the trial, from wholly unreliable witnesses, and in the attempt to precipitate the trial while passion was still hot, the misbehavior of the people was grave. In all this no leader was more eager than Samuel Adams, and in no time in his career, probably, does he more plainly lay himself open to the charge of being a reckless demagogue, a mere mob-leader, than at this moment.

Captain Preston and six of the soldiers, who were tried for murder, were acquitted; two of the soldiers, convicted of manslaughter, were branded on the hand and then released. The most important testimony in the case was that of the celebrated surgeon, John Jeffries, who attended Patrick Carr, an Irishman, fatally wounded in the affray. It is as follows: "He said he saw many things thrown at the sentry; he believed they were oyster shells and ice; he heard the people huzza every time they heard anything strike that sounded hard. He then saw some soldiers going down towards the custom-house; he saw the people pelt them as they went along. I asked him whether he thought the soldiers would fire; he said he thought the soldiers would have fired long before. I then asked him if he thought the soldiers were abused a great deal; he said he thought they were. I asked him whether he thought the soldiers would have been hurt if they had not fired; he said he really thought they would, for he heard many voices cry out, 'Kill them!' I asked him, meaning to close all, whether he thought they fired in self-defence or on purpose to destroy the people; he said he really thought they did fire to defend themselves; that he did not blame the man, whoever he was, that shot him. He told me he was a native of Ireland; that he had frequently seen mobs, and soldiers called to quell them. Whenever he mentioned that, he called himself a fool; that he might have known better; that he had seen soldiers often fire on people in Ireland, but had never in his life seen them bear so much before they fired."

John Adams, in his plea in defence of the soldiers, said: "We have been entertained with a great variety of phrases to avoid calling this sort of people a mob. Some called them shavers, some called them geniuses. The plain English is, they were probably a motley rabble of saucy boys, negroes, mulattoes, Irish teagues, and outlandish Jack-tars, and why we should scruple to call such a set of people a mob, I can't conceive, unless the name is too respectable for them."

Chief-Justice Lynde, eminent for his judicial integrity and impartiality, said on the announcement of the verdict: "Happy am I to find, after much strict examination, the conduct of the prisoners appears in so fair a light, yet I feel myself deeply affected that this affair turns out so much to the disgrace of every person concerned against them, and so much to the shame of the town in general."

In 1887, at the instigation of John Boyle O'Reilly and the negroes of Boston, the Legislature passed a bill authorizing the expenditure of $10,000 for the purpose of erecting a monument to the memory of the "victims of the Boston Massacre." The monument was erected on Boston Common, notwithstanding the fact that the Massachusetts Historical Society, and the New England Historic Genealogical Society, voted unanimously against it. "That it was a waste of public money, that the affray was occasioned by the brutal and revengeful attack of reckless roughs upon the soldiers, while on duty, who had not the civilian's privilege of retreating, but were obliged to contend against great odds, and used their arms only in the last extremity; that the killed were rioters and not patriots, and that a jury of Boston citizens had acquitted the soldiers." A joint committee, composed of members of both societies, presented the resolutions to Governor Ames, and requested him to veto the bill. He admitted that "the monument ought not to be erected, but if he vetoed the bill it would *cost the Republican party the colored vote.*" When the monument was erected and uncovered, it presented such an indecent appearance that the City Council immediately voted $250 for a new capstone. It now represents an historical lie, and is a sad commentary on the intelligence and art taste of the citizens of Boston. To be sure monuments of stone will not avail to perpetuate an error of history, as witness the monument erected to commemorate the Great Fire of London. The inscription on that monument, embodying a gross perversion of history, was effaced in 1831, after it had stood there one hundred and fifty years, but the just resentment, the ill-feeling, the grief and shame which it engendered during that period, had been evils of incalculable magnitude. The time will surely come when the monument on Boston Common will be removed for the same reason.

On the 18th of March, 1766, the Stamp Act was repealed. It had remained in force but one year, and was then repealed in an effort to pacify the colonists. A duty was placed on tea and other imports which the colonists had always admitted to be a valid act of the Parliament. Whatever might be said of the Stamp Act, the tea duty was certainly not a real grievance to Americans, for Parliament had relieved the colonists of a duty of 12d. in the pound which had hitherto been levied in England, and the colonists were only asked, in compensation, to pay a duty of 3d. in the pound on arrival of the tea in America. The measure, therefore, was not an act of oppression, but of relief, making the price of tea in the colonies positively cheaper by 9d. per pound than it had been before. But the turbulent spirits were not to be satisfied so easily. They organized an immense boycott against British goods and commercial intercourse with England, and appointed vigilance committees in many communities to see that the boycott was rigidly enforced. Hutchinson, in describing them, says: "In this Province the faction is headed by the lowest, dirtiest, and most abject part of the community, and so absurdly do the Council and House of Representatives reason, that they justify this anarchy, the worst of tyranny, as necessary to remove a single instance of what they call oppression; they have persecuted my sons with peculiar pleasure." August 26, 1770, he wrote to William Parker, of Portsmouth: "You certainly think right when you think Boston people are run mad. The frenzy was not higher when they banished my pious great-grandmother, when they hanged the Quakers, when they afterwards hanged the poor innocent witches, when they were carried away with a Land Bank, or when they all turned "New Lights," than the political frenzy has been for a twelve-month past."*

In December, 1773, three ships laden with tea, private property of an innocent corporation, arrived at Boston, and on the 16th of that month, forty or fifty men, disguised as Mohawk Indians, under the direction of Samuel Adams, John Hancock, and others, boarded the vessels, posted sentinels to keep all agents of authority off at a distance, and flung the three cargoes, consisting of three hundred and forty-two chests, into the harbor. How can we, law-abiding citizens, applaud the "Boston Tea Party" and condemn the high-handed conduct of strike-leaders of the present time? In this transaction some respectable men were engaged, and their posterity affects to be proud of it. But they were not proud of it at the time. In their disguise as Indians they were not recognized, and the few well-known names among them were not divulged till the rebellion became a successful revolution. It probably made no "patriots." We have proof that it afterwards turned the scales against the patriot cause with some who had sympathized with it and taken part in it.

Looking back to those times during later years, John Adams wrote: "The poor people themselves, who, by *secret manoeuvres, are excited to insurrection*, are seldom aware of the purposes for which they are set in motion or of consequences which may happen to themselves; and *when once heated and in full career, they can neither manage themselves nor be managed by others.*"

The illegal seizure of the tea was in a certain sense parallel to the so-called "respectable" mob which on the 11th of August, 1834, destroyed the Charlestown convent, and, a year later, nearly killed Garrison and made the jail his only safe place of refuge. Had slavery triumphed, that mob would at this day be the object and the subject of popular glorification; every man who belonged to it, who was present abetting and encouraging it, would claim his share of the glory, and a roll of honor would have been handed down for a centennial celebration in which every slaveholder in the land would have borne a part. But now that slavery is dead, and the statue of Garrison has its place in the

* "Life of Hutchinson," page 195.

BOSTONIANS PAYING THE EXCISEMAN, OR TARRING AND FEATHERING.

A Cartoon published in London in 1774, showing how the authority of the government was wholly disregarded in Boston.

fashionable avenue of Boston, there is no longer any merit in the endeavor to buttress the fallen cause. Had the Revolution failed, the disgrace of the men who threw the tea overboard would never have been removed, and the best that history could say of them would be that, like the Attucks mob, they were enthusiasts without reason.

John Hancock, one of the principal leaders of the Tea Party Mob, and the owner of the sloop "Liberty," which was seized for smuggling, and later the first to sign the Declaration of Independence, inherited £70,000 from his uncle, who had made a large part of it by importing from the Dutch island of St. Eustacia great quantities of tea, in molasses hogsheads, and, by the importation of a few chests from England, had freed the rest from suspicion, and not having been found out, had borne the reputation of a "fair trader." Partly by inattention to his private affairs, and partly from want of sound judgment, John Hancock became greatly involved and distressed, and his estate was lost with much greater rapidity than it had been acquired by his uncle.*

John Adams had very positive opinions concerning the mobs of the Revolution. In a letter to his wife he says:

"I am engaged in a famous cause. The cause of King of Scarborough *versus* a mob that broke into his house and rifled his papers and terrified him, his wife, children and servants, in the night. The terror and distress, the distraction and horror of this family, cannot be described in words, or painted upon canvas. It is enough to move a statue, to melt a heart of stone, to read the story. A mind susceptible of the feelings of humanity, a heart which can be touched with sensibility for human misery and wretchedness, must relent, must burn with resentment and indignation at such outrageous injuries. These private mobs I do and will detest."†

Concerning the Loyalists, he says: "A notion prevails among all parties that it is politest and genteelest to be on the side of the administration, that the better sort, the wiser few, are on one side, and that the multitude, the vulgar, the herd, the rabble, the mob, only are on the other."‡

As regards his own actions towards the Loyalists, he writes in his later years as follows:

"Nothing could be more false and injurious to me than the imputation of any sanguinary zeal against the Tories, for I can truly declare that through the whole Revolution, and from that time to this, I never committed one act of severity against the Tories." ‖

At the time of the shedding of the first blood at Lexington, Hancock was respondent, in the admiralty court, in suits of the crown to recover nearly half a million of dollars, as penalties alleged to have been incurred for violation of the statute-book. It was fit that he should be

* His. Mass. Bay, page 207.
† Letters of John Adams to his wife, Vol. I., pages 12, 13.
‡ Letters of John Adams to his wife, Vol. I., page 12.
‖ Diary of John Adams, page 413.

the first to affix his name to an instrument which, if made good, would save him from financial ruin.

One-fourth of the signers of the Declaration of Independence were bred to trade or to the command of ships, and more than one of them was branded with the epithet of "smuggler."*

In 1773 John Hancock was elected treasurer of Harvard college. "In this they considered their patriotism more than their prudence." The amount of college funds paid over to him was upwards of fifteen thousand and four hundred pounds, and, like his friend, Samuel Adams, he, too, proved to be a defaulter. For twenty years the corporation begged and entreated him to make restitution. They threatened to prosecute him and also to put his bond in suit, as Adams' was, but it was all of no avail. He turned a deaf ear to their entreaties, and it was only after his death, in 1793, that his heirs made restitution to the college, when a settlement was made, in 1795, in which the college lost five hundred and twenty-six dollars interest."

Josiah Quincy, the president of Harvard college, in referring to this matter, says:

"From respect to the high rank which John Hancock attained among the patriots of the American Revolution, it would have been grateful to pass over in silence the extraordinary course he pursued in his official relation to Harvard college, had truth and the fidelity of history permitted. But justice to a public institution which he essentially embarrassed during a period of nearly twenty years, and also to the memory of those whom he made to feel and to suffer, requires that these records of unquestionable facts which at the time they occurred were the cause of calumny and censure to honorable men, actuated in this measure solely by a sense of official fidelity, should not be omitted. In republics, popularity is the form of power most apt to corrupt its possessor and to tempt him, for party or personal interests, to trample on right to set principle at defiance. History has no higher or more imperative duty to perform than, by an unyielding fidelity, to impress this class of men with the apprehension that although through fear or favor they may escape animadversion of contemporaries, there awaits them in her impartial record, the retribution of truth."†

The action of the tea mob was the culmination of mob violence in Boston. It brought the king and parliament to decide that their rebellious subjects in Boston must be subdued by force of arms, and that mob violence should cease. General Thomas Gage was to have at his command four regiments and a powerful fleet. He arrived at Boston, May 13, 1774, and was appointed to supersede Governor Thomas Hutchinson, as governor, who had succeeded Governor Sir Francis Bernard in 1771. General Gage was now in the prime of life. He had served with great credit under several commanders, at Fontenoy and Culloden,

* Sabine, Vol. I., page 13.
† "History of Harvard University," by Josiah Quincy, Vol. II., pp. 182-209.

and had fought with Washington, under Braddock, at Monongahela, where he was severely wounded, and carried a musket ball in his side for the remainder of his life as a memento of that fatal battle. An intimacy then existed between him and Washington, which was maintained afterwards by a friendly correspondence, and which twenty years later ended regretfully when they appeared, opposed to each other, at the head of contending armies, the one obeying the commands of his sovereign and the other upholding the cause of his people. How many cases similar to this occurred, eighty-six years later, when brother officers in arms faced each other with hostile forces, and friendship and brotherly love were changed to deadly hatred.

The claim has been set up by American historians, and accepted as true by those of Great Britain, that hostilities were commenced at Lexington and by the British commander. This is not so. The first act of hostilities was the attack upon the government post of Fort William and Mary at Newcastle, in Portsmouth harbor, New Hampshire. The attack was deliberately planned by the disunion leaders, and executed by armed and disciplined forces mustered by them for that purpose.* The fort contained large quantities of government arms and ammunition, and being garrisoned by but a corporal's guard, it was too tempting a prize to be overlooked by Samuel Adams and his colleagues.

Sir John Wentworth, governor of New Hampshire, tells us that the raiding party was openly collected by beat of drum in the streets of Portsmouth, and that, being apprised of their intent to attack a government fort, he sent the chief justice to warn them that such an act "was short of rebellion," and entreated them not to undertake it, "but all to no purpose." They embarked in three boats, sailed to the fortress and "forced an entrance in spite of Captain Cochrane, the commander, who defended it as long as he could. They then secured the captain triumphantly, gave three cheers, and hauled down the king's colors."*

Thomas Coffin Amory, in his "Military Service of General Sullivan," says (p. 295) that "the raiding force consisted of men whom Sullivan had been drilling for several months; that they captured 97 kegs of powder and a quantity of small ammunition which were used against the British at Bunker Hill."

The attack on this fort is worthy of far more consideration than has been given to it, for not only did it occur prior to the conflict at Concord, but was the direct cause of that conflict. It was as much the commencement of the Revolutionary war as was the attack on Fort Sumpter by the disunionists, in 1861, the commencement of the Civil War, and had precisely the same effect in each case. When the news reached London that a government fort had been stormed by an organized force, its garrison made prisoners and the flag of the empire torn down, the ministers seem to have become convinced that it was the determination of the colonists to make war upon the government. To tolerate such a pro-

* Letter of Governor Wentworth, New Eng. His. Gen. Reg., 1869, page 274.

ceeding would be a confession that all law and authority was at an end. Some vindication of that authority must be attempted. An order was dispatched to General Gage to retake the munitions that had been seized by the disunion forces, and any other found stored that might be used for attacking the government troops; surely a very mild measure of reprisal. It was in obedience to this order that the expedition was dispatched to Concord, that brought about the collision between the British and colonial troops and the so-called "Battle of Lexingon."

In Rhode Island, a revenue outrage of more than common importance occurred at this time. A small schooner named the Gaspee, in the government service, with a crew of some 25 sailors, commanded by Lieutenant Duddingston, while pursuing a suspected smuggler on June 6, 1772, ran aground on a sand-bar near Providence, and the ship which had escaped brought the news to that town. Soon after a drum was beat through the streets, and all persons who were disposed to assist in the destruction of the king's ship were summoned to meet at the home of a prominent citizen. There appears to have been no concealment or disguise, and shortly after 10 at night eight boats, full of armed men, started with muffled oars on the expedition. They reached the stranded vessel in the deep darkness of the early morning. Twice the sentinel on board vainly hailed them, when Duddingston himself appeared in his shirt upon the gunwale and asked who it was that approached. The leader of the party answered with a profusion of oaths that he was the sheriff of the county, come to arrest him, and while he was speaking one of his men deliberately shot the lieutenant, who fell, badly wounded, on the deck. In another minute the "Gaspee" was boarded and taken without any loss to the attacking party. The crew was overpowered, bound and placed upon the shore. Duddingston, his wounds having been dressed, was landed at a neighboring house. The party set fire to the "Gaspee," and while its flames announced to the whole county the success of the expedition, they returned, in broad daylight to Providence. Large rewards were offered by the British government for their detection, but though they were universally known, no evidence could be obtained, and the outrage was entirely unpunished. It is to be observed that this act of piracy and open warfare against the government was committed by the citizens of a colony that had no cause for controversy with the home government, and whose constitution was such a liberal one that it was not found necessary to change one word of it when the province became an independent republic.

General Gage, being informed that powder and other warlike stores were being collected in surrounding towns for the purpose of being used against the government, he sent, on Sept. 1, 1774, two hundred soldiers up the Mystic river, who took from the powder house 212 barrels of powder, and brought off two field-pieces from Cambridge. On April 18, 1775, at 10 o'clock at night, eight hundred men embarked from Boston Common and crossed the Charles river in boats to the

Cambridge shore. At the same time Paul Revere rowed across the river, lower down, and landed in Charlestown, and then, on horseback, went in advance of the troops to alarm the country. He was pursued, and with another scout named Dawes, was captured by the troops. At the dawn of day Lexington was reached, 12 miles distant from Boston, where the troops were confronted on the village green by the Lexington militia, which was ordered by the commander of the British expedition to disperse, but failing to do so they were fired on by the troops, and several of them killed. The militia dispersed without firing a shot.

The troops gave three cheers in token of their victory, and continued their march to Concord, their objective point, where they were informed munitions of war were being collected. They arrived there at 9 o'clock, and after destroying the stores collected there, they took up their march for Boston. But now the alarm had spread through the country. The troops had hardly commenced marching, when, crossing the North Bridge they were fired upon by the Americans; one soldier was killed and another wounded.*

Captain Davis and Abner Hosmer, two Americans, were killed by the British fire. On the march towards Boston the troops were met by the fire of the Americans from the stonewalls on either side of the highway, along the skirt of every wood or orchard, and from every house or barn or cover in sight. The troops, exposed to such a galling attack in flank and rear, must have surrendered had they not been met with reinforcements from Boston. This very emergency had been anticipated, and General Gage had sent out a brigade of a thousand men, and two field-pieces, under Earl Percy. The forces met at Lexington about 2 o'clock in the afternoon. After a short interval of rest and refreshment, the troops took up their line of march for Boston. At every point on the road they met an increasing number of militia, who by this time had gathered in such force as to constitute a formidable foe. It was a terrible march. Many were killed, on both sides, and it was with the greatest difficulty that Lord Percy was able at last, about sunset, to bring his command to Charlestown Neck under cover of the ships of war. The troops lost that day in killed, wounded, and missing, 273; the Americans, 93. The war of the Revolution had commenced. The fratricidal struggle was entered into, between men of the same race and blood who had stood shoulder to shoulder in many a hard-fought field; brothers, fathers and sons, were to engage in a deadly struggle that should last for years, and which, eighty-six years afterwards, was to be repeated over again in the war between the North and South.

* As the wounded soldier was crawling away he was met by a boy who had been chopping wood, and who, inflamed by the spirit of the hour, killed him with his axe. The two soldiers lay buried near the stonewall where they fell. More than a century later a young woman came here recently from Nottinghamshire, who was a relative of one of them. She went to the graves and placed upon them a wreath, singing as she did so, " God save the King!"

CHAPTER V.
THE LOYALISTS OF MASSACHUSETTS.

At the outbreak of the American rebellion the great majority of men in the colonies could be regarded as indifferent, ready to stampede and rush along with the successful party. Loyalty was their normal condition; the state *had* existed and *did* exist, and it was the disunionists who must do the converting, the changing of men's opinion to suit a new order of things which the disunionists believed necessary for their welfare. Opposed to the revolutionists were the crown officials, dignified and worthy gentlemen, who held office by virtue of a wise selection. Hardly to be distinguished from the official class were the clergy of the Established Church, who were partially dependent for their livings upon the British government. The officers and clergy received the support of the landowners and the substantial business men, the men who were satisfied with the existing order of things. The aristocracy of culture, of dignified professions and callings, of official rank and hereditary wealth, was, in a large measure, found in the Loyalist party. Such worthy and talented men of high social positions were the leaders of the opposition to the rebellion. Supporting them was the natural conservatism of all prosperous men. The men who had abilities which could not be recognized under the existing regime, and those that form the lower strata of every society and are every ready to overthrow the existing order of things, these were the ones who were striving to bring about a change—a revolution.

The persecution of the Loyalists by the Sons of Despotism, or the "Sons of Liberty," as they called themselves, was mercilessly carried out; every outrage conceivable was practiced upon them. Freedom of speech was suppressed; the liberty of the press destroyed; the voice of truth silenced, and throughout the colonies was established a lawless power. As early as 1772 "committees of correspondence" had been organized throughout Massachusetts. Adams exclaimed in admiration: "What an engine! France imitated it and produced a revolution."* Leonard, the Loyalist, with "abhorrence pronounced it the foulest, subtlest and most venomous serpent ever issued from the egg of sedition."† Insult and threat met the Loyalist at every turn. One day he was, perhaps, set upon a cake of ice to cool his loyalty,‡ and was then in-

---

* John Adams' Letters. Vol. X., page 197.
† "Massachusettsensis."
‡ "Moor's Diary." Vol. I., page 359.

formed that a certain famous liberty man had sworn to be his butcher. Next he was told that he might expect a "sans benito" of tar and feathers, and even an "auto da fe." The committee sent "Patriot" newspapers and other propaganda to the wavering or obstinate, but seldom failed to follow this system of conversion with a personal interview if the literature failed. Such were the means that were used by the "Sons of Despotism" to bring over the mass of the people to the disunion cause.

In the courts of law, not even the rights of a foreigner were left to the Loyalist. If his neighbors owed him money he had no legal redress until he took an oath that he favored American independence. All legal action was denied him. He might be assaulted, insulted, blackmailed or slandered, though the law did not state it so boldly, yet he had no recourse in law. No relative or friend could leave an orphan child to his guardianship. He could be the executor or administrator of no man's estate. He could neither buy land nor transfer it to another; he was denied his vocation and his liberty to speak or write his opinions. All these restrictions were not found in any one place, nor at any one time, nor were they always rigorously enforced. Viewed from the distance of one hundred years, the necessity of such barbarous severity is not now apparent.

When this ostracism was approved by a large majority of the inhabitants of a town the victim was practically expelled from the community. None dared to give him food or comfort. He was a pariah, and to countenance him was to incur public wrath.

On January 17, 1777, Massachusetts passed an Act punishing with death the "Crime of adhering to Great Britain." The full extent of this law was not carried into effect in Massachusetts, but it was in other colonies. The "Black List" of Pennsylvania contained the names of 490 persons attainted of high treason. Only a few actually suffered the extreme penalty. Among these were two citizens of Philadelphia—Mr. Roberts and Mr. Carlisle. When the British army evacuated Philadelphia, they remained, although warned of their danger. They were at once seized by the returning disunionists and condemned to be hanged. Mr. Roberts's wife and children went before congress and on their knees supplicated for mercy, but in vain. In carrying out the sentence the two men, with halters around their necks, were walked to the gallows behind a cart, "attended with all the apparatus which makes such scenes truly horrible." A guard of militia accompanied them; but few spectators.*

At the gallows Mr. Roberts' behavior, wrote a loyal friend, "did honor to human nature," and both showed fortitude and composure.

Roberts told his audience that his conscience acquitted him of guilt; that he suffered for doing his duty to his sovereign; that his blood would

---

* "Penn Packet," Nov. 17, 1778. "Penn Archives," Vol. VIII., page 22. "Dallis," Vol. I., pp. 39, 42; "Gallowway's Examinatio...", page 77.

one day be required at their hands. Turning to his children he charged and exhorted them to remember his principles for which he died, and to adhere to them while they had breath. "He suffered with the resolution of a Roman," wrote a witness.

After the execution, the bodies of the two men were carried away by friends and their burial was attended by over 4000 in procession.*

Some of the more heartless leaders of the rebellion defended this severity of treatment and thought "hanging the traitors" would have a good effect and "give stability to the new government." "One suggested that the Tories seemed designed for this purpose by Providence."* The more thoughtful leaders, however, denounced the trial of Loyalists for treason, and Washington feared that it might prove a dangerous expedient. It was true, he granted, that they had joined the British after such an offence had been declared to be treason; but as they had not taken the oath, nor entered into the American service, it would be said that they had a right to choose their side. "Again," he added, "by the same rule that we try them may not the enemy try any natural-born subject of Great Britain taken in arms in our service? We have a great number of them and I, therefore, think we had better submit to the necessity of treating a few individuals who may really deserve a severer fate, as prisoners of war, than run the risk of giving an opening for retaliation upon the Europeans in our service." †

American writers never fail to tell of the "brutal and inhuman treatment" of the American prisoners by the British in the prisons and prison-ships at New York, where about five thousand prisoners were confined. We are informed that their sufferings in the prison-ships were greater than those in the prisons on land; that "every morning the prisoners brought up their bedding to be aired, and after washing the decks, they were allowed to remain above till sunset, when they were ordered below with imprecations and the savage cry, "Down, rebels! Down!" The hatches were then closed, and in serried ranks they lay down to sleep," etc.‡ That many died from dysentery, smallpox and prison fever, there is no doubt; but there is not any record that *they were starved to death*. Compare the above treatment of prisoners by the British with that of the Loyalists by the disunionists! In East Granby, Connecticut, was situated an underground prison which surpassed the horrors of the Black Hole of Calcutta. These barbarities and inhumanities were the portion of those who had been guilty of loyalty to their country, a social class distinguished by both their public and private virtues. It seemed almost incredible that their fellow-countrymen should have confined them in a place unfit for human beings.

This den of horrors, known as "Newgate Prison," was an old worked-out copper mine, sixty feet under ground, in the hills of East

* "Records of North Carolina," Vol. XI., page 561.
† "Washington's Writings," Vol. VI., page 241.
‡ Lossing, "Field Book of the Revolution," Vol. II., page 661.

Granby. The only entrance to it was by means of a ladder down a shaft which led to the caverns under ground. The darkness was intense; the caves reeked with filth; vermin abounded; water trickled from the roof and oozed from the sides of the cavern; huge masses of earth were perpetually falling off. In the dampness and the filth the clothing of the prisoners grew mouldy and rotted away, and their limbs became stiff with rheumatism.

During the Revolutionary war Loyalists of importance were confined in this place of horrors, then of national importance, although now but seldom referred to by American writers. Loyalists were consigned to it for safe keeping by Washington himself. In a letter dated December 11, 1775, addressed to the Committee of Safety, Simsbury, Conn., he informed them that the "charges of their imprisonment will be at the Continental expense," and "to confine them in such manner so that they cannot possibly make their escape."*

Driven to desperation the Loyalists rose against their guards. About 10 o'clock at night, on the 18th of May, 1781, when all the guards but two had retired to rest, a wife of one of the prisoners appeared, to whom permission was given to visit her husband in the cavern. Upon the hatches being removed to admit her passing down, the prisoners who were at the door, and prepared for the encounter, rushed up, seized the gun of the sentry on duty, who made little or no resistance, and became master of the guard-room before those who were asleep could be aroused to make defence. The officer of the guard who resisted was killed, and others wounded. The guard was easily overcome, a few sought safety in flight, but the greater number were disarmed by the prisoners. The prisoners, numbering twenty-eight persons, having equipped themselves with the captured arms, escaped, and, with few exceptions avoided recapture."†

The heart sickens at the recital of the sufferings of the Loyalists, and we turn in disgust from the views which the pen of faithful history records.

After the legislation of 1778 every grievance the colonists had put forward as a reason for taking up arms had been redressed, every claim they had presented had been abandoned, and from the time when the English parliament surrendered all right of taxation and internal legislation in the colonies, and when the English Commissioners laid their propositions before the Americans, the character of the war had wholly changed. It was no longer a war for self-taxation and constitutional liberty. It was now an attempt, with the assistance of France and Spain, to establish independence by shattering the British empire.

There were brave and honest men in America who were proud of the great and free empire to which they belonged, who had no desire to shirk the burden of maintaining it, who remembered with gratitude

* "History of Simsbury and Granby," page 125.
† "History of Simsbury and Granby," pp. 123, 124.

that it was not colonial, but all English blood that had been shed around Quebec and Montreal in defence of the colonies. Men who with nothing to hope for from the crown were prepared to face the most brutal mob violence and the invectives of a scurrilous press; to risk their fortunes, their reputation, and sometimes even their lives, in order to avert civil war and ultimate separation. Most of them ended their days in poverty and exile, and, as the supporters of a beaten cause, history has paid but a scanty tribute to their memory. But they comprised some of the best and ablest men America has ever produced, and they were contending for an ideal which was at least as worthy as that for which Washington fought.

It was the maintenance of one great, free, industrial, and pacific empire, comprising the whole British race, holding the richest plains of Asia in possession, blending all that was most venerable in an ancient civilization with the abundant energies of a youthful social combination likely in a few generations to outstrip every commercial competitor, and to acquire an indisputable ascendency among the nations. Such an ideal was a noble one, and there were Americans who were prepared to make any personal sacrifice to realize it. These men were the LOYALISTS of the Revolution. Consider what the result would be today had not this "Anglo-Saxon Schism," as Goldwin Smith calls it, taken place. There would be a great English-speaking nation of 130,000,000 that could dominate the world. They would in all substantial respects be one people, in language, literature, institutions, and social usages, whether settled in South Africa, in Australia, in the primitive home, or in North America.

Because the Revolution had its origin in Massachusetts, and the old Bay State furnished a large part of the men and the means to carry it to a successful issue,* it seems to have been taken for granted that the people embraced the popular side almost in a mass.

A more mistaken opinion than this has seldom prevailed. At the evacuation of Boston, General Gage was accompanied by eleven hundred Loyalists, which included the best people of the town. Boston at that time had a population of 16,000. "Among these persons of distinguished rank and consideration there were members of the council, commissioners, officers of the customs, and other officials, amounting to one hundred and two; of clergymen, eighteen; of inhabitants of country towns, one hundred and five; of merchants and other persons who resided in Boston, two hundred and thirteen; of farmers, mechanics and traders, three hundred and eighty-two." †

Cambridge lost nearly all her men of mark and high standing; nearly all the country towns were thus bereft of the very persons who had been the most honored and revered. With the exiles were nearly one hundred graduates of Harvard college.

* The Southern States furnished 59,330 men; the Middle States 54,116, and New England 118,355, of which number Massachusetts furnished 67,907. (General Knox's Report.")
† Sabine, "Loyalists of the Revolution," Vol. I., page 25.

Among the proscribed and banished were members of the old historic families, Hutchinson, Winthrop, Saltonstall, Quincy, the Sewells, and Winslows, families of which the exiled members were not one whit behind those that remained, in intelligence, social standing and moral worth.

At the evacuation of New York and Savannah no fewer than 30,000 persons left the United States for Nova Scotia and New Brunswick. From northern New York and Vermont the Loyalists crossed over into Upper Canada, and laid the foundations of that prosperous province under the vigorous leadership of Governor Simcoe, who, during the war, commanded a regiment of Loyalist rangers which had done efficient service. Many of the Southern Loyalists settled in Florida, the Bahamas and the West India Islands.

Familiar New England names meet one at every turn in the maritime provinces, especially Nova Scotia. Dr. Inglis, from Trinity church, New York, was the first bishop, and Judge Sewell, of Massachusetts, the first chief justice there. The harshness of the laws and the greed of the new commonwealth had driven into exile men who could be ill spared, and whose absence showed itself in the lack of balance and of political steadiness which characterized the early history of the republic, while the newly-founded colonies, composed almost exclusively of conservatives, were naturally slow, but sure, in their development. The men who were willing to give up home, friends and property, for an idea, are not men to be despised; they are, rather, men for us to claim with pride and honor as American—men of the same blood, and the same speech as ourselves; Americans who were true to their convictions and who suffered everything except the loss of liberty, for their political faith. We look in vain among the lists of voluntary and banished refugees from Massachusetts for a name on which rests any tradition of disgrace or infamy, to which the finger of scorn can be pointed. Can this be said of the Revolutionary leaders of Massachusetts, the so-called patriots, to whom the Revolution owes its inception? If the reader has any doubts on this subject, then let him compare the lives of the Loyalists, as given in this work, with those of Samuel Adams, John Hancock, and other Revolutionary leaders. The Loyalists were generally people of substance; their stake in the country was greater, even, than that of their opponents; their patriotism, no doubt, fully as fervent. "There is much that is melancholy, of which the world knows but little, connected with this expulsion from the land they sincerely loved. The estates of the Loyalists were among the fairest, their stately mansions stood on the sightliest hill-brows, the richest and best-tilled meadows were their farms; the long avenue, the broad lawn, the trim hedge about the garden, servants, plate, pictures, for the most part these things were at the homes of the Loyalists. They loved beauty, dignity and refinement." The rude contact of town meetings was offensive to their tastes. The crown officials were courteous, well-born and congenial gentlemen.

"The graceful, the chivalrous, the poetic, the spirits over whom these feelings had power, were sure to be Loyalists. Democracy was something rude and coarse, and independence to them meant a severance of those connections of which a colonist ought to be proudest."

"Hence when the country rose, many a high-bred, honorable gentleman, turned the key in his door, drove down his tree-lined avenue with his refined dame and carefully-guarded children at his side, turned his back on his handsome estate, and put himself under the shelter of the proud banner of St. George. It was a mere temporary refuge, he thought, and he promised himself a speedy return when discipline and loyalty should have put down the rabble and the misled rustics."

"But the return was never to be. The day went against them; they crowded into ships, with the gates of their country barred forever behind them. They found themselves penniless upon shores sometimes bleak and barren, always showing scant hospitality to outcasts who came empty-handed, and there they were forced to begin life anew. Consider the condition of Hutchinson, Apthorp, Gray, Clarke, Faneuil, Sewell, Royal, Vassall, and Leonard, families of honorable note bound in with all that was best in the life of the Province." "Who can think of their destiny unpityingly."*

A man suspected of loyalty to the crown was not left at peace, but was liable to peremptory banishment unless he would swear allegiance to the "Sons of Liberty," and if he returned he was subject to forcible deportation, and to death on the gallows if he returned a second time.

One of the first acts of the revolutionary party when they returned to Boston after the British evacuation, was to confiscate and sell all property belonging to Loyalists and apply the receipts to supply the public needs. The names and fate of a considerable proportion of these Loyalists and those that preceded and succeeded the Boston emigration, will be found in succeeding pages. Most of them went to Halifax, Nova Scotia, and St. John, New Brunswick, where they endured great privation. Many, however, subsequently went to England and there passed the remainder of their lives. We find seventy or more of the Massachusetts Loyalists holding offices of greater or less importance in the provinces, and many of them were employed in places of high trust and large influence in various parts of the Empire. They and their sons filled for more than half a century the chief offices in the Nova Scotia and New Brunswick judiciary, and they and their descendants must have contributed in a degree not easily estimated to the elevation and progress of those provinces.

"Men whose fathers, mocked and broken
  For the honor of a name,
Would not wear the conqueror's token,
  Could not salt their bread with shame.

* Hosmer's "Life of Hutchinson," pages 321, 322.

> Plunged them in the virgin forest
>   With their axes in their hands,
> Built a Province as a bulwark
>   For the loyal of the lands.
>
> Won it by the axe and harrow,
>   Held it by the axe and sword,
> Bred a race with brawn and marrow,
>   From no alien over-lord.
> Gained the right to guide and govern;
>   Then with labor strong and free
> Forged the land a shield of Empire,
>   Silver sea to silver sea.
>
> —Duncan C. Scott.

In this way the United States, out of their own children, built upon their borders a colony of rivals in navigation and the fisheries, whose loyalty to the British crown was sanctified by misfortune. It is impossible to say how many of these Loyalists would have been on the Revolutionists' side had the party opposed to the crown been kept under the control of its leaders. But they were, most of them, of the class of men that would have the least amount of tolerance for outrage and rapine, and when we consider how closely they were identified with the institutions of their native province, and how little remains on record of anything like rancor or malignity on their part, there can be little doubt that a considerable proportion of them would have been saved for the republic but for the very acts which posterity has been foolish enough to applaud, and for their loss Massachusetts was appreciably the poorer for more than one or two generations.

It is also admitted by those who are authorities on the subject, that if it had not been for the brutal and intolerant persecution of the Loyalists, the ruthless driving of these unfortunate people from their homes, with the subsequent confiscation of property, the attempt to throw off the authority of Great Britain at the time of the Revolutionary War would not have succeeded; that is, people entirely or at least reasonably content with the previous political condition were terrorized into becoming patriots by the fear of the consequences that would follow if they remained Loyalists.

The fact is, that, as far as the Americans were in it, the war of the Revolution was a civil war in which the two sides were not far from equality in numbers, in social conditions, and in their manners and customs. The Loyalists contended all through the war that they were in a numerical majority, and if they could have been properly supported by British forces, the war might have ended in 1777, before the French alliance had given hope and strength to the separatist party. Sabine computes that there were at least 25,000 Americans in the military service of the King, at one time or another, during the wars. In New York, New Jersey, the Carolinas, and Georgia, the Loyalists outnumbered the Revolutionists. Even in New England, the nursery of the Revolution, the number was so large and so formidable, in the opinion of the Revolutionary leaders, that in order to suppress them there was established a reign of terror, anticipating the famous "Law of the Suspected" of the French Revolution. An irresponsible tyranny was established, of town and country committees, at whose beck and call were the so-called "Sons of Liberty." To these committees was entrusted absolute power over the lives and fortunes of their fellow citizens, and they proceeded on principles of evidence that would have shocked and scandalized a grand inquisitor.*

The rigorous measures adopted by the new governments in New England States, and the activity of their town committees, succeeded in either driving out these Loyalist citizens, or reducing them to harmless inactivity. In New York, Pennsylvania, New Jersey, the Carolinas and Georgia, they remained strong and active throughout the war, and loyalty was in those states in the ascendancy.

If the Loyalists were really a majority, as they claimed to be, the disunionists were determined to break them up. Loyalists were tarred and feathered and carried on rails, gagged and bound for days at a time; stoned, fastened in a room with a fire and the chimney stopped on top; advertised as public enemies, so that they would be cut off from all dealings with their neighbors; they had bullets shot into their bedrooms, their horses poisoned or mutilated; money or valuable plate extorted from them to save them from violence, and on pretence of taking security for their good behavior; their houses and ships burned; they were compelled to pay the guards who watched them in their houses, and when carted about for the mob to stare at and abuse, they were compelled to pay something at every town. For the three months of July, August and September of the year 1776, one can find in the American archives alone over thirty descriptions of outrages of this kind, and all this done by so-called "patriots" in the name of liberty! In short, lynch law prevailed for many years during the Revolution, and the habit became so fixed that it has never been given up. It was taken from the name of the brother of the man who founded Lynchburgh, Virginia.

Wherever the disunionists were most successful with this reign of terror, they drove all the judges from the bench, and abolished the courts, and for a long time there were no courts or public administration of the law, notably in New England.

To the mind of the Loyalists, all this lynching proceeding were an irrefragible proof not only that the disunionist party were wicked, but that their idea of independence of a country free from British control and British law were silly delusions, dangerous to all good order and civilization. That such a people could ever govern a country of their own and

* "Essays in American History," 180-181.

have in it that thing they were crying so much about, "liberty," was in their opinion beyond the bounds of intelligent belief. A recent American writer says: "The revolution was not by any means the pretty social event that the ladies of the so-called 'patriotic' societies suppose it to have been. It was, on the contrary, a rank and riotous rebellion against the long-established authority of a nation which had saved us from France, built us up into prosperity, and if she was ruling us today would, I am entirely willing to admit, abolish lynch-law, negro burning, municipal and legislative corruption, and all the other evils about which reformers fret." The same writer also says: "All that saved this country from complete annihilation was the assistance after 1778 of the French army, fleet, provisions, clothes, and loans of money, followed by assistance from Spain, and, at the last moment, by the alliance of Holland, and even with all this assistance the cause was, even as late as the year 1780, generally believed to be a hopeless one."* "In fact, Washington, at this time, was prepared to become a guerilla." In case of being further pressed, he said: "We must retire to Augusta County, in Virginia. Numbers will repair to us for safety, and we will then try a predatory war. If overpowered, we must cross the Allegheny Mountains."†

The question will naturally be asked why, if they were so numerous, were they not more successful, why did they yield to popular violence in New England, and desert the country while the contest was going on, Why did they not hold the Southern States, and keep them from joining the others in the Continental Congresses, and in the war?

In the first place, a negative attitude is necessarily an inactive one, and in consequence of this, and the fact that they could not take the initiative in action, the Loyalists were put at a disadvantage before the much better organization of the Revolutionary leaders. Though these were few in number in the South, they were of families of great social influence, and in the North were popular agitators of long experience. They manipulated the committee system so carefully that the colonies found themselves, before they were aware of the tendency of the actions of their deputies, involved in proceedings of very questionable legality, such as the boycotting agreement known as the "American Association," and other proceedings of the Continental Congress.‡ In regard to the subject of legal attainder and exile, Mr. Sabine remarks, very moderately and sensibly: "Nor is it believed that either the banishment or the confiscation laws, as they stood, were more expedient than just. The latter did little towards relieving the public necessities, and served only to create a disposition for rapacity, and to increase the wealth of favored individuals. Had the estates which were seized and sold been judiciously or honestly managed, a considerable sum would have found

---

* " The American Revolution and Boer War," By Sidney Fisher, 1902.
† Irving's " Life of Washington," Vol. II., chap. xli.
‡ " Essays in American History," 179. See also " Royalists' Archives," Mass. State House.

its way to the treasury; but, as it was, the amount was inconsiderable. Some of the wisest and purest Whigs of the time hung their heads in shame because of the passage of measures so unjustifiable, and never ceased to speak of them in terms of reprobation. Mr. Jay's disgust was unconquerable, and he never would purchase any property that had been forfeited under the Confiscation Act of New York.*

Judge Curwen, a Salem Loyalist, says: "So infamously knavish has been the conduct of the commissioners, that though frequent attempts have been made to bring them to justice and to respond for the produce of the funds resting in their hands, so numerous are the defaulters in that august body, the *General Court*, that all efforts have hitherto proved in vain. Not two pence on the pound have arrived to the public treasury of all the confiscation."†

"The Loyalists, to a great extent, sprung from and represented the old gentry of the country. The prospect of seizing their property had been one great motive which induced many to enter the war. The new owners of the confiscated property now grasped the helm. New men exercised the social influence of the old families, and they naturally dreaded the restoration of those whom they had dispossessed."

At the close of the war, the Revolutionists committed a great crime. Instead of repealing the proscription and banishment acts, as justice and good policy required, they manifested a spirit to place the humbled and unhappy Loyalists beyond the pale of human sympathy. Hostilities at an end, mere loyalty should have been forgiven. When, in the civil war between the Puritans and the Stuarts, the former gained the ascendancy, and when at a later period the Commonwealth was established, Cromwell and his party wisely determined not to banish nor inflict disabilities on their opponents, and so, too, at the restoration of the monarchy, so general was the amnesty act in its provisions that it was termed an act of oblivion to the *friends* of Charles, and of grateful remembrance to his *foes*. The happy consequences which resulted from the conduct of *both* parties, and in both cases, were before the men of their own political and religious sympathies, the Puritans of the North and the Cavaliers of the South in America, but neither of them profited by it, at that time; but since then the wisdom of it has been exemplified by the happy consequences which have resulted to both parties engaged in the war of secession, where the United States wisely determined not to banish, confiscate, or inflict any disabilities on their opponents in the late seceded states.

The crime having been committed, thousands ruined and banished, new British colonies founded, animosities to continue for generations made certain, the violent Revolutionists of Massachusetts, New York and Virginia, were satisfied; all this accomplished and the statute-book was divested of its most objectionable enactments, and a few of the Loyal-

* "North American Review," LIX., page 289.
† The "Journal and Letters of Samuel Curwin," 147.

ists returned to their old homes, but by far the greater part died in banishment.

No one who studies the history of the American Revolution can fail to be convinced that the persecution of the Loyalists had for its final result the severance of the North American continent into two nations. The people who inhabited Nova Scotia prior to the Revolution were largely New England settlers, who dispossessed the Acadians, and who for the most part sympathized with the revolutionary movement. But for the banishment of the Loyalists, Nova Scotia would have long continued with but a very sparse population, and certainly could never have hoped to obtain so enterprising, active, and energetic a set of inhabitants as those who were supplied to it by the acts of the several states hostile to the Loyalists. The same can also be said of Upper Canada. The hold of the British government upon the British provinces of North America which remained to the crown, would have been slight indeed, but for the active hostility of the Loyalists to their former fellow-countrymen. They created the state of affairs which consolidated British power on this continent, and built it up into the Dominion of Canada, which in another century will probably contain one hundred million inhabitants.

The treaty of peace with Great Britain, like other documents of its kind, contained provisions of give and take. After signature by the commissioners in Paris it was ratified with due consideration by the Continental Congress. The advantages which it secured were not merely of a sentimental nature, but material. It was justly regarded by enlightened citizens of the states as a triumph of diplomacy. The credit of Britain in the bargain was more of the heart than of the head. She was willing to concede substantial and important benefits in order to secure the lives and property of the Loyalists who had clung to her and had sustained her arms. Looking at the matter now, in a cool light, she blundered into sacrifices that were altogether needless, even with this aim in view, and knowledge of the knavery that was to follow.

The game was played, and she had lost. North America, in the eyes of her statesmen, was a strip of eastern seaboard; the great lakes were but dimly understood; the continent beyond the Mississippi was ignored. She gave much more than she needed to have given both in east and west, to attain her honorable end, and what was more immediately distressing, she received little or no value in return for her liberal concession.

"That each party should hold what it possesses, is the first point from which nations set out in framing a treaty of peace. If one side gives up a part of its acquisitions, the other side renders an equivalent in some other way. What is the equivalent given to Great Britain for all the important concessions she has made? She has surrendered the capital of this state (New York) and its large dependencies. She is to surrender our immensely valuable posts on the frontier, and to yield to us a vast tract of western territory, with one-half of the lakes, by which we shall command almost the whole fur trade. She renounces to us her claim to the navigation of the Mississippi and admits us to share in the fisheries even on better terms than we formerly enjoyed. As she was in possession, by right of war, of all these objects, whatever may have been our original pretensions to them, they are, by the laws of nations, to be considered as so much given up on her part. And what do we give in return? We stipulate that there shall be no future injury to her adherents among us. How insignificant the equivalent in comparison with the acquisition! A man of sense would be ashamed to compare them, a man of honesty, not intoxicated with passion, would blush to lisp a question of the obligation to observe the stipulation on our part."* In return for these advantages which Hamilton informs us Great Britain gave to the States, Congress had most solemnly undertaken three things, and people, wearied by the sufferings of our eight years' war, would have gladly purchased the blessings of peace at a much higher price. The first of these conditions was that no obstacle or impediment should be put in the way of the recovery of debts due to British subjects from the citizens of the Republic; the second that no fresh prosecution or confiscation should be directed against Loyalists; the third, that Congress should sincerely recommend to the legislatures of the various states a repeal of the existing acts of confiscation, which affected the property of these unfortunate persons. On the last no stress could be laid, but the first and second were understood by every man, honest or dishonest, in the same sense as when peace was joyfully accepted. The American states took the benefits of peace which the efforts of Congress had secured to them, they accepted the advantages of the treaty which their representative had signed, they watched and waited until the troops of King George were embarked in transports at New York for England, and then proceeded to deny, in a variety of tones, all powers in the central government to bind them in the matter of the *quid pro quo*. It was not a great thing which Congress had undertaken to do, or one which could be of any material advantage to their late enemy. All their promises amounted to was that they would abstain from the degradation of a petty and personal revenge, and this promise they proceeded to break in every particular.

As Hamilton wisely and nobly urged, the breach was not only a despicable perfidy, but an impolitic act, since Loyalists might become good citizens and the state needed nothing more urgently than population. But no sooner was danger at a distance, embarked on transports, than the states assumed an attitude of defiance. The thirteen legislatures vied with one another in the ingenuity of measures for defeating the recovery of debts due to British creditors. They derided the recommendation to repeal oppressive acts, and to restore confiscated property, and proceeded, without regard either for honor or consequences, to pass new acts of wider oppression and to order confiscation on a grander scale. There

* The Works of Alexander Hamilton, by H. C. Lodge, 2d edition, Vol. IV., page 239.

was a practical unanimity in engaging in fresh persecutions of Loyalists, not merely by the enactment of oppressive civil laws, but by even denying them the protection afforded by a just enforcement of the criminal laws. In many districts these unfortunate persons were robbed, tortured, and even put to death with impunity, and over a hundred thousand driven into exile in Canada, Florida and the Bahamas.

Measures were passed amid popular rejoicing to obstruct the recovery of debts due to British merchants and to enable the fortunate Americans to revel unmolested in the pleasure of stolen fruits. It is remarkable how at this period public opinion was at once so childish and rotten, and one is at a loss whether to marvel most at its recklessness of credit or its unvarnished dishonesty; it was entirely favorable to the idea of private theft, and the interest of rogues was considered with compassion by the grave and respectable citizens who composed the legislatures of the various states. It was the same spirit which had violated the Burgoyne convention at Saratoga, the same which in later days preached the gospel of repudiation, greenbackism, silver currency, violated treaties with the Indians, that produced a "Century of Dishonor."

Meanwhile the policy of breach of faith was producing its natural crop of inconvenience. Dishonest methods were not the unmixed advantages which these adherents had supposed, when they engaged upon them in a spirit of light-hearted cunning. For in spite of all the ill-feeling, a large demand arose for British goods. For these, specie had to be paid down on the nail in all cases where wares or material were not taken in exchange, since no British merchant would now give one pennyworth of credit, out of respect to the measures of the various states for the obstruction of the payment of British debts. It was true that Britain was in no mood to embark upon a fresh war for the punishment of broken promises. She had surrendered the chief hostage when she evacuated her strategical position at New York, but she declined to hand over the eight important frontier posts which she held upon the American side of the line between Lake Michigan and Lake Champlain. These posts were much in themselves, and as a symbol of dominion to the Indian tribes. They were much also as a matter of pride, while their retention carried with it the whole of the valuable fur trade, which consequently, until 1795, when they were at last surrendered, brought considerable profits to British merchants.

To the short-sighted policy which banished the Loyalists may be traced nearly all the political troubles of this continent, in which Britain and the United States have been involved. "Dearly enough have the people of the United States paid for the crime of the violent Whigs of the Revolution, for to the Loyalists who were driven away, and to their descendants, we owe almost entirely the long and bitter controversy relative to our northeastern boundaries, and the dispute about our right to the fisheries in the colonial seas."

CHAPTER VI.
THE REVOLUTIONIST.

The American Revolution, like most other revolutions, was the work of an energetic minority who succeeded in committing an undecided and fluctuating majority to courses for which they had little love; leading them, step by step, to a position from which it was impossible to recede. To the last, however, we find vacillation, uncertainty, half measures, and, in large classes, a great apparent apathy. There was, also, a great multitude, who, though they would never take up arms for the king; though they, perhaps, agreed with the constitutional doctrines of the revolution, dissented on grounds of principle, policy, or interest, from the course they were adopting.

That the foregoing is a correct presentation of the case is shown by a letter written by John Adams, when in Congress, to his wife. He says:

"I have found this congress like the last. When we first came together, I found a strong jealousy of us from New England, and the Massachusetts in particular—suspicions entertained of designs of independency, an American republic, Presbyterian principles, and twenty other things."*

It was an open question with many whether a community liable to such outbreaks of popular fury did not need a strongly repressive government; and especially when the possibilities of a separation from the mother country was contemplated, it was a matter of doubt whether such a people were fit for self-government. Was it not possible that the lawless and anarchical spirit which had of late years been steadily growing, and which the "patriotic" party had actively encouraged, would gain the upper hand, and the whole fabric of society would be dissolved?

In another letter of John Adams to his wife at this time, he gives us an idea of what the opinion was of the Loyalists concerning the doctrines taught by the disunionists, and which, he says, "Must be granted to be a likeness." "They give rise to profaneness, intemperance, thefts, robberies, murders, and treason; cursing, swearing, drunkenness, gluttony, lewdness, trespassing, mains, are necessarily involved in them. Besides they render the populace, the rabble, the scum of the earth, insolent and disorderly, impudent and abusive. They give rise to lying, hypocrisy, chicanery, and even perjury among the people, who are drawn to such artifices and crime to conceal themselves and their companions from prosecution in consequence of them. This is the picture drawn by the Tory pencil, and it must be granted to be a likeness."†

* Letters of John Adams to His Wife, Vol. I., p. 45.
† Letters of John Adams to His Wife, Vol. I., p. 8.

There are several passages in the writings of John Adams that seem to indicate that he at times had doubts of the righteousness of the course he had pursued. They were written in his later years, though one refers to an incident alleged to have occurred during his early manhood. In a letter to a friend in 1811, he thus moralizes: "Have I not been employed in mischief all my days? Did not the American Revolution produce the French Revolution? And did not the French Revolution produce all the calamities and desolations to the human race and the whole globe ever since?" But he justifies himself with the reflection: "I meant well, however; my conscience was as clear as crystal glass, without a scruple or doubt. I was borne along by an irresistible sense of duty." In his diary Mr. Adams recalls to mind one incident which occurred in 1775. He mentions the profound melancholy which fell upon him in one of the most critical moments of the struggle, when a man whom he knew to be a horse-jockey and a cheat, and whom, as an advocate, he had often defended in the law courts, came to him and expressed the unbounded gratitude he felt for the great things which Adams and his colleagues had done. "We can never," he said, "be grateful enough to you. There are now no courts of justice in this province, and I hope there will never be another." "Is this the object," Adams continued, "for which I have been contending?" said I to myself. Are these the sentiments of such people, and how many of them are there in the country? Half the nation, for what I know; for half the nation are debtors, if not more, and these have been in all the countries the sentiments of debtors. If the power of the country should get into such hands—and there is great danger that it will—to what purpose have we sacrificed our time, health and everything else?"*

Misgivings of this kind must have passed through many minds. To some may have come the warning words of Winthrop, the father of Boston, uttered one hundred and fifty years before these events occurred, in which he said: "Democracy is, among most civil nations, accounted the meanest and worst of all forms of government, and histories record that it hath always been of least continuance and fullest of trouble."

There was a doubt in the minds of many people, which we have often heard uttered in recent times, with reference to the French people in their long series of revolutions, and equally so with the Spanish-American republics with their almost annual revolutions, whether these words of Winthrop were not correct, and that the people were really incapable of self-government. It was a doubt which the revolution did not silence, for the disturbing elements which had their issue in the Shay Rebellion, The Whiskey Insurrection and the mutiny of the Pennsylvania Line, in 1781, were embers of a fire, smothered, not quenched, which rendered state government insecure till it was welded into the Federal Union. There was a widespread dislike to the levelling principles of New Eng-

* Adams' Works, Vol. II., 420.
† Life of Winthrop, Vol. II., 427.

land, to the arrogant, restless and ambitious policy of its demagogues; to their manifest desire to invent or discover grievances, foment quarrels and keep the wound open and festering.*

Those who rebelled in good faith did so because they feared that the power of Parliament to tax them moderately to raise money for their own defence might be used sometime in the future for a less worthy purpose, and then they would all be "slaves." Their argument led to mob rule and anarchy, till the adoption of the Federal Constitution, after the close of the Revolutionary War.

The opinion of such an authority as Lecky on our revolutionary movements must be worthy of thoughtful attention; and his opinion is this: "Any nation might be proud of the shrewd, brave, prosperous and highly intelligent yeomen who flocked to the American camps; but they were very different from those who defended the walls of Leyden, or immortalized the field of Bannockburn. Few of the great pages of history are less marked by the stamp of heroism than the American Revolution and perhaps the most formidable of the difficulties which Washington had to encounter were in his own camp."† And he concludes his survey of the movement with these words: "In truth the American people, though in general unbounded believers in progress, are accustomed, through a kind of curious modesty, to do themselves a great injustice by the extravagant manner in which they idealize their past. It has almost become as commonplace that the great nation which in our own day has shown such an admirable combination of courage, devotion and humanity in its gigantic Civil War, and which since that time has so signally falsified the prediction of its enemies and put to shame all the nations of Europe by its unparalleled efforts in paying off its national debt, is of far lower moral type than its ancestors at the time of the War of Independence. This belief appears to me essentially false. The nobility and beauty of Washington can, indeed, hardly be paralleled. Several of the other leaders of the Revolution were men of ability and public spirit, and few armies have ever shown a nobler self-devotion than that which remained with Washington through the dreary winter at Valley Forge. But the army that bore those sufferings was a very small one, and the general aspect of the American people during the contest was far from heroic or sublime. The future destinies and greatness of the English race must necessarily rest mainly with the mighty nation which has arisen beyond the Atlantic, and that nation may well afford to admit that its attitude during the brief period of its enmity to England has been very unduly extolled. At the same time, the historian of that period would do the Americans a great injustice if he judged them only by the revolutionary party, and failed to recognize how large a proportion of their best men had no sympathy with the movement."‡

* See Adams' Works, Vol. II., pp. 350, 410.
† Lecky, " American Revolution," p. 230.
‡ Lecky,s " American Revolution," p. 375.

Our native historians and the common run of Fourth of July orators have treated their countrymen badly for a hundred years. They have given the world to understand that we are the degenerate children of a race of giants, statesmen, and moralists, who flourished for a few years about a century ago and then passed away. An impartial examination of the records would show that we are wiser, better, more benevolent, quite as patriotic and brave as the standard heroes of 1776. We may give our ancestors credit for many admirable virtues without attempting to maintain that a multitude of unlettered colonists, scattered along the Atlantic coast, hunting, fishing, smuggling, and tilling the soil for a slender livelihood, and fighting Indians and wild beasts to save their own lives, possessed a vast fund of political virtue and political intelligence, and left but little of either to their descendants. The public is beginning to tire of this tirade of indiscriminate eulogy, and the public taste is beginning to reject it as a form of defamation. And so the ripening judgment of our people is beginning to demand portraits of our ancestors painted according to the command that Cromwell gave the artist; to paint his features, warts, blotches, and all, and to demand an account of our forefathers in which we shall learn to speak of them as they were.

Sabine, in his valuable work, "Loyalists of the American Revolution," says: "I presume that I am of Whig descent. My father's father received his death-wound under Washington, at Trenton; my mother's father fought under Stark at Bennington. I do not care, of all things, to be thought to want appreciation of those of my countrymen who broke the yoke of colonial vassalage, nor on the other hand, do I care to imitate the writers of a later school, and treat the great and the *successful* actors in the world's affairs as little short of divinities, and as exempt from criticism. Nay, this general statement will not serve my purpose. Justice demands as severe a judgment of the Whigs as of their opponents, and I shall here record the result of long and patient study. At the Revolutionary period the principles of unbelief were diffused to a considerable extent throughout the colonies. It is certain that several of the most conspicuous personages of those days were either avowed disbelievers in Christianity, or cared so little about it that they were commonly regarded as disciples of the English or French school of sceptical philosophy. Again, the Whigs were by no means exempt from the lust of land hunger. Several of them were among the most noted land speculators of their time, during the progress of the war, and, in a manner hardly to be defended, we find them sequestering and appropriating to themselves the vast estates of those who opposed them. Avarice and rapacity were seemingly as common then as now. Indeed, the stock-jobbing, the extortion, the forestalling of the law, the arts and devices to amass wealth which were practised during the struggle, are almost incredible. Washington mourned the want of virtue as early as 1775, and averred that he "trembled at the prospect"—soldiers were stripped of their miserable pittance that contractors for the army might become rich in a single campaign. Many of the sellers of merchandise monopolized (or "cornered") articles of the first necessity, and would not part with them to their suffering countrymen, and to the wives and children of those who were absent in the field, unless at enormous profit. The traffic carried on with the army of the king was immense. Men of all descriptions finally engaged in it, and those who at the beginning of the war would have shuddered at the idea of any connection with the enemy, pursued it with increasing avidity. The public securities were often counterfeited, official signatures forged, and plunder and jobbery openly indulged in. Appeals to the guilty from the pulpit, the press, and the halls of legislature were alike unheeded. The decline of public spirit, the love of gain of those in office, the plotting of disaffected persons, and the malevolence of factions, became widely spread, and in parts of the country were uncontrollable. The useful occupations of life and the legitimate pursuits of commerce were abandoned by thousands. The basest of men enriched themselves, and many of the most estimable sank into obscurity and indigence. There were those who would neither pay their debts nor their taxes. The indignation of Washington was freely expressed. "It gives me sincere pleasure," he said, in a letter to Joseph Reed, "to find the Assembly is so well disposed to second your endeavor in bringing those murderers of our cause to condign punishment. It is much to be lamented that each state, long ere this, has not hunted them down as pests of society and the greatest enemies we have to the happiness of America. No punishment, in my opinion, is too great for the man who can build his greatness upon his country's ruin."

In a letter to another, he drew this picture, which he solemnly declared to be a true one: "From what I have seen, heard, and in part known," said he, "I should in one word say, that idleness, dissipation, and extravagance seem to have laid fast hold on most; that speculation, peculation, and an insatiable thirst for riches, seem to have got the better of every other consideration, and almost every order of men, and that party disputes and personal quarrels are the great business of the day."

In other letters he laments the laxity of public morals, the "distressed rumors, and deplorable condition of affairs," the "many melancholy proofs of the decay of private virtue." "I am amazed," said Washington to Colonel Stewart, "at the report you make of the quantity of provision that goes daily into Philadelphia from the County of Bucks." Philadelphia was occupied at that time by the British army, who paid in hard money and not in "continental stuff," and mark you! this was written in January of that memorable winter which the American army passed in nakedness and starvation at Valley Forge. There was always an army—on paper. At the close of one campaign there were not enough troops in camp to man the lines. At the opening of another "scarce any state in the Union," as Washington said, had an "eighth part of its quota" in service. The bounty finally paid to soldiers was enormous. The price for a single recruit was as high sometimes as seven hundred and fifty, and one thousand dollars, on enlistment for the war, besides the bounty and emoluments given by Congress. One hundred and fifty dollars "in specie" was exacted and paid for a term of duty of only five months. Such were the extraordinary inducements necessary to tempt some men to serve their country when its vital interests were at issue. Making every allowance for the effects of hunger and want, for the claims of families at home, and for other circumstances equally imperative, desertion, mutiny, robbery, and murder are still high crimes. There were soldiers of the Revolution who deserted in parties of twenty and thirty at a time, and several hundred of those who then abandoned the cause fled to Vermont and were among the early settlers of that state. A thousand men, the date of whose enlistment had been misplaced, perjured themselves in a body, as fast as they could be sworn, in order to quit the ranks which they had voluntarily entered. In smaller parties, hundreds of others demanded dismissals from camp under false pretexts, and with lies upon their lips. Some also added treason to desertion, and joined the various corps of Loyalists in the capacity of spies upon their former friends, or as guides and pioneers. Many more enlisted, deserted, and re-enlisted under new recruiting officers for the purpose of receiving double bounty, while others who placed their names upon the rolls were paid the money to which they were entitled, but refused to join the army; and others still who were sent to the hospitals returned home without leave after their recovery, and were sheltered and secreted by friends and neighbors, whose sense of right was as weak as their own. Another class sold their clothing, provisions, and arms to obtain means of indulgence in revelry and drunkenness; while some prowled about the country to rob and kill the unoffending and defenceless. A guard was placed over the grave of a foreigner of rank, who died in Washington's own quarters, and who was buried in full dress, with diamond rings and buckles, "lest the soldiers should be tempted to dig for hidden treasure." Whippings, drummings out of the service, and even military executions were more frequent in the Revolution than at any subsequent period of our history.

If we turn our attention to the officers we shall find that many had but doubtful claims to respect for purity of private character, and that some were addicted to grave vices. There were officers who were destitute alike of honor and patriotism, who unjustly clamored for their pay, while they drew large sums of public money under pretext of paying their men, but applied them to the support of their own extravagance; who went home on furlough and never returned to the army; and who, regardless of their word as gentlemen, violated their paroles, and were threatened by Washington with exposure in every newspaper in the land as men who had disgraced themselves and were heedless of their associates in captivity, whose restraints were increased by their misconduct. At times, courts-martial were continually sitting, and so numerous were the convictions that the names of those who were cashiered were sent to Congress in long lists. "Many of the surgeons"—are the words of Washington—"are very great rascals, countenancing the men to sham complaints to exempt them from duty, and often receiving bribes to certify indisposition with a view to procure discharge or furlough"; and still further, they drew as for the public "medicines and stores in the most profuse and extravagant manner for private purposes." In a letter to the governor of a state, he affirmed that the officers who had been sent him therefrom were "generally of the lowest class of the people," that they "led their soldiers to plunder the inhabitants and into every kind of mischief." To his brother, John Augustine Washington, he declared that the different states were nominating such officers as were "not fit to be shoeblacks." Resignations occurred upon discreditable pretexts, and became alarmingly prevalent. Some resigned at critical moments, and others combined together in considerable number for purposes of intimidation, and threatened to retire from the service at a specified time unless certain terms were complied with. Many of those who abandoned Washington were guilty of a crime which, when committed by private soldiers, is called "desertion," and punished with death. Eighteen of the generals retired during the struggle, one for drunkenness, one to avoid disgrace for receiving double pay, some from declining health, others from weight of advancing years; but several from private resentments and real or imagined wrongs inflicted by Congress or associates in the service.

John Adams wrote in 1777: "I am worried to death with the wrangles between military officers, high and low. They quarrel like cats and dogs. They worry one another like mastiffs, scrambling for rank and pay like apes for nuts."*

"The abandoned and profligate part of our army," wrote Washington, "lost to every sense of honor or virtue as well as their country's good, are by rapine and plunder spreading ruin and terror wherever they go, thereby making themselves infinitely more to be dreaded than the common enemy they are come to oppose. Under the idea of Tory property, or property that may fall into the hands of the enemy, no man is secure in his effects, and scarcely in his person."† American soldiers were constantly driving innocent persons out of their homes by an alarm of fire, or by actual incendiarism, in order more easily to plunder the contents, and all attempts to check this atrocious practice had proved abortive. The burning of New York was generally attributed to New England soldiers. The efforts of the British soldiers to save the city were remembered with gratitude, and there is little doubt that in the city, and in the country around it, the British were looked upon not as invaders, but as deliverers.

"Wherever the men of war have approached, our militia have most manfully turned their backs and run away, officers and men, like sturdy fellows, and these panics have sometimes seized the regular regiments. . . . You are told that a regiment of Yorkers behaved ill, and it may be true; but I can tell you that several regiments of Massachusetts men behaved ill, too. The spirit of venality you mention is the most dreadful

* Sabine, Vol. I., pp. 139-150.
† Washington's Works, IV., 118, 119; Lecky, 257.

and alarming enemy America has to oppose. It is as rapacious and insatiable as the grave. This predominant avarice will ruin America. If God Almighty does not interfere by His grace to control this universal idolatry to the mammon of unrighteousness, we shall be given up to the chastisement of His judgments. I am ashamed of the age I live in."*

Nor was the public life of the country at that time more creditable. In the course of the war, persons of small claims to notice or regard obtained seats in Congress. By force of party disruptions, as was bitterly remarked by one of the leaders, men were brought into the management of affairs "who might have lived till the millennium in silent obscurity had they depended upon their mental qualifications." Gouverneur Morris was, no doubt, one of the shrewdest observers of current events in his day, and the purity of the patriotism of John Jay entitled him to stand by the side of Washington. One day, in a conversation, thirty years after the second Continental Congress had passed away, Morris exclaimed: "Jay, what a set of damned scoundrels we had in that second Congress!" And Jay, as he knocked the ashes from his pipe, replied: "Yes, we had."

Near the close of 1779, Congress, trying to dispel the fear that the continental currency would not be redeemed, passed a resolution declaring: "A bankrupt, faithless republic would be a novelty in the political world. The pride of America revolts at the idea. Her citizens know for what purpose these emissions were made, and have repeatedly pledged their faith for the redemption of them." The rest of the resolution is too coarse for quotation, even for the sake of emphasis. In a little more than three months from the passage of that resolution a bill was passed to refund the continental currency by issuing one dollar of new paper money for forty of the old, and the new issue soon became as worthless as the former emission. Indeed, the patriots repudiated obligations to the amount of two hundred million dollars, and did it so effectually that we still use the expression, "not worth a continental" as a synonym for worthlessness.

It is a common belief that scurrilous and indecent attacks upon public men by American journalists is an evil of modern growth; but this is an error. A century ago such attacks exceeded in virulence anything that would be possible today. Among the vilest of the lampooners of that age were a quartette of literary hacks who for some years were engaged in denouncing the federalist party and government. Philip Freneau owned "*The National Gazette*," a journal that Hamilton declared disclosed "a serious design to subvert the government." He was among the most virulent assailants of Washington's administration, denouncing not only the members of the cabinet, except Jefferson, but the chief himself. Among other charges brought against him, Washington was accused of "debauching the country" and "seeking a crown," "and all the while passing himself off as an honest man." Benjamin F. Bache was a grandson of Dr. Benjamin Franklin. He inherited all his ancestor's duplicity, love of in-

* Letter of John Adams to His Wife, Vol. I., p. 171.

trigue, and vindictiveness, but none of his suavity and tact. Sullen and malevolent of disposition, scarcely could he keep in accord with men of his own party. He owned and edited "The Aurora," a paper which in depth of malice and meanness exceeded the journal of Freneau. He also made vicious attacks upon Washington, both in the "Aurora" and other publications. Washington's "fame" he declared to be "spurious"; he was "inefficient," "mischievous," "treacherous," and "ungrateful." His "mazes of passion" and the "loathings of his sick mind" were held up to the contempt of the people. "His sword," it was declared, "would have been drawn against his country" had the British government given him promotion in the army. He had, it was asserted, "cankered the principles of republicanism" "and carried his designs against the public liberty so far as to put in jeopardy its very existence."

William Duane, a man of Irish parentage, assisted Bache in the conduct of the "Aurora," and upon his death, in 1798, assumed full control of it. He was responsible for some of the most virulent attacks upon Washington, published in that paper. Bache and Duane both received severe castigations, administered in retaliation for abusive articles.

James Thompson Callender, who disgraced Scotland by his birth, was a shameless and double-faced rascal. A professional lampooner, his pen was at the service of any one willing to pay the price. He, too, had a fling at the President, declaring that "Mr. Washington had been twice a traitor," and deprecating "the vileness of the adulation" paid him.

In this quartette of scoundrels may be added the notorious Thomas Paine, who, after exalting Washington to the seventh heaven of excellence, upon being refused by him an office that to confer upon him would have disgraced the nation, showered upon him the vilest denunciation. "As for you, sir," he wrote, addressing him, "treacherous in private friendship, and a hypocrite in public life, the world will be puzzled to decide whether you are an apostate or an impostor; whether you have abandoned good principles, or whether you ever had any." That these attacks upon members of the government were the direct results of the teachings of Jefferson there is no room for doubt. That he encouraged and supported their authors has been proved beyond a doubt. He was one of the worst detractors of Great Britain. For fifty years he employed his pen in reviling the mother country. Then occurred one of the most remarkable instances of political death-bed repentance that the annals of statecraft have to show. He who had so often asserted that Great Britain was a nation powerless, decrepit, lost to corruption, eternally hostile to liberty, totally destitute of morality and good faith, and warned his countrymen to avoid intercourse with her lest they become contaminated by the touch; he who had yearned for her conquest by a military despot, and proposed to burn the habitations of her citizens, like the nests of noxious vermin, is suddenly found proclaiming "her mighty weight," lauding her as the protector of free government, and exhorting his fellow citizens to "sedulously cherish a cordial friendship with her." This change of heart was brought about by the announcement by Great Britain of the so-called "Monroe Doctrine." In Jefferson's letter to Monroe of October 24, 1823, he said: "The question presented by the letters you have sent me (the letters of Mr. Rush, reciting Mr. Canning's offer of British support against the attempt of the "Holy Alliance" to forcibly restore the revolted Spanish-American colonies to Spain), is the most momentous that has ever been offered to my contemplation since that of Independence. And never could we embark under circumstances more auspicious. By acceding to Great Britain's proposition we detach her from the bonds, bring her mighty weight into the scale of free government, and emancipate a continent at one stroke. With her on our side we need not fear the whole world. With her then we should most sedulously cherish a cordial friendship."

Alexander Hamilton was a soldier of fortune of the highest type. He was born on the island of Nevis, in the West Indies. He was of illegitimate birth; his father was Scotch and his mother French. Endowed with a high order of intellect, possessed of indomitable energy and passionate ambition, he went forth into the world determined to win both.* Chance threw him into the colonies at a time when the agitation for independence was at its height. He landed at Boston in October, 1772; thence he went to New York, where in his sixteenth year he entered King's (now Columbia) College. At first he affiliated with the Loyalists, but soon deserted to the Disunionists, which gave him greater opportunities of realizing his ambitious dream. As a Loyalist the world would never have heard of him, but as John Marshall informs us, he ranks next to Washington as having rendered more conspicuous service to the United States than any other man in the Revolution. A great orator, a talented lawyer, a good soldier, "master of every field he entered, punctilious and haughty of temperament, he scorned to bend even to the proud spirit of Washington. His position on Washington's staff was literally a secretaryship more civil than military. It was "the grovelling condition of a clerk," which his youthful genius revolted at. This caused him to resign his staff appointment. Alexander Hamilton was the deviser and establisher of the government of the United States. He it was that framed the Constitution, who urged and secured its adoption by the original thirteen states at a time when but a rope of sand bound them together. To Hamilton, more than any other man, is due the fact that the United States to-day form a nation. He lived long enough to see the nation to which he gave political stability submitting itself in entire respect and confidence to the declaration contained in the most remarkable document ever written.

Like many of his contemporaries he was an *intrigaunt*, injuring his health and impairing the sanctity of his home, and was destined to meet his death at the hands of a man more dissolute than himself, and destitute of his honorable traits of character.

Professor Sumner says: "It is astonishing how far writers kept from

* In a letter written by Hamilton when he was but thirteen years of age, employed as a clerk, he declared: " I condemn the grovelling condition of a clerk to which my future condition condemns me, and would willingly risk my life, though not my character, to exalt my station."

the facts and evidence. This is so much the case that it is often impossible to learn what was really the matter. The colonists first objected to internal taxes, but consented to import duties. Then they distinguished between import duties to regulate commerce, and import duties for revenue. They seem to have changed their position and to be consistent in one thing only, to pay no taxes and to rebel." After patiently examining their pamphlets and discussions, Sumner concludes: "The incidents of the trouble offer occasion at every step for reserve in approving the proceedings of the colonists." We therefore come to the conclusion that the Revolutionary leader made a dispute about the method of raising a small amount of revenue a pretext for rending an empire which, if united, might civilize and wisely govern the fairest portion of the globe."

The foregoing statements are more than corroborated by a letter written to Washington by Rev. Jacob Duche, a former rector of Christ Church, Philadelphia, a man of great learning, eloquence, and piety, who was appointed chaplain to the first Congress. His prayer at the opening of the session was pronounced not only eloquent, but patriotic in the extreme. While it was being uttered there was but one man in that whole assembly who knelt, and that man was George Washington. When Washington received the letter he immediately transmitted it to Congress. The letter was in part as follows:—

Philadelphia, 8th October, 1777.

"Sir—If this letter should find you in council or in the field, before you read another sentence I beg you to take the first opportunity of retiring and weighing its important contents. You are perfectly acquainted with the part I formerly took in the present unhappy contest. I was, indeed, among the first to bear my public testimony against having any recourse to threats, or indulging a thought of an armed opposition.

The current, however, was too strong for my feeble efforts to resist. I wished to follow my countrymen as far only as virtue and the righteousness of their cause would permit me. I was, however, prevailed on, among the rest of my clerical brethren of this city, to gratify the pressing desires of my fellow citizens by preaching a sermon, and reluctantly consented. From a personal attachment of nearly twenty years' standing and a high respect for your character, in private as well as public life, I took the liberty of dedicating this sermon to you. I had your affectionate thanks for my performance in a letter, wherein was expressed, in the most delicate and obliging terms, your regard for me, and your wishes for a continuance of my friendship and approbation of your conduct. Further than this I intended not to proceed. My sermon speaks for itself, and wholly disclaims the idea of independence. My sentiments were well known to my friends. I communicated them without reserve to many respectable members of Congress, who expressed their warm approbation of it then. I persisted to the very last moment to use the prayers for my Sovereign, though threatened with insults from the violence of a party.

"Upon the declaration of independence I called my vestry and solemnly put the question to them whether they thought it best for the peace and welfare of the congregation to shut up the churches, or to continue the service without using the prayers for the Royal Family. This was the sad alternative. I concluded to abide by their decision, as I could not have time to consult my spiritual superiors in England. They determined it most expedient, under such critical circumstances, to keep open the churches that the congregations might not be dispersed, which we had great reason to apprehend.

"A very few days after the fatal declaration of independence I received a letter from Mr. Hancock, sent by express to Germantown, where my family were for the summer season, acquainting me I was appointed Chaplain to the Congress, and desired my attendance next morning at nine o'clock. Surprised and distressed as I was by an event I was not prepared to expect, obliged to give an immediate attendance without the opportunity of consulting my friends, I easily accepted the appointment. I could have but one motive for taking this step. I thought the churches in danger, and hoped by this means to have been instrumental in preventing those ills I had so much reason to apprehend. I can, however, with truth declare I then looked upon independence rather as an expedient, and hazardous, or, indeed, thrown out in *terrorem,* in order to procure some favorable terms, than a measure that was seriously persisted in. My sudden change of conduct will clearly evince this to have been my idea of the matter.

"Upon the return of the Committee of Congress appointed to confer with Lord Howe I soon discerned their whole intentions. The different accounts which each member gave of this conference, the time they took to make up the matter for public view, and the amazing disagreements between the newspaper accounts, and the relation I myself had from the mouth of one of the Committee, convinced me there must have been some unfair and ungenerous procedure. This determination to treat on no other strain than that of independence, which put it out of his lordship's power to mention any terms at all, was sufficient proof to me that independence was the idol they had long wished to set up, and that rather than sacrifice this they would deluge their country with blood. From this moment I determined upon my resignation, and in the beginning of October, 1776, sent it in form to Mr. Hancock, after having officiated only two months and three weeks; and from that time, as far as my safety would permit, I have been opposed to all their measures.

"This circumstantial account of my conduct I think due to the friendship you were so obliging as to express for me, and I hope will be sufficient to justify my seeming inconsistencies in the part I have acted.

"And now, dear sir, suffer me in the language of truth and real affection to address myself to you. All the world must be convinced you are engaged in the service of your country from motives perfectly disinterested. You risked everything that was dear to you, abandoned the sweets of domestic life which your affluent fortune can give the uninterrupted enjoyment of. But had you, could you have had, the least idea of matters being carried to such a dangerous extremity? Your most intimate friends shuddered at the thought of a separation from the mother country, and I took it for granted that your sentiments coincided with theirs. What, then, can be the consequences of this rash and violent measure and degeneracy of representation, confusion of councils, blunders without number? The most respectable characters have withdrawn themselves, and are succeeded by a great majority of illiberal and violent men. Take an impartial view of the present Congress, and what can you expect from them? Your feelings must be greatly hurt by the representation of your native province. You have no longer a Randolph, a Bland or a Braxton, men whose names will ever be revered, whose demands never ran above the first ground on which they set out, and whose truly glorious and virtuous sentiments I have frequently heard with rapture from their own lips. Oh, my dear sir, what a sad contrast of characters now presents! others whose friends can ne'er mingle with your own. Your Harrison alone remains, and he disgusted with the unworthy associates.

"As to those of my own province, some of them are so obscure that their very names were never in my ears before, and others have only been distinguished for the weakness of their undertakings and the violence of their tempers. One alone I except from the general charge; a man of virtue, dragged reluctantly into their measures, and restrained by some false ideas of honor from retreating after having gone too far. You cannot be at a loss to discover whose name answers to this character.

"From the New England provinces can you find one that as a gentleman you could wish to associate with, unless the soft and mild address of Mr. Hancock can atone for his want of every other qualification necessary for the seat which he fills? Bankrupts, attorneys, and men of desperate fortunes are his colleagues. Maryland no longer sends a Tilghman and a Carroll. Carolina has lost her Lynch, and the elder Middleton has retired. Are the dregs of Congress, then, still to influence a mind like yours? These are not the men you engaged to serve; these are not the men that America has chosen to represent her. Most of them were chosen by a little, low faction, and the few gentlemen that are among them now are well known to lie on the balance, and looking up to your hand alone to turn the beam. 'Tis you, sir, and you only, that supports the present Congress; of this you must be fully sensible. Long before they left Philadelphia their dignity and consequence were gone; what must it be now since their precipitate retreat? I write with freedom, but without invective. I know these things to be true, and I write to one whose own observation must have convinced him that it is so.

"After this view of the Congress, turn to the army. The whole world knows that its only existence depends upon you, that your death or captivity disperses it in a moment, and that there is not a man on that side—the question in America—capable of succeeding you. As to the army itself, what have you to expect from them? Have they not frequently abandoned you yourself in the hour of extremity? Can you have the least confidence in a set of undisciplined men and officers, many of whom have been taken from the lowliest of the people, without priniciple, without courage? Take away them that surround your person, how very few there are you can ask to sit at your table! As to your little navy, of that little what is left? Of the Delaware fleet part are taken, and the rest must soon surrender. Of those in the other provinces some are taken, one or two at sea, and others lyig unmanned and unrigged in your harbors.

"In America your harbors are blocked up, your cities fall one after another; fortress after fortress, battle after battle is lost. A British army, after having passed unmolested through a vast extent of country, have possessed themselves of the Capital of America. How unequal the contest! How fruitless the expense of blood! Under so many discouraging circumstances, can virtue, can honor, can the love of your country prompt you to proceed? Humanity itself, and sure humanity is no stranger to your breast, calls upon you to desist. Your army must perish for want of common necessaries or thousands of innocent famiiies must perish to support them; wherever they encamp, the country must be impoverished; wherever they march, the troops of Britain will pursue, and must complete the destruction which America herself has begun. Perhaps it may be said, it is better to die than to be made slaves. This, indeed, is a splendid maxim in theory, and perhaps in some instances may be found experimentally true; but when there is the least probability of a happy accommodation, surely, wisdom and humanity call for some sacrifices to be made to prevent inevitable destruction. You well know there is but one invincible bar to such an accommodation; could this be removed, other obstacles might readily be removed. It is to you and you alone your bleeding country looks and calls aloud for this sacrifice. Your arm alone has strength sufficient to remove this bar. . May Heaven inspire you with this glorious resolution of exerting your strength at this crisis, and immortalizing yourself as friend and guardian to your country! Your penctrating eye needs not more explicit language to discern my meaning. With that prudence and delicacy, therefore, of which I know you possessed, represent to Congress the indispensable necessity of rescinding the hasty and ill-advised declaration of independence. Recommend, and you have an undoubted right to recommend, an immediate cessation of hostilities. Let the controversy be taken up where that declaration left it, and where Lord Howe certainly expected to find it left. Let men of clear and impartial characters, in or out of Congress, liberal in their sentiments, heretofore independent in their fortunes—and some such may be found in America—be appointed to confer with His Majesty's Commissioners. Let them, if they please, propose some well-digested constitutional plan to lay before them at the commencement of the negotiation. When they have gone thus far I am confident the usual happy consequences will ensue—unanimity will immediately take place through the different provinces, thousands who are now ardently wishing and praying for such a measure will step forth and declare themselves the zealous advocates for constitutional liberty, and millions will bless the hero that left the field of war to decide this most important contest with the weapons of wisdom and humanity.

"O sir, let no false ideas of worldly honor deter you from engaging in so glorious a task! Whatever censure may be thrown out by mean, illiberal minds, your character will rise in the estimation of the virtuous and noble. It will appear with lustre in the annals of history, and form a glorious contrast to that of those who have fought to obtain conquest and gratify their own ambition by the destruction of their species and the ruin of their country. Be assured, sir, that I write not this under the eye of any British officer or person connected with the British army or ministry. The sentiments I express are the real sentiments of my own heart, such as I have long held, and which I should have made known to you by letter before had I not fully expected an opportunity of a private conference. When you passed through Philadelphia on your way to Wilmington I was confined by a severe fit of the gravel to my chamber; I have since continued much indisposed, and times have been so very distressing that I had neither spirit to write a letter nor an opportunity to convey it when written, nor do I yet know by what means I shall get these sheets to your hands.

"I would fain hope that I have said nothing by which your delicacy can be in the least hurt. If I have, I assure you it has been without the least intention, and therefore your candor will lead you to forgive me. I have spoken freely of Congress and of the army; but what I have said is partly from my own knowledge and partly from the information of some respectable members of the former and some of the best officers of the latter. I would not offend the meanest person upon earth; what I say to you I say in confidence to answer what I cannot but deem a most *valuable purpose*. I love my country; I love you; but to the love of truth, the love of peace, and the love of God, I hope I should be enabled if called upon to the trial to sacrifice every other inferior love.

"If the arguments made use of in this letter should have so much influence as to engage you in the glorious work which I have warmly recommended, I shall ever deem my success the highest temporal favor that Providence could grant me. Your interposition and advice I am confident would meet with a favorable reception from the authority under which you act.

"If it should not, you have an infallible recourse still left—negotiate for your country at the head of your army. After all, it may appear presumption as an individual to address himself to you on a subject of such magnitude, or to say what measures would best secure the interest and welfare of a whole continent. The friendly and favorable opinion you have always expressed for me emboldens me to undertake it, and which has greatly added to the weight of this motive. I have been strongly impressed with a sense of duty upon the occasion, which left my conscience uneasy and my heart afflicted till I fully discharged it. I am no enthusiast; the course is new and singular to me; but I could not enjoy one moment's peace till this letter was written. With the most ardent prayers for your spiritual as well as temporal welfare, I am your most obedient and humble friend and servant, Jacob Duche."

The estimation in which Mr. Duche was held before he wrote this letter, by John Adams, who was not particularly friendly to Episcopalians, who as a class were Loyalists (although Washington was one), is here shown. Adams says: "Mr. Duche is one of the most ingenuous men, and of best character, and greatest orator in the Episcopal order upon this continent; yet a zealous friend of liberty and his country.*

In the cold light of truth it now seems quite clear that Americans took up arms before they were in any real danger of oppression, and George III. was persuaded to concede more than all their reasonable demands, but yielded too late to save the integrity of the empire.

We are taught in many of our histories that George III. was a tyrant, seeking to establish despotism, and that Washington rescued and preserved Anglo-Saxon liberty, not only in America, but wherever it existed in the British domains; but this is too extravagant a compliment to the king. We may admit that he was a respectable man in private life, that he acted on principle, as he understood it, in his public career, and that he had some princely accomplishments, but was far from a great man. Certainly he was not in the class of conqueror, nor was he able to commit "a splendid crime." His mother was ever croaking in his ears: "George, be a king!" Thackeray gives us a touching account of the king's last years. All history, he tells us, presents no sadder picture. It is too terrible for tears. Driven from his throne, buffeted by rude hands, his children in revolt, his ending was as pitiful and awful as that of King Lear. "In a lucid moment the Queen entered his room and found him singing and playing on a musical instrument. When he had finished he knelt and prayed for her and for his family, and for the nation, and last for himself. And then tears began to flow down his cheeks, and his reason fled again. Caesar, Henry VIII., and Napoleon tried to establish a dynasty of despots, and failed. As we glance at the figure of George III. and recall the traits of his character, we see that Anglo-Saxon civilization or liberty was in no danger of permanent injury from the last king of England who tried to reign.

"As we review the conflict we are apt to forget that the Americans were not alone in their efforts to throw off the restraint of law and authority of the government during the twenty years preceding the surrender at Yorktown; Wilkes, 'Junius,' and Lord George Gordon surpassed the efforts of Patrick Henry, Sam Adams, and Crispus Attucks, to make life unpleasant for King George. Mobs surged about the streets of London as they did in Boston, defying the law, destroying property, and disturbing the public peace. The house of Lord Mansfield, chief justice of Eng-

* Letters of John Adams to His Wife, Vol. I., p. 24.

land, was wrecked and burned to the ground in the same manner as the home of Thomas Hutchinson, chief justice of Massachusetts, was wrecked and pillaged. Both mobs claimed to act "on principle," and there is a curious likeness in the details of these two acts of violence. It was an age of insurrection, with no political genius able, or in a position, to direct the storm. During the Wilkes riots, in 1768, the civil power in England was reduced to extreme weakness. Lecky tells us "there were great fears that all the bulwarks of order would yield to the strain," and Franklin, then in London, said that if Wilkes had possessed a good character and the king a bad one, Wilkes would have driven George III. from the throne. In 1780, during the Gordon riots, chaos came again to London, and all England was threatened with anarchy. The time was out of joint on both continents, and George III. was not born to set it right. We may be sure there is something more serious than glory in all this turmoil that embittered the most beneficent of civilizing races. Whoever examines the dispute with impartial care, will probably perceive that the time had come for a new adjustment of the constitutional relations of the several parts of the British Empire, but the temper of George III. and the disorderly elements, active both in England and America, were unfavorable to rational treatment of the great problem.

Early in the Revolution it was considered necessary, in order to insure its success, to obtain aid and recognition from the French.

Mr. Silas Deane, of Connecticut, and three agents, were sent to France to feel the pulse of the king and nation upon the subject. They, however, neither acknowledged the agents nor directed them to leave the kingdom.

It was not so with individuals, among whom was M. Beaumarchais, who, on his own account and credit, furnished the United States with twenty thousand stand of arms and one thousand barrels of powder of one hundred pounds weight each. Ten thousand of the muskets were landed at Portsmouth, N. H., and the remainder in some southern State. The first opportunity of testing the qualities of the new French muskets occurred September 19, 1777, which engagement led up to the battle of Saratoga October 7, which terminated in the convention with Burgoyne October 17, 1777. Major Caleb Stark, the eldest son of Gen. John Stark, who was present in these actions, says: "I firmly believe that unless these arms had been thus timely furnished to the Americans, Burgoyne would have made an easy march to Albany. What then? My pen almost refuses to record the fact that these arms have never been paid for to this day. When the war ended, application was made to Congress for payment, which was refused on the frivolous pretext that they were a present from the French king. The claim was referred to the United States attorney-general, who reported in substance that he could find no evidence of their having been paid for, or that they were presented as a gift by the court of France.

Supposing the most favorable plea of Congress to be true, that there was an underhand connivance by France to furnish the arms, or the king had thought proper to deny it, is it just or magnanimous for the United States to refuse payment? Suppose the arms were clearly a "gift" bestowed upon us in our poverty, ought not a high-minded people to restore the value of that gift with ten-fold interest, when their benevolent friend has become poor, and they have waxed wealthy and strong?

Congress, skulking behind their sovereignty, still refused payment. Yet the cries of Beaumarchais, reduced to poverty by the French Revolution, have not been heeded."*

The action of Congress concerning the Saratoga Convention was equally base. The whole number of prisoners surrendered by Burgoyne was 5791. The force of the Americans was, according to a statement which Gates furnished to Burgoyne, 13,222. The terms of the Convention was that Burgoyne's troops were to march out of their camp with all the honors of war, the artillery to be moved to the banks of the Hudson, and there to be left, together with the soldiers' arms; that a free passage should be granted the troops to Great Britain, on condition of their not serving again during the war; that the army should march to the neighborhood of Boston by the most expeditious and convenient route, and not delayed when transport should arrive to receive them; that every care should be taken for the proper subsistence of the troops till they should be embarked. Although Congress ratified the terms of the Convention entered into by General Burgoyne and Gates, yet they violated them in the most perfidious manner. Many Americans now regard this as the most disgraceful act ever perpetrated by the United States. There was not the slightest excuse for this treachery. When the British ministry charged Congress with positive perfidy, Congress added insult to injury by charging the ministry with "meditated perfidy," for they "believed the British would break their parole if released." After the arrival of the troops at Boston they were quartered at Cambridge, where they were subjected to the most cruel and inhuman treatment. Officers and soldiers were shot down and bayoneted in the most cold-blooded manner without the slightest provocation. If the officers resented any insults, they were sent to Worcester and treated as felons. They were charged the most exorbitant prices for food. Burgoyne alone was allowed to go home on parole; all the other officers and men were marched into the interior of Virginia, where they were kept in confinement for five years.†

There is probably not one American in a thousand that knows the origin and meaning of Washington's advice to his countrymen against entering into "entangling foreign alliances," and the often quoted phrase: "French Spoliation Claims," and yet the two are inseparably connected, and form a most important phase in the early history of the United States. American historians have passed over this episode, fearing that

* Memoir of Gen. John Stark, by his son Caleb Stark, pp. 356-7-8.
† "Travels Through the Interior Parts of America," by Thomas Aubury.

it would bring odium on the "Fathers of the Revolution." By the treaty made by Franklin with France, in which she recognized the United States and by which means American independence was secured, it was agreed that the United States should assist France in foreign complications in which she might be involved, and furthermore to protect her possessions in the West Indies. This was the first treaty made by the United States. When the time came for putting these pledges into force, the United States refused to act.

"The expense of the war of the Revolution was as much, if not more, to France, than to the United States, and it is a matter of historical truth that the expenses incurred in this war by France bankrupted the nation and hurried on the terrible events which convulsed the world from the commencement of the French Revolution until the battle of Waterloo. During all this distress and disaster, the Americans were chuckling in their sleeves, and wasting the treasures of the old world to embellish the half-fledged cities of the new world. Gratitude is a virtue often spoken of with apparent sincerity, but not so frequently exhibited in practice." This is the language of a well-known Revolutionary officer.* Therefore, the United States acted in a most shameful and disgraceful manner in violating the first treaty she ever entered into, through which she secured her independence; she did not give the French that assistance she had agreed to give by treaty, but remained neutral and indifferent, while England seized upon the larger part of the French colonies in the West Indies. The base ingratitude of the United States exasperated the French, so they issued orders to seize and destroy American property wherever found. Several naval engagements between the late allies ensued, and 898 vessels were seized by the French government or were destroyed by its cruisers, prior to the year 1800. Hence, when Ellsworth, Van Murray and Davie, the commissioners appointed by the United States to negotiate with France, and to settle the dispute, asked for damages for the seizure and destruction of American vessels, the French foreign minister turned upon them with the assertion that in performing her part of the Franklin treaty of 1778, France had spent $28,000,000, and had sacrificed the lives of thousands of her people, simply for the purpose of gaining the independence for the United States. All it had asked had been the friendship and assistance of the United States in the manner provided in this treaty. Instead of meeting these claims and requiting the generosity of France in the way such conduct deserved, the United States had ignored its obligations, and now came forward and advanced a petty claim for money, utterly forgetful of how much France had sacrificed in its behalf.

As might be supposed, there was no answer that could be made to this assertion, and hence the new treaty then drawn up, in which the two states agreed to renounce respectively whatever pretensions they might have had to claims one against the other, was ratified by the Senate, and

* "Letter of Major Caleb Stark in Memoir of General John Stark," p. 364.

promulgated by President Jefferson December 21, 1801, thus relieving France of all responsibility for damages caused by her cruisers prior to 1800, and throwing the responsibility of liquidating these demands upon the United States government—a responsibility it succeeded in avoiding for a hundred years, as it succeeded in avoiding the demands which the French government could and did make upon it to defend French West India possessions. These were the "entangling foreign alliances" referred to by Washington.

Bills granting payment of these claims, which originally amounted to $12,676,000, passed Congress twice, and were vetoed first by President Polk and then by President Pierce. If ever there was a just claim brought before Congress, these French spoliation claims deserve the title, and it is a historical disgrace to the government of the United States that the payment of them was delayed for nearly a hundred years.*

* During Cleveland's administrations a bill was passed allowing claimants to present claims for adjudication to the amount of their face value. If interest was added, they would exceed $100,000,000. The owners of the 898 vessels destroyed, who were called upon to make this sacrifice as a means of relieving the government from a great responsibility, in many cases were reduced to poverty by the duplicity of the government, and even now with this scant justice, there are many that find it very difficult to prove their claim, so long a time has elapsed, and many are dead witout legal representation.

CHAPTER VII.

INDIANS IN THE REVOLUTION.

The writers of American histories severely condemn the British government for employing Indians in the war of the Revolution as well as in 1812, and give unstinted praise to the Americans for humanity in refusing to make use of the warlike but undisciplined and cruel Indian as an ally in the activities of a military campaign. Either an attempt is made to suppress the whole truth of this matter, or the writers have failed in their duty to thoroughly investigate sources of history easily accessible to the honest historian. .

The fact is, that in the incipient stage of the Revolutionary war, overtures were made by the political disturbers and leading instigators of trouble to win over to the side of the American party the fiercest, if not the most numerous Indian nation on the North American continent.

From Concord, on the fourth of April, 1775, the Provincial Congress thought fit, with cunning prudence, to address the sachem of the Mohawks, with the rest of the Iroquois tribes, in the following words:

"Brother, they have made a law to establish the religion of the pope in Canada, which lies near you. We much fear some of your children may be induced, instead of worshipping the only true God, to pay his due to images, made with their own hands."*

Here, then, a religious reason was advanced, in lieu of the real one, why the Indians should oppose the British, by whom they had always been generously treated. The response to the insinuating address was not encouraging. May it not be assumed that these Indians had already experienced some of the same kind of love, generosity and good faith, as later every tribe has received from every government at Washington, from the days of the first president to the latest, through the past "century of dishonor."

Before the 19th of April, the Provincial Congress had authorized the enlistment of a company of Stockbridge (Massachusetts) Indians. These Indians were used by the Americans during the siege of Boston. A letter, dated July 9, 1775, says: "Yesterday afternoon some barges were sounding the Charles River near its mouth, but were soon obliged to row off by our Indians, fifty in number, who are encamped near that place."

On the 21st of June, two of the Indians killed four of the regulars with their bows and arrows, and plundered them. Frothingham says

* American Archives, series 1, p. 1350.

COLONEL MIFFLIN'S INTERVIEW WITH THE CAUGHNAWAGA INDIANS.

At Watertown during the siege of Boston, the Revolutionists endeavored to obtain their assistance.

the British complained, and with reason, of their mode of warfare.

Lieut. Carter, writes July 2, 1775: "Never had the British army so ungenerous an enemy to oppose. They send their riflemen, five or six at a time, who conceal themselves behind trees, etc., till an opportunity presents itself of taking a shot at our advanced sentries, which done, they immediately retreat."*

During the siege of Boston, John Adams visited Washington's camp at Watertown, and wrote the following letter to his wife, which goes to prove the efforts made by the Americans to enlist the Canadian Indians in their cause, and which they afterwards complained so bitterly of the British for doing:

"Watertown, 24 January, 1776.

"I dined at Colonel Mifflin's with the general and lady, and a vast collection of other company, among whom were six or seven sachems and warriors of the French Caughnawaga Indians, with several of their wives and children. A savage feast they made of it, yet were very polite in the Indian style. One of the sachems is an Englishman, a native of this colony, whose name was Williams, captivated in infancy, with his mother, and adopted by some kind squaw."†

Many attempts were made by the Americans to use the Indians. Montgomery made use of them in his Canadian expedition.

In April, 1776, Washington wrote to Congress, urging their employment in the army, and reported on July 13th that, without special authority, he had directed General Schuyler to engage the Six Nations on the best terms he and his colleagues could procure, and again submitting the propriety of engaging the Eastern Indians. John Adams thought "we need not be so delicate as to refuse the assistance of Indians, provided we cannot keep them neutral." A treaty was exchanged with the Eastern Indians on July 17, 1776, whereby they agreed to furnish six hundred for a regiment, which was to be officered by the whites. As a result of this, the Massachusetts Council subsequently reported that seven Penobscot Indians—all that could be procured—were enlisted in October for one year.‡ It is interesting to remember, in this connection, that the courteous and chivalrous Lafayette raised a troop of Indians to fight the British and the Tories, though his reputation has been saved by the utter and almost ludicrous failure of his attempt. ‖

When all this had been done, it needed the forgetfulness and the blind hypocrisy of passion to denounce the king to the world for having "endeavored to bring on the inhabitants of our frontiers, the merciless Indian savage." Yet Americans have never had the self-respect to erase this charge from a document generally printed in the fore-front of the

* American Archives, Series 1, p 1350.
† Frothingham Siege of Boston, p. 212. "Letters of John Adams to his Wife Vol. I., p. 79.
‡ Windsor Nar. and Crit. His. Vol. VI., 655, 657.
‖ Essays in American History, 178.

Constitution and Laws, and with which every schoolboy is sedulously made familiar.

The Revolutionists failed to enlist the Indians in their cause, for the Indian and the Colonist were bitter and irreconcilable foes. The Indian had long scores to pay, not upon the English nation or the English army, but upon the American settler who had stolen his lands, shot his sons, and debauched his daughters. It is well here to remember the speech of Logan, the Cayuga chief, on the occasion of the signing of the treaty of peace in 1764, at the close of the Pontiac Conspiracy. Logan said: "I appeal to any white man to say if ever he entered Logan's cabin hungry and he gave him not meat; if ever he came cold and naked and he clothed him not. Such was my love of the white man that my countrymen in passing my cabin said: 'Logan is the friend of the white man.' I have even thought to have lived with you but for the injuries you did me last spring, when in cold blood and unprovoked, you murdered all the relations of Logan, not sparing even my women and children. There runs not a drop of my blood in the veins of any living creature. This called for revenge. I have sought it I have killed many. I have fully glutted my vengeance." Logan's family, being on a visit to a family of the name of Greathouse, was murdered by them and their associates under circumstances of great brutality and cowardice. It is known that in revenge, Logan took over 30 scalps with his own hand. And others than Indians had old scores to wipe out. Many loyalists who desired to be left alone in peace had been tarred and feathered by their former friends and fellow-townsmen; were driven from their homes and hunted like wild beasts; imprisoned, maimed, and compelled to suffer every kind of indignity. In many cases fathers, brothers and sons were hanged, because they insisted on remaining loyal to their country. Therefore it is not to be wondered at that many of these loyalists sought a terrible revenge against those who had maltreated them. If the loyalists of New York, Georgia and the Carolinas resolved to join the Indians and wreak vengeance on their fellow countrymen at Wyoming and Cherry Valley, and to take part in the raids of Tyron and Arnold, there was a rude cause for their retaliating. Their actions have been held up to the execration of posterity as being exceptionally barbarous, and as far surpassing in cruelty the provocative actions of the revolutionists, Sullivan's campaign through the Indian country being conveniently forgotten. There was not much to choose between a cowboy and a skinner, and very little difference between Major Ferguson's command and that of Marion and Sumpter. There were no more orderly or better behaved troops in either army than Simcoe's Queen's Rangers. There can be no doubt that the action of the loyalists have been grossly exaggerated, or at least dwelt upon as dreadful scenes of depravity, to form a background for the heroism and fortitude of the "patriotic" party whose misdeeds are passed lightly over. The methods of the growth of popular mythology have been the same in America as in Greece or Rome. The

CARTOON ILLUSTRATING FRANKLIN'S DIABOLICAL SCALP STORY.

From an old print in the possession of the Bostonian Society.

gods of one party have become the devils of the other. The haze of distance has thrown a halo around the American leaders—softening outlines, obscuring faults, while those of the British and the loyalists have grown with the advanced years.*

The following brief entry in a diary, will show that among the American forces savage customs found place: "On Monday, the 30th, sent out a party for some dead Indians. Toward morning found them, and skinned two of them from their hips down, for boot legs; one pair for the major, the other for myself."†

It has been the policy of American historians and their echoes in England to bring disrepute upon the Indians and the British government who employed them, and not only to magnify actual occurrences, but sometimes, when facts were wanting, to draw upon imagination for such deeds of ferocity and bloodshed as might serve to keep alive the strongest feelings of indignation against the mother country, and thus influence men to take the field for revenge who had not already been driven thither by the impulse of their sense of patriotism. Dr. Franklin himself did not think it unworthy of his antecedents and position to employ these methods to bring disrepute on the British. The "deliberate fiction for political purposes," by Franklin, were written as facts. Never before was there such diabolical fiction written as his well known scalp story, long believed and recently revived in several books purporting to be "authentic history." The details were so minute and varied as to create a belief that they were entirely true. For a century supposed to be authentic, it has since been ascertained to be a publication from the pen of Dr. Franklin for political purposes. It describes minutely the capture from the Seneca Indians of eight bales of scalps, which were being sent the governor of Canada, to be forwarded by him as a gift to the "Great King." The description of the contents of each bale was given with such an air of plausibility as to preclude a suspicion that it was fictitious. The following are a few brief abstracts from this story: "No. 1 contains forty-three scalps of Congress soldiers, also sixty-two farmers, killed in their houses in the night time. No. 2 contains ninety-eight farmers killed in their houses in the day time. No. 3 contains ninety-seven farmers killed in the fields in the day time. No. 4 contains 102 farmers, mixed, 18 burnt alive, after being scalped; sixty-seven being greyheads, and one clergyman. No. 5 containing eighty-eight scalps of woman's hair, long-braided in Indian fashion. No. 6 containing 193 boys' scalps of various ages. No. 7, 211 girls' scalps, big and little. No. 8, this package is a mixture of all the varieties above mentioned, to the number of 122, with a box of birch bark, containing twenty-nine infants' scalps of various sizes."‡

With the bales of scalps was a speech addressed to the "Great King." One of the most cruel and bloodthirsty acts of the Americans was

* Essays in American History, 176, 177.
† Proceedings, N. J. His. Soc. II, 31.
‡ Life of Brandt. Appendix No. 1, Vol. I.

the massacre of the Moravian Indians. "From love of peace they had advised those of their own color who were bent on war to desist from it. They were also led from humanity, to inform the white people of their danger, when they knew their settlements were about to be invaded. One hundred and sixty Americans crossed the Ohio and put to death these harmless, inoffensive people, though they made no resistance. In conformity with their religious principles these Moravians submitted to their hard fate without attempting to destroy their murderers. Upward of ninety of these pacific people were killed by men who, while they called themselves Christians, were more deserving of the names of savages than were their unresisting victims."[*]

[*] Dr. Ramsay's His. U. S., Vol. II., Chapter XIX, pp. 330, 332.

CHAPTER VIII.

THE EXPULSION OF THE LOYALISTS AND THE SETTLEMENT OF CANADA.

The Huguenots and the proscribed of the French Revolution found sanctuary as welcome guests in England and the English colonies.

The Moors were well treated when banished from Spain; the Revocation of the Edict of Nantes was civil death to all Huguenots; the Americans made the treaty of peace of 1783 worse than civil death to all Loyalists.

The Americans, at the inception and birth of their republic, violated every precept of Christianity and of a boasted civilization, even to confiscating the estates of helpless women. For all time it is to be a part of American history that the last decade of the eighteenth century saw the most cruel and vindictive acts of spoliation recorded in modern history.

At the treaty of peace, 1783, the banishment and extermination of the Loyalists was a foregone conclusion. The bitterest words ever uttered by Washington were in reference to them: "He could see nothing better for them than to recommend suicide." Neither Congress nor state governments made any recommendation that humane treatment should be meted out to these Loyalists. John Adams had written from Amsterdam that he would "have hanged his own brother had he taken part against him."*

At the close of the war the mob were allowed to commit any outrage or atrocity, while the authorities in each state remained apparently indifferent. An example of Loyalist ill-treatment is to be found in a letter written October 22, 1783, to a Boston friend, and preserved in New York City manual, 1870:—

"The British are leaving New York every day, and last week there came one of the d——d refugees from New York to a place called Wall Kill, in order to make a tarry with his parents, where he was taken into custody immediately. His head and eyebrows were shaved, tarred and feathered, a hog-yoke put on his neck, and a cowbell thereon; upon his head a very high hat and feathers were set, well plumed with tar, and a sheet of paper in front with a man drawn with two faces, representing the traitor Arnold and the devil."

Some American writers have been extremely severe upon Americans who served in the royal armies. Such condemnation is certainly illogical and unjust. They must have reasoned they were fighting to save their

* Address to the "United Empire Loyalists," by Edward Harris, Toronto, 1897.

country from mob rule, from the domination of demagogues and traitors, and to preserve to it what, until then, all had agreed to be the greatest of blessings, the connection with Great Britain, the privilege of being Englishmen, heirs of all the free institutions which were embodied in a "great and glorious constitution." If the Loyalists reasoned in this manner, we cannot blame them, unless we are ready to maintain the proposition that the cause of every revolution is necessarily so sacred that those who do not sympathize with it should abstain from opposing it.

Very early in the Revolution the disunionists tried to drive the Loyalists into the rebel militia or into the Continental army by fines, and by obliging them to hire substitutes. The families of men who had fled from the country to escape implication in the impending war were obliged to hire substitutes, and they were fined for the misdeeds of the mercenary whom they had engaged. Fines were even imposed upon neutral and unoffending persons for not preventing their families from entering the British service. If the fines were refused, the property was recklessly sold to the amount of the fine and costs of action. Loyalists convicted of entering the enemy's lines could be fined as high as 2000 pounds, and even the unsuccessful attempt to enter might be punished by a fine of 1000 pounds.* If the property of the offender failed to answer for his offence, he became subject to corporal punishment, whipping, branding, cropping of ears, and exposure in the pillory being resorted to in some of the states.

The Disunionists had early a covetous eye upon the property of the Loyalists. The legislative bodies hastened to pass such laws as would prevent those suspected of Loyalism from transferring their property, real or personal, by real or pretended sale. Friends who tried to guard the property of refugees nailed up the doors that led to the room containing valuable furniture, but were obliged by bullying committeemen to remove their barricades and give up their treasures.

The members of one wealthy refugee's family were reduced in their housekeeping to broken chairs and teacups, and to dipping the water out of an iron skillet into a pot, which they did as cheerfully as if they were using a silver urn. The furniture had been removed, though the family picture still hung in the blue room, and the harpsichord stood in the passage way to be abused by the children who passed through. These two aristocratic ladies were obliged to use their coach-house as a dining-room, and the "fowl-house" as their bed chamber. The picture continues: "In character the old lady looks as majestic even there, and dresses with as much elegance as if she were in a palace."† This mansion was General Putnam's headquarters at the battle of Bunker Hill, and was afterward confiscated.

When the treaty of peace was signed, the question of amnesty and compensation for the Loyalists was long and bitterly discussed. Even

* "Acts of New Jersey," Oct. 8, 1778, p. 60.
† James Murray, Loyalist, p. 245, 253.

the French minister had urged it. John Adams, one of the commission, favored compensating "the wretches, how little soever they deserved it, nay, how much soever they deserve the contrary."*

The commission hesitated "to saddle" America with the Loyalists because they feared the opposition at home, especially by the individual states. The British demand had been finally met with the mere promise that Congress would recommend to the states a conciliatory policy with reference to the Loyalists. This solution neither satisfied the Loyalists nor the more chivalrous Englishmen. They declared that the provision concerning the Loyalists was "precipitate, impolitic," and cruelly neglectful of their American friends.† But all of this cavilling was unreasonable and hasty, for England had gotten for the Loyalists the utmost attainable in the treaty, and later proved honorable and generous in the highest degree by compensating the Loyalists out of her own treasury—an act only excelled in the next century by the purchase and emancipation of all the slaves in the British Empire, for which the people of Great Britain taxed only themselves—the most generous act ever performed by any nation in the history of mankind.

In spite of the recommendation of Congress which had been made in accordance with the terms of the treaty, confiscation still went on actively. Governors of the states were urged to exchange lists of proscribed persons, that no Loyalists might find a resting-place in the United States, and in every state they were disfranchised, while in many localities they were tarred and feathered, driven from town and warned never to return again. Some were murdered and maltreated in the most horrible manner. Thousands of inconspicuous Loyalists did, nevertheless, succeed in remaining in the larger cities, where their identity was lost, and they were not the objects of jealous social and political exclusion as in the small town. In some localities where they were in the majority, the hostile minority was not able to wreak its vengeance.

With the treaty of peace there came a rush for British American territory. The numbers were increased in Canada to some 25,000 during the next few years, and those in Nova Scotia and other British territory swelled the number to 60,000.

Most of these exiles became, in one way or another, a temporary expense to the British government, and the burden was borne honorably and ungrudgingly. The care began during the war. The Loyalists who aided Burgoyne were provided with homes in Canada, and before the close of 1779 nearly a thousand refugees were cared for in houses and barracks and given fuel, household furniture, and even pensioned with money. After the peace, thousands of exiles at once turned to the British government for temporary support. The vast majority had lost but little, and asked only for land and supplies to start life with. The minority

* John Adams' Works, Vol. IX., p. 516.
† Stevens' "Facsimiles," 1054.

who had lost lands, offices and incomes, demanded indemnity. As for the members of the humbler class, the government ordered that there should be given 500 acres of land to heads of families, 300 acres to single men, and each township in the new settlements was to have 2000 acres for church purposes and 1000 for schools. Building material and tools, an axe, spade, hoe and plow, were furnished each head of a family. Even clothing and food were issued to the needy, and as late as 1785 there were 26,000 entitled to rations. Communities were equipped with grindstones and the machinery for grist and saw mills. In this way $5,000,000 were spent to get Nova Scotia well started, and in Upper Canada, besides the three million acres given to the Loyalist, some $4,000,000 were expended for this benefit before 1787.

But there was a far greater burden assumed by the British government in granting the compensation asked for by those who had sacrificed everything to their loyalty. Those who had lost offices or professional practice were, in many cases, cared for by the gift of lucrative offices under the government, and Loyalist military officers were put on half pay. It is said with truth that the defeated government dealt with the exiled and fugitive Loyalists with a far greater liberality than the United States bestowed upon their victorious army.

After, the peace, over five thousand Loyalists submitted claims for losses, usually through agents appointed by the refugees from each American colony. In July of 1783, a commission of five members was appointed by Parliament to classify the losses and services of the Loyalists. They examined the claims with an impartial and judicial severity. The claimant entered the room alone with the commissioners and, after telling his services and losses, was rigidly questioned concerning fellow claimants as well as himself. The claimant then submitted a written and sworn statement of his losses. After the results of both examinations were critically scrutinized, the judges made the award. In the whole course of their work, they examined claims to the amount of forty million of dollars, and ordered nineteen millions to be paid.

If to the cost of establishing the Loyalists in Nova Scotia and Canada we add the compensation granted in money, the total amount expended by the British government for their American adherents was at least thirty million dollars. There is evidence that the greatest care that human ingenuity could devise was exercised to make all these awards in a fair and equitable manner. The members of the commission were of unimpeachable honesty. Nevertheless there was much complaint by the Loyalists because of the partial failure of giving the loyal exiles a new start in life. The task was no easy one—to transfer a disheartened people to a strange land and a trying climate, and let them begin life anew. But when, years later, they had made of the land of this exile a mighty member of the British empire, they began to glory in the days of trial through which they had passed.

At a council meeting held at Quebec, November 9, 1789, an order was passed for "preserving a register of the Loyalists that had adhered to the unity of the empire, and joined the Royal Standard previous to the treaty of peace in 1783, to the end that their posterity may be distinguished from future settlers in the rank, registers, and rolls of the militia of their respective districts, as proper objects for preserving and showing the fidelity and conduct so honorable to their ancestors for distinguished benefit and privileges."

Today their descendants are organized as the United Empire Loyalists, and count it an honor that their ancestors suffered persecution and exile rather than yield the principle and idea of union with Great Britain.

The cause of the Loyalists failed, but their stand was a natural one and was just and noble. They were the prosperous and contended men —the men without a grievance. Conservatism was the only policy that one could expect of them. Men do not rebel to rid themselves of prosperity. Prosperous men seek to conceive prosperity. The Loyalist obeyed his nature, but as events proved, chose the ill-fated cause, and when the struggle ended, his prosperity had fled, and he was an outcast and an exile.

If, when George III. and his government recognized the independence of the thirteen colonies, the Loyalists had been permitted to remain here and become, if they would, American citizens, the probabilities are that, long before this time, an expansion would have taken place in the national domain which would have brought under its control the entire American continent north of the United States, an extension brought about in an entirely peaceful and satisfactory manner. The method of exclusion adopted peopled Canada, so far as its English-speaking inhabitants were concerned, with those who went from the United States as political exiles, and who carried with them to their new homes an ever-burning sense of personal wrong and a bitter hatred of those who had abused them.

The indifference shown to treaty obligations by Congress and the states, and the secret determination to eradicate everything British from the country, is now known to have been the deliberate, well-considered policy of the founders of the Republic.

This old legacy of wrongdoing has been a barrier in the way of a healthful northern development of the United States. The contentions which gave rise to these hostile feelings have been forgotten, but the feelings themselves have long outlived the causes which gave rise to them.

CHAPTER IX.
THE WAR OF 1812 AND THE ATTEMPTED CONQUEST OF CANADA.

When the Revolutionary War had ended came the long twenty-three years' war in which Great Britain, for the most part, single-handed, fought for the freedom of Europe against the most colossal tyranny ever devised by a victorious general. No nation in the history of the world carried on a war so stubborn, so desperate, so costly, so vital. Had Great Britain failed, what would now be the position of the world? At the very time when Britain's need was the sorest, when every ship, every soldier and sailor that she could find was needed to break down the power of the man who had subjugated all Europe except Russia and Great Britain, the United States, the land of boasted liberty, did her best to cripple the liberating armies by proclaiming war against Britain in the hour of her sorest need.

Napoleon was at the height of his power, with an army collected at Boulogne for the invasion of England. England was growing exhausted by the contest. Her great Prime Minister, Pitt, had died broken hearted. Every indication was favorable to the conquest of Canada by the United States and therewith the extinction of all British interests on the western continent.

In the motherland it seemed, to the popular imagination, that on the other side of the Atlantic lived an implacable enemy, whose rancor was greater than their boasted love of liberty. Fisher Ames, who was regarded by his party as its wisest counsellor and chief ornament, expresses this general feeling on their part in a letter to Mr. Quincy, dated Dedham, Dec. 6, 1807, in which he says: "Our cabinet takes council of the mob, and it is now a question whether hatred of Great Britain and the reproach fixed even upon violent men, if they will not proceed in their violence, will not overcome the fears of the maritime states, and of the planters in Congress. The usual levity of a democracy has not appeared in regard to Great Britain. We have been steady in our hatred of her, and when popular passions are not worn out by time, but argument, they must, I should think, explode in war."*

The action of the United States in declaring war against Great Britain when she was most sorely pressed in fighting for the liberty of mankind is best set forth in the famous speech of Josiah Quincy, delivered before Congress on the 5th of January, 1813. It was, as he himself says of it, "most direct, pointed and searching as to the motive and conduct of our rulers. It exposed openly and without reserve or fear the iniquity of

* Life of Josiah Quincy, p. 119.

the proposed invasion of Canada. I was sparing of neither language nor illustration." Its author, on reading it over in his old age, might well say that "he shrunk not from the judgment of after times." Its invective is keen, its sarcasm bitter, its denunciations heavy and severe, but the facts from which they derive their sting or their weight are clearly stated and sustained.

As a means of carrying on the war, he denounces the invasion of Canada as "cruel, wanton, senseless, and wicked—an attempt to compel the mother country to our terms by laying waste an innocent province which had never injured us, but had long been connected with us by habits of good neighborhood and mutual good offices." He said "that the embarrassment of our relations with Great Britain and the keeping alive between this country and that of a root of bitterness has been, is, and will continue to be, a main principle of the policy of this American Cabinet."

The Democratic Party having attained power by fostering the old grudge against England, and having maintained itself in power by force of that antipathy, a consent to the declaration of war had been extorted from the reluctant Madison as the condition precedent of his nomination for a second term of office."

When war against Great Britain was proposed at the last session, there were thousands in these United States, and I confess to you I was myself among the number, who believed not one word of the matter, I put my trust in the old-fashioned notions of common sense and common prudence. That a people which had been more than twenty years at peace should enter upon hostilities against a people which had been twenty years at war, the idea seemed so absurd that I never once entertained it as possible. It is easy enough to make an excuse for any purpose. When a victim is destined to be immolated, every hedge presents sticks for the sacrifice. The lamb that stands at the mouth of the stream will always trouble the water if you take the account of the wolf who stands at the source of it. We have heard great lamentation about the disgrace of our arms on the frontier. Why, sir, the disgrace of our arms on the frontier is terrestrial glory in comparison with the disgrace of the attempt. Mr. Speaker, when I contemplate the character and consequences of this invasion of Canada, when I reflect on its criminality and its danger to the peace and liberty of this once happy country, I thank the great Author and Source of all virtue that, through His grace, that section of country in which I have the happiness to reside, is in so great a degree free from the iniquity of this trangression. I speak it with pride. The people of that section have done what they could to vindicate themselves and their children from the burden of their sin.

Surely if any nation had a claim for liberal treatment from another, it was the British nation from the American. After the discovery of the error of the American government in relation to the repeal of the Berlin and Milan Decrees in November, 1810, they had declared war against her on the supposition that she had refused to repeal her orders in council after the French Decrees were in fact revoked, whereas it now appears that they were in fact not revoked. Surely the knowledge of this error was followed by an instant and anxious desire to redress the resulting injury. No, sir, nothing occurred. On the contrary the question of impressment is made the basis of continuing the war. They renewed hostilities. They rushed upon Canada. Nothing would satisfy them but blood.

I know, Mr. Speaker, that while I utter these things, a thousand tongues and a thousand pens are preparing without doors to overwhelm me, if possible, by their pestiferous gall. Already I hear in the air the sound of "Traitor," "British Agent," "British Gold!" and all those changes of calumny by which the imagination of the mass of men are affected and by which they are prevented from listening to what is true and receiving what is reasonable. *

As will be noticed in the foregoing extract from Josiah Quincy's celebrated speech, New England refused to take any part in the war. In fact, it must be said in their favor that they refused absolutely to send any troops to aid in the invasion of Canada. They regarded the pretexts on which the war had been declared with contemptuous incredulity, believing them to be but thin disguises of its real object. That object they believed to be the gratification of the malignant hatred the slave-holding states bore toward communities of free and intelligent labor, by the destruction of their wealth and prosperity.

A town meeting was held in Boston at Faneuil Hall on June 11, 1812, at which it was "Resolved: That in the opinion of this town, it is of the last importance to the interest of this country to avert the threatened calamity of war with Great Britain," etc. A committee of twelve was appointed to take into consideration the present alarming state of our public affairs, and report what measures, in their opinion, it is proper for the town to adopt at this momentous crisis.

The committee reported in part as follows: "While the temper and views of the national administration are intent upon war, an expression of the sense of this town, will of itself be quite ineffectual either to avert this deplorable calamity or to accelerate a return of peace, but believing as we do that an immense majority of the people are invincibly averse from conflict equally unnecessary and menacing ruin to themselves and their posterity, convinced as we are that the event will overwhelm them with astonishment and dismay, we cannot but trust that a general expression of the voice of the people would satisfy Congress that those of their representatives who had voted in favor of war, have not truly represented the wishes of their constituents, and thus arrest the tendency of their measures to this extremity."

Had the policy of government been inclined towards resistance to the pretentions of the belligerants by open war, there could be neither pol-

* Life of Josiah Quincy, pp. 256, 280, 281, 282, 283, 286, 287, 288, 289, 291.

icy, reason or justice in singling out Great Britain as the exclusive object of hostility. If the object of war is merely to vindicate our honor, why is it not declared against the first aggressor? If the object is defense and success, why is it to be waged against the adversary most able to annoy and least likely to yield? Why, at the moment when England explicitly declares her order in council repealed whenever France shall rescind her decrees, is the one selected for an enemy and the other courted as a conqueror? "Under present circumstances there will be no scope for valor, no field for enterprise, no chance for success, no hope of national glory, no prospect but of a war against Great Britain, in aid of the common enemy of the human race, and in the end an inglorious peace."

The resolution recommended by the committee was adopted and it was voted that the selectmen be requested to transmit a copy thereof to each town in this commonwealth."

At a town meeting held August 6, 1812, the following resolutions were passed: "That the inhabitants of the town of Boston have learned with heartfelt concern that in the City of Baltimore a most outrageous attack, the result of deliberate combinations has been made upon the freedom of opinion and the liberty of the press. An infuriated mob has succeeded in accomplishing its sanguinary purpose by the destruction of printing presses and other property, by violating the sanctuary of dwelling houses, breaking open the public prison and dragging forth from the protection of civil authority the victims of their ferocious pursuit, guilty of no crime but the expression of their opinions and completing the tissue of their enormities by curses, wounds and murders, accompanied by the most barbarous and shocking indignities."

"In the circumstances attending the origin, the progress, and the catastrophe of this bloody scene, we discern with painful emotion, not merely an aggravation of the calamities of the present unjust and ruinous war, but a prelude to the dissolution of all free government, and the establishing of a reign of terror. Mobs, by reducing men to a state of nature, defeat the object of every social compact. The sober citizen who trembles in beholding the fury of the mob, seeks refuge from its dangers by joining in its acclamations. The laws are silenced. New objects of violence are discovered. The government of the nation and the mob government change places with each other. The mob erects its horrid crest over the ruins of liberty, of property, of the domestic relations of life and of civil institutions."*

The foregoing is a fair example of the feelings shown in New England towards this unjustifiable war, and which culminated in the famous Hartford convention which was accused of designing an organized resistance to the general government, and a separation of the New England states from the Union if the war was not stopped. The resolutions condemning the Baltimore mob also show the change in public opinion that had taken place in Boston during the thirty-seven years that had elapsed

* Boston Town Records, City Document No. 115, pp. 317, 318, 319, 320, 321, 322.

since the commencement of the Revolution in Boston, which was inaugurated by mob violence, participated in by many who, by the strange irony of fate, by these resolutions condemned their own actions.

Mr. Quincy did not stand alone among his countrymen of that day in a general championship of Great Britain in the hour of her extremity. The Reverend John Sylvester, John Gardner, rector of Trinity church, Boston, a man of great scholarship, among others lifted up his voice in protest against unfair treatment of Great Britain by the government and people of the United States.

In a sermon at this time he said: "Though submissive and even servile to France, to Great Britain we are eager to display our hatred and hurl our defiance. Every petty dispute which may happen between an American captain and a British officer is magnified into a national insult. The land of our fathers, whence is derived the best blood of the nation, the country to which we are chiefly indebted for our laws and knowledge is stigmatized as a nest of pirates, plunderers and assassins. We entice away her seamen, the very sinews of her power.

"We refuse to restore them on application; we issue hostile proclamations; we interdict her ships of war from the common rights to hospitality; we have non-importation acts; we lay embargoes; we refuse to ratify a treaty in which she has made great concessions to us; we dismiss her envoy of peace who came purposely to apologize for an act unauthorized by her government; we commit every act of hostility against her in proportion to our means and station. Observe the conduct of the two nations and our strange conduct. France robs us and we love her; Britain courts us and we hate her."

It was during the summer of 1812, when Jefferson truly stated that every continental power of importance, except Russia, was allied with Napoleon, and Great Britain stood alone to oppose them, for Russia could not aid her if she would—her commerce paralyzed, her factories closed, commerce and her people threatened with famine. It was at this moment of dire extremity that Madison chose to launch his war message. His action was eagerly supported by Jefferson, Clay and Calhoun, and the younger members of his party.

Jefferson wrote to Duane: "The acquisition of Canada this year (1812) as far as the neighborhood of Quebec, will be a mere matter of marching, and will give us experience for the attack on Halifax, the next and the final expulsion of England from the American continent. Perhaps they will burn New York or Boston. If they do, we must burn the city of London, not by expensive fleets of Congreve rockets, but by employing a hundred or two Jack-the-painters, whom nakedness, famine, desperation and hardened vice will abundantly furnish from among themselves."*

---

* "Jack-the-painter" was a miscreant employed by Silas Deane, one of the U. S. Commissioners to France, and the colleague of Dr. Franklin, to burn the docks at Bristol. He partially succeeded and was hanged for the crime, a far less infamous one than that advocated by Jefferson, the champion of the rights of man.

BURNING OF NEWARK, CANADA, BY UNITED STATES TROOPS.

In retaliation for the destruction of the Public building at Toronto and Newark, and other villages, the public building at Washington was burned.

Three months after making this prediction, the surrender of the United States invading force to the British General Brock, or as Jefferson preferred to style it, "the detestable treason of Hull," "excited," he writes, "a deep anxiety in all breasts." A few months later we find him lamenting that "our war on the land was commenced most inauspiciously. This has resulted, he thinks, from the employment of generals before it is known whether they will "stand fire" and has cost us thousands of good men and deplorable degradation of reputation.‡ "The treachery, cowardice, and imbecility of the men in command has sunk our spirits at home and our character abroad."*

At the commencement of the war of 1812, the whole number of British troops in Canada was 4450, supplemented by about four thousand Canadian militia. With this corporal guard it was necessary to protect a frontier of over 1600 miles in length. Any part of this line was liable to an invasion of United States troops whose lines of communication were far superior. Moreover Great Britain was unable to send reinforcements until after the fall of Napoleon in June, 1814, when the war was nearly fought out.

American writers have always severely criticised the British for burning the public buildings when they captured Washington. Ex-President Jefferson, who proposed that the criminal classes of London should be hired to burn that city, stigmatized the burning of Washington as "vandalism," and declared it would "immortalize the infamy" of Great Britain. He who could contemplate with equanimity the fearful horrors that must have resulted from the putting in practice of his monstrous proposition to burn a city crowded with peaceful citizens, professed to be horrified at the destruction of a few public buildings by which no man, woman or child, was injured in person or property. With equal hypocrisy he professed to believe that no provocation for the act was given by the United States commanders. Upon this point he was taken to an account by an open letter from Dr. John Strachan, afterwards Bishop of Toronto. This letter should be preserved as long as there lives a British apologist for the acts of the United States in the War of 1812. In part is was as follows:

"As you are not ignorant of the mode of carrying on the war adopted by your friends, you must have known it was a small retaliation after redress had been refused, for burnings and depredations not only of public but private property, committed by them in Canada. In July, 1812, General Hull invaded Upper Canada and threatened by proclamation to exterminate the inhabitants if they made any resistance. He plundered those with whom he had been in habits of intimacy for years before the war. Their linen and plate were found in his possession after his surrender to General Brock. He marked out the loyal subjects of the king as objects of peculiar resentment, and consigned their property to pillage and conflagration.

* Jefferson's Works, Vol. VI., pp. 99, 193, 104.

In April, 1813, the public buildings at York (now Toronto) the capital of Upper Canada, were burned by the troops of the United States contrary to the articles of capitulation. Much private property was plundered and several homes left in a state of ruin. Can you tell me, sir, the reason why the public buildings and library at Washington should be held more sacred than those at our York?

In June, 1813, Newark came into possession of your army, and its inhabitants were repeatedly promised protection to themselves and property by General Dearborne and General Boyd. In the midst of their professions the most respectable of them, almost all non-combatants, were made prisoners and sent into the United States. The two churches were burned to the ground; detachments were sent under the direction of British traitors to pillage the loyal inhabitants in the neighborhood and to carry them away captive. Many farm-houses were burned during the summer and at length, to fill up the measure of iniquity, the whole of the beautiful village of Newark was consigned to flames. The wretched inhabitants had scarcely time to save themselves, much less any of their property. More than four hundred women and children were exposed without shelter on the night of the tenth of December, to the extreme cold of a Canadian winter, and great numbers must have perished, had not the flight of your troops, after perpetrating their ferocious act, enabled the inhabitants of the country to come to their relief. General McClure says he acted in conformity with the order of his government.

In November, 1813, your friend General Wilkinson committed great depredations through the eastern district of Upper Canada. The third campaign exhibits equal enormities. General Brown laid waste the country between Chippewa and Fort Erie, burning mills and private houses. The pleasant village of St. David was burned by his army when about to retreat. On the 15th of May a detachment of the American army pillaged and laid waste as much of the adjacent country as they could reach. They burned the village of Dover with all the mills, stores, distillery, and dwelling houses in the vicinity, carrying away such property as was portable, and killing the cattle.

On the 16th of August, some American troops and Indians from Detroit surprised the settlement of Port Talbot, where they committed the most atrocious acts of violence, leaving upwards of 234 men, women and children in a state of nakedness and want.

On the 20th of December, a second excursion was made by the garrison of Detroit, spreading fire and pillage through the settlements of Upper Canada. Early in November, General McArthur, with a large body of mounted Kentuckians and Indians, made a rapid march through the western part of the London districts, burning all the mills, destroying provisions and living upon the inhabitants. Other atrocities committed by the American troops, among them the wanton destruction of a tribe of Indians, unarmed and helpless, are detailed by Dr. Strachan. He adds, addressing Jefferson: "This brief account of the conduct of your govern-

BURNING OF JAY IN EFFIGY.

For signing the Treaty of 1797 Jay was burned in effigy. Hamilton was stoned and the British Minister at Philadelphia insulted.

ment and army will fill the world with astonishment at the forbearance of Great Britain."

After two years and a half had been expended in vain and puerile attacks on the "handful of soldiers" with which Great Britain was able to resist its invasion, combined with such assistance as the patriotic Canadians were able to afford, it was found that not only Canada could not be conquered, but that much of the territory of the United States had passed into the hands of the enemy, with not one foot of that enemy's territory in their own hands to compensate for the loss.

When the arms of the United States had suffered many reverses and it became plain that they must accept the best terms from Great Britain that they could procure, John Adams declared that he "would continue the war forever rather than surrender one iota of the fisheries as established by the third article of the treaty of 1783." He boasted that he had saved the fishermen in that year, and now in 1814 he learned with dismay that they were again lost to his country, their relinquishment being one of the terms insisted on by the British commission as the price of peace.

The Federalists also were not easily satisfied. They admitted that peace was a happy escape for a country with a bankrupt treasury, and all resources dissipated. "But what," they asked, "have we gained by a war provoked and entered into by you with such a flourish of trumpets? Where are your 'sailors' rights?' Where is the indemnity for our impressed seamen? How about the paper blockade? The advantages you promised us we have not obtained. But we have lost nothing? Have we not? What about Grand Manan and Moose Island and the fisheries and our West Indian commerce? So severely did Boston suffer that there were sixty vessels captured at the entrance to the harbor by one small fishing smack of Liverpool, Nova Scotia, cruising in Massachusetts Bay.

All who were concerned in the passage of the treaty were the subjects of the popular wrath. Jay was declared to be an "arch traitor," a "Judas who had betrayed his country with a kiss," and was burned in effigy in a dozen cities. Hamilton was stoned; the name of Washington was hooted, and the British flag dragged in the mud.

Edmund Quincy, in the life of his father, says, "The fall of Bonaparte, although it occasioned as genuine joy to New England as to the mother country herself, did not bring with it absolutely unalloyed satisfaction. There was reason to apprehend that the English administration, triumphant over its gigantic foe, its army and navy released from the incessant service of so many years, might concentrate the whole of the empire upon the power which it regarded as a volunteer ally of its mighty enemy, and administer an exemplary chastisement. No doubt many Englishmen felt, with Sir Walter Scott," that "it was their business to give the Americans a fearful memento, that the babe unborn should have remembered," and there is as little question that infinite damage might have been done to our cities and seacoast and to the banks of our great rivers, had Great Britain employed her entire naval and military forces for that purpose. But happily the English people wisely refrained from an expenditure of blood and gold which could have no permanent good result, and which would only serve to exasperate passions and to prolong animosities which it was far wiser to permit to die out. It is not unlikely that the attention of English people had been so absorbed by the mighty conflict going on at their very doors that they had not much to spare for the distant and comparatively obscure fields across the Atlantic, and indeed the sentiments of the English people and the policy of English governments have never exhibited a spirit of revengefulness. The American war was but a slight episode in the great epic of the age. At any rate the English ministry were content to treat with the American commissioners at Ghent and to make a peace which left untouched the pretended occasion for the war. over in expressive silence, and peace was concluded,, leaving "sailors' rights" the great watchword of the war party, substantially as they stood before hostilities began, except that our fishermen were deprived of the valuable privilege they enjoyed of catching and curing fish on the shores of the Gulf of the St. Lawrence.*

The news of peace was received in Boston with great joy. It was a day given up to rejoicing; salutes were fired; the bells rang out their merriest peals; the volunteer companies with their bands filled the streets; the school boys took a holiday; the wharves so long deserted were thronged, and the melancholy ships that rotted along side them were once more gay with flags and streamers. Thus rejoicing extended all along the seaboard and far inland, making glad all hearts and none more glad than those of the promoters of the war in high places and low.†

And so the "war of 1812" ended amid a general joy, not for what it had accomplished, for the American forces were defeated in their invasion of Canada, and the United States did not acquire one foot of additional territory, or the settlement of any of the questions which were the pretext for the war.

Much that occurred during the war of 1812 has been conveniently forgotten by American historians, and much that had not occurred, remembered. By degrees failure was transformed into success. The new generations were taught that in that war their fathers had won a great victory over the whole power of Great Britain single handed and alone. This amazing belief is still cherished among the people of the United States, to the astonishment of well informed visitors who meet with evidence of the fact.

* Life of Josiah Quincy, p. 358.
† Life of Josiah Quincy, pp. 360, 361.

CHAPTER X.

THE CIVIL WAR AND THE PART TAKEN BY GREAT BRITAIN IN SAME

For the first fifty years after the Revolution, the wealthy aristocratic slave-holding Southern states governed the Union and controlled its destiny. The acquisition of Florida and the Louisiana purchase doubled the area of the United States, and the territory derived from the Mexican War doubled it again. It was the intention of the South to extend slavery over this immense territory, but they were checked in the northern part of it by the enormous European immigration that poured into it and prevented it from becoming slave territory. Then came the "irrepressible conflict," the border war in Missouri and "bleeding Kansas," the battle of Ossawatomie and Harper's Ferry raid, and the constant pin-pricking of the abolition societies in the North, the headquarters of which were in Boston.

The presidential election of 1860 showed the South that they had lost control of the government and that the free states were increasing enormously in wealth and population, and that, following the example of Great Britain, it would be only a question of time before they would insist on abolishing slavery. Then it was that the Southerners decided to do what their fathers had done eighty-five years before, secede and become Dis-unionists. They could not believe that there would be any opposition to their leaving, especially from Massachusetts, that place that had always been foremost in disunion sentiments. Besides, had not the Abolitionists said repeatedly in Faneuil Hall, "The Cradle of Liberty," that if they would leave the Union they would "pave their way with gold" to get rid of them, and did not the New York Tribune, which had been the organ of the Abolitionists, and which now declared that "if the cotton states wished to withdraw from the Union they should be allowed to do so"; that "any attempt to compel them to remain by force would be contrary to the principles of the Declaration of Independence, and to the fundamental idea upon which human liberty is based," and that "if the Declaration of Independence justified the secession from the British Empire of three million subjects in 1776, it was not seen why it would not justify the secession of five million of Southerners from the Union in 1861." This was quite consistent with the remark of a leading Abolitionist paper in Boston that "the Constitution was a covenant with hell." The South also contended that even if they were not justified in becoming Dis-unionists in 1776, they had established their right to independence by force of arms and that when they had entered into a confederation with the other seceding colonies, they had never assigned any of their rights which they had fought for, that they were sovereign, independent states, and that the bond that bound them together was simply for self-protection and was what the name signified "United States," and not a nation. In proof of this they stated that when the convention met in Philadelphia in May, 1787, for the purpose of adopting a constitution for a stronger form of government, the first resolution presented was, "Resolved, That it is the opinion of this committee that a national government ought to be established, consisting of a supreme legislature, executive and judiciary. This was followed by twenty-three other resolutions as adopted and reported by the committee in which the word "national" occurred twenty-six times. Mr. Ellsworth, of Connecticut moved to strike out the word "national" and to insert the words "Government of the United States." This was agreed to unanimously, and the word "national" was stricken out wherever it occurred, and nowhere makes its appearance in the Constitution finally adopted. The prompt rejection of this word "national" is obviously much more expressive of the intent of the authors of the Constitution than its mere absence from the Constitution would have been. It is a clear indication that they did not mean to give any countenance to the idea that the government which they organized was a consolidated nationality instead of a confederacy of sovereign members. The question of secession was first raised by men of Massachusetts, the birthplace of secession. Colonel Timothy Pickering was one of the leading secessionists of his day. He had been an officer in the Revolution; afterwards Postmaster General, Secretary of War, Secretary of State in the cabinet of General Washington and senator from Massachusetts.

Writing to a friend on December 24, 1803, he says: "I will not despair. I will rather anticipate a new confederacy exempt from the corrupt and corrupting influence and oppression of the aristocratic Democrats of the South. There will be (and our children, at farthest, will see it) a separation. The white and black population will mark the boundary."*

In another letter, written in January 29, 1804, he said: "The principles of our Revolution point to the remedy—a separation. This can be acomplished and without spilling one drop of blood, I have little doubt. It must begin in Massachusetts."*

In 1811, on the bill for the admission of Louisiana as a state of the Union, the Hon. Josiah Quincy, a member of Congress from Massachusetts, said: "If this bill pass, it is my deliberate opinion that it is virtually a dissolution of this Union; that it will free the states from other moral obligations, and as it will be the right of all, so it will be the duty of some definitely to prepare for a separation, amicably, if they can, violently if they must."

The war between the North and the South produced an abundant crop of bitter prejudices against the mother country. This sentiment

* Life of Cabot, p. 491.

was shared by the South as well as by the North. Each imagined it had been unfairly treated by the British Government.

Americans continually point to the period of the Civil war and triumphantly declare that Englishmen were unfriendly to the United States at that time. So they were. And Englishmen were unfriendly to the Confederate states during that time. In fact, Englishmen did exactly what Americans did at that time—some took the side of the North and others took the side of the South. This it was their privilege to do. They simply asserted the right of free men to think as they pleased, and to express those thoughts freely. But that in so doing they showed hostility to the United States it is false and foolish to assert. There was neither unfriendliness nor malice. This hostility to the South, so far as it existed, was based solely upon the existence of slavery there. That which existed against the North was based solely upon the belief that a stronger power was taking advantage of its strength to trample upon the political rights of a weaker one. Any person living either North or South at that time cannot deny that they met many examples of both of these opinions among their respective acquaintances in both these sections.

At the commencement of the Civil War, the Queen issued a proclamation of neutrality, forbidding the sale of munitions of war to either party, warning her subjects against entering any blockaded port for purposes of trade under penalty of forfeiture of vessel and cargo if captured by either contestant.

Great Britain, as well as all other civilized powers, granted to the Confederacy belligerent rights, the same as had been accorded to them by the United States. Many, through cupidity, were tempted to enter into an illegal traffic with the seceded states.

A writer at that time says: "It is to the disgrace of our country that some of the goods smuggled into the Confederacy via Nassau were from Northern ports, as for example, shiploads of pistols brought from Boston in barrels of lard." There was also a considerable trade between Boston and Confederate ports via Halifax during the war, as well as an immense amount of contraband trade along the border even by the United States officials, as for example, the exploits of General Benjamin F. Butler while in command at Norfolk, Va., in 1864. If citizens of the United States, even those of Massachusetts, the home of the abolitionists, entered into this traffic, what could be expected of Great Britain with her mills closed and thousands of operatives obliged to resort to the poor rates for subsistence, because she was prevented from buying cotton with which the wharves of the Southern states were loaded down awaiting shipment. It was claimed by Unionists that the British ministry and aristocracy, from political and commercial considerations, openly and heartily sympathized with the South, and that, under the friendly flag of Great Britain, secessionists and blockade-runners were welcomed and assisted in the nefarious traffic; that this unfriendliness of the British government at that time furnished a solid foundation upon which the rebellion rested their hopes, thereby protracting the war. It should not be forgotten, however, that the Queen and the royal family stood faithfully by the Union in the days of its sorest peril, and refused to listen to the importunities of the French emperor, to recognize the Southern Confederacy and open the southern ports.

France, having taken advantage of the Civil War, set the Monroe Doctrine at defiance and conquered Mexico. Her remaining there depended on the success of the Confederacy, as after events proved. Had Great Britain listened to France and joined her in recognizing the Southern Confederacy, the South would have surely succeeded. It is generally admitted that the strict blockade of the Southern ports is what defeated the Confederacy. It is due to Great Britain that the United States is not dismembered. It should be remembered that during the Civil War the great body of British workmen were on the side of the North. Even in the cotton famine districts they preferred to starve rather than have the Southern ports opened whereby they could obtain an abundance of cotton, thereby relieving their sore necessities.

It is also true that the Confederacy had many friends in Great Britain; that Gladstone, the great Liberal Chancellor of the Exchequer, so far forgot what was due to his position as to make a speech in which he said "he expected the liberation of the slaves by their own masters sooner than from the North; that Jefferson Davis and the leaders of the South have made an army; they are soon, I understand, to have a navy, but greater than all this, they have made a nation."

It must be admitted that in building a navy the government connived at the building of cruisers, such as the Alabama, in British shipyards, for which they had to pay dearly afterwards. In answer to this speech of Gladstone, the robust yet tender tones of John Bright's voice rang out for the Northern cause in the darkest hour of the Civil War. His voice was heard with no uncertain sound when he uttered his indignant protest at anything like a reception being tendered Mason and Slidell on their release. John Bright for a long time sustained the enormous loss of keeping his mills open at least half time with no material to work with. There he stood, all Quaker as he was, praying that the North might not stay its hand till the last slave was freed, even if no bales of cotton were sent to relieve his grievious losses protesting against outside interference. When the day came that marked the passing away of this venerable patriot, one of earth's greatest and best, an attempt was made in Congress to pass a vote of sympathy to his family and to the shame and disgrace of the United States it must be said that Congress refused to pay even this poor tribute to the memory of the best friend the United States had in the whole wide world in the hour of her great distress. This was done because it would be "offensive to the Irish." John Bright could see no difference between dis-union in the United States and dis-union in the United Kingdom. He had written to Mr. Gladstone concerning Parnell, Dillon, O'Brien, etc., saying, "You deem them patriots; I hold them not to be patriots, but conspirators against the crown and government of the

United Kingdom." These men were afterwards found guilty of criminal conspiracy and Parnell was received with honor on the floor of Congress.

Henry Ward Beecher stated that during the American Civil War there were thousands of mass meetings held in Great Britain in favor of the Union cause, and not one in favor of the Confederacy.

Jefferson Davis complained bitterly of the action of Great Britain. He says "The partiality of Her Majesty's government in favor of our enemies was further evinced in the marked difference of its conduct on the subject of the purchase of supplies by the two belligerents. This difference was conspicuous from the commencement of the war."* Great Britain endeavored to deal justly with both parties in the contest, but pleased neither and was blamed by both. This is probably the best evidence that can be given to show the impartiality of Great Britain in the great Civil War, and it is safe to say that there were ten times more British subjects serving in the Northern armies than there were in the Southern.

As previously stated, Great Britain has been greatly blamed by American historians for her treatment of American prisoners of war during the Revolution, and at Dartmouth prison in the war of 1812. In view of these facts it will be interesting to see how the Americans treated their prisoners when at war between themselves in the Civil War of 1861. One of the worst cases recorded in the history of the world is that of Andersonville. The first prisoners were received there in March, 1864. From that time till March, 1865, the deaths were 13,000 out of a total of 50,000 or 26 per cent. This enormous loss of life was due to the fact that in order to subjugate the South their crops were destroyed, their fields devastated, their railroads broken up, which interrupted their means of transportation, which reduced their people, troops and prisoners to the most straitened condition for food. If the troops in the field were in a half-starved condition, certainly the prisoners would fare worse.† The Confederates have been blamed for this enormous loss of life, but when the facts are examined it is found that it was due to the cold-blooded policy of the Federal Government, who would not exchange prisoners for the atrocious reason set forth in the dispatch from General Grant to General Butler, dated West Point, August 18, 1864.

General Grant says: "On the subject of exchange, however, I differ from General Hitchcock. It is hard on our men in Southern prisons not to exchange them, but it is humanity to those left in the ranks to fight our battles. Every man released on parole or otherwise becomes an active soldier against us at once, either directly or indirectly. If we commence a system of exchange, which liberates all prisoners taken, we will have to fight on till the whole South is exterminated. If we hold those caught, they amount to no more than dead men. At this particular time to release all rebel prisoners North would insure Sherman's defeat and would compromise our safety."

What brought forth this letter was a statement made by the Confederate government concerning the excessive mortality prevailing among the prisoners of Andersonville. As no answer was received, another communication was sent on Aug. 22, 1864 to Major General E. A. Hitchcock, United States Commissioner of Exchange, concerning the same proposal. But again no answer was made. One final effort was made to obtain an exchange. Jefferson Davis sent a delegation of prisoners from Andersonville to Washington. "It was of no avail. They were made to understand that the interest of the government required that they should return to prison and President Lincoln refused to see them. They carried back the sad tidings that their government held out no hope of their release."*

Up to this time the mortality among the prisoners had been far greater in the Northern prisons than in the Southern prisons, notwithstanding there was an abundance of food and clothing and medical supplies in the North. In proof of this it is only necessary to offer two facts. First, the report of the Secretary of War, E. M. Stanton, made on July 19, 1866, shows that of all the prisoners held by the Confederates during the war, only 22,576 died, while of the prisoners held by the Federal government, 26,246 died.

Second, the official report of Surgeon General Barnes, an officer of the U. S. Government, stated that the number of Confederate prisoners in their hands amounted to 220,000. The number of U. S. prisoners in Confederate hands amounted to 270,000. Thus out of 270,000 held by the Confederates 22,000 died, and of the 220,000 Confederates held in the North, 26,000 died. Thus 12 per cent of the Confederates died in Northern prisons and only 9 per cent U. S. prisoners died in the South.†

* Rise and Fall of the Confederate Government, Vol. II., p. 606.
† Rise and Fall of the Confederate Government, Vol. II., p. 606.

CHAPTER XI.

RECONCILIATION. THE DISMEMBERED EMPIRE RE-UNITED IN BONDS OF FRIENDSHIP. "BLOOD IS THICKER THAN WATER."

It is well known and now acknowledged that for the past hundred years it has been the deliberate and well considered policy of the United States to eradicate everything British from the country to the north of us.

During the Canadian rebellion of 1837, as well as during the Fenian raid of 1866, the American frontier was openly allowed to be made a base of operation against British North America.

Canada has always claimed that she has been deprived of enormous areas of territory by the United States through sharp practice and unjustifiable means, especially in Oregon, Maine and Alaska. The most notable case of duplicity on the part of the United States was that of the Northeast boundary settled under the Ashburton Treaty of Washington in 1842. After a bitter controversy it was left out to arbitration for the King of the Netherlands to decide. The award was accepted by Great Britain and rejected by the United States. The question remained in abeyance for two years, during which there was imminent danger of a collision and of war. Military posts were simultaneously established and rashly advanced into the wild country which both parties claimed as their own. Redoubts and blockhouses were erected at several points. Reinforcement of troops from either side poured in. The public mind in the United States became inflamed by the too ready cry of "British outrage," proclaimed in all quarters by the reckless politicians of both parties in order to lash the national spirit into fury. The people in the whole length and breadth of the Union were, to a man, convinced of the justice of their claim and of the manifest wrong intended by Great Britain. The Nation at large was ready and anxious for war, and had a skirmish taken place on the frontier involving the death of a dozen men during the so-called "Aroostook War," the whole country would have rushed to war and plunged the two nations into hostilities, the end of which no man then living could have foreseen.

During this trouble, the English people were quite calm and almost apathetic. With a vague notion of the locality of the disputed territory, a total ignorance of the merits or demerits of the dispute, and a profound contempt of the blustering and abuse of American politicians and newspapers, they were perfectly content to leave affairs in the hands of the government.

Finally a joint commission was appointed from the States of Maine and Massachusetts (both having rights in the disputed territory) and sent to Washington to negotiate a treaty with Lord Ashburton, a nobleman well adapted to the occasion from his connection by marriage, and property in the United States.

The odds were greatly against the British negotiator. His principal adversary was Daniel Webster, Secretary of State, who in one of his letters said: "I must be permitted to say that few questions have arisen under this government in regard to which a stronger or more general conviction was felt that the country was in the right than this question of the northeast boundary." He reiterated his own belief in "the justice of the claim which arose from our honest conviction that it was founded in truth and accorded with the intention of the negotiators of the treaty of 1783." The whole of the disputed territory amounted to 6,750,000 acres. At last a compromise was effected which granted to Great Britain 3,337,000 acres, and to the United States 3,413,000 acres, and acknowledged the title of England to all the military positions upon the frontier, and 700,000 acres more was awarded her than was assigned to her by the King of the Netherlands.

But the decision of the Commissioners suited neither party. The factions in England pronounced Lord Ashburton to have been sold, and those in America declared that Webster had been bought. The most violent opposition to the treaty was made; every part of it was denounced, and it became at last doubtful if the Senate would ratify it. That final consummation was, however, suddenly effected in a most remarkable manner, the Senate coming to its decision by an unexpected majority of thirty-nine to nine, after several days of secret debate. The sanction of the Queen and the British government had been given without hesitation and the people on both sides of the Atlantic were well satisfied with the termination of the long and virulent dispute, and the Northeastern Boundary Question would have sunk into the archives of diplomatic history, but truth like murder will out, and it so happened that Mr. Thomas Colley Grattan, British Consul for Massachusetts* who, at the request of the commissioners, had accompanied them to Washington to assist them in their negotiation, had the fortune to discover after the treaty was signed, the duplicity of the Senate during their secret debates leading to the ratification of the treaty. He says: "My informant gave unmeasured expression to his indignation, which he assured me was fully shared in by his friends, Judge Story and Dr. Channing. Judge Story expressed himself without reserve on Webster's conduct as a 'most disgraceful proceeding.'" Other gentlemen of Boston entirely coincided in these opinions.

"It is obvious to all persons familiar with boundary disputes that the most important evidence in such disputes is founded on surveys and maps. Early in the controversy there was a strange disappearance of the one in the archives of the State Department, that had been transmitted by Frank-

---

* For full particulars see his work, "Civilized America," Vol. I., Chap. XXI, XXII, XXIII.

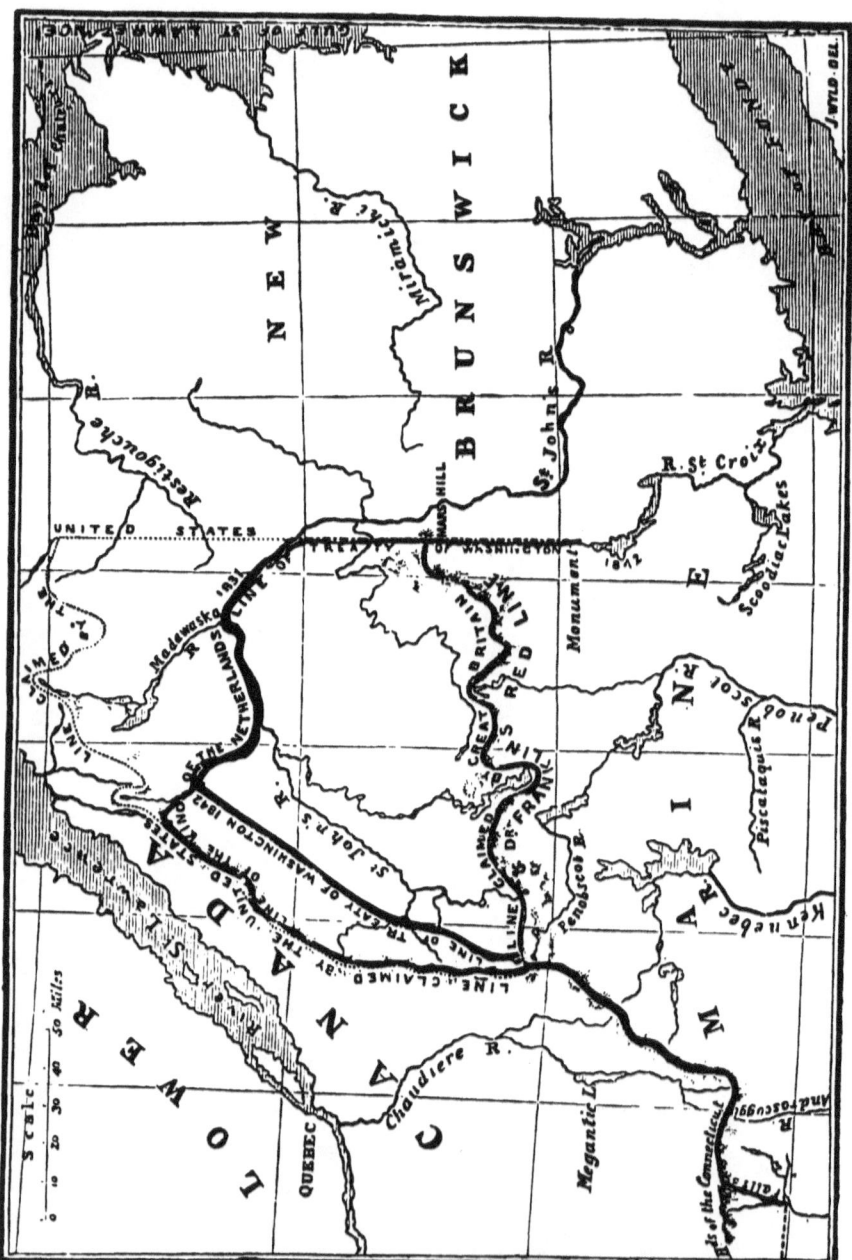

Map of the Boundary Line between Maine and New Brunswick.

lin to Jefferson in October, 1790, with the true boundary line traced on it. It was, therefore, with great astonishment that I learned from the confidential communication just alluded to that during the whole of the negotiations at Washington, while the highest functionaries of the American Government were dealing with Lord Ashburton with seeming frankness and integrity, pledging their faith for a perfect conviction of the justice of their claim to the territory which was in dispute. Mr. Webster had in his possession and had communicated to them all—President, Cabinet, Commissioners and Senate—the highest evidence which the case admitted, that the United States had never had a shadow of right to any part of the territory which they had so pertinaciously claimed for nearly fifty years. This evidence, as my conscientious informant told me, was nothing less than a copy of an original map presented by Dr. Franklin to Count de Vergennes, the Minister of Louis XVI, on December 6, 1782 (six days after the preliminaries of the treaty of Paris of 1783 were signed) tracing the boundary, as agreed upon by himself and the other commissioners, with a strong red line south of the St, John, and exactly where a similar line appears in an unauthenticated map discovered in London subsequent to Lord Ashburton's departure on his mission."

Public attention being aroused by the statements made by the British Consul to his government, the injunction of secrecy imposed by the Senate on its members was dissolved, and permission was given for the publication of the speeches made in secret session of August 17-19, 1842, The most important of those speeches was that of Mr. Rives, chairman of the Committee on Foreign Affairs. His principal argument was that if they did not sign the treaty, the dispute would be referred to a second arbitration with very great danger of their losing the whole, Mr. Webster, the Secretary of State, having sent to him to be laid before the Senate a communication and a copy of the map presented by Dr. Franklin to Count de Vergennes. In short, it is exactly the line contended for by Great Britain except that it concedes more than is claimed. When this communication was read, Senator Benton informed the Senate that he could produce a map of higher validity than the one referred to. He accordingly repaired to the library of Congress and soon returned with a map which there is no doubt was the one sent by Franklin to Jefferson already alluded to as having been surreptitiously removed from the archives of the State Department some years before. The moment it was examined it was found to sustain, by the most precise and remarkable correspondence in every feature, the map communicated by Mr. Webster. Mr. Benton then stated that "if the maps were really authentic the concealment of them was a fraud on the British, and that the Senate was insulted by being a party to the fraud," and further that "if evidence had been discovered which deprived Maine of the title to one-third of its territory, honor required that it should be made known to the British."

The sudden acceptance of the treaty was in consequence of the evidence of the maps, and the conviction of all concerned that a discovery of their existence before the conclusion of a treaty would have given irresistible strength to the English claims.

Calhoun said: "It would be idle to suppose that these disclosures would not weigh heavily against the United States in any future negotiations."

The settlement of the Oregon boundary question again showed American hatred of England to be chronic. The question finally resolved itself into whether the threat of 54.40 or fight should be carried out, (a threat to deprive Canada of access to the Pacific Ocean and the possession of most of the enormous wheat fields now being developed in the northwest) or to fight Mexico and extend its boundaries to the South instead of the north. This latter scheme suited the slaveholders best who were then in power. The United States government then entered into a war with Mexico, one of the most unjustifiable contests ever entered into by a civilized nation. By this war of conquest the United States nearly doubled its territory. It must be said to the credit of New England that she would not take any part in this war any more than she did in the war of 1812.

When confederation of the Canadian provinces occurred in 1867, there was placed on record in the House of Representatives at Washington that it was disapproved and that the House regarded the Act of Confederation as a menace to the United States. For a hundred years after the Revolution it had been the policy of the United States to force Canada into annexation, and it was considered that she would be more likely to come into the Union if she was harrassed by a high tariff, boundary and fishing disputes, but now it is known to have been all wrong. The factors worked out just the reverse. Conditions have arrived that were little foreseen until within ten years. The American people have recognized the fact that a great change has taken place in Canada which materially effects the relation between Canada and the United States. Mr. Root, U. S. Secretary of State, recently said:

"Canada is no longer the outlying northern country in which a fringe of descendants of royalists emigrating from the colonies when they became independent of Great Britain, lived and gained a precarious subsistence from a fertile soil. It has become the home of a great people increasing in population and wealth. The stirrings of a national sentiment are to be felt. In their relations to England one can see that while still loyal to their mother country, still a loyal part of the British Empire, they are growing up, and, as the boy is to his parents when he attains manhood, they are a personality of themselves. In their relations to us they have become a sister nation. With their enormous national wealth, with their vigor and energy following the pathway that we have followed, protecting their industries as we have protected ours, proud of their country as we are proud of ours, they are no longer the little remnants upon our borders; they are a great and powerful sister nation."

For years after the Civil War there came from the press, from the lecture platform, and from the political rostrum, the most relentless abuse of Great Britain and everything British. Lecturers gave their audiences vivid descriptions of the Revolution and the war of 1812, in which American valor was always rated high and British brutality was held up to scorn. These lectures were frequently of thrilling interest because the speakers were not handicapped by matters so paltry as facts of history. But the most formidable batteries of wrath were trained against everything British from the political stump. The iron-lunged orators told of the iniquity of England, of its infamous tariff laws, the oppression of Ireland, etc. He was but a poor speaker who could not enliven a political meeting by twisting the tail of the British lion. All this is now changed. It was brought about by President Cleveland's Venezuelan message of December, 1895, and the Spanish War. When the Venezuelan episode occurred, England was believed to be isolated and without an ally. It proved that war could be declared against Great Britain at any time, in ten minutes, upon any pretext. The insolent message fell upon every one in England, from Lord Salisbury down, as a bolt from the blue sky. Englishmen were as innocent as babes of intentional offence to the United States. They had no conception that there existed in the United States such latent irritation or antagonism as under the first provocation would lead to an almost open avowal of national enmity. It, however, happily disclosed the fact that there still existed in the United States a numerous highly educated and conservative element (not dissimilar to the vanished Loyalists of the last century) in which one seldom finds a trace of antagonism to the old mother country. Following the message, magazine reviews, the public press, and the pulpit overflowed with a brilliant series of public utterances and these soon checked the noisy approving outbursts of a reckless half-educated majority to obtain whose votes at the next election undoubtedly prompted the presumptuous interference of the chief of the Republic and the unfriendly tone of his message.

Within three years after the message a wonderful change came over the people of the United States. The Spanish War had taken place and instead of finding Great Britain to be the hereditary enemy of the United States, which they had been taught in the school histories to believe, it was found that among the great powers of the world, Great Britain was the only friend which the United States had, and that "blood was thicker than water." It was discovered that the nations were envious of the great Republic, and that Britain alone was proud of her eldest daughter. It was remarked to the writer by a Spanish officer shortly after the surrender of Porto Rico: "But mind you, this from an old man who has studied history. You would never have had these islands had not England stepped in at the beginning of the trouble and said to all the nations of the world, 'Allow me to present my daughter, America.'" It was found, too, that the "traditional friendship" of Russia was of but little account at that time.

It was Russia that eagerly became the spokesman for envious Europe and gave voice to the words: "Now is the time for us to combine and crush this huge American monster before she becomes too strong for all of us, as she is already too strong for any one of us." It was Russia that planned to have the "concert of Europe" warn us that we were not to pose as champion of any other American people against any form of misrule by Europe—and that we were not to dare to meddle in Europe on any pretext.

She failed because England refused to join the league, or to enter with the other powers into a naval demonstration before Cuba, but so long as the war lasted with Spain the Russian diplomats kept pounding at every backdoor in Europe with an insistence that something be done to cut our comb, or make trouble or lose us the friendship of England. Our people in Washington know all this. They know also the behavior of the Russian minister at Washington who thought to poison us against England in the very days when we were buying in that country and shipping in secret from that country the vital necessities which the war demanded and which we had not got; when great steamers were found abandoned off New York loaded with contraband of war, cannon, arms, ammunition, etc., and towed into port by United States warships; when coal and ammunition were left on desert islands in the Philippines by British warships for the use of the United States navy; when England's fleet at Manila stood ready to take sides with Dewey and to open fire, to begin war on the Germans should occasion arise. American naval officers who were there know these facts to be true, and it is very significant that the Navy Department has not published the correspondence between it and Admiral Dewey at that time. We are hated all over the continent of Europe. Paris made a fete day when she imagined Sampson's fleet was destroyed.

The Germans hate us for taking 3,000,000 fighting men away from them, and also because we prevented them from purchasing the Philippines from Spain, and because the Monroe doctrine prevents them from obtaining colonies or naval stations in the Western Hemisphere. The Austrians hate us for humiliating Spain. There is not a country to the south of us but what hates us. Every republic in South America would put a knife in our back if the opportunity occurs.

Very significant, too, was the reception and banquet given at Windsor Castle in 1896 by Queen Victoria to the Ancient and Honorable Artillery Company of Boston—the oldest military organization in the Western Hemisphere—and the grand reception they received everywhere they went in England. It was a revelation to the Americans, as every one of them acknowledged, to receive such marked expression of kindliness and brotherhood at the old home. It was something they did not expect. The company more than reciprocated when the parent company, The Honourable Artillery of London, visited Boston in 1903. Once more were seen armed British sailors and soldiers marching through Boston's streets under the British flag, the buildings along the entire route beautifully decorated, and the visitors received with vociferous welcome wherever they went. We will hope that something even better and more substantial may yet come to us, when the United States and Great Britain will be allied in amity as firm as that which now holds together these federal states. "Old prejudices should be cast aside; the English-speaking states recognizing their kinship, should knit bonds together around the world, forming a kingly brotherhood inspired by beneficence, to which supreme dominion in the earth would be sure to fall; for whatever may be said today for other stocks, the 135,000,000 of English-speaking men have been able to make themselves masters of the world to an extent which no people has thus far approached.

"If love would but once unite, the seas could never sever. Earth has never beheld a co-mingling of men, so impressive, so likely to be frought with noble advantages through ages to come, as would be the coming together of English-speaking men in one cordial bond."*

The statesmen of Britain and America can do no worthier service than to find a way by which their strength may be combined to secure the peace of the world and the betterment of mankind. It is not necessary that their governments should be unified, or even that any hard and fast treaty obligation incurred. It is only necessary that they should agree to be friends and to stand by each other in all that will further these great objects. They alone of all the nations can do this and that they ought to do it few will deny. Both must forget certain bitterness born of the past and certain jealousies growing out of the greatness of both.

What Great Britain is doing for the many peoples under her care and what this nation is doing for the few outside our borders that we have in hand we might unitedly do for a great portion of the globe and its inhabitants. This combination must be strong enough to check certain highwaymen in international relations and to install a wholesome regard for human rights. Such an outcome of present friendliness will not be achieved in a day or generation. But it will come; it must come. Asia and the continent of Europe may become Chinese or Cossack, but the English-speaking race shall rule over every other land and all the islands and every sea.

The present time is a critical period in the life of the American Republic, and therefore in the life of the world. The impotence of the federal government to stop strike disturbances, lynchings and disfranchisements, the growing power of an oligarchial and plutocratic Senate, and the perils of imperialism are disquieting enough, but worst of all is the evil of party rule and party strife.

Washintgon abhorred party and regarded it as a disease which he hoped to avert by putting federalists and anti-federalists in his cabinet together. The intuition of the founders of the Republic was that the president should be elected by a chosen body of select and responsible citizens, but since the Jacksonian era, nomination and election have been completely in the hands of the Democracy at large, and the election has been

* Short History of Anglo-Saxon Freedom.

performed by a process of national agitation and conflict which sets at work all the forces of political intrigue and corruption on the most enormous scale, besides filling the country with persons almost as violent and anti-social as those of the Civil War.

The qualification for public office from that of president down to that of a member of a city council in national, state or city politics is not a question of which man is most worthy of public confidence. It is no longer eminence but availability. The great aim of each party is to prevent the country from being successfully governed by its rival. Each will do anything to catch votes and anything rather than lose them. Government consequently is at the mercy of any organization which has votes on a large scale to sell, or corporations that will freely contribute its funds. The Grand Army of the Republic is thus enabled to levy upon the nation tribute to the amount of a hundred and fifty million dollars each year, thirty-six years after the war, although General Grant at the close of the war said that the pensions should never exceed seven millions each year. And now both parties in their platform promise their countenance to this exaction.

The recent exposures of the millions contributed by the trusts, tariff protected industries, life insurance companies, etc., to the campaign funds has astonished the world. The history of the most corrupt monarchies could hardly furnish a more monstrous case of financial abuse, to say nothing of the effect upon national character.

Each party machine has a standing army of wire pullers with an apparatus of intrigue and corruption to the support of which holders of office under government are assessed. The boss is a recognized authority, and mastery of unscrupulous intrigue is his avowed qualification for his place. The pest of partyism invades all the large cities of the country. New York is made the plunder of the thieves of one party and Philadelphia of thieves of the other. It is surely impossible that any nation should endure such a system forever. A nation which deliberately gives itself up to government by faction, under the name of party, signs its own doom. The end may be delayed but it is sure. The American people undoubtedly have the political wisdom and force to deal with this crisis, but there is no evidence that these qualities are being brought to bear on the situation nor is there any great man arisen to lead the reform.

PART II.

BIOGRAPHICAL SKETCHES

of the

LOYALISTS OF MASSACHUSETTS

with

The Addresses to Governor Hutchinson. The Conspiracy Act; and Resolution, relating to the banishing and confiscation of the estates of the Absentees, and Refugees, and a list of the Loyalists that went to Halifax on the evacuation of Boston.

The Loyalists of Massachusetts

WHO WERE THE INHABITANTS OF THE NEW ENGLAND COLONIES AT THE TIME OF THE REVOLUTION?

The first and second chapters of this work treated of the settlement of Massachusetts and the framing and establishing of that social system and form of government which through successive generations, the settlers and their descendants took part, which culminated in the Revolution. The founders of Massachusetts and of all New England, were almost entirely Englishmen. Their emigration to New England began in 1620, it was inconsiderable till 1630, at the end of ten years more it almost ceased. A people consisting at that time of not many more than twenty thousand persons, thenceforward multiplied on its own soil, in remarkable seclusion from other communities, for nearly two centuries. Such exceptions to this statement are of small account. In 1651 after the battle of Dunbar, Cromwell sent some four or five hundred of his Scotch prisoners to Boston, but very little trace of this accession is left. After the revocation of the Edict of Nantes in 1685, about one hundred and fifty families of French Huguenots came to Massachusetts; their names and a considerable number of their posterity are yet to be found. A hundred and twenty Scotch-Irish families, came over in 1719 and settled in Boston, and New Hampshire. Some slight emigrations from it took place at an early date, but they soon discontinued, and it was not till after the Revolution that those swarms began to depart, which have since occupied so large a portion of the territory of the United States. During that long period their identity was unimpaired. No race has ever been more homogeneous than this, at the outbreak of the Revolution, and for many years later. Thus the people of New England was a singularly unmixed race. There was probably not a county in England occupied by a population of purer English blood than theirs. Down to the eve of the war in 1775, New England had little knowledge of the communities which took part in that conflict with her. Till the time of the Boston Port Bill, Massachusetts and Virginia, the two principal English settlements, had with each other scarcely more relations of acquaintance, business, mutual influence, or common action, than either of them had with Bermuda or Barbados.

During the latter part of the nineteenth century vast numbers of Irish, and next to them German, came to New England, so at the time of writing, 1908, it is claimed that one half of the inhabitants of Boston are Irish, or of Irish parentage. During the past ten years the places of the Irish are being taken by the Italians, Jews, Portuguese, Greeks, Armenians, French Canadians, and others. The reader will see from the foregoing that the contestants in Massachusetts during the Revolutionary war were a race representing a peculiar type of the Englishmen of the seventeenth century who, sequestrated from foreign influences, formed a distinct character by their own discipline, and was engaged in a work within itself, on its own problem, through a century and a half, and which terminated in the Revolutionary War, that dismembered the Empire. That the foregoing statement concerning the purity of the race at the time of the Revolution is a correct one, is shown in the following biographies of the Loyalists of Massachusetts, for in nearly every case their ancestry date back to that of the first settlers, through several generations.

The Addressers.

The importance of the following addressers is out of all proportion to their apparent significance. They are an indispensable genesis to the history of the Loyalists. For the next seven years the Addressers were held up to their countrymen as traitors and enemies to their country. In the arraignments, which soon began, the Loyalists were convicted not out of their mouths, but out of their addresses. The ink was hardly dry upon the parchment before the persecution began against all those who would not recant, and throughout the long years of the war, the crime of an addresser grew in its enormity, and they were exposed to the perils of tarring and feathering, the horrors of Simbury mines, a gaol or a gallows.

ADDRESS OF THE MERCHANTS AND OTHERS OF BOSTON TO GOV. HUTCHINSON.

Boston, May 30, 1774.

We, merchants and traders of the town of Boston, and others, do now wait on you, in the most respectful manner, before your departure for England, to testify, for ourselves, the entire satisfaction we feel at your wise, zealous, and faithful administration, during the few years that you have presided at the head of this province. Had your success been equal to your endeavors, and to the warmest wishes of your heart, we cannot doubt that many of the evils under which we now suffer, would have been averted, and that tranquility would have been restored to this long divided province; but we assure ourselves that the want of success in those endeavors will not abate your good wishes when removed from us, or your earnest exertions still on every occasion to serve the true interest of this your native country.

While we lament the loss of so good a governor, we are greatly relieved that his Majesty, in his gracious favor, hath appointed as your successor a gentleman who, having distinguished himself in the long command he hath held in another department, gives us the most favorable prepossessions of his future administration.

We greatly deplore the calamities that are impending and will soon fall on this metropolis, by the operation of a late act of Parliament for shutting up the port on the first of next month. You cannot but be sensible, sir, of the numberless evils that will ensue to the province in general, and the miseries and distresses into which it will particularly involve this town, in the course of a few months. Without meaning to arraign the justice of the British Parliament, we could humbly wish that this act had been couched with less rigor, and that the execution of it had been delayed to a more distant time, that the people might have had the alternative either to have complied with the conditions therein set forth, or to have submitted to the consequent evils on refusal; but as it now stands, all choice is precluded, and however disposed to compliance or concession the people may be, they must unavoidably suffer very great calamities before they can receive relief. Making restitution for damage done to the property of the East India Company, or to the property of any individual, by the outrage of the people, we acknowledge to be just; and though we have ever disavowed, and do now solemnly bear our testimony against such lawless proceedings, yet, considering ourselves as members of the same community, we are fully disposed to bear our proportions of those damages, whenever the sum and the manner of laying it can be ascertained. We earnestly request that you, sir, who know our condition, and have at all times displayed the most benevolent disposition towards us, will, on your arrival in England, interest yourself in our behalf, and make such favorable representations of our case, as that we may hope to obtain speedy and effectual relief.

May you enjoy a pleasant passage to England; and under all the mortifications you have patiently endured, may you possess the inward and consolatory testimonies of having discharged your trust with fidelity and honor, and receive those distinguishing marks of his Majesty's royal approbation and favor, as may enable you to pass the remainder of your life in quietness and ease, and preserve your name with honor to posterity.

William Blair,	John Greenlaw,	Theophilus Lillie,
James Selkrig,	Benjamin Clark,	Miles Whitworth,
Archibald Wilson,	William McAlpine,	James McEwen,
Jeremiah Green,	Jonathan Snelling,	William Codner,
Samuel H. Sparhawk,	James Hall,	James Perkins,
Joseph Turill,	William Dickson,	John White,
Roberts & Co.,	John Winslow, jr.,	Robert Jarvis,

William Perry,
Jas. & Pat. McMasters,
William Coffin,
Simeon Stoddard, jr.,
John Powell,
Henry Laughton,
Eliphalet Pond,
M. B. Goldthwait,
Peter Hughes,
Samuel Hughes,
John Semple,
Hopestill Capen,
Edward King,
Byfield Lynde,
George Lynde,
A. F. Phipps,
Rufus Green,
David Phips,
Richard Smith,
George Spooner,
Daniel Silsby,
William Cazneau,
James Forrest,
Edward Cox,
John Berry,
Richard Hirons,
Ziphion Thayer,
John Joy,
Joseph Goldthwait,
Samuel Prince,
Jonathan Simpson,
James Boutineau,
Nathaniel Hatch,
Martin Gay,
Joseph Scott,
Samuel Minot,
Benjamin M. Holmes,
Archibald McNiel,
George Leonard,
John Borland,
Joshua Loring, jr.,
William Jackson,
James Anderson,
David Mitchelson,
Abraham Savage,
James Asby,
John Inman,
John Coffin,
Thomas Knight,
Benjamin Green, jr.,
David Green,
Benjamin Green,
Henry H. Williams,
James Warden,
Nathaniel Coffin, jr.,
Silvester Gardiner,
John S. Copley,
Edward Foster,
Colbourn Burrell,
Nathaniel Greenwood,
William Burton,
John Winslow,
Issac Winslow, jr.,
Thomas Oliver,
Henry Bloye,
Benjamin Davis,
Isaac Winslow,
Lewis Deblois,
Thomas Aylwin,
William Bowes,
Gregory Townsend,
Francis Green,
Philip Dumaresq,
Harrison Gray,
Peter Johonnot,
George Erving,
Joseph Green,
John Vassall,
Nathaniel Coffin,
John Timmins,
William Tailor,
Thomas Brinley,
Harrison Gray, jr.,
John Taylor,
Gilbert Deblois,
Joshua Winslow,
Daniel Hubbard,
Hugh Turbett,
Henry Lyddell,
Nathaniel Cary,
George Brinley,
Richard Lechmere,
John Erving, jr.,
Thomas Gray,
George Bethune,
Thomas Apthorp,
Ezekial Goldthwaite,
Benjamin Gridley,
John Atkinson,
Ebenezer Bridgham,
John Gore,
Adino Paddock.

ADDRESS OF THE BARRISTERS AND ATTORNEYS OF MASSACHUSETTS TO GOV. HUTCHINSON, MAY, 30, 1774.

A firm persuasion of your inviolable attachment to the real interest of this your native country, and of your constant readiness, by every service in your power, to promote its true welfare and prosperity, will, we flatter ourselves, render it not improper in us, barristers and attorneys at law in the province of Massachusetts Bay, to address your Excellency upon your removal from us, with this testimonial of our sincere respect and esteem.

The various important characters of Legislator, Judge and first Magistrate over this province, in which, by the suffrages of your fellow-subjects, and by the royal favor of the best of kings, your great abilities, adorned with a uniform purity of principle, and integrity of conduct, have been eminently distinguished, must excite the esteem and demand the grateful acknowledgements of every true lover of his country, and friend to virtue.

The present perplexed state of our public affairs, we are sensible, must render your departure far less disagreeable to you than it is to us,—we assure you, sir, we feel the loss; but when, in the amiable character of your successor, we view a fresh instance of the paternal goodness of our most gracious sovereign; when we reflect on the probability that your presence at the court of Great Britain, will afford you an opportunity of employing your interests more successfully for the relief of this province, and particularly of the town of Boston, under their present distresses, we find a consolation which no other human source could afford. Permit us, sir, most earnestly to solicit the exertion of all your distinguished abilities in favor of your native town and country, upon this truly unhappy and distressing occasion.

We sincerely wish you a prosperous voyage, a long continuation of health and felicity and the highest rewards of the good and faithful.

We are, sir, with the most cordial affection, esteem and respect,
Your Excellency's most obedient and very humble servants,

Robert Achmuty,	Andrew Cazneau,	David Ingersoll,
Jonathan Sewall,	Daniel Leonard,	Jeremiah D. Rogers,
Samuel Fitch,	John Lowell,	David Gorham,
Samuel Quincy,	Daniel Oliver,	Samuel Sewall,
William Pynchon,	Sampson S. Blowers,	John Sprague,
James Putnam,	Shearjashub Brown,	Rufus Chandler,
Benjamin Gridley,	Daniel Bliss,	Thomas Danforth,
Abel Willard,	Samuel Porter,	Ebenezer Bradish,

From the Essex Gazette of June 1, 1775.

Salem, May 30, 1775.

Whereare we the subscribers did some time since sign an address to Governor Hutchinson, which, though prompted to by the best intentions, has, nevertheless, given great offence to our country: We do now declare, that we were so far from designing by that action, to show our acquiescence in those acts of Parliament so universally and justly odious to all America, that on the contrary, we hoped we might in that way contribute to their repeal; though now to our sorrow we find ourselves mistaken. And we do now further, declare, that we never intended the offence which this address occasioned; that if we had foreseen such an event we should never have signed it; as it always has been and now is our wish to live in harmony with our neighbors, and our serious determination is to promote to the utmost of our power the liberty, the welfare, and happines of our country, which is inseparably connected with our own.

John Nutting,	N. Sparhawk,	Thomas Barnard,
N. Goodale,	Andrew Dalglish,	Nathaniel Dabney,
Ebenezer Putnam,	E. A. Holyoke,	William Pickman,
Francis Cabot,	William Pynchon,	C. Gayton Pickman,

In Committee of Safety, Salem, May 30, 1775.—The declaration, of which the above is a copy, being presented and read, it was voted unanimously that the same was satisfactory; and that the said gentlemen ought to be received and treated as real friends to this country.

By order of the Committee,

RICHARD DERBY, JR., Chairman.

ADDRESS OF THE INHABITANTS OF MARBLEHEAD TO GOV. HUTCHINSON.

Marblehead, May 25, 1774.

His Majesty having been pleased to appoint his Excellency the Hon. Thomas Gage, Esq., to be governor and commander-in-chief over this province, and you, (as we are informed,) begin speedily to embark for Great Britain: We, the subscribers, merchants, traders, and others, inhabitants of Marblehead, beg leave to present your our valedictory address on this occasion; and as this is the only way we now have of expressing to you our entire approbation of your public conduct during the time you have presided in this province, and of making you a return of our most sincere and hearty thanks for the ready assistance which you have at all times afforded us, when applied to in matters which affected our navigation and commerce, we are induced from former experience of your goodness, to believe that you will freely indulge us in the pleasure of giving you this testimony of our sincere esteem and gratitude.

In your public administration, we are fully convinced that the general good was the mark which you have ever aimed at, and we can, sir, with pleasure assure you, that it is likewise the opinion of all dispassionate thinking men within the circle of our observation, notwithstanding many publications would have taught the world to think the contrary;

and we beg leave to entreat you, that when you arrive at the court of Great Britain, you would there embrace every opportunity of moderating the resentment of the government against us, and use your best endeavors to have the unhappy dispute between Great Britain and this country brought to a just and equitable determination.

We cannot omit the opportunity of returning you in a particular manner our most sincere thanks for your patronizing our cause in the matter of entering and clearing the fishing vessels at the custom-house, and making the fishermen pay hospital money; we believe it is owing to your representation of the matter, that we are hitherto free from that burden.

We heartily wish you, sir, a safe and prosperous passage to Great Britain, and when you arrive there may you find such a reception as shall fully compensate for all the insults and indignities which have been offered you.

Henry Saunders,	John Fowle,	Thomas Lewis,
Richard Hinkly,	Robert Hooper, 3d,	Sweet Hooper,
Samuel Reed,	John Gallison,	Robert Hooper,
John Lee,	John Prince,	Jacob Fowle,
Robert Ambrose,	George McCall,	John Pedrick,
Jonathan Glover,	Joseph Swasey,	Richard Reed,
Richard Phillips,	Nathan Bowen,	Benjamin Marston,
Issac Mansfield,	Thomas Robie,	Samuel White,
Joseph Bubler,	John Stimson,	Joseph Hooper,
Richard Stacy,	John Webb,	John Prentice,
Thomas Procter,	Joseph Lee,	Robert Hooper, jr.

ADDRESS TO GOVERNOR HUTCHINSON FROM HIS FELLOW TOWNSMEN IN THE TOWN OF MILTON.

This document which was printed recently in the "History of Milton," was not a matter of record, and had never been printed before, it had also failed to meet the searching eye of the antiquarian, and the author said "it has come down to us in its original manuscript yellow with age."

It will be noticed the signers were obliged to recant, so as to save their property from being destroyed by the mob, and from personal injury and insult such as tarring and feathering, etc. It was with such doings that the "Sons of Despotism" amused themselves, and made converts to the cause of "liberty." It, however, did not save James Murray and Stephen Miller, who were banished, and Miller's estate confiscated.

To THOMAS HUTCHINSON *Esquire Late Gov. &c.*

SIR,—We the Select Men, the Magistrates and other principal Inhabitants of the Town of Milton, hearing of your speedy Embarkation for England, cannot let you leave this Town which you have so long honored by your Residence without some publick Expression of our sincere wishes for your health and happiness.

We have been Eye Witnesses, Sir, of your amiable private and useful publick Life; We have with concern beheld you, in the faithful and prudent Discharge of your Duty exposed to Calumnies, Trials and Sufferings, as unjust as severe; and seen you bearing them all with becoming Meekness and Fortitude.

As to ourselves and Neighbours in particular; altho many of us, in future Perplexities will often feel the Want of your skillful gratuitous advice, always ready for those who asked it, we cannot but rejoice for your Sake Sir, at your being so seasonably relieved by an honourable and worthy Successor, in this critical and distressful period from the growing Difficulty of the Government of your beloved native Province. And we see your Departure with the less Regret, being convinced that the Change at present will contribute to your and your Family's Tranquility: possessed as you are of the applause of good men, of the favour of our Sovereign, and the Approbation of a good Conscience to prepare the Way to Rewards infinitely ample from the King of Kings; to whose Almighty protection, We, with grateful hearts commend you and your family.

Signed

SAML. DAVENPORT	STEPHEN MILLER	BENJAMIN HORTON
JA. MURRAY	JOSIAH HOW	ZEDAH. CREHORE

REPLY OF GOVERNOR HUTCHINSON.

GENTLEMEN

I have received innumerable marks of respect and kindness from the Inhabitants of the Town of Milton, of which I shall ever retain the most grateful Remembrance. I leave you with regret. I hope to return and spend the short remains of my life among you in peace and quiet and in doing every good office to you in my power.

THO. HUTCHINSON.

Milton, Sept. 21, 1774.—Messrs. Davenport Miller and How were taken to Task by the Town Meeting for having signed the above address altho it was never presented or published. They were required by next day to make an acknowledgement of their offence—And a Committee of fifteen was chosen to treat with them and Mr. Murray.

Sept. 22. These Culprits attended and made the following acknowledgement, of which the Committee accepted, requiring them to sign it and to read it severally before the Town Meeting on the green. This done the Meeting by some Majority voted it not satisfactory. The offenders all but Capt. Davenport went home without making any other.

ACKNOWLEDGEMENT.

Whereas We the Subscribers did sign and endeavour to promote among the Inhabitants of our Town of Milton an Address to Gov. Hutchinson a few days before his Embarkation for England, which Address contained Compliments to the Gov. that we did and do still, in our consciences, believe to be justly due to him; and Whereas we did further believe that it would be very acceptable to the Town to give them such an Opportunity of showing their gratitude to the Governor.

Now since the Temper of the Times is such, that what we meant to please has eventually displeased our Neighbours, We, who desire to live in peace and good will with them are sorry for it. Witness our hands this 22d. day of Sept. 1774.

Signed

JA. MURRAY   SAML. DAVENPORT.
STEPHEN MILLER   JOSIAH HOW

After the departure of the first three of these, the meeting insisted on Capt. Davenport's making the following acknowledgement, and that the committee should have the rest to make it at or before the next town-meeting on Monday, 3d October:—

Whereas We the Subscribers have given the good People of this Town and Province in General just Cause to be offended with each of us, in that unguarded action of ours in signing an address to the late Governor Hutchinson, for which we are heartily sorry and take this opportunity publickly to manifest it, and declare we did not so well consider the Contents. And we heartily beg their forgiveness and all others we may have offended: Also that we may be restored to their favour, and be made Partakers of that inestimable blessing, the good Will of our Neighbours, and the whole Community.

Witness our hands

Milton 22d Sept. signed SAML. DAVENPORT
   24 Sept. ——— JOSIAH HOW
   25 Sept. ——— JA. MURRAY
   25 Sept. ——— STEPHEN MILLER

Address presented to His Excellency Governor Gage, June 11th, 1774, on his Arrival at Salem.

To his Excellency Thomas Gage, Esq., Captain-General, Governor and Commander-in-Chief of the Province of Massachusetts Bay in New England, and Lieutenant-General of his Majesty's Forces.

May it please your Excellency:

We, merchants and others, inhabitants of the ancient town of Salem, beg leave to approach your Excellency with our most respectful congratulations on your arrival in this place.

We are deeply sensible of his Majesty's paternal care and affection to this province, in the appointment of a person of your Excellency's experience, wisdom and moderation, in these troublesome and difficult times.

We rejoice that this town is graciously distinguished for that spirit, loyalty, and reverence for the laws, which is equally our glory and happiness.

From that public spirit and warm zeal to promote the general happiness of men, which mark the great and good, we are led to hope under your Excellency's administration for everything that may promote the peace, prosperity, and real welfare of this province.

We beg leave to commend to your Excellency's patronage the trade and commerce of this place, which, from a full protection of the liberties, persons and properties of individuals, cannot but flourish.

And we assure your Excellency we will make it our constant endeavors by peace, good order, and a regard for the laws, as far as in us lies, to render your station and residence easy and happy.

John Sargent,	John Prince,	Benjamin Lynde,
Jacob Ashton,	George Deblois,	William Browne,
William Wetmore,	Andrew Dalglish,	John Turner,
James Grant,	Joseph Blaney,	P. Frye,
Henry Higginson,	Archelaus Putnam,	Francis Cabot,
David Britton,	Samuel Porter,	William Pynchon,
P. G. Kast,	Thomas Poynton,	John Fisher,
Weld Gardner,	Samuel Flagg,	John Mascarene,
Nathaniel Daubney,	Nathan Goodale,	E. A. Holyoke,
Richard Nicholls,	William Pickman,	Jos. Bowditch,
William Cabot,	C. Gayton Pickman,	Ebenezer Putnam,
Cabot Gerrish,	Nathaniel Sparhawk,	S. Curwen,
William Gerrish,	William Vans,	John Nutting,
Rowland Savage,	Timothy Orne,	Jos. Dowse,
William Lilly,	Richard Routh,	Benjamin Pickman,
Jonathan Goodhue,	Stephen Higginson,	Henry Gardner.

The "Loyal Address from the Gentlemen and Principal Inhabitants of Boston to Governor Gage on his departure for England, October 6, 1775," was signed as follows:

John Erving,
Thomas Hutchinson, jr.,
Silvester Gardiner,
Wm. Bowes,
John Timmins,
Nathaniel Coffin,
John Winslow, jr.,
Alexander Bymer,
Robert Hallowell,
Robert Jarvis,
David Phips,
John Tayler,
Archibald McNeal,
Francis Green,
Benjamin Davis,
Thomas Courtney,
John Sampson,
William Tayler,
John Inman,
Wm. Perry,
John Gore,
Isaac Winslow, jr.,
William Dickerson,
William Hunter,
Robert Semple,
John Joy,
Gregory Townsend,
Isaac Winslow,
Byfield Lyde,
John Love,
Hugh Tarbett,
Nathaniel Perkins,
John Powell,
James Selkrig,
Archibald Cunningham,
William Cazneau,
David Barton,
John Semple,
Henry Lawton,
William Brattle,
John Troutbeck,
Stephen Greenleaf,
William Walter,
James Perkins,
Phillip Dumaresque,
Joshua Loring, jr.,
Henry Lloyd,
William Lee Perkins.
George Leonard,
Thomas Brinley,
Daniel Hubbard,
Samuel Fitch,
John Atkinson,
Joseph Turill.
Samuel Hirst Sparhawk,
Ebenezer Brigham,
William Codner,
Jonathan Snelling,
Benjamin Gridley,
Gilbert Deblois,
Edward Hutchinson,
Miles Whitworth,
Daniel McMasters,
John Hunt, 3d,
James Lloyd,
William McAlpine,
John Greecart,
Richard Clarke,
Benjamin Fanieul, jr.,
Thomas Amory,
George Brindley,
Ralph Inman,
Edward Winslow,
Benjamin M. Holmes,
William Jackson,
Richard Green,
James Murray,
Joseph Scott,
Peter Johonnot.
Nathaniel Cary,
Martin Gay,
Samuel Hughes,
William Coffin, jr.,
Adino Paddock,
Andrew Cazneau,
Henry Lindall,
Theophilus Lillie,
Henry Barnes,
M. B. Goldthwait,
Lewis Gray,
Nathaniel Brinley,
John Jeffries, jr.,
Archibald Bowman,
Jonathan Simpson,
Nathaniel Tayler,
James Anderson,
Lewis Deblois,

The Loyal Address to Governor Gage on his departure, October 14, 1775, of those Gentlemen who were driven from their Habitations in the Country to the Town of Boston, was signed by the following persons:

John Chandler,
James Putnam,
Peter Oliver, sen.,
Seth Williams, jr.,
Charles Curtis,
Samuel Pine,
David Phips,
Richard Saltonstall,
Peter Oliver, jr.,

Jonathan Stearns, Thomas Foster, Edward Winslow, jr.,
Ward Chipman, Pelham Winslow, Nathaniel Chandler,
William Chandler, Daniel Oliver, James Putnam, jr.

List of the inhabitants of Boston, who on the evacuation by the British, in March, 1776, removed to Halifax with the army. Taken from a paper in the handwriting of Walter Barrell from the Proceedings of the Mass. Hist. Soc., Vol. 18, page 266.

Lieutenant-Governor Oliver and servants	6

Council, &c.

Peter Oliver and niece	2
Harrison Gray and family	5
Timothy Ruggles and sons	3
Foster Hutchinson and family	13
Josiah Edson	1
John Murray and family	7
Richard Lechmere	12
John Erving	9
Nathaniel Ray Thomas and son	2
Abijah Willard and two sons	3
Daniel Leonard and family	9
Nathaniel Hatch	7
George Erving	6

Custom House.

Henry Hulton	12
Charles Paxton	6
Benjamin Hallowel	7
Samuel Waterhouse, *Secretary*	7
James Porter, *Comptroller Gen'l*	1
Walter Barrell, *Inspector Gen'l*	6
James Murray, *Inspector*	7
William Woolen, *Inspector*	2
Edward Winslow, *Collector, Boston*	1
Charles Dudley, *Collector, Newport*	2
George Meserve, *Collector, Piscataq.*	1
Robert Hallowel, *Comptroller, Boston*	6
Arthur Savage, *Surveyor, &c.*	6
Nathaniel Coffin, *Cashier*	4
Ebenezer Bridgham, *Tide Surveyor*	8
Nathaniel Taylor, *Dep'y Naval Officer*	2
Samuel Mather, *Clerk*	3
Samuel Lloyd, *Clerk*	6
Christopher Minot, *Land Waiter*	1
Ward Chipman, *Clerk Sol.*	1
Robert Bethel, *Clerk Col.*	1
Skinner, Cookson, and Evans *Clerks*	3
James Barrick, *Clerk Insp.*	5
John Ciely, *Tidesman*	4
John Sam Petit, *Tidesman*	6
John Selby, *Clerk*	2
Edward Mulhall, *Tidesman*	1
Hammond Green, *Tidesman*	1
John Lewis, *Tidesman*	6
Elkanah Cushman, *Tidesman*	1
Edmund Duyer, *Messenger*	3
Samuel Chadwel, *Tidesman*	1
Samuel Sparhawk, *Clerk*	5
—— Chandler, *Land Waiter*	1
—— Patterson, *Land Waiter*	1
Isaac Messengham, *Coxwain*	1
Owen Richard, *Coxwain*	1

Refugees.

Ashley, Joseph	1
Andros, Barret	1
Atkinson, John, *Merchant*	4

134 THE LOYALISTS OF MASSACHUSETTS

Atkins, Gibbs	1
Ayres, Eleanor	3
Allen, Ebenezer	8
Bowes, William, *Merchant*	4
Brinley, Thomas, *Merchant*	3
Burton, Mary, *Milliner*	2
Bowen, John	2
Blair, John, *Baker*	1
Bowman, Archibald, *Auctioneer*	1
Broderick, John	3
Butter, James	2
Brown, Thomas, *Merchant*	6
Byles, Rev'd Doctor	5
Barnard, John	1
Black, John	7
Baker, John, Jun'r	1
Badger, Rev'd Moses	1
Beath, Mary	4
Butler, Gilliam	1
Brandon, John	2
Brattle, William	2
Coffin, William	2
Cazneau, Andrew, *Lawyer*	1
Cednor, William	1
Connor, Mrs.	2
Cummins, A. and E. *Milliners*	3
Coffin, William, Jun'r, *Merchant*	4
Cutler, Ebenezer	1
Campbel, William	1
Caner, Rev'd Doctor	1
Cook Robert	1
Chandler, John, Esq'r	1
Chandler, Rufus, *Lawyer*	2
Chandler, Nathaniel	1
Chandler, William	1
Carver, Melzer	1
Cooley, John	4
Courtney, Thomas	11
Carr, Mrs.	3
Deblois Gilbert	5
Doyley, John	4
Dunlap, Daniel	1
Danforth, Thomas	1
Dumaresq, Philip, *Merchant*	8
De Blois, Lewis	3
Duncan, Alexander	1
Doyley, Francis	1
Dickenson, Nathaniel	1
Draper, Margaret	5
Dougherty, Edward	2
Dechezzan, Adam	7
Duelly, William	3
Emerson, John	1
Etter, Peter	7
Fisher, Wilfree	4
Foster, Thomas	1
Faneuil, Benjamin, *Merchant*	3
Fitch, Samuel, *Lawyer*	7
Foster, Edward, *Blacksmith*	7
Full, Thomas	5
Foster, Edward, Jun'r	5
Forest, James	7
Flucker, Mrs.	6
Gilbert, Thomas	1
Gallop, Antill	1
Gray, Andrew	1
Gray, John	3
Goldsbury, Samuel	3
Gardiner, Doctor Sylvester	8
Gridley, Benjamin	1
Grison, Edmund	2
Gay, Martin	3
Gilbert, Samuel	1
Grozart, John	1
Gray, Mary	1
Green, Francis	8
Greenwood, Samuel	5
Grant, James	1
Griffith, Mrs.	3
Gore, John	3
Griffin, Edmund	4
Hill, William	17
Hallowel, Rebecca	4
Hall, Luke	1
Henderson, James	5
House, Joseph	1
Hughes, Samuel	1
Hooper, Jacob	2
Hicks, John, *Printer*	1
Hurlston, Richard	1
Holmes, Benjamin Mulberry	11
Hatch, Hawes	1

Hale, Samuel	1	McMullen, Alexander	1
Hester, John	6	Mitchel, Thomas	1
Hutchinsen, Mrs.	7	Mills, Nathaniel	2
Horn, Henry	7	McClintock, Nathan	1
Hefferson, Jane	1	Nevin, Lazarus and wife	2
Heath, William	1	O'Neil, Joseph	4
Jones, Mary	6	Oliver, William Sanford	1
Jarvis, Robert	1	Oliver, Doctor Peter	1
Inman, John	3	Powel, John	8
Joy, John	8	Philips, Martha	3
Ireland, John	2	Phipps, David	11
Jefferies, Doctor John	6	Pelham, Henry	1
Johannot, Peter	1	Putnam, James	7
Jones, Mrs.	4	Paine, Samuel	1
Knutter, Margaret	4	Perkins, Nathaniel	1
King, Edward and Samuel	7	Patterson, William	3
Lazarus, Samuel	1	Philipps, Ebenezer	1
Lovel, John, Sen'r	5	Paddock, Adine	9
Leonard, George	9	Pollard, Benjamin	1
Liste, Mrs.	5	Patten, George	3
Lillie, Theophilus	4	Perkins, William Lee	4
Lutwiche, Edward Goldston	1	Price, Benjamin	2
Lyde, Byefield	5	Page, George	1
Leddel, Henry	4	Rummer, Richard	3
Laughton, Henry	5	Rogers, Jeremiah Dummer	2
Lloyd, Henry	10	Rogers, Samuel	1
Linkieter, Alexander	4	Richardson, Miss	1
Lowe, Charles	2	Rose, Peter	1
Loring, Joshua, Jun'r	1	Read, Charles	1
Murray, William	3	Ramage, John	1
Moody, John, Jun'r	1	Roath, Richard	6
McKown, John	1	Rhodes, Henry	5
McAlpine, William	2	Russell, Nathaniel	3
Moody, John	4	Richards, Mrs.	3
McKown, John (of Boston)	5	Ruggles, John and Richard	2
Macdonald, Dennis	1	Smith, Henry	6
Mackay, Mrs.	1	Sullivan, George	1
Mitchelson, David	2	Serjeant, John	1
McNeil, Archibald	13	Scoit, Joseph	3
Marston, Benjamin	1	Simonds, William	3
Moore, John	1	Stow, Edward	4
Miller, John	5	Sterling, Elizabeth	1
Mulcainy, Patrick	4	Sterling, Benjamin Ferdinand	1
MacKinstrey, Mrs.	12	Simpson, John	5
Morrison, John	1	Simpson, Jonathan, Jun'r	2
McMaster, Patrick and Daniel	3	Semple, Robert	4

136 THE LOYALISTS OF MASSACHUSETTS

Stayner, Abigail	3	Winslow, Edward	1
Stearns, Jonathan	1	Williams, Seth	1
Savage, Abraham	1	Willis, David	4
Saltonstal, Leveret	1	Wittington, William	3
Service, Robert	5	Warden, William	2
Snelling, Jonathan	6	Williams, Job	1
Sullivan, Bartholomew	2	Warren, Abraham	1
Smith, Edward	4	Willard, Abel	4
Spooner, Ebenezer	1	Warden, Joseph	3
Selknig, James	6	Willard, Abijah	1
Scammel, Thomas	1	Whiston, Obadiah	3
Shepard, Joseph	2	Wheelwright, Joseph	1
Thompson, James	1	Winnet, John, Jun'r	1
Taylor, Mrs.	5	Wright, Daniel	2
Terry, Zebedee	1	Welsh, Peter	1
Terry, William	4	White, Gideon	1
Taylor, William	2	Wilson, Archibald	1
Winslow, Isaac	11	Welsh, James	1
Winslow, Pelham	1	Worral, Thomas Grooby	5
Winslow, John	4		
Winslow, Mrs. Hannah	4		[927] 926

For Mr. Samuel B. Barrell
From his friend and kinsman,
Theodore Barrell

Saugerties Ulster Co.,
New York, Aug. 16, 1841.

MANDAMUS COUNSELLORS.

Salem, Aug. 9, 1774. The following were appointed by his majesty, counsellors of this province by writ of mandamas,* viz:—

Col. Thomas Oliver, Lieut. Governor, President; Peter Oliver, *Thomas Flucker, Foster Hutchinson.* Thomas Hutchinson, Jr., *Harrison Gray,* Judge Samuel Danforth, Col. John Erving, Jr., James Russell, Timothy Ruggles, *Joseph Lee, Isaac Winslow,* Israel Williams, Col. George Watson, Nathaniel Ray Thomas, Timothy Woodbridge, William Vassall, *William Browne,* Joseph Greene, *James Boutineau,* Andrew Oliver, Col. Josiah Edson, Richard Lechmere, *Commodore Joshua Loring,* John Worthington, Timothy Paine, *William Pepperell,* Jeremiah Powell, Jonathan Simpson, Col. John Murray, Daniel Leonard, Thomas Palmer, Col. Isaac Royall, Robert Hooper, Abijah Willard, *Capt. John Erving, Jr.*

* Those whose names are in italics alone took the oath of office.

BANISHMENT ACT OF THE STATE OF MASSACHUSETTS.

An Act to prevent the return to this state of certain persons therein named, and others who have left this state or either of the United States, and joined the enemies thereof.

Whereas Thomas Hutchinson, Esq., late governor of this state, Francis Bernard, Esq., formerly governor of this state, Thomas Oliver, Esq., late lieutenant governor of this state, Timothy Ruggles, Esq., of Hardwick, in the county of Worcester, William Apthorp, merchant, Gibbs Atkins, cabinet maker, John Atkinson, John Amory, James Anderson, Thomas Apthorp, David Black, William Burton, William Bowes, George Brindley, Robert Blair, Thomas Brindley, James Barrick, merchant, Thomas Brattle, Esq., Sampson Salter Blowers, Esq., James Bruce, Ebenezer Bridgham, Alexander Brymer, Edward Berry, merchants, William Burch, Esq., late commissioner of the customs, Mather Byles, Jun., clerk, William Codner, book-keeper, Edward Cox, merchant, Andrew Cazneau, Esq., barrister at law, Henry Canner, clerk, Thomas Courtney, tailor, Richard Clark, Esq., Isaac Clark, physician, Benjamin Church, physician, John Coffin, distiller, John Clark, physician, William Coffin, Esq., Nathaniel Coffin, Esq., Jonathan Clark, merchant, Archibald Cunningham, shop-keeper, Gilbert Deblois, merchant, Lewis Deblois, merchant, Philip Dumaresque, merchant, Benjamin Davis, merchant, John Erving, Jun. Esq., George Erving, Esq., Edward Foster and and Edward Foster, Jun., blacksmiths, Benjamin Faneuil, Jun., merchant, Thomas Flucker, Esq., late secretary for Massachusetts Bay, Samuel Fitch, Esq., Wilfret Fisher, carter, James Forrest, merchant, Lewis Gray, merchant, Francis Green, merchant, Joseph Green, Esq., Sylvester Gardiner, Esq., Harrison Gray, Esq., late treasurer of Massachusetts Bay., Harrison Gray, Jun., clerk to the treasurer, Joseph Goldthwait, Esq., Martin Gay, founder, John Gore, Esq., Benjamin Hallowell, Esq., Robert Hallowell, Esq., Thomas Hutchinson, Jun., Esq., Benjamin Gridley, Esq., Frederick William Geyer, merchant, John Greenlaw, shop-keeper, David Green, merchant, Elisha Hutchinson, Esq., James Hall, mariner, Foster Hutchinson, Esq., Benjamin Mulbury Holmes, distiller, Samuel Hodges, book-keeper, Henry Halson, Esq., Hawes Hatch, wharfinger, John Joy, housewright, Peter Johonnot, distiller, William Jackson, merchant, John Jeffries, physician, Henry Laughton, merchant, James Henderson, trader, John Hinston, yeoman, Christopher Hatch, mariner, Robert Jarvis, mariner, Richard Lechmere, Esq., Edward Lyde, merchant, Henry Lloyd, Esq., George Leonard, miller, Henry Leddle, book-keeper, Archibald McNeil, baker, Christopher Minot, tide-waiter, James Murray, Esq., William McAlpine, bookbinder, Thomas Mitchell, mariner, William Martin, Esq., John Knutton, tallow-chandler, Thomas Knight, shop-keeper, Samuel Prince, merchant, Adino Paddock, Esq.,

Charles Paxon, Esq., Sir William Pepperell, baronet, John Powell, Esq., William Lee Perkins, physician, Nathaniel Perkins, Esq., Samuel Quincy, Esq., Owen Richards, tide-waiter, Samuel Rogers, merchant, Jonathan Simpson, Esq., George Spooner, merchant, Edward Stowe, mariner, Richard Smith, merchant, Jonathan Snelling, Esq., David Silsby, trader, Samuel Sewall, Esq., Abraham Savage, tax-gatherer, Joseph Scott, Esq., Francis Skinner, clerk to the late council, William Simpson, merchant, Richard Sherwin, saddler, Henry Smith, merchant, John Semple, merchant, Robert Semple, merchant, Thomas Selkrig, merchant, James Selkrig, merchant, Robert Service, trader, Simon Tufts, trader, Arodi Thayer, late marshal to the admiralty court, Nathaniel Taylor, deputy naval officer, John Troutbeck, clerk, Gregory Townsend, Esq., William Taylor, merchant, William Vassal, Esq., Joseph Taylor, merchant, Joshua Upham, Esq., William Walter, clerk, Samuel Waterhouse, merchant, Isaac Winslow, merchant, John Winslow, jr., merchant, David Willis, mariner, Obadiah Whiston, blacksmith, Archibald Wilson, trader, John White, mariner, William Warden, peruke-maker, Nathaniel Mills, John Hicks, John Howe, and John Fleming, printers, all of Boston, in the county of Suffolk, Robert Auchmuty, Esq., Joshua Loring, Esq., both of Roxbury, in the same county, Samuel Goldsbury, yeoman, of Wrentham, in the county of Suffolk, Joshua Loring, jr., merchant, Nathanial Hatch, Esq., both of Dorchester, in the same county, William Brown, Esq., Benjamin Pickman, Esq., Samuel Porter, Esq., John Sargeant, trader, all of Salem, in the county of Essex, Richard Saltonstall, Esq., of Haverhill, in the same county. Thomas Robie, trader, Benjamin Marston, merchant, both of Marblehead, in said county of Essex, Moses Badger, clerk, of Haverhill, aforesaid, Jonathan Sewall, Esq., John Vassal, Esq., David Phipps, Esq., John Nutting, carpenter, all of Cambridge, in the county of Middlesex. Isaac Royall, Esq., of Medford, in the same county, Henry Barnes, of Marlborough, in said county of Middlesex, merchant, Jeremiah Dummer Rogers, of Littleton in the same county, Esq., Daniel Bliss, of Concord, in the said county of Middlesex, Esq., Charles Russell, of Lincoln, in the same county, physician, Joseph Adams, of Townsend, in said county of Middlesex, Thomas Danforth, of Charlestown, in said county, Esq., Joshua Smith, trader of Townsend, in said county, Joseph Ashley, jr., gentleman, of Sunderland, Nathaniel Dickenson, gentleman, of Deerfield, Samuel Bliss, shopkeeper, of Greenfield, Roger Dickenson, yeoman, Joshah Pomroy, physician, and Thomas Cutler, gentleman, of Hatfield, Jonathan Bliss, Esq., of Springfield, William Galway, yeoman, of Conway, Elijah Williams, attorney at law, of Deerfield, James Oliver, gentleman, of Conway, all in the county of Hampshire, Pelham Winslow, Esq., Cornelius White, mariner, Edward Winslow, jr., Esq., all of Plymouth, in the county of Plymouth, Peter Oliver, Esq., Peter Oliver, jr., physician, both of Middleborough, in the same county, Josiah Edson, Esq., of Bridgewater, in the said county of Plymouth, Lieutenant Daniel Dunbar, of Halifax, in the same county, Charles Curtis, of Scituate, in the said county of Plymouth, gentleman, Nathaniel Ray Thomas, Esq., Israel Tilden, Caleb Carver, Seth Bryant, Benjamin Walker, Gideon Walker, Zera Walker, Adam Hall, tertius, Isaac Joice, Joseph Phillips, Daniel White, jr., Cornelius White, tertius, Melzar Carver, Luke Hall, Thomas Decrow, John Baker, jr., all of Marshfield, in the said county of Plymouth, Gideon White, jr., Daniel Leonard, Esq., Seth Williams, jr., gentleman, Solomon Smith, boatman, all of Taunton, in the county of Bristol, Thomas Gilbert, Esq., Perez Gilbert, Ebenezer Hathaway, jr., Lot Strange, the third, Zebedee Terree, Bradford Gilbert, all of Freetown, in the same county, Joshua Broomer, Shadrach Hathaway, Calvin Hathaway, Luther Hathaway, Henry Tisdel, William Burden, Levi Chace, Shadrach Chace, Richard Holland, Ebenezer Phillips, Samuel Gilbert, gentleman, Thomas Gilbert, jr., yeoman, both of Berkley, in the said county of Bristol, Ammi Chace, Caleb Wheaton, Joshua Wilbore, Lemuel Bourn, gentleman, Thomas Perry, yeoman, David Atkins, laborer, Samuel Perry, mariner, Stephen Perry, laborer, John Blackwell, jr., laborer, Francis Finney, laborer, and Nehemiah Webb, mariner, all of Sandwich, in the county of Barnstable, Eldad Tupper, of Dartmouth, in the county of Bristol, laborer, Silas Perry, laborer, Seth Perry, mariner, Elisha Bourn, gentleman, Thomas Bumpus, yeoman, Ephraim Ellis, jr., yeoman, Edward Bourn, gentleman, Nicholas Cobb, laborer, William Bourn, cordwainer, all of Sandwich, in the county of Barnstable, and Seth Bangs, of Harwich, in the county of Barnstable, mariner, John Chandler, Esq., James Putnam, Esq., Rufus Chandler, gentleman, William Paine, physician, Adam Walker, blacksmith, William Chandler, gentleman, all of Worcester, in the county of Worcester, John Walker, gentleman, David Bush, yeoman, both of Shrewsbury, in the same county, Abijah Willard, Esq., Abel Willard, Esq., Joseph House, yeoman, all of Lancaster, in the said county of Worcester, Ebenezer Cutler, trader, James Edgar, yeoman, both of Northbury, in the same county, Daniel Oliver, Esq., Richard Ruggles, yeoman, Gardner Chandler, trader, Joseph Ruggles, gentleman, Nathaniel Ruggles, yeoman, all of Hardwick, in the said county of Worcester, John Ruggles, yeoman, of said Hardwick, John Eager, yeoman, Ebenezer Whipple, Israel Conkay, John Murray, Esq., of Rutland, in said county of Worcester, Daniel Murray, gentleman, Samuel Murray, gentleman, Michael Martin, trader, of Brookfield, in the said county of Worcester, Thomas Beaman, gentleman, of Petersham, in the same county, Nathaniel Chandler, gentleman, John Bowen, gentleman, of Princeton, in the said county of Worcester, James Crage, gentleman, of Oakham, in the same county, Thomas Mullins, blacksmith, of Leominster, in the said county of Worcester, Francis Waldo, Esq., Arthur Savage, Esq., Jeremiah Pote, mariner, Thomas Ross, mariner, James Wildridge, mariner, George Lyde, custom house officer, Robert Pagan, merchant, Thomas Wyer, mariner, Thomas Coulson, merchant, John Wiswall, clerk, Joshua Eldridge, mariner, Thomas Oxnard, merchant, Edward Oxnard, merchant, William Tyng, Esq., John Wright, merchant, Samuel Longfellow, mariner, all of Falmouth, in the county of Cumberland, Charles Callahan, of Pownalborough, in the county of Lincoln, mariner, Jonas Jones of East Hoosuck, in the county of Berkshire, David Ingersoll, of Great Barrington, Esq., in the same county, Jonathan Prindall, Benjamin Noble, Francis Noble, Elisha Jones, of Pittsfield, in the said county of Berkshire, John Graves, yeoman, Daniel Brewer, yeoman, both of Pittsfield, aforesaid, Richard Square, of Lanesborough, in the said county of Berkshire, Ephraim Jones, of East Hoosuck, in the same county. Lewis Hubbel, and many other persons have left this state, or some other of the United States of America, and joined the enemies thereof and of the United States of America, thereby not only depriving these states of their personal services at a time when they ought to have afforded their utmost aid in defending the said states, against the invasions of a cruel enemy, but manifesting an inimical disposition to the said states, and a design, to aid and abet the enemies thereof in their wicked purposes, and whereas many dangers may accrue to this state and the United States, if such persons should be again admitted to reside in this state:

Sect. 1. Be it therefore enacted by the Council and House of Representatives, in general court assembled, and by the authority of the same, that if either of the said persons, or any other person, though not specially named in this act, who have left this state, or either of said states, and joined the enemies thereof as aforesaid, shall, after the passing this act, voluntarily return to this state, it shall be the duty of the sheriff of the county, and of the selectmen, committees of correspondence, safety, and inspection, grand jurors, constables, and tythingmen, and other inhabitants of the town wherein such person or persons may presume to come, and they are hereby respectively empowered and directed forthwith to apprehend and carry such person or persons before some justice of the peace within the county, who is hereby required to commit him or them to the common gaol within the county, there in close custody to remain until he shall be sent out of the state, as is hereinafter directed; and such justice is hereby directed to give immediate information thereof to the board of war of this state: and the said board of war are hereby empowered and directed to cause such person or persons so committed, to be transported to some part or place within the dominions, or in the possession of the forces of the king of Great Britain, as soon as may be after receiving such information: those who are able, at their own expense, and others at the expense of this state, and for this purpose to hire a vessel or vessels, if need be.

Sect. 2. And be it further enacted by the authority aforesaid, that if any person or persons, who shall be transported as aforesaid, shall voluntarily return into this state, without liberty first had and obtained from the general court, he shall, on conviction thereof before the superior court of judicature, court of assize and general gaol delivery, suffer the pains of death without benefit of clergy.—[*Passed, September,* 1778.]

WORCESTER RESOLUTIONS RELATING TO THE ABSENTEES AND REFUGEES.

The following votes were passed by the citizens of Worcester, May 19, 1783, and contain the substance of their doings relative to the refugees:

Voted,—That in the opinion of this town, it would be extremely dangerous to the peace, happiness, liberty and safety of these states, to suffer those who, the moment the bloody banners were displayed, abandoned their native land, turned parricides, and conspired to involve their country in tumult, ruin and blood, to become subjects of and reside in this government; that it would be not only dangerous, but inconsistent with justice, policy, our past laws, the public faith, and the principles of a free and independent state, to admit them ourselves, or have them forced upon us without our consent.

Voted,—That in the opinion of this town, this commonwealth ought, with the utmost caution, to naturalize or in any other way admit as subjects a common enemy, a set of people who have been by the united voice of the continent, declared outlaws, exiles, aliens and enemies, dangerous to its political being and happiness.

Voted,—That while there are thousands of the innocent, peaceable and defenceless inhabitants of these states, whose property has been destroyed and taken from them in the course of the war, for whom no provision is made, to whom there is no restoration of estates, no compensation for losses; that it would be unreasonable, cruel and unjust, to suffer those who were the wicked occasion of those losses, to obtain a restitution of the estates they refused to protect, and which they abandoned and forfeited to their country.

Voted,—That it is the expectation of this town, and the earnest request of their committees of correspondence, inspection and safety, that they, with care and diligence, will observe the movements of our only remaining enemies; that until the further order of government, they will, with decision, spirit and firmness, endeavor to enforce and carry into execution the several laws of this commonwealth, respecting these enemies to our rights, and the rights of mankind; give information should they know of any obtruding themselves into any part of this state, suffer none to remain in this town, but cause to be confined immediately, for the purpose of transportation according to law, any that may presume to enter it.

CONFISCATION ACT.

CONSPIRACY ACT.

An Act to confiscate the estates of certain notorious conspirators against the government and liberties of the inhabitants of the late province, now state, of Massachusetts Bay.

Whereas the several persons hereinafter mentioned, have wickedly conspired to overthrow and destroy the constitution and government of the late province of Massachusetts Bay, as established by the charter agreed upon by and between their late majesties William and Mary, late King and Queen of England, etc., and the inhabitants of said province, now state, of Massachusetts Bay; and also to reduce the said inhabitants under the absolute power and domination of the present king, and of the parliament of Great Britain, and, as far as in them lay, have aided and assisted the same king and parliament in their endeavors to establish a despotic government over the said inhabitants:

Sect. 1. Be it enacted by the Council and House of Representatives, in General Court assembled, and by the authority of the same, that Francis Bernard, baronet, Thomas Hutchinson, Esq., late governor of the late province, now state, of Massachusetts Bay, Thomas Oliver, Esq., late lieutenant governor, Harrison Grey, Esq., late treasurer, Thomas Flucker, Esq., late secretary, Peter Oliver, Esq., late chief justice, Foster Hutchinson, John Erving, jr., George Erving, William Pepperell, baronet, James Boutineau, Joshua Loring, Nathaniel Hatch, William Browne, Richard Lechmere, Josiah Edson, Nathaniel Rae Thomas, Timothy Ruggles, John Murray, Abijah Willard, and Daniel Leonard, Esqs., late mandamus counsellors of said late province, William Burch, Henry Hulton, Charles Paxon, and Benjamin Hallowell, Esqs., late commissioners of the customs, Robert Auchmuty, Esq., late judge of the vice-admiralty court, Jonathan Sewall, Esq., late attorney general, Samuel Quincy, Esq., late solicitor general, Samuel Fitch, Esq., solicitor or counsellor at law to the board of commissioners, have justly incurred the forfeiture of all their property, rights and liberties, holden under and derived from the government and laws of this state; and that each and every of the persons aforenamed and described, shall be held, taken, deemed and adjudged to have renounced and lost all civil and political relation to this and the other United States of America, and be considered as aliens.

Sect. 2. Be it enacted by the authority aforesaid, that all the goods and chattels, rights and credits, lands, tenements, and hereditaments of every kind, of which any of the persons herein before named and described, were seized or possessed, or were entitled to possess, hold, enjoy, or demand, in their own right, or which any other person stood or doth stand seized or possessed of, or are or were entitled to have or demand to and for their use, benefit and behoof, shall escheat, enure and accrue to the sole use and benefit of the government and people of this state, and are accordingly hereby declared so to escheat, enure and accrue, and the said government and people shall be taken, deemed and adjudged, and are accordingly hereby declared to be in the real and actual possession of all such goods, chattels, rights and credits, lands, tenements and hereditaments, without further inquiry, adjudication or determination hereafter to be had: any thing in the act, entitled, "An act for confiscating the effects of certain persons commonly called absentees," or any other law, usage, or custom to the contrary notwithstanding; provided always, that the escheat shall not be construed to extend to or operate upon, any goods, chattels, rights, credits, lands, tenements or hereditaments, of which the persons afore named and described, or some other, in their right and to their use, have not been seized or possessed, or entitled to be seized or possessed, or to have or demand as aforesaid, since the nineteenth day of April, in the year of our Lord one thousand seven hundred and seventy-five.—[*Passed April 30, 1779. Not revised.*]

STATE OF MASSACHUSETTS.

An Act for confiscating the estates of certain persons commonly called absentees.

Whereas every government hath a right to command the personal service of all its members, whenever the exigencies of the state shall require it, especially in times of an impending or actual invasion, no member thereof can then withdraw himself from the jurisdiction of the government, and thereby deprive it of the benefit of his personal services, without justly incurring the forfeiture of all his property, rights and liberties, holden under and derived from that constitution of government, to the support of which he hath refused to afford his aid and assistance: and whereas the king of Great Britain did cause the parliament thereof to pass divers acts in direct violation of the fundamental rights of the people of this and of the other United States of America; particularly one certain act to vacate and annul the charter of this government, the great compact made and agreed upon between his royal predecessors and our ancestors; and one other act, declaring the people of said states to be out of his protection; and did also levy war against them, for the purpose of erecting and establishing an arbitrary and despotic government over them; whereupon it became the indispensable duty of all the people of said states forthwith to unite in defence of their common freedom, and by arms to oppose the fleets and armies of the said king; yet nevertheless, divers of the members of this and of the other United States of America, evilly disposed, or regardless of their duty towards their country, did withdraw themselves from this, and other of the said United States, into parts and places under the acknowledged authority and dominion of the said king of Great Britain, or into parts and places within the limits of the said states, but in the actual possession and under the power of the fleets or armies of the said king; thereby abandoning the liberties of their country, seeking the protection of the said king, and of his fleets or armies, and aiding or giving encouragement and countenance to their operations against the United States aforesaid:

Sect. 1. Be it enacted by the Council and House of Representatives, in General Court assembled, and by the authority of the same, that every inhabitant and member of the late province, now state, of Massachusetts

Bay, or of any other of the late provinces or colonies, now United States of America, who, since the nineteenth day of April, Anno Domini one thousand seven hundred and seventy-five, hath levied war or conspired to levy war against the government and people of any of the said provinces or colonies, or United States; or who hath adhered to the said king of Great Britain, his fleets or armies, enemies of the said provinces or colonies or United States, or hath given to them aid or comfort; or who, since the said nineteenth day of April, Anno Domini one thousand seven hundred and seventy-five, hath withdrawn, without the permission of the legislative or executive authority of this or some other of the said United States, from any of the said provinces or colonies, or United States, into parts and places under the acknowledged authority and dominion of the said king of Great Britain, or into any parts or places within the limits of any of the said provinces, colonies, or United States, being in the actual possession and under the power of the fleets or armies of the said king; or who, before the said nineteenth day of April, Anno Domini one thousand seven hundred and seventy-five, and after the arrival of Thomas Gage, Esq., (late commander-in-chief of all his Britannic Majesty's forces in North America,) at Boston, the metropolis of this state, did withdraw from their usual places of habitation within this state, into the said town of Boston, with an intention to seek and obtain the protection of the said Thomas Gage and of the said forces, then and there being under his command: and who hath died in any of the said parts or places, or hath not returned into some one of the said United States, and been received as a subject thereof, and (if required) taken an oath of allegiance to such states, shall beheld, taken, deemed and adjudged to have freely renounced all civil and political relation to each and every of the said United States, and be considered as an alien.

Sect. 2. And be it further enacted by the authority aforesaid, that all the goods and chattels, rights and credits, lands, tenements, hereditaments of every kind, of which any of the persons herein before described were seized or possessed, or were entitled to possess, hold, enjoy or demand, in their own right, or which any other person stood or doth stand seized or possessed of, or are or were entitled to have or demand to and for their use, benefit and behoof, shall escheat, enure and accrue to the sole use and benefit of the government and people of this state, and are accordingly hereby declared so to escheat, enure and accrue.— [*Passed April* 30, 1779. *Not revised.*]

BIOGRAPHIES
OF THE
LOYALISTS OF MASSACHUSETTS

THOMAS HUTCHINSON.
GOVERNOR OF MASSACHUSETTS 1771-4.

Among all the loyalists of the revolted colonies, there was none so illustrious, through his position and abilities, as Thomas Hutchinson, Governor of Massachusetts. No public man of this State was ever subject to more slander, personal abuse, and misrepresentation than he, and no son of Massachusetts ever did so much to benefit and advance the best interests of the State; beyond all question he was the greatest and most famous man Massachusetts has ever produced.

Descended from one of the oldest and most noted of Massachusetts families, he was not one of the first members of it to acquire prominence, that distinction belongs to the celebrated Ann Hutchinson, wife of William Hutchinson who came over in 1634, " that woman of ready wit and bold spirit," more than a match for her reverend and magisterial inquisitors, and who won to her side men even of such power as John Cotton and Sir Henry Vane. She was finally banished and with her followers went to live under the protection of the Dutch, at Long Island where she and all of her family except one child were killed by the Indians*, her husband having died the year previous.** Her grandson, Elisha Hutchinson, became the first chief justice under the old charter and afterwards assistant and commander of the town of Boston. His son, Col. Thomas Hutchinson, was of scarcely less note. He it was who seized Captain Kidd when he resisted the officers of justice sent against him, and was the father of Governor Thomas Hutchinson. He was a wealthy merchant, and councillor who made his native town a sharer in his prosperity by founding the North End Grammar School. He lived in the North Square in the finest house in Boston. Here his son, the future governor, was born Sept. 9, 1711 and the two, father and son, occupied it for more than sixty years, till it was sacked by the mob in 1765.

* This was Colonel Edward H. Hutchinson who was killed by the Indians during King Philip's war. He was father of Elisha Hutchinson.

** William Hutchinson was the first grantee of East Milton, where the Governor afterwards resided. He settled in Boston on the "Old Corner Bookstore" lot, corner of School and Washington streets. William Hutchinson was the grandson of John Hutchinson, Mayor of Lincoln, England.

When five and a half years old the boy was sent to the school established by his father, and at the age of twelve went thence to Harvard College. He graduated in 1727, and three years after he took the degree of Master of Arts. He then became a merchant—apprentice in his father's counting room. At the age of twenty-one, he had amassed by his own efforts £500. He married Margaret Sanford, daughter of the Governor of Rhode Island. In 1735 he joined the church, in 1737 he became selectman of Boston, and four months later, was elected Representative to the General Court. At the age of twenty-six, he entered upon his wonderful career, so strangely and sadly varied. When he stepped into leadership, he seemed simply to come to his own, for since the foundation of Massachusetts Bay there had been no time when some of his name and line had not been in the front.

From the first he is set to deal with questions of finance; as early as June 3, 1737, he is appointed to wrestle with a tax bill, and before the end of the year he is settling a boundary dispute with New Hampshire, and it was a mark of confidence when in 1740 he was appointed, being then 29, to go to England to represent the case to men in power. A far more memorable service than this had already been entered upon by him, and was resumed upon his return in which he was thoroughly successful in spite of great difficulties, it also having a close relation with the coming into being of the United States.

New England was at this time cursed with an irredeemable paper currency. Democracies never appear to so poor advantage as in the management of finances, and no more conspicuous instance in point can be cited, than that of provincial New England, throughout the first half of the 18th century. The Assembly, the members of which were simply the mouthpieces of the towns, surrendered their private judgment and became submissive to the "Instruction" which they received at the time of their election, was uniformly by a large majority, in favor of an irredeemable paper currency. Before the enormous evils which early became apparent and constantly grew in magnitude, the Assembly was impotent. Widows and orphans, classes dependent on fixed incomes, were reduced to distress, creditors found themselves defrauded of their just dues, till almost nothing was left, a universal gambling spirit was promoted. The people saw no way to meet the evil but by new, and ever new issues of the wretched script, until with utter callousness of conscience, men repudiated contracts voluntarily entered upon, and recklessly discounted the resources of future generations by placing upon them the obligations their own shoulders should have borne. The action of the Council in which the higher class was represented was uniformly more wise, and honorable, than that of the lower House during this period of financial distress, and it is especially to be noted that King and Parliament threw their influence on the right side, and sought repeatedly to save the poor blind people from themselves. The right of the home government to interfere in colonial affairs was then never questioned.

Massachusetts would dodge if she could, the government mandates, but the theories of a later time, that Parliament had no jurisdiction over sea and that the King, having granted the charter, had put it out of his power to touch the provincial policy, in these days found no expression.

The Revolution was now preparing, the Colonies were chafing under restrictions imposed beyond the ocean for their own benefit. It is now generally admitted, that this was one of the first causes of the Revolution, perhaps the most potent of all causes. In all this time of distress, no figure is apparent so marked with traits of greatness as that of Thomas Hutchinson. All the Colonies were infected with the same craze, but no other man in America saw the way out. Franklin, level headed though he was, elaborately advocated paper money, turning a good penny in its manufacture.* The father of Samuel Adams was one of the directors of the iniquitous "Land Bank" and the part taken by Hutchinson in causing Parliament to close it, was what led to the undying hatred of Samuel Adams towards Hutchinson, and the Government. When "Instructions" were reported in Town Meeting, Hutchinson was immediately on his feet, and declared he would not observe them, there were immediately cries "Choose another Representative." This could not be done during the session; he consistently threw his influence on the hard money side, and so far lost popularity that he was dropped in 1739. He was, however, elected again in 1742, and was Speaker in 1746-7-8.

What saved the province from financial ruin at this time was the capture of Louisburg. This warlike enterprise of Shirley led the country to increase its debt to between two and three million dollars, but the paper money was so depreciated at the close of the war that £1,200 was equal to only £100 sterling. Parliament very generously voted to reimburse the Province for the expense it had gone to in this war, and voted to pay £183,649, 2s 7 1-2d sterling.

Mr. Hutchinson. who was then Speaker of the House of Representatives, considered this to be a most favorable opportunity for abolishing bills of credit, the source of so much iniquity, and for establishing a stable currency of gold and silver for the future. £2,200,000 would be outstanding in bills in the year 1749 £180,000 sterling at eleven for one, which was the rate at that time, would redeem all but £220,000. It was therefore proposed that Parliament should ship to the Province Spanish dollars, and apply same to redeem the bills, and that the remainder of the bills should be met by a tax on the year 1749. This would finish the bills. The Governor approved of the bill prepared by Mr. Hutchinson but when the Speaker laid the proposal before the House, it was received with a smile; for a long time the fight was hopeless, many weeks were spent in debating it.

The large class of debtors preferred paper to anything more solid. Others claimed that though the plan might have merit, the bills must be put an end to in a gradual way, a "fatal shock" would be felt by so sudden

* A Modest Inquiry into the Nature and Necessity of a Paper Currency.

a return to a specie basis. When the vote was taken the bill was decisively rejected. The chance of escaping from bondage seemed to be irrecoverably gone. A motion to reconsider having been carried, the conviction overtook some men of influence, and the bill for a wonder passed. The Governor and Council were prompt to ratify, and while the people marvelled, it was done. The streets were filled with angry men and when it was reported that Hutchinson's home was on fire there were cries in the street "Curse him, let it burn." His fine home at Milton, a recent purchase, many thought should be protected by a guard. The infatuation was so great, the wish was often expressed that the ship bringing the treasure might sink. Many doubted whether the treasure would really be sent, and this uncertainty perhaps helped the adoption of the bill.

But the treasure came, seventeen trucks were required to cart from the ship to the Treasury, two hundred and seventeen chests of Spanish dollars, while ten trucks, conveyed one hundred casks of coined copper. At once a favorable change took place. There was no *shock* but of the pleasantest kind, a revulsion of popular feeling followed speedily, until Hutchinson, from being threatened at every street corner, became a thorough favorite. Twelve years after this time Hutchinson wrote, "I think I may be allowed to call myself the father of the present fixed medium." There is no doubt of it. He alone saw the way out of the difficulty, and nothing but his tact, and persistency, pushed the measure to success. This is admitted by his enemy, John Adams, who thirty years after Hutchinson's death said, "If I was the witch of Endor, I would wake the ghost of Hutchinson, and give him absolute power over the currency of the United States, and every part of it, provided always that he should meddle with nothing but the currency. As little as I revere his memory, I will acknowledge that he understood the subject of coin and commerce better than any man I ever knew in this country He was a merchant, and there can be no scientific merchant, without a perfect knowledge of a theory of a medium of trade."* Hutchinson, in the third volume of his history of Massachusetts, remarks that the people of Massachusetts Bay were never more easy and happy, than in 1749 when, through the application of the Louisburg reimbursement to the extinction of the irredeemable bills, the currency was in an excellent condition. It excited the envy of the other colonies where paper was the principal currency.

In 1750 he was again elected to the Assembly and "he was praised as much for his firm" as he had before been abused for "his obstinate perseverance." He was made chairman of a commission to negotiate a treaty with the Indians of Casco Bay. He also settled the boundary question with Connecticut, and Rhode Island, as he had done previously with New Hampshire. Massachusetts became greatly the gainer by this settlement of its boundaries. The present boundaries of Massachusetts are those established by Hutchinson. In 1752 he was appointed Judge of Probate, and Justice of the Common Pleas, for the County of Suffolk.

* Curwen's Journal p. 456.

In the spring of 1754 he lost his wife. With her dying voice and with eyes fixed on him she uttered three words, "Best of husbands." He loved her tenderly; twenty years later, taking thought for her grave, as we shall see later on in this article (where his countrymen could not let her bones rest in peace, but they must desecrate her grave on Copps Hill.)

"In 1754 he was sent as delegate to the Convention held in Albany, for the purpose of Confederating the Colonies, the better to protect themselves from the French. Hutchinson and Franklin were the leading minds of the body. To these two the preparation of important papers was confided and plans made to prevent the "French from driving the English into the sea."

In 1758 Hutchinson became Lieutenant Governor. The excellent financial condition produced by Hutchinson's measure ten years previous, still continued, and was made even better than before. Quebec had fallen, and Canada was conquered by the English, and the mother country, made generous by success, sent over large sums of money to reimburse the Colonies for the share they had taken in bringing about the brilliant success, the result was that the taxes became a burden of the lightest ever before known.

In 1760 Chief Justice Sewall died. Hutchinson was appointed his successor by Governor Bernard. James Otis, Sr., then Speaker of the Assembly, desired the place. James Otis, Jr., a young vigorous lawyer, who was soon to arrive at great distinction, vigorously espoused his father's cause. Hutchinson warned the Governor of trouble, in case the Otises were disappointed. Bernard however, saw the risk of this, and declared he would in no case appoint Otis, but named Hutchinson instead. At once the younger Otis vowed vengence, a threat which he soon after proceeded to execute by embarrassing the Governor, including the new Chief Justice also in his enmity. Though before friends of government, the Otises now became its opposers, and as the younger man presently developed power as an unequalled popular leader, he became a most dangerous foe. "From so small a spark," exclaimed Hutchinson, "a great fire seems to have been kindled." Henceforth the two men are to have no feelings for each other, but dread and hatred. An agitation began between these two men, destined before it closes, to affect most profoundly the history of the whole future human race.

In February, 1761, Hutchinson just warming to his work as Chief Justice, was a principal figure in the disturbance about "Writs of Assistance" or "Search Warrants." The customs taxes were evaded the whole country over, in a way most demoralizing. The warehouses were few indeed in which there were no smuggled goods. The measures taken for tariff enforcement were no more objectionable than those employed today. Freedom to be sure is outraged when a custom-officer invades a man's house, his castle, but high tariff cannot exist without outrages upon freedom. A change had come about; the government had declared the laws must be enforced, and it lay upon Hutchinson to interpret the laws and see to this enforcement. The position of the Chief Justice was an embarrassing one. His own proclivities were for free trade; his friends had been concerned in contraband commerce, according to the universal practice in the term of slack administration. Hutchinson was as yet a novice in the Chief Justiceship, but he made no mistake in postponing his decision, and have the Court wait till the English practice could be known. When news came from England, a form was settled on as near to that employed in England, as circumstances would permit. Writs were issued to custom-house officers, for which application should be made to the Chief Justice by the Surveyor-General of the customs.* Before this determination was reached James Otis made his memorable plea against "Writs of Assistance," one of the epoch-making events in the history of America. John Adams afterward said, "I do say in the most solemn manner, that Mr. Otis's oration against Writs of Assistance breathed into this nation the breath of life."

Hutchinson's popularity from now begins to wane, and the main hand in this was no doubt the teachings of James Otis whose phrase "no taxation without representation" was used as a rallying cry. Boston at once elected him as its Representative in the Assembly, and his leadership thus was scarcely broken even when he became insane. At last he became a great embarrassment to his party, from the fact that, although his wits were gone, the people would still follow him. Peter Oliver, who succeeded Hutchinson as Chief Justice is quoted by John Adams as saying to him, that Otis would at one time declare of the Lieutenant Governor, "that he would rather have him than any man he knows in any office"; and the next hour represent him as the greatest tyrant and most despicable creature living."**

Hutchinson was now known as a "prerogative man," ready to defer to the home government in important things, but there was as yet no definite line drawn between prerogative men and patriots. Otis always scouted the idea of independence of the Colonies as disloyal folly, his successor, Samuel Adams, was the first to preach disloyalty and secession. Otis, as Moderator in Town Meeting in Boston, in 1763, spoke eloquently of the British empire and constitution. He said, "The true interests of Great Britain and her plantations are mutual, and what God in his providence has united, let no man dare pull asunder." As to parliamentary supremacy, Otis was much more emphatic than Hutchinson. He said, "the power of Parliament is uncontrollable, but by themselves, and we must obey. Forcibly resisting the Parliament and the King's laws is high treason. Therefore let the Parliament lay what burdens they please upon us; we must, it is our duty, to submit, and patiently to bear them till they will be pleased to relieve us."***

Otis conceded to Parliament supremacy, but insisted that the Col-

* For further matter concerning the Writs of Assistance and James Otis see p. 34.
** Adams' Diary, June 5th, 1762.
*** Rights of the British Colonies.

onies should have representatives there. Hutchinson considered representation there impracticable, and while conceding supremacy, thought it should be kept well in the background, while the Colonies managed for themselves. Great Britain has really always held to this position even to the present day—"Although the general rule is that the legislative assembly has the sole right of imposing taxes in the Colony, yet when the imperial legislature chooses to impose taxes according to the rule of law they have a right to do it." So decided the English judge Blackburn in 1868 in a case when Jamaica was involved.* Mansfield's position that the Colonies were *virtually* represented in Parliament was an entirely reasonable one. Parliamentary supremacy in the British empire is, indeed kept well in the background at the present moment, but let any great emergency arise, such as some peril to the mother country. If the Colony should remain apathetic, or in any way render aid and comfort to the enemy, the dependency would be as arbitrarily ridden over by the fleets, and armies, as in the days of George III. So long as America remained dependent, parliamentary supremacy was necessary. It would only be got rid of by such a declaration as that of 1776. This, Hutchinson was not ready for nor any other person in the Colonies until many years after this time, except one man, Samuel Adams, who said taxation without representation was tyranny and representation was impossible.

The correctness of the position of Hutchinson in the case of the Writs of Assistance have been maintained and exhibited in detail by so high an authority as the late Horace Gray, Esq., for many years Chief Justice of the Supreme Court of Massachusetts and at the time of his decease justice of the Supreme Court of the United States.** A currency dispute took place in 1762 as regarde the parity between gold and silver. Hutchinson represented the Council and Otis the House, the former, true to the policy which had already been of such advantage, set himself once more against a course certain to lead to a disastrous depreciation. This financial controversy led to further unpopularity, and lost him not only a great number of friends, but the House while reducing the allowance to the Superior Court in general, refused to make any allowance to him whatever as Chief Justice. After the great war with France, which was waged mainly for the benefit of the Colonies, it was found that England had a debt of £140,000,000 instead of £70,000,000 which it had before the war. England also had paid the Colonies vast sums of money as previously stated, expenses incurred in protecting themselves from the French. The American civil and military establishments before the war was £70,000 per annum, it was now £350,000. George Grenville, Chancellor of the Exchequer thought that the Colonies ought to contribute towards it; he did not expect them to raise the whole, but a portion of it, and did not intend to charge them with any interest on the national debt, although it was largely incurred on their behalf.

* Yonge Const. His. of Eng. p. 66. See also Todd, Parl. Gov. in the British Colonies 1899.
** See Quincy, Massachusetts Reports 1761-1772. Appendix 1.

In February, 1765, he laid a bill before Parliament for further defraying the expenses of protecting the colonies and he proposed to charge certain stamp duties in said colonies. The agents of the several colonies had an interview with him and tried to dissuade him from it. He replied that he had considered the whole case and believed the colonies should contribute something to the mother country to pay for their protection, every penny of which would be spent in the colonies, and that he knew of no better way than a stamp tax. "If," he said, "you can tell of a better, I will adopt it." Benjamin Franklin, proposed that the demand for money should be made in the old constitutional way in the form of a requisition to the Assembly of each province. Can you agree, rejoined Grenville, on the proportion that each colony should raise. The question touched the heart of the difficulty, the agents were obliged to answer in the negative, and the interview speedily closed, a few days later the fatal Bill passed,—one of the most momentous legislative Acts in the history of mankind.

The position of Hutchinson was a trying one; he favored neither the issuance of the Writs of Assistance nor the Stamp Act. The whole course of the government he disapproved of he had been ready to cross the ocean to remonstrate for the Colony, against the impolitic treatment. On the other hand, the disloyal tone which daily grew rife about him, was utterly against his mind, he saw no outcome for it but independence, a most wise forecasting of the situation, in fact there was no middle ground. Independence seemed to him and to every man then, except Sam Adams, a calamity. If that was to be avoided, there was nothing for it but to admit the supremacy of Parliament.* But the Province, to which he had been like a father, was growing away from him, and before the summer ended, he was to receive a blow as ruthless, and ungrateful, as it was possible to give. He was at this time a Judge of the highest Judicial Court, a member of the Council, and Lieutenant Governor at the same time. He had performed the duties of these incompatible offices to the satisfaction of the community, as is shown in the writings of John Adams before he became Hutchinson's enemy. He says, "Has not his merits been sounded very high by his countrymen for twenty years? Have not his countrymen loved, admired, revered, rewarded, nay, almost adored him? Have not ninety-nine in a hundred of them really thought him the greatest and best man in America? Has not the perpetual language of many members of both Houses and of a majority of his brother-counselors been, that Mr. Hutchinson is a great man, a pious, a wise, a learned, a good man, an eminent saint, a philosopher etc? Nay, have not the affections and the admiration of his countrymen arisen so high as often to style him the greatest and best man in the world, that they never saw, nor heard, nor read of such a man—a sort of apotheosis like that of Alexander and that of Cæsar while they lived?"**

* For further Information concerning the Stamp Act, see p. 37.
** John Adams, Diary, March 17, 1766.

It is not possible to give a more glowing eulogy in the English language of a person, than this written by John Adams, the successor of Washington as second President of the United States, but it could scarcely be less. The regularity of his life, his sympathy for the distressed, his affability, his integrity, his industry, his talents for business, and the administration of affairs, his fluency, and grace, as public speaker. His command of temper, and courteousness under provocation, united to form a rare man, and to give him influence. In a country where literary enterprise was very uncommon, he had devoted a great part of his life to investigating the history of his native province, busy though he was in so many places, in behalf of the public, he found time to carry it forward. In 1764 was published in Boston the first volume of his "History of Massachusetts Bay," a carefully studied work quite unparalleled in the meagre colonial literature, and is still, and will always remain, of the first authority respecting the beginning of New England. In 1767 came the second volume. He had access to original papers such as no person now possesses which were of the highest historical value. Writing to a friend in England in 1765, he said, "I think from my beginning the work until I had completed it, which was about twelve months, I never had time to write two sheets at a sitting without avocations by public business, but forced to steal a little time in the morning and evening while I was in town, and leave it for weeks together so I found it difficult to keep any plan in my mind."

In his third volume, written twenty years later and not published till 1828, more than forty years after his death, the heat of the fight is still in the heart beating behind the pen, in painting the portraits of his contemporaries, Otis, Sam Adams, Hancock and others, the men who bore him down after the fiercest possible struggle. His portrait drawing is by no means without candor, and one wonders that the picture is no darker. His presentment is always clear and dignified; his judgment of men and events are just. It is the work of the thoughtful brain whose comments on politics, finance, religion, etc., are full of intelligence and humanity.

And now Hutchinson approaches the most crucial period of his life. As seen in a previous chapter after the passing of the Stamp Act, and the adoption of the Patrick Henry Resolves, the people grew riotous and treason was talked of openly. The first great riot was on August 14, 1765. In the morning the effigies of Andrew Oliver, the Stamp agent, and Lord Bute the former prime minister, were hung on an elm tree, on the corner of what is now Washington and Essex streets, in the evening they were taken down, carried as far as Kilby street, where a new government building was torn down by the mob, who, taking portions of the wood-work with them, proceeded to Fort Hill, where they burnt the effigies in front of the home of Mr. Oliver and committed gross outrages on his premises which were plundered and wrecked.*

* See page 40 for a more full description.

On the evening of the 26th the riots recommenced with redoubled fury. Lieutenant Governor Hutchinson, also Chief Justice, the second person in rank in the colony and a kinsman of Oliver, was made a mark for the most unmeasured outrage. The story is best told in the words of the victim in a letter to a friend.

To Richard Jackson,   Boston, Aug. 30, 1765.

My Dear Sir—I came from my house at Milton the 26 in the morning. After dinner it was whispered in the town there would be a mob at night, and that Paxton, Hallowell, the custom house, and admiralty officers' houses would be attacked; but my friends assured me that the rabble were satisfied with the insult I had received, and that I was become rather popular. In the evening, whilst I was at supper and my children round me, somebody ran in and said the mob were coming. I directed my children to fly to a secure place, and shut up my house as I had done before, intending not to quit it; but my eldest daughter repented her leaving me, hastened back and protested that she would not quit the house unless I did. I couldn't stand against this, and withdrew with her to a neighboring house, where I had been but a few minutes before the hellish crew fell upon my house with the rage of devils, and in a moment with axes split down the doors and entered. My son being in the great entry heard them cry 'Dam him, he is upstairs, we'll have him.' Some ran immediately as high as the top of the house, then filled the rooms below and the cellar, and others remained without the house to be employed there. Messages soon came one after another to the house where I was to inform me the mob were coming in pursuit of me, and I was obliged to retire through yards and gardens to a house more remote, where I remained until 4 o'clock, by which time one of the best finished houses in the Province had nothing remaining but the bare walls and floors.

Not content with tearing off all the wainscot and hangings, and splitting the doors to pieces, they beat down the partition walls; and although that alone cost them near two hours, they cut down the cupola or lanthorn and they began to take the slate and boards from the roof, and were prevented only by the approaching daylight from a total demolition of the building. The garden house was laid flat, and all my trees, etc., broke down to the ground. Such ruin was never seen in America. Besides my plate and family pictures, household furniture of every kind, my own, my children, and servants, apparel, they carried off about £900 sterling in money and emptied the house of everything whatsoever, except a part of the kitchen furniture, not leaving a single book or paper in it, and have scattered or destroyed all the manuscripts and other papers I had been collecting for thirty years together, besides a great number of public papers in my custody. The next evening, I intended to go to Milton with my children, but meeting two or three small parties of the ruffians who I suppose had concealed themselves in the country, and my coachman hearing one of them say, 'There he is'! my daughters were terrified, and said they should never be safe, and I was forced to shelter them that night at the Castle.*

Josiah Quincy, then twenty-one years old, writing in his diary Aug. 27, 1765, says that Hutchinson's life "it is more than probable, was saved by his giving way to his eldest daughter and leaving the house." He described "the coming into court the next day of the stripped Chief

Governor Hutchinson's House Destroyed by the Mob.

Justice, clothed in a manner which would have excited compassion from the hardest heart. Such a man in such a station, thus habited, with tears starting from his eyes, and a countenance which strongly told the inward anguish of his soul,—what must an audience have felt, whose compassion had before been moved by what they knew he had suffered, when they heard him pronounce the following words which the agitation of his mind dictated, "Gentlemen,—There not being a quorum of the Court

* Mass. His. Soc. Vol. XXVI., p. 146.

without me, I am obliged to appear. Some apology is necessary for my dress; indeed, I had no other. Destitute of everything,—no other shirt; no other garment but what I have on; and not one in my whole family in a better situation than myself. The distress of a whole family around me, young and tender infants hanging about me, are infinitely more insupportable than what I feel for myself, though I am obliged to borrow part of *this* clothing.

"Sensible that I am innocent, that all the charges against me are false, I can't help feeling: and although I am not obliged to give an answer to all the questions that may be put to me by every lawless person, yet I call God to witness—and I would not, for a thousand worlds, call my Maker to witness to a falsehood—I say I call my Maker to witness, that I never, in New England or Old, in Great Britain, or America, neither directly or indirectly, was aiding, assisting or supporting—in the least promoting or encouraging—what is commonly called the Stamp Act; but, on the contrary, did all in my power, and strove as much as in me lay, to prevent it. This is not declared through timidity, for I have nothing to fear. They can only take away my life, which is of but little value when deprived of all its comforts, all that was dear to me, and nothing surrounding me but the most pressing distress.

"I hope the eyes of the people will be opened, that they will see how easy it is for some designing, wicked man to spread false reports to raise suspicion and jealousies in the minds of the populace, and enrage them against the innocent, but if guilty, this is not the way to proceed. The laws of our country are open to punish those who have offended. This destroying all peace and comfort and order of the community—all will feel its effects; and all will see how easily the people may be deluded, inflamed and carried away with madness against an innocent man. I pray God give us better hearts." The Court then adjourned to October 15th.

Why Hutchinson should have fallen into such great disfavor, it is not easy to say. Gordon, a writer of Whig leaning, but a fair minded witness of all that occurred suggests that there were some who still entertaining rancor towards him for doing away with paper money in 1748, for, as we have seen, his position in 1762 on the currency was not popular. Moreover the mob was led on to the house by a secret influence, with a view to the destruction of certain public papers known to be there relating to the grant of the New Plymouth Company on the Kennebec River.* Hutchinson himself speaks on having given rise to animosity against him for having taken certain depositions in the interest of government, before him in his character of Chief Justice to which his name was signed. They were purely official acts: for the depositions he had no responsibility whatever, but the unreasoning mass of the people confused him with others. There was nothing in his course at the time of the Writs of Assistance, at which the people needed to feel aggrieved. He

* His. of Am. Rev. Vol. I., p. 180.

was with the people in opposing the external taxes, also in disapproving the Stamp Act. Now that they were imposed, he to be sure thought nothing would answer but submission, but certainly in his declaration here he was nothing like so emphatic as James Otis, who still remained the popular idol. Otis had said in May, "It is the duty of all humbly and silently to acquiesce in all the decisions of the supreme legislature." In private talk he was still more vigorous in his utterances. He said to Hallowell, "That Parliament had a right to tax the Colonies, and he was a d—d fool who denied it and that this people never would be quiet till we had a Council from home, till our charter was taken away, and till we had regular troops quartered upon us.* Hutchinson had never expressed his thoughts anywhere near so definitely as this.

The inhabitants of Boston and the Province were generally ashamed of the outrage upon Hutchinson, but the mob still dared to show its hand. Though in the first rush of feeling many of the rioters were sent to jail, they were afterwards set free. The chief actor seems to have been a shoemaker, named Mackintosh, who, though arrested, was presently discharged; Hutchinson declares this was through the interference of men of good position, who feared that a confession from him would implicate them. Hutchinson's demand of the legislature for compensation for the destruction of his home, was at last effectual. He is said to have received £3,194, 17s 6d., a fair indemnity. The Act had attached to it for a "rider" pardon to all who had taken part in the disturbance connected with the Stamp Act. Bernard hesitated to sign the Act; but was finally induced to do so by his earnest wish to have Hutchinson receive justice. When the Act was sent to England, the King disallowed it; such lawlessness could not be condoned, even that a faithful official might receive his rights. But the money had been paid before the news of the King's displeasure arrived.

A period of lawlessness now followed. Riots were absolutely unpunished, for no jury would convict the rioters. Governor Bernard wrote that his position was one of utter, and humiliating impotence, and that the first condition of the maintenance of English authority in Massachusetts was to quarter a powerful military force at Boston.

Two regiments arrived Sept. 28, 1768. Shortly before their arrival the people gathered together in an immense meeting, and voted that a standing army could not be kept in the province without its consent. On the arrival of the troops everything was done by the people to provoke and irritate them. A perfect reign of terror was directed against all who supported the government. Soldiers could not appear in the streets without being the objects of the grossest insults. A press eminently scurrilous and vindictive was ceaselessly employed in abusing them. They had become as Samuel Adams boasted 'the objects of the contempt even of woman, and children.' Every offence they committed was maliciously exaggerated and vindictively prosecuted, while in the absence of martial

* John Adams' Diary, Jan. 16, 1776.

law, they were obliged to look passively on the most flagrant insults to authority. At one time the "Sons of liberty" in a procession a mile and a half long marched around the State House, to commemorate their riots against the Stamp Act, and met in the open fields to chant their "liberty song" and drink "strong halters, firm blocks, and sharp axes, to such as deserve them." At another an informer, who was found guilty of giving information to revenue officers, was seized by a great multitude, tarred and feathered, and led through the streets of Boston, which was illuminated in honor of the achievement.

A printer who had dared to caricature the champions of freedom was obliged to flee from his house, to take refuge among the soldiers, and ultimately to escape from Boston in disguise. Merchants who had ventured to import goods from England were compelled by mob violence to give them up to be destroyed, or to be re-embarked. A shopkeeper who sold some English goods, found a post planted in the ground with a hand pointing to his door, and when a friend tried to remove it, he was stoned by a fierce mob through the streets. A popular minister delighted his congregation by publicly praying "that the Almighty would remove from Boston the English soldiers."*

These outrages led to the so-called Boston Massacre, more fully described in a previous chapter.** None of the mobs of that time of mobs was more brutal and truculent than that which provoked the firing of the group of baited men, standing their ground with steady discipline, among the clubs and missles resorted to now, to enforce the usual foul and blasphemous abuse. Lieutenant Governor Hutchinson fulfilled at this time with complete adequacy the functions of chief magistrate, for Governor Bernard was at this time in England. Hutchinson was at once in the street, in imminent danger of having his brains dashed out, expostulating, entreating that order might be preserved.*** It was a fine exhibition of power and courage. His standing in the east balcony of the State House, with the snow reddened beneath by the blood of the killed, with the regiments kneeling in rank ready for street firing, and several thousand of enraged men on the other side on the point of rushing into the fight, he was able to hold both parties in check. His prompt arrest of Captain Preston and the squad which had done the killing, was his full duty; and it is to the credit of the troops that the officer and his men in the midst of the exasperation gave themselves quietly into the hands of the law. Instead of a bloody battle, there was substituted a well-ordered civil process, due delay being observed that the passion of both sides might subside and the evidence, pro and con be calmly weighed. A mild and just verdict was the outcome, to which all submitted. Men they were, all of the same stock, for the time being fallen into antagonism, seeing things

*Lecky's Am. Rev. Chapt. XI., p. 127.
** Boston Mobs, page 43.
*** Mass. A. His. Vol. XXXI., p. 491. Witness at the trial of the soldiers said "He stood close behind him, and one of the mob lifted up a large club over my head, and was going to strike, but he seized him by the arm and prevented it."

differently. All, however, bore themselves like Englishmen, showing the quality which has made the Anglo-Saxon race a mighty one.

Since the departure of Bernard there had been no session of the legislature. In March one took place that was the cause of a new dispute between the Lieutenant Governor and the legislature, which was destined to be long and important. It was as to how far the chief magistrate could be bound by royal instruction. Hutchinson says the Assembly was prorogued to meet at Boston March 14th, 1770, but before the time arrived there came a further signification of the King's pleasure that it should be held at Cambridge, unless the Lieutenant Governor had more weighty reasons for holding it at Boston, than those which were mentioned by the Secretary of State against it.* On the 15th of March therefore the legislature met in the "Philosophy Room" in Harvard College, in Cambridge.

Remonstrances were passed by the Council and the House against the removal to which Hutchinson replied "That the King by his prerogative could remove the legislature from the 'Town House in Boston' did not in his mind admit of a doubt and therefore he disregarded the remonstrance." Soon after the Massacre, Hutchinson begged the Earl of Hillsborough, the Colonial Secretary, to allow him to resign. He said, "I must humbly pray that a person of superior powers of body and mind may be appointed to the administration of the government of this Province. I shall faithfully endeavor to support such person according to the best of my abilities, and I think it not improbable that I may be capable of doing his Majesty greater service in the Province, even in a private station than at present."** Instead of accepting his resignation he was appointed Governor in March, 1771, and his wife's brother-in-law, Andrew Oliver, being at the same time commissioned Lieutenant Governor, and Thomas Flucker Secretary.

At his inauguration while the Assembly and the Congregational ministers were silent, there were many congratulations, among them Harvard College. The students singing in Holden Chapel the anthem, "Thus saith the Lord from henceforth, behold! all nations shall call ye blessed; for thy rulers shall be of thine own kindred, your nobles shall be of yourself, and thy governors shall proceed from the midst of thee."

April 1, 1771, he writes to Colonel Williams of Hatfield. "It's certain all the valuable part of the town have shown me as much respect personally, as in my public character, as I could desire. Two Adamses, Phillips, Hancock, and two or three others, who, with the least reason have been the most injurious, are all of any sort of consideration who stand out."*** Again on April 19, 1771, in a letter to Hillsboro, referring to the Town Meeting he says, "In these votes, and in most of the public proceedings of the town of Boston, persons of the best character and estate

* Hutchinson His. Vol. III., p. 280.
** M. A. Hist. Vol. XXVI. Mar. 27 to Hillsboro.
*** M. A. Hist. Vol. XVII., p. 131.

have little or no concern. They decline attending Town Meetings where they are sure of being outvoted by men of the lowest order, all being admitted, and it being very rare that any scrutiny is made into the qualification of voters."*

The hopes Hutchinson and the friends of government were never brighter since the troubles began with the government, than in the spring of 1771. Among Hutchinson opponents men like Andrew Eliot, thought "it might be as well not to dispute the legal right of Parliament." Otis too, pursued a strong reactionary course and when on May 29 the legislature met, at his instance, while the remonstrance was passed as had become usual, against the removal of the legislature from Boston, the clause was struck out which denied to the crown the right to remove. The principle so long contended for was then sacrificed, the right of prerogative to infringe the charter at this point was acknowledged, and it would be easy to proceed on the ground that the crown might take what liberties it pleased with the charter. Otis's change was indeed startling. Samuel Adams was going on in the old road, when Otis started up, and said they had gone far enough in that way, the Governor had an undoubted right to carry the court where he pleased, and moved for a committee to represent the inconveniences of sitting there, and for an address to the Governor. He was a good man; the minister said so, and it must be so; and moved to go on with the business, and the House voted everything he moved for.**

"Serious as was the defection of James Otis that of Hancock was even more so. His wealth, popular manners and some really strong qualities made his influence great. Samuel Adams had exploited Hancock, with all his consumate art ever since his appearance in public life, making him a powerful pillar of the popular cause. Contemptuous allusions to Hancock as little better than an ape, whom Samuel Adams led about according to his will, have come down from those times."*** Such things were flying in the air and Hancock was feeble enought to be moved by them, if they came to his ears. Whatever may have been the reason, Hancock forsook his old guide, voted with the party of Otis for the acknowledgment of Hutchinson's right to convene the legislature where and when he choose. Hancock's defection at this time from the Whig cause seemed imminent, and when Hutchinson fled to England, three years later and his papers fell into the hands of his enemies, it was found necessary to suppress certain documents, belonging to this time as it is supposed they compromised Hancock, who in 1774 was once more firmly on the side of the Colonies.

Samuel Adams probably never experienced a greater mortification than when, as a member of a committee, he waited, by command of the House, upon Hutchinson to present an address acknowledging the right

* M. A. Hist. Vol. XXVII., p. 151.
** John Adams' Works, Vol. II., p. 266.
*** Hosmer's Life of Thomas Hutchinson, p. 213.

of the Governor to remove the General Court "to Housantonic in the western part of the Province," if he desired, nor, on the other hand, did the Governor ever enjoy a greater triumph. Hutchinson must have felt that he was even with his chief adversary for the humiliation of the preceding year, the driving out of the regiments. Adams felt his defeat keenly, but gave no sign of it, he saw his influence apparently on the wane, but was as unremitting as ever in his attempts to retrieve lost ground. But for him the revolutionary cause at this time must have gone by the board.

The revulsion was not long in coming. Before Hutchinson had time to restore the repentant legislature to the town house in Boston, the hearts of the members became hardened against him. When it became known that the decision of the king had been made for the support of the Massachusetts town officials from the revenue of the Colony by warrants drawn on the Commission of Custom, the wrath of the people became heavy, and the voice of Samuel Adams led the discontented. The Governor was paid £1500 sterling, instead of £1000, annually, which he was paid when dependent on the people. Hutchinson now plainly announced that he should now receive his salary from the King. The House protested in its usual temper, the set of the opposition being so powerful that several of the Loyalists withdrew disheartened. But in the midst of the fault-finding "Sons of Liberty", he received a mark of confidence from the General Court at which he was greatly pleased, as he had a right to be. We have already seen him as the principal figure in settling the boundary lines on the sides of New Hampshire, Rhode Island and Connecticut. The boundary line on the side of New York, not settled in 1767, and still in dispute, were equally in need of adjustment, and although his principles were popularly denounced, and the scheme was already in progress which was to drive him from his native land and deprive him of all his possessions in it, yet none but he could be trusted to undertake the delicate negotiations upon which the welfare of the Province depended.*

The journal of the proceedings in the handwriting of the Governor, is still extant. With William Brattle, Joseph Hawley, and John Hancock, Hutchinson journeyed to Hartford, where on May 18, 1773, they discussed the matter with Governor Tyron, John Watts, William Smith, R. R. Livingston, and William Nicoll, Commissioners from New York. The New York men, although more compliant than the negotiators of seven years ago, were still disposed to exact hard concessions, to which all the commissioners but Hutchinson were about prepared to agree. Hutchinson, however, while diplomatic, was unyielding, insisting upon what had been substantially the demand of 1767. At last it was conceded, establishing for all time as a part of the Bay State the beautiful county of Berkshire. This alone should entitle him to a monument by the State of Massachusetts. He alone, it is said, prevented the giving up by Massachusetts of

* The details are in Mass. Archives marked Colonial, Vol. IV., pp. 335-344.

her claim to western lands; these were retained and afterwards sold for a large sum.*

It was a great victory for the Governor, the Massachusetts Commissioners had been left free to do what seemed to them best, but they cordially acknowledged that success belonged to him.

On the return to Boston, the legislature was in session and the assembly authorized him to transmit the settlement to Lord Dartmouth, Secretary of State, at once, without formally laying it before them. They trusted him entirely. Hutchinson with some pride declared that "no previous instance of a like confidence of our Assembly in a Governor can be found in Massachusetts history."** This transcient favor, and trust, aggravated for him the force of the blow he was so soon to receive. How bitter the home coming of Hutchinson was, the following extract from a letter to Sir Francis Bernard, the late Governor will show:

June 29, 1773. "After every other attempt to distress me they have at last engaged in a conspiracy which has been managed with infinite art, and succeeded beyond their own expectation. They have buzzed about for three or four months a story of something that would amaze everybody as soon as the elections were over, it was said in the House something would appear in eight and forty hours, which, if improved aright, the Province might be as happy, as it was fourteen or fifteen years ago. These things were spread through all the towns of the Province, and everybody's expectations were raised. At length upon motion the gallery was ordered to be cleared and the doors shut. Mr. Samuel Adams informed the House that seventeen original letters had been put in his hands, written to a gentleman in England by several persons from New England, with an intention to subvert the constitution. They were delivered to him on condition that they should be returned, not printed, and no copies taken. If the House would receive them on these terms, he would read them. They broke through the pretended agreement, printed the resolves, and then the letters, which effrontery was never known before. The letters are mere narratives which you well know to be true, as respects remarks upon the Colonies, and such proposals as naturally follow from the principles which I have openly avowed; but by every malversation, which the talents of the party in each House, could produce they have raised the prejudices of the people against me, and it is generally supposed all the writers were concerned in one plan, though I suppose no one of them ever saw or knew the contents of the letters of any others unless by accident."

After three weeks spent, the House resolved to address the King, to remove the Governor and Lieutenant Governor.*** The name of the person to whom the letters were written was erased from all of them, but they appear to be all Mr. Thomas Whatley's six from the Governor,

* N. E. His. and Gen. Reg., Vol. 1, p. 310.
** Hutchinson His. Vol. III., p. 391, 392.
*** M. A. His., Vol. XXVII., p. 502, etc.

four from the Lieutenant-Governor, one from Rogers, and one from Auchmuty and the remainder from Rhode Island and Connecticut.

The affair of the Hutchinson Letter created great excitement both in America and England, an affair in which the best men of Massachusetts Bay were concerned, including Franklin, then the agent of his native Province, although a citizen then of Pennsylvania; a shade has rested therefrom upon the character of Franklin, which cannot yet be said to have been explained away. Is it creditable that those wary, able men, Franklin, Samuel Adams, Bowdoin, John Adams, Samuel Cooper, and others, really thought the very quiet statements contained "in the letters in which there was no sentiment which the Governor had not openly expressed in his addresses to the Legislature, was a danger and menace to the welfare of the colony?"* The only explanation is that they had persuaded themselves that Hutchinson was so dangerous that if conduct thoroughly above board would not answer, he must be cast out by questionable means. Mr. Winthrop justifies their conduct by believing that it may be classed among what Burke calls "irregular things done in the confusion of mighty troubles, not to be justified on principle."* When the printed copies of the letters arrived in England they excited great astonishment. Thomas Whatley was dead. William Whatley, his brother, and executor was filled with a very natural consternation, at a theft which was likely to have such important consequences, and for which public opinion was inclined to make him responsible. He in turn suspected a certain Mr. Temple, who had been allowed to look through the papers of his deceased brother, for the purpose of perusing one relating to the colonies, and a duel ensued in which Whatley was severely wounded. Mr. Temple continued to be suspected. A letter of Jan. 4, 1774, says: "Although when they first came abroad his own brother said: Whoever sent them was a d—d villian."**

Franklin then for the first time, in a letter to a newspaper, disclosed the part he had taken. He stated that "he, and he alone, had obtained and transmitted to Boston the letters in question, that they had never passed into the hands of William Whatley, and that, therefore, it was impossible, either that Whatley could have communicated them, or that Temple could have taken them, from his papers." There is some reason to believe that the original owner had left them carelessly in a public office, whence they had been stolen, but the mystery was never decisively solved.

"In England Franklin's conduct was regarded with the utmost severity. For the purpose of ruining honorable officials it was said, their most confidential letters, written years before to a private member of Parliament, who had at that time no connection with Government, had been deliberately stolen; although the original thief was undiscovered, the full weight of the guilt and dishonor rested upon Franklin. He was

* New Eng. Hist. and Gen. Reg. I., p. 307.
** Hosmer's Life of Hutchinson, p. 274.

perfectly aware that the letters had been written in the strictest confidence, that they had been dishonestly obtained without the knowledge of the person who received them, or the person who wrote them, and that their exposure would be a deadly injury to the writers. Under these circumstances he sent them to a small group of politicians whom he knew to be the bitterest enemies of the Governor, and one result was a duel in which the brother of the man whose private papers had been stolen, was nearly killed. Any man of high and sensitive honor, it was said, would sooner have put his hand into the fire than have been concerned in such a transaction."*

When the petition for the removal of Hutchinson and Oliver arrived the Government referred it to the Committee of the Privy Council that the allegations might be publicly examined with counsel on either side. The case exerted an intense interest which had been rarely paralleled. No less than thirty-five Privy Councillors attended; among the distinguished strangers who crowded the Bar were Burke, Priestley and Jeremy Bentham, Dunning and Lee, who spoke for the petitioners; they appear to have made no impression; while on the other side Wedderburn, the Solicitor-General, made one of his most brilliant but most virulent speeches, which was received with boundless applause."

After a brief but eloquent eulogy of the character and services of Hutchinson he passed to the manner in which the letters were procured, and turning to Franklin, who stood before him he delivered an invective which appeared to have electrified his audience. How the letters 'came into the possession of anyone but the right owner's,' he said, "is still a mystery for Dr. Franklin to explain, and they could not have come into his hands by fair means. Nothing will acquit Dr. Franklin of the charge of obtaining them by fraudulent or corrupt means, for the most malignant of purposes, unless he stole them from the person who stole them. I hope, my Lords, you will brand this man for the honor of this country, of Europe, and of mankind. . . . Into what country will the fabrication of this iniquity hereafter go with unembarrassed face? Men will watch him with a jealous eye. They will hide their papers from him, and lock up their escritoires. Having hitherto aspired after fame by his writings, he will henceforth esteem it a libel to be called a man of letters—*homo trium literarum*. But, he not only took away those papers from our brother, he kept himself concealed, till he nearly occasioned the murder of another. It is impossible to read his account, expressive of the coolest, and most deliberate malice, without horror."

The scene was a very strange one, and it is well suited to the brush of an historical painter. Franklin was now an old man, sixty-seven, the greatest writer, the greatest philosopher America had produced, a member of some of the chief scientific societies in Europe, the accredited representative of the most important of the colonies of America, and for nearly an hour, and in the midst of the most distinguished of living

* Lecky's Am. Rev., pp. 149, 150.

Englishmen, he was compelled to hear himself denounced as a thief or the accomplice of thieves. He stood there conspicuous, and erect, and without moving a muscle, amid the torrent of invective, but his apparent composure was shared by few who were about him. Fox, in a speech which he made as late as 1803, reminded the House how on that memorable occasion, "all men tossed up their hats, and clapped their hands, in boundless delight, at Mr. Wedderburn's speech." The committee at once voted that the petition of the Massachusetts Assembly was "false, groundless, and scandalous and calculated only for the seditious purpose of keeping up a spirit of clamor and discontent in the province." The king and Council confirmed the report and Franklin was ignominiously dismissed from his office of Postmaster.* From this time Franklin and his friends had a deep personal grudge against the British Government.

As the autumn deepened Hutchinson interpreted as favorable to himself the symptoms he perceived of the mood of the people. Oct. 16, 1773, he writes, "I now see so great a change in the people wherever I travel about the country, that I have reason to think I shall rather gain than lose by the late detestable proceedings, and my friends express stronger attachments to me than ever." This was only a brief Indian summer of favor before the outbreak, not now distant, of a storm more cold and pitiless than ever, for a crisis was now at hand more threatening than any that had preceded it. As shown in a previous chapter,* after the repeal of the Stamp Act in order to pacify the colonists, a duty was placed on tea, and other imports, which the colonists had always admitted to be a valid Act of the Parliament. No revenue probably had ever been expected from it. It was felt that the principle that Parliament might tax must be maintained; the cost of collection was greater than the proceeds. Instead of paying 12d per pound export duty from England, only 3d per pound was to be charged, when imported by the East India Company to the Colonies, thereby making a saving to the colonists of 9d per pound which would make tea cheaper than that smuggled in from the Dutch colonies.**

The project of sending the tea, was decided on in May, 1773, and Massachusetts was the Colony where the crisis was to come. The consignees were important persons. Two of them were Thomas and Elisha Hutchinson, sons of the Governor, a third was the Governor's nephew Richard Clarke, father-in-law of Copley, the painter, a fourth was Benjamin Faneuil, a nephew of Peter Faneuil, deceased, a fifth Joshua Winslow, also of a memorable family. These held bravely to the task that had been set for them, putting their property and lives in jeopardy until finally they were driven to seek refuge in the Castle. Of those opposed to them Samuel Adams was the chief, followed by Hancock, Bowdoin, Dr. Thomas Young, Dr. Joseph Warren, Dr. Benjamin

* Lecky's Am. Rev. pp. 150, 151, 152.
** See pp. 47, for further information concerning the Stamp Act and the Tea Tax.

Church, Josiah Quincy, John Scollay, and others who lent their hands to action and their heads to counsel. Historic truth also compels the statement that the man put forward to do the disreputable work for them was "Captain Mackintosh" leader of the South End toughs in street fights with the North Enders, leader of the rioters in the destruction of the Governor's home in August, 1765. For his part in that affair he had never been punished, and now seems to have been rather a popular pet. He was styled the "First Captain-General of Liberty-Tree," and managed the illumination, hanging of effigies, etc. Long afterwards, in speaking of the Tea Party he said, "It was my chickens that did the job."*

An attempt was made to cause the consignees to resign their commissions under "Liberty Tree;" this they refused to do and in consequence they were mobbed in their houses, windows and doors were smashed and amid a tempest of missles their lives and persons were in great danger. Hutchinson set himself against the "Sons of Liberty," "his course not showing one sign of vacillation from first to last, but throughout bearing the marks of clear, cold, passionless inflexibility."**

Another American writer says, "To candid men, the letters he wrote in those days of struggle ought to have interest, as well as the declarations of those who have portrayed him as the disgraced minion of a tyrant."*** Another writer, referring to his action at this time, says, "We can at this day well afford to mete out this tardy justice to a man, whose motives and conduct have been so bitterly and unscrupulously vilified and maligned as have been those of Thomas Hutchinson.****

At last, in December, 1773, three ships laden with tea arrived at Boston, and what followed has been told a thousand times, with all possible elaborations by those who fully sympathize with the tea mob. The cold facts are that "Captain Mackintosh" and "his chickens," disguised as Mohawk Indians, instigated by Samuel Adams, John Hancock***** and other leading "patriots" flung the whole cargo consisting of 342 chests, into the harbor. In the course of the violent proceedings this year the Council, the militia, and the company of cadets, had been vainly asked to assist in maintaining the law and order. The sheriff was grossly insulted, the magistrates could do nothing, and as usual, the crowning outrage of the destruction of the tea was accomplished with perfect impunity, and not a single person engaged in it was in any way molested, but every soul in Boston knew the penalty must fall, as certain as night follows day. "The news of these events convinced most intelligent Englishmen, that war was imminent, and that taxation of America could only be enforced by the sword. Popular opinion in England, which had

* Francis Drake. "Tea Leaves." Introd. p. CXXVII.
** Richard Frothingham.
*** Hosmer's Life of Hutchinson, p. 299.
**** Francis S. Drake. Tea Leaves. Int. LXIII.
***** Hancock's uncle made his large fortune by smuggling tea. See Hutchinson His., Vol. III., p. 297.

supported the repeal of the Stamp Act, was now opposed to further concession, England, it was said, had sufficiently humiliated herself. The claim and the language of the colonial agitators excited profound and not unnatural indignation, and every mail from America brought news that New England at least was in a condition of virtual rebellion, that Acts of the British Parliament were defied and disobeyed with the most perfect impunity, that the representatives of the British Government were habitually exposed to the grossest insults, and reduced to the most humiliating impotence."

The time for temporising, it was said, was over. It was necessary to show that England possessed some real power of executing her laws and the ministers were probably supported by a large majority of the English people, when they resolved to throw away the scabbard, and to exert all the power of Parliament to reduce Massachusetts to obedience.* The measures that were taken were very stringent. By one Act, the harbor of Boston was legally closed. "The Custom House officers were removed to Salem. All landing, lading, and shipping of merchandise in Boston harbor was forbidden, and English men-of-war were appointed to maintain the blockade. The town which owed its whole prosperity to its commercial activity was debarred from all commerce by sea and was to continue under this ban, till it had made compensation to the East India Company for the tea which had been destroyed, and had satisfied the crown that trade would for the future be safely carried on in Boston, property protected, laws obeyed, and duties regularly paid."** By another Act, Parliament was to remodel the charter of Massachusetts, the Council or Upper Chamber was now to be appointed as in most of the other colonies of America by the crown. The judges and magistrates of all kinds, including the sheriffs, were to be appointed by the royal governor. Jurymen were to be summoned by the Sheriffs. That these Acts of the British Parliament at this time was necessary is beyond question, for there was a mob in revolutionary Boston at this time, scarcely less foul-mouthed, pitiless, unscrupulous, than that which roared for the blood of the Bourbons in revolutionary Paris, or that of the Commons of later times. Mackintosh and his crew were unmistakably in evidence, certainly not restrained, but connived at by the better men, so that those just as conscientious and patriotic, who tried by lawful ways to oppose, found destruction for their property imminent; and could feel that their lives were secure only when they had fled down the harbor to the Castle.

John Adams was one of the very few "patriots" who really disowned and opposed mob violence; not only did he defend the soldiers for killing some of the mob, but in a letter to his wife, he said: "mobs I do and will detest."***

* Lecky's Am. Rev., pp. 154, 164, 165, 166.
** 14 George III., c. 19, 45.
*** Letters of John Adams, Vol. 1., p. 13.

On May 10th, 1774, news reached Boston of the passing of the Boston Port Bill, and the penalties the Tea-Party had brought upon the town. General Gage, who was to command four regiments and a powerful fleet arrived three days later. A military governor was now to succeed the civilian, it being understood that Hutchinson, after the disturbances were

(View from Governor Hutchinson's Field.)

quelled, should return to power; in the meantime he was to go to England, and help the King with personal counsel."* Hutchinson's work in America was done. It may be asked, why did he remain in office in all these years up to this time, enforcing laws with which he had no sympathy, the instrument of a policy he disliked, wrecking in the minds of many of his countrymen the honorable name which for forty years he had been establishing. It was certainly not for emolument. It was not for fame, for instead of credit he had long received only abuse. He kept hoping against hope, that the home government would become wiser, that the supremacy of Parliament, having once been recognized, should be allowed to sink out of sight, the Colonies being allowed to control themselves as British Colonies do at the present time. He hoped that in his own land the question of taxation would be less hotly contested by the people. These things gained, the glorious empire of England might remain undivided, mother and daughter remaining in peace together, an

* Hutchinson Hist. Vol. III., p. 458.

affectionate headship dwelling in one, a filial and loving concession of precedence in the other. To attain such a consummation seemed to the Governor a thing worth suffering and striving for. To bring this about, as is shown by all his acts, and all his words, he contended year after year, sacrificing to his aim his reputation, his fortune, at last, hardest of all, his citizenship, dying in exile of a broken heart.

Before leaving Boston he received a most complimentary address signed by the principal inhabitants of that and other towns endorsing this course and conduct; they were known as "Addressers," and were afterwards persecuted and subjected to many indignities from their fellow townsmen.

June the 1st, 1774, he turned away from his beautiful mansion and extensive farm, and walked down Milton Hill, to the Lower Mills, nodding and smiling to his neighbors on this side and that, it is said, whether Whig or Tory, he was good friends with all. He was in a cheerful mood on that day when he left his home forever, for had not the best people of the Province approved of him, and had shown him strong marks of favor in their addresses. It is very evident, as shown in all his writing, that he was greatly attached to his beautiful country home and to his Milton neighbors, with whom he was a favorite. He mingled with them in social life, and worshipped with them in the same church. His residence on Milton Hill is situated in one of the pleasantest places in the vicinity of Boston. It is the same to-day as it was when the Governor resided there, with the exception that the house has been remodeled, and the surrounding estates, now the homes of millionaires, have been greatly improved by art. It is situated on the crest of Milton Hill—a drumlin—to the south of which, across a beautiful valley are the Blue Hills, called by the Indians the "Massachusetts" or the place of the great hills, and from which the state has derived its name. They appear like mountains rising through the atmosphere charged with fragrant mist from the intervening blossoming fields, which give them a blue appearance, and soften all their ruggedness into beauty.

The mansion faces the north on the road leading to Plymouth; across the road in front of the home is an extensive field sloping towards the green waving marshes that line the banks of the beautiful Neponset river, winding its course to the harbor, which bears upon its bosom many picturesque islands, and in the remote distance is seen the rocky Brewsters, on which is situated the white lighthouse, marking the edge of the ocean.*

On that beautiful spring morning as the Governor walked down the hill he had no thought of a lasting absence, though martial law for a time was to be tried he was still Governor; meantime his salary was continued and he was about to give an account of his stewardship to his royal master. At the foot of the hill he crossed the river and there met

* Several wealthy citizens of Milton have recently purchased this field and donated it to the State as a public reservation to be known as the "Governor Hutchinson Field."

his carriage, next year to be confiscated, and appropriated to the use of Washington. In it he rode to what is now South Boston Point; then embarking in a boat, he was rowed to the Castle, on Castle Island, the last bit of Massachusetts earth to feel his footfall. From here he embarked on the warship Minerva, which was to convey him to England,

(Governor Hutchinson's House on Milton Hill.)

where he arrived July 1st,· and was immediately received by the King, who during the interview said, "I believe you generally live in the country, Mr. Hutchinson, what distance are you from town?" Mr. Hutchinson replied, "I have lived in the country, Sir, in the summer for 20 years, but except the winter after my house was pulled down, I have never lived in the country in the winter until the last. My house is 7 or 8 miles from Town, a pleasant situation, and most gentlemen from abroad say it has the finest prospect from it they ever saw, except where great improvements have been made by art to help the natural view."*

He often afterwards was at Court, and was treated with

* Hutchinson Diary, Vol. II., pp. 164, 165.

the greatest kindness by both King and Queen. A baronetcy was offered him, which he declined because of insufficient means to support the title, his property in America having been confiscated. He was however handsomely pensioned. He does indeed write under date of September 1st, 1778, "The changes in the last four or five years of my life make the whole scene, when I look back upon it appear like a dream, or other delusions. From the possession of one of the best houses in Bos-

(Inland View from Governor Hutchinson's House.)

ton, the pleasantest house and farm at Milton, of almost any in the world and one of the best estates in the Colony of Rhode Island, with an affluent income, and a prospect of being able to make a handsome provision for each of my children at my death—,I have not a foot of land at my command, and personal estate of £7000 only, depending on the bounty of Government for a pension, which, though it affords a present ample provision for myself, and enables me to distribute £500 a year among my children, yet is precarious, and I cannot avoid anxiety. But I am still distinguished by a kind Providence from my suffering relations, friends, and countrymen in America as well as from many of them in England, and have great reason to be thankful that so much money is yet continued to me."*

The Governor's diary in England is a profoundly pathetic record of a man broken-hearted by his expatriation. His sons and daughters and their families to the number of twenty-five were all dependent upon him. "He is glad he has a home for them, when so many fellow-exiles are

* Diary and Letters of H. Vol. II., p. 216.

in want." As Hutchinson was by far the ablest and most eminent of his party, so his sufferings were especially sharp. His name was held to be a stigma. Hutchinson Street in Boston became Pearl Street. The town of Hutchinson in the heart of the Commonwealth, cast off its title as that "of one who had acted the part of a traitor and parricide," substituting for it that of Barre, the liberal champion in Parliament.

The honorable name he had made through forty years of self-denying wisely directed public service, was blotted out, for generations it was a mark for obloquy. His great possession and large estate were confiscated, and to the shame of his countrymen be it said, they did not spare even his family tomb. It was sold by the State and the bones of his ancestors, some of the greatest men of the colony, and those of his wife and children were thrown out. The old stone with the Hutchinson crest on it still remains over the tomb in Copp's Hill burial ground with the name of the new owner of the tomb rudely marked on it. Could the governor have had a premonition of what was going to happen when he wrote to his son, Feb. 22, 1775, that he wished to have a new tomb built at Milton, and the remains of his wife, deceased twenty-one years, to be tenderly removed from Copp's Hill and deposited therein, with space for himself, and bade him "leave the wall or any ornament or inscription till I return, and the sooner it is finished the better."

His son Thomas had left Milton and retired to Boston before he received his father's letter. Hostilities immediately followed, and were succeeded by the confiscation of the estates of the loyalists. Hence this cherished design of the governor was never carried out. Again on May 15th, 1779, he writes in his diary, "And though I know not how to reason upon it, I feel a fondness to lay my bones in my native soil and to carry those of my dear daughter with me." Again he writes, "The prospect of returning to America and laying my bones in the land of my forefathers for four preceding generations, and if I add the mother of W. H. it will make five, is less than it has ever been." Then at last this entry is found. "Sept. 16, 1779. Stopped at Croydon, went into the church, looked upon the grave of my dear child, inquired whether there was room for me, and was informed there was." He was indeed sinking fast, and his end was rapidly approaching. A few months later, June 3, 1780, as he was walking down the steps of his house to his coach, going for his morning drive, he fell into the arms of his servant, and with one or two gasps he resigned his soul to God, who gave it. He was buried at Croydon on the 9th of June. It would scarcely be possible for a human life to close among circumstances of deeper gloom. Utter destruction had overtaken his family. His daughters and his son dispirited, dropped prenaturely at the same time with him into the grave. His son "Billy" died on Feb. 20. A child of Elisha's died on June 25th, and his daughter Sarah died on the 28th. In daily contact with him was a company of Loyalist exiles, once men of position and wealth, now discredited, disheartened, and in danger of starvation. The country he loved and had suffered so much for, had nothing for him but contumely. To a man like Hutchinson public calamity would cause a deeper pang than private sorrow. No more threatening hour for England has probably ever struck than that in which the soul of this great and good man passed away. It had become apparent that America was lost, a separation that might be fatal to the empire, and which her hereditary enemies were hastening to make the most of. To America herself the rending seemed to many certain to be fatal.

While the members were thus being torn away, destruction seemed to impend at the heart. At the moment of his death, London was at the mercy of the mob, in the Gordon riots. The city was on fire in many places, a drunken multitude murdered, right and left, laying hands even upon the noblest of the land. Lord Mansfield, Chief Justice of England, because he had recommended to the mercy of a jury, a priest arrested for celebrating mass, saved his life with difficulty, his home with all his possessions going up in flames. What a remarkable coincidence this was with what happened to the governor when he was Chief Justice of Massachusetts. The exile's funeral passed on its way through smoke, and uproar, that might easily have been regarded as the final crash of the social structure. No one foresaw then what was immediately to come; that England was to make good her loss twice over, that America was to become the most powerful of nations, that the London disorders were on the surface merely, and only transient. In Hutchinson's latest consciousness, every person, every spot, every institution dear to his heart must have seemed to be overwhelmed in catastrophe. Such was the end of a life thoroughly dutiful and honorable."*

On the death of Cromwell, his body was buried in Henry VII chapel, and after the restoration it was disinterred and gibbeted at Tyburn, and then buried under the gallows, the head being placed on a pike over Westminster Hall, where Cromwell had Charles I condemned to death. And now nearly two and one-half centuries since this event occurred a beautiful monument of Cromwell has been erected by Parliament on the lawn a few feet from Westminster Hall where the above events took place. Will the city of Boston ever do likewise and erect a statue to Governor Hutchinson in some public place as a slight atonement for the oboloquy cast upon his name, the desecration of his family tomb, and as a recognition of the great services he rendered his native state, for certainly he was one of the worthiest sons that Massachusetts has ever produced, and there should be some memorial in the place of his birth, to record his private virtues, his historical labors, his high station, his commanding influences, and his sorrows, which have an interest, which none acquainted with his life can fail to feel.

The following list of estates belonging to Thomas Hutchinson situated at, and near Boston, taken from him under the Conspiracy and Confiscation Acts comprises nineteen parcels of land. The state received

* Hosmer's Life of Hutchinson, p. 349.

for them £98,121, 4s or about $490,000. His mansion house on the corner of Fleet and Hanover Streets brought £33,500. The Governor owned other valuable real estate in Rhode Island and other parts of Massachusetts, particularly in that part now the State of Maine. He was probably the wealthiest person in the state of Massachusetts at the commencement of the Revolutionary War. The author is indebted to the late John T. Hassam, A. M., for the list of Confiscated Estates in Suffolk County contained in this work, giving the name of the purchaser at the sale, the Lib. and folio of the record and a brief description of the confiscated estates. It was originally printed in the proceedings of the Mass. His. Soc. for May, 1895.

LIST OF GOVERNOR HUTCHINSON'S CONFISCATED ESTATES IN SUFFOLK COUNTY AND TO WHOM SOLD.

To Joseph Veasey, Dec. 27, 1779; Lib. 131, fol. 21; Land and dwelling-house in Boston, Fish St. W.; land purchased by Thomas Stephenson N.; passageway E.; heirs of William Graves S.

To Samuel Broome, July 24, 1780; Lib. 131, fol. 233; Land, 43 A. 2 qr. 34 r., in Milton, a back lane E.; Mr. Ivers and Milton River N.; Stephen Badcock and a brook N.W.; lane to Stephen Badcock S.W.; road to Milton meeting-house S.E.———Land, 33 A. 1 r., mansion house and barn in Milton road to Braintree E.; heirs of William Badcock S.E. and S.W.; road to Milton meeting-house N.W.———14 A. 3 qr. 3 r. in Milton, road to Braintree S.W.; Robert Williams S.E.; heirs of William Badcock N.; Milton River N.E.———Woodland, 48 A. 1 qr. 9 r., in Milton, road by Moses Glover's N.W.; Braintree town line S.E.; John Bois S.W.; John Sprague N.E.———Tillage land, 17 A. 2 qr. 27 r., and salt marsh, 16 A. 14 r. adjoining, in Dorchester, lower road from Milton bridge to Dorchester meeting-house W.; Hopestill Leeds N.E.; John Capen and others E.; Amariah Blake and the river N.; Ebenezer Swift, Daniel Vose and a creek S.———Salt marsh, 2 A. 3 qr. 9 r., near the Hummucks in Dorchester, Levi Rounsavel N.; Robert Swan and Madam Belcher S.; the river W.———Salt marsh, 7 A., in Dorchester, Billings Creek S. and W.; Robert Spurr N.; Henry Leadbetter S.E. and E.———One undivided third of 8 A. salt marsh in Dorchester, held in common with Timothy Tucker and Joseph Tucker, Billings Creek S.; Nathan Ford W.———Woodland, 33 1-2 A. 9 r., in Braintree.

To John Hotty, Aug. 8, 1780; Lib. 131, fol. 247; Land and dwelling-house in Boston, Fish St. W.; land purchased by Parsons and Sargeant N.; passageways E. and S.

To Ebenezer Parsons, Daniel Sargent, Feb. 25, 1783; Lib. 137, fol. 95; Land and dwelling-house in Boston, Fish St. W.; passageways N. and E.; land purchased by Thomas Stephenson S.———Land and dwelling-house, Fish St. W.; land purchased by John Hancock N.; Thomas Hutchinson E.; land purchased by John Hotty S.———Land, store, block-maker's shop, and other work places near the above, passageways S.; W. and E.; Thomas Hutchinson N.———Flats, dock, wharf and stores near the above, passage W.; dock N.; sea E.; dock S.———Flats, dock and wharf adjoining the above-described wharf, John Brick S.; passageways W. and N.; dock N.; the sea E.

To Ebenezer Parsons, Daniel Sargeant, Feb. 25, 1783; Lib. 137, fol. 99; Land and dwelling-houses in Boston, Fish St. W.; land purchased by said Parsons and Sargeant S.; passage N.; passage E.; land purchased by said Parsons and Sargeant S.; passage W.; then running W. and S.

To Thomas Stephenson, Mar. 13, 1783; Lib. 137, fol. 161; Land and dwelling-house in Boston, Fish St. W.; land purchased by Parsons and Sargent N.; passage E.; land purchased by Joseph Veasey S.

To Enoch Brown, Oct. 14, 1784; Lib. 145, fol. 126; Land and brick dwelling-house in Boston, Middle St. W.; Fleet St. N.; street from Clark's Square to Fleet St. E.; Lady Franklin S.

THOMAS HUTCHINSON.

Eldest son of Governor Hutchinson. He was born in Boston in 1740. He married Oct. 10, 1771, Sarah, daughter of Lieut. Governor Andrew Oliver. He was Judge of the Probate Court for the County of Suffolk. He was Mandamus Councillor, and an Andresser of General Gage. He and his family were in Boston during the blockade, and bombardment. At the evacuation, they went aboard ship with their two children, when the third child was born, as they were leaving for England. Dr. Peter Oliver, the second son of Chief Justice Oliver, refers to this matter in his Diary, as follows: "We remained blocked up in Boston till the beginning of March, 1776, when we were ordered to embark. Tommy Hutchinson's family and mine went aboard the Hyde Pacquet for England, March 25th, 1776, we set sail for England. The day before we set sail from Nantasket, Tommy's wife was delivered of a boy which had not a drop of milk during the whole passage, was much emaciated, and no one thought it would have lived. The lady well. As to myself, I was sick 21 days without any support; reduced almost to a skeleton. Seven children on board ship, and the eldest not 6 years old."

The child born aboard ship was baptised Andrew, after its mother's father, Lieut. Gov. Andrew Oliver. It grew up, married, left children, was an eminent surgeon, and after a long life, died Dec. 23, 1846, aged 70 years. He was the father of the late Peter Orlando Hutchinson, great grandson of the Governor who edited the two volumes of the Diary of Governor Hutchinson, published in 1883. He was a local antiquary, of local repute, and a gentleman of great kindness of heart. He was a bachelor, and died at Sidmouth, Devon, Oct. 1st, 1897, aged 87, and was the last of his generation.

His last words at the end of the second volume, are as follows: "If in these volumes, I have anywhere said anything of my American friends that is untrue, or too harsh for the occasion, I regret it should have been so, and I willingly withdraw it altogether. I need not apologise for any unkind remarks that may have been made by the Governor, though most concerned, for he made none; and when they have made reparation for all the slander and misrepresentation which they have persistently heaped upon him during the last 120 years, then—we shall be quits. It is time to bury the hatchet. Farewell."

Thomas Hutchinson, the subject of this sketch, writing to his brother under date of Nov. 15th, 1788, alluded to the trying position in which the Loyalists were placed, he says, "We will give a little attention to a large and suffering body of people whose only crime had been that of fidelity to the Mother country. Driven out of the land of their adoption, they fled back to the land of their ancestors, where most of them were strangers. Some pressed their claims for relief from the English Government; others applied to the American Courts for recovery of the estates themselves, while others despairing of success, gave up everything for lost, and sat down resigned to their fate. Sir Francis Bernard lost the valuable Island of Mount Desert, and Sir William Pepperell lost miles of coast line, stretching away from Kittery Point to Saco, extending miles into the interior."

"These unfortunate people were very difficultly placed— if they had joined the American party, they would have been Rebels to England, but when the war was over and they applied for the restitution of their estates, they were told they were Rebels to America."

Writing again under date of 1789, he said: "We proceeded to Exeter, and I have taken a house at a mile from the town, but in the neighborhood, the house furnished, and has every convenience about it, with about six acres of land—mowing, orchard, and garden stocked with fruit trees. I could have had my house and garden without the land, at £45, and am to pay £60 per ann. for the whole. The last year my orchard produced 20 hhds of cyder."

Thus the family became settled in a respectable looking old house built in the Queen Anne style, known as East Wonford near Heavitree church, where it still stands. The rent appears to be extraordinarily low. He would not bind himself to a lease, for he still had hopes of returning to America, but the return was never to be. The Hutchinsons had very little chance of a favorable hearing in Massachusetts, and their large fortune there was forever lost to them. The family seems to have been content with their new home, for in another letter to his brother of May 19, 1791, Thomas says:—"After eighteen months residence, we continue to think this a very agreeable part of England; and perhaps I could not have made a better pitch than I have done."

Thomas Hutchinson, son of the Governor, died in 1811, and his wife in 1802. They were deposited in a vault in the middle of Heavitree church. The church was pulled down in 1843 and a new one erected on the same site.

Thomas, his eldest son, grandson of the Governor, was born in America in 1772, brought to England by his father in 1776, he was a Barrister-at-Law, resided during the early years of his career at No. 14 New Boswell Court, Lincoln's Inn, London, and after that in Magdalen Street, Exeter. He married twice, had three sons and one daughter. He is buried in the N. W. corner of Heavitree churchyard. A stone with the following inscription marks the spot: "Underneath this stone Lie the mortal remains of Thomas Hutchinson, Barrister-at-Law, who departed this life the 12th of November 1837, aged 65."

Mary Oliver Hutchinson, daughter of Thomas Hutchinson, and granddaughter of the Governor, was born in America, Oct. 14, 1773, and was brought to England by her father in 1776, married Captain W. S. Oliver, R. N., grandson of Lieut. Governor Andrew Oliver, at Heavitree, in Oct. 1811. She died at East Tergnmouth, Devon, July 11th, 1833, leaving one son and two daughters of whom more presently.

William Hutchinson, son of Thomas and grandson of the Governor, was born in England, June 14, 1778. He entered the church and was pastor for some time at Heavitree and Colebrook, Devon. He had two sons and three daughters. Rev. William Hutchinson, died May 3rd, 1816.

ELISHA HUTCHINSON.

Son of Governor Hutchinson, was born Dec. 24, 1745, at Boston. He graduated at Harvard College in 1762. His wife Mary was the eldest daughter of Colonel George Watson of Plymouth, Mass. He was the commercial partner of his brother Thomas. They were the consignees of one-third of the tea. Their names were given to the East India Company by a London correspondent, who solicits the consignment for them, without mentioning their connection with the Governor, although the historian Bancroft falsely asserts that he had a pecuniary interest in the shipment, of which there is not the slightest evidence.* He accompanied his father to England in 1774, leaving his wife in America, with the intention of rejoining her in a few months, but it was three years before she could join him in England. Having reached his 80th year he died at Tutbury, June 24, 1824, having had issue three daughters and two sons. His son John, born Sept. 21, 1793, was perpetual curate of Blurton near Trentham, Co. Staff. Percentor and Canon of Lichfield, Editor of Vol. 3 of Gov. Hutchinson Hist. of Mass., in 1828. He married his cousin Martha Oliver Hutchinson, May 10th, 1836. He died April 27, 1865, at Blurton, having had issue two daughters and one son, John Rogers, born March 6, 1848, who married Ruth Hombersley, Oct. 19, 1882, at Kirk Ireton, Derbyshire.

FOSTER HUTCHINSON.

Was brother of Governor Hutchinson, and one of the last judges of the supreme court of Massachusetts. He graduated at Harvard University in 1743. He accepted the appointment of mandamus councillor in 1774 and soon after was compelled to take refuge in Boston. He was proscribed and banished and his estates were confiscated. He left Boston at the evacuation in 1776, and with his family of twelve persons went to Halifax. He died in Nova Scotia in 1799. His son, Foster, an Assistant Judge of the Supreme Court of that Colony died in 1815, and his daughter Abigal deceased at Halifax, July 1843, aged seventy-four years. Foster and his brother Thomas had a dry goods store in 1765 below the "Swing Bridge" near what is now the corner of Hanover and Salem streets.

* Tea Leaves, p. 324.

CONFISCATED ESTATES BELONGING TO FOSTER HUTCHINSON ET AL IN SUFFOLK COUNTY AND TO WHOM SOLD.

To Ebenezer Parsons, Daniel Sargent, Feb. 25, 1783; Lib. 137, fol. 95; Land and dwelling-house in Boston, Fish St. W.; passageways N. and E.; land purchased by Thomas Stephenson S.———Land and dwelling-house, Fish St. W.; land purchased by John Hancock N.; Thomas Hutchinson E.; land purchased by John Hotty S.———Land, store, block-maker's shop and other work places near the above, passageways S.; W. and E.; Thomas Hutchinson N.———Flats, dock, wharf and stores, near the above, passage W.; dock N.; sea E.; dock S.——— Flats, dock and wharf adjoining the above described wharf, John Brick S.; passageways W. and N.; dock N.; the sea E.

To John Codman, Jr., Sept. 25, 1783; Lib. 140, fol. 4; Land, wharf and dock in Boston, Town Dock N.; heirs of William Clarke deceased W.; heirs of Benjamin Andrews S.; passage from the Town Dock to Green's Wharf E.

ELIAKIM HUTCHINSON.

As previously stated, the ancestor of Governor Hutchinson who emigrated to Boston was William Hutchinson, grandson of the Mayor of Lincoln; he had a brother Richard in business in London whose son Eliakim also settled at Boston. There is nothing to show that Richard ever came to this country, and when William and his wife Anne was expelled from Boston, the lot which had been granted to him in 1634, now known as the "Old Corner Bookstore," which then extended to the City Hall lot, was sold by his son Edward to Richard Hutchinson of London, linen-draper. This was the father of Eliakim. The subject of this notice was the great grandson of the emigrant. He was born in 1711 and married Elizabeth, eldest daughter of Governor Shirley. He was a member of the Governor's Council and Chief Justice of the Court of Common Pleas for Suffolk County. In 1764 he purchased from his father-in-law "Shirley Hall," the finest estate in Roxbury. In 1746 Governor Shirley bought thirty-three acres of land and erected this palatial mansion on it. Its oaken frame and other materials, even the bricks, it is said, were brought from England, at a vast expense. It has been removed from its original location, and is now occupied as a tenement house, yet, notwithstanding the vicissitudes it has undergone, it is extremely well preserved. One of the peculiarities of "Shirley Place," as the governor styled it, is its double front. From the upper windows a fine view is obtained of the city, harbor and islands. Each front was approached by a flight of stone steps flanked by an iron railing of an antique and rustic pattern. Entering the northern or proper front, you find yourself in a spacious hall of grand proportions. To the right a broad staircase leads to a balcony extending around to the left where two doors open into the guest chambers in which Washington, Lafayette, Franklin, Daniel Webster and many other celebrated men have from time to time been accommodated. From the balcony the musicians entertained the company at the table in the hall. The carved balusters around the staircase and gallery are of three different patterns, and the rail surmounting them is inlaid at the top. The base of the balustrade and staircase, is also adorned with a carved running vine. To the right and left of the hall are doors leading into the reception room, parlors, etc. Upon great occasions the two halls were thrown into one by opening the folding doors between. Washington paid a visit to Governor Shirley in March 1756, to relate to him the circumstances of his son's death who was killed at the battle of the Monongahela. In a letter to his friend and patron Lord Fairfax, he says, "I have had the honor of being introduced to several governors, especially Mr. Shirley, whose character and appearance, have perfectly charmed me." The next time Washington visited "Shirley Place" it was not as a guest, but as an enemy.

Governor Shirley was a man of great industry and ability, thoroughly able, enterprising, and deservedly popular. He was a strong advocate of perogative, and in 1756 advised the ministry to impose a stamp tax in America. In February, 1755, he was made a major-general, with superintendence of military operations in the Northern Colonies. It was then, after the disastrous defeat and death of General Braddock, that Major Washington came to report it to him, and he was superseded both in his command and his government, and ordered to England. Triumphantly vindicating himself from the charges against him, he was made a lieutenant-general in 1759, and was governor of the Bahamas from 1758 to June 1769 when he returned to Roxbury, residing with his son-in-law in the mansion built by him until his death, March 24, 1771, and was interred in the burying ground of King's Chapel, which edifice he caused to be built while governor.

Judge Eliakim Hutchinson died in June, 1775. He had a high standing at the bar, being well versed in his profession, and enjoyed a good reputation as a general scholar, and as a man of high moral and religious principles. He was early imbued with principles favorable to the government, but was never a bitter, nor even a warm partisan.

His patrimonial inheritance, aided by industry enabled him to acquire a handsome fortune, one of the largest in the province. He adhered to government from the beginning of the controversy, but the moderation of his conduct, his superior fitness for his office, and the confidence in his integrity, secured him public favor through the stormy period, which commenced soon after his appointment to the Governor's Council. But this was an unpardonable offence in the eyes of the "Sons of Despotism." It was however unsolicited, unexpected and accepted with great reluctance, and although he died before actual hostilities had scarcely commenced, yet his large and valuable estate was confiscated. That portion of it in Suffolk County was inventoried at £21,400, Shirley Place with eighty acres of land was valued at £12,000. During the siege of Boston the mansion was used as a barracks by the Revolutionary troops and was greatly injured thereby.

It was purchased from the State by John Read, and then passed through many hands, and in 1819 was purchased by Governor Eustis, who passed the remainder of his days there, dying in 1825. Among the guests that accepted his hospitality was John Quincy Adams, Henry Clay, Daniel Webster, Aaron Burr, and John Calhoun.

Judge Hutchinson's wife left Boston at the evacuation, and went to England. She died at London in 1790.

WILLIAM HUTCHINSON, son of Eliakim Hutchinson, graduated at Harvard College in 1762. He went to the Bahamas when his grandfather Shirley became Governor of same. In 1771 William Hutchinson was appointed Judge of the Admiralty Court of the Bahama Islands. He died in England in 1790.

LIST OF CONFISCATED ESTATES BELONGING TO ELIAKIM HUTCHINSON IN SUFFOLK COUNTY AND TO WHOM SOLD.

To William McNeill, Archibald McNeill, Feb. 21, 1782; Lib. 134, fol. 27; Land in Boston, Cow Lane E.; Howe's ropewalk S.; W. and S.; Milk St. W.; Palmer's pasture N.

To Edward Compton Howe, June 17, 1782; Lib. 135, fol. 22; Land in Boston, Milk St. N.; Mr. McNeil E. and S.; McNeil's ropewalk E.; Cow Lane S.; ropewalk of Ferister and Torrey W.

To John Read, Sept. 9, 1782; Lib. 135, fol. 196; Land 37A., in Roxbury, bounded by the road from Roxbury to Dorchester, the brook and salt water creek between Roxbury and Dorchester, the way to the clay pit and by the lands of John Howes, John Humphrey, John Williams, Aaron White, James White, Caleb Williams, Samuel Warren, Joseph Clapp, Isaac Williams and Benjamin Williams.——Woodland 13 A., in Roxbury, Elijah Wales S.; widow Bourne and heirs E.; Noah Davis W. and N.——Right of William Shirley Esq., to the clay pits above mentioned called the Town of Roxbury clay pits.——23 1-2 A. in Roxbury, John Williams N.; Aaron White, Samuel Cheney, John Hawes, widow Warren and heirs of Joseph Warren W.; Nehemiah Munroe S.; town way from Dorchester brook to Braintree road E.——Pasture land, 19 A., in Roxbury, Daniel Holbrook N.; Braintree road W.; James White S.W.; said town way S. and E.——22 A., in Roxbury, said town way N.W.; John Williams and Swan S.; John Humphrey E.; John Williams N.E.——Salt marsh and upland, 20 A., in Roxbury, heirs of Benjamin Williams S.W.; town creek between Roxbury and Dorchester S.E.; Joseph Curtis N.

To John Lucas, Edward Tuckerman, Oct. 4, 1782; Lib. 136, fol. 22; Land in Boston, on Dock Square and Cooper's Alley, bounded by lands of Thomas Green, Joshua Blanchard, widow Apthorp, John Newell, William Greenleaf, Jonathan Simpson and heirs of Thomas Young.

To Nathan Spear, March 1, 1783; Lib. 137, fol. 131; Land in Boston, passageway from the Town Dock to Green's wharf W.; Jonathan Williams, William Hyslop, Nathaniel Correy, Alexander Hill, heirs of John Gould, of Anthony Stoddard, and of John Walker deceased N.; the end of the wharf E.; the dock between said wharf and Green's wharf S.

To Francis Bigelow, April 3, 1783; Lib. 137, fol. 260; Land in Boston on Milk St.; bounded by a passageway and by land of said Bigelow, said Hutchinson and Mr. Bourne.

To Joseph Russell, July 12, 1783; Lib. 139, fol. 75; Land in Boston near Fort Hill, Gridley's Lane S.; Cow Lane E.; land of Town of Boston and of heirs of Andrew Oliver N.; Thomas Palmer W.

To Thomas Green, Feb. 18, 1784; Lib. 141, fol. 136; Land in Boston, Dock Square S.; Eliakim Hutchinson W.; Mr. Blanchard N.; Thomas Green E.; N. and E.

To Thomas Walley, Aug. 28, 1784; Lib. 144, fol. 172; Land and buildings in Boston, Cross St. S.; Thomas Walley W.; widow Holmes N.; Samuel Ellinwood E.

To Samuel Emmons, Jr., Victor Blair, Dec. 24, 1792; Lib. 174, fol. 183; Land in Boston, Milk St. and Cow Lane, between a highway and ropewalk of Farreter and Torrey.

To Jeffery Richardson, May 17, 1793; Lib. 176, fol. 8; Land in Boston, Cow Lane S.E.; Samuel Emmons N.E.; Thomas Davis S.W.; extending towards Milk St. N.W.

To Jeffery Richardson, Dec. 15, 1795; Lib. 182, fol. 27; Confirmation of above.

To Martin Brimmer, Apr. 13, 1796; Lib. 183, fol. 37; Flats and wharf in Boston, Minot's T N.; flats towards the town W.; wharf and flats of William Davis S.; the channel E.

ANDREW OLIVER.
Born in Boston, 1707.   Lieutenant Governor 1770-4.   Died in Boston, March, 1774.

ANDREW OLIVER.

LIEUTENANT GOVERNOR OF MASSACHUSETTS 1770-1774.

The Oliver family are among the most prominent of the early colonial families. Thomas Oliver came from Bristol in 1632. He was one of the founders, and Elder of the First Church in Boston.* His son Peter born in England in 1622 and died in Boston in 1670, was a prominent merchant, and commander of the Ancient and Honorable Artillery Company in 1669 and was one of the founders of the Old South Church. Peter's son Daniel married Elizabeth, the daughter of Andrew Belcher, who was the father of Governor Jonathan Belcher.

ANDREW OLIVER, son of Daniel Oliver, a member of the Council, and brother of Peter Oliver, the Chief Justice. He graduated at Harvard College in 1724. He was a representative from Boston, member of the council and Secretary of the Province. In 1765, soon after receiving the appointment of Stamp Collector, without his solicitation, he not approving of the Act, he became very unpopular. The rough population which abounded about the wharves and shipyards, whose movements were directed by persons of higher rank and larger views of mischief, grew riotous, and with the usual want of discrimination shown by mobs, were not slow to lift their hands against even their best friends. The houses of the Custom and Admiralty officials were attacked, which culminating in an extraordinary outrage against Andrew Oliver, which led John Adams to exclaim, "Has not the blind undistinguishing rage of the rabble done that gentleman irreparable injustice"?** He was hung in effigy, a drunken crowd carrying the effigy through the Town House, even while the Governor and Council were in session. The building he had fitted for the transaction of business was destroyed. Taking a portion of it for a fire, the mob proceeded to Fort Hill where Mr. Oliver lived and burned his effigy in a bonfire before his home; they then went to work on the barn, fence, garden, and dwelling house. After breaking all the windows they entered the house and damaged and destroyed his furniture, completely wrecking this beautiful mansion. The business being finished, the "Sons of Despotism" proceeded to the Province-house, gave three huzzas and dispersed. On the day following the riot, Mr. Oliver resigned his office. In writing to a friend he says, "I was presuaded to yield in order to prevent what was coming on the second night." This action of the mob caused intense suffering both to himself and family.***

In 1770, Mr. Oliver was appointed Lieutenant Governor. In 1773, several letters which he had written to persons in England, and which were obtained surreptitiously by Franklin and sent to Boston, created much ex-

*He lived on Washington Street; his lot extended north from Spring Lane, including the head of Water Street.

** John Adams' Diary, Aug. 15, 1765.

*** See page 40 for account of the riot.

citement and abuse of the writers.* In addition to the assaults at home, he was accused in England by Arthur Lee who signed himself Junius Americanus with the grave crime of perjury. "Scarce any man ever had a more scrupulous and sacred regard for truth, and yet, to such a degree did the malignant spirit of party prevail as to cause this man in the public papers in England, to bring against him a charge of perjury. The Council of Massachusetts Bay, from whose votes and resolves this writer attempted to support the charge, by vote which they caused to be printed, repaired the injury as well as they could, but a consciousness of his innocence and integrity, however, together with the reproaches most injuriously cast upon him by the resolves of the council and house, in which he was treated as the determined enemy of the liberties of his country, the interest whereof according to the best of his judgment (which was much superior to that of his most virulent persecutors) he always had at heart, affected his spirits and evidently accelerated his death."** Mr. Oliver was now advanced in life, and unable to endure the disquiet and misery caused by his position in affairs at so troubled a period, soon sunk under the burden. After a short illness he died at Boston in March 1774, aged 67. By the testimony of foes as well as friends, he was a most useful and estimable man, modest, indefatigable, well-cultured, soundly sensible. He had been the most beloved member of a family greatly beloved, and no charge could be brought against him except that in his political principles he sided with the Government. He was a liberal benefactor to his ALMA MATER in books, ancient manuscripts, and anatomical preparations. At his funeral the mob was again in evidence. The House of Representatives withdrew from the procession because a certain punctilio was neglected. The mob of Boston ran after the funeral train hooting and in an unseemly way hilarious, gave three cheers when the mourners came out of the graveyard, his brother the Chief Justice, intrepid as he was, did not dare to be present, because his life was threatened. Had he died before this violent spirit was raised, he would have been revered by all orders and degrees of men in the Province.

He was a man of large wealth for those days. The inventory of his real estate was as follows:

The Mansion House and Buildings situated near Fort Hill.
The Brick School House near Griffin's Wharf.
A Warehouse on Long Wharf.
A right in said Wharf.
The Buildings and Land etc., on Oliver's Dock.
A Brick House on Union Street with a small Wooden Shop adjoining and Land belonging thereto.
A Dwelling House and about three Acres of Land at Dorchester.

* See page 162, 163 concerning Hutchinson and other letters abstracted by Franklin.
** Curwin's Journal, pp. 462, 463.

ANDREW OLIVER MANSION, WASHINGTON STREET, DORCHESTER.
Lieutenant Governor of Massachusetts, 1770-1774.

The last named building is the only one now in existence, and the following description of it at the time of writing, may be interesting to the reader.

Lieut. Governor Oliver's country house in Dorchester is situated on the corner of Washington and Park streets. In the old deeds it is described as being "On the Road leading to Milton." The house appears the same as in the olden times. Not one whit has the estate changed outside of the interior of the great house. The broad acres that surround it still spread out before and behind it, the same drives are lined with great English Elms as in the old days; no finer old mansion house of the colonial period is to be found in New England, none is richer in memories of olden times. Here Lieut. Gov. Andrew Oliver entertained the finest of the land, where gentlemen in powdered wigs and ladies in fine old silks used to dance the minuet, and where the negro slaves used to be happy in their own way. It was sold by John J. Spooner, administrator of the estate of Andrew Oliver, to Col. Benjamin Hichborn, and was used by him as a summer residence. In 1817 it went into the hands of his brother, Samuel Hichborn, who entertained there Gen. Lafayette, and Presidents Jefferson, and Munroe. For many years it was owned and occupied by the famous chocolate manufacturer, Walter Baker. At the descease of Mrs. Baker, it was purchased by the Colonial Club who now occupy it as a club house.

THOMAS OLIVER.

Lieutenant-Governor of Massachusetts, 1774-1775.

Thomas Oliver was born in Antigua and graduated at Harvard College in 1753, he was the son of Robert Oliver, a wealthy planter from Antigua who settled in Dorchester. His parentage is unknown, there were Olivers in Dorchester as early as 1637, and he may have descended from them.* He brought with him from Antigua his wife Anne and one son, Thomas, the subject of this notice. He purchased a number of pieces of land of which 30 acres had been the property of Comfort Foster, on this homestead lot he built in 1745 a fine mansion, on what is now known as Edward Everett square. Tradition records that he brought many slaves with him, and when they were given wheelbarrows in which to carry the dirt, in ignorance of their proper use they carried them upon their heads, in just the same manner as the writer has seen negroes at the present time carry burdens on their heads on the "Pope's Head" estate in Antigua where these slaves came from. In Dorchester Robert Oliver had born to him sons, Isaac and Richard, and a daughter, Elizabeth, who became the wife of John Vassall, Jr. He died December 20, 1762. "The Post Boy" contained the following brief obituary: "Thursday morning

* Sabine says Dorchester. Dorchester Record says Thomas Oliver, the son of Robert Oliver, Esqr., and Ann, his wife, was born Jan. 5, 1733-4 at ye Island of Antigua.

last died at his seat in Dorchester, in the 63d year of his age, Col. Robert Oliver. A Gentleman of extensive Acquaintance, remarkable for his Hospitality to All, was kind to the Poor, and in his Military Character, beloved and esteem'd, his Family and Neighbours, have met with a great Loss in this Bereavement; His Remains are to be interr'd Tomorrow at 3 o'clock in the Family Tomb at Dorchester." About two years before this Thomas, his eldest son, had married Elizabeth, daughter of Col. John Vassall of Cambridge, making a double connection by marriage between these two families. Closely allied with them by marriage were the Royalls, all three families being probably originally of New England, then resident in Antigua and Jamaica, and returning here to enjoy their acquired wealth. All three families built houses which have lasted to our time: Royall in Medford, Vassall in Cambridge and Oliver in Dorchester.

Thomas Oliver remained for several years in Dorchester after his father's death. He inherited a large estate from his grandfather, James Brown, and from his great-uncle, Robert Oliver. He then began life under the most favorable auspices. His father-in-law was John Vassall of Cambridge, who married the daughter of Lieutenant-Governor Spencer Phips. Being a man of fortune he did not mingle in the stormy political contests of that period until a day fatal to his peace and quiet, when he accepted the office of Lieutenant-Governor. He has been represented as a mild, peaceable person, and gentlemanly in deportment. In 1766 he removed to Cambridge and built the fine mansion recently occupied by James Russell Lowell. He sold his Dorchester mansion to Richard Lechmere, who was the uncle by marriage of Oliver's wife, he having married May Phips, whose sister Elizabeth married Col. John Vassall, who died in 1741. In 1771 the mansion passed into the hands of John Vassall, a son of the Colonel, who was a Loyalist, and his property was confiscated. It was sold by the State to John Williams; it afterwards passed into the possession of Oliver Everett in 1792, and here his son Edward Everett was born in 1794. The house was torn down in 1900 and the square in front of it, previously known as the Five Corners, was named Edward Everett Square. On the opposite side of the square on a part of the same estate in a small park is situated a house built by one of the earliest settlers, about 1640, owned and occupied by the Dorchester Historical Society.

Thomas Oliver was the last Royal Lieutenant-Governor and President of the Council of Massachusetts. He received his appointment from the Crown in 1774, after the decease of Andrew Oliver, who was of a totally distinct family; it is understood that the King thought he was appointing Chief Justice Peter Oliver, a brother of Andrew, a much more active man in the politics of the times.

His appointment as Councillor was by the King's writ of mandamus which was held, was contrary to the charter. This made him an object of popular resentment. He detailed the course pursued against him, in consequence of being sworn into office in the following narrative dated

THOMAS OLIVER AND JOHN VASSALL MANSION, DORCHESTER.

It stood on the north side of Edward Everett square. A bronze tablet marks its site. Edward Everett was born here April 11, 1794. (See p. 182.)

September 7, 1774, which as throwing light on the transaction of the times is inserted entire:

"Early in the morning" (of September 2d), said he, "a number of inhabitants of Charlestown called at my house to acquaint me that a large body of people from several towns in the county were on their way coming down to Cambridge; that they were afraid some bad consequences might ensue, and begged I would go out to meet them, and endeavor to prevail on them to return. In a very short time, before I could prepare myself to go, they appeared in sight. I went out to them, and asked the reasons of their appearance in that manner; they respectfully answered, they 'came peaceably to inquire into their grievances, not with design to hurt any man.' I perceived they were landholders of the neighboring towns, and was thoroughly persuaded they would do no harm. I was desired to speak to them; I accordingly did, in such a manner as I thought best calculated to quiet their minds. They thanked me for my advice, said they were no mob, but sober, orderly people, who would commit no disorders; and then proceeded on their way. I returned to my house. Soon after they had arrived on the Common at Cambridge, a report arose that the troops were on their march from Boston; I was desired to go and intercede with his Excellency to prevent their coming. From principles of humanity to the country, from a general love of mankind, and from persuasions that they were orderly people, I readily undertook it; and is there a man on earth, who, placed in my circumstances, could have refused it? I am informed I am censured for having advised the general to a measure which may reflect on the troops, as being too inactive upon such a general disturbance; but surely such a reflection on a military man can never arise but in the minds of such as are entirely ignorant of these circumstances. Wherever this affair is known, it must also be known it was my request the troops should not be sent, but to return; as I passed the people I told them, of my own accord, I would return and let them know the event of my application (not, as was related in the papers, to confer with them on my own circumstances as President of the Council). On my return I went to the Committee, I told them no troops had been ordered, and from the account I had given his Excellency, none would be ordered. I was then thanked for the trouble I had taken in the affair, and was just about to leave them to their own business, when one of the Committee observed, that as I was present it might be proper to mention a matter they had to propose to me. It was, that although they had a respect for me as Lieutenant-Governor of the Province, they could wish I would resign my seat. I told them I took it very unkind that they should mention anything on that subject; and among other reasons I urged, that, as Lieutenant-Governor, I stood in a particular relation to the Province in general, and therefore could not hear anything upon that matter from a particular county. I was then pushed to know if I would resign when it appeared to be the sense of the Province in general; I answered, that when all the other Councillors had resigned, if it appeared to be the sense of the Province I should resign, I would submit. They then called for a vote upon the subject, and, by a very great majority, voted my reasons satisfactory. I inquired whether they had full power to act for the people, and being answered in the affirmative, I desired they would take care to acquaint them of their votes, that I should have no further application made to me on that head. I was promised by the Chairman, and a general assent, it should be so. This left me entirely clear and free from any apprehensions of a farther application upon this matter, and perhaps will account for that confidence which I had in the people, and for which I may be censured. Indeed, it is true, the event proves I had too much; but reasoning from events yet to come, is a kind of reasoning I have not been used to. In the afternoon I observed large companies pouring in from different parts; I then began to apprehend they would become unmanageable, and that it was expedient to go out of their way. I was just going into my carriage when a great crowd advanced, and in a short time my house was surrounded by three or four thousand people, and one quarter part in arms. I went to the front door, where I was met by five persons, who acquainted me they were a Committee from the people to demand a resignation of my seat at the Board. I was shocked at their ingratitude and false dealings, and reproached them with it. They excused themselves by saying the people were dissatisfied with the vote of the Committee, and insisted on my signing a paper they had prepared for that purpose. I found that I had been ensnared, and endeavored to reason them out of such ungrateful behavior. They gave such answers, that I found it was in vain to reason longer with them; I told them my first considerations were for my honor, the next for my life; that they might put me to death or destroy my property, but I would not submit. They began than to reason in their turn, urging the power of the people, and the danger of opposing them. All this occasioned a delay, which enraged part of the multitude, who, pressing into my back yard, denounced vengeance to the foes of their liberties. The Committee endeavored to moderate them, and desired them to keep back, for they pressed up to my windows, which then were opened; I could from thence hear them at a distance calling out for a determination, and, with their arms in their hands, swearing they would have my blood if I refused. The Committee appeared to be anxious for me, still I refused to sign; part of the populace growing furious, and the distress of my family who heard their threats, and supposed them just about to be executed, called up feelings which I could not suppress; and nature, ready to find new excuses, suggested a thought of the calamities I should occasion if I did not comply: I found myself giving way, and began to cast about to contrive means to come off with honor. I proposed they should call in the people to take me out by force, but they said the people were enraged, and they would not answer for the consequences. I told them I would take the risk, but they refused to do it. Reduced to this extremity, I cast my eyes over the paper, with a hurry of mind and

REVOLUTIONISTS MARCHING TO CAMBRIDGE.

To oblige Lieutenant-Governor Thomas Oliver to resign from the Council Board.

conflict of passion which rendered me unable to remark the contents, and wrote beneath the following words: 'My house at Cambridge being surrounded by four thousand people, in compliance with their commands, I sign my name, THOMAS OLIVER.' The five persons took it, carried it to the people, and, I believe, used their endeavors to get it accepted. I had several messages that the people would not accept it with those additions, upon which I walked into the court-yard, and declared I would do no more, though they should put me to death. I perceived that those persons who formed the first body which came down in the morning, consisting of the landholders of the neighboring towns, used their utmost endeavors to get the paper received with my additions; and I must, in justice to them, observe, that, during the whole transaction, they had never invaded my enclosures, but still were not able to protect me from other insults which I received from those who were in arms. From this consideration I am induced to quit the country, and seek protection in the town."

The document presented to Mr. Oliver on the 2d of September, and which he signed, was as follows: "I, Thomas Oliver, being appointed by his Majesty to a seat at the Council Board, upon, and in conformity to the late Act of Parliament, entitled an 'Act for the better regulation of the Province of Massachusetts Bay,' which being a manifest infringement of the Charter rights and privileges of this people, I do hereby, in conformity to the commands of the body of this county now convened, most solemnly renounce and resign my seat at said unconstitutional Board, and hereby firmly promise and engage, as a man of honor and a Christian, that I never will hereafter, upon any terms whatsoever, accept a seat at said Board on the present novel and oppressive plan of Government." To this, the original form, he added the words above recited. Judge Danforth and Judge Lee, who were also Mandamus Councillors, and Mr. Phipps, the sheriff, and Mr. Mason, clerk of the county, were compelled to submit to the same body, and make written resignations.

Governor Oliver, as stated by himself, went into Boston, and made assurances both to General Gage and to the Admiral on the station, which prevented a body of troops from being sent to disperse the large body of people who assembled at Cambridge on this occasion; and to these assurances it was owing, undoubtedly, that the day passed without bloodshed. But for the peaceable demeanor of those whom he met in the morning,—the landholders of the neighboring towns,—the first collision between the King's troops and the inhabitants of Massachusetts, would have occurred, very likely, at Cambridge, and not at Lexington. A detachment was sent to the former town the day before, to bring off some pieces of cannon, and from this circumstance arose, principally, the proceedings related by Governor Oliver. Indignant because the "redcoats" had been sent upon such an errand, thousands from the surrounding country assembled in the course of the day, (September 2d,) armed with guns, sticks, and other weapons; and when the Lieutenant-Governor's promise on his return from Boston, rendered it certain that they would not be opposed by the troops, they exacted from every official who lived at Cambridge full compliance with their demands, as has been stated.

From this period Governor Oliver lived in Boston, until March, 1776, when at the evacuation he accompanied the Royal Army to Halifax, and took passage thence to England.

His mansion near Mt. Auburn is the house in which he resided at the time he was mobbed by four thousand Disunionists. When Benedict Arnold with his Connecticut Company arrived at Cambridge just after the fight at Lexington, they were quartered in this house. After Bunker Hill the house became a hospital and the dead were buried in the opposite field. The mansion was afterwards the residence of Governor Gerry, and at a later period was owned and occupied by Prof. James Russell Lowell, which made it still more famous under the name of "Elmwood."

He was proscribed and banished in 1778 and in the year following was included in the Conspiracy Act, and his large estate confiscated. Though he forfeited his estates in Massachusetts, he was better situated financially than most of his fellow sufferers, for he was wealthy from his possessions in the West Indies, still owned by his descendants. He was a studious man and lived in retirement in England. He died at Bristol, Nov. 29, 1815, aged 82, and left six daughters.

PETER OLIVER.

CHIEF JUSTICE OF MASSACHUSETTS.

Peter Oliver, son of Daniel Oliver and brother of Andrew Oliver, the Lieutenant Governor, born in 1713, married Mary, daughter of William Clark. His son Peter, Jr., married Sarah, daughter of Governor Hutchinson. Peter Oliver, Sr., graduated from Harvard College in 1730. He received the degree of LL. D. He was appointed to the supreme bench of the province, September 15, 1756.

An affair happened at the close of the year 1773, which drove Adams and all his factions into madness. It was a grant from the King of a salary to the judges of the Supreme Court. The Assembly had endeavoured to keep the judges in absolute dependance upon their humor and because they found them rather too firm to coincide with their views in the subversion of government, they made them the object of their resentment. The judges of the Court had the shortest allowance from the General Assembly of any publick officers, even their Doorkeeper had a large stipend. The judges' travel on their circuits were from 1100 to 1500 miles in a year. Their circuit business engrossed seven months of the year during the extremes of heat and cold in a severe climate. For all their service, the highest grant made to them was £120 sterling per year, and it had been much less; the Chief Justice had £30 sterling more.

His Majesty taking the cases of the judges into consideration, and from his known justice and benevolence, ordered their salaries to be paid out of his revenues in America, such salaries as would keep them above want, and below envy. The judges upon hearing of His Majesty's intention of such a grant had agreed to accept it, but four of them who lived at and near the focus of tarring and feathering, the town of Boston flinched in the day of battle, they were so pelted with soothings one day, and with curses and threatenings the next, that they prudentially gave the point up. The Chief Justice was now left alone in the combat, his brethren had but lately been seated on the Bench. He had been 17 years in the service, and had sunk more than £2000 sterling in it. He had offered not to accept of the grant (if His Majesty would permit him to do so), provided the Assembly would reimburse him one-half of his loss in their service, and for this he would resign his seat on the Bench. The Chief Justice very luckily lived at Middleborough, about 30 miles from Boston, or perhaps he would have followed suit of his brethren in giving up the King's grant. A message was sent to him by the Lower House signed "Samuel Adams, Clerk," requiring him to make explicit answer whether he would accept of the King's grant, or of their grant. He replied that he should accept the King's grant. Nothing less than destruction now awaited him. Col. Gardner, who was afterwards killed at Bunker Hill, declared in the General Assembly, that he himself would drag the Chief Justice from the Bench, if he should sit upon it.

The Assembly voted that he had rendered himself obnoxious to the people, as an enemy, and immediately presented a petition for his removal. Articles of impeachment for high crimes and misdemeanors were exhibited, which Gov. Hutchinson refused to countenance. The grand jury at Worcester on April 19th following, presented to the court a written refusal to serve under the Chief Justice, considering it illegal for him to preside until brought to answer to the above mentioned charges. He became a refugee in 1775, and died at Birmingham, England, in October 1791, aged 79.* Of the five judges of the Superior Court of Massachusetts at the commencement of the Revolution, four remained loyal, viz., Peter Oliver, Edmund Trowbridge, Foster Hutchinson, and William Browne. The Revolutionary member of the Court was William Cushing. Judges at this time wore swords, ermine robes, etc., while on the Bench.

DR. PETER OLIVER. Second son of Chief Justice Oliver, of Massachusetts, graduated at Harvard University in 1761. He dwelt at Middleborough, Plymouth County. He had practised in Scituate in early life, was one of the eighteen country gentlemen who were driven into Boston and who were Addressers of General Gage in 1775. He was proscribed and banished in 1778, and became a refugee in England, where he died at Shrewsbury, in Sept. 1822, aged eighty-one.

DANIEL OLIVER, son of Chief Justice Oliver, a learned and accomplished lawyer of Worcester County, graduated at Harvard College in

* Curwin's Journal, p. 516.

1762. A refugee loyalist of the Revolution, he died at Ashted, Warwickshire, May 6, 1826, aged 82. His father was an antiquarian, and copied with his own hand Hubbard's manuscript History of New England, which the son refused the loan of to the Massachusetts Historical Society for publication in their Collection.*

Sabine says that it was Doctor Oliver who refused to lend his copy or at least to permit a transcript of such parts of it as were missing in the American manuscript. In consequence, we have "Hubbard" mutilated at the beginning, and at the end. At this time, 1814, when the Massachusetts Historical Society with the aid of the Legislature desired to publish that work, there was a very bitter feeling towards the United States on account of the war at that time existing between the two countries.

ANDREW OLIVER of Salem, son of Lieutenant Governor Oliver, graduated at Harvard College in 1749. Studied law. Was often a representative to the assembly and a judge of the Court of Common Pleas. He was one of the founders of the American Academy of Arts and Sciences, and a member of the American Philosophical Society at Philadelphia; he was considered one of the best scholars of his day, and possessed fine talents. Judge Oliver was never fond of public life, but ardently attached to his books and friends. He was honored with a commission of mandamus councillor, which he declined. He married Mary, daughter of Chief Justice Lynde, and many of his descendants are now living here, for although Judge Oliver was a loyalist, he was the only member of his family that was not driven out of his country in consequence of the Revolution.

PETER OLIVER of Salem, the son of Lieutenant Governor Andrew Oliver, was an Addresser of Gage in 1775 and was proscribed and banished in 1778. He became a surgeon in the British Army, and died at London in April, 1795. His widow afterwards married Admiral Sir John Knight, and died in 1839.

BRINLEY SYLVESTER OLIVER, another son of Andrew Oliver, graduated at Harvard in 1774. Later became a surgeon in the British service; was also purser on the Culloden at the battle of the Nile. He died in 1828.

A third son, WILLIAM SANFORD OLIVER, in 1776 accompanied the Royal Army to Halifax. He settled at St. John, New Brunswick, at the peace, and was the first Sheriff of the county. His official papers are dated at Parr or Parr-town, by which names St. John was then known. In 1792, he held the office of Marshal of the Court of Vice-Admiralty of New Brunswick. At the time of his death, he was Sheriff of the County of St. John, and Treasurer of the Colony. He died at St. John in 1813, aged 62. His son, William Sanford Oliver, was a grantee of St. John in 1783, but left New Brunswick about 1806, and entered the Royal Navy. He rose to the position of Captain and was married at Heavitree, in October, 1811, to Mary Oliver Hutchinson, the daughter of

* Curwin's Journal, p. 510.

SIR FRANCIS BERNARD.

Born in 1712 at Brightwell, England. Governor of Massachusetts from 1760 to 1769. Died in England June 16, 1779. From Copley's painting, in Fiske's American Revolution.

Thomas Hutchinson, Jr., who was brought to England in 1776 by her father and mother, when she was but three years of age. He was put on the retired list in 1844, and died in England the next year, aged 71.

SIR FRANCIS BERNARD.

Governor of Massachusetts from 1760 to 1769.

Sir Francis Bernard was descended from Godfrey Bernard of Wansford in Yorkshire, who in the 13th century was a large landowner, whose clearly defined armorial bearings were the first of the family entered in the Heralds College.

Francis, the only child of the Rev. Francis Bernard was baptized July 12th, 1712, in the church of Brightwell in Berkshire. He was unfortunate in losing his father three years later. He became a scholar of St. Peter's College in 1725, and was admitted as a student to Christ Church, Oxford, later. In 1733 he entered himself a member of the Middle Temple and was called to the Bar in 1737, and soon after settled at Lincoln as a provincial counsel. Four years later he married Amelia, daughter of Stephen Offley, Esq., of Norton Hall, Derbyshire. In 1744 he was elected Steward of the City of Lincoln and Deputy Recorder of Boston. In 1745 he was appointed Receiver-General of the Dean and Chapter of Lincoln. In 1750 he was admitted Proctor of the Consistory Court of the Diocese. The years that Francis Bernard spent at Lincoln were probably some of the happiest in his life. He was fortunate in his domestic relations, was doing well in his profession, and his many accomplishments which were always at the service of his friends, rendered him a general favorite in society.

In 1758 Mr. Bernard decided to seek a larger field for the support of his now large family. He was on intimate terms with the second Viscount Barrington, and his brothers and sisters; they were his wife's first cousins. It was thus through his influence that Francis Bernard received the office of Governor of New Jersey. The new world afforded an opening for his sons which meant much to the father. Mr. and Mrs. Bernard and four of their children left England in April, 1758. On his arrival in New Jersey, he entered into negotiations with the Indians. The war at the time raged between England and France rendering the positions of the Indians peculiarly important. By his address and tact he conciliated the Indians, and kept them steadfast in their allegiance to England, Governor Pownall of Massachusetts being appointed to South Carolina. Mr. Bernard was appointed as his successor. His residence in New Jersey was remembered as a time of happiness by the governor and his wife. His life was gladdened by a sense of the good he was able to achieve, and he was hopeful for the future, the page written by Thomas Bernard, his son, of this period reads like a pleasant fairy tale, but it was soon ended. Notwithstanding the supposed indignity offered to the colony of Massachusetts by the appointment of three officers of State by the Crown, the Constitution remained exceedingly democratic. Thomas Bernard gives a sketch of its leading features in which he depicts the colony as forming one of the freest communities in the world.

Governor Bernard reached Boston August 2nd, 1760. He was received with great parade and ceremony. At Dedham he was met by Lieutenant-Governor Hutchinson, several of the Council, and Brigadier-General Isaac Royal and the troops escorted him to his residence at the Province House in Boston. The Militia was drawn up in the main streets, and salutes were fired from all the forts and ships in the harbor, and the Governor and his family were entertained at a great dinner at Fanueil Hall, was then escorted to the State House, and to the Kings Chapel where the Governors were in the habit of attending.

Governor Bernard's nine years' administration in Massachusetts was during one of the most interesting periods in American history. When he arrived at Boston he found affairs on an apparently peaceful and prosperous footing. He stayed till all was in turmoil, and left only just before the storm broke. The first part of his administration was very agreeable. Soon after his arrival Canada was surrendered. The General Court in an address to the Governor declared that without the assistance of England the colonies must have fallen a prey to the power of France, and that without the money sent from England the burden of the war would have been too great to bear. For this relief the colonists gave warm thanks to the king and to parliament, and made the Governor a present of the great island of Mount Desert, and voted a costly monument in Westminster Abbey to Lord Howe, who had fallen in the campaign against Canada.

Much harmony prevailed for two or three years, but this happy and prosperous commencement did not continue. Governor Bernard was soon classed with those who were desirous of strengthening the authority of the government.

Shortly after Bernard's appointment, Chief Justice Sewall died on September 11. He was a great loss to the Province and it was a misfortune that his death occurred just at this time. Colonel Otis, as he was generally called, desired to succeed to this office. It was believed that he and his son were not friendly to the government. Governor Bernard, who had no doubt studied the affairs in Massachusetts, considered Colonel Otis to be wholly unsuited to the position of a Chief Justice, and determined not to appoint him. Thomas Hutchinson, the Lieutenant-Governor, an able and intelligent man, was appointed to the important office of Chief Justice. Governor Bernard had at once realized Hutchinson's qualities and said many years later, when they were both living in England, that he had never repented appointing Hutchinson Chief Justice.*

* Hutchinson's Diary & Letters. Vol. 1. p. 195.

Lynde, the senior judge, who did not care particularly to succeed Sewall, appears to have been satisfied with the appointment of Hutchinson, also Gridley, the leader of the Bar, and apparently all possible rivals, save Colonel Otis. Hutchinson discharged the duties of his new office in the most satisfactory manner. He proved himself to be efficient, and always kind, as evinced by his special attention to the claims of the helpless.

At this time, there were mutterings of a possible storm, and at this critical moment, in October of 1760, George II died. Just previous to his death Mr. Pitt, Secretary of State, sent a dispatch to the Governor touching on the trade of England and her American colonies. The organized system of smuggling that existed in the Colonies caused the Custom House officers to apply for the "writs of assistance," that were frequently employed in England.

So far the Governor's course had been hampered only by factious opposition from the chief offenders, but this opposition assumed formidable dimensions when the question of "writs of assistance" was brought forward. The rights of the Custom House officers to demand such help was tried before the Supreme Court of Massachusetts. "The verdict was in their favor, but public opinion was strongly excited, and James Otis, the lawyer who opposed the Custom House officers, gained great popularity."* Notwithstanding Otis' eloquence, the case as already said was decided against his clients on the point of law. Governor Bernard was only performing his duty when he was active in promoting seizures for illicit trade.

In speaking of his early life in Boston, Julia Bernard, Governor Bernard's youngest daughter, mentions their home in Boston as "the Government House." She says that they employed both black and white servants, and speaks of the formalities that existed while the family lived there. "In Boston, none of the family, grown up brothers excepted, ever walked out in the town. We had a large garden, but it seemed rather a confinement." She also speaks of her father's home at Jamaica Pond. "This residence we usually moved to in May I think, and here we enjoyed ourselves extremely. We ran pretty much at liberty; there was no form or ceremony. My father was always on the wing on account of his situation. He had his own carriage and servants, my mother hers; there was a town coach, and a whiskey for the young men to drive about. I was used from a child to ride on horseback, and from childhood none of us had any fear of anything." Speaking of these days she says, they "all seemed great, enlightened, and enjoyable."

In describing her parents Julia Bernard says: "My father, though not tall, had something dignified and distinguished in his appearance and manner; he dressed superbly on all public occasions. My mother was tall, and a very fine woman. Her dresses were ornamented with gold and silver, ermine, and fine American sable."

* Doyle's History of America, Ch. XVIII.

The Province House was visited about the middle of the ninteenth century by Nathaniel Hawthorne, who has written interesting but melancholy pages on the subject.*

The Province or Government House occupied by Sir Francis Bernard was situated nearly opposite the head of Milk street. It was purchased by the Colonial Legislature in 1716, of the widow of Peter Sargent, who built it. It was a magnificent building, no pains had been spared to make it not only elegant, but also spacious and convenient. It stood back some distance in its ample lot, and had the most pleasant and agreeable surroundings of any mansion in town. It was of brick, three stories in height, with a high roof and lofty cupola. The house was approached over a stone pavement and a high flight of massive stone steps, and through a magnificent doorway. Two stately oaks of very large size, reared their verdant tops on either side of the gate separating the grounds from the highway, and cast a grateful shade over the approach, through the beautiful grass lawn in front of the mansion.

After the evacuation of Boston the Province House and all other Government property was confiscated and became the property of the State. In 1811 the State gave the property to the Massachusetts General Hospital who leased it for ninety-nine years. Stores were erected in front of it. In 1864 it was destroyed by fire and only the walls are all that remain of the Old Province House. The engraving shown here was made from a sketch of it taken a short time before it was leased and altered. The Royal Arms, and the Indian vane are on exhibition in the Old State House.

Sir Francis Bernard's country mansion was situated on the southwest side of Jamaica Pond, fronting on Pond street, now a part of the Boston Park system. This was and still is a most lovely spot. The mansion house was surrounded with an estate of sixty acres. Here, but for the gathering clouds which darkened the political horizon, the remaining years of this scholarly and able representative of the government might have been passed in the enjoyment of all that seemed the most enjoyable in life— a delightful home, set in a lovely landscape, and the esteem and regard of the people he had governed. His extensive and beautiful grounds were filled with choice fruit trees, plants and shrubs including one hundred orange and lemon trees, besides fig, cork, cinnamon and other rare exotics.

After Bernard went to England, it was occupied by the second Sir William Pepperell, until he too was driven out by the disunionists. Then came the siege and the occupation of loyalist dwellings by the revolutionists, this being the quarters of Col. Miller of Rhode Island, in the summer of 1775. Afterwards it was used as a hospital for the camp at Roxbury. The soldiers who died were buried on elevated ground some distance back from the buildings. The governor's hot house was taken by Major Crane and converted into a magazine for the artillery. Confiscated by the

---

* For description of House, see "The Bernards of Abington and Nether Winchendon," by Mr. N. Higgins. Vol. I. p. 285.

OLD PROVINCE HOUSE.

State in 1779, it was bought by Martin Brimmer, a Boston merchant, who died here in 1804. Capt. John Prince purchased it in 1806, in 1809 took down the old house, a part of which had stood one hundred and forty-one years, and no doubt many a bumper of good wine had been drunk to the health of the seven sovereigns of Great Britain, who had reigned during that period.

Captain Prince made a road through the property from Pond to Perkins street, now known as Prince street; the whole estate was divided up into good sized building lots, on which many elegant residences have since been erected. In front of one of them are some fine large English elms probably planted by Gov. Bernard. One of them measures twenty-five feet in circumference.*

Governor Bernard soon after his arrival in Massachusetts became much interested in Harvard College, and his interests extended far beyond the formalities required of him in his official capacity. "Having regard to the Governor's delight in Latin verse, it is not surprising that he should have endeavored to refine and soften the somewhat rugged type of student which Harvard then produced." He suggested that the college should follow the custom established in the English universities, of writing poetical tributes in commemoration of public events. Thirty-one poems were written. Of these nine were by the Governor himself in Greek and Latin, and the others owed their existence to the stimulus of prizes offered by him. It was a difficult undertaking for him to start this custom. A recent writer (Mr. Goddard) styles this volume, indeed, "the most ambitious typographical and literary work attempted on the continent previous to the Revolution, etc."

Governor Bernard's interest and exertion for the development of the material resources of his province should have won him lasting gratitude. He encouraged with all his power the manufacture of potash, the cultivation of hemp and flax on waste lands, and the carriage of lumber to British markets.

The Province prospered under Bernard during these years preceding the Stamp Act, and peace came through his ability and guidance. Mr. Hutchinson writes: "If at the expiration of that term he had quitted the government, he would have been spoken of as one of the best of the New England Governors." His son Thomas, also remarked upon his popularity during these five out of the nine years he presided as Governor of Massachusetts. The House of Representatives, conscious that Mr. Bernard had expended a considerable sum of his own money in improving the castle, and for other public benefits, passed a resolution that the island of Mount Desert, lying on the northeastward of Penobscot Bay, be granted to him and his heirs and assigns. The Council at once concurred in the grant. The confirmation of the Assembly's grant of Mount Desert was contained in a letter from the English Lords of Trade, dated May 21, 1763.

* The Town of Roxbury. Francis S. Drake.

In July, 1763 [writes Thomas Bernard], orders were transmitted to the American Governors for carrying into strict execution the laws of trade, at the same time notifying the new authority which had been delegated to commanders of the King's ships stationed in America, to seize all vessels concerned in any prohibited commerce. These were followed by further orders for improvement of the revenue, and for suppression of all clandestine and illicit trade with foreign nations; with directions for the Governors to transmit such information as they had to communicate on the subject.*

Governor Bernard was compelled in the discharge of his official functions to enforce these commands, but he lost no time in remonstrating. His letter to the Earl of Egremont, Secretary of State, contains a plea for the indulgence granted, or tacitly allowed up to that time, with regard to wine and fruit, especially lemons, which he considered necessary to health in the climate of Massachusetts. This letter was followed by another addressed to the Lords Commissioners for Trade and Plantations, in which he entreats that the duties imposed by the Molasses Act may at least be reduced in the interest of England as well as of America, since it had been, and would be evaded, and its end to a large extent defeated." He continues: "this Act has been a perpetual stumbling block to the Custom House officers, and it will be most agreeable to them to have it in any way removed."**

It was not until Bernard left America that the colonists knew of his protest to the government. A large number evidently were satisfied at his good will and perhaps suspected that he interceded in their favour, so their regard for him survived the trial of the new orders from England.

In the midst of this agitation, the smallpox broke out in the capital, and the Governor was compelled to move the General Assembly to Cambridge. Here in January, 1764, another misfortune occurred. Harvard Hall was burned to a heap of ruins, the only one of the ancient buildings which still remained. Of five thousand volumes, only a hundred were saved, and of John Harvard's books, but a single one.

The Governor at once appealed to the Assembly and obtained a vote for reconstruction. He set the example of contributing towards a new library by the gift of some of his own books; he also drew the architectural design for the new building and superintended its execution. Subscriptions were made both in England and America for the erection of the new hall.

In June. 1763, a confederation of several Indian tribes had suddenly and unexpectedly swept over the whole western frontier of Pennsylvania and Virginia, had murdered almost all the English settlers, and through unusual skill captured every British fort between the Ohio and Lake Erie, and had closely blockaded Fort Detroit and Pittsburg. After desperate

* Life of Sir Francis Bernard.
** The Bernards of Abington and Nether Winchendon," by Mr. Napier Higgins.

fighting, the troops under Amherst succeeded in repelling the invaders and secured the three great fortresses of Niagara, Detroit and Pittsburg. The severe fighting appears to have been done by the English troops. Massachusetts seemed to be fatigued from the late war and could give no help when aid was asked. Connecticut finally sent 250 men. Peace was signed in September, 1764, the war having lasted fourteen months, months of extreme horror. The credit of the war belonged to the English soldiers, another great service rendered to the colonies by England.

England felt that the colonies should help share the great expense of the late wars. George Grenville as First Lord of the Treasury, and Chancellor of the Exchequer, signalized his period of administration by the Stamp Act. On the 10th of March the House of Commons on the motion of the Minister, passed a variety of resolutions respecting certain duties on foreign goods imported into the British colonies of America.

Grenville remarked in his honest way to the colonial agents in London, "I am not, however, set upon this tax. If the Americans dislike it, and prefer any other method, I shall be content. Write therefore, to your several colonies, and if they choose any other mode, I shall be satisfied, provided the money be but raised."*

The British Government gave the colonies a year to deliberate, and the House of Representatives trusted Governor Bernard to plead for the colonists. When the members met again on January 10, 1765, the Governor honestly stated how much he had done. On January 14 began in the British Parliament the vehement and eloquent debates, ending in a majority of both Houses declaring in favour of the Stamp Act. The Ministry seems to have paid no attention to Governor Bernard's suggestion. His "Principles of Law and Polity" were ignored and also the Petition of the Assembly. On March 22, 1765, the Stamp Act received the Royal Assent, and England and her colonies were divided.

When the Colonists learned that the hated act had been passed, they became defiant. Riots soon took place in Boston, and Secretary Oliver, who was appointed by the British government as Stamp Distributor, was hung in effigy. This was during the summer of 1765 when the first cargo of stamps was daily expected. Then came the attack upon Mr. Oliver's house, and the complete destruction of Mr. Hutchinson's home.**

During the warm months the Governor and his family were in the habit of residing at the castle. They were there when the stamps were expected and during the riotous times in Boston. The night that Hutchinson's home was destroyed seems to have made a deep impression on Julia Bernard, then in her sixth year. She afterwards wrote:

"While the family was resident at Castle William, my father came one night in his barge from Boston and brought Lieutenant-Governor Hutchinson, his sister, and two daughters, whom he had thus rescued from the fury of the mob. They had forced the house; the family fled

* Samuel Adams (Hosmer) Ch. VI.

** For further information concerning the Stamp Act, see pp. 40, 41, 42.

for their lives; my father's barge was in waiting for him and he took them under his protection. The house was stripped of everything, and pulled down that night. They had nothing but what they had on. I can remember my mother getting them out clothes, and ordering beds to be prepared. Terror and distress sat upon their countenances."

Governor Bernard assured the people he had their interest at heart, but his road was a difficult one, and he was greatly worried over the performance of his duty. Because he represented the government, he was abused and insulted, and finally felt that he had no real authority, but was totally in the hands of the people. His son quotes his father's words: "Although I have never received any orders concerning the Stamp Act until this day, nor even a copy of the Act, I have thought it my duty to do all I could to get it carried into execution. And I must say in so doing I have exerted all possible spirit and perserverance. . . I have made great sacrifices to his Majesty's service upon this occasion. My administration, which before was easy, respectable, and popular, is rendered troublesome, difficult, and dangerous, and yet there is no pretext to charge me with any other offence than endeavoring to carry the Stamp Act into execution; but that is here an high crime never to be forgiven." The struggle was carried on without intermission, but towards the end of April, Boston was delighted by the news of the repeal of the Stamp Act. "Letters published in England," writes Hutchinson, "Allowed that Governor Bernard's letters to the Ministry, and the petition from the Council and House in 1764, which had been drawn by the Lieutenant-Governor, forwarded the repeal. But they had no merit with the prevailing party, because they solicited the repeal as a matter of favour, and not as a claim of right."

Great rejoicings now took place in the city and for a while Governor Bernard's life became a little easier.

In August 1768, the King offered the Governor a Baronet's title, which he accepted. Rule and order was vanishing in Massachusetts. On September 28, 1768, two regiments from Halifax with artillery, arrived off Boston, and the vessels which brought them, cast anchor in Nantasket Roads, a few miles below Castle William. The troops were landed on Saturday, October 1, and on Saturday, October 15, General Gage arrived with his officers to look after the quartering of the troops himself, a difficult problem to solve in this divided community. Thus was the Governor placed, trying to fulfil his duty to England, and yet always with the best interest of the people at heart. Commodore Hood wrote to Mr. Stephens, Secretary to the Admiralty on November 25, 1768, stating that "The General [Gage] and Governor Bernard have been lately burnt in effigy, in a most public manner."

All through the next winter a fierce controversy raged in the newspapers regarding England and her colonies. Samuel Adams was the most prolific and forcible writer, and his contributions went also to newspapers at a distance. In the spring of this year the Governor became

"Sir Francis Bernard of Nettleham, in the county of Lincoln, Baronet." The patent bears the date April 5, 1769. The King had ordered the expense of the patent to be paid out of his privy purse, and this according to the Governor's son, was a compliment seldom offered.

The grant of the baronetcy was accompanied by an order summoning Sir Francis Bernard to proceed to England and there report on the state of his province. Ere long the Governor and the whole body of loyalists were struck with consternation by the intelligence that General Gage had ordered the removal of the troops from Boston. They considered this extremely dangerous.

On the 4th of January, 1770, a town meeting was held by which every one was declared an enemy who had in any way assisted in obtaining or retaining troops. Sir Francis Bernard was making preparations for his departure, and this of course, was intended as a parting shot. He yielded to the advice of friends to attend the Harvard Commencement as usual and Mr. Hutchinson says that, "When he had gone through it without any insult worth notice from the rude people, who always raise more or less tumult on that day, he thanked his friends for their advice." It is satisfactory to think that his last public appearance in Massachusetts was at Harvard, the institution he had always felt such a deep interest in.

A few days before the Governor departed, he received a circular from the Earl of Hillsborough announcing the intended repeal of the duties on glass, paper and paint, and one of his last acts of administration consisted in making this intention known, and the assurance of the good will of the British Government for the American colonies. Governor Bernard then bequeathed the administration to Lieutenant-Governor Hutchinson and made his last farewells.

"He embarked on board the Rippon, a man-of-war ordered from Virginia to convey him, and sailed for England. Instead of the marks of respect commonly shown, in a greater or less degree, to governors upon their leaving the province, there were many marks of public joy in the town of Boston. The bells were rung, guns were fired from Mr. Hancock's wharf, Liberty Tree was covered with flags, and in the evening a great bonfire was made upon Fort Hill."* The Governor sailed on August 1, 1769, a sad ending to nine years of laborious and anxious administration. Perhaps there were some staunch friends with him to the last in whose sympathy he found consolation for sights and sounds which must have jarred upon his feelings, and were of set purpose arranged to aggravate his sorrow in parting, for an indefinite time, from his nearest and dearest. Hosmer, the biographer and eulogist of Samuel Adams, speaks of Francis Bernard as "an honourable and well-meaning man, and by no means wanting in ability."

Thomas Bernard, who accompanied his father, states that he was

* Hutchinson Hist. Mass., Vol. III. p. 253.

graciously received in England and by George III. A petition arrived from the colonies asking for a new governor, it concludes:

"Wherefore we most humbly entreat your Majesty that his Excellency Sir Francis Bernard, Baronet, may be forever removed from the government of this province, and that your Majesty would be graciously pleased to place one in his stead worthy to serve the greatest and best Monarch on earth."

The Governor's resignation soon followed. His life was filled with much anxiety for the financial welfare of his family as during his eleven years of residence in America, his private fortune had not been increased. He received a pension, but many troubles arose which greatly taxed his physical and mental strength. Mrs. Bernard and the remaining members of her family, moved from their country home at Jamaica Pond, which was afterwards occupied by Sir William Pepperell, to a new residence called the Cherry House, which the Governor caused to be built on a lot of land containing about 30 acres on the "Road leading to Castle William" at Dorchester Neck, now South Boston. The Governor probably selected this locaton on which to build his house on account of its nearness to Castle Island, to which he and his family could take refuge in case of mob violence.* John Bernard's name continued for some time to head the list of proscribed traders and his position, entailing loss, insult, and even danger, must have been a constant source of apprehension to his relatives. After learning that her husband had definitely resigned, Lady Bernard prepared to join him in England. Many of their household possessions were sold at the Province house on September 11. Just before the vessel sailed, young Francis Bernard died November 20, 1770, at the age of twenty-seven, and is probably buried beside his brother Shute in the burial ground of the King's Chapel at Boston. Mrs. Bernard was accompanied by four of her children, Amelia, William, Scrope and Julia.

Sir Francis took a house in the vicinity of Hampstead and for a while the family was united, the children from America joining those in England. The two youngest had never seen their eldest sisters, Jane and Frances, who had remained in the mother country. A short time later, Sir Francis suffered from a paralytic stroke and his recovery was partial and imperfect. Realizing this, he applied for leave to resign his appointment to Ireland, having been appointed to the Irish Board of Commissioners. This was granted him in 1774, and his former pension

---

* One lot of 26½ acres was purchased of John Baker et al. in 1762. Lib. 98, Fol. 113. Another lot adjoining same, of 3 acres of James Baker in 1764. Lib. 102, Fol. 39. During a raid made by the "Ministerial Troops" from the Castle on Feb. 13th, 1776, nearly all the houses on the Neck were burnt; among them was "An House and Stable and Barn belonging to Francis Bernard burnt; valued at £100.00," also damage done "by our Soldiers," £40.00. (See New Eng. Gen. Reg. Jan. 1897.) This tract of land extended from Fourth street (Way leading to Castle William) to Dorchester Bay, M street running through the center of it. The writer's father in 1858 purchased a portion of this land, and it was here he spent his boyhood days. After the war another house was erected on the site of the one burnt; its location was on Fourth street between M and N streets. The writer remembers that a boyhood companion that lived there picked up in the garden an English guinea.

restored to him. The vigor of his mental faculties is evinced by the fact that on July 2, 1772, he went to Oxford and received the degree of D. C. L. and from Christ Church the honour of having his picture by Copley among other illustrious students in the Hall of that society.

After a stay at Nether Winchendon, the family removed to the Prebendal House at Aylesbury, and now for a short period enjoyed comparative peace. The colonies were in open revolt. Soon after Governor Hutchinson's arrival in England, he resumed his habits of friendly intercourse with Sir Francis Bernard and his family. Thomas Bernard studied for the Bar, and William and Scrope were sent to Harrow. Jane, the eldest daughter, married Charles White, a barrister, in 1774. Fanny, the third daughter, became greatly attached to her newly found sister Julia, and proved herself very capable with her pen. Scrope later entered Christ Church at Oxford and William embarked for Canada. John left England for America probably in 1775. William, who was a Lieutenant in the army, was drowned before reaching Canada. He was on board a provision ship bound for Quebec which took fire, and he, with some others, took to a boat which overset and they all were drowned. This cast a gloom over the family, from which the father and mother never fully recovered.

A London visit of Sir Francis and Lady Bernard in March, 1777, is mentioned by Governor Hutchinson.

"8th.—Sir Francis and Lady came to town last evening, and dined with us to-day, with Paxton, Dr. Caner, Chandler, and Boucher."

Later came Lady Bernard's death and Hutchinson in his "Dairy," 1778, says:

"2nd.—Lady Bernard died last week, the 26th. [May], at Aylesbury. Paxton was there on a visit. She had been in poor health several months, but took an airing the day before the night in which she died, or rather towards morning."

This remarkable woman was married to Sir Francis Bernard thirty-seven years and had shared every vicissitude of his career. She had felt the cares of his agitated public life in America and had seen him gradually broken down by much trouble, not the least of which was the final blow received in England at the hands of supposed friends.

Thomas, who was now eight and twenty, relieved his father from business cares, and became a worthy head to the family. News reached England of the act of banishment. John Bernard had reached America before the Declaration of Independence and lived in a remote part of Maine, but his name does not appear among the proscribed. News of the Confiscation Act did not reach Sir Francis before his death, and Thomas says that his last days were free from anxiety on that ground. He died believing in the honesty of America.

The engagement of Julia Bernard about this time to the Rev. Joseph Smith, brought a gleam of happiness into the family.

On June 21. Hutchinson writes:

"A gentleman, who knew me and asked how I had been since he last saw me, informed me Saturday morning, as I was taking my morning walk, that he went to Aylesbury a day or two before, and that Sir Francis Bernard died Wednesday night, the 16. [1779], which has since been confirmed."

He suffered from several complaints, and an epileptic fit more violent than any he had had before, hastened the end. He died surrounded by his children, within a month of completing his sixty-seventh year, and was buried by the side of Lady Bernard in a vault under Aylesbury church. Sir Francis Bernard's memory was held in high honor by his children, and by none more tenderly than Thomas, his father's companion and confidant. After his father's death, Thomas wrote:

"May his children contemplate with pleasure and confidence, the talents and probity of their father, and, soothed with the memory of his virtues, forget the return which those virtues have received! And may they, by retracing the events of his life, strengthen and fortify their minds, that if ever they should be called to such a trial as he underwent, they may imitate him in the conscientious and honourable discharge of their duty, and in integrity of life."*

Sir John Bernard, on the death of his father, succeeded to the Baronetcy in 1779. When, in 1769, Sir Francis was recalled from the government, he possessed a large landed estate in Maine of which the large island of Mount Desert, which was given him by the Colony, and afterwards confirmed by the Crown, was a part. He also owned Moose Island, now Eastport, and some territory on the mainland. John, at the time of his departure, had an agency for the sale and settlement of these and other lands, and until the war commenced, was in comfortable circumstances. In order to hold his property and prevent its confiscation, he remained in the country, and therefore it could not be claimed that he was an absentee, or a refugee, and as he did not take any part in the controversy, it could not be claimed that he was an enemy to the new government. His place of residence during the war appears to have been at Bath, Machias, and at Pleasant Point, a few miles from Eastport. An unbroken wilderness was around him. The only inhabitants at the head of the tidewater of the St. Croix were a few hunters and Indians. He lived in a small hut built by himself, with no companions but a dog. Robbinston and Perry were uninhabited, Eastport contained but a single family, yet at the spot now occupied by the remnant of the Passamaquoddy Indians, he attempted to make a farm. He had been bred in ease and refinement, had hardly done a day's laborious work in his life, yet he believed he could earn a competence by labor. He told those who saw him that "other young men went into the woods, and made themselves farms, and got a good living, and he saw no reason why he could not." But he cut down a few trees, became discouraged, and after the confiscation of the property of Sir Francis in 1778, he was in abject poverty, and

* Life of Sir Francis Bernard, by One of his Sons.

the misfortune of himself and family seemed to have unsettled his mind. After the peace, he lived at Pleasant Point, and occasionally went to Boston. His abject condition in mind and estate rendered him an object of deep commiseration, and his conduct during hostilities having entitled him to consideration, the Legislature of Massachusetts restored to him one half of his father's estate, which included one half of the island of Mount Desert, and an estate in Boston consisting of wharves, land, and flats, which he sold for £600 to Wm. Allen. Of his subsequent history while he continued in the United States, but little is known. Later in life he held offices under the British Crown at Barbadoes and St. Vincent. He died in the West Indies in 1809 in his sixty-fifth year, without issue, and was succeeded by his brother Thomas.

SIR THOMAS BERNARD, the third surviving son of Sir Francis, succeeded his brother John to the Baronetcy. He took his degree from Harvard College in 1767. After he took up his residence in England, much of his time was devoted to institutions of benevolence in London, and he wrote several essays with a design to mitigate the sorrows, and improve the condition of the humbler classes of English society. The University of Edinburgh conferred on him the degree of Doctor of Laws. He married a lady of fortune who died in 1813 while preparing to go to church.

Sir Thomas' account of his father's life makes him stand out perhaps the most prominent of Sir Francis' children. His death occurred in England in 1818. The Baronetcy of Sir Francis Bernard now stands in the name of Morland.

The following is a list of Sir Francis Bernard's confiscated property in Suffolk County situated in what is now South Boston, and Jamaica Plain, together with the name of the purchasers. He had also much property in Maine, including one half of Mount Desert island, that was confiscated.

CONFISCATED PROPERTY OF SIR FRANCIS BERNARD SITUATED IN SUFFOLK COUNTY.

To Martin Brimmer, Aug. 18, 1779; Lib. 130 fol. 178; Farm, 50 A., mansion house and barn in Roxbury, highway to Benj. Child S.E.; Jamaica Pond N.E.; Joseph Winchester N.W.; Samuel Griffin and school lands S.W.; the hill N.; Samuel Griffin W.; S.W.; W. and S.W. —— Wood lot in Roxbury, 12 A. 3 qr. 36 r., Sharp and Williams S.; land of heirs of William Douglas deceased W.; land of heirs of Edward Bromfield deceased N.; land of heirs of Elizabeth Brewer deceased E. —— Wood lot in Roxbury, 2A. 1 qr. 17 r., highway W.; Capt. Baker S.; John Harris E.; Mr. Walter N. —— Salt marsh in Roxbury, 3 A. 1 qr., John Williams S., creek N.W.; Robert Pierpoint N.; creek to Dorchester E.

To William Allen, Jan. 2, 1781; Lib. 132 fol. 76; Land in Dorchester, 25 A. 3 r., road to Point of Dorchester Neck N.; land of town of Dorchester and Richard Withington deceased E.; said Withington, James Baker, Samuel Blake deceased and James Blake S.; Jonathan [Clap] W. —— Salt marsh in Dorchester, 2 A. 3 qr., Sir Francis Bernard N.; salt marsh of Richard Withington deceased E.; James Blake W.; the sea S.

SIR WILLIAM PEPPERELL.

Baronet of Kittery, Maine.

William Pepperell was a native of Tavistock near Plymouth in Devon, who at the age of twenty-two, about the year 1676, emigrated to the Isle of Shoals, and became a fisherman. He acquired property and removed to Kittery on the mainland, where he died in 1734, leaving an only son of his own name, who continued the business of fishing, amassed great wealth, and arrived at great honors. It is interesting and instructive to trace the rising steps of the Pepperell family, from a destitute young fisherman to the princely affluence and exalted station, civil, political, and military, to which his son arrived. It throws light upon the early history of the infant colonies, the character of the early settlers, the nature of their occupations, their commerce, the condition, and relative importance of places of trade, and the influence of the times, and events, in forming the character and shaping the fortunes of the illustrious subject of this memoir. The name once so celebrated, has in America long since become extinct, and but for its record in the page of history, would ere this have passed into oblivion. To account for this curious fact, it will be necessary to give a more extended notice of the history of the family than would otherwise seem necessary.

While a fisherman at the Isle of Shoals, Pepperell had frequent occasion to sail to Kittery Point for the purpose of traffic, and for the purchase and repair of boats. A shipwright there named John Bray welcomed him to his home, and supplied his wants. He had a daughter Margery, who had arrived at the age of seventeen when she first saw Mr. Pepperell, who was smitten with her youthful charms. At the time of this marriage Mr. Pepperell removed from the Shoals to Kittery Point, where Mr. Bray gave him the site of the present Pepperell mansion. The south part of this structure was built by him and the north part by his son Sir William, who was born here in 1696, and here dwelt the two families till the decease of the father in 1734, which left the son's family sole occupants till 1759. The home has since been curtailed in its dimensions by the removal of ten feet from each end of the building. It was during this period of little more than half a century that the largest fortune, then known in New England, was gradually accumulated. The principal business of the Pepperells was done in the fisheries. They sometimes had more than one hundred small vessels at a time on the Grand Banks. Ship-building was also a very extensive branch of industry on the Pascataqua, and its tributary streams. The Pepperells built many vessels and sent them to the West India islands, laden with lumber fish, oil, and live stock, to exchange for cargoes of rum, sugar, and molasses, for home consumption; others to European markets to exchange for dry goods, wine, and salt, and to sell both vessel and cargo. To the

Southern colonies fish was sent in exchange for corn, tobacco, and naval stores. Mills were erected by them on the small rivers, and lumber and ship-timber, were floated down to Kittery Point, and Newcastle, to be shipped to European and American ports.

Sir William was his only son. About 1727 he was elected a member of the Council of Massachusetts, and held a seat in that body by annual election for thirty-two years, until his death. He was also selected to command a regiment of militia, and being fond of society, rich, and prosperous, was highly popular, and possessed much influence. With a vigorous frame, firm mind, and great coolness, when in danger, he was well fitted for his residence in a country exposed to ferocious enemies.

The Treaty of Utrecht which secured Nova Scotia to the British Crown, gave France undisputed right to Cape Breton. Here they built the city of Louisburg at enormous cost, and protected it with fortresses of great strength. The walls of the defences were formed with bricks brought from France, and they mounted two hundred and six pieces of cannon. The city had nunneries, and Palaces, gardens, and squares, and places of amusement, and was designed to become a great capital, and to perpetuate French dominion, and the Catholic faith in America. Twenty-five years of time and six million dollars in money were spent in building, arming, and adorning this city, "The Dunkirk of the New World." That such a plan existed, at so early a period of our history, is a marvel, and the lovers of the wonderful may read the works of Parkman which contain accounts of its rise, and ruin, and be satisfied that "truth is sometimes stranger than fiction."

The possession of this stronghold by the French was a source of continual annoyance to the New England fishermen, and at last became intolerable. Situated as it was directly off the fishing grounds, it meant destruction to the fishing interest every time there was a war with France. At last its capture was seriously conceived and undertaken. Governor Shirley, in 1744, listening to the propositions made to him on the subject, submitted them to the Legislature of Massachusetts, and that body in secret session, the first ever held in America, authorized a force to be raised, equipped, and sent against it, and the command was conferred upon Colonel William Pepperell. His troops consisted of a motley assemblage of fishermen, and farmers, sawyers, and loggers, many of whom were taken from his own vessels, mills, and forests. Before such men, and others hardly better skilled in war, in the year 1745, Louisburg fell. The achievement is the most memorable in the Colonial annals. For this great service Colonel Pepperell was created a Baronet in 1746. After the fall of Louisburg, he went to England and was presented at Court. In 1759 he was appointed Lieutenant-General. He died the same year at his seat at Kittery, aged sixty-three years, and was buried in the large and beautiful tomb erected in 1734 which was placed near the mansion home. His children were two, Andrew, a son who graduated at Harvard University in 1743, and died March 1, 1751, aged twenty-five, and a daughter,

Elizabeth, who married Colonel Nathaniel Sparhawk. Lady Pepperell, who was Mary Hirst, daughter of Grove Hirst of Boston, and granddaughter of Judge Sewall of Massachusetts, survived until 1789. Mrs. Sparhawk bore her husband five children, namely Nathaniel, William Pepperell, Samuel Hirst, Andrew Pepperell, and Mary Pepperell. Sir William, her father, soon after the decease of her brother, executed a will, by which after providing for Lady Pepperell, he bequeathed the bulk of his remaining property to herself, and her children. Her second son was made the residuary legatee, and inherited a large estate. By the terms of his grandfather's will he was required to procure an Act of the Legislature to drop the name of Sparhawk, and assume that of Pepperell. This he did on coming of age, and was allowed by a subsequent Act, to take the title of Sir William Pepperell, Baronet. He received the honors of Harvard University in 1766, subsequently he visited England, and became a member of the Council of Massachusetts. In 1774 when that body was recognized under the Act of Parliament, he was continued, under the mandamus of the King, and thereby incurred the wrath of the disunionists, who at a county congress, held at Wells, York County, Maine, on the 16th of Nov. 1774, declared a boycott against him, and denounced him in the following manner: "The said William Pepperell, Esq., hath, with purpose to carry into force, Acts of the British Parliament, made with apparent design to enslave the free and loyal people of this country, accepted, and now holds, a seat in the pretended Board of Councillors in this Province, as well as in direct repeal of the charter thereof, as against the solemn compact of kings, and the inherent right of the people. It is therefore Resolved, that said William Pepperell, Esq. hath thereby justly forfeited the confidence, and friendship of all true friends to American liberty, and with other pretended councillors, now holding their seats in like manner, ought to be detested by all good men, and it is hereby recommended to the good people of this country, that as soon as the present leases made to any of them by said Pepperell, are expired, they immediately withdraw all connection, commerce, and dealings, from him, and they take no further lease, or conveyance of his farms, mills, or appurtenances thereunto belonging (where the said Pepperell is the sole receiver and appropriator of the rents and profits), until he shall resign his seat, pretendedly occupied by mandamus. And if any persons shall remain, or become his tenants, after the expiration of their present leases, we recommend to the good people of this country, not only to withdraw all connections, and commercial intercourse with them, but to treat them in the manner provided by the third resolve of this Congress."

The Baronet not long after this denouncement retired to Boston. His winter residence was on Summer street, near Trinity church, and his country residence was an estate on the southerly side of Jamaica Pond containing sixty acres, which he leased from Sir Francis Bernard. In 1775 he arrived in England under circumstances of deep affliction. Lady

Pepperell, who was Elizabeth, daughter of Hon. Isaac Royall, of Medford, having died on the passage. In 1778 he was proscribed and bannished, and the year following was included in the Conspiracy Act. In May, 1779, the Committee on confiscated estates offered for sale "his large and elegant house, gardens, and other accommodations, &c., "pleasantly situated on Summer street, Boston, a little below Trinity church." His vast domain in Maine, the largest owned by any individual in New England, though entailed upon his heirs, was confiscated. This estate extended from Kittery to Saco, with a coast line of upwards of thirty miles, and extending back many miles into the interior, and, for the purposes of farming and lumbering, was of great value, and the water power and mill privileges, rendered it even at the time of the sequestration, a princely fortune. His possessions were large in Scarboro, Elliot, Berwick, Newington, Portsmouth, Hampton and Hubbardston. In Saco alone he owned 5,500 acres, including the site of that populous town and its factories. A large portion of this property was purchased by Thomas Cutts who had served as a clerk in Sir William's counting room. He was active during the revolution, was a noted merchant, president of a bank, colonel of a regiment, senator in the Massachusetts Legislature, and one of the founders of the Massachusetts General Hospital. He died in 1821.

All of Sir William's brothers were loyalists and were forced to leave the country, and their vast domains passed into other hands. A life interest or dower right in the Saco lands was enjoyed by Lady Mary Pepperell, the widow of the first Sir William and her daughter, Mrs. Sparhawk, which was devised to them by the Baronet's will. In exchange for the right thus arising, the State afterwards assigned two-ninths in absolute property to Lady Pepperell and her daughter, by a deed executed in 1788. This small porion of this great estate was saved through these ladies residing in the country during the war, the "sons of despotism" could hardly tar and feather two defenceless women, or drive them forth as they did their sons, and brothers, and make absentees or refugees of them.

Thus the princely fortune of Pepperell, that required a century to construct, from the foundation laid by John Bray the shipwright to the massive structure raised by the fisherman William Pepperell and completed by his son Sir William, fastened and secured though it was, by every instrument that his own skill and the best legal counsel could devise to give stability and perpetuity, was in a brief hour overthrown, and demolished by the confiscation act of 1778. So complete was the wreck that two of his daughter's grandsons, were saved from the almshouse by the bounty of some persons on whom they had no claim for favor.

Never before in the history of this country has there been a more conspicuous fall of a family from a high estate. There has always been a doubt as to the legality of the Confiscation Act, as far as the remainder or reversionary interest, of the first Sir William was concerned, since it is apparently clear that the life-interest of the second Sir William could only be, or by the statute actually was, diverted and passed to the State.*

After the death of the first Sir William, his widow, Lady Pepperell, caused a neat house to be erected near that of her daughter, and the village church which still remain. Here she died in 1789 after being a widow thirty years.

This house came into the possession of Captain Joseph Cutts. He was a large ship owner and a successful merchant. Ruined by Mr. Jefferon's embargo, and the war of 1812, he lost his reason, and his two sons also went insane. One fell by his own hand in Lady Pepperell's bedchamber, the other was so violent at times that it was necessary to chain him. Under these misfortunes the daughter Sally's reason gave way. The town allowed a small sum for the board of her father, and her brother. Her home even was sold to satisfy a Government claim for duties owed by her father. It would seem that the doom of the Pepperells was transmitted to all who should inhabit this house. Surely a blight seemed to have fallen upon it which consumed the lives and fortunes of a family until its evil destiny was fully accomplished.

The old mansion built by the first Colonel Pepperell, and enlarged by his son, is plain in its architecture, and contained a great many rooms before it was curtailed ten feet from each end. It was well adapted to the extensive domains and hospitalities of its former owners. The lawn in front extends to the sea, and the restless waves over which Sir William successively sought fortune and fame, still glitter in the sunbeams, and dash around the disconsolate abode. The fires of hospitality are extinguished. It is now occupied by the families of poor fishermen who do not like to be troubled with visitors or strangers. The hall is spacious and well finished; the ceiling is ornamented, and the richly carved bannisters bear traces of former elegance. The large hall was formerly lined with some fifty portraits of the Pepperell and Sparhawk families, and of the companions in arms of Sir William, such as Admiral Sir Peter. Warren, Commodore Spry and others. We have now no sympathy with the joyous acclamations once bestowed on these successful victors returning from the field of glory to be crowned with laurels. The American people feel no desire to perpetuate the fame of their achievements, although characterized at the time by patriotism as pure, and disinterested as any exhibited since this government was formed. Patriotism in those days implied loyalty and fidelity to the king of England, but how changed the meaning

*This question was decided in the case of Roger Morris of New York who married Mary, daughter of Frederick Phillips, who it is said had previously refused George Washington, the estate which belonged in right to his wife was confiscated, and that the whole interest should pass under the Act Mrs. Morris was included in the attainder. Humanity is shocked that a woman was attainted of treason, for no crime but that of clinging to the fortunes of the husband whom she had vowed on the altar never to desert. However, in the year 1809, their son, Captain Henry Gage Morris of the Royal Navy, in behalf of himself and his two sisters, sold their reversionary interest to John Jacob Astor of New York for the sum of £20,000 sterling. In 1828 Mr. Astor made a compromise with the State of New York by which he received for the rights thus purchased by him, the large sum of five hundred thousand dollars, having obtained a judgment of the Supreme Court of the United States affirming the validity and perfectibility of his title.

of that word in New England after the Declaration of Independence? Words and deeds before deemed patriotic, were now traitorous, and so deeply was the idea of their moral turpitude impressed on the public mind, as to have tainted popular opinion concerning the heroic deeds of our ancestors performed in the king's service, in the French wars, but criticism of this is apt to produce what Coleridge declared the cold waters of reason thrown on the burning embers of democracy inevitably produced—namely a hiss. The Revolution absorbed and neutralized all the heroic fame

THE PEPPERELL MANSION.

of the illustrious men that preceded it. The extinction of their fame was not more remarkable than the wreck of their fortunes. The Penns, Fairfaxes, Johnsons, Phillips, Robinsons and Pepperells were stripped of their immense possession, by confiscation, who up to that time had been but little less than hereditary noblemen and viceroys of boundless demains.

During the Revolution the Baronet was treated with great respect and deference by his fellow exiles in England. His home in London was open for their reception, and in most cases in which the Loyalists from New England united in representations to the ministry or to the throne, he was their chairman or deputed organ of communication. He was allowed

£500 sterling per annum by the British Government, and this stipend, with the wreck of his fortune, consisting of personal effects, rendered his situation comfortable, and enabled him to relieve the distress of the less fortunate. And it is to be recorded in respect for his memory, that his pecuniary benefactions were not confined to his countrymen who were in banishment, for their loyalty, but were extended to his countrymen who were disloyal, who languished in England in captivity sharing with them the pension which he received from the government, after their government had despoiled him of all his great possessions. It is to be remembered, too, that his private life was irreproachable, and that he was among the founders of the British and Foreign Bible Society.

In 1779 the Loyalists then in London formed an Association, and Sir William was appointed President. The first meeting was held at Spring Garden Coffee House, May 29th, 1779, and the next at the Crown and Anchor, in the Strand on the 26th. About ninety persons met at this place composed of Loyalists from each Colony. A Committee appointed at this meeting, on July 6th, reported an Address to the King. In this document it is said, that, "notwithstanding your Majesty's arms have not been attended with all the effect which those exertions promised, and from which occasion has been taken to raise an indiscriminate charge of disaffection in the Colonists, we beg leave, some of us from our own knowledge, and others from the best information, to assure your Majesty that the greater number of your subjects in the Confederated Colonies, notwithstanding every art to seduce, every device to intimidate, and a variety of oppressions to compel them to abjure their sovereign, entertain the firmest attachment and allegiance to your Majesty's sacred person and government. In support of those truths, we need not appeal to the evidence of our own sufferings; it is notorious that we have sacrificed all which the most loyal subjects could forego, or the happiest could possess. But, with confidence, we appeal to the struggles made against the usurpations of Congress, by Counter Resolves in very large districts of country, and to the many unsuccessful attempts by bodies of the loyal in arms, which have subjected them to all the rigors of inflamed resentment; we appeal to the sufferings of multitudes, who for their loyalty have been subjected to insults, fines, and imprisonments, patiently enduring all in the expectation of that period which shall restore to them the blessings of your Majesty's Government; we appeal to the thousands now serving in your Majesy's armies, and in private ships-of-war, the former exceeding in number the troops enlisted to oppose them; finally, we make a melancholy appeal to the many families who have been banished from their once peaceful habitations; to the public forfeiture of a long list of estates; and to the numerous executions of our fellow-citizens, who have sealed their loyalty with the ⸺ blood. If any Colony or District, when covered or possessed by your Majesty's troops had been called upon to take arms, and had refused; or, if any attempts had been made to form the Loyalist militia, or otherwise, and it had been declined, we should not on this occasion have presumed thus to address your Majesty; but if, on the contrary, no general measure to the above effect was attempted, if petitions from bodies of your Majesty's subjects, who wished to rise in aid of Government, have been neglected, and the representations of the most respectable Loyalists disregarded, we assure ourselves that the equity and wisdom of your Majesty's mind will not admit of any impressions injurious to the honor and loyalty of your faithful subjects in those Colonies."

Sir William Pepperell, Messrs. Fitch, Leonard, Rome, Stevens, Patterson, Galloway, Lloyd, Dulaney, Chalmers, Randolph, Macknight, Ingram, and Doctor Chandler, composing a committee of thirteen, were appointed to present this Address. At the same meeting it was resolved, "That it be recommended to the General Meeting to appoint a Committee, with directions to manage all such public matters as shall appear for the honor and interest of the Loyal in the Colonies, or who have taken refuge from America in this country, with power to call General Meetings, to whom they shall from time to time report." Of this Committee, Sir Egerton Leigh, of South Carolina, was Chairman. This body was soon organized. On the 26th of July, Mr. Galloway, of Pennsylvania, who was a member of it, reported rules for its government, which, after being read and debated, were adopted. The proceedings of this Committee do not appear to have been very important; indeed, to meet and sympathize with one another, was probably their chief employment. On the 2d of August, it was, however, "Resolved, That each member of the Committee be desired to prepare a brief account of such documents, facts, and informations, as he hath in his power, or can obtain, relating to the rise, progress, and present state of the rebellion in America, and the causes which have prevented its being suppressed, with short narratives of their own, stating their facts, with their remarks thereon, or such observations as may occur to them; each gentleman attending more particularly to the Colony to which he belongs, and referring to his document for the support of each fact." This resolution was followed by another, having for its design to unite with them the Loyalists who remained in America, in these terms: "Resolved, That circular letters be transmitted from the Committee to the principal gentleman from the different Colonies at New York, informing them of the proceedings of the General Meeting, the appointment and purposes of this Standing Committee, and requesting their co-operation and correspondence."

August 11, 1779, at a meeting of the Committee, report was made that General Robertson had been "so obliging as to undertake the trouble of communicating to our brethren in New York our wishes to have an institution established there on similar principles to our own, for the purpose of corresponding with us on matters relative to the public interests of British America." Whereupon it was resolved, that, in place of the circular letter resolved upon on the 2d, "a letter to General Robertson, explanatory of our designs and wishes, and entreating his good offices to the furtherance of an establishment of a Committee at New York, be drawn up and transmitted." At the same meeting, (August 11th,) Sir William Pepperell stated that Lord George Germain had been apprised of the proceedings of the "Loyalists for considering of American affairs in so far as their interests were concerned, and that his Lordship had been pleased to declare his entire approbation of their institution."

The framing of the letter to General Robertson, above mentioned, seems to have been, now, the only affair of moment, which, by the record, occupied the attention of the Association. It may be remarked, however, that agreeably to the recommendation above stated, a Board of Loyalists was organized at New York, composed of delegates from each Colony. Another body, of which the Baronet was President, was the Board of Agents constituted after the peace, to prosecute the claims of Loyalists to compensation for their losses by the war, and under the Confiscation Acts of the several States. Sir James Wright, of Georgia, was first elected, but at his decease, Sir William was selected as his successor, and continued in office until the Commisioners made their final report, and the commission was dissolved. Sir William's own claim was of difficult adjustment, and occupied the attention of the Commissioners several days. In 1788, and after Mr. Pitt's plan had received the sanction of Parliament, the Board of Agents presented an Address of thanks to the King for the liberal provision made for themselves and the persons whom they represented, which was presented to his Majesty by the Baronet. On this occasion, he and the other Agents were admitted to the presence, and "all had the honor to kiss his Majesty's hand." As this Address contains no matter of historical interest, it is not here inserted. But some mention may be made of West's picture, the "Reception of the American Loyalists by Great Britain in 1783," of which an engraving is here shown. The Baronet is the prominent personage represented, and appears in a voluminous wig, a flowing gown, in advance of the other figures, with one hand extended and nearly touching the crown, which lies on a velvet cushion on a table, and holding in the other hand, at his side, a scroll or manuscript half unrolled.

The full description of this picture is as follows: "Religion and Justice are represented extending the mantle of Britannia, whilst she herself is holding out her arm and shield to receive the Loyalists. Under the shield is the Crown of Great Britain, surrounded by Loyalists. This group of figures consists of various characters, representing the Law, the Church, and the Government, with other inhabitants of North America; and as a marked characteristic of that quarter of the globe, an Indian Chief extending one hand to Britannia, and pointing the other to a Widow and Orphans, rendered so by the civil war; also, a Negro and Children looking up to Britannia in grateful remembrance of their emancipation from Slavery. In a Cloud, on which Religion and Justice rest, are seen in an opening glory the Genii of Great Britain and of America, binding up the broken fasces of the two countries, as emblematical of the treaty of peace and friendship between them. At the head of the group of Loyalists are likenesses of Sir William Pepperell, Baronet, one of the Chairmen of their Agents to the Crown and Parliament of Great Britain; and William Franklin, Esq., son of Dr. Benjamin Franklin, who, having his Majesty's commission of Governor of New Jersey, preserved his fidelity and loyalty

RECEPTION OF THE AMERICAN LOYALISTS IN ENGLAND.

to his Sovereign from the commencement to the conclusion of the contest, notwithstanding powerful incitements to the contrary. He was arrested by order of Congress and confined for two years, when he was finally exchanged. The two figures on the right hand are the painter, Mr. West, the President of the Royal Academy, and his lady, both natives of Pennsylvania."

Sir William continued in England during the remainder of his life. He died in Portman Square, London, in December, 1816, aged seventy. William, his only son, deceased in 1809. The baronetcy was inherited by no other member of the family, and became extinct. His daughters were Eliza-

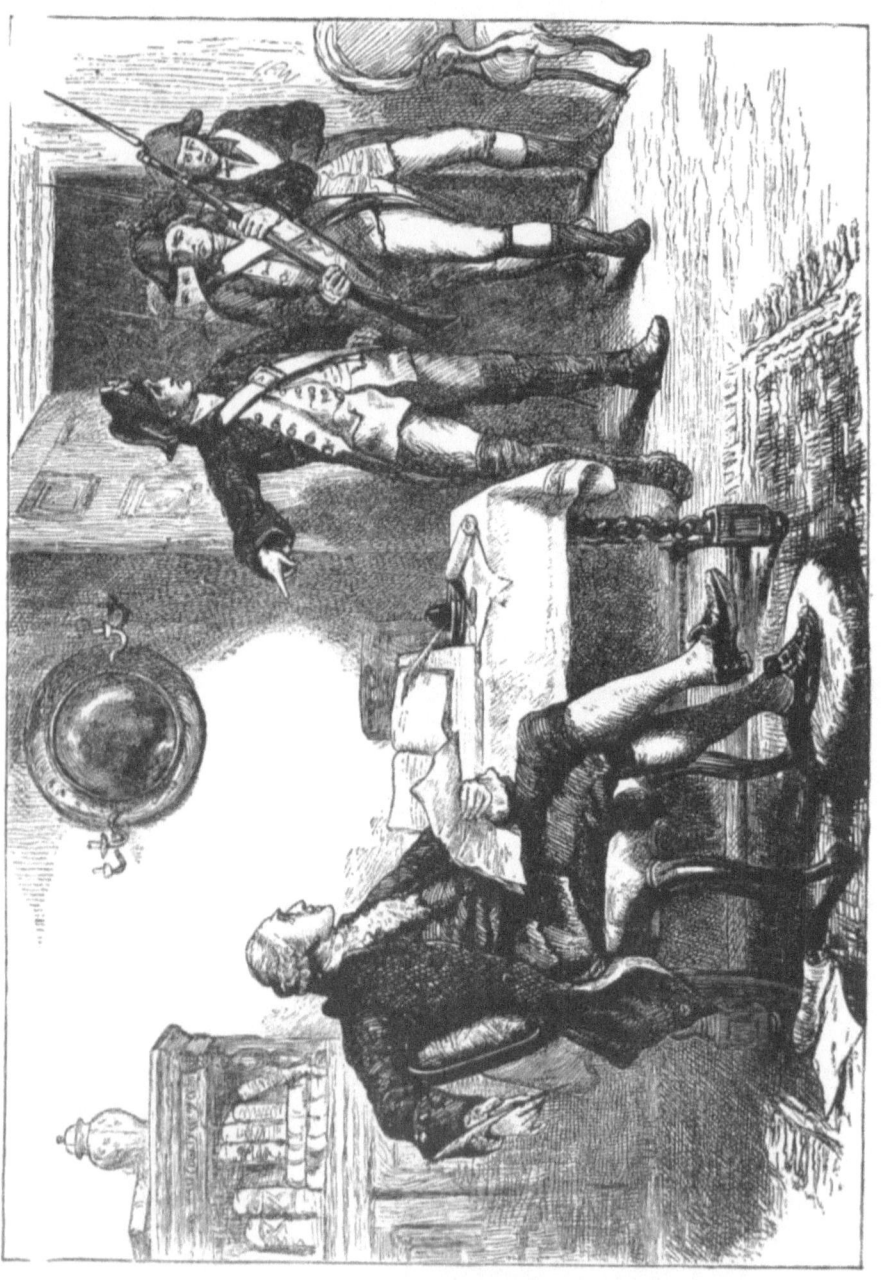

ARREST OF WILLIAM FRANKLIN BY ORDER OF CONGRESS
THE LAST ROYAL GOVERNOR OF NEW JERSEY, SON OF BENJAMIN FRANKLIN

beth, who married the Rev. Henry Hutton, of London; Mary, the wife of Sir William Congreve; and Harriet, the wife of Sir Charles Thomas Palmer, Baronet.

NATHANIEL SPARHAWK, brother of the second Sir William Pepperell, was born August, 1744. Graduated at Harvard University in 1765. He was an Addresser to Gov. Gage and went to England where he remained till 1809, when he returned, and died in Kittery, 1814. His two sons never married, and were by the kindness of their neighbors saved from the almshouse, on account of their noble ancestor, being great grandsons of the elder Sir William Pepperell.

SAMUEL HIRST SPARHAWK, also brother to Sir William Pepperell, graduated at Harvard University in 1771, an Addresser to both Hutchinson and Gage. Subsequently he went to England with his family of four persons. He died at Kittery, August 29, 1789, aged thirty-eight. He left an only daughter, Miss Harriot Hirst Sparhawk, who at his request, was adopted by his sister in Boston, wife of Dr. Jarvis, with whom she lived till the death of that lady in 1815. She afterwards lived at Portsmouth, and expended one hundred dollars in repairing the old Pepperell tomb. She was the last Sparhawk living of Pepperell blood, in America.

ANDREW SPARHAWK, the fourth son of Colonel Sparhawk, married a Miss Turner. Was a Loyalist and went to England with his brothers, where his wife died soon after their arrival, and he died there in 1783, leaving no children.

MARY PEPPERELL SPARHAWK, married Dr. Charles Jarvis of Boston, and after his death, she passed the remainder of her days at Kittery Point, near the village church, and nearly opposite the residence of her grandmother, Lady Pepperell's dwelling, built after the Baronet's death. She died in 1815.

LIST OF CONFISCATED ESTATES BELONGING TO SIR WILLIAM PEPPERELL IN SUFFOLK COUNTY AND TO WHOM SOLD.

To Thomas Russell, Jan. 2, 1783; Lib. 136, fol. 203; Land and dwelling-house in Boston, Summer St. S.; Benjamin Goldthwait E.; heirs of Benjamin Cunningham deceased N.; Samuel Whitwell W.———Land and Buildings, Summer St. N.; widow Jones W. and N.; Joseph Balch W.; John Rowe and Thomas Thompson S.; said Thompson W.; John Rowe S.; Zachariah Brigdon E.

JOHN SINGLETON COPLEY

AND HIS SON

Lord Lyndhurst, Lord Chancellor of England.

John Singleton Copley of Boston was the son of Richard Copley of County Limerick, who married Mary Singleton, of Deer Park, County Clare. Her father was of a Lancashire house of that name which had settled in Ireland in 1661.

Richard and Mary came to Boston in 1736, and their son John was born July 3rd, 1737. The father went to the West Indies and died there about the time of the birth of his son.

The widow of Richard Copley married Peter Pelham, an engraver and artist, by whom she had one son, Henry Pelham, who followed his father's profession. Peter Pelham died in 1751. John S. Copley became one of the most famous painters of his time. Without instruction, or master, he drew and painted, and "saw visions" of beautiful forms and faces which he transferred to canvass. His pictures show up the features and the figures of the aristocracy of Boston, of a time when there were aristocrats here, so that it has been frequently said that one of these ancestral portraits is a Bostonian's best title of nobility.

Major George Washington visited Boston in 1755 and sat to young Copley for a miniature. In 1766 Copley sent, without name or address, an exquisite portrait of his half brother, Henry Pelham, known as the "Boy and the Flying Squirrel," to Benjamin West, a fellow countryman then settled in London with a request to have it placed in the Exhibition Rooms of the Society of British Artists. The attention and admiration excited by this wonderful painting were such that the friends of the artist wrote most warmly to persuade him to go to England for the pursuit of his vocation, and West extended to him a pressing invitation to his own home. In 1769 he married Susannah Farnum, daughter of Richard Clarke, a wealthy merchant of Boston, and agent of the East India Company for their trade in that town. The tie between the artist and his wife was peculiarly close. We constantly meet her familiar lineaments through the whole course of Copley's works. Now Mary by the manger, with the Divine Infant at her breast, in "The Nativity," again in "The Family Picture" and in the fabled scene of Venus and Cupid, or in the female group in "The Death of Major Pierson," dissolved in an agony of grief, and fear, as they escape from the scene of violence and death.

The locality associated with his married life in Boston was a solitary house on Beacon Hill, chosen with his keen perception of picturesque beauty. His prophecy has been fully verified that the time would come when that situation would become the favorite site for the homes of the wealthy. Singular as it may appear the site selected by Copley was the same as that selected by William Blackstone, the first settler of Boston. In after years Copley's thoughts fondly reverted to his early home--his farm, he called it—which contained 11 acres on the southwest side of Beacon Hill, now bounded by Charles, Beacon, Walnut, and Mt. Vernon streets, Louisburg Square and Pinckney street.

In 1771 Copley wrote that he was earning a comfortable income. At this time, he moved in the best society, where his courtly manners and genial disposition made him a general favorite. He was now approaching the crucial period of his life. He saw the approaching storm that was soon to break and deluge his country in blood. He was peculiarly situated, and in a trying position. It is said that his sympathies were at first with the revolutionists, and he acted as an intermediary between them and his father-in-law, Richard Clarke,* to whom the tea was consigned, but when the infuriated mob destroyed the tea, and attacked the warehouse, and residence of Mr. Clarke, forcing him to flee for his life, Copley could no longer tolerate mob rule. His case was like that of many others of whom it is said "persecution made half of the king's friends." These outrages occurred in December 1773. Less than two years afterwards he wrote to his wife, from Italy, July 1775: "You know "years ago I was right in my opinion that this would be the result of "the attempt to tax the colony; it is now my settled conviction that all "the power of Great Britain will not reduce them to obedience. Unhappy "and miserable people, once the happiest, now the most wretched. How "warmly I expostulated with some of the violent 'Sons of Liberty' "against their proceedings, they must remember; and with how little "judgment, in their opinion, did I then seem to speak! But all this is "past; the day of tribulation is come, and years of sorrow will not dry "the orphan's tears, nor stop the widow's lamentations, the ground will "be deluged in the blood of its inhabitants before peace will again as- "sume its dominion in that country."** Copley embarked for England, June 1774, six monhs after his father-in-law was driven out of Boston by the mob, and one year before the conflict with the mother country commenced. Leaving his aged mother, his favorite brother, his wife and children behind him, he went to prepare a place of refuge for them from the impending storm. Probably the desire to visit Europe and behold the work of the great masters of the art he loved so well had something to do with leaving his native land, to which he was never to return. After travelling and studying two years on the Continent, he went back to London, and was soon joined by his family. Then began a career of uninterrupted success. He became the fashion, and many of the nobility sat to him as did also three of the princesses, daughters of George III. Following the fashion of the day he took up historical painting, which included the death of Major Pierson and the death of Chatham (both now in the English National Gallery); The

* Tea Leaves 322, 323, 327, 329.
** Life of Copley, p 62.

siege of Gibraltar, now in the Guild Hall of London, and Charles I demanding in the House of Commons, the surrender of the five impeached members, which now hangs in the Boston Public Library. "The death of Major Pierson" in repelling the attack of the French at St. Helier's, Jersey, on the 6th of January 1781, was painted in 1783 for Alderman Boydell, for his gallery. When this was dispersed it was bought back by Copley, and remained in the house in George Street till Lord Lyndhurst's death, when it was purchased for the National Gallery for 1500 guineas. The woman flying from the the crowd in terror, with the child in her arms, was painted from the nurse of Mr. Copley's family; the figure between her and the wall, with the upraised arm, is Mrs. Copley; the boy running by the nurse's side is young Copley.

Copley was an Addresser of Hutchinson in 1774, the year he left Boston, and in 1776, on his return from Italy to London, he became a member of the Loyalist club, for weekly conversation and a dinner. He died at his residence in George Street, London, Sept. 9, 1815, aged seventy-eight and was buried in the tomb belonging to Governor Hutchinson's family in the parish church at Croydon, near London. Copley had one son and two daughters who lived to maturity.

JOHN SINGLETON COPLEY, the younger, was born in Boston May 20, 1772, was early destined for his fathers profession, and, accordingly he attended the lectures of Sir Joshua Reynolds, and Barry, at the Royal Academy. He, however, had no inclination to follow in his father's footsteps. He threw off his instructors, impatiently declaring that he would not be known as the "son of Copley the painter" but it should be "Copley, the father of the Lord Chancellor." So early did he prognosticate his own future eminence. He was entered 1790 at Trinity College, Cambridge. In the mathematical tripos of 1794, was second wrangler, sickness alone preventing him from obtaining the highest honor of the year. He was also Smith's Prizeman, won the King William prize, and, the following year, was appointed a "travelling bachelor" with a grant for three years of a £100 a year, and, a month later, was elected a fellow of Trinity, improved the opportunity to visit Boston, the town of his birth, with the ulterior view of regaining the family estates on Beacon Hill, owned by his father before leaving Boston, more than twenty years before. For although Copley was an Absentee, or Refugee, and therefore had laid himself liable to the confiscation of his property, yet, through his well known sympathy with the Revolutionists before the commencement of open war, and through the assistance of some of his friends, his property, which consisted of the largest landed estate in Boston, had not been confiscated. There were however several real estate speculators who had profited largely by purchasing the confiscated estates of the Loyalists for a mere trifle who determined to possess themselves of Copley's property. Jonathan Mason, and Harrison Grey Otis, made a contract with Gardiner Green, who was Copley's agent, to purchase the same, without adequate authority from the owner. When the deed was sent to

JOHN SINGLETON COPLEY.
Born in Boston July 3, 1737. Painter to the King. Died in London Sept. 9, 1815.

him for execution he refused to sign it. A bill in equity was bought to enforce the contract of sale. Copley executed a power of attorney to his son, when he went to Boston, giving him authority to settle the case. He arrived in Boston Jan. 2nd, 1796, and wrote to his father: "The business cannot come on till May. If you can make yourself a subject of the United States you are clear. If otherwise I am not yet sufficiently informed to say what may be the result, if you are decreed an alien, but take courage." He wrote again in February 27, 1796, saying, "I have, my dear sir, concluded my negotiations with Messrs. Mason, Otis, and others. I have acted for the best. I was very strongly of the opinion that the event of the contest would be in favor of the plaintiffs. Your counsel agreed with me in their sentiments upon that head.* A compromise became, therefore, necessary, and for the consideration of $18,450 a deed of release was given, dated February 22, 1796, recorded in Lib 182, fol 184, Suffolk Deeds."**

No deed of any lands in Boston within a century will compare with this in importance and interest. Taking into consideration the upland, beach, and flats, this purchase is at a considerably less rate than $1,000 per acre. That the son acted wisely his letters prove, but the transaction was one of deepest regret to the whole family, and embittered the remainder of the artist's life.

In a letter to his mother from Boston, the young man says: "Shall I whisper a word in your ear? The better people are all aristocrats. My father is too rank a Jacobin to live among them. Samuel Adams is superannuated, unpopular and fast decaying in every respect." Again he wrote to his mother from Philadelphia: *"I have become a fierce Aristocrat.* This is the country to cure your Jacobins. Send them over and they will return quite converted. The opposition here are a set of villains. Their object is to overset the government, and all good men are apprehensive lest they should be successful. A great schism seems to be forming, and they already begin to talk of a separation of the States north of the Potomac from those on the southern side of the river.*** He was a visitor at Mount Vernon and spent a week as a guest of the first President of the young Republic.

After nearly two years spent in the new United States, John Singleton Copley, the younger, returned to what had now become the settled home of the Copley family. He commenced a long course of study and systematic preparation for a life which was to become of the most distinguished, among the most famous men of the first half of the 19th century. Called to the bar in 1804 he, with no other influence than that of his own commanding talents, soon ranked among the leading men of his profession and that at a time when an unusually large number of great advocates were at the English bar.

* Life of Copley, p 141.
** Gleaner Articles, p 196.
*** Life of Copley, p 140, 145.

But it was not at the bar only, or when on the bench at the head of the judiciary of England that this son of Boston distinguished himself. In both houses of Parliament, as Copley or Lyndhurst, he was an acknowledged leader of men.

Copley took his seat in the House of Commons as member for Yarmouth in the Isle of Wight, in March 1818, and until his removal to the House of Lords, nine years later, sat continuously as a member. Meanwhile promotion, professionally and politically, was constantly growing. In 1819, he was made a king's sergeant (at large) and chief justice of Chester. In June of the same year he was appointed Solicitor General (with knighthood), five years later became Attorney General. In 1826 he succeeded Lord Gifford as Master of the Rolls, a high judicial office, which at that time and for many years after did not compel the vacating of a seat in Parliament.

The town Council of Bristol unanimously elected him in the same year Recorder of that city.

In April 1827 in his 55th year on the retirement of Lord Chancellor Eldon, the ambition of his life was realized. The great prize of the legal profession was offered to him by the express desire of the king and with it of course a peerage. Sir John Singleton Copley became Baron Lyndhurst of Lyndhurst in the County of Hampshire and, for nearly forty years thereafter remained to adorn the House of Lords by his high talents, his noble character, and his fervid eloquence.

Lyndhurst's first Chancellorship, was not of long duration. From 1830 to 1834 we find him occupying the chiefship of the Court of Exchequer. He a strong tory, had been honored by a whig ministry, in his appointment to the office of Lord Chief Baron. This dignified and permanent position he resigned again to became Chancellor following the passing of the Reform Bill. As Lord Chancellor once more, and for the third time, from 1841 to 1846 he was a member of the ministry of Sir Robert Peel. The fame of the great jurist and statesman had become as precious to the citizens of Boston, as it was to the mother country. Here in Massachusetts he was born, and from his American parents received the first vivid impression of childhood. The reminiscences of his youth however, were always accompanied by a heartfelt effusion of gratitude that his lot was cast in England. To London he was especially attached, and used to say "that every product known to man, every wonder of art, and skill, which the civilized world produced, could be found there."*

He was called the "Nestor of the House of Lords." His speeches were remarkable for their clearness, vigor, and force, even when he had reached nearly to his ninetieth year. A portrait of Lord Lyndhurst in his Chancellor robes is in the portrait gallery of the New York Historical Society. Lord Lyndhurst died October, 1863, in his 92nd year. Leaving no male heirs, his title died with him.

He married Sarah Geray, daughter of Charles Brunsden, and widow

* Life of Copley, p 126.

LORD LYNDHURST, LORD HIGH CHANCELLOR OF ENGLAND.
Born in Boston May 20, 1772.   Son of John Singleton Copley.   Died in London Oct. 12, 1863.

of Lieutenant-Colonel Thomas, who fell at Waterloo. He was the father of Sarah Elizabeth, Susan Penelope, and Sophia Clarence. His second wife, Georgiana, daughter of Lewis Goldsmith, bore him a single child, Georgiana Susan.

His Lordship's eldest sister, Elizabeth Clarke, born in Boston, 1770, was educated at a boarding school at Clapham, London, and married Gardiner Greene of Boston, a man of high social standing and business position, who had come to Boston from Demerara after the Revolution, where he had accumulated a large fortune. While on a visit to London in July, 1800, he married Miss Copley. She died at Boston in 1866, aged 95 years. In her will she left to Harvard College a collection of proof copies of all of Copley's historical paintings. Her daughter, Martha B. Greene, born in 1812, married Charles Amory and wrote the Life of John Singleton Copley, and to this valuable work we are indebted for much of the information we have given in this biographical notice. She died in 1880 leaving many descendants.

KING HOOPER OF MARBLEHEAD.

Marblehead is a rough peninsular, projecting into the Bay, with craggy shores, and a narrow harbor a mile and a half in length and a half mile wide. It is distant about eighteen miles from Boston.

From its peculiar adaptation to fisheries and commerce, though very limited in territory, this place was once famous for the hardihood and daring enterprise of its citizens. It was the principal fishing port in all the colonies, and now it does not contain one single fisherman that goes to the "Banks," but it has since become the principal yachting centre in the United States if not in the world; frequently there will be seen gathered here more than five hundred yachts of all classes and descriptions.

It was naturally a wilderness of rock, with here and there a green valley or glade just fitted for a little garden, where the mariner perched his pretty nest, on the adjacent cliff. No herds or flocks ranged on this barren place. A Marbleheader ploughed only the deep for his living, his pasture lay afar off on the Banks of Newfoundland, or the Georges, and his harvest whitened the shores with their wide spread fish flakes. Even at this day, with its cluster of antique dwellings and rough trapesian streets, this seaport has an odd look, like some ancient town in England. But in this secluded spot, where stands the dilapidated fortresses of Sewall and Lee, several eminent men, merchants, mariners and lawyers, were born and educated, who became staunch loyalists. They were sincere in their convictions and had the courage to declare them in defiance of a rough and turbulent population. They could not view the revolutionary proceedings of their townsmen without deep concern, and doing all in their power to dissuade their fellow-citizens from the course they had taken, they protested that the entire policy of the colonies was suicidal and that the town had been guilty of treason by its action. With a sincere belief that these rebellious acts of the colonists must sooner or later bring disaster and ruin upon the country, and death and imprisonment to the leaders, they entreated their friends and neighbors to recede from their position before it was too late, but in vain. It was voted in town meeting that they "ought not to be indulged in their wickedness" and that a committee should be chosen to attend to the conduct of these ministerial tools and Jacobites, that effectual measures might be taken "either for silencing them or expelling them from the community". What brought about this action of the Revolutionists was the address to Governor Hutchinson on his departure for England signed by thirty-three of the principal citizens of the town. Among these names there were five of the name of Hooper, chief of whom was "King Hooper," the principal merchant in the town. He had a high reputation for honor and integrity in his business dealings and for his benevolence.

ROBERT HOOPER, the first to appear in Marblehead, is first mentioned in Massachusetts records as master of a shallop hired of Mr. Moses Maverick, a wealthy business man of Marblehead, in 1663. From a deposition he made in court, he was born about 1606. This would make him old enough to have been the father of John, Robert and Henry Hooper, the other very early residents of Marblehead. He died after 1686.

ROBERT HOOPER, supposed to be the son of the aforesaid, was born as early as 1655. Married Dec. 4, 1684, Anna, daughter of Peter and Hannah Greenfield. Hannah was a daughter of John and Ann Devereux. He was an inn keeper and died about 1689.

GREENFIELD HOOPER, son of the aforesaid, was born about 1686. He resided at Marblehead, was a merchant. He also had a "workshop," with loom for weaving. He married, Jan. 16, 1706, Alice, daughter of Andrew Tucker, Sr., and received a share of his real estate. He died about October 1, 1747.

ROBERT HOOPER, known as "King Hooper," was born at Marblehead, June 26, 1709, son of the aforesaid Greenfield Hooper. He was married four times. Was a merchant who rose from poverty to apparently inexhaustible wealth, engrossing for years a large part of the foreign fishing business of Marblehead, which was very extensive about the year 1760. For awhile he purchased all the fish brought into that port, sent it to Bilboa and other parts of Spain and received gold and silver in return, with which he purchased goods in England. He owned lands in Marblehead, Salem, Danvers, and an extensive tract at Lyndeborough, N. H., and elsewhere. He had a large and elegant house at Marblehead, and also a mansion at Danvers, where he did "royal" entertaining, rode in a chariot like a prince, and was ever after known as "King Hooper." He was

*Hooper Genealogy. Curwen's Journal. History of Marblehead.

KING HOOPER MANSION, DANVERS.

At his elegant mansion in Danvers, Robert Hooper entertained General Gage, who made it his headquarters in 1774.

one of the wealthiest and most benevolent men in the colony. He presented Marblehead with a fire engine in 1751.*

At his elegant house in Danvers he entertained General Gage for some time in 1774, and was an Addresser of Hutchinson the same year. He was appointed representative to the General Court in 1775, and declined a seat in the Governor's council in 1759 on account of deafness. He was one of thirty-six persons appointed as mandamus councillors of the province in 1774, at the beginning of the agitation that led to the Revolution, and was one of the twelve that did not accept of the honor, his deafness previously referred to being probably the reason, for he was a staunch loyalist. This, together with his age and known generosity, prevented his being driven forth from the town; it however did not prevent the loss of his great property, for when he died in 1790 he was insolvent. In a letter dated Marblehead, March 17, 1790, addressed to his granddaughter Ruth, the wife of Lewis Deblois, a Boston loyalist residing at St. John, N. B., he says: "But as you justly observe we have been and still are 300 miles distance from each other and my advanced age makes it doubtful whether I may ever see you more in this world, your parting from me was next to burying you, there is nothing would give more pleasure than to hear of the health and prosperity of every branch of my family." This truly great and honorable man died, a little more than a month after writing this letter. He died May 20, 1790, aged 81 years.

JOSEPH HOOPER, son of the aforesaid, was born at Marblehead, May 29, 1743, married Oct. 30, 1766, Mary, daughter of Benjamin and Lucy (Devereux) Harris of Newburyport, Nov. 20, 1746. She died at Newburyport Oct. 3, 1796.

He graduated from Harvard College in 1763, was a merchant in his native town, carrying on a foreign trade. He built the mansion in Marblehead afterwards occupied by Chief Justice Sewall. He was an Addresser of Governor Hutchinson in 1774. Being an ardent loyalist he was forced to leave his home in 1775 and go to England. He became a paper manufacturer at Bungay, Suffolk, England, where he died in 1812. The Marblehead Revolutionary committee recorded May 8th, 1781, that "they believed he had voluntarily gone over to our enemies," that is he was a loyalist, and proceeded to administer on his affairs. One third share was set off to his wife June 9, 1783, and the balance confiscated and sold. He had two sons and two daughters.

ROBERT HOOPER, son of King Hooper, was born at Marblehead, Feb. 9, 1746, married May 23, 1769, Anna, daughter of Richard and Jemima Corwell. He was an Addresser of Governor Hutchinson, but evidently made peace with the Revolutionists and was allowed to remain. He died about 1781 at Marblehead. "He had usually traded beyond the sea."

SWEET HOOPER, son of King Hooper. Married at Boston, Aug. 4, 1779, Mary, daughter of Hector McNeil. He was an Addresser of Governor Hutchinson, but was allowed to remain. He was a merchant at Marblehead, died October, 1781.

ROBERT HOOPER, 3d, as described in the Addressers to Governor Hutchinson, was probably a son of Deacon Robert Hooper, cousin to the aforesaid Hoopers. He was born at Marblehead 1757, and married Sept. 21, 1777, Elizabeth, daughter of Rev. Nathaniel Whittaker of Salem. In 1794 he sold his two-sixths of the mansion house, etc., which had belonged to his father, the late Deacon Robert Hooper. He removed to Lexington, Maine, was master of Limerick Academy. He died May 11, 1836.

WILLIAM BOWES.

Nicholas Bowes of Cambridge, Mass., married 26 June, 1684, Sarah Hubbard, who died 26 Jan. 1686, and for second wife married 6 May, 1690, Dorcas Champney, and a third wife, Martha Remington, of Cambridge, June 21, 1718. It is claimed that he was descended from Sir Martin Bowes, Lord Mayor of London. Nicholas Bowes, son of the preceding was born at Boston, Nov. 2nd, 1706. He graduated at Harvard College as M. A., was minister at Bedford from 1730 to 1754. He married Lucy Hancock, the aunt of John Hancock, the Revolutionary Governor of Massachusetts. Their son

WILLIAM BOWES, was born at Boston, 3 December 1734. He married Ann Whitney, March 22, 1761, who died Jan. 2, 1762. His second wife was Mary Stoddard, whom he married Oct. 30, 1769, and who died 9 May, 1774. He was a merchant and had inherited in 1764 a large property from his uncle, Thomas Hancock, one of the wealthiest merchants in Boston. He was an Addresser of Governor Hutchinson in 1774, and of General Gage in 1775. At the evacuation of Boston he went to Halifax with his family of four persons. In 1788 he was proscribed and banished, and his estates confiscated. He died near London, April, 1805. His eldest son,

WILLIAM BOWES, born at Boston, 15 Oct., 1771, lived in England and died near London 10 June, 1850, aged 79. He married Harriet Troutbeck, daughter of Rev. John Troutbeck, born at Boston 1 Oct. 1768, and died in England, 14 January, 1851, aged 82. Their children were Emily Bowes born 1806, Edmund Elford Bowes, born 1808, M. A. Trinity College, Cambridge. Arthur Bowes, born 1813. All born and living in England in 1856.

Sarah Bowes, daughter of William Bowes, Sr., was born at Boston, Jan. 31, 1773, and died in England, July 1850, unmarried.

LIST OF CONFISCATED ESTATES BELONGING TO WILLIAM BOWES IN SUFFOLK COUNTY AND TO WHOM SOLD.

To Richard Driver, Feb. 16, 1782; Lib. 134 fol. 23; Land in Boston, Fitch's Alley W.; Margaret Phillips N.; Corn Court E.; Andrew Oliver S.
To Mungo Mackey, June 11, 1783; Lib. 139, fol. 16; One fourth of land, brick distill house and other buildings in Boston, Cambridge St. N.; George St. E.; heirs of John Guttridge deceased S.; Belknap St. W.
To Robert Jenkins, Feb. 16, 1784; Lib. 141 fol. 132; Land and buildings in Boston, Wilson's Lane W.; Dock Square N.; Arnold and Samuel Wells E.; heirs of Charles Hammock deceased S.
To James Welch, Nov. 6, 1784; Lib. 145 fol. 250; Land in Boston, Wings Lane N.; Nathan Frazier and heirs of Charles Apthorp deceased E.; said heirs S.; E.; S. and W.

GENERAL TIMOTHY RUGGLES.

THOMAS RUGGLES of Nazing, Essex County, England, was born in Sudbury, Suffolk County, England, in 1584. He came to Roxbury, Massachusetts, in 1637 and was freeman May 22, 1639. He married in Nazing, England, Mary Curtis. He died in Roxbury, November 16, 1644, and his wife died in 1674, leaving four children.

His son Samuel was many years selectman, representative, and captain of the Roxbury company. His son Samuel succeeded his father in the several offices named and in company with seven other persons purchased, Dec. 27, 1686, for £20, from John Nagers and Lawrence Nassawano, two noted Indians, a tract of land containing by estimation 12 miles long north and south and eight miles wide east and west. This purchase is now known as the town of Hardwick, Mass. His son, the Rev. Timothy Ruggles, was born in Roxbury, Massachusetts, November 3, 1685, and married Mary White, the daughter of Benjamin and Susanna White. He graduated from Harvard College in 1707, and was ordained pastor of the Rochester church in 1710, which office he held until his death which occurred October 26, 1768. He was a great worker in the community and much beloved.

GENERAL TIMOTHY RUGGLES, born in Rochester, Mass., October 20, 1711, eldest son of Rev. Timothy Ruggles, one of the fifth generation of Ruggles in America, graduated at Harvard College in 1732 and commenced practicing law in Rochester. He represented his native town in the provincial assembly at the age of 25, and procured the passing of a bill still in force prohibiting sheriffs from filing writs. He removed to Harwich about 1753 on to the lands bought by his grandfather from the Indians. In 1757 he was appointed judge and in 1762 Chief Justice of the Court of Common Pleas, which he held till the Revolution. He was also surveyor-general of the king's forest, an office of profit, attended with but little labor. Besides professional employment he was engaged in military and political occupation.

In 1756 almost immediately before Mr. Ruggles' appointment to the bench, he accepted a Colonel's Commission in the forces raised by his native province for service on the frontier of Canada. In the campaign which followed, he served under the command of Sir William Johnson, and did good service in the expedition against Crown Point. In September of the same year he was second in command under that leader at the battle of Lake George, in which the French under Baron Dieskau, met a signal defeat, after very severe fighting, in which he distinguished himself for coolness, courage and ability, and so highly were his services esteemed on that occasion that he was promoted to the position of General of Brigade and placed under the command of the Commander-in-Chief.

In 1758 he commanded the Third Division of the Provisional troops under Abercrombie, in the unsuccessful attack upon Ticonderoga. He also served with distinction and courage in the campaign of 1759-1760. In the winter of 1762 while the belligerent forces on both sides were in winter quarters, he had the honor to be chosen speaker of the House of Representatives. On the passing of the Stamp Act in 1765 delegates were chosen by the legislature of the various colonies, to seek out some relief from immediate and threatened evils, by a representation of their grievances to the king and parliament. Gen. Ruggles was chosen as one of the delegates from Massachusetts. The Stamp Act Congress met at New York, Oct. 19, 1765, and General Ruggles was elected president of same. An address to the king was voted and certain resolves framed setting forth the rights of the colonies, and claiming an entire exemption from all taxes excepting those imposed by the local assemblies. Gen. Ruggles refused his concurrence in the proceedings for which he was censured on his return by the House of Representatives, and was reprimanded by the speaker who occupied his place. John Adams, who claimed relationship with Ruggles before his defection found nothing in his character but what was noble and grand. "Ruggles' grandeur" he wrote, consists in the quickness of his apprehension, steadiness of his attention, the boldness and strength of his thoughts and his expressions, his strict honor, conscious superiority, contempt of meanness, etc." He was, he said, a man of genius and great resolution. At an early period of the Disunion propaganda, Ruggles, conceiving that the course of the British Government was neither politic nor just, and believing that the Disunion leaders honestly intended to bring about a reform, joined hands with them and as previously stated he was elected President of the Stamp Act Congress, but on the discovery of the real aim of that body, he refused to proceed any further on the road to Disunion and left the Congress. Adams then suddenly discovered, "an inflexible oddity about him, which has gained him a character for courage and probity, and that at Congress." "His behavior was very dishonorable" and governed by "pretended scruples and timidities" and ever since he was "held in utter contempt and derision by the whole continent." But fifty years later, when no advantage could be gained by blackening the character of this brave and honest man, he remembered he was a high-minded man, an exalted soul acting in scenes he could not comprehend.* General Ruggles was a staunch, independent and fearless supporter of the government, a son of Massachustts of which she should be proud.

An extract from the "History of the County of Annapolis, Nova Scotia," says, "The conduct of Mr. Ruggles as a military commander has been highly praised by most competent judges. Few men in the province were more distinguished and few more severely dealt with in the bitter controversies preceding the Revolution. His appearance was commanding and dignified, being much above the common size; his wit was ready and brilliant; his mind clear, comprehensive and penetrating; his judgment was profound and his knowledge extensive; his abilities as a public speaker placed him among the first of the day; and had he embraced the popular sentiments of the times, there is no doubt he would have ranked among the leading characters of the Revolution.

By pen and tongue, in the halls of the Legislature, and on the platform, he declared against rebellion and bloodshed; General Ruggles was a good scholar and possessed powers of mind of a very high order. Many anecdotes continue to be related of him in the town of his nativity, which show his shrewdness, his sagacity, his military hardihood and bravery. As a lawyer he was an impressive pleader and in parliamentary debate able and ingenious. He remained in the army until 1760, the last three years being Brigadier General under Lord Amherst.

As the Revolutionary quarrel progressed he became one of the most violent supporters of the ministry and he and Otis as leaders of the two opposing parties were in constant collision in the discussion of the popular branch of government. In 1774 he was named a Mandamus Councillor, which increased his unpopularity to so great a degree that his house was attacked by night and his cattle were maimed and poisoned, General Ruggles tried to form a plan of combining the Loyalists against the Disunionists after the model of similar associations formed in other colonies. On December 22, 1774, he sent a communication to the "Printers of the Boston Newspaper" concerning the forming of an Association "and if attended to and complied with by the good people of the province might put it in the power of anyone very easily to distinguish such loyal subjects to the king and are to assert their rights to freedom, in all respects consistent with the laws of the land from such rebellious ones as under the pretence of being friends of liberty, are frequently committing the most enormous outrages upon the persons and the property of such of his Majesty's peaceable subjects who for want of knowing whom to call upon, in these distracted times for assistance, fall into the hands of bandits, whose cruelties surpass those of savages."

The "Association" consisted of a preamble and six articles. The principal were the first and third, which provided "That we will upon all occasions, with our lives and fortunes, stand by and assist each other in the defence of life, liberty and property, whenever the same shall be attacked

* Diary and Letters of John Adams.

or endangered by any bodies of men, riotously assembled upon any pretence, or under any authority not warranted by the laws of the land." And "That we will not acknowledge or submit to the pretended authority of any Congress, Committees of Correspondence, or any other unconstitutional assembly of men, but will at the risk of our lives if need be, oppose the forcible exercise of all such authority."

The Association did not succeed, the Loyalists were not inclined to such organization, nor fitted for secret intrigue without which it could not have succeeded in combatting the measures of the Disunionists. They were slow to join, and inefficient in action. No good was accomplished by this association and the Disunionists proceeded on their way triumphant.

When the appeal to arms had been finally decided on by the Disunionists, the popular excitement was at a fearful height, and all those who had counselled moderation, either in demand or action, were declared to be enemies to their country and traitors to the cause of liberty, and as such worthy of death. No man in Massachusetts was regarded as so inimical to the cause of rebellion as General Ruggles, whose known and recognized ability, great energy, and unflinching courage made him an object of fear as well as dislike.

They denounced him as malignant and openly threatened his life. In consequence of this violence he was forced, with his family and such of his neighbors as remained loyal, to seek safety and refuge from his dwelling house which he had built in Harwich by joining the British forces in Boston. On the very day of the battle of Lexington, a body of Loyalists formed in Boston, composed of tradesmen and merchants. They are spoken of as "the gentlemen volunteers," or Loyal American Association. They were placed under the command of Brigadier General Ruggles. During the seige of Boston they were joined by other Loyalist companies, Loyal Irish Volunteers, Captain James Forrest, Royal Honorable Americans, Colonel Gorham. After the evacuation of Boston he was in Long Island for a while and in 1783 he was an exile from his native province in his old age, but still as vigorous as he was loyal. His extensive estates in Harwich were confiscated, but were made up to him subsequently by the crown. He was living at Digby or Annapolis in the year of 1783, and made an application for a grant of land in that portion of the province. "In the following year the grant was issued. The undismayed grantee commenced a labor at the age of more than seventy years, which few, if any of the young men of to-day would voluntarily undertake. The work of chopping down the forests and clearing the lands for crops and of preparation for building went on simultaneously and rapidly under his direction.

"Two young men, Stromach and Fales, were employed to work with him for a limited number of years and receive their pay in land. They did their work, and he paid them, and their descendants are now the occupiers of many a fair home in the beautiful township of Wilmot."

General Ruggles' four daughters were married before the Revolution broke out and their husbands probably adhered to the Colonial side, for they never came to Novia Scotia. Three of his sons followed him into exile and settled in that country, Timothy, John, and Richard. It may not be without use to remark that for much the greater part of his life, General Ruggles ate no animal food, and drank no spirituous or fermented liquors, small beer excepted, and that he enjoyed health to his advanced age. This remarkable leader of men died in 1795. The "Royal Gazette" in August, 1795, said of him that "the district of county in which he lived will long feel the benefits resulting from the liberal exertions he made to advance the agricultural interests of the Province." It was also said of General Timothy Ruggles that he was one of the best soldiers in the colonies.

He was buried to the eastward of the chancel of the (then new) church, lately known as the "Pine Grove Church," in Central Wilmot, near the present village of Middleton,—a church toward the erection of which he was a considerable contributor.

Numerous descendants of General Ruggles are to be met with in Nova Scotia. There is a street and church in Roxbury named after this illustrous family.

JOHN RUGGLES, son of General Ruggles of Harwich, Mass., was proscribed and banished in 1778. He settled in Nova Scotia and died there in 1795. His widow Hannah, only daughter of Dr. Thomas Sackett of New York, died at Wilmot, N. S. in 1839, aged 76. His only son, CAPTAIN TIMOTHY AMHERST RUGGLES of the Nova Scotia Fencibles died at the same place in 1838 at the age of 56.

TIMOTHY RUGGLES, another son of the General, was a member of the House of Assembly of Nova Scotia for many years. He died at N. S. in 1831. Sarah, his widow, died at that place in 1842, aged 92.

RICHARD RUGGLES, son of the General, was born at Rochester, Mass., in 1774 and died at Annapolis in 1832.

THE FANEUIL FAMILY OF BOSTON.

The Faneuils were Huguenot refugees from La Rochelle, France. When they came to America they brought with them considerable wealth in jewels and money. From their coat of arms we should judge they dated back as far as the crusades, as the crossed palm branches can have no other meaning.

There is a paper extant in the French language and written by Benjamin Faneuil the elder. It is a family record in which he states that in 1699 he married Ann Bureau; then follows the birth of Peter Faneuil, afterwards the birth of three daughters. This paper was left by Benjamin Faneuil the younger, and is now in the possession of his great-grand-son George A. Bethune, M. D., Boston (1884). They first settled near New Rochelle, N. Y., and in 1699 Benjamin Faneuil was given the freedom of the city of New York. In Valentine's "History of New York," P. 219, we read in a list of the principal merchants of the city the name of Benjamin Faneuil the third in the list.

Andrew, the brother of Benjamin settled in Boston and made an immense fortune as a merchant. His wife was born in Holland and was a very beautiful woman.

Andrew Faneuil had no children that lived to maturity. He adopted two sons of his brother Benjamin of New York—Peter, born in 1701, and Benjamin the younger, born in 1702. Benjamin Faneuil the younger, married the daughter of Dr. John Cutler from a noted German family. Andrew Faneuil was offended about this marriage and left most of his fortune to his nephew Peter Faneuil. Peter Faneuil died five years after his uncle and left no will, and his brother Benjamin was declared sole heir to his fortune.

Benjamin Faneuil the elder is buried on the north side of Trinity church in New York City and the gravestone is in good preservation. His brother Andrew lived in a splendid house at the corner of Somerset and Beacon Streets, Boston; the house after his death was owned and occupied by Gardner Greene. From that home in Boston Andrew Faneuil was buried, having a most imposing funeral. (See Memorial Hist. of Boston). His tomb is in the graveyard at the south side of the common.

Benjamin Faneuil the younger, and Mary Cutler, had two sons neither of whom left descendants, and a daughter. He lived at one time in Boston at the corner of Washington and Summer Streets, and later in Brighton. He was stone blind for twenty years and lived to be eighty-four years of age. He was an admirable character and greatly beloved. His daughter entertained General Washington at their home during the seige of Boston, and General Lee was with him. Benjamin Faneuil admired Washington and he told him so, emphatically, whether a Whig or not. But he also told General Lee who was an Englishman that he had his "head in the noose" for he was a very decided old man and had to state his opinions under any circumstances.

Peter Faneuil possessed his uncle's estate only about five years but during that time he lived in sumptuous style at the corner of Somerset and Beacon Streets in the house that Andrew built. He gave great sums to charity and Faneuil Hall was but one of his gifts to the city. Every charity of that day has his name down for a large sum. To Trinity church he gave a £100 for an organ and a donation to support the families of the deceased clergy of that church. It became so large that it was divided between Trinity church and Kings Chapel, and has done much good. There is a fine portrait of Peter Faneuil still extant; it was given to the Antiquarian Society of Boston by his niece, Miss Jones, and is a better picture than the one in Faneuil Hall.

Peter Faneuil was a careful business man, but was always generous. At the time of the erection of Faneuil Hall there was no market house then in the town, and so he erected a building one hundred feet in length by forty feet in width. Besides the market there were several rooms for town officers, and a hall which would contain one thousand persons. On the completion of the building the first public oration held there was a funeral eulogy delivered in honor of its donor, Peter Faneuil, March 14, 1743 by Master Lovell of the Latin School, and was "Recorded by Order of Town."* The Hall was dedicated to Liberty and Loyalty to the King in the following words, "May Liberty always spread its Joyful Wings over this Place. And may Loyalty to a King under whom we enjoy this Liberty ever remain our Character." That the building should ever be used by conspirators against the King, and become synonymous for disloyalty to the King, was the very last purpose that its founder intended it to be used for, yet by the strange irony of fate Faneuil Hall became known to the world as the "Cradle of Liberty" in which the Revolution was rocked. The town also voted to purchase the "Arms of Peter Faneuil and Fix them up in Faneuil Hall." Only a few years passed when the very people he had so benefited by his bounty tore down his "Arms" and portraits, and showed the most violent marks of disrespect to the memory of him who had been their best friend, but it was unreasonable violence that moved the mob who called themselves patriots. Faneuil Hall is a permanent memorial of the Huguenots of Boston and with the exception of a few crumbling gravestones it is the only visible monument of their residence here.

Peter Faneuil died in 1742 and left his vast fortune to his two nephews, Peter and Benjamin Faneuil the younger, the latter being an eminent merchant and was one of the consignees of the tea that was destroyed by the mob. The following letter sent to him by the "patriots" at that time undoubtedly expresses the feelings and the sentiment of those who formed the "Boston Tea Party." The letter he said was found in his entry.

"Gentlemen, It is currently reported that you are in the extremest anxiety respecting your standing with the good people of this Town and Province, as commissioners of the sale of the monopolized and dutied tea. We do not wonder in the least that your apprehensions are terrible, when the most enlightened humans and conscientious community on the earth view you in the light of tigers or mad dogs, whom the public safety obliges them to destroy. Long have this people been irreconcilable to the idea of spilling human blood, on almost any occasion whatever, but they have lately seen a penitential thief suffer death for pilfering a few pounds, from scattering individuals you boldly avow a resolution to bear a principal part in the robbing of every inhabitant of this country, in the present and future ages of every thing dear and interesting to them. Are there no laws in the Book of God and nature that enjoin such miscreants to be cut off from among the people, as troublers of the whole congregation. Yea, verily, there are laws and officers to put them into execution, which you can neither corrupt, intimidate, nor escape, and whose resolu-

* See Boston Town Records 1742 to 1757. Pp. 14, 15, 16. Printed by the City of Boston.

tion to bring you to condign punishment you can only avoid by a speedy imitation of your brethren in Philadelphia. This people are still averse to precipitate your fate, but in case of much longer delay in complying with their indispensable demands, you will not fail to meet the just rewards of your avarice and insolence. Remember, gentlemen, this is the last warning you are ever to expect from the insulted, abused and most indignant vindicators of violated liberty in the Town of Boston.

Thursday evening 9 o'clock,
Nov. 4, 1773.   O. C. Secy. per order.
To Messrs. the Tea Commissioners,
Directed to B—— —F—— Esq."*

The Faneuils did not lack patriotism. They counselled prudence until the country was prepared for action in a constitutional way. They were entirely opposed to mob violence, and their patriotism took a reasonable practical form, looking to the best interests of all. Further they had no angry feelings against the English; they had too recently been received and protected by them when their own country turned them out. They always spoke of the English as a great nation. They admired their liberality as to religious opinions in which France was wanting.

BENJAMIN FANEUIL the elder previously referred to, the father of Peter and Benjamin, the younger, and Mary died at Cambridge in 1785 aged 84.

PETER FANEUIL his son, who shared with his brother the vast fortune left them by their uncle went to Canada at the outbreak of the Revolution and then to the West Indies.

BENJAMIN FANEUIL found that it was necessary for his safety to leave Boston. He went to Halifax with the fleet when Boston was invaded on March 17, 1776, he afterwards went to England where he had $300,000 in English funds, with which he entertained his friends, the less fortunate refugees. In writing to a friend he said, "When we shall be able to return to Boston I cannot say, but hope and believe it will not exceed one year, for sooner or later America will be conquered, that you may depend on." He, however, was destined never to return but was proscribed and banished. He resided at Bristol where he died in 1785. His wife Jane was the daughter of Addington Davenport. The Faneuil name has become extinct; there are, however, numerous descendants through the female. Mary Faneuil, daughter of Benjamin Faneuil the elder became the wife of George Bethune, Oct. 13. 1754, and died in 1797, leaving many descendants. Mary Ann Faneuil, sister of Peter, who built the hall, married John Jones, who died at Roxbury in 1767, and whose son Edward died in Boston in 1835 at the age of 83. She was a loyalist, and resided for some time in Windsor, Nova Scotia. A letter from her son dated at Boston, June 23, 1783, advising her if de-

* Tea Leaves, pp. 292-3.

sirous of returning, not to come directly to Boston, as the law was still in force; but first to some other State and thence to Boston.*

THE COFFIN FAMILY OF BOSTON.

ADMIRAL SIR ISAAC COFFIN, SIR THOMAS ASTON COFFIN, ADMIRAL FROMAN H. COFFIN, GENERAL JOHN COFFIN.

The name of Coffin is widely spread over this continent; thousands take pride in tracing their descent from Tristram Coffin of Alwington, which extends along the Severn Sea, south of the boundary between Somerset and Devon, fronting the broad Atlantic.

The Coffins came over with William the Conqueror and settled there in 1066. It is said that the name Coffin was a corruption or translation of Colvinus, signifying a basket or chest, and that from the charge of the King's treasure, such employment, like royalty itself, being hereditary, the name became attached to the family. In 1085, according to the "Doomsday Book," Alwington was possessed by David De la Bere, and that the heiress of that name brought it to the Coffins. On a subject less grave this might be suspected for a jest but the authority is proof. Tristram came over to New England in 1642 and settled at Salisbury, and also at Haverhill and Newbury. He resided at these places for sixteen years and then went to Nantucket, which at that time was a dependency of New York. For 80 pounds he and his associates bought of the Indians a large part of the island. Tristram's third son, James, was Judge of the Court of Common Pleas and of Probate. James' son, Nathaniel, married the daughter of William Gayer, and niece of Sir John Gayer. William, the eldest son of Nathaniel, born 1699, removed to Boston and became proprietor of the Bunch of Grapes Tavern in 1731. It was situated on King street at the corner of Mackerel lane, the site now occupied by the Exchange building, on the corner of State and Kilby streets. It was a tavern from 1640 to 1760, when the Great Fire swept everything away.

The Coffins were strong in numbers and near neighbors, along the principal thoroughfare, now Washington street, dwelt twenty families, descended from William Coffin, or their near kinfolk, who lived in constant intercourse. The patriarch, at four score, his vigor hardly abated, lived on this street near his son's house. His daughter, Elizabeth, married her cousin, Thomas C. Amory, who had bought the house opposite her father's, at the corner of Hollis street, built by Governor Belcher for his own use. He was one of the organizers of Trinity church in 1734 and was one of the first wardens of same. He lived in honor and affluence till he died in 1774, just before the war broke out, which saved him from witnessing the exile and widespread confiscation that awaited his

* Dealings with the Dead, p. 510.

sons. His children and their children counted about sixty when he died, but of his descendants bearing the name of Coffin, all have died out in Massachusetts. He had four sons, all staunch Loyalists, William, Nathaniel, John and Ebenezer. The daughters, Mrs. De Blois, Mrs. Amory, and Mrs. Dexter, married into the best families of Boston, and through love for their husbands took the other side. The sons were proscribed and banished by an Act of the Massachusetts Legislature.

WILLIAM COFFIN, JR., the eldest son of William, was born in Boston, April 11th, 1723. He was an Addresser of General Gage, was proscribed and banished. He accompanied the Royal Army to Halifax in 1776 on the evacuation of Boston.

SIR THOMAS ASTON COFFIN, Baronet, son of William, Jr., was born at Boston, March 31, 1754. He graduated at Harvard College in 1772. He was for a long time Secretary to Sir Guy Carleton, by whose side he sat in the last boat which left Castle Garden on the evacuation of New York, 25th Nov., 1783. When Sir Guy Carleton became Lord Dorchester and Governor of Quebec, 1784, Coffin accompanied him and by his influence was appointed in 1804 Secretary and Comptroller of Accounts of Lower Canada. At another part of his life he was Commissary General in the British Army. He went to England and died in London in 1810, very wealthy. He was grandfather to Mrs. Bolton, wife of Col. Bolton, R. A., who took an active part in the Red River Expedition of 1870.

WILLIAM COFFIN, the second son of William Coffin, Jr., was born in Boston, 1758, and died at Kingston, Canada, in 1804.

EBENEZER COFFIN, the third son of William Coffin, Jr., was born at Boston, 1763, went to South Carolina where he acquired property as a merchant and planter and was the father of Thomas Aston Coffin of Charleston, South Carolina, whose descendants, with an hereditary instinct, distinguished themselves by their chivalrous devotion to a failing cause in the late Confederate war.

NATHANIEL COFFIN, second eldest son of William, was born in Boston in 1725, graduated at Harvard College in 1744, received in 1750 an honorary degree at Yale. Brought up a merchant, he was early appointed King's Cashier of the Customs and acquired considerable property. He resided on the corner of Essex and Rainsford Lane, now Harrison avenue. The tide washed up to the garden wall. Near by in front, on what is now called Washington street, was the "Liberty Tree," where Captain Mackintosh and his "chickens," met to plan outrages upon loyal citizens.

In August, 1767, a flagstaff was erected which went through and above it highest branches. A flag hoisted on this was the notice for the assembling of the "Sons of Liberty" for action. In 1775, his son Nathaniel, and his friends cut it down, much to the disgust of Mackintosh who was known as the "First Captain General of Liberty Tree." On the building occupying its site is a stone bas-relief of the tree with an inscription on it. Nathaniel Coffin held one of the most lucrative positions under the crown, his acquaintances and friends were naturally among the government officials and the better class of the community. He had much to lose if he severed from his fealty to the mother country and, banishment and confiscation would be the penalty, if the disunionists succeeded.

NATHANIEL COFFIN was the last Receiver General and Cashier of his Majesty's Customs at the Port of Boston, he was an addresser of Hutchinson in 1774 and of Gage in 1775. With his family of three persons he accompanied the Royal Army to Halifax in 1776 and in July of that year embarked for England in the ship Aston Hall. In May, 1780, while returning, he died the day before the vessel arrived at New York. His wife was Elizabeth, daughter of Henry Barnes of Boston.

NATHANIEL COFFIN, JR., son of the aforesaid, was born in Boston in 1749. Was an Addresser of Hutchinson in 1774 and a Protester against the disunionists the same year. He was brought up to the bar, and succeeded well in his profession. As he took a prominent part on the side of the Government; and caused the "Liberty Tree" to be cut down, he was obliged to fly, or he would have been tarred and feathered. He employed a negro to assist him in cutting it down. A thousand dollars reward was offered by the Revolutionists for the offender, the darky informed against him, and he had to leave.* He was at New York in 1783, and was one of the petitioners for lands in Nova Scotia. At a subsequent period he was appointed Collector of Customs at the island of St. Kitt's and filled that position for thirty-four years. He died in London in 1831, aged 83.

WILLIAM COFFIN, second son of Nathaniel, the Cashier. An Addresser of Hutchinson in 1774; went to Halifax in 1776, proscribed and banished, 1778. Assisted his brother in destroying the "Liberty Tree." He had three sons in the British service. After the peace, he was at St. John, New Brunswick, a prosperous merchant.

GENERAL JOHN COFFIN, the third son of Nathaniel, the Cashier, was born in Boston, 1756, was sent to sea at a very early age, and at the age of eighteen was in command of a ship. In 1775, while his ship was in England, she was engaged by the government to take troops to America. He had on board nearly a whole regiment with General Howe in command of the troops, who was ordered out to supersede General Gage at Boston. The vessel arrived at Boston June 15th. Mr. Coffin landed the regiment on June 17th at Bunker Hill, and the action having already commenced, he was requested by the Colonel, "to come up and see the fun," the only weapon at hand being the tiller of his boat; he immediately, to use a nautical phrase, "unshipped it," and with equal determination, commenced "laying about" him, and "shipped" the musket, powder and belt of the first man he knocked down. He bore an active part and distinguished himself during the rest of the action. In consideration of his gallant conduct he was presented to General Gage after the battle and made an ensign on the field, shortly after he was promoted to a lieutenancy,

* "Memoir of General John Coffin." By Captain Henry Coffin, R. N., 1880, p. 17.

but still retained the command of his ship. He was promised by General Howe on his arrival at Boston the command of 400 men, if he would go to New York and raise them. He accordingly went to New York when Boston was evacuated March 17, 1776, where he raised among the Loyalists a mounted rifle corps, called the "Orange Rangers," of which he was made Commandant, and from which he exchanged into the New York Volunteers in 1778. He took part in the defeat of Washington in the battle of Long Island in 1777 and went with that corps to Georgia in 1778. Here he raised a corps of partisan cavalry, composed chiefly of loyal planters. At the battle of Savannah, at that of Hobkerk's Hill, and the action of Cross Creek near Charleston, and on various other occasions, his conduct won the admiration of his superior.

At the battle of Eutaw Springs which he opened on the part of the King's troops, his gallantry and good judgment attracted the notice and remark of General Greene, the Revolutionary leader, one of General Washington's ablest lieutenants. Major Coffin with 150 infantry and 50 cavalry averted the advance on Eutaw. Colonel William Washington, a distinguished partisan leader, with numerous cavalry rashly dashed forward; he lost most of his officers and many of his men, and his horse was shot under him, and he would have been slain had not Major Coffin interposed, who took him prisoner. These two men, who had known each other well in private life, rode back to camp to share the same meal and the same tent.

In the Southern colonies the Revolutionists and Loyalists, waged a war of extermination, the partisans on both sides, seldom gave quarter or took prisoners. At the close of the conflict in Virginia Lord Cornwallis made him a gift of a handsome sword, accompanied by a letter conferring on him the rank of Major Brevet. Whilst Coffin was attached to Cornwallis, he was able to be of great service to him, but the bravery, not to say the extraordinary sagacity mingled with audacity of one man, could not save the army. Lord Cornwallis' army cooped up in Yorktown by a superior army of French and Americans, and blockaded by a French fleet, was in danger of starvation, and Coffin stood almost alone in successful forays, in which he frequently eluded the whole American and French army, and returned laden with the fruits of his success. In one of these raids he accidently came to the house of a wealthy planter whose daughter was to be married that day. He quietly surrounded the house with his troops and knocking at the door, sent in word that he wished to speak with the proprietor. On presenting himself, the gentleman was courteously made aware of his condition. He was told not to make any noise, but to order sufficient turkeys, ham, wine and other provisions to be put up, to satisfy his men; if this was done no harm would happen, but on the contrary, if any resistance was attempted, everything and everybody in the house would be destroyed. Coffin's character and resolution were well known, so the planter thought it best to graciously comply with the mandate. A large quantity of provisions was thus secured.

Captain Coffin supped with the wedding party, danced with the bride, and left in safety, taking care that no alarm should be given, and reached Cornwallis without accident by daylight.

Even when the enemy held Charleston, during which time he ran very great risks of being taken prisoner, he went to see Miss Ann Matthews, daughter of William Matthews, Esq., of St. John's Island, to whom he was eventually married in 1781. On the occasion of one visit, the house was searched for him by authority, and the gallant soldier took refuge under Miss Matthews' ample dress. At that time ladies wore hoops and they must have been of considerable size, when Major Coffin, who stood six feet two and was proportionately stout, could successfully conceal himself under one. At the surrender of Cornwallis at Yorktown, that portion of his army consisting of native Americans, he failed to obtain special terms for, in the articles of capitulation. He, however, availed himself of the conceded privilege of sending an armed ship northerly, without molestation, to convey away the most obnoxious of them. Major Coffin determined not to be taken by the Revolutionists who had offered $10,000 for his head, so he cut his way through the lines, and reached Charleston, attracted by the charms of Miss Matthews. When Charleston was evacuated Major Coffin made his way up to New York, crossed the Hudson, having eluded all attempts at his capture and presented himself at headquarters, to the great astonishment of his friends in the British Army. Sir Guy Carleton, Commander-in-chief, appointed him Major of the King's American Regiment, vacant by the death of Major Grant.

Previous to the evacuation of New York, and probably in view of it, Major Coffin and others who were feared and disliked by the victorious Revolutionists, and were, therefore, thrust out beyond the pale of redemption, were sent by the British Government, to New Brunswick. At twenty-seven he laid down his sword and took up his axe, accompanied by a wife delicately nurtured in a wealthy family and a warm climate, and four negroes, one woman and three men, all brought from Charleston. They arrived in October, 1783, when there were but two persons in or near the harbor of St. John. Mr. Symonds and Mr. White, fur-traders, kindly supplied the newcomers with provisions, and they immediately commenced clearing and felling timber. During the first winter they suffered great hardships, particularly Mrs. Coffin. His first mishap was the loss of his boots in crossing a swamp, now the market place of the city of St. John. Having selected some lots of ground fronting the harbor, he proceeded to explore the interior of the country. An ascent of about twelve miles up the beautiful St. John, opened out a rich and lovely landscape-hill and dale, magnificent woods, rivers and lakes, swarming with game and fish.

In this fine and fertile locality Major Coffin purchased for a trifle a tract of land from Colonel Grazier, to whom it had been granted by Government. Four men were sent up there to build a house, and in the following May, 1784, he and his wife and four black servants, took possession of their new residence, and called it Alwington Manor, after the family estate in Devonshire, which belonged to them in the time of William the Conqueror. Two of the men, and the woman, proved to be good and faithful servants, and when the slaves were emancipated, still remained with the family.

Settlers soon flocked into the province. Ten years' residence, with Major Coffin's activity, aided by his willing men, made it a respectable and desirable settlement. He was made a Magistrate of the county and in due time a Member of the Provincial Parliament, and of the Legislative Council, which offices he filled till within a few years of his death.

In June, 1794, His Royal Highness, the Duke of Kent, the father of Queen Victoria, who was then Governor of Nova Scotia, stopped at Alwington Manor.

Although retired from active employ, he still remained in the service on half pay, and in 1804 he was advanced to the rank of Lieutenant Colonel. In 1805 he went to England, where he was received with much distinction, and was presented to the King by the commander-in-chief.

The war of 1812 aroused all the warlike instincts of the old partisan; he snuffed the battle afar off, and at once offered to raise a regiment for home service. He soon had 600 men ready for service, which enabled the Government to send the 104th regiment to Canada, then hardly pressed by invasion. At the peace of 1815 he was promoted to the rank of Major-General, and the regiment disbanded and General Coffin returned to half pay once more.

He for many years alternated in his residence between England and New Brunswick. He was the oldest General in the British Army when he died in 1838, aged 82, at the house of his son, Admiral T. Coffin, in King's County, New Brunswick.

Those who knew the General well in his later days, recall with affectionate recollection the noble presence and generous character of the chivalrous old soldier, a relic of the days in which giants were in stature and in heart, true to his king and country, a humble Christian and an honest and brave man, who united to the heroism of a Paladin the endurance of the pioneer, and when he could no longer serve his Prince in the field, served him still better by creating a new realm of civilization and progress in the heart of primeval forest. His name will ever be held in honor in New Brunswick.

Eight of the children of General and Mrs. Coffin, all natives of New Brunswick, lived to make their way in the world, thanks to a grateful government and helpful country. The eldest son, General Guy Carleton Coffin, died in 1856, a General of the Royal Artillery; John Townsend Coffin, the second eldest, entered the British Navy as midshipman in 1799 and became admiral in 1841. Under the will of his uncle, Sir Isaac Coffin, he became the owner of the Magdalen Islands in the Gulf of St. Lawrence. He died in 1882. Henry Edward Coffin, the third son, became a lieutenant

ADMIRAL SIR ISAAC COFFIN.

Born in Boston, 1759. Died in England, June 23, 1839. From a painting in possession of the Boston Atheneum.

in the British Navy in 1814 and an Admiral in 1856. He died in 1881. The eldest daughter, Caroline, married the Hon. Charles Grant of Canada, afterwards Baron de Longueuil; their son, the present Baron, married a daughter of Lewis Trapmane of Charleston, S. C. The second daughter married General Sir Thomas Pearson, K. C. B., an officer much distinguished in Canada during the war of 1812.

A third married Colonel Kirkwood of the British Army and went to live in Bath, England.

A fourth married John Barnett, Esq., also an officer in the British Army, who subsequently occupied a high official position in the Island of Ceylon.

The fifth, Mary, married Charles R. Ogden, Esq., Attorney-General, Lower Canada.

ADMIRAL SIR ISAAC COFFIN was the fourth son of Nathaniel, the Cashier. He was born in Boston in 1759. At eight years of age he entered the Boston Latin School. He was a diligent student in a class that embraced numerous celebrities and when in Parliament he acknowledged himself indebted to the methods and discipline of the Boston schools for his apt classical quotations, then a mode much in vogue in that august assemblage. His constitution was, however, too vigorous, his animal spirits too buoyant for scholarship alone to mark his schoolboy days. He led the sports of the playground and was the leader on the 5th of November, the anniversary of the Gunpowder plot. Boston was a pleasant place to dwell in, broad stretches of tree or turf, sloping pastures, and blooming gardens, surrounded the abodes of the wealthy. Tide water fresh from the ocean, spread nearly around the peninsular. Beyond these basins, wooded heights of considerable elevation lifted themselves above boundless tree tops. For fishing, or shooting, rowing, sailing, or swimming, coasting or skating, Boston with its environs of lake, and orchards, was then the paradise for boys. It was a capital school for his play hours, and the old Latin,—the oldest school in the country,—dating from 1635, for his studies of a graver sort. There fifteen of his cousins were his school mates, a host of his own celebrities and four—Scheaffe, Moreland, Mackay, and Ochterlony—who became baronets, or generals by military service in England, he was well placed for development nor were his opportunities neglected. At the commencement of the Revolution Isaac was too young to enter into it, or to realize what it meant, but long before he entered, at the age of fourteen, the British navy, he no doubt had formed opinions of his own.* It was doubtless of advantage to him, quickening his faculties and maturing his character, that such events were transpiring about him at this plastic period. His sense of justice and right

* It is a singular fact that all persons of American birth that were in the navy remained loyal. Washington came very near entering the navy as midshipman and going with his brother Lawrence under Admiral Vernon to the attack on Cartagena. His trunk was packed and he was all ready to depart when his mother prevailed upon him to remain. Had he gone he would have remained loyal, or his case would have been the exception.

and of what freedom signified, proved in his subsequent career that these advantages had not been without effect.

At the age of fourteen Isaac entered the Royal navy under the auspices of Rear Admiral Montague. By him he was confided to the care of Lieutenant William Hunter, at that time commanding the Brig Gaspee and who then spoke of his pupil, "Of all the young men I ever had the care of, none answered my expectations equal to Isaac Coffin. He pleased me so much that I took all the pains in my power to make him a good seaman, and I succeeded to the height of my wishes, for never did I know a young man acquire so much nautical knowledge in so short a time." After serving on the Gaspee he served as midshipman on the Kingfisher, Captain, Diligent, Fowey, Le Pincon and the Sybl, frigate. In 1779 Coffin, now Lieutenant, went to England and joined the Adamant. His next appointment was to the London of 98 guns, the flagship of Rear Admiral Graves on the coast of America, from her he removed into the Royal Oak where he acted as signal lieutenant in the action off Cape Henry, March 16, 1781. By following such traces the naval histories of Great Britain afford of these several ships, we can reasonably conjecture the part Coffin took in the Revolutionary War. We learn what duties were performed by him on each of them, and we have no reason to doubt, from his rapid promotions, of his efficiency and zeal. We know that his patron, Admiral Montague, protected the rear of Howe's retreat from Boston in 1776, that the ships were often engaged with the enemy, and that they captured several valuable prizes in which action he participated. The events of the first four years of the war from 1775 to 1779 are sufficiently familiar. D'Estraing's repulse at Savannah and Prescott's evacuation of Newport in 1779, its reoccupation by Tiernay in July 1780. The reduction of Charleston, defeat of Gates at Camden. Capture at sea of Henry Laurens, president of Congress. After the surrender of Cornwallis at Yorktown to the combined French and American armies and French fleet. De Grasse hastened to the West Indies intending to join the Spaniards, and capture Jamaica and drive the English out of the West Indies. After the battle of March 16 at Cape Henry, on the return to New York, the Royal Oak took several valuable prizes, and then went to Halifax for repairs. In the middle of June a vessel arrived from Bristol with the remains of his father, who died the day before. Having held an important government position, his obsequies in New York on Broadway showed due regard to his memory. Isaac was placed soon after in command of Avenger, the advanced post of the British up the North River, which he held during the autumn till he exchanged with Sir Alexander Cochrane, for the Pocahontas and joined Admiral Hood at Barbados and served on his flagship, the Barfleur. Soon after Coffin joined him he learned that De Grasse was at St. Kitts, after an engagement there in which the French lost one thousand men, Hood joined Lord Rodney's fleet.

For two days the hostile fleets manoeuvered in sight of each other near Dominica. In number the fleets were equal, in size and complement of crew the French were immensely superior; they had twenty thousand soldiers on board to be used in the conquest of Jamaica; a defeat at this time would be England's ruin. The English Admiral was aware that his country's fate was in his hands. It was one of those supreme moments which great men dare to use and weak ones tremble at. At seven in the morning, April 12, 1782, the signal to engage was flying at the masthead of the Formidable Rodney's flagship. The Admiral lead in person and in passing through the enemy's line engaged the Glorieux, a 74, at close range. He shot away her masts and bowsprit and left her a bare hull. All day long the cannons roared and one by one the French ships struck their flags or fought till they sank. The carnage on them was terrible, crowded as they were with troops. Fourteen thousand were reckoned as killed besides the prisoners. The Barfleur, Hood's flagship, on which was Coffin engaged the "Ville de Paris," the flagship of the French Admiral, the pride of France, and the largest ship in the world. After fighting valiantly all day, after all hope was gone, and a broadside from the Barfleur had killed sixty men, she surrendered. Her decks above and below were littered over with mangled limbs and bodies. It was said when she struck there were but three men on the upper deck unhurt, the Count was one. The French fleet was totally destroyed, and so on that memorable day Yorktown was avenged, and the British empire was saved. Peace followed but it was peace wth honor. The American Colonies were lost but England kept her West Indies. The hostile strength of Europe all combined had failed to wrest Britannia's ocean sceptre from her. She sat down, maimed and bleeding, but the wreath had not been torn from her brows. She was and is still the sovereign of the seas. After the battle Captain Coffin went in his sloop to Jamaica, where through the influence of Hood, he was appointed by Lord Rodney captain of the Shrewsbury, of 74 guns; he was then only 22 years of age. This indicated the estimate of both Hood and Rodney of the value of his services in the late famous battle. Peace soon came, but there was much to discourage him. His family was broken up. The remains of his father lay in their last resting place in New York. The Shrewsbury was paid off, and he was put out of commission. He was his own master with abundance of prize money. Many of his family and friends from Boston had taken up their abode in London, and the refugee loyalists formed there a large circle. They all liked Isaac, a handsome young fellow with pleasant ways, generous and unpretending and loaded with laurels. He was held in high estimation by the great naval celebrities and by the public, their attention might have turned the head of one less sensible.

Sir Guy Carleton, who had been created Lord Dorchester, could hardly have saved Canada for the Crown in 1775 without the aid of the Coffins, was now appointed Governor of Canada. It was probably at his request that Isaac was appointed to the command of the Thisbe, to take him and his family and suite to Quebec in 1786. While on his way up the river to Quebec the Thisbe was becalmed off the Magdalen Islands, and struck by their appearance, perhaps the more attractive from the autumnal splendor, Coffin requested, probably not in very serious earnest, that Lord Dorchester as representative of the Crown, would bestow them on him. This request seemed reasonable to the governor, and eventually letters patent were granted to him on the Islands. The records recite the grant of the islands to him for his zeal and unremitting persevering efforts in the public service. At Sir Isaac's death he left the island by will to his nephew, Admiral John T. Coffin, who died in 1882. On his return to Europe he was employed in many branches of the service. In 1794 he was in charge of the Melampus frigate, in 1796 he was resident commissioner of Corsica. From Elba he removed to Lisbon, to take charge of the naval establishment there for the next two years. He was then dispatched to superintend the arsenal at Port Mahon when Minorca fell into the hands of the British, and from there to Nova Scotia, in the Venus frigate. At Halifax and afterwards at Sheerness, as resident commissioner, he was employed till April 1804, when appointed rear admiral he hoisted his flag on the Gladiator, and the following month was created a baronet.

March, 1811, he married Elizabeth Browne, but within a few years satisfied of their utter incompatibility, they very amicably, on both sides, arranged for independence of each other. She was said to be addicted to writing sermons at night to the disturbance of the slumber of her rollicking spouse. The fault was certainly not hers, for she was a clever and exemplary woman. She lived nearly as long as he did, but they rarely met, though he made repeated overtures to reconcilliation, some rather amusing. It is the reasonable ambition of all Englishmen, whose conditions and circumstances justify such aspirations, to be permitted to take part in the legislation and government of the country, and when Sir Isaac's health and peace rendered active service in the navy no longer desirable, his wish was gratified by his return to Parliament in 1818 for the borough of Ilchester for which he sat till 1826. His reputation and experience, gave considerable weight to his opinion when he took part as he frequently did in debates on naval affairs. He was tall, robust, but of symmetrical proportions, his voice powerful, and his countenance expressive and noble. Sir Isaac died at Cheltenham in Gloucestershire, June 23, 1839, at the age of 80. Lady Coffin preceded him to the tomb on the 27th of January that year. His brother, General John Coffin, died the year previous, June 12, 1838, in New Brunswick. Sir Isaac made frequent visits to his native town, having made more than thirty voyages to and from America. The many brilliant gentlemen of Boston in professional life, or among its merchant princes, affluent and convivial, were pleased to have him as their guest. Loyalty to the mother country died out slowly, and a Boston born boy, who had attained great distinction, whose kinsfolk had ample means for hospitality, had much attention paid him. His kinsman, Thomas C. Amory writes, "Often when at my father's, who resided in Park street, where now is the Union Club house, the festal entertainments extended into the small hours, and those upon whom it devolved to sit up to receive the roisters, would gladly welcome from for off his shout of 'Home ahoy!' breaking the silent watches of the night."

His prize money amounted to considerable. This he entrusted to his cousin Amory in Boston, and the income finally equalled the original deposit.

He was very generous to his native land. Soon after the war ended he established a schoolship in Massachusetts waters, for mates and skippers to learn the art of navigation. The barge Clio which he purchased for the purpose, was commanded by his kinsman, Captain Hector Coffin, who was imprudent enough in 1826 to go up in her to Quebec with the American flag flying and act in a very indiscreet manner, and when his brother, General John Coffin, of New Brunswick, urged him to abandon what gave umbrage at home, he acquiesced in giving up what had cost him several thousand pounds. He also sent over to the land of his birth famous race horses and cattle to improve the breed; also fish, rare fruit and plants.

He was warmly attached to Nantucket, where his ancestors and their descendants had dwelt for many generations. He visited the place and became acquainted with his kinsfolk and in 1826 appropriated $12,000 afterwards increased till now it is upwards of $60,000, as a fund for a school for the instruction of the posterity of Tristram. This includes nearly every native born child of the island. The Duke of Clarence, William the Fourth, who succeeded his brother George to the throne, through his long connection with the navy, attached to him the officers who had grown old with him. It is said the King had Sir Isaac upon his list as Earl of Magdalen and intended to make him Governor of Canada, and the only obstacle that prevented it was the attachment he had for the land of his birth.

This memoir of a Boston boy, who by dint of his own native energy attained a title, and the highest rank in the British navy, and a generous benefactor, whose works still bear witness to the noble impulse that prompted them, will ever be kindly remembered and cherished by his countrymen.

Jonathan Perry Coffin, Sir Isaac's youngest brother, born in Boston in 1762, was a barrister of repute in London.

JOHN COFFIN, the third son of William and Ann Coffin, was born in Boston, August 19, 1729, and was brother of Nathaniel, the Cashier, and uncle of General John, and Admiral, Sir Isaac Coffin. In the confiscation Act he was described as distiller, and combined this business, no doubt, with that of merchant and ship owner. Loyal to the core, and knowing that he was a marked man, he resolved early in 1775, to place his family in safety. Embarking, therefore, his household goods, his wife and eleven children, on board his own schooner, the Neptune, he brought them around safely to Quebec where on the 23d August, 1775, he bought from "La Dame Veuve Lacroix" a piece of land at the *pres de ville*, well known during the siege which followed as the "Potash." He went to work with characteristic energy to establish a distillery, when his work was interrupted by that celebrated event. In the autumn the Revolutionary forces under Arnold and a former British officer, Montgomery, invaded the Province, and Quebec was invested. Late in the year John Coffin joined the Quebec enrolled British militia and the building he had designed for a distillery, became a battery for the defence of the approach from Wolfe's cove. The battery was armed with the guns of a privateer frozen in for the winter. Her commander, Barnsfare, and his seamen handled the pieces, and by his side John Coffin, the Boston Loyalist, shared the merit of the defence.

Before that battery, on the memorable morning of the 1st January, 1776, fell, General Montgomery, and the chief officers of his staff, and with them the last hopes of the Revolutionary cause in Canada.

In a paper prepared by his nephew, Lieutenant-Colonel Coffin of Ottawa, read before the Literary and Historical society of Quebec Dec. 18, 1872, it is shown on the testimony of Sir Guy Carleton, then Governor of Canada, and of Colonel Maclean, Commandant of Quebec, "that to the resolution and watchfulness of John Coffin, in keeping the guard at the *pres de ville* under arms, awaiting the expected attack, the coolness with which he allowed the rebels to approach, the spirits which his example kept up among the men, and to the critical instant when he directed Captain Barnsfare's fire against Montgomery and his troops, is to be ascribed the repulse of the rebels from that important post where, with their leader, they lost all heart."

There can be no question but that the death of Montgomery and the repulse of this attack, saved Quebec, and with Quebec, British North America to the British Crown, and that of the brave men who did this deed John Coffin was one of the foremost.

John Coffin died September 28, 1808, aged 78, as the record of his burial has it, "One of His Majesty's Justices of the Peace of the City of Quebec and Inspector of Police for said City."

He had thirteen children born to him, 11 survived him. Directly, or indirectly, all throve under the fostering protection of the Crown and a grateful government. The eldest daughter, Isabella, married Colonel McMurdo. Her sons served in India, a grandson was captain in the Royal Canadian Rifles, when that fine regiment disbanded at Kingston in 1870.

The second daughter, Susannah, married the Hon. John Craigie of Quebec, Provincial Treasurer, a brother of Lord Craigie, Lord of Sessions in Scotland. One son, Admiral Craigie, died in 1872. A daughter married Captain Martin, who led one of the storming parties at the capture of Fort Niagara in 1814.

MARGARET, the youngest daughter, married her cousin, Roger Hale

Sheaffe. At the time of the marriage he was major in Brock's regiment. That gallant officer was slain at Queenstown Heights at 7 o'clock in the morning. At noon Colonel Sheaffe moved up from Niagara, attacked the American forces and hurled them from the rocks into the river. For this great service he was made a Baronet.

Of John Coffin's sons, the oldest, JOHN, born in Boston in 1760, died Deputy Commissary-General at Quebec, March, 1837.

WILLIAM, the second son, born in Boston, 1761, obtained a commission in the 1st Battalion of the King's Royal Regiment. Subsequently through the kind influence of His Royal Highness, the Duke of Kent, he obtained a commission in the regular army and served half the world over. He retired from the service in 1816 a captain in the 15th Regiment and Brevet Major, and died in England in 1836. His son WILLIAM FOSTER COFFIN, was Commissioner of Ordnance and Admiralty, Land Department of the Interior, Canada. This gentleman married, in 1842, MARGARET, second daughter of Isaac Winslow Clarke, of Montreal, who, in 1774, was the youngest member of the firm of Richard Clarke and Sons of Boston, to which was consigned the historical cargo of tea. He rose to the rank of Deputy Commissary General, and after 50 years service died in 1822.

The third son, THOMAS COFFIN, born in Boston, 1762, was a member of the Legislative Council of Lower Canada, and Lieutenant-Colonel of Militia. He married a Demoiselle de Tonancour and lived and died at Three Rivers, 1841. A son of his was for many years Prothonotary for the District of Montreal.

The fifth son, FRANCIS HOLMES COFFIN, born in Boston, 1768, entered the Royal Navy and served during the long war with France, and died an Admiral in 1835. His eldest son, General Sir Isaac Coffin, K. C. Star of India, died at Black Heath, October, 1872.

The fourth son, NATHANIEL COFFIN, born in Boston, 1766, lived and died in Upper Canada. In the war of 1812 he joined the volunteer companies and was aide-de-camp to Sir Roger Sheaffe at the battle of Queenstown Heights, where General W. Scott was taken prisoner. He became Adjutant General of Militia in Upper Canada. He died at Toronto in 1835.

The sixth son, JAMES, born in Boston, 1771, died at Quebec in 1835, Assistant Commissary-General.

These Boston men and women, sons and daughters of brave John Coffin, are all living instances of the loyal faith in which they were born, and of its honorable and just reward of a grateful and kind government, and is but one case of many which goes to show that the Americans who were loyal, as a body fared infinitely better than the Revolutionists who were successful. It is proverbial that republics are ungrateful.

Today their descendants are organized as the United Empire Loyalists and count it an honor that their ancestors suffered persecution and exile rather than yield the principals and the ideal of union with Great

Britain. They have made of the land of their exile a mighty member of the great British empire, they begin to glory in the days of trial through which they passed.

LIST OF JOHN COFFIN'S CONFISCATED ESTATES IN SUFFOLK COUNTY AND TO WHOM SOLD.

To Christopher Clark, Aug. 9, 1783; Lib. 139 fol. 151; Land in Boston, Essex St. S.; Short St. W.; Joseph Ford E.; Thomas Snow N.

To Moses Wallack, Mar. 12, 1785; Lib. 146 fol. 260; Land in Boston, Essex St. S.; said Wallack W.; S. and W.; Blind Lane N.; Thomas Downes and Samuel Bradley E.

To Edward Jones, Feb. 13, 1786; Lib. 155 fol. 111; Land in Boston, Essex St. N.; the sea S.; sugar house and land of heirs of Thomas Child deceased E.; Mary Pitman and heirs of Samuel Bradley W.; with flats to low water mark.

JUDGE SAMUEL CURWEN.

The paternal ancestry of Samuel Curwen, the subject of this sketch were for many centuries amongst the leading families in the county of Cumberland, in the north of England, where the family seat Workington Hall still remains, George Curwin his immediate ancestor was an early emigrant to New England, having established his residence in Salem in 1638. He was highly esteemed for his active, and energetic character, and for several years represented Salem in the "General Court" or Legislature of. the colony. He also commanded a squadron of horse in the Indian wars and assisted in checking the inroads of the savage enemy. He died at Salem in 1685 at the age of 74 years, leaving a large estate. His son Jonathan was of the provincial council named in the second charter granted by William and Mary in 1691, and a judge of the superior court of the province. He married a daughter of Sir Henry Gibbs and their son George was the father of the subject of this sketch. George Curwin graduated at Harvard College in 1701 and was pastor of a church at Salem. He died in 1717 at the early age of thirty-five years. The subject of this memoir was born in 1715 and graduated at Harvard College in 1735. In 1738 he traveled in England and the Continent. On his return he engaged in commercial pursuits with success. His business was subsequently interrupted by the depredation of French cruisers fitted out from Louisburg. In 1744-5 Mr. Curwin as a captain and his brother as a commissary joined an expedition for the reduction of that stronghold. The result of the expedition was completely successful, and reflected great credit on the participators in it.

Annexed is a cut of the Curwin House, Salem, erected by Captain Curwin in 1642, now known as the witch house. The unfortunate persons arrested during the witchcraft delusion were examined in this house by Justices Jonathan Curwin and Hawthorn before being committed.

At the commencement of the Revolution Samuel Curwin was Judge of Admiralty and had been in the commission of the peace for thirty years. He was one of the signers of the address to Governor Hutchinson when he went to England. This gave great offence to the disunionists, they attempted to compel him to make public recantations in the newspapers. This he refused to do, saying that the prescribed

CURWIN HOUSE, SALEM. ERECTED IN 1642.

recantation contained more than in conscience he could own, and that to live under the character of reproach, which the fury of the mob might throw upon him, was too painful a reflection to suffer for a moment. He therefore resolved to withdraw from the impending storm. He accordingly embarked for Philadelphia on the 23rd of April, 1775, and thence to London on the 13th of the following month. While in exile he kept a journal, which has been published. No work extant contains so much information of the unfortunate Loyalists while aboard. The journal commences at Philadelphia, May 4th, 1775, and says: "Since the unhappy affairs at Concord and Lexington, finding the spirit of the people to rise on every fresh alarm, (which has been almost hourly) and their temper to get more and more soured and malevolent against all moderate men, who they see fit to reproach as enemies of their country by the name of tories, among whom I am unhappily (although unjustly) ranked, and unable longer to bear their undeserved reproaches and menace, hourly denounced against myself, and others, I think it a duty I owe to myself to withdraw for a while from the storm, which to my foreboding mind is approaching. Having in vain endeavored to persuade my wife to accompany me, her apprehensions of danger from an incensed soldiery, a people licentious, and enthusiastically mad, and broke loose from all the restraints of law or religion, being less terrible to her than a short passage on the ocean, and being moreover encouraged by her, I left my late peaceful home (in my sixtieth year) in search of personal security, and those rights which by the laws of God I ought to have enjoyed undisturbed there, and embarked at Beverly on board the schooner Lively, Captain Johnson, bound hither, on Sunday the 23rd ultimo, and have just arrived. Hoping to find an asylum among quakers and Dutchmen, who I presume from former experience have too great a regard for ease and property to sacrifice either at this time of doubtful disputation on the altar of an unknown goddess or rather doubtful divinity."

On landing he writes I went in pursuit of lodgings, and on enquiring at several houses, ascertained they were full or for particular reasons would not take me in; and so many refused, as made it fearful whether like Cain I had not a discouraging mark upon me, or a strong feature of toryism. The whole city appears to be deep in congressional principles and inveterate against *"Hutchinson Addressers."* Under date of May 9th, 1775, he writes, "Dined with Stephen Collins. Passed the evening at Joseph Reed's in company with Col. Washington (a fine figure and of most easy and agreeable address) Richard Henry Lee, and Col. Harrison, three of the Virginia delegates. Besides Mr. and Mrs. Reed, were Mrs. Deberatt, Dr. Shippen and Thomas Smith. I staid till twelve o'clock, the conversation being chiefly on the most feasible and prudent method of stopping up the channel of the Deleware to prevent the coming up of any large ships to the city. I could not perceive the least disposition to accommodate matters." He wrote, "Having had several intimations that my residence here would be unpleasant, if allowed at all, when it shall be known that I am what is called *'an addresser'* I have therefore consulted the few friends I think it worth while to advise with, and on the result am determined to proceed to London in the vessel in which I came here."

Following is a brief description of the journal, which Curwin kept while in England, the four hundred and more pages contain matters of the deepest interest to those who are interested in the lives of those Loyalists who returned to England, July 3, 1775. "On landing at Dover, visited the Castle. Next day arrived at the New England Coffee House, Threadneedle Street. Visited Westminster Hall with my friend Benjamin Pickering. Went to old Jewery meeting-house where I met Gov. Hutchinson, and his son and daughter, and received a cordial reception and invitation to visit him. There is an army of New Englanders here. Evening to Vauxhall Gardens. Spent the day at Hempstead in company with Isaac Smith, Samuel Quincy, David Greene, and P. Webster. I am just informed of the most melancholy event, the destruction of Charlestown by the King's troops, of great carnage among the officers. My distress and anxiety for my friends and countrymen embitter every hour. By invitation dined at Grocers' Company feast, at their hall in the Poultry. Dined with Governor Hutchinson in company with Mr. Joseph Green, Mr. Manduit and Mr. Ward Nicholas Boylston. It is a capital mistake of our American friends to expect insurrections here, there is not a shadow of hope for such an event. It is said most vigorous measures will take place in the spring, if no offer be made on the part of the colonies. Visited Hampton Court, and Gardens. Thence to Windsor. From the terrace we saw almost under out feet Eaton college. Saw Mr. Garrick in Hamlet at Drury Lane. To the Herald's office where Parson Peters, with his friend Mr. Punderson lodges, the latter has lately arrived from Boston. It seems he was harshly dealt with by the *sons of liberty*, being obliged to make two confessions to save his life notwithstanding which he was hunted, pursued, and threatened, and narrowly escaped death (or the Simsbury mines to which he was finally adjudged, and he thinks with the loss of his eyes) which would have been his fate but for his seasonable and providential retreat.* At Chapel Royal, St. James, saw the king and queen, who joined in the service with becoming devotion. Bishop of London preached. To the Adelphia, Strand, where by appointment met twenty-one of my countrymen, who have agreed on a weekly dinner here, viz., Messrs. Richard Clark, Joseph Green, Jonathan Bliss, Jonathan Sewell, Joseph Waldo, S. S. Blowers, Elisha Hutchinson, Wm. Hutchinson, Samuel Sewell, Samuel Quincy, Isaac Smith, Harrison Grey, David Green, Jonathan Clark, Thomas Flucker, Joseph Taylor, Daniel Silsbee, Thomas Brindley, William Cabot, John S. Copley and Nathaniel Coffin, Samuel Porter, Edward Oxnard, Benj. Pickman, Jno. Amory, Judge Robert Auchmuty and Major Urquhart, absent, are members of this New England club, as is also Gov. Hutchinson. At Parson Peters saw Mr. Troutbeck, lately arrived from Halifax, and Mr. Wiswall, mutually invited each other to visit and gave cards. Drank tea at Mr. Green's in company with Gov. Hutchinson, whom I had not seen for some weeks, and who expressed an uneasiness at my neglect to call. I called at Mr. Copley's to see Mr. Clark and the family who kindly pressed my staying to tea. Was presented to Mr. West, a Philadelphian, a most masterly hand in historic painting. Mr. West is the king's history painter. Called on my friend

* For description of Simsbury mines see pp. 56-57.

Browne. He acquainted me with some facts relative to the unfortunate abandonment of Boston by the king's troops, which has all the appearance of being forced. Would to God this illjudged, unnatural quarrel was ended.

"Went to Shepton Mallet.* Walked to the market-cross, an open structure supported by Gothic arches and pillars, and ornamented in front by a few mutilated statues, but whether of saints or heroes of antiquity, I know not. A few gentlemen of fortune live here, but many worthy clothiers. Walked with Mr. Morgan over the hills to the remains of Roman-way, the ditch continues, although in an imperfect state, and carried over the Meridep hills, running from north to south and from shore to shore. Rode to Bath. Met Col. Saltonstall who with Mr. Boyleston has taken lodgings here for sometime past. Visited Glastonbury Abbey ruins. In the Bristol Gazette is the following: "Gov. Howe has landed the British army and taken possession of New York on the 15th of September, the provincials had fled from the city with great precipitation, towards Kingsbridge.' There have been some discouraging accounts from France, respecting the intention of that court to assist the colonies, and advices from Spain say their ports are open to the English colonists. Received a letter informing me of my wife's health, and that she had been obliged to pay ten pounds sterling to find a man for the American army in my stead. Dec. 14. This day, General Burgoyne's mortifying capitulation arrived in town. We all know the General's bravery, and skill. He did not surrender whilst there was a possibility of defence. On confirmation of the American news, Manchester offered to raise a thousand men at their own expense, to be ready for service in America in two months, and was soon followed after by Liverpool. It is said there are to be proposals for raising two thousand men out of each parish through the kingdom.

"Lord North has proposed terms of reconciliation, but nothing short of independency will go down with the colonies. France will support them, all thoughts of conquest, of unconditional submission, be assured are given up. 'I am fully convinced the colonies will never find any good purpose answered by independence. God only knows what is before us. I cannot review the state of Great Britain four years since, and regard the present crisis without horrer, without trembling. France and Spain are armed from head to foot at all points ready to sally forth. Heard the dreaded sound, war declared against France.

Exeter, Sept. 6. Am informed that I am suspected to be an American spy disaffected to government. Have heard that Paul Jones in the French king's service, has taken a forty-four gun frigate, and entered the harbor of Hull and destroyed sixteen ships.

Visited Col. Erving and family, afterwards dined and took tea with my worthy friend Judge Sewall, his company Mr. and Mrs. Faneuil. From thence I went to see Mrs. Gardner, her husband the doctor, and

* The native town of the author, J. H. Stark.

their daughter Love Eppes. Meeting Colonel Oliver, late lieutenant-governor of Massachusetts, he informed me of his residence.

Visited Mr. Lechmere, drank tea with Judge Sewall, Captain Carpenter, young Jonathan Gardner, both of Salem, and a Mr. Leavitt, having arrived in a cartel ship from Boston, dined and passed the afternoon and evening. From them I obtained much information relating to our country and town. Those who five years ago were the *"meaner people"* are now by a strange revolution become the only men of power, riches and influence. Those who, on the contrary, were leaders in the highest line of life, are glad at this time to be unknown, and unnoticed, to escape insult, and plunder, the wretched condition of all who are not violent, and adopters of republican principles. The Cabots of Beverly, who you know, had but five years ago a very moderate share of property, are now said to be by far the most wealthy in New England. It is a melancholy truth that whilst some are wallowing in undeserved wealth, that plunder and rapine has thrown into their hands, the wisest, most peaceable and most deserving such as you and I know are now suffering want, accompanied by many indignities that a licentious, lawless people can pour forth upon them.

The number of Americans in Bristol are compiled in the following list: Col. Oliver and six daughters. Mr. R. Lechmere, his brother Nicholas, with wife and two daughters. Mr. John Vassal, wife and niece, Miss Davis, Mr. Barnes, wife and niece, Miss Arbuthnot, Mr. Nathaniel Coffin, wife and family. Mr. Robert Hallowell, wife and children. Judge Sewell, wife, sister, and two sons. Samuel Sewall with his kinsman. Mr. Faneuil, and wife. Mr. Francis Waldo and Mr. Simpson, together with Mrs. Borland, a son and three daughters.

April 24, 1780. This day, five years are completed since I abandoned my house, estate, effects and friends. God only knows whether I shall ever be restored to them, or they to me. Party rage, like jealousy and superstition is cruel as the grave;—that moderation is a crime and in times of civil confusions, many good, virtuous and peaceable persons now suffering banishment from America are the wretched proofs and instances. By letter from Salem from our friend Pynchon, all our friends there are well and longing, but almost without hope, for the good old times as is the common saying now except among those as he expresses it, whose enormous heaps have made them easy and insolent, and to wish for a continuance of those confusions by which they grow rich.

London, Oct. 30th, 1781. To Samuel Sewell, Esq., You wish me to write you favorable news from America. Would to God such was to be found written in the book of fate. The French you know are in possession of the Chesapeake, with a much superior fleet to that of Great Britain, for they reckon thirty-six capital ships to our twenty-four, even after Digby's junction. General Cornwallis's royal master is in the utmost distress for him, who, all the world here fears to hear will have been *Burgoyned* and therefore an end to this cursed, ill-omened quarrel, though not in a way they wish, for which the instigators and continuers deserve execution. At New England Coffee House heard the glorious news of Admiral Rodney's defeat and capture of the French Admiral de Grasse, with five capital ships and one sunk.

London, March 17, 1783. Before the preliminaries are ratified or hostilities ceased in the channel, an American ship laden with oil, with thirteen stripes flying, came into the river from Nantucket. The ship, Captain Holton Johnson of Lynn, with whom I came from America, was, by a revolution common at such periods translated into a legislator in our Massachusetts Assembly, being about two months in London, told me that had not his interests and efforts prevailed, my name would have been inserted in the banishment list, and my estate confiscated, the reason, if any, must be private spite and malice, no public crime was ever alleged, but merely leaving the country in her distress. If success is justification, I confess my guilt. Read a Boston newspaper, where I saw poor Coomb's estate in Marblehead advertised for sale. I really pity my poor fellow refugee and think him cruelly treated by his savage townsmen. At New England Coffee House to read the papers filled with relations of the rising spirit of Americans against the refugees, in their towns and assemblies. Intoxicated by success under no fear of punishment, they give an unrestrained loose to their angry, malevolent passions attribute to the worst of causes the opposition to their licentious, mobbish violation of all laws human and divine; and even some of the best of the republican party seem to think at least their practice squints that way, that the supposed goodness of their cause will justify murder, rapine, and the worst of crimes. But cool impartial posterity will pass a better judgment, and account for the violence of the times from party rage which knows no bounds.

London, Aug. 9, 1783. By the newspapers from America, particularly our quarter, I find there but slender grounds of hope for success in attempting the recovery of debts or estates; a general shipwreck is seemingly intended of all absentees' property—the towns in their instructions to the representatives making it a point to prevent the return of them, and consequent confiscations of all their property, notwithstanding the provision in the fifth preliminary article. These lawless people regard not any obstacle when the gratification of their angry passions or the object of gain are in view. For an explicit answer, "Do you propose to spend the remainder of your days abroad?" The wished for period of my return is not arrived, it is a subject I consider with some indifference, age and infirmities having made such inroads on my constitution as leave me but little to hope, or fear from the result of public councils, or the imprudence of private conduct. I am free to declare my apprehension that the lower, illiterate classes, narrow-minded and illiberal all over the world, have too much influence. Oct. 6. This day was proclaimed peace with France, Spain, and Holland. At New England Coffee House

SAMUEL CURWEN.
Born at Salem in 1715. Judge of Admiralty. Died at Salem in 189..

in company with Mr. Nathaniel Gorham, lately arrived from Boston, whom I had well known. He is a native of Charlestown, late a member of Congress, and of the Massachusetts Assembly, and who is now here on the score of obtaining a benevolence for the sufferers at the destruction of that town June 17, 1775, by the king's troops, which all things considered, carries with it such a face of effrontery as is not to be matched. Invited him to tea; received a letter from my wife's brother, James Russell. To him he replied, I thank you for your favor of the 21st of August, the first from you since my unhappy abandoning my former home in April, '75. In truth, were your sister (Mrs. Curwin) no more, there would need no act of Massachusetts, or any other assembly, or senate to prohibit my return. To his wife he writes: If it was not for your sake, or that you would follow my fortune or accompany my fate, I should not hesitate for a moment taking up my future abode, the limits of the republican government. Wishes for the welfare of my friends still warm my heart, as to the rest, I read with cold indifference which cannot possibly be but of short continuance, somewhere out of the insurrection in Pennsylvania, and the carryings-on in the late English colonies, having lost local attachment. If your fortitude has increased in the proportion that your health and spirits have improved, perhaps you will not find it an insurmountable difficulty to resolve on a land tour to Canada, or a voyage to some other English settlement. Whatever shall be the result of your thoughts let me be made acquainted therewith as soon as convenient. Should a final expulsion be concluded on, you will no longer hesitate. Captain Nathaniel West brings me a message from the principal merchants and citizens of Salem proposing and encouraging my return which instance of moderation I view as an honor to the town and respectful to myself. It affords me pleasure, and I would cheerfully accept the offer, but should the popular dislike rise against me, to what a plight should I be reduced, being at present (out for how long is a painful uncertainty) on the British government list for £100 a year (a competency for a single person exercising strict economy) to surrender this precarious allowance without public assurance of personal security. Imagine to yourself the distress of an old man, without health under such adverse circumstances, and you will advise me to wait with resignation till the several Assemblies shall have taken decisive measures. Went to the Treasury and there received the agreeable information that the commissioners had granted my petition to appoint an agent to receive my quarterly allowance, after my departure from England, on making satisfactory proof of my being alive at the successive periods of payment. From this date an end to my doubts respecting my embarkation, its issue time must reveal. I know not in what employment I am to pass the small remainder of my days, should Providence permit my safe return home, but I shall not think part of it ill-bestowed in directing and assisting the studies and pursuits of my niece's children who are just of an age to receive useful ideas—with regard to the English, Latin, and Greek tongues. Sept. 25, 1784. Arrived at Boston at half past three o'clock. Landed at the end of Long Wharf after an absence of nine years and five months, occasioned by a lamented civil war. By plunder and rapine some have accumulated wealth, but many more are greatly injured in their circumstances. Some have to lament over the wreck of their departed wealth and estates, of which pitiable number I am, my affairs sunk into irretrievable ruin. On Sunday, being the day following, I left for Salem, where I alighted at the house of my former residence, and not a man, woman, or child, but expressed a satisfaction at seeing me, and welcomed me back. The melancholy derangement of my affairs has so entirel yunsettled me, that I can scarcely attend to anything. I think it very unlikely that my home can be saved.* Salem, Nov. 22, 1784. Judge Curwin wrote to his friend Judge Sewall, Bristol, England, saying: "I find myself completely ruined. I confess I cannot bear to stay and perish under the ruins of my late ample property and shall therefore as soon as I can recover my account-books, left in Philadelphia on my departure from America and settle my deranged affairs, retreat to Nova Scotia, unless my allowance be taken from me. He however remained at Salem where he passed the remainder of his days dying in 1802 at the age of eighty-six. The foregoing brief abstracts from Curwin's Journal give some of the things which he saw and heard, and the hopes and fears which agitated him and his fellow exiles. He left no children. Samuel Curwin Ward, a grandson of his brother George, at the request of Judge Curwin, took his name by an act of the Legislature, and his descendants are all that now bear the name in New England.

JAMES MURRAY.

James Murray was a direct descendant of Sir John Murray of Philiphaugh, Scotland, who sat in Parliament for the County of Selkirk in 1612. Sir John's second son, was John Murray of Bowhill. This John Murray was the father of John Murray of Unthank, born in 1677, who in turn was the father of James Murray, the subject of this notice, who was born in 1713 at Unthank. Here on this ancestral estate he passed the first fifteen years of his life, after the wholesome manner of Scotch lads—porridge-fed, bare legged—he protested in after life against his grandson wearing stockings. The people amongst whom he lived had married, thriven and multiplied until the population had become one vast cousinship, bound together by that clannish loyalty which, quite apart from pride of name, is ineradicable in the Scots to the present day. Through the influence of Sir John Murray he was apprenticed to William Dunbar of London, a merchant in the West India trade. On

* It was saved from confiscation by his wife remaining in it during the war, and her furnishing a substitute for her husband to serve in the army.

the death of his father, he received a thousand pounds as his share of the estate. With this small patrimony he decided to try his fortune in the New World. His objective point in his new venture was the Cape Fear Region in North Carolina. The Carolinas having shaken off their proprietary rule were now entering, it was hoped, upon a more prosperous period as dependencies of the Crown. Gabriel Johnson, a Scotchman who had been a physician and professor at St. Andrews University, had been recently appointed Governor. This made some stir in Scottish circles, a fact which directed James Murray's desire to this particular Colony. With letters of recommendation to Governor Johnson, he embarked at Gravesend, September 20, 1735, for Charleston. He settled at Wilmington, on the Cape Fear River, and purchased a house in town and a plantation of 500 acres and Negro slaves. He was also appointed collector of the Port, and in 1729 he was appointed a member of the Board of Councillors. In 1737 Mr. Murray received news of the death of his mother. This necesitated a journey to Scotland to settle her estate. On returning he brought with him his younger brother and his sister Elizabeth, not quite fourteen years of age. She was installed as his housekeeper, and then began that affectionate intimacy between them which was perhaps the most vital and enduring element in the life of each. James Murray prospered as a planter and merchant. He imported from England such goods as the colonists required and in exchange sent to England naval stores, tar, pitch, and turpentine.

In 1744 he returned to Scotland with his sister Elizabeth, married his cousin, Barbara Bennet, and remained in England and Scotland for five years. On his return in 1749, accompanied by his wife and daughter and his sister Elizabeth, their ship put into Boston, and he returned alone to Wilmington, leaving his family in Boston, because, as he wrote, "they had an opportunity of spending three of the most disagreeable months of this climate in that poor Healthy Place, New England—their health they owe to God's goodness, their poverty to their own bad policy and to their Popular Government." His sister Elizabeth remained in Boston and married Thomas Campbell, a Scotchman, merchant and trader. Their married life was short, for the husband died in a few years.

A comfortable, prosperous figure in Boston at that time was Mr. James Smith, a Scotchman, a sugar-baker, whose refinery had been in working since 1729 or before and who had amassed wealth as well as years. His home on Queen Street, now Court Street, was central in position, surrounded by other residences of its kind, yet conveniently near his sugar house, which stood in Brattle Street, between the old church and what was known as Wing's Lane. At the same time it was not far from King's Chapel. As one of the Church Wardens of King's Chapel and a generous contributor to its needs Mr. Smith stood high in the esteem of his fellow townsmen and the few allusions to him in the records and traditions of his day indicate that he was no less genial a friend than an open handed citizen. Mr. Smith married Mrs. Campbell in 1760. "I can assure you," wrote James Murray in 1761, "they both enjoy a happiness which is rarely met with in a match of such disparity." Her brother rejoiced in this marriage, which he declared placed her "in the best circumstances of any of her sex in the town." Prosperity for one member of the family must help for all. Boston thus became a second home for the Murrays in America.

COUNTY RESIDENCE OF JAMES SMITH, BRUSH HILL, MILTON. BUILT IN 1734.

Shortly after his sister's marriage he lost his wife and all his children but two, owing to the unhealthy climate. This caused him to leave the South and his opinion of New England was changed, for he wrote at this time, 1760, "you cannot well imagine what a land of health, plenty and contentment this is among all ranks, vastly improved within these ten years. The war on this continent has been a blessing to the English subjects and a calamity to the French, especially in the Northern Colonies, for we have got nothing by it in Carolina."

In 1761 Mr. Murray married Miss Thompson, a daughter of Mrs. Mackay, who lived on King Street. The marriage proved to be a fortunate one for Mr. Murray's two daughters as well as for the two most concerned. Mr. Smith was withdrawing from the sugar business and wished Mr. Murray to take it up. He was, however, in no haste to be off from his plantation, which he really loved, but at last the break was made and in 1765 he removed to Boston to cast in his lot permanently. Mr. Murray had warm friends in Boston and felt himself in congenial surroundings. He occupied Mr. Smith's home on the corner of Queen Street, the Smiths reserving a portion of it for themselves, though their permanent residence was now at Brush Hill, Milton. Mr. Smith had purchased in 1734, and subsequently, 300 acres at Brush Hill and erected the mansion house now owned and occupied by Murray Howe.

Mr. Smith's long life came to an end on the 4th of March, 1769. He died at Brush Hill and was buried from his home on Queen Street. Mrs. Smith returned to Scotland and before leaving she made over to her brother the Brush Hill Farm, in trust for his daughters, Dorothy and Elizabeth. This was very fortunate, as it afterwards turned out, for it saved it from confiscation. Mr. Murray, with much content, established himself there, hoping to "run off the dregs of his days" in peace. Of the farm he had given his brother, some years before, a graphic description; it was in many respects as pleasantly situated as Governor Hutchinson's. It had, he said "a good house, well furnished, good garden and orchards, meadows and pasturage, in 300 acres. A riverlet washed it and by several windings lost itself between two bushy hills, before it ran into the great bay. Of this bay, often covered with sails, and of the light-house, there is a fair prospect from the house which stands on an eminence and overlooks also a pleasant country round. It is in short one of the pleasantest and most convenient seats I see in the country."

Dorothy Murray, who, family traditions say, had grown to be a beautiful and fascinating young lady, accepted the hand of Rev. John Forbes, a clergyman then settled at St. Augustine, Florida. Their marriage occurred in 1769. The Forbes of Milton are the descendants.

The political turmoil in the midst of which Mr. Murray found himself upon his removal to Boston, in 1765, filled him with surprise and dismay. He had hoped, on leaving North Carolina, that he was turning his back upon rebellion, but here he had alighted upon the very seat of disorder. By force of circumstances, as well as by inclination, it was inevitable that in North Carolina, and afterwards in Massachusetts, his associates should have been those whose sympathies were on the side of law and order. The Boston of the disunionists, of Otis, Hancock, and the "brace of Adams" he never knew. "He shared so completely Hutchinson's convictions that the best interests of America were being sacrificed" by the very men who maintained they were asserting their rights and although, like those who sided with the Government, he incurred suspicion and hatred, he never to the end of his life could see himself as an enemy to the land he helped to build.*

To such men as him, men who were averse to partisanship and whose interests centered wholly within the domestic circle, yet who could take

* James Murray, Loyalist: pp. 152, 154, 155.

a large impersonal view of passing events, the inevitable ban under which, as Tories, they afterward fell, bore all the sting of injustice. He wrote in 1766, "the truth is we are all the children of a most indulgent Parent, who has never asserted his authority over us, until we are grown almost to manhood and act accordingly; but were I to say so here before our Chief Ruler, the Mob, or any of their adherents, I should presently have my house turned inside out."

When the troops sent by General Gage from New York arrived in Boston and were refused shelter in various places under control of the disunionists, Mr. Murray came forward and the sugar house was opened to them for barracks. Thenceforth "Murray's Barracks" or "Smith's Barracks," as they were indiscriminately called, were a source of irritation to the disloyal section of the town. Moreover, his willingness to lodge British soldiers, and a free hospitality shown to British officers (among others who frequented his house was General Mackay, a relative, probably, of his wife) marked Mr. Murray as a King's man. His appointment in 1768 as a Justice of the Peace drew him still further into public notice. Popular displeasure in fact, so far distinguished him as to make him, in the autumn of the next year, the victim of a mob. The condition of affairs was rapidly growing worse. The troops were called from Murray's barracks to protect the guard on King's Street from the fury of the mob and this brought about the so-called "State Street Massacre." Then followed the Lexington affair and Bunker Hill and the siege of Boston by Washington's army. During this time Mr. Murray remained in Boston. His daughter, Mrs. Forbes, had returned from Florida and with her sister Elizabeth, lived on the farm at Brush Hill. His sister, Elizabeth Smith, had married Ralph Inman of Cambridge and while her husband remained in Boston, she stayed in the Cambridge mansion to prevent its being confiscated. Communications between Milton and Boston were carried on by vessels sailing up the Neponset.

Mr. and Mrs. Murray visited Brush Hill in this manner and Mrs. Inman even journeyed back and forth between Cambridge, Boston and Milton in this way. Finally the evil day came when the evacuation of Boston became a necessity. The consternation was indescribable. Men who had lived all their lives in Boston and were a part and parcel of it found themselves suddenly compelled to take leave of friends, old associations and property and to flee with the army to Nova Scotia. The departure of General Howe was hampered and delayed by the necessity of caring for the removal of the Loyalists. All the transports which were at hand, assisted by such other vessels as could be procured, were inadequate for the purpose. The refugees, on their part, were in a state of distraction between the impossibility of taking with them more than a small part of their possessions. Mr. Murray, like the rest, had no recourse but to sail with the troops for Halifax. The parting he must have believed to be only temporary, but it was final.

A lady writing from Brush Hill under date of May 17th, 1776, and signing herself E. F., gives a graphic description of the condition in which the Murray family were left. She writes, "This amiable family are going to be involved in new troubles. Did I fear for myself alone, I should he happy compared with what I now suffer, for I have nothing to fear from the malevolence of man, but when I see the few but valuable friends I have remaining upon the point of becoming destitute like myself my heart sinks within me, and I can not avoid exclaiming "Great God!" Surely for all these things people shall be brought to judgment. I am hunted from one retreat to another, and since I left your Ark, like Noah's dove I can find no resting place. The Committee at Cambridge have left Mrs. Inman's farm, in spite of all assiduity to prevent it and the same tribe of demons have been here to take this into possession during the life of Mr. Murray. When this affair will end, God knows. Nature is all blooming and benevolent around us. I wish to Heaven that she could inspire the breasts of this deluded people with the same affectionate glow towards each other. *May eternal curses fall on the heads of those who have been instrumental to this country's ruin.*"

Again under the date of June 16th she writes, "Rejoice with me, my dear Aunt, *this infernal crew cannot succeed in taking the farm from this amiable family. The Almighty Father of infinite perfection will not permit them to prosper in all their wickedness.*"*

James Murray now began the weary life of banishment, the pathos of which was so many times repeated in the history of the Loyalist exiles. He first went to Halifax; there he established himself with his wife and his sister, Mrs. Gordon, but he could not be content to stay so far from his sister and his children, who remained in Boston to prevent their property from being confiscated, and soon, as he puts it, he came "creeping towards" them, hoping at least to be able more easily to communicate with them and to serve them by sending occasional supplies. He visited Newport, New York and Philadelphia. He found himself, however, no nearer the accomplishment of his wishes in New York than in Halifax and to Halifax, in 1778, after some two years spent in profitless wanderings, he returned. There he remained the rest of his life. In his last letter to his daughter dated Halifax, February 17th, 1781, he said "A man near seventy, if in his senses, *can want but little here below, nor want that little long.* Therefore the withdrawing of my salary for some time past gives me but little concern." In this letter he seems to have had a premonition of his death, for he died a few months later. The salary that he refers to was that which he received from England for several years after leaving Boston—about 150 Pounds a year as inspector of imports and exports, many sufferers received from 50 to 300 Pounds a year in addition to their salary for their present subsistence. Mrs. Inman, his sister, survived her brother but a few years

* James Murray, Loyalist; pp. 248, 249, 251.

and those were sad ones. Her friends were scattered, her means reduced and her health undermined. She died May 25, 1785.

ELIZABETH MURRAY, his daughter, married Edward Hutchinson Robbins, who in 1780, when but twenty-two years of age, became a member of the disloyal government and who occupied the position of Speaker of the House of Representatives, Lieutenant Governor and Judge of Probate. Brush Hill afterwards passed into the possession of her son, James Murray Robbins, who lived here until his death in 1885. It then passed into the possession of his nephew, James Murray Howe, its present occupant.

As previously stated, the only thing that prevented the confiscation aunt had given it had remained on the property during the war and would not leave it, although every effort was made to drive them off it by their of this estate was that Elizabeth and Dorothy Murray, to whom their disloyal neighbors. Their father was proscribed and banished under the Act of 1778, he was forbidden to return to Massachusetts and for a time did not even dare to write to his family. A daughter of Mary Robbins married a son of Paul Revere. Two of their sons fell upon the battlefield in the war for the Union, fighting on the loyal side in support of their government, giving to their country on the one hand lives derived from the disunionists and on the other from their loyal ancestor.

Rev. John Forbes wrote to his wife in 1783, just previous to his death, as follows: "Upon hearing of the peace, having all my property in Florida, I thought of going immediately to England. I might be of use to myself either by giving a short representation of the importance of retaining the province under the Crown of Great Britain or in finding early what hopes I might entertain of being in a situation of remaining in England with my united family, when the boys might be educated under my eye." After Mr. Forbes' death his wife, Dorothy Forbes, hoping to recover something from his estate as well as from her father's, made a trip to Wilmington and St. Augustine. The land which Mr. Forbes owned in Florida, which had been given over to the Spaniards, she received compensation for from the British Government. In Wilmington, however, she did not succeed, for when her father went to Boston he turned over his Cape Fear estate, which he valued at that time at £3000, to his nephew, Thomas Clark, who had recently come over from England. After the war commenced, the whole of Mr. Murray's property was confiscated. It was then claimed by Thomas Clark, who presented an account for more than the assessed value of the property for his salary for caring for it. As he had joined the disunionists it was ultimately made over to him by act of the Legislature. Mrs. Forbes tried to recover some of her patrimony, but without success. She did not even see her cousin, who wrote from his plantation that floods prevented his leaving his estate to visit Wilmington but that if she would come to him he would be happy to see her and did not doubt of being able to convince her that he had acted for the best in what he did.

SIR BENJAMIN THOMPSON.

BENJAMIN THOMPSON, otherwise known as Count Rumford was one of the most distinguished men of his age. He came on both sides of his parentage from the original stock of the first colonists of Massachusetts Bay. JAMES THOMPSON, one of the original settlers of Woburn, was prominent among those who fixed their residence in that part of the town now known as North Woburn. Little is known of his English antecedents except that he was born in 1593, his wife's name was Elizabeth and by her he had three sons and one daughter all probably born in England. As early as 1630 when he was thirty-seven he joined the company of about fifteen hundred persons who under lead of Gov-

BIRTHPLACE OF BENJAMIN THOMPSON, NORTH WOBURN.

ernor Winthrop landed on New England shores during the eventful year. He was one of the first settlers of Charlestown and belonged to sturdy yeomanry of the country. He was among the few adventurers who early pushed their way into an unknown region and fixed their home in the wilderness, with Henry Baldwin and a few others, in that part of Charlestown Village now known as North Woburn. James Thompson was twice married. Elizabeth died November 13, 1643, and he married February 15, 1644, Susannah Blodgett, widow of Thomas Blodgett of Cambridge. The descendants of this early settler are now very numerous in the country.

Jonathan Thompson, son of the former had a son Jonathan who had a son Ebenezer. Captain Ebenezer Thompson and Hannah Converse were the grandparents, Benjamin Thompson, the son of the last, and Ruth Simonds were the father and mother of the celebrated Count Rumford. His mother was the daughter of an officer who performed distinguished service in the French and Indian wars, which were in progress at the time of the birth of his eminent grandson. The parents were married in 1752, and went to live at the house of Captain Ebenezer Thompson. Here under his grandfather's roof, the future Count Rumford was born, March 26, 1753, in the west end of the strong substantial farm-house. The father of the little boy died November 7, 1754, in his twenty-sixth year, leaving his wife and her child to the care and support of the grandparents. In March, 1756, when the child was three years old, his widowed mother was married to Josiah Pierce, the younger, of Woburn. Mr. Pierce took his wife and her child to a new home, which, now removed, stood but a short distance from the old homestead.

Ellis in his "Life of Count Rumford" says, that Benjamin Franklin and Benjamin Thompson were the two men most distinguished for philosophical genius of all that have been produced on the soil of this continent. "They came into life in humble homes within twelve miles of each other, under like straits and circumstances of frugality and substantial thrift. They both sprang from English lineage, of an ancestry and parentage yeoman of the soil on either continent, to be cast, as their progenitors had been, upon their own exertions, without dependence upon inherited means, or patronage, or even good fortune. Born as subjects of the English monarch, they both, at different periods of their lives, claimed their privileges as such, visiting their ancestral soil, though under widely unlike circumstances, and their winning fame and distinction for services to humanity. We almost forget the occasion which parted them in the sphere of politics, because they come so close together in the more engrossing and beneficent activity of their genius." It is not known whether these two men ever met together, or sought each other's acquaintance, or even recognized each other's existence, though they were contemporaries for more than thirty years.

Benjamin Thompson in his youth attended the village grammar school. Later he was apprenticed to Mr. John Appleton, an importer of British goods at Salem, and later still was for a short time a clerk in a dry goods store in Boston where he was when the "Massacre" occurred. It was while at Salem he first displayed his fondness for experimental philosophy, when accidentally his face was somewhat marked by a pyrotechnical explosion. He used to steal moments to play the fiddle as he was passionately fond of music. Lacking taste for trade he engaged in the study of medicine with Dr. Hay of Woburn, meanwhile in company with his friend and neighbor, Loammie Baldwin, walking to and fro from Cambridge, in order to attend scientific lectures at Harvard College. At length he became a teacher, first in Wilmington, then in Bradford and then in a more permanent and lucrative position in Concord, New Hampshire, then a part of Essex County, Massachusetts; once known as Penacook but at this time as Rumford. His more public and noticeable life now began. Here he married at the early age of nineteen Sarah, the widow of Colonel Rolfe and the daughter of the Rev. Timothy Walker. When he went to Concord as a teacher he was in the glory of his youth, and his friend Baldwin describes him as of a fine manly make and figure, nearly six feet in height, of handsome features, bright blue eyes, and dark auburn hair. He had the manners and polish of a gentleman, with fascinating ways, and an ability to make himself agreeable. His diligent study and love of learning also added to his attractions. He was married about November, 1772, and his wife brought to him a fortune. It was at about this time that Benjamin Thompson met Governor Wentworth,—an event which led to that series of difficulties and troubles which resulted in his leaving the country. The governor was struck by the young man's commanding appearance, and a vacancy having occurred in a majorship in the Second Provincial Regiment of New Hampshire, Governor Wentworth at once commissioned Thompson to fill it. Thus the young man received an appointment over the heads of other officers of age and experience. It was a mistake on the part of the governor and a mistake for him to accept the office. The veteran officers over whom he had been appointed so suddenly and unexpectedly from the plain life of a civilian were very angry as was to be expected.

Young Thompson manifested in early manhood the tastes, aptitudes and cravings which prompt their possessor, however humbly born, and under whatever repression from surrounding influence, to push his way in the world by seeking and winning the patronage of his social superiors, who have favor and distinctions to bestow. He was regarded from his boyhood as being above his position; he had also a noble and imposing figure, with great personal beauty, and with those whose acquaintance he cultivated he was most affable and winning in his manners. His marriage enabling him to give over the necessity of school keeping, furnished him the means for making excursions at his pleasure. Besides his acquaintance with Governor Wentworth at Portsmouth, he had also on visits with his wife to Boston, been introduced to Governor Gage and several of the British officers, and had partaken of their hospitalities. Two soldiers, who had deserted from the army in Boston, finding their way to Rumford (Concord), had been employed by him upon his farm. Wishing to return to their ranks and comrades, they had sought for the intervention of their employer to secure them immunity from punishment. Thompson addressed a few lines for this purpose to General Gage asking at the same time that his own agency in their behalf should not be disclosed. Besides his acquaintance with the royal governors, the patronage he had received from one of them, the intimacy in which he was supposed to stand with others, the return of the deserters, and his independent spirit, as shown in speaking his mind with freedom, in a way to check the rising spirit of rebellion, and in distrust of the ability and success of the disunionists, caused him to be distrusted, and unpopular by the inflammable materials around him. He therefore became a suspected person in Rumford, where there were watching enemies, and tale-bearers, as well as jealous committees, who soon brought their functions to bear in a most searching and offensive way against all who did not attend revolutionary assemblies. It was well known as it was observable that Thompson took no part in these. He had occasion to fear any indignity which an excited and reckless county mob, directed by secret instigators might see fit to inflict upon him, whether it were by arraying him in tar and feathers, or by riding him upon a rail to be jeered at by his former school-pupils. If ill usage stopped short of these extremes, the condition of escape and security was a public recantation, unequivocally and strongly expressed, involving a confession of some act, or word, in opposition to the will of the disunionists, and solemn pledge of future uncompromising fidelity to them.

There was something exceedingly humiliating and degrading to a man of independent and self-respecting spirit, in the conditions imposed upon him by the "Sons of Despotism" in the process of clearing himself from the taint of "Loyalism." The Committees of "Correspondence and of Safety" whose services stand glorified to us through their most efficient agency in a successful struggle, delegated their authority to every witness or agent who might be a self-constituted guardian of the disloyal cause or a spy, or an eaves-dropper, to catch reports of suspected persons. It was this example, followed a few years later that led to such terrible results in the French Revolution.

Major Thompson insisted from the first, and steadfastly to the close of his life, affirmed that he had never done anything hostile to the revolutionary cause up to this time. He demanded first in private, and then in public, that his enemies should confront him with any charges they could bring against him, and he promised to meet them and defend himself against all accusations. He resolved, however, that he would not plead except against explicit charges, nor invite indignity by self-humiliation. Major Thompson was summoned before a Committee of the people of Rumford (Concord), in the summer of 1774 to answer to the suspicion of "being unfriendly to the cause of Liberty." He positively denied the charge and boldly challenged proof. The evidence, if any such was offered, was not a sort to warrant any proceedings against him, and he was discharged. This discharge, however, though nominally an acquittal, was not effectual in relieving him from popular distrust and in assuring for him confidence. Probably his own reluctance to avow sympathy with the disloyal cause, and make professions in accordance with the wishes of his enemies, left him still under a cloud. A measure less formal and more threatening than the examination before a self constituted tribunal, was secretly planned by the "Sons of Despotism." This was a visit to his comfortable home, the most conspicuous residence in the village. It was carried into effect in November, 1774. A mob gathered at the time agreed on, around his dwelling, and after a serenade of hisses, hootings and groans, demanded that Major Thompson should come out before them. The feeling must have been intense and was of a nature to feed its own flames. Had Thompson been within, he would inevitably have met wth foul handling. The suspicion that he was hiding there would have led to the sacking of his dwelling, and the destruction of his goods, though the daughter of their venerated minister was its mistress, and she was the mother, not only of Thompson's infant, but of the only child of their former distinguished townsman, Colonel Benjamin Rolfe. Mrs. Thompson and her brother, Colonel Walker, came forth and with their assurance that her husband was not in town, the mob dispersed.

Having received a friendly warning that this assault was to be made upon him, his brother-in-law and other friends advised him to quit the place, for although his family connections, beginning with the minister, and the squire of the town, were, the most powerful set among the inhabitants, yet they were unable to vindicate him and protect him from outrage, and we may infer that his apprehensions were not in vain, notwithstanding his own consciousness of rectitude.

Mr. Thompson therefore had secretly left Rumford just before the mob came to his home. He thought it was to be only a temporary separation from the place, for all his friends were there, and his wife and infant child; but he was never to see that pleasant home again, nor anyone of those whom he left there, except that he had a brief and troubled visit from his wife and infant, and met the latter again only after an interval of twenty-two years. He made a hasty effort to collect some dues which belonged strictly to himself, but he scrupulously avoided taking with him anything that belonged to others, or even to his wife. What of his own he left there was soon subjected to the process of confiscation.

Thompson sought refuge in his former home at Woburn with his mother. Here for a short time, he sought to occupy himself in quiet retirement with his favorite pursuits of philosophical study and experiment. But popular suspicion found means to visit its odium upon him there, and seeking a new refuge, he found temporary shelter in Charlestown, with a friend, nine miles from Woburn and one from Boston. In compliance with an earnest appeal, his wife with her infant joined him at his mother's home in Woburn, though it required of them a ride of more than fifty miles in winter. They remained with him till the end of May, 1775, after which he never saw his wife again. Thompson offered his services to the patriot army but his enemies interposed their veto. Ellis says, "There is no record, or even tradition of unwise or unfriendly expressions dropped by Mr. Thompson which could be used against him even when he challenged proof of his alleged disaffection to the cause of his country. However he was young and he had an independent spirit. His military promotion by pure favoritism, and, what he insisted was simply an act of humanity, his seeking immunity for two returning deserters, were enough in themselves to assure him zealous enemies."

Through all this trouble Thompson had a staunch and loyal friend. Colonel L. Baldwin was an ardent patriot, but stood faithfully by his old friend and fellow-student, believed in him and protected him from violence. At last Thompson's pride was so wounded and he felt the humiliation so keenly that in the hot impulse of youth and a naturally proud spirit, he embraced an opportunity to leave a land which he honestly thought to be ungrateful and cruel. It is not true as has often been said that Benjamin Thompson lost his interest in his family and country. Some of the most tender and most touching letters were written by him to his mother and his family still in Concord who believed in his integrity. Some of these letters have never been published, others after the lapse of nearly a century appeared in the "life of Count Rumford" by Dr. Ellis. These errors as to matters of fact may persuade us that the early predilection of Thompson for the loyalist cause, and the opening of opportunities, more than any settled purpose, decided the course of this forlorn and ill-treated young husband and father, adrift on the world, when he found himself loosed from all home ties and that there was nothing secret or disguised in the plans he formed for seeking in a foreign land and among strangers at the risk of homelessness and poverty, the peace and protection which he could not find in his own dwelling. He did not privately steal away; he remained in and about Woburn two months after writing his last letter to his friend, Mr. Walker, in which he so deliberately avowed his intentions. He settled his affairs with his neighbors, collecting dues and paying debts, well assured that his wife and child would lack none of the means of a comfortable support. Having made all his preparations he started from Woburn October 13, 1775, in a country vehicle, accompanied by his step-brother, Josiah Pierce, who drove him to the shores of Narragansett Bay where he was taken aboard of the British frigate Scarborough, in the harbor of Newport. The vessel very soon came round to Boston and remained till the evacuation, of which event he was undoubtly the bearer of the tidings to England in despatches from General Howe. From henceforth we are to know Benjamin Thompson till the close of the war as an ardent loyalist, and in council and in arms an opponent to the revolutionary cause. He must have done appreciable service in the four or five months he was in Boston, in order to have won so soon the place of an official in the British government. Thenceforward the rustic youth became the companion of gentlemen of wealth, and culture, of scientific philosophers, of the nobility and of princes. The kind of influences which he at once began to exert, and the promotion which he so soon received in England, answers to a class of services rendered by him of a nature not to be misconceived. They had not in England at that time much exact information about the state

SIR BENJAMIN THOMPSON.

Born in North Woburn, March 26, 1753. In the uniform of a British Officer. Known as Count Rumford. Died at Paris, Aug. 21, 1814.

of the country. Thompson thoroughly understood the matter. He could give trustworthy information about the topography, and about the events of the war in which he had played a part. He was not slow in winning the confidence of Lord George Germaine, Secretary of State for the Colonies, who was sadly deficient in his knowledge of the American Colonies. Major Thompson was immediately admitted to a desk in the Colonial office. He of course proffered and showed he could impart "information." The young man became such a favorite with Lord George that he was daily in the habit of breakfasting, dining and supping with him at his lodgings and at his country seat, Stoneland. Apart from the discharge of his duties as a private secretary, he made the most and the best use of his opportunities in acquainting himself with London and seeking introductions alike to men in public station and to those engaged in scientific pursuits; nothing of interest would escape his keen observation, and no means of personal improvement or acquisition through men or things, would fail to yield him advancement.

He was elected a Fellow of the Royal Society, and became one of the most active and honored members of the Society. In 1780 he was made "Under Secretary of State for the Northern Department." The oversight of all the practical details for recruiting, equipping, transporting, and victualling the British forces, and of many other incidental arrangements was then committed to him. Major Thompson, who had always clung to that title, though its provisional commission gave him no rank in the regular army, was now honored with the commission in the regular army of a Lieutenant Colonel; though now at the age of only twenty-eight, not yet a veteran, he wished for, and meant to do, full military duty. He needed a command. Where should he find a regiment. He provided for himself, and resolved to secure a following from those in his native land, who had been loyal to the government. They were known as the "Loyal American Regiments" and for the most part, they were the most desperate, and hated of any of the combatants, they had suffered the loss of their homes, and endured the most cruel treatment from their neighbors, and countrymen, and when the opportunity occurred they often retaliated. In this partisan warfare quarter was neither given or taken. In the early part of January, 1782, Lieutenant Colonel Thompson arrived at Charleston, South Carolina, General Green's army at that time invested the city. Becoming desperate in their need of supplies, a sortie was made under Thompson's command, an attack was made by him on the partisan forces under the command of Marion, the famous partisan leader, near the Santee. When the brigade was first attackd it was under the command of Colonel Horrey, and though Marion came in season to take part in the action, he had the mortification of witnessing the discomfiture of his band with the loss of many men and munition.*

Rivington's New York Gazette, under date of Feb. 18th, 1782, says

* Memoir of the war in the Southern Department of the United States. By Henry Lee, p. 397.

"A detachment of the Royal Americans went on service against Greene," March 27th. A person who left the Southern Army Feb. 13th, says Lieutenant Colonel Thompson has taken command of the British cavalry under Colonel Leslie. "A considerable force of cavalry and infantry commanded by Colonel Thompson sallied out from Charleston on the side opposite the American camp and surprised and dispersed a party of militia. The British retreated before Greene could send reinforcements.

Charleston, March 2. Lieutenant Colonel Thompson moved Sunday, Feb. 24 from Daniel's Island, with the cavalry, Cunningham's and Young's troops of mounted militia, Yagers, and Volunteers of Ireland, with one three pounder, and a detachment of the Thirtieth Regiment. By the spirited exertion of his troops, and by the Colonel's mounting the infantry occasionally on the dragoon horses, he carried his corps thirty-six miles without halting. Having secured the American scouts to prevent information being given he drove in Horrey's regiment. They were pursued by Major Doyle with mounted militia. On seeing the enemy, Colonel Thompson sounded a charge and dashed forwards. Marion's marque and men refreshed our soldiers. Colonel Thompson marched back driving the cattle, etc. The admirable conduct of the officer who commanded can be equalled by the spirit with which his orders were executed. (Rivington, April 17). In the war of posts, of desultory skirmishes, and of raids into the farming country, to which the struggle at the South was reduced, there was indeed little opportunity for Thompson to win laurels. He made use of his energetic and methodical skill in doing what he could to organize and discipline such materials as he had before him.

Towards the end of the war he was sent to New York to organize a regiment out of the broken and scattered bands of Loyalists on Long Island. "Recruits for the King's American Dragoons, likely and spirited young lads who were desirous of serving their King and country, and who prefer riding to going on foot, were offered ten guineas each, if volunteers." Such was the advertisement. His ability in organizing this regiment was a great achievement. He commanded at Huntington, Long Island in 1782-3 where he caused a fort to be built. In August, 1782, near Flushing, standards were presented to his corps, with imposing ceremonies. Prince William came forward to the center of the regiment, received the colors from Admiral Digby, and presented them with his own hand to Lieutenant Colonel Thompson. On a given signal the whole regiment gave three shouts, the music played "God save the King", the artillery fired a royal salute and the ceremony ended.

An ox was roasted whole, to grace this occasion. He was spitted on a hickory sapling, twelve feet long, supported on crutches, and turned by handspikes. An attendant dipped a swab in a tub of salt and water to baste the ox, and moderate the fire. Each soldier then sliced off for himself a piece of juicy beef.*

* The barbecue is still in vogue in the Southern States at all large social gatherings.

The Prince who officiated on this occasion was the King's third son, afterwards William IV. He had sailed on board the Prince George under Admiral Digby, to qualify himself for rank in the Royal Navy.

Returning to England Thompson, as a commissioned officer of high rank now on half pay, obtained leave to travel on the Continent. He left England in September, 1783, with no anticipation of the ultimate result of what was to him in intent mainly a trial of fortune. On his arrival at Strasburg, Prince Maximilian, who became Elector of Bavaria in 1799 and King in 1805, was attracted by the young man's appearance. On acquaintance he soon realized that the Englishman was a man of remarkable intelligence and later Thompson received an earnest invitation to enter into the service of the elector. Thompson therefore returned to England to receive the necessary permission from the king. The king not only granted the permission but also conferred on him the honor of Knighthood on February 23, 1784.

Returning to the continent Thompson became a fast friend of the Elector of Bavaria. His great mind was put to useful service in a country that needed his wisdom, philanthropy and personal help. Many honors were conferred upon him and he was admitted to several academies. In 1788 the Elector made him Major-General of Cavalry and Privy Councillor of State. He was also put at the head of the War Department. His constant study in science and philosophy, and the great problems of the day, made him an invaluable help to the people, besides his ability as a statesman. In Munich, where beggary had been reduced to a system and had become an intolerable curse, he received from all classes multiplied tokens of most grateful regard for his acts of disinterested benevolence. Both in England and on the continent he was held in the highest esteem for the broad and wise plans for the amelioration of the condition of the poor which he devised and executed, He dealt with those who lived in the filthiest order and it was his aim to show them that virtue came from cleanliness, and he worked unceasingly that their surroundings might first be clean.

Honors of all kinds were heaped upon this worker for mankind, but nothing so deeply moved him or was so tenderly cherished in his memory, as that scene, when once he was dangerously ill, the poor of Munich went publicly in a body, in processions, to the cathedral, and offered public prayers for his recovery. And on another occasion four years later, when he was again dangerously ill at Naples, these people of their own accord, set apart an hour each evening, after they had finished their work in the Military Work-house, to pray for him. On his return, after an absence of fifteen months, the subjects of his benevolence gave him a most affecting reception. He in response, provided for them a festival in the English Gardens which his own skill and taste had laid out where before was an unhealthy marsh. Here eighteen hundred poor people of all ages enjoyed themselves, in presence of above eighty thousand visitors. Thompson says, "Let him imagine, I say, my feelings, upon hearing the confused noise of the prayers of a multitude of people who were passing by in the streets, upon being told that it was the poor of Munich, many hundreds in number, who were going in procession to the church to put up public prayers for me;—public prayers for me!—for a private person!—a stranger!—a Protestant!"

"Such testimonies as these were more valuable than all his military honors, all his scientific reputation, his diplomas of Knighthood in England, and in Poland, and his decoration as a count of the Holy Roman Empire and there is reason to believe that he so regarded them himself."*

He was accused of being selfish and devoid of all honor, coarse and cruel. That he married another woman while his wife was alive and was always a tyrant! The records of Concord give the date of his wife's death as January 19, 1792, while the register of Paris gives the date of his second marriage as October 24, 1805.

Sarah, the only child of Count Rumford, who was born in the Rolfe Mansion in Concord, Oct. 18, 1774, remained in the care of her mother until the latter's death. Her father had taken great interest in her and never forgot his family, and he made provision also for his mother. After his wife's death, Sarah accepted her father's invitation to rejoin him in Europe where she shared his honors both in London and on the Continent. She received her title as countess and her pension both of which she enjoyed to the close of her life.

While the countess was on a return visit to her old home she gained the first news of her father's coming marriage through his letters to her. Father and daughter kept up a continual correspondece, and from these letters which have since been published much of their private life is revealed.** Count Rumford married the widow of General Anthony Laurence Lavosier at Paris in 1805, but the marriage soon proved unhappy and he retired to the Villa Auteuil, within the walls, but removed from the noise of the great city. Count Rumford never returned to his old home in Massachusetts though it was his wish to do so. The United States government through its ambassador, Hon. Rufus King, then resident of London, formally invited him to return, assured of his loyalty and great ability, and offered him the responsible position of superintendent of the proposed American Military Academy and of inspector-general of artillery. Though to the mutual regret of both parties concerned, the count was not able to accept the invitation of the American government, he gave in order to assist in the equipment of the Military Academy, some of his very valuable models and drawings and offered to give his whole rich collection of military books, plans, drawings, and models, provided they would be acceptable.

The Count's last days were spent near Paris, as that climate was best

* Memorial of James Thompson of Charlestown, Mass., and Woburn, Mass., by Leander Thompson, A. M.

** See "Life of Count Rumford," by George Ellis.

suited to him. He lived a very retired life spending most of his days in philosophical pursuits and experiments, almost secluded from the world. Constant friendship between Colonel Baldwin and Benjamin Thompson remained until the end, and the latter was always grateful for the interest and care his old friend had bestowed upon his daughter during their separation.

Thompson published essays and papers on his work and that he could have been great in theoretical science is shown by his experiment at Munich in 1798, and his clear reasoning upon it which was in advance of the prevailing scientific opinion by half a century. When he was in London in 1800 he projected the Royal Institute of Great Britain.

Besides a great number of communications to scientific journals, he published four volumes of essays, political, economical, experimental, and philosophical. He was ever a great friend to Harvard College. When the Colleges were converted into barracks, during the siege of Boston, he was instrumental in preserving the library and philosophical apparatus from destruction by the revolutionists who regarded the College as a hotbed of toryism. By his will he laid the foundation of that professorship to Harvard University, which has rendered his name justly esteemed with his friends. He bequeathed an annuity of one thousand dollars and the reversion of another of four hundred dollars, also the reversion of his whole estate, which amounted to twenty-six thousand dollars, "for the purpose of founding a new institution and professorship, in order to teach by regular courses of academical and public lectures accompanied with proper experiments, the utility of the physical and mathematical science for the improvement of the useful arts, and for the extension of the industry, prosperity, happiness and well being of society. In 1796 he remitted five thousand dollars in three per cent. stocks, to the American Academy of Arts and Sciences, the income to be appropriated as a premium to the author of the most important discovery on light and heat.

This great, useful and influential life came to a close on August 21, 1814. He was just about to depart for England to which country, as long as he lived, he retained the most devoted attachment. His death resulted from a nervous fever at Auteuil, about four miles from Paris and he is buried within the limits of that city. In the Monthly Magazine or British Register (London) for September, 1814, appeared the following:

"At his seat near Paris, 60, died, August 21, that illustrious philosopher, Benjamin Thompson, Count Rumford, F. R. S., Member of the Institute, &c., an American by birth, but the friend of man, and an honor to the whole human race."

Many testimonies were given in remembrance of Benjamin Thompson throughout the civilized world. In Munich the king erected at his own cost a bronze statue of Count Rumford, and it stands in the Maximillian Strasse, the finest street of Munich, perhaps of any city of Europe. The new and beautiful library which was erected in Woburn,

Massachusetts, has paid tribute also to this man's memory. A bronze monument of heroic size stands boldly out upon the library lawn, and the inscription was written by President Eliot of Harvard College. The Rumford Historical Association was organized in 1877 with the simple desire to do justice to Count Rumford's transcendent abilities as a great scientist and to his marked usefulness as one of the greatest philanthropists of his age. A portrait of Count Rumford by Page after one Kellerhofer hangs in Memorial Hall, Cambridge.

Sarah, the Countess of Rumford, after living in Paris and London several years returned to her old home in Concord, where she spent her last years. She possessed many memorials and pictures which she was fond of exhibiting to visitors. She was eccentric but had a quick and vigorous mind and idolized America. She was never married and her death occurred December 2, 1852, at the age of seventy. In her will she left $15,000 and her homestead, worth $5,000, for the endowment of an institution for widows and orphans of Concord, the homestead to be the site of the institution, to the New Hampshire Asylum for Insane in Concord she left $15,000, to the Concord Female Charitable Society who have under their care a school for poor children, called the Rumford School, she left $2,000, and the rest of her property, estimated at from $75,000 to $100,000, to distant relatives.

COLONEL RICHARD SALTONSTALL.

The ancestors of Sir Richard Saltonstall resided for centuries in the parish of Halifax, in the West Riding of Yorkshire, England, and the earliest date at which we find this name recorded is in 1276. Thomas de Saltonstall of the West Riding of Yorkshire is the first name of whom any record is preserved. Sir Richard Saltonstall, born in 1521 was knighted by Queen Elizabeth in 1598. After holding several prominent offices under the crown he became Lord Mayor of London in 1597-8. He was the uncle of Sir Richard Saltonstall who was born in 1586 at Halifax and was one of the patentees of the Colony of the Massachusetts Bay and was appointed First Assistant. He came over with the Winthrop fleet, and arrived in Salem aboard of the Arabella, June 12, 1630, "bringing out the charter with them." He returned to England, and at his death, left a legacy to Harvard College. He dissented from the action of the tyrannical rulers who were his associates, who inflicted punishment on such as differed from them, but slightly in their notion of policy, and requested that his dissent should be entered upon the records, which stand much to his honor and credit. After his return to England he wrote to Mr. Cotton and Mr. Wilson, the ministers in Boston "that it did not a little grieve his spirit to hear what sad things were reported daily of the tyranny and persecution in New England, as that they fined, whipped and imprisoned men for their consciences." His son Richard, born in 1610, settled at Ipswich, Massachusetts, returned to England, and died there in 1694. His son Nathaniel, born about 1639 and died in 1707, settled at Haverhill, Mass., of which he is called the father. He married Elizabeth, the daughter of the first minister, Rev. John Ward, who gave the young couple the land for their home, on which was erected the Saltonstall mansion which remained in the possession of the Saltonstall family for several generations. In the early part of the last century it was purchased by Major James Duncan, who erected the present mansion which is now owned and occupied by the Haverhill Historical Society. Nathaniel had a son Richard, who also had a son Richard born June 24, 1703. He graduated from Harvard College in 1722 and became Colonel in 1726. In 1736 he became judge of the Superior Court and died in 1756. His eldest son, Richard Saltonstall, the subject of this notice, was the sixth generation from Sir Richard the First Assistant, and the fourth of the family in succession who held the office of Colonel. He graduated from Harvard College with high honors and delivered the Latin Oration at Commencement.

His acceptance from Governor Shirley of the commission of Colonel, so soon after leaving college, evinced a spirit which was not long after to be tried in arduous service for his country. During the French war he was Major in the army and was one of the unfortunate prisoners at the capitulation of Fort William Henry. He escaped being massacred by the Indians by concealing himself in the woods where he lay for many hours, and when at last he reached Fort Edward was nearly exhausted with fatigue and hunger. He remained in active service until the close of the war, and later was appointed Sheriff to the County of Essex.

Colonel Saltonstall was always a steady loyalist in principle and never for a moment wavered in his devotion to the flag which he had so bravely fought under and which he had so often sworn to support. "The proceedings (of the Government) were in his opinion extremely inexpedient, but he never doubted their right to tax the Colonies."

"He was much beloved by the people of Haverhill, and its vicinity. He resided on the beautiful family estate in Haverhill known as 'the Saltonstall Place,' where he lived in a liberal style of hospitality, sustaining the character of a truly upright man, and an accomplished gentleman. It was long before he lost his popularity, but in 1774 a mob assembled from the West Parish of Haverhill and Salem, N. H., for the purpose of proving themselves *Sons of Liberty* by attacking him. By a word he could have collected a great part of the inhabitants of the village to his defence, but he would not, though urged by some of his friends. The rioters marched to his home and paraded before it, armed with clubs and other offensive instruments, when he came to the door and addressed them with great firmness and dignity He told them he was under the oath of allegiance to the king, that he was bound to discharge the duties of the office he held under him, that he did not think the people were pursuing a wise or prudent course but that he was as great a friend to the country as any of them, and had exposed his life in its cause, etc. He then ordered some refershment for the *gentlemen,* who soon began to relent, when he requested them to go to the tavern and call for entertainment at his expense. They then huzzard to the praise of Colonel Saltonstall, and never attempted to mob him again."

Colonel Saltonstall left Haverhill in the fall of 1774 and embarked for England. He did not enter the British service, saying, if he could not conscientiously engage on the side of his native country he never would take up arms against her. If he had joined the continental army he undoubtedly would have held an office of high command. The king granted him a pension and he passed the remainder of his life in England, where he died. In one of his last letters in which he expressed great affection for the *"delightful place of his nativity,"* he wrote, "I have no remorse of conscience for my past conduct. I have had more satisfaction in a private life here than I should have had in being next in command to General Washington, where I must have acted in conformity to the dictates of others, regardless of my own feelings."

In Haverhill Colonel Saltonstall was much beloved and had a great influence from his integrity, benevolence of disposition and his superior understanding and knowledge of the world. In England he was hospitably received by his remote family connections, who paid him every kind and generous attention while living, and erected a monument to his memory in Kensington church, on which is the following inscription:

"Near this place are interred the remains of Richard Saltonstall, Esq., who died October, 1785, aged fifty-two. He was an *American loyalist,* from Haverhill in Massachusetts, where he was descended from a first family, both for the principal share it had in the early erecting as well as in rank and authority in governing that province, and wherein he himself sustained, with unshaken loyalty and universal applause, various important trusts and commands under the Crown both civil and military, from his youth till its revolt; and throughout life maintained such an amiable private character, as engaged him the esteem and regard of many friends. As a memorial of his merits this stone is erected.

Colonel Saltonstall was not married. He was Proscribed and Banished by the law of 1778. His mansion home at Haverhill passed into the hands of his brother, Dr. Nathaniel Saltonstall who joined the Disunionists, at a time when his brothers remained true to those principals of loyalty in which they had been educated. He however did not take up arms against the government. At his death he left three sons and four daughters, the only family of that name in Massachusetts.

LEVERETT SALTONSTALL, youngest son of Judge Saltonstall was born in 1754 and at the commencement of the war had nearly completed his term of service with a merchant of Boston, when Col. Saltonstall came to that place for protection from mob violence. Being in the habit of looking up to him for advice and direction, he embraced the same political opinion, and becoming acquainted with the British officers he was fascinated with their profession. After the passing of the Act of Disunion July 4, 1776 he unlike his brothers decided to enter the British service and fight for his government. He was in many battles, and commanded a company in the army of Lord Cornwallis. He died at the close of the war at New York, 1782. His brother-in-law, the Rev. Moses Badger, who was also a loyalist, in a letter to Dr. Nathaniel Saltonstall concerning his sickness (consumption), says, "It may be some consolation to you and his mother to hear, that his behaviour in the regiment endeared him to every officer, and the soldiers who had so frequent opportunities to see his intrepidity, coolness and gallantry in action, absolutely revered him. He was agreeable to people of all ranks. He was exceedingly cautious in speaking, seldom uttering a word without reflection and was never heard to speak ill of any one and reprobated the man or woman who indulged themselves in this infirmity. He never fell into the scandalous and fashionable vice of profaneness. In short, I looked upon him to be as innocent a young man as any I have known since I have been capable of making observations on mankind."*

REV. MATHER BYLES.

JOSIAH BYLES, a saddler by trade, came from Winchester, Hants county. He was in Boston in 1695 and joined the church October 11, 1696; seven years later he married the pastor's daughter.

He had four children by his wife Sarah. His second wife, Elizabeth, he married October 6, 1703; she was the widow of William Greenough and the daughter of Increase Mather.

Mather Byles, D. D., son of Josiah and Elizabeth, was born in Boston in 1706. He graduated from Harvard University in 1725 and was ordained first pastor of the Hollis street church in 1733. This church was built on land given by Governor Belcher in 1733, the site is now occupied by the Hollis street Theatre. He married, February 14, 1733, Mrs. Anna Gale; the ceremony took place in the state room of the Province House, Rev. Thomas Prince of the Old South officiating. By this marriage he had six children born, all of whom died young except Elizabeth. His second wife was Rebecca, daughter of Lieutenant Governor Hon. William Tailor; the ceremony was performed by Rev. Joseph Sewell, D. D. By his second wife he had four children. He was created Doctor of Divinity at Aberdeen in 1765. He lived happily with his parish until 1776 when the connection was dissolved and never renewed. Of the Congregational clergy he stood alone against the revolution.

Mather Byles is one of the most interesting men of this period. He was a scholar and a great wit. Pope, Lansdowne and Watts were among

* Mass. His. Coll. 2, series Vol. IV, pp. 167, 168.

his correspondents. In his pulpit he avoided politics and on being asked the reason, replied: "I have thrown up four breastworks, behind which I have entrenched myself, neither of which can be enforced. In the first place I do not understand politics; in the second place, you all do, every man and mother's son of you; in the third place you have politics all the week, pray let one day in seven be devoted to religion; in the fourth place, I am engaged in work of infinitely greater importance; give me any subject to preach on of more consequence than the truth I bring you, and I will preach on it the next Sabbath."

The preacher became known as the "celebrated Dr. Byles.". He wrote in poetry and prose very well, and some of his sermons are still extant. Also several of his essays, in the New England Weekly Journal, a poem on the death of George I; and the accession of George II, in 1727. A sort of memorial address to Governor Belcher, on the death of his wife, and a poem called the conflagration, and a volume of metrical matters published in 1744.

The serious writings of Dr. Byles are singularly free from everything suggestive of frivolous association. In his pulpit there was none of it, while out of it, unless on solemn occasions, there was very little else. One of that day said his wit at times was quite as clever as Jonathan Swift or Sydney Smith.

Mather Byles and his family were staunch loyalists. News of the repeal of the stamp act arrived in Boston May 16, 1766. The nineteenth of May was appointed for merry-making. "At one in the morning the bell of the Hollis street church began to ring," says a zealous writer of that day. "The slumbers of the pastor, Dr. Byles, were disturbed of course, for he was a tory, though a very pleasant tory, after all." In 1777 he was denounced in town meeting, and having been by a subsequent trial pronounced guilty of attachment to the Royal cause, was sentenced to confinement, and to be sent to England with his family. This Byles steadfastly refused to do and the doom of the banishment was never enforced, and he was permitted to remain in Boston. The substances of the charges against him were that he continued in Boston during the siege; and that he prayed for the king and the safety of the town.

For a time he was kept a prisoner in his own house. On one occasion while under guard he persuaded the sentinel to go on an errand for him, promising to perform sentinel's duty himself; and to the great amusement of all gravely marched before his own door with a musket on his shoulder, until his keeper returned. This was after his trial; and alluding to the circumstances that he had been kept prisoner, that his guard had been removed and replaced again, he said, that "he had been guarded, re-guarded, and disregarded.

Near his house, in wet weather, was a very bad slough. It happened that two of the selectmen who had the care of the streets, passed that way driving in a chaise, stuck fast in this hole, and were obliged to get out in the mud to extricate their vehicle. Dr. Byles came out, and making

REV. MATHER BYLES, D. D.

Born in Boston in 1706. "A man of infinite wit." Died in Boston July 5, 1788.

them a respectful bow, said: "Gentlemen, I have often complained to you of this nuisance, without any attention being paid to it, and I am very glad to see you 'stirring' in this matter now."

Dr. Byles' wit created many a laugh and many an enemy. In person he was tall and commanding. His voice was strong and harmonious and his delivery graceful. He was intimate with General Knox, who was a bookseller before the war. When the American troops took possession of the town after the evacuation, Knox, who had become quite corpulent, marched in at the head of his artillery. As he passed on Byles thought himself privileged, on old scores, exclaimed, loud enough to be heard, "I never saw an ox fatter in my life." When confined in his own house and quite poor and had no money to waste on follies, he caused the little room in which he read and wrote to be painted brown, that he might say to every visitor, "You see, I am in a brown study."

From the time of the stamp act in 1765 to the period of the revolution the cry had been repeated in every form of phraseology, "that our grievances should be redressed." One fine morning the multitude had gathered on the common to see a regiment of redcoats parade there, who had recently arrived. "Well," said the doctor, gazing at the spectacle, "I think we can no longer complain that our grievances are not reddressed." "True," said one of his neighbors who were standing near, "but you have two d's, Dr. Byles." "To be sure, sir, I have," the doctor instantly replied, "I had them from Aberdeen in 1765."

Some visitors called one morning, and Mrs. Byles unwilling to be found at her ironing board, and desiring to hide herself, as she would not be so caught by those ladies, the doctor put her in a closet, and buttoned her in. After a few remarks the ladies expressed a wish to see the doctor's curiosities, which he proceeded to exhibit; and after entertaining them very agreeably for some time, he told them he had kept the greatest curiosity to the last; and proceeding to the closet, unbuttoned the door and exhibited Mrs. Byles.

He had at one time a remarkably stupid and literal Irish girl as a domestic. With a look and voice of terror he said to her in haste, "Go and say to your mistress, Dr. Byles has put an end to himself." The girl ran upstairs and with a face of horror, screamed, "Dr. Byles has put an end to himself." The astonished wife and daughter ran into the parlor—and there was the doctor, calmly waltzing about with a part of a cow's tail, that he had picked up in the street, tied to his coat or cassock behind.

On the celebrated Dark-day in 1780 a lady who lived near the doctor, sent her young son with her compliments, to know if he could account for the uncommon appearance. His answer was, "My dear, you will give my compliments to your mamma, and tell her that I am as much in the *dark* as she is." He paid his addresses unsuccessfully to a lady who afterwards married a gentleman of the name of Quincy; the doctor on meeting her said: "So madam, it appears that you prefer a

Quincy to Byles." "Yes, for if there had been anything worse than *biles*, God would have afflicted Job with them."

Mather Byles had two daughters by his second wife, Mary born in 1750 and Katherine born in 1753. They were famous for their hospitality and their stout, unflinching loyalty to the throne, to the last hours of their existence. This thread of life was spun out more than half a century after the Royal government had ceased in these States; yet they retained their love of, and strict adherance to monarch and monarchies, and refused to acknowledge that the Revolution had transferred their allegiance to new rulers. One of these ladies of a by-gone age, wrote to William the Fourth, on his accession to the throne. They had known the "sailor-king" during the Revolution and now assured him that the family of Doctor Byles always had been, and would continue to be, loyal to the rightful sovereign of England.

Dr. Byles continued to live in Boston after the Revolution, the last twelve years of his life being spent in retirement. He died of paralysis July 5th, 1788 at the age of 82. As Dr. Byles refused to be driven out and made a refugee, or absentee, he therefore saved his property from confiscation, and his two daughters, maiden ladies, lived and died in the old family house at the corner of Tremont and Nassau street, now Common street. They were repeatedly offered a great price for their dwelling, but would not sell it, nor would they permit improvements or alterations. In the course of improvements in Boston a part of the building had to be removed in widening the street. This had a fatal influence upon the elder sister; she mourned over the sacrilege, and, it is thought, died its victim. "That," said the survivor, "is one of the consequences of living in a Republic. Had we been living under a king, he would have cared nothing about our little property, and we could have enjoyed it in our own way as long as we lived. But," continued she, "there is one comfort, that not a creature in the States will be any better for what we shall leave behind us." She was true to her promise, for the Byles estate passed to relatives in Halifax at their decease. One of them died in 1835, the other in 1837. They worshipped in Trinity church under which their bodies were buried, and on Sundays wore dresses almost as old as themselves. Among their furniture, was a pair of bellows two centuries old, a table on which Franklin drank tea on his last visit to Boston, a chair which more than a hundred years before the Government of England had sent as a present to their grandfather, Lieutenant-Governor Tailer. They showed to visitors commissions to their grandfather, signed by Queen Anne, and three of the Georges. They talked of their walks arm-in-arm, on Boston Common, with General Howe, and Lord Percy, while the British Army occupied Boston. They told of his Lordship's ordering his band to play under their window for their gratification. They took pleasure in exhibiting the many heirlooms which were in the possession of the family and enjoyed hearing a recitation of the bright stories of the day. The works of Watts were sent to Byles by the author from time to time and among the treasures highly prized by the family was a presentation copy, in quarto from Pope, of his translation of the Odyssey. At the sale of the library of Dr. Byles a large folio Bible in French, was purchased by a private individual. This Bible had been presented to the French-Protestant church in Boston, by Queen Anne, and at the time when it came into the hands of Dr. Byles was the last relic of that church, whose visible temple had been erected in School Street about 1716.*

The bible is now preserved in the library of the Divinity School at Cambridge and was presented in 1831 by the widow of the late Samuel Cobb of Boston, who had bought it at the sale of Mather Byle's library.

MATHER BYLES, JR., D. D., a son of Rev. Mather Byles by his second wife, was born in 1734, and married Rebecca, daughter of Rev. N. Walter of Roxbury in 1761. He graduated in 1751 at Harvard University. In 1757 at the age of twenty-three he was ordained at New London; his father preached the sermon. Eleven years after, his ministry came to an abrupt termination. Without previous intimation, he called a meeting of his church and requested dismission, that he might accept an invitation to become Rector of the North Episcopal, or Christ Church, Salem street, Boston. His change to Episcopacy was soon a matter of discussion all over New England. Among the reasons he gave in the course of the discussion that ensued, were, that "another minister would do much better for them than he had done or could do, for his health was infirm, and the position of the church very bleak, the hill wearisome, he was not a country minister, and his home and friends were all in Boston." The debate was long and warm, and produced total alienation. April 12, 1768, the record is "The Rev. Byles dismissed *himself* from the church and congretion." Before the close of 1768, he was inducted into the desired rectorship; and of Christ Church, was the third in succession. He continued to discharge his ministerial duties until 1775, when the force of events compelled him to abandon his flock. He was a staunch loyalist, and resigned the rectorship of Christ Church on Easter Tuesday, 1775, meaning to go to Portsmouth, in New Hampshire, but political tumults there, making that impossible, he remained in Boston, and performed the duty of chaplain to some of the regiments, until the evacuation in 1776, when he left Boston. Accompanied by his family of four persons, he went to Halifax. In 1778 he was proscribed and banished. He settled at St. John, New Brunswick, after the war, and was Rector of the city, and Chaplain of the Province. He died at St. John in 1814.

His daughter Rebecca, born in 1762, married W. J. Almon, M. D., Surgeon to the Ordnance and Artillery, and died at Halifax in 1853.

MATHER BYLES (3) born in 1764, went to the British West Indies, was Commissary General at Grenada. He married June, 1799, Mary, eldest daughter of Chief Justice Bridgewater of Grenada. The writer was at St. George, Grenada, in 1907, and saw there in the Episcopal

* For further information about these French Protestants see the "Memoir" by Dr. Holmes, or to Vol. XXII, p. 62, of Massachusetts Historical Collections.

Church a marble tablet erected to the memory of Mather Byles of Boston, by his Brother Belcher. He died Dec. 17, 1802.

ELIZABETH, born in 1767, married William Scoville, Esq., of St. John, and died in 1808.

ANNA, born at Boston, married General Thomas DesBrisay, Lieut. General in the Army, Commandant at Halifax in 1799.

BELCHER was born in 1780 at Halifax, and died in England in 1815.

MATHER BROWN, was a grandson of Rev. Mather Byles (1). His mother was "Elizabeth, born in 1737, who married in 1760 Gawler Brown and died in 1763.

Mather Brown went to Europe in 1780, with a letter of introduction from his grandfather to Harrison Gray, Esq., London, a firm friend of the family. Mr. Copley had likewise been intimate with Dr. Byles before he left Boston. He also gave him a letter addressed by the old patriarch "'To Mr. Copley in the Solar system." In a letter dated Paris 23, 1781, he writes: "Dr. Franklin has given me a pass, and recommendatory letter to the famous Mr. West. He treats me with the utmost politeness; has given me an invitation to his home. I delivered him my grandfather's message, he expressed himself with the greatest esteem and affection for him, and has since introduced me at Versailles, as being grandson to one of his most particular friends in America."

In his first letter from London, 1781, he writes: "In consequence of the recommendation of Dr. Franklin, who gave me letters to his fellow townsman, the famous Mr. West of Philadelphia, I practice gratis with this gentleman, who affords me every encouragement, as well as Mr. Copley, who is particularly kind to me, welcomed me to his home, and lent me his pictures, etc. At my arrival Mr. Treasurer Gray carried me and introduced me to Lord George Germaine." In a letter in 1783 he wrote: "I have exhibited four pictures in the exhibition; the king and queen were there yesterday." In 1784: "I have painted several Americans. Yesterday I had two pictures shown his royal highness, the Prince of Wales. They were carried to the palace by his page. He criticised them, and thought them strong likenesses. I believe I never told you that the king knew a picture of mine in the last exhibition, of the keeper of Windsor Castle, and took particular notice of Mr. Gray's picture; asked him who it was, and who did it, and what book he had in his hand. Mr. West told him it was the treasurer of Boston painted by his pupil, a young man, Mr. Brown of America. The king asked him what part. He told him Massachusetts." In 1785 he writes: "Among other great people I have painted, Sir William Pepperell and family, and Hon. John Adams, ambassador to His Britannic Majesty. On the 20th of June, I had the honor to be introduced to the Duke of Northumberland at his palace; his Grace received me with the utmost politeness."

Mather Brown became afterwards artist to the king, a worthy successor to Copley. And thus two Boston-born boys filled this honorable position.

THE HALLOWELL FAMILY OF BOSTON.

ROBERT HALLOWELL arrived in Boston from London, in 1764 and entered upon his duties as Comptroller of the Customs. He was Collector of the Customs at Portsmouth, New Hampshire before the age of twenty-five. In 1765, Sabine says, "A mob surrounded his elegant house in Hanover Street, tore down his fences, broke his windows, and forcing the doors at last destroyed furniture, stole money, scattered books and papers, and drank of the wines in the cellar to drunkenness."

In 1768 Hallowell ordered Hancock's vessel, the *Liberty*, seized for smuggling wine, to be removed from the wharf to a place covered by the guns of the *Romney* frigate; and in the affray which occurred, received wounds and bruises that at the time seemed fatal.

He removed his office to Plymouth, June 1, 1774, when the port of Boston was closed. In 1775, he was an Addresser of Gage; and the year following with his family of five persons, he accompanied the British Army to Halifax. In 1778 he was proscribed and banished. He went to England and resided at Bristol. Hallowell came to the United States in 1788 and in 1790—as the executor of his own father and of his wife's father. In 1792 he removed to Boston with his family, and lived in the homestead on Batterymarch Street, which because of his mother's life interest, had not been confiscated. He was kindly received and became intimate with some distinguished citizens.

In 1816, when failing in health, he went to Gardiner, Maine to reside with his son, and died there April, 1818, in his seventy-ninth year. His wife was Hannah, daughter of Doctor Sylvester Gardiner. His two daughters, Hannah and Anne, died unmarried. His son, the Hon. Robert Hallowell, became a gentleman of great wealth and a highly respected citizen. Two of Mr. Hallowell's sisters died in England; Sarah, wife of Samuel Vaughan, in 1809; and Anne, widow of General Gould, in 1812.

The towns of Hallowell and Gardiner on the Kennebec River are named after their families.

BENJAMIN HALLOWELL of Boston, brother of Robert Hallowell, was Commissioner of the Customs. In early life he commanded a small armed vessel, and during the war ending in the conquest of Canada, commanded the province twenty-gun ship, "King George," rendering essential service notably at the retaking of Newfoundland.

Captain Hallowell's acceptance of the office of Mandamus Councillor made him a special object of public detestation.

On September 2, 1774, while the mob were assembled on Cambridge Common to receive the resignations of Danforth, Lee, and Oliver as Mandamus Councillors, Hallowell passed on his way to Roxbury. About one hundred and sixty horsemen pursued him at full gallop. Some of the leaders however, prudently dissuaded them from proceeding and they returned and dismounted, except for one man who followed Hallowell to Roxbury and caused him much annoyance. Through the action of the mob he was obliged to seek protection in Boston and leave his mansion which was built in 1738. It was used afterwards by the disunion forces as a hospital for the camp at Roxbury and his pleasure grounds were converted into a place of burial for the soldiers who died there.

In March, 1776, Captain Hallowell accompanied the British army to Halifax with his family of six persons. In July, 1776, he sailed for England in the ship Aston Hall. While at Halifax he wrote: "If I can be of the least service to either army or navy I will stay in America until the Rebellion is subdued."

The British Government granted him lands in Manchester, and two other towns in Nova Scotia, and a township in Upper Canada, which bears his name. He was a large proprietor of lands on the Kennebec, Maine, prior to the Revolution, but in 1778, he was proscribed and banished and included in the Conspiracy Act a year later, and his entire estate confiscated. His mansion house in Roxbury was seized and sold by the State, but as the fee was in Mrs. Hallowell, her heirs sued to recover of the person who held under the deed of the Commission of Confiscation and obtained judgement in 1803 in the United States Circuit Court, by which she recovered the property.

In 1784, when Mrs. Adams, the wife of the first minister from the United States was in England, she relates that both Mr. Hallowell and his wife treated her with respect and kindness. They also urged her to take lodgings with them, but this she declined. She records, too, that they lived in handsome style but not as splendidly as when in Boston. She accepted an invitation to "an unceremonious family dinner" as Mrs. Hallowell called it and met the Rev. Dr. Walter, Rector of Trinity Church, and two other gentlemen who belonged to Massachusetts.

On visiting Boston in 1796, Captain Hallowell was accompanied by his daughter, Mrs. Emsley, whose husband had just been appointed Chief Justice of Upper Canada. During his stay the odium which attached to his official relations to the Crown seemed to have been forgotten, since he was received by his former associates with the greatest kindness and hospitality. He died at York (Toronto) Upper Canada, in 1799, aged seventy-five, and was the last survivor of the Board of Commissioners.

Captain Hallowell had two sons, both of whom changed their names. WARD NICHOLAS HALLOWELL'S name was changed to Boylston. He was born in Boston in 1749. Sabine says: "I have before me the original license bearing the signature of George III by which he was authorized to change his name;" it recites—"That Nicholas Boylston, his uncle by his mother's side has conceived a very great affection for him, the petitioner, and has promised to leave him at his death, certain estates which are very considerable, etc." In early life he made a tour of Europe, visiting Italy, Turkey, Syria, Palestine, Egypt and along the coast of Barbary; and arrived in England in 1775 through France, and Flanders. He dined at Governor Hutchinson's, London, with some fellow Loyalists, July 29, 1775, and entertained the company with an account of his travels, and, at subsequent periods, exhibited the curiosities which he brought from the Holy Land, Egypt, and other countries to the unhappy exiles from his native state.

In the Autumn of the next year, he was in lodgings at Shepton Mallet. He became a member of the Loyalist Association, formed in London in 1799. In 1800 he returned to Boston and laid claim to his father's estate that had been confiscated and sold, as being the property of his mother in her own right. Having assumed her name of Boylston, he obtained the estate by due process of law, as previously stated. In 1810 he presented Harvard College with a valuable collection of medical and anatomical works and engravings. He took his mother's name of Boylston, and thus claimed the family estate. He died at his seat in Roxbury, January 7, 1828.

He was a gentleman of education and took an active interest in the Roxbury schools. His liberality is commemorated by a school, and a street named after him, Boylston street being one of the principal streets in Boston.

SIR BENJAMIN HALLOWELL (Carew), another son of Captain Hallowell, who, succeeding to the estates of the Carews of Beddington, assumed the name and arms of that family. He was one of the eight Boston boys who subsequently attained high rank in the British service. Admiral Sir Isaac Coffin, Sir Benjamin Hallowell (Carew), John Singleton Copley, the younger, who became Lord Lyndhurst, Lord Chancellor of England, General Sir John Coffin, Hugh Mackay Gordon, Sir David Ochterlony, Sir Roger Hale Sheaff, Sir Aston Coffin.

Entering the royal navy during the American war he was at the time of his death in 1834, an admiral of the Blue in the British Navy, G. C. B., K. St. F. M. His commission as Lieutenant, bears date August, 1781; as Captain, in 1793; as Rear-Admiral, in 1811; as Vice-Admiral, in 1819. He was made a Knight Commander of the Bath in 1819, and was promoted to the rank of Grand Cross in 1831.

His employments at sea were various and arduous. He was with Rodney in the memorable battle with De Grasse; also at the siege of Bastia; and in command of a ship-of-the-line under Hotham, in the encounter with the French off the Hieres Islands. He served as a volunteer on board the *Victory*, in the battle of Cape St. Vincent. In the battle, Admiral Jarvis took his official post on the quarter deck of the Victory. Calder, the captain of the fleet kept bringing reports of the increasing numbers, observed till he reached twenty-seven, and said something of the disparity. Enough of that, said Jarvis, the die is cast and if there are fifty sail, I will go through them. Hallowell could not contain himself. He slapped the great admiral on the back, crying "That's right, Sir John, and by God, we'll give them a damned good licking." He was in command of the *Swiftsure* of seventy-four guns, and contributed essentially to Nelson's victory in the battle of the Nile. From a part of the mainmast of L'Orient, which was picked up by the *Swiftsure*, Hallowell directed his carpenter to make a coffin, which was sent to Nelson with the following letter:

"Sir, I have taken the liberty of presenting you a coffin made from the mainmast of L'Orient, that when you have finished your military career in this world, you may be buried in one of your trophies. But that that period may be far distant is the earnest wish of your sincere friend,
BENJAMIN HALLOWELL."

Southey, in his "Life of Nelson," remarks: "An offering so strange and yet so suited to the occasion, was received in the spirit in which it was sent. And, as if he felt it good for him, now that he was at the summit of his wishes, to have death before his eyes, he ordered the coffin to be placed upright in his cabin. An old favorite servant entreated him so earnestly to let it be removed, that at length he consented to have the coffin carried below; but he gave strict orders that it should be safely stowed, and reserved for the purpose for which its brave and worthy donor had designed it."

In 1799, Sir Benjamin was engaged in the attacks on the castles of St. Elmo and Capua, and was honored with the Neapolitan Order of St. Ferdinand and Merit. Two years later he fell in with the French squadron, and surrendered his ship—the Swiftsure—after a sharp contest. During the peace of Amiens, he was stationed on the coast of Africa. He was with Hood in the reduction of St. Lucia and Tobago; with Nelson in the West Indies; in command of the convoy of the second expedition to Egypt; with Martin, off the mouth of the Rhone, where he assisted in driving on shore several French ships-of-war; and in the Mediterranean. His last duty seems to have been performed on the Irish station. He died at Beddington Park, in 1834, at the age of seventy-three. His wife was a daughter of Commissioner Inglefield, of Gibraltar Dock-yard. His son and heir, Charles Hallowell Carew who at the time of his decease, had attained the rank of Captain in the Royal Navy, and who married Mary, the daughter of Sir Murray Maxwell, C. B., died at the Park, in 1848. In 1851 his fifth son, Robert Hallowell Carew, late captain in the 36th Regiment, married Ann Roycroft, widow of Walter Tyson Smythes.

LIST OF CONFISCATED ESTATES BELONGING TO BENJAMIN HALLOWELL IN SUFFOLK COUNTY, AND TO WHOM SOLD.

To Samuel Gardner Jarvis, July 24, 1780; Lib. 131, fol. 230 Farm, 7 1-2 A., and dwelling-house in Roxbury, Jamaica Plain N.W.; road by widow Parker's N.E.; Joseph Williams S.E.; heirs of Capt. Newell, deceased, S. W.

To John Coffin Jones, Mar. 15, 1782; Lib. 134, fol. 60; Land and brick dwelling-house in Boston, Hanover St. N.; heirs of Alexander Chamberlain, deceased, and heirs of Miles Whitworth, deceased, W.; land in occupation of Samuel Sumner S. and W.; said Sumner and Joseph Scott, an absentee, S.; said Scott and, heirs of Benjamin Andrews, deceased, E.

To John Coffin Jones, Mar. 15, 1782; Lib. 134, fol. 62; Land and dwelling-house in Boston, land purchased by said Jones N.; Joseph Scott E.; S. and E.; said Scott and Sampson Mason S. and E.; Masons Court S.; heirs of Miles Whitworth, deceased, W.

THE OLD VASSALL HOUSE, CAMBRIDGE.

Occupied during the siege of Boston by Dr. Benjamin Church, Surgeon-General, who was arrested and confined here until his trial.

THE VASSALLS.

JOHN VASSALL, the first member of this illustrious family of which anything is definitely known, was an alderman of London, and in 1588 fitted out and commanded two ships of war to oppose the Spanish Armada. He was descended from an ancient French family traced back to about the eleventh century of the house of Du Vassall, Barons de guerdon, in Querci, Perigord.

John Vassall had two sons, Samuel and William. Samuel was one of the original patentees of lands in Massachusetts in 1628. His monument in King's Chapel, Boston, erected by Florentinus Vassall, his great grandson, in 1766, sets forth that he was "a steady and undaunted asserter of the liberties of England in 1628, he was the first who boldly refused to submit to the tax of tonnage and poundage, an unconstitutional claim of the crown arbitrarily imposed for which to the ruin of his family, his goods were seized and his person imprisoned by the star chamber court, the Parliament in July, 1641, voted him £10,445:12:2 for his damages, and resolved that he should be further considered for his personal sufferings."

His name headed the subscription list to raise money against the rebels in Ireland, and his whole life was indicative of the energy and liberality which characterized many of his descendants.

His son, WILLIAM VASSALL, born about 1590, was the first of his name who came to America. He was an assistant in the Massachusetts Bay Company and one of the original patentees of New England. In June, 1635, he embarked with his wife and six children on board the Blessing, for New England. He undoubtedly settled at first in Roxbury, for in the church record of that town is the following entry: "Mrs. Anna Vassaile, the wife of Mr. Willia Vassaile. Her husband brought five children to this land, Judith, Frances, John, Margaret, Mary." Also one other, Anne, who afterwards married Nicolas Ware.

William Vassall removed later to Scituate, where he proved himself to be an ever staunch Episcopalian. The Puritans had strong suspicion of him always as "inclining to the Bishops." While he lived in Scituate he was regarded as a highly respectable citizen and of "a busy and factious spirit." He was proprietor of a large estate, which bore the name of Newland. In 1646 he sailed to England for the redress of wrongs in the government and never returned, but in 1648 removed to Barbados and resided in the parish of St. Michael, where he died in 1655, aged 65 years. He bequeathed to his son John one-third of his real estate and the remainder to his five daughters. His Scituate estate consisted of about 120 acres, with house, barns, and the privilege of "making an oyster bed in North River," before his house. The estate was conveyed by Joshua Hubbard to John Cushen and Mathyas Briggs for £120.

His daughter Judith married Resolved White, the eldest brother of

Peregrine White, at Scituate, 1640. Frances married James Adams at Marshfield 1646. Ann married Nicholas Ware of Virginia. Margaret married Joshua Hubbard of Scituate. Mary was unmarried and alive at Barbados in 1655.

JOHN VASSALL, only son of William Vassall, born about 1625. In 1643 his name is on the militia roll of Scituate, and later bore the rank of captain. In 1652 he sold his house in Boston for £59. In 1661 he sold his Scituate estates and removed, it is supposed, to Cape Fear, N. C., and later to the West Indies.

JOHN VASSALL, the only son of Samuel, whose monument is in King's Chapel, married Ann, the daughter of John Lewis, an English resident of Geno. He went to Jamaica shortly after it was taken in 1655, and laid the foundation of the great estate which his posterity enjoyed until the emancipation in 1834. He had two sons, William and Leonard, from whom descended all of the name of which there is any subsequent record.

LEONARD VASSALL, son of said William, was born in Jamaica, 1678, and was twice married. His first wife was Ruth Gale, of Jamaica by whom he had seventeen children. She died in Boston in 1733. His second wife was widow Phebe Goss, by whom he had one daughter. He removed to Boston previous to 1723. He was early connected with Christ Church. In 1730 he was instrumental in founding Trinity church. The original building was built on land which he had purchased of William Speakman, baker, 1728, for £450. The lot covered by the church was bounded by Seven-starr Lane (Summer street), 86 feet and 169 feet on Bishop's Lane (Hawley street), and is nearly opposite the estate which he purchased in 1727 of Simeon Stoddard, and where he resided until his death. He had large and valuable estates in Braintree and Jamaica.

John and William Vassall, two of Major Leonard's sons, were important men in Boston, and added much to the prosperity of the town.

JOHN VASSALL, the elder brother of William, was born in the West Indies, Sept. 7, 1713, and graduated from Harvard college in 1732. In 1734 he married Elizabeth, the daughter of Lieut. Gov. Spencer Phips by whom he had four children, and later he married Lucy, the daughter of Jonathan Barron of Chelmsford by whom he had one child. He resided in Cambridge most of his life and died there November 27, 1747. December 30, 1741, John Vassall conveyed to his brother Henry (a planter who had married Penelope the daughter of Isaac Royal of Antigua), in consideration of £9050 over seven acres of land in Cambridge, with dwelling house, barn and outhouses. During the Revolution, no doubt, this house was the headquarters of the Surgeon-General and perhaps a hospital. Dr. Benjamin Church, after he was detected in correspondence with the enemy, was arrested here and confined to his quarters until trial, and left a record of his occupation of the house by his name, cut with a penknife on one of the doors of his chamber, which is still legible though since covered with several coats of paint.

After the death of John Vassall, his son, who was also known by the name of John, erected the house in Cambridge, which has since become famous through Washington's connection with it, as during the Revolution it was used as his headquarters, and afterwards it was the home of Prof. Henry W. Longfellow.

MAJOR JOHN VASSALL, the grandson of Leonard Vassall, was born in Cambridge, June 12, 1738, and graduated from Harvard College in 1757. He erected a beautiful edifice on the estate inherited from his father and occupied it until driven from it by the rage of the mob. The estate was confiscated in 1774 and he removed to Boston for protection, and in that city continued to dwell upon the estate adjoining that of his uncle, William Vassall, on Pemberton Hill, until 1776.

At the commencement of the Revolution he was obliged to flee with his family to England. He had large possessions in Cambridge, Boston and Dorchester,* all of which were confiscated and himself exiled, soon after he departed from home. He joined the British army in Halifax, and from there sailed to England. He died there suddenly, October 2, 1796. An obituary published in the "Gentleman's Magazine" said of him, "he had a very considerable property in America where he lived in princely style. Sometime after the disturbances took place, having taken a very active part and spared no expense to support the royal cause, he left his possessions there to the ravagers, and having fortunately very large estates in Jamaica, he came with his family to England. He carried his loyalty so far as not to use the family motto, "Soepe pro rege, semper pro republica."

In 1774 he had been addresser of Hutchinson and for this great offence to the mobs, he was driven from his home, his property was confiscated and he was exiled. During his residence in England, he seems to have lived near Bristol and died at Clifton. A part of the Jamaica grant was still in the family, and his several children inherited a competence. His wife Elizabeth, sister of Lieut.-Gov. Thomas Oliver, died at Clifton, in 1807. His children were John, who died at Lyndhurst, in the year 1800; Thomas Oliver, who died in England in 1807; Elizabeth; Robert Oliver, who became a member of the Council of Jamaica, and died at Abington Hall, in that island in 1827; a second Elizabeth, who married a Mr. Lemaistre and died at Cheltenham, in 1856; Leonard and Mary, who alone was born in England, who married Mr. Archer, and who with her only child, deceased, at Clifton, in 1806.

SPENCER THOMAS VASSALL, son of the aforesaid John Vassall, born at Cambridge, Mass., 1764. Entered the British Army as Ensign at the age of twelve years. He rose to the command of the 38th regiment, and was regarded as one of the bravest officers in the service. He was mortally wounded at the storming of Monte Video, in 1807. His remains were taken to England and buried in St. Paul's church, Bristol, where there is a monument to his memory. His son, Spencer Lambert Hunter, who died in 1846, was a Knight and a captain in the Royal Navy. His other son,

*See p. 184 concerning his mansion in Dorchester.

Rawdon John Popham, was a colonel in the Royal Artillery. His youngest daughter Catherine married Thomas L. Marchant Saumerez, son of the admiral.

WILLIAM VASSALL, brother of Major John Vassall, was born in Jamaica, November 23, 1715, and graduated at Harvard College in 1733. In 1774 he was appointed Mandamus Councillor, but was not sworn. He was also sheriff of Middlesex County. He owned considerable property, and was the possessor of a fine estate near Bristol, R. I. He was prominent among the Loyalists of Boston, and was singled out early as an enemy to the Revolutionary cause. He was proscribed and banished and obliged to flee with his family to England. Mr. Vassall was for many years connected with King's Chapel, Boston, and in 1785 protested by proxy against the change in the Liturgy and the unauthorized ordination of James Freeman.

The confiscation of his estate gave rise to a singular suit. As the Federal Constitution was adopted, a State could be sued; and, at Mr. Vassall's instance, proceedings against Massachusetts were commenced in the court of the United States; and Hancock, who was governor, was summoned as defendant in the case; he however declined to appear, and soon after the eleventh amendment to the Constitution put an end to the right of Loyalists to test the validity of the Confiscation Acts of the Revolution. Mr. Vassall died at Battersea Rise, England, in 1800, aged eighty-five. He was upright, generous, and loving. Church and society lost in him an eager, zealous advocate, an upright Christian, of an honorable and unblemished reputation. His first wife, Ann Davis, bore him Sarah, four named William, two named Fanny, Francis, Lucretia, Henry and Catherine. His second wife, Margaret Hubbard, was the mother of Margaret, Ann, Charlotte, Leonard and Nathaniel. Each wife had twins. Nathaniel, the youngest son, a captain in the Royal Navy, died in London in 1832.

WILLIAM VASSALL, son of the preceding William Vassall, was born in Boston in 1753, and graduated at Harvard College in 1771. He was a Loyalist and went to England. He inherited the bulk of his father's property in the West Indies, which descended to his nephew, Rev. William Vassall, rector of Hardington, England, "but so burdened and deteriorated in consequence of emancipation of the slaves that it was not worth anything," and that gentleman declined to administer upon it. He died at the Weston House, near Totness, December 2, 1843. Ann, his widow, died at the same place October 1846, aged seventy-five years.

FLORENTINUS VASSALL was the son of William Vassall and a great-grandson of Samuel, to whose memory he erected the beautiful marble monument in King's Chapel, when he was in Boston in 1766. He was here again in 1775 and in that year went to England. He was born in Jamaica, and lived there the greater part of his life. He died in London in 1778.

Of the immense domain fifteen miles wide on both sides of the Kennebec River, extending from the vicinity of Merry Meeting Bay to the

COLONEL JOHN VASSALL'S MANSION, CAMBRIDGE.

Washington's headquarters during the siege of Boston afterwards known as the Craigie and Longfellow House.

southerly line of the town of Norridgwock, he was the owner of one twenty-fourth part. In his will, executed in 1776, he gave to his son Richard and to Richard's daughter, Elizabeth, life estate in these lands, and then devised them in entail to his male children. The bequest proved of little value to either. After the lapse of years the rights of Elizabeth and her son Henry were transferred separately to parties in Boston, to test the title which was claimed by squatters. Three of them were sued in the name of the son. The cases were carried up to the United States Supreme Court, where it was decided that during his mother's life, he could not maintain an action. After her decease, suit against one settler was renewed, but on intimation by the court that fifty years' possession was sufficient to presume a grant, or title without consideration, another point, namely, whether the right of the plaintiff to recover was barred by the statute of limitation. The defendant paid a small sum for the land he occupied, and each party his own costs. Thus in 1851 terminated litigation, which for a long time was the subject of great interest on the Kennebec, and elsewhere in Maine. This granddaughter Elizabeth was a remarkable woman. Those who knew her speak of her as brilliant and witty, as possessed of queenly grace of manner, as well informed, of wonderful tact, and of excellent sense. Her first husband was Sir Godfrey Webster, Bart. By this marriage she was the mother of Sir Godfrey Vassall Webster, Bart., who died in 1836, of Lieut-Col. Sir Henry Vassall Webster, K. T. S., of the British Army, who died in London in 1847, aged 54, and of Harriet, who married Admiral Sir Fleetwood B. Reynolds, C. B. K. C. H., who died at Florence in 1849, leaving an only child, the wife of the son and heir of the Earl of Oxford. Another son, Charles Richard Fox, whose father was Lord Holland, married Mary Fitzclarence, second daughter of King William IV., and who, in 1845 was a colonel in the army, and aide-de-camp to Queen Victoria.

In 1797 Lady Webster married Lord Holland, who took by sign-manual the surname of Vassal which, however, was not assumed by his children. As Lady Holland, she was the mother of three children, who died young, of Henry Holland, who became at the death of his father, Lord Holland, of Mary Elizabeth, wife of Lord Lilford, and of Georgianna Anne who died in 1819.

The friendly feelings of Bonaparte towards Lady Holland, especially after the peace of Amiens, is well known, and that in return "for the many acts of kindness, which she had bestowed upon him" he left her a gold snuff box which had been presented to him by Pope Pius VI., containing a card with these words: "L'Empereur to Lady Holland, temoigne de satisfaction et d'estime." She died at London, in 1845, aged 75. Among her bequests were the income of an estate, about £1500 per annum, to Lord John Russill, for his life, and a legacy of £100 to Macaulay the historian.

"The Vassall family has ever been distinguished for enterprise, magnanimity, and noble bearing. If some of this name were not only often, but always, for their king it must be admitted that they made as great sacrifices to loyalty as did their forefathers to liberty."

The Vassals were connected by marriage and business dealings with the Olivers and Royalls. All three families had acquired great wealth in the West Indies, and although they lost their great possessions in New England, by the Confiscation Act, yet they were much better situated than their fellow sufferers as they retained their West Indian estates till they, too, became worthless, after the emancipation of the slaves.

LIST OF CONFISCATED ESTATES BELONGING TO JOHN VASSAL IN SUFFOLK COUNTY AND TO WHOM SOLD.

To John Williams, Sept. 25, 1781; Lib. 133, fol. 110; Land 3 1-2 A., and buildings in Dorchester, the high road S. and W.; Ebenezer and Lemuel Clap N.; Zebadiah Williams E.—— 1-2 A. South of the above, Mr. Jeffries E.; the high road on the other side.

To Isaiah Doane, Jan. 8, 1784; Lib. 141, fol. 2; Land and buildings in Boston, Tremont St. E.; heirs of John Jefferies deceased S.; heirs of Jeremiah Allen deceased, William Vassall and heirs of Joseph Sherburne W.; William Vassall and land of the old brick church N.

GENERAL ISAAC ROYALL.

WILLIAM ROYALL, the first member of this family of which there is anything definitely known, emigrated to Salem probably during the year of 1629. He had a grant of land there known as "Royall's side" or "Ryall's Neck." He married, at Boston or Malden, Phoebe Green. He was in Casco Bay as early as 1635. His house was built on the south side of what was afterwards known as Royall's River, near its mouth, in North Yarmouth. Here he lived until the troubles with the neighboring Indians, which induced him to remove to Dorchester in 1675, accompanied by his son William, who was born probably at the Casco settlement in 1640. He was a carpenter by occupation, and died in 1724, in the 85th year of his age, and is buried in the tomb built by his son Isaac in the Dorchester burying ground.

Isaac Royall, son of the aforesaid William, born probably at the settlement in Casco Bay about 1672. He early settled at Boston, and engaged in trade, making frequent voyages to Antigua and other West India Islands. He married, according to Boston records, on July 1, 1697, Elizabeth, daughter of Asaph Eliot, and grandniece of the apostle to the Indians of that name. His wife was the widow of one Oliver, probably of Dorchester.

For a period of forty years Isaac Royall was a resident of Antigua, although his frequent presence in Boston during that time is evinced by his signature to conveyances. His name first appears on the Suffolk records in a mortgage deed given by himself and wife on the 24th August, 1697, he then being styled a "merchant of Boston." His trading operations between 1704 and 1710 with the West Indies, proved the foundation of his fortune.

On December 26, 1732, he purchased of the heirs of Lieutenant Governor Usher the estate in Charlestown (Medford) containing about five hundred acres. The large Mansion house was built by Usher, but has since become widely known as the Royall Mansion. It was one of the finest and most pretentious residences of the time within the suburbs of Boston. It is described by a visitor at that time as "A fine Country Seat belonging to Mr. Isaac Royall, being one of the grandest in N. America." This mansion was greatly added to, and almost rebuilt by the wealthy West Indian planter. He petitioned the General Court in December, 1737, that he might not be taxed on the twenty-seven slaves which he brought with him from Antigua. "That he removed from Antigua with his family, and brought with him among other things, and chattels, a parcel of negroes, designed for his own use, and not any of them for merchandise."

Isaac Royall, the builder of this mansion, did not live long to enjoy his princely estate, dying in 1739, not long after its completion. His widow, who survived him eight years, died in this house, and was interred from Colonel Oliver's in Dorchester April 25, 1747. The pair share the same tomb in the old Dorchester burying place. His daughter Penelope married Colonel Henry Vassall of Cambridge in 1742. He died in 1769, and she died in Boston in 1800, aged 76.

GENERAL ISAAC ROYALL, a son, who was born in Antigua, probably in 1719, married Elizabeth McIntosh in 1738, but lived mostly in Boston. He became an extensive purchaser of lands in various parts of the State, and was one of the original proprietors of the township of Royalston in Worcester County. He was a member of the Artillery Company of Boston in 1750, was made a brigadier general in 1761, the first of that title among Americans. He was elected by the House a Councillor of the Province, and served in that office until 1774, completing twenty-three years of consecutive service.

Much has been written of this man's position at the time of the colonial disturbances in 1774. Possessed of large wealth, and the influence that riches and education carried with them, his course was watched by the people with intense anxiety. He was known to have much in common with the faithful band of Loyalists, who were gathered about Cambridge and Boston, yet he was still faithful to the people's church, and most of his family ties held him to the popular cause. A long letter, written by him to Lord Dartmouth, dated in January of 1774, exists in the archives of the Massachusetts Historical Society's Proceedings, 1873-1875, page 179. Harris says, "there can be no good reason for doubting the sincerity of his sympathy with the people, and although, when the time came to make a choice, he was prevailed upon to adhere to the side of the government, there is abundant evidence of his continued love towards New England and his desire to return and end his days here." How much harder was it then for a man in his position to make the great sacrifices he did, to give up his loved home and his property, all for the cause of his King.

He wrote to Lord Dartmouth, "I am conscious that in all public affairs I have made the honor of my king and the real Interests and Peace of my country the ultimate end of all my transactions. I am so to live in this world as that I may be happy in another, and no man more ardently wishes and earnestly prays to the God of Peace for the Restoration of those happy days, which formerly subsisted between us and our mother country than I do."

Three days before the battle of Lexington, Colonel Royall took his departure from Medford. He drove in his chariot, which was one of the few in this vicinity, to Boston, and never again returned.

The mansion itself was indeed one of the finest of colonial residences, standing, as it did, in the midst of elegant surroundings. In the front, or what is now the west side, was the paved court. Reaching farther west were the extensive gardens, opening from the courtyard, a broad path leading to the summer house. The slave quarters were at the south. The brick slave quarters have remained unchanged, and are the last visible relics of slavery in New England. The deep fireplace where the slaves prepared their food is still in place, and the roll of slaves has certainly been called in sight of Bunker Hill, though never upon its summit.

The interior woodwork of the house is beautifully carved, especially the drawing room, guest chamber, and staircase. The walls are panelled, and the carving on either side of the windows is very fine, that in the guest chamber being the most elaborate.

One interested in colonial architecture may wander for hours through this noble house, and yet feel that there is more to learn. The dark cellar, full of passages, the garret with its corners, and the secret staircase so often searched for, yet undiscovered, all furnish good material for imaginary pictures of the Revolutionary days of our ancestors.

The Royall mansion is now owned and occupied by "The Royall House Association" and is open for the public.

When Colonel Royall left his mansion he had prepared to take passage from Salem to Antigua, but, having gone into Boston, the Sunday previous to the battle of Lexington, and remained there until that affair occurred, he was, by the course of events, shut up in the town. He sailed for Halifax very soon, still intending, as he says, for Antigua, but on the arrival of his son-in-law, George Erving, and his daughter, with the troops from Boston, he was by them persuaded to sail for England, whither his other son-in-law, Sir William Pepperell, had preceded.

Upon his arrival in England, he exchanged visits with Governors Pownall, Bernard, and Hutchinson, Colonel Royall, after the loss of some of his nearest relatives and of his own health, requested that he be allowed to return "home" to Medford and to be buried by the side of his wife, his father and mother, and the rest of his friends. He would fain have lived

GENERAL. ISAAC ROYALL'S MANSION, MEDFORD.

He was kind to his slaves, charitable to the poor and friendly to everybody.

in amity with all men and with his king too, but the Revolution engulfed him. But he is not forgotten. He died in England 1781, his large hearted benevolence showed itself in many bequests to that country that had driven him forth and to which he was an alien. He bequeathed upwards of two thousand acres of land in Worcester County to found the first Law Professorship of Harvard University and his other bequests were numerous and liberal. He has a town (Royalston) in Massachusetts named for him, and is remembered with affection in the place of his former abode. His virtues and popularity at first saved his estate, as his name was not included with those of his sons-in-law, Sir William Pepperell and George Erving, in the "conspirators act," but on the representation of the selectmen of Medford *"that he went voluntarily to our enemies"* his property was taken under the confiscation act and forfeited. It was held by the State until 1805, when it was released by the Commonwealth, owing to the large bequests that Colonel Royall made to the public. It was then purchased by Robert Fletcher, who divided the estate up into house lots and sold them to various persons.

General Royall's mansion was the centre of great festivities, and the most noted families of Boston and vicinity were entertained there. He was noted for his hospitality and was always generous and charitable to the poor, and an excellent citizen. Brooks in his "History of Medford" says hospitality was almost a passion with him. No home in the Colony was more open to friends, no gentleman gave better dinners, or drank costlier wines. As a master he was kind to his slaves, charitable to the poor, and friendly to everybody.

He was a most accurate man and in his daily journal minutely described every visitor, topic, and incident and even descended to recording what slippers he wore and when he went to bed. Some one said in speaking of Colonel Isaac Royall, "it is not that he loved the colonies less but England more." Among his bequests was a legacy of plate to the first church of Medford, and legacies to the clergymen, and while a member of the House of Representatives, he presented the chandelier which adorned its hall.

After the departure of General Royall from his beautiful home, it was taken possession of by the rebels who came pouring into the environs of Boston and laid seige to same. Colonel, afterwards General, John Stark,* made the mansion his headquarters, and his New Hampshire troops pitched their camp in the adjacent grounds. It was afterwards occupied by General Lee, who took up his quarters in the mansion, whose echoing corridors suggested to his fancy the name of Hobgoblin Hall.

Elizabeth, the wife of Isaac Royall, died at Medford, July, 1770, and

---

* General John Stark's brother Colonel William Stark, was a man of great bravery and hardihood. Before the Revolution he was a much greater man than his brother John. He commanded New England troops in the capture of Ticonderoga, Crown Point, Louisburg and Quebec. In West's picture, "The Death of Gen. Wolf," he is shown as holding Wolf in his arms. William Stark remained loyal and became a colonel in the Royal Army. He was killed from a fall from his horse at the battle of Long Island.

was buried in the marble tomb in Dorchester. Their daughter Elizabeth, the wife of Sir William Pepperell, died at sea upon the voyage to England in 1775.*

It is said that the male line of the Royalls has ceased to exist in Maine and Massachusetts. The writer knows not of a single living individual bearing the surname who has descended from the stock that in the beginning of the settlement was so vigorous, and promised to be so prolific. This statement will also apply to many other Loyalists' families that were driven from their homes at the commencement of the Revolution.

GENERAL WILLIAM BRATTLE.

Thomas Brattle, the forefather of the Brattle family that settled in Boston, was at his death accounted the wealthiest man in the Colony. Though we have no information concerning the family prior to the coming of Thomas Brattle to New England, it is only reasonable to believe that he was descended from an educated and intelligent line. Only four generations bearing the name existed here, and it is a notable circumstance that all the male representatives of those four generations were men of remarkable powers and distinguished abilities.

THOMAS BRATTLE was born about 1624, and was a merchant of Boston. He was a member of the Artillery Company and captain in the militia, and the commander of several expeditions against hostile Indians. He was one of the founders of the Old South Church. He married Elizabeth, the daughter of Captain William Tyng, by whom he had seven children. His death occurred in 1683.

THOMAS BRATTLE, the son of the former, was born in 1658, and was a graduate of Harvard College. He was a very intelligent man, and was treasurer of Harvard College for twenty-five years. He was one of the founders of the Brattle Street church, and gave an organ to the King's Chapel when it was rebuilt in 1710, the first organ used in Boston in a church. He was a steadfast opposer of the proceedings of the courts during the witchcraft delusion in 1692. He was a Fellow of the Royal Society, and died in 1713. President Quincy says of him: "He was distinguished for his private benevolences and public usefulness."

WILLIAM BRATTLE graduated from Harvard college, and for over twenty years was pastor of the Cambridge church. He was also a member of the Royal Society of London.

WILLIAM BRATTLE, son of the former, was baptized by his father in 1706. He graduated from Harvard College in 1722, and was a member

---

* For an account of the Pepperell family see New Eng. Gen. Reg. xx. 4. Those descended from him comprise probably a hundred families holding the highest social positions including dignitaries in church and state, baronets, presidents of colleges, D. D's., and bishops, and others of exalted rank, perhaps more numerous than can be found in any one family in the British realms.

of the Ancient and Honorable Artillery Company. He was a theologian, and as a physician he was widely known, and no higher tribute to his eminence as a barrister need be sought than in the years 1736-7, when, only thirty years of age, he was elected by the House and Council to the office of Attorney General.

He possessed strong peculiarities, and Sabine says of him that "A man of most eminent talents and of greater eccentricities has seldom lived." He inherited a large and well invested property, and had ample means to cultivate those tastes to which, by his nature and education, he was inclined. He was for many years Major General of the Province, and afterwards Brigadier General. His large and beautifully situated house, which now exists in Cambridge, though greatly transformed, known as the "Old Brattle House" was the resort of the fashion and style of this section of the country. At the age of twenty-one he married Katherine, the daughter of Governor Gurdon Saltonstall. She died at Cambridge in 1752, and he married again in 1755, Mrs. Martha, widow of James Allen, and daughter of Thomas Fitch. General Brattle seems to have inherited from his father the same love for and interest in the welfare of his Alma Mater, which so characterized the beloved minister of the church in Cambridge. He was long one of her overseers, and in 1762 was appointed by the Council one of a committee for the erection of Hollis Hall, a task which was satisfactorily completed.

When the Revolution broke out in 1775, he was holding a very honorable office under the crown. Harris says he was "on terms of friendship with many of the regular army officers quartered in Boston and vicinity. His cultivated and refined tastes tending always to draw him to court, rather than plebeian society, were, no doubt, inducements for him to remain loyal. Certain it was, while studiously endeavoring to preserve friendly and peaceful relations with his townsmen and neighbors, he was openly opposed to their principles. He was an Addresser of Gen. Gage and approved of his plans, but at last public excitement reached such a height that he deemed it wise to withdraw from Cambridge, and leaving his house and property in the hands of his only daughter, Madame Wendell, at that time a widow, he quietly joined the Royal army in Boston, and at the evacuation in 1776, sailed with the forces to Halifax, where he died in October of the same year. It is said that his gravestone is still to be seen in the churchyard in that city." There is a portrait of William Brattle in the possession of his descendants, which was painted by Copley, being one of the first productions of that eminent artist. Of his nine children, only two lived to maturity, Katherine in whom the line but not the name was perpetuated, and Thomas.

Katherine was married to John Mico Wendell, a merchant of Boston, in 1752, who was of Dutch origin. After the death of her husband, Katherine removed to Cambridge and resided there until her death in 1821, at the age of nearly ninety-one years. The house was situated near the corner of what afterwards became Wendell street, and North ave. The Centinel of February 10, 1821, contained a memoir from which we gain some knowledge of her character.

"Descended from honorable families, she possessed the virtues and and maintained the honors of her ancestors. . . . During the war of the Revolution, both her talents and virtues were put to severe tests, and by her wisdom and discretion, her energy, and integrity, her benevolence, and charity, she conciliated the favor of men in power, civil and military; secured to herself personal respect, and rescued the paternal inheritance from the hazard of confiscation. It was by her means that the portion of the estate that fell to her brother Thomas, then in England, was in a like manner preserved. . . . . Her contributions aided in the translation of the Bible into the languages of the East, and in the diffusion of Christian knowledge among the poor and destitute of our own country."

She had five children, but three of them died before reaching maturity. Governor James Sullivan, who knew Thomas Brattle well, wrote of him: "Major Brattle exercised a deep reverence for the principles of government, and was a cheerful subject of the laws. He respected men of science, as the richest ornament of their country. If he had ambition, it was to excel in acts of hospitality, benevolence, and charity. The dazzling splendor of heroes, and the achievements of political intrigues, passed unnoticed before him, but the character of the man of benevolence filled his heart with emotions of sympathy." . . . "In his death, the sick, the poor and the distressed have lost a liberal benefactor, politeness an ornament, and philanthropy one of its most discreet and generous supporters."

THOMAS BRATTLE, the youngest and only surviving son of General William and Katherine Saltonstall Brattle, was born at Cambridge in 1742. He graduated from Harvard College in 1760, and not long afterwards visited England and the Continent, for the double purpose of study and travel.

When the war broke out, he was still abroad, and being informed of the position taken by his father, he conceived to be the most prudent course to remain in England. While abroad he traveled over various parts of Great Britain, and made a tour through Holland and France, and was noticed by persons of distinction. Returning to London, he zealously and successfully labored to ameliorate the condition of his countrymen, who had been captured and were in prison. This restored to him his estates, for he was included in the Confiscation, Proscription and Banishment Act of 1778. He returned to America in 1779, and 1784 the enactments against him in Massachusetts were repealed, and he took possession of his patrimony. He found his mansion home at Cambridge had been thoroughly ransacked and damaged by the Continental troops, who had occupied it during the war. The neglected estate was restored to its former beauty, and improved by the erection of a green-house, probably one of the earliest known in this part of the country. He lived here for many years, and became well known for his charities. He died, universally lamented and beloved, on the seventh of February, 1801, and was laid to rest in the family tomb, the last of his name. He was never married.

The only descendants of General William and Katherine Saltonstall Brattle, are through their daughter Katherine, who married John Mico Wendell.

CONFISCATED ESTATE OF WILLIAM BRATTLE IN BOSTON, AND TO WHOM SOLD.

To James Allen, May 12, 1781; Lib. 132 fol. 202; Land and buildings in Boston, Tremont St. W.; John Rowe and Henry Caner, an absentee, S.; Nathaniel Holmes E.; George Bethune N. and E.; John Andrew and heirs of Samuel Pemberton deceased N.; Robert McElroy W. and N.; passageway W. and W. [N.]

JOSEPH THOMPSON.

JOSEPH THOMPSON was the son of Joseph and Sarah (Bradshaw) Thompson, who were located in Medford as early as 1772, coming from Woburn, and descended from the same family as Sir Benjamin Thompson (Count Rumford). They lie buried side by side in the little burial ground on Salem street, Medford. Joseph, the subject of this sketch, was born May 16, 1734. He was married in Boston, 1759, to Rebecca Gallup, whom Isaac Royall refers to in his will as a kinswoman of his wife.

In addition to the double portion assigned to him out of his father's estate, he added to it from time to time by the purchase of several estates. His occupation is mentioned in the deeds as that of merchant. In June, 1775, news reached the Provincial Congress, that the Ervings, of Boston, had fitted out, under color of chartering to Thompson, a schooner of their own, to make a volage to New Providence (Nassau, Bahama Islands), to procure "fruit, turtle and provisions of other kinds for the sustenance and feasting of those troops who are, as pirates and robbers, committing daily hostilities and depredations on the good people of this colony and all America." Congress therefore resolved that Captain Samuel McCobb, a member, "be immediately dispatched to Salem and Marblehead, to secure said Thompson, and prevent said vessel from going said voyage, and cause the said Thompson to be brought before this Congress." Thompson, however, escaped, and afterwards went to England. On June 3, 1780, on the petition of Rebecca Thompson, asking leave be granted her to rejoin her husband in England on the first convenient opportunity, and to also return again to this state, the General Court, and the committee of Inspection for Medford, were directed to see that she carried no letters nor papers that might be detrimental to this, or any of the United States of America.*

James Prescott, Joseph Hosmer and Samuel Thatcher, Esq., were

* Medford Historical Register, Vol. viii, p. 50.

ordered to make sales of certain estates situated in the county of Middlesex, confiscated to the use of the government, belonging to Joseph Thompson, merchant. Six acres of salt marsh on Medford river were sold to Ebenezer Hall, Jr., for £70; a dwelling house and yard bounded south on the great road, to Thomas Patten for £295; 1 1-2 rods of land (part of the dower estate of his mother), with 3-16 of the dwelling house, 1-4 of an acre of mowing land, 20 rods of plow land, to Samuel Kidder for £24.15; a pew in the meeting house to Susanna Brooks, widow, for £10; 8 acres of land bounded south on the great road and west on Proprietor's Way, and situated near the Hay Market, to Jonathan Foster for £252.10, and about 10 poles of land with a joiner's shop thereon, bounded north on the road to Malden, to Ebenezer Hall for £40.5, making a total of £692.5.

A Mr. Thompson died in England during the war, probably the same.

COLONEL JOHN ERVING.

The Erving family was one of the oldest and most respected families in Boston. Hon. John Erving, the father of the colonel, was one of the most eminent merchants in America, and was a member of the Council of Massachusetts for twenty years. The Hon. Robert C. Winthrop, his great-grandson, in a public address in 1845, thus refers to him: "A few dollars earned on a commencement day, by ferrying passengers over Charles River, when there was no bridge—shipped to Lisbon in the shape of fish, and from thence to London in the shape of fruit, and from thence brought home to be reinvested in fish, and to be re-entered upon the same triangular circuit of trade—laid the foundations of the largest fortunes of the day, a hundred years ago." Mr. Erving, by his wife Abigail, had a large family. He died in Boston in 1786, aged ninety-three.

COLONEL JOHN ERVING, eldest son of the preceding, was born in Boston, June 26, 1727, was a colonel of the Boston regiment of militia, a warden of Trinity church. He graduated at Harvard University in 1747. In 1760 he signed the Boston Memorial, and was thus one of the fifty-eight who were the first men in America to array themselves against the officers of the Crown, but like many others that did not favor many acts of the government, he could not tolerate mob rule, and therefore threw his lot in on the side that represented law and authority.

When Hancock's sloop Liberty was seized for smuggling in 1768, by the commissioners, the fury of the mob became great. They fell upon the officers, several of whom barely escaped with their lives. Mr. Erving, besides having his sword broken, was beaten with clubs and sticks, and considerably wounded. He was not concerned with the seizure of the sloop.

In 1774 he was an addresser of Hutchinson, and the same year appointed mandamus councillor. On the evacuation of Boston, he

MAJOR GENERAL SIR DAVID OCHTERLONY.

Born in Boston Feb. 12, 1758. There is erected in Calcutta a monument to him, which is one of the notable sights of that city. Died at Meerut, India in 1825.

and his family of nine persons accompanied the army to Halifax, and from there he went to England. In 1778 he was proscribed and banished. He died at Bath, England, June 17, 1816, aged eighty-nine. His wife, Maria Catherina (youngest daughter of Governor Shirley), with whom he lived sixty years, died a few months before him. A daughter of Mr. Erving married Governor Scott of the island of Dominica and died at that island February 13, 1768. His son, Dr. Shirley Erving, entered Harvard College in 1773, but his education was cut short by the Revolution. He became a prominent physician at Portland, Maine, and died at Boston in 1813, aged fifty-five. His widow survived him for many years. They left two sons and one daughter. The Erving mansion house was on Milk street, and was confiscated.

GEORGE ERVING was a prominent merchant of Boston. He was one of the fifty-eight memorialists who were the first men in America to array themselves against the officers of the Crown, but he could not take part with the mobs in their lawless and brutal actions. He was an Addresser of Hutchinson in 1774, was proscribed under the Act of 1778, and his estate was confiscated under the Conspiracy Act of 1779. He went to Halifax with his family of five persons, and thence to England. He died in London in 1806 at the age of seventy. His wife was a daughter of General Isaac Royall of Medford.

CONFISCATED ESTATES BELONGING TO COLONEL JOHN ERVING AND TO WHOM SOLD.

To James Lloyd, May 4, 1787; Lib. 160 fol. 105; Land and buildings in Boston, Kilby St., formerly Mackerel Lane, E.; heirs of John Erving deceased N.; heirs of Samuel Hughes W.; Joseph Winthrop S.
To John Codman, Jr., July 2, 1787; Lib. 160, fol. 201; Land and messuage in Boston, Newbury St., W.; John Crosby N.; E. and N., John Soley E. and S.; passage or alley S. — Land 14 A., in Walpole, road from Walpole to the sign of the Black Lamb in Stoughton N.; Nathaniel Preble S.E.; Philip Bardin S.W. and N.W.
To Nathaniel Appleton, Feb. 13, 1789; Lib. 164 fol. 149; Land, 14 A., in Walpole, road from Walpole to the sign of the Black Lamb in Stoughton N.; Nathaniel Preble S.E.; Philip Bardin S.W. and N.W.
To John Deming, May 6, 1789; Lib. 166 fol. 11; Land and messuage in Boston, Newbury St. W.; John Crosby N.; E. and N.; John Soley E. and S.; passage or alley S.

MAJOR GENERAL SIR DAVID OCHTERLONY.

CAPTAIN DAVID OCHTERLONY, the father of the subject of this memoir, was born in Forfarshire, Scotland, and was descended from one of the most ancient families in that country. In 1226 the land of "Othirlony" was exchanged by his ancestors for those of Kenney in Forfarshire possessed by the Abbey of Aberbrothock. Kenney had been bestowed on the Abbey by its founder, King William, the Lion King of Scotland.

David, was a captain in the merchant service, and resided for a while at Montrose. Boston was one of the many ports visited by him in his voyages. Five years after his first appearance in Boston, June 4, 1757, his intention of marriage was published, to Katherine, daughter of Andrew Tyler of Boston, by his wife Miriam, a sister of Sir William Pepperell. On 27th of June, 1762, he purchased a brick house with about 1500 square feet of land on Back street, which at that time was that part of Salem street from Hanover to Prince street. Meanwhile three sons and a daughter were born. The eldest of these, MAJOR GENERAL SIR DAVID OCHTERLONY, born 12 Feb. 1758, who was to revive the name in a new locality: Captain Ochterlony, the father, continued his career as a mariner, but a few years after locating in Boston, he died in 1765, at St. Vincent, W. I. His widow went to England, where she married Sir Isaac Heard of London, Norroy and Garter King of Arms, and gentleman of the Red Rod, to the order of the Bath.

The son David was a scholar at the Latin School in Boston, when his father died. At the age of eighteen he entered the army and went to India, as a cadet, and in 1778 received an appointment as Ensign. In 1781 he was Quartermaster to the 71st Regiment of Foot. During the twenty years that succeeded, he was exposed to all the danger and fatigue of incessant service in the East. He attained the rank of Major in 1800, and of Lieutenant-Colonel in 1803, and Colonel in 1812. His commission of Major General bears date June 1, 1814. In 1817 he received the thanks of both Houses of Parliament. His health, after nearly fifty years of uninterrupted military duty in a tropical climate, became impaired, and he resigned a political office in India with the intention of proceeding to Calcutta, and thence to England. This plan he did not live to execute. He died at Meerut in 1825, while there for a change of air. He was Deputy-Adjutant-General at the Battle of Delhi, after which he was sent as envoy to the Court of Sha Alum. For his conduct in the Nepaulese war, he was created a Knight Commander of the Bath, and May 7, 1816, was made a baronet. After his death there was erected in Calcutta a monument to him, which is one of the notable signs of the city. Sir David never married. His title descended to Charles Metcalf Ochterlony, and was succeeded in it by his son, the present baronet, Sir David Ferguson Ochterlony. Gilbert Ochterlony, the second son of Captain David, died Jan. 16, 1780, aged 16, at the home of his step-father, Isaac Heard, Esq., at the college of arms.* Alexander, the third son, died in 1803, and Catherine in 1792.

Captain David's will, made at the time of his marriage, was probated March 7, 1766, and left everything to his wife Katrin, but his estate was not settled till after the peace, 1791, and then it was insolvent, the sum then obtained to close up the estate paid a dividend of only six and a half pence on the pound. The name of Ochterlony in New England became extinct.

* It was Sir Isaac Heard that took such pains in searching out the pedigree of the Washington family.

JUDGE AUCHMUTY'S FAMILY.

ROBERT AUCHMUTY first of the American family of that name was descended from an ancient Scottish family, holding a barony in the north of that country. His father settled in England early in the eighteenth century, and Robert studied law at the Temple, London, and came to America and settled in Boston about the year 1700. He was a profound lawyer and possessed remarkable talents and wit, but when he was admitted to practice does not appear. He was in practice soon after 1719 and the profession owed much to his character and system and order which now began to distinguish its forms of practice. His talents were extraordinary, "Old Mr. Auchmuty says a contemporary would sit up all night at his bottle, yet argue to admiration next day, and was an admirable speaker." He was sent to England to settle a boundary dispute between Massachusetts, New Hampshire, and Rhode Island. His services were so valuable, that on December 1738, he received from the former a grant of two hundred acres of land. He was judge of the Court of Admirality for New England from 1733 until 1747. While he was in England he advocated the expedition to Cape Breton in an ably written pamphlet published in 1744. This tract probably gave to the historian Smollett the erroneous impression that Auchmuty was the originator of that brilliant enterprise, the credit of which belongs to Governor Shirley.

Judge Auchmuty held his office until 1747 when he was superseded by Chambers Russell. His home was in Roxbury, Massachusetts, and many anecdotes of him have been handed down from generation to generation. He was "greatly respected and beloved in public and private life. His memory is held in high veneration by the bar in Massachusetts and his opinions are still respected.

Judge Auchmuty died in April, 1750, leaving several children. His daughter married Judge Pratt of New York and his son, Judge Robert Auchmuty, followed in his father's footsteps and became a noted lawyer in Massachusetts. Although he had not the advantage of a collegiate education he became an able lawyer. As an advocate he was eloquent and successful. "Among his contemporaries were Otis, Quincy, Hawley, and judges Paine, Sargent. Bradbury, R. Sewall, W. Cushing and Sullivan and though less learned than some of these he was employed in most of the important jury trials."

"It was when together with that class of lawyers above named that the profession owed the respectability which since his day has characterized the bar of Massachusetts."* He held the office of Advocate of the Court of Admiralty from August 2, 1762, until his appointment as judge, having been originally appointed in the place of Mr. Bollan, to

*Updike History of Narragansett church.

hold the office during his absence. Chambers Russell was appointed in the place of the elder Auchmuty as judge of the Admiralty for Massachusetts, New Hampshire and Rhode Island in 1747. He held the office until his death in 1767, and Robert Auchmuty, the younger, was appointed by the governor to fill his place. This was in April, but on the sixth of July he was duly commissioned as Judge of the Admiralty for all New England with a salary of £300 a year. His commission was received in March, 1769, when his salary was increased to £600 per annum. Judge Auchmuty continued to hold this office as long as the authority of the British was recognized, as he was a zealous Loyalist.

Robert Auchmuty was one of the commissioners with Governor Wanton of Rhode Island, Samuel Horsemanden, Chief Justice of New York, Frederic Smythe, Chief Justice of New Jersey, and Peter Oliver, Chief Justice of Massachusetts, to inquire into the destruction of the Gaspee, in 1772.* He was a colleague of Adams and Quincy in defence of the British soldiers tried for participation in the "Boston Massacre."** He appeared once after his appointment in defence of Captain Preston and his soldiers, and his argument was described as so memorable and persuasive, "as almost to bear down the tide of prejudice against him, though it never swelled to a higher flood."

The Auchmuty house in Roxbury stands at the corner of Cliff and Washington Streets. It was build about 1761 by the younger Judge Auchmuty, who resided there until the outbreak of the revolution. Here as a convenient halting place between the Province House and the Governor's country seat at Jamaica Plain, and the Lieutenant Governor residence at Milton, met the crown officers to make plans to stem the rising tide of disloyalty and lawlessness of the mobs, and their secret leaders. Here Bernard Hutchinson, Auchmuty, Hallowell, and Paxton discussed the proposed alterations in the charter, and the bringing over of British troops to preserve the peace. Letters of Judge Auchmuty to persons in England were sent to America with those of Governor Hutchinson by Franklin in 1773 and created much commotion.***

At the Declaration of Independence in 1776 he left his native country and settled in England. At one period he was in very distressed circumstances. He never returned to the United States and his estate was confiscated. His mansion in Roxbury became the property of Governor Increase Sumner and was occupied by him at the time of his decease. Auchmuty Lane was that part of Essex Street between Short and South Street in Boston. Robert Auchmuty died in London an exile from his native land in November, 1778.

HONORABLE JAMES AUCHMUTY, son of the elder Robert, was a storekeeper in the Engineer Department. At the peace he removed to Nova Scotia where he became an eminent lawyer, and was appointed judge. He

*See page 52 for description of same.
**Ibid 45.
***See page 162.

BRITISH TROOPS PREVENTING THE DESTRUCTION OF NEW YORK

On its evacuation by Washington; it was set on fire, it was saved by the summary execution of all incendiaries by the British.

had a son, a very gallant officer in the British Army, who was killed in the West Indies.

REVEREND SAMUEL AUCHMUTY, another son of the elder Judge Auchmuty who settled in New York, was born in Boston in 1725. He graduated from Harvard college in 1742 and was taken by his father to England, where he was ordained a minister in the Episcopal church. The degree of D. D. was conferred on him by Oxford. He was appointed by the Society for the Propagation of the gospel, an assistant minister of Trinity church in New York. He married in 1749 a daughter of Richard Nichols, governor of that province. In 1764 at the death of the Rector of Trinity church he was appointed to succeed him and took charge of all the churches in the city, performing his arduous duties with faithfulness until the revolution. In 1766 he received the degree of S. T. D. at Oxford. Dr. Auchmuty opposed the revolution and when the Americans took possession of New York City in 1777, it is said a message was sent him from Lord Sterling by one of his sons, "that if he read a prayer for the King the following Sunday, he would send a band of soldiers and take him out of the desk." His son, knowing his father's indomitable spirit did not deliver the message, but with some of his classmates from Columbia college attended the church with arms concealed under their gowns and sat near the pulpit for his protection. His conscience would not allow him to omit these prayers without violating his ordination vows. As soon as he commenced reading, Lord Sterling marched into the church with a band of soldiers and music playing Yankee Doodle. The Doctor's voice never faltered and he finished his prayer and the soldiers marched up one aisle and down another, and went out again without violence. After the service Dr. Auchmuty sent for the keys of Trinity and its chapels, and ordered that they should not be opened again until the liturgy could be performed without interruption, and took them to New Jersey. When the British took possession of New York he resolved at once to return to his loved flock and applied for leave to pass the American lines. This was denied him. With the unfailing energy which marked his character he determined to return on foot through circuitous paths to avoid the American lines. After undergoing great hardships, sleeping in the woods and great exposure, he reached the city. On its evacuation by Washington's Army it had been set on fire, and it was only by using the most drastic means,—the summary execution of all incendiaries by the British—that the city was saved from total destruction. Nearly one thousand buildings were burned in the western part of the city and among them Trinity church, the Rector's home, and the Charity School. Through the exertions of the British troops, St. Paul's and King's College barely escaped. The Vestry of Trinity reported their loss at £22,000, besides the annual rent of 246 lots of ground on which the buildings had been destroyed. After the fire, Dr. Auchmuty searched the ruins of his church and of his large and elegant mansion; all of his papers and records had been destroyed; he found no articles of value except the church plate and his own. His personal loss he estimated at upwards of $12,000.

The Sunday following Dr. Auchmuty preached in St. Paul's church for the last time. The hardships which he had undergone terminated in an illness which resulted in his death after a few days. This venerable and constant worker for mankind died March 4, 1777 in his fifty-second year, and was buried under the altar of St. Paul's. Interesting notices of his labors and sufferings and death may be found in Hawkins' "Historical Notices of the Missions of the Church of England, in the North American Colonies," London, 1845. By the old inhabitants of the city Dr. Auchmuty was much respected and beloved and was spoken of as Bishop Auchmuty. He had seven children. Jane, one of his daughters, married Richard Tylden of Milstead, of county Kent in England. One of her sons was Sir John Maxwell Tylden, who was in the army for twenty years in which he greatly distinguished himself. Another, William Burton Tylden was a major in the Royal Engineers. Dr. Auchmuty had two other daughters of which there is no account, save that they were married.

SIR SAMUEL AUCHMUTY, the eldest son of the Rev. Dr. Auchmuty, was a Lieutenant General in the British Army. At the beginning of the Revolution he was a student at Kings College and was intended by his father for the ministry. His own inclinations were military from his boyhood and soon after he graduated he joined the Royal army under Sir William Howe as an ensign in the 45th regiment and was present at most of the actions in that and the following year. In 1783 he commanded a company in the 75th Regiment, in the East Indies, and was with Lord Cornwallis in the first siege of Seringaptarn. In 1801 he joined the expedition to Egypt, and held the post of adjutant-general. He returned to England in 1803 and three years after was ordered to South America, where as brigadier-general, he assumed the command of the troops; and in 1807 assaulted and reduced—after a most determined resistance—the city and fortress of Montevideo. In 1809 he was transferred to India. Subsequently he succeeded Sir D. Baird as chief of staff in Ireland. He was knighted in 1812, his nephew, Sir John Maxwell Tylden, lieutenant-colonel of the 52 regiment being his proxy. He twice received the thanks of Parliament, and was presented with a service of plate by that body and by the East India Company. His seat was Syndale House, in Kent, near Feversham. He died in Ireland suddenly in 1822 at the age of 64.

ROBERT NICHOLIS AUCHMUTY, another son of the Rev. Dr. Auchmuty graduated at Kings College, New York and in the revolution served as a volunteer in the British army. His wife was Henrietta, daughter of Henry John Overing and he died at Newport, Rhode Island in 1813. His daughter Maria M., widow of Colonel E. D. Wainwright of the United States Marines, died at Washington, D. C., Jan. 1861, aged 71.

RICHARD HARRISON AUCHMUTY, brother of the above, was a surgeon in the British Army. Taken prisoner in the storming of Stony Point. With Cornwallis at Yorktown, and died soon after the surrender, while on parole.

"It is regretted that men as distinguished in their day as were the Auchmuty's, father and sons, so few memorials new remain." They were men who adorned their profession and "left a distinct and honorable impresion upon their age."

LIST OF CONFISCATED ESTATES BELONGING TO ROBERT AUCHMUTY ET AL, IN SUFFOLK COUNTY, AND TO WHOM SOLD.

To Samuel Clark, Feb. 26, 1780; Lib. 131 fol. 58; Land and dwelling-house in Boston, School St. S.; the town's land W.; John Rowe N.; Joseph Green E.—— Garden land near the above, Cook's Alley W.; Leverett Saltonstall N.; William Powell E.; S. and E.; Leverett Saltonstall S. [Description corrected in margin of record.]

To Josiah Waters, Jr., April 13, 1782; Lib. 134, fol. 164; Discharge of mortgage Fillebrown et al. to Auchmuty dated Feb. 10, 1766.

To Increase Sumner, July 31, 1783; Lib. 139, fol. 122; 6 A. 3 qr. 10 r. land and dwelling-house near the meeting-house in Roxbury, the road N.; Jonathan Davis E.; S. E.; and S.; the lane and Increase Sumner W.

COLONEL ADINO PADDOCK.

Robert Paddock was one of the Pilgrim Fathers, he was one of the early settlers of Plymouth, and was a smith by trade. He had a son, Zachariah, born in 1636, who was the ancestor of the subject of this sketch. Robert Paddock was probably a relative of Captain Leonard Peddock who was master of one of the ships that came to Plymouth in 1622, it being frequently the case in those times that names were mis-spelled. This is the origin of the name of Peddock's Island at the entrance of Boston Harbor. Branches of this family at the Revolutionary period were to be found in various parts of New England, New Jersey, and South Carolina. Adino Paddock was the son of John and Rebecca (Thatcher) Paddock; was born March 14, 1727, and was baptized in the First Church, Harwich, March 31, 1728.

His father died in 1732 and his mother removed soon after to Boston, where her name appears as a communicant in Brattle Square church "from Church East Yarmouth" December 5, 1736. Adino Paddock was married in Boston, June 22, 1749, to Lydia Snelling, daughter of Robert and Lydia (Dexter). He settled in Boston, where he manufactured chaises and transacted his business near the head of Bumstead Place. He lived opposite the burying ground, on the east side of Long-Acre Street. Adino Paddock was the first coach-maker of the town, and was a man of substance and character. His name is best known in connection with the famous Paddock elms. Mr. James Smith, a prosperous sugar baker, whose house was on Queen Street,—now Court Street,—when in London, was struck by the beauty of the elms in Brompton Park. The story goes that Mr. Smith procured young trees of the same kind, and had them planted in his nursery, on his beautiful farm, Brush Hill, in Milton. The fame of these trees spreading, one of his friends, Mr. Gilbert Deblois, asked for some, saying that he would in return name his new-born son for Mr. Smith. The bargain was struck, and James Smith Deblois, baptized May 16, 1769, bore witness to its fulfilment. Other elms of this stock were also planted, but those received by Mr. Gilbert Deblois became the most celebrated. These were set out in front of the granary, just opposite Mr. Deblois' house in Tremont Street. As Adino Paddock's shop window looked out upon them, Mr. Deblois enjoined Mr. Paddock to have an eye to their safety.

It is related that on one occasion, Paddock offered the reward of a guinea, for the detection of the person who "hacked" one or more of the trees. He guarded the infant elms very carefully and the "Gleaner" tells of his darting across the street upon one occasion and vigorously shaking an idle boy who was making free with one of the sacred saplings. The elms were thought to have been planted in 1762. They grew to magnificent proportions, and withstood the axe for more than a century. They escaped in 1860, but were cut down a few years later. The largest was one that stood near the Tremont House. Its circumference near the sidewalk was nearly seventeen feet. This was the largest of all the trees belonging to the public walks of the city, excepting the great American elm on Boston Common that was destroyed by the tornado of 1869.

Adino Paddock was in 1774 captain of the train of artillery belonging in Boston of which John Erving was colonel. This company was particularly distinguished for its superior discipline and the excellence of its material. The gun house stood at the corner of West and Tremont Streets, separated by a yard from the school house. In this gun house was kept two brass three-pounders, which had been recast from two old guns sent by the town to London for that purpose, and had the arms of the province engraved upon them. They arrived in Boston in 1768, and were first used at the celebration of the King's birthday, June 4th, when a salute was fired in King Street.

When the mobs began to be in evidence Captain Paddock expressed an intention to turn them over to General Gage, for safe keeping, some of the men that composed the company, resolved, that it should not be so, they met in the school-room, and watching their opportunity they crossed the yard, entered the building and, removing the guns from their carriages, carried them to the school-room where they were concealed in a box in which fuel was kept. They were finally taken to the American lines, in a boat, and were in actual service during the whole war. The two guns were called the "Hancock" and "Adams," and were in charge of the Ancient and Honorable Artillery Company, until presented in 1825 by the State to the Bunker Hill Monument Association. They are now suspended in the chamber at the top of Bunker Hill Monument, with a suitable inscription on each.

Before Mr. Paddock's departure from Boston he was entitled to the higher military appellation of Colonel. As an active officer, and for a time commander of the Boston train of artillery, he felt himself particularly honored, as he was then in a position of great usefulness, for, in fact his lessons in military matters while in the Train, were productive of much good, as laying the foundation of good soldiership, in the Province, by giving thorough instruction to many who afterwards became distinguished officers in the revolutionary war.

Ardently attached to the interests of the government he was one of the foremost of the loyalist party. He left Boston at the evacuation, March 17, 1776. There were nine in his family. They went to Halifax and in the following June he embarked with his wife and children for England.

In 1778 he was proscribed and banished. From 1781 until his death he resided on the Isle of Jersey and for several years held the office of Inspector of Artillery Stores with rank of Captain. Colonel Paddock received a partial compensation for his losses as a Loyalist, and died March 25, 1804, aged seventy-six years. Lydia, his wife died at the Isle of Jersey, in 1781, aged fifty-one.

Colonel Paddock's house was situated on the south corner of Bromfield and Tremont Streets, formerly Common Street and Ransom Lane. Thomas Bumstead, a coach-maker, purchased the estate when it was confiscated and carried on the coach-making business there. Bumstead Place was laid out in 1807 on the site of the home, and was closed in 1868. Gilbert Deblois occupied the opposite corner, on which was built Horticultural Hall, the trustees of the new office building recently erected there, at the suggestion of Alex S. Porter, named the new building the "Paddock Building" who said "I think that we ought to do all we can to preserve the memory of those good old citizens who by their influence and hard labor did so much in laying the foundation of our beloved city."

Adino Paddock and Lydia Snelling had thirteen children, nine of them died in infancy, and John a student at Harvard College was drowned while bathing in Charles River in 1773.

ADINO PADDOCK, the younger, accompanied his father to Halifax in 1776 and in 1779 followed his father to England, where he entered upon the study of medicine and surgery. Having attended the different hospitals of London and fitted himself for practice, he returned to America before the close of the Revolution, and was surgeon of the King's American Dragoons. In 1784 he married Margaret Ross of Casco Bay, Maine, and settling at St. John, New Brunswick, confined his attention to professional pursuits. In addition to extensive and successful private practice he enjoyed from Government the post of surgeon to the ordinance of New Brunswick. He died at St. Mary's, York County in 1817, aged 58. Margaret his wife died at St. John in 1815 at the age of 50. The fruit of this union was ten children, of whom three sons, Adino, Thomas and John were educated physicians. Adino commenced practice in 1808 at Kingston, New Brunswick. Thomas married Mary, daughter of Arthur

McLellan, Esq., of Portland, Maine, and died at St. John, deeply lamented in 1838, aged 47.

LIST OF CONFISCATED ESTATES BELONGING TO ADINO PADDOCK IN SUFFOLK COUNTY AND TO WHOM SOLD.

To Thomas Bumstead, Aug. 1, 1782; Lib. 135, fol. 139; Land and buildings in Boston, Common St. W.; land of the Commonwealth S.; heirs of Gillum Taylor deceased E. and S.; Thomas Cushing E.; N. and E.; Rawson's Lane N.

THEOPHILUS LILLIE.

Edward Lillie by the recorded births of his children appears to have been in Boston as early as 1663. As he was devoted to the Church of England, it may be presumed that he came from that country, and the date of his eldest child's birth makes it likely that he was born before 1640. This branch of the Lillie family probably lived for a while in Newfoundland, and if so, they are likely to have been of the Devonshire or West-of-England stock, which supplied the first settlers for that Province. They became possessed of real estate at St. John's during the latter half of the seventeenth century, described as "a plantation"—a term signifying full proprietorship.

Edward Lillie married about 1661, Elizabeth, whose maiden name is unknown. He was one of the well known citizens of the town of Boston when its estimated population was from five to seven thousand inhabitants. In 1687 he was one of the sixty citizens whose property was rated at £50 or more,—taking rank with such contemporaries as Elisha and Eliakim Hutchinson, Adam Winthrop, Samuel and Anthony Checkley, and Simon Lynde.* Edward Lillie carried on a large business as "cooper," at that period one of the most important industries of New England in its connection with commerce.

Prior to 1670 Edward Lillie had land "in his tenure and occupation" at the North End. He purchased July 8, 1670, an estate at what was then the South End of the town,—a dwelling-house and land. This estate was situated on the south-east corner of Washington and Bedford Streets, and it is in part now (1907) the site of R. H. White's dry-goods establishment. In January 1674 he purchased of Captain Thomas Savage land on Conduit (now North) Street and erected theron in 1684 a brick dwelling-house. The estate was valued in inventory at £1300.

Edward Lillie's will was dated December 24, 1688, and proved January 7, 1688-9. His wife was probably the "Mrs. Lily" whose death, according to town records, took place January 4, 1705. They had six children.

Samuel Lilly, born March 20, 1663, was the eldest child. June 4, 1683, he married at the age of twenty Mehitable Frary, daughter of Captain and

*Memorial Hist. of Boston, II. 8. Record Com. Report VII. 69.

Deacon Theophilus Frary, one of the founders of the Old South Church. Her mother was the daughter of Jacob Eliot, and the niece of John Eliot, the "Apostle to the Indians." Mehitable, was born February 4, 1665-6, and as her father had no sons, his estate was divided between the daughters.

Samuel Lillie, like his father, was a "cooper," but early in life became interested in commerce, sending as early as May 23, 1684, merchandise to the island of Nevis. For the next twenty-three years he was widely engaged in commercial transactions, and was uniformly styled "merchant" in formal documents. After his father's death he bought and occupied the latter's premises at the North End, enlarging them by other purchases.

Mrs. Royall, wife of Isaac Royall and mother of the Loyalist was a cousin of Mrs. Samuel Lillie. During his latter years Samuel Lillie was absent from America quite frequently. It is not likely that he was in Boston from 1708 till shortly before his death.* Mrs. Lillie died March 4, 1723. They had eleven children, born in Boston and baptized (except one or two) in the Second church, each a few days after birth.

Theophilus Lillie, the fourth child of Samuel and Mehitable Lillie, was baptized August 24, 1690. He married July 8, 1725, Hannah Ruck (Rev. Cotton Mather officiating.) Seems to have done much in settling his father's affairs, but was not engaged in active business.

On the 28th of July, 1732, in Town Meeting, he with others, was appointed a committee to receive proposals, touching the demolishing, repairing, or leasing out the old buildings belonging to the town in Dock Square. The committee to give their attendance at Mr. William Coffin's, the Bunch of Grapes tavern, on Thursdays weekly, from six to eight o'clock in the evening. In 1736 he appears as one of the subscribers to Prince's Chronological History of Boston, the list containing, according to Drake, the names of persons most interested at that period in literary concerns.

Hannah Ruck, his wife, was born December 4, 1703 and was the daughter of John Ruck, a successful merchant, a citizen active in municipal affairs and holding municipal offices. Her mother was Hannah Hutchinson, daughter of Colonel Elisha Hutchinson, and aunt of Thomas Hutchinson, the last Royal Governor. A close friendship existed between the two families, and their homes were near together at the North End. This friendship was continued in Halifax, after the Loyalist exodus in 1776.

Theophilus Lillie sold the family estate at the corner of Newbury and Pond Streets, March 9, 1754. Before this sale he had removed to the Ruck homestead "near the old North Meeting House." Mr. Lillie died late in March, 1760. He left but little property. His eldest son Samuel, died young and John and Theophilus Lillie were his father's sole heirs.

THEOPHILUS LILLIE, the youngest son, was born August 18, 1730.

*"The Lillie Family of Boston" by Edward L. Pierce.

He married late in 1757 (intentions of marriage published October 27, 1757) Ann Barker, who had been a shop-keeper, in company with Abiel Page, "near Rev. Mr. Mather's meeting-house." He was educated as a merchant and was in retail trade as early as 1758, as shown by the numerous collection suits brought by him, and his advertisements in the Boston "Gazette" May 22 of that year. His store was on "Middle (Hanover) Street, near Mr. Pemberton's meeting-house." His stock was miscellaneous English Dry Goods and Groceries.

When it was determined to resist the tax on imports, a non-importation agreement was entered into in August, 1768, by the merchants of Boston, many were forced to sign it through fear of offending the mob, the agreement ended in 1769 and some of those who had been forced into it were determined to proceed in their regular business, and would pay no attention to a renewal of it, among these was Theophilus Lillie. They were proscribed and persecuted for several weeks by the rabble collecting to interrupt customers, passing to and from their shops, and houses, by posts erected before their shops with a hand pointed towards them, and by many marks of derision. At length on February 22nd, 1770, a more powerful mob than common, collected before the house of Theophilus Lillie and set up a post on which was a large Wooden Head, with a board faced paper, on which was painted the figures of four of the principal importers. One of the neighbors, Ebenezer Richardson found fault with the proceedings which provoked the mob to drive him into his home for shelter. Having been a custom house officer, he was peculiarly obnoxious to the mob. They surrounded his house, threw stones and brick-bats through the windows, and, as it appeared upon trial were forcing their way in, when he fired upon them, and killed a boy eleven or twelve years of age. He was soon seized, and another person, George Wilmot with him, who happened to be in the house. They were in danger of being sacrificed to the rage of the mob, being dragged through the streets, and a halter having been prepared, but some more temperate than the rest, advised to carry him before a justice of peace, who committed him to prison.

The boy that was killed was Christopher Snider, the son of a poor German. The event was taken advantage of by Sam Adams, and other revolutionary leaders to raise the passion of the people, and thereby strengthen their cause. A grand funeral therefore was judged to be the proper course to pursue. In the *Evening Post* of 26 Feb. is a very minute account of the affair, which had a very great deal to do with subsequent events. The corpse was set down under 'Liberty Tree' whence the procession began. About 50 school boys preceded, and there was "at least 2000 in the procession, of all ranks, amid a crowd of spectators." The pall was supported by six youths chosen by the parents of the deceased. On the Liberty Tree and upon each side and foot of the coffin were inscriptions well calculated to excite sympathy for the deceased, and at the same time indignation against him, who occasioned his death.

On the 20th of April following the two culprits were tried for their lives. Richardson was brought in guilty of murder, but Wilmot was acquitted. Drake says "In this account of the case of Richardson and Wilmot, it must be borne in mind that it is almost entirely made up from the facts detailed by their enemies. Richardson was no doubt insulted beyond endurance, which caused his rashness, in a moment of intense excitement he fired on the mob. These facts doubtless had their weight with the court, for the Chief Justice Thomas Hutchinson, viewed the guilt of Richardson as everybody would now, a clear case of justifiable homicide, and consequently refused to sign a warrant for his execution, and, after lying in prison two years, was, on application to the King pardoned and set at liberty."*

After the affair of the Wooden Figure at Lillie's, there was constant trouble in Boston between the soldiers and roughs of the town, until the 5th of March, when occurred the affray between the Mob and the Soldiers known as the "Boston Massacre."**

Mr. Lillie had taken no part in the affair that happened near his store, but popular feeling was influenced by that occurrence against him. Mr. Lillie's full statement of the interference with his business by the illegal committee of citizens, will be found in the 'Massachusetts Gazette," January 11, 1770. An extract will show his attitude towards the affair.

"Upon the whole, I cannot help saying—although I have never entered far into the mysteries of government, having applied myself to my shop and my business—that it always seemed strange to me that people who contend so much for civil and religious liberty should be so ready to deprive others of their natural liberty; that men who are guarding against being subject to laws [to] which they never gave their consent in person or by their representative should at the same time make laws, and in the most effectual manner execute them upon me and others, to which laws I am sure I never gave my consent either in person or by my representative. But what is still more hard, they are laws made to punish me after I have committed the offence; for when I sent for my goods, I was told nobody was to be compelled to subscribe; after they came, I was required to store them. This in no degree answered the end of the subscription, which was to distress the manufacturers in England. Now, my storing my goods could never do this; the mischief was done when the goods were bought in England; and it was too late to help it. My storing my goods must be considered, therefore, as punishment for an offence before the law for punishing it was made.

"If one set of private subjects may at any time take upon themselves to punish another set of private subjects just when they please, it's such a sort of government as I never heard of before; and according to my poor notion of government, this is one of the principal things which gov-

*Drake's History of Boston, p. 777.
**See pages 43 and 44 for account of the "Massacre."

ernment is designed to prevent; and I own I had rather be a slave under one master (for I know who he is. I may perhaps be able to please him) than a slave to a hundred or more whom I don't know where to find, nor what they will expect of me."

In 1770 Mr. Lillie removed to Oxford in Worcester County,—a removal induced probably by his recent experiences in Boston. His domicile is stated to be in that town in actions brought by him in Suffolk County. On account of his political views his new residence did not prove to be any more congenial than Boston had been.

In 1772 he attached for a debt the house of Dr. Alexander Campbell and the people of Oxford took umbrage, and threatened him with violence. In the same year he sold his place in Oxford, and returned to Boston. He bought in 1774 an estate in Brookfield, but it does not appear that he lived upon it at any time. Until the political troubles Mr. Lillie seems to have been in good circumstances, and to have kept up in his manner of dress the fashions of the period, according to family traditions. He left Boston in March, 1776 with the British troops for Halifax. His family thus embarking numbered four persons—himself and wife, and one of the other two being, doubtless, a negro servant.

Mr. Lillie's death occurred in Halifax two months after leaving Boston, on May 12. His property in Massachusetts was confiscated. Jacob Cooper, of Boston, administered on his estate. Mrs. Lillie continued to live at Halifax, and notwithstanding the confiscation proceedings, she undertook to collect, by suits in Massachusetts in 1784-85, some of the debts due to her husband. The Confiscation Act however, was a bar to any recovery.

Mrs. Lillie survived her husband eighteen years. Her funeral is registered on the records of St. Paul's church, Halifax, as being on September 16, 1794, at the age of seventy-nine. Her will dated December 10, 1791, and August 5, 1794 (appointing Foster Hutchinson, the younger, Executor) was proved September 20, 1794, on the oath of John Masters and Foster Hutchinson, the younger. Certain provisions of the will show a particular interest in a colored servant. The will provides: "It is also my will and intention that my black man Caesar be free, and that the sum of ten pounds be retained and left in the hands of my hereinafter named executor, to be applied to the use of said Caesar in case of sickness, or other necessity, at the discretion of said executor." She also bequeathed to him "a suit of mourning cloths suitable for a man in his situation in life; and in a later codicil, "the feather-bed and bedstead whereupon he usually sleeps, and also the bedclothes and bedding belonging thereto." Mr. Lillie's confiscated personal effects indicate that he lived in a liberal style. At the time of his death, Governor Hutchinson, then in England, wrote in his Diary, July 24, 1776:

When I came home I heard of Mr. Lillie's death at Halifax. What numbers have been brought to poverty, sickness, and death by refusing to concur with the present measures of America!

Theophilus Lillie died childless. Search was made in July, 1895, by Edward Lillie Pierce and his son George, in the old graveyard at Halifax, but no stone for him or his wife was discovered, although her funeral had been duly recorded in the church register. The stones of Foster Hutchinson and his family were well preserved; and the Lillie stone if ever set up, would be likely to be found near them.

Mr. Lillie's personal property in Massachusetts was disposed of and his three pieces of real estate were sold at public auction. His debts were small and the whole amount turned into the treasury, £595, valued at £446 in sterling money. The public gain was considerable.

JOHN LILLIE, the only surviving brother of Theophilus was born August 8, 1728. He is described as a "mariner" in public documents, but no details of his career on the sea have been transmitted. He married in Trinity church, August 16, 1754 Abigail Breck (born June 19, 1732.) She was the daughter of John and Margaret Breck. John Lillie died April, 1765, and his will was proved on the 19th. He left six children. John Lillie, his son, became a Major in the Continental Army and served in many engagements with great bravery during the war. General Washington certified that Major Lillie "conducted himself on all occasions with dignity, bravery, and intelligence." He was married to Elizabeth Vose, January 20, 1785, and was survived by several children.

Mehitable and Ann Lillie, two of John Lillie's daughters (the mariner) have always with their descendants been well known.

LIST OF CONFISCATED ESTATES BELONGING TO THEOPHILUS LILLIE IN SUFFOLK COUNTY AND TO WHOM SOLD.

To John Greenough, May 26, 1781; Lib. 132, fol. 216; Land and buildings in Boston, Middle St. E.; Samuel Ridgeway S.; Thomas Greenough W.; Thomas Greenough and Edward Foster, an absentee, N.

To Samuel Howard, Aug. 3, 1781; Lib. 133, fol. 5; One undivided third of land and large brick dwelling-house in Boston, Sun Court St. N.; Joseph Hemmingway and others E.; John Leach and others S.; Market Square W.

DR. SYLVESTER GARDINER.

Sylvester Gardiner was born in South Kingston, Rhode Island, in 1707. He was descended from the first emigrant of the name to the Narragansett country. His father was William Gardiner, the son of Benoni, the son of Joseph, an English emigrant. Sylvester was the fourth son of William Gardiner and was educated by his brother-in-law, the Rev. Dr. McSparran, for the medical profession. He studied eight years in England and France, and returning to Boston, entered and pursued a successful professional career. He established a store for the importation of drugs and acquired a fortune. He accumulated much real estate in Maine and became proprietor of one-twelfth part of the "Plymouth Purchase," so-called, on the Kennebec River. At one time he owned 100,000 acres and was grantor of much of the land in ancient Pittston. "His efforts to settle the large domain were unceasing from the year 1753 to the Revolution. He was made perpetual moderator of the proprietors at all their meetings; he executed their plans, built mills, houses, stores and wharves, cleared lands, made generous offers to emigrants; established an episcopal mission, and furnished the people of that region with their first religious instruction. And most of all this was accomplished with his own money.* He erected houses and mills at Swan Island, Pownalborough and other places, and was the author of the beginnings of many settlements. He was a public spirited man of great zeal and energy, broad and liberal in his views.

Dr. Gardiner was married three times. His first wife was Anne, daughter of Doctor John Gibbons of Boston; his second, Abigail Eppes of Virginia; his third, Catharine Goldthwaite. In Boston he was respected by all classes. Of the "Government Party," he entertained as guests, Sir William Pepperell, Governor Hutchinson, Earl Percy, Admiral Graves, Major Pitcairn, General Gage, Major Small and others. He was an Addresser of the Royal Governors in 1774 and the year following he became identified with the Royal cause. In 1776, at the evacuation, he abandoned all and found temporary shelter at Halifax. When he left his native country close to the age of three score and ten, he took only about £400 with him. The vessel in which he embarked was destitute of common comforts, poorly supplied with provisions, and the cabin, which he and several members of his family occupied, was small and crowded with passengers. In 1778 he was proscribed and banished and settled in Poole, England. His property in Boston and Maine was confiscated and all goods that could be found were sold at public auction. A library containing five hundred volumes, was sold in 1778-79 at auction by William Cooper. His books and other personal effects amounted to £1658.18.

The estates on the Kennebec were confiscated but the Attorney-General found that the action was illegally prosecuted and instituted new proceedings. Before they were brought to a close peace was declared and the proceedings stayed. The heirs of Dr. Gardiner learned these facts and obtained the property. Had there not been a flaw in the first suit this would not have been the case.

"In 1785 Doctor Gardiner returned to the United States. For a part of his losses he petitioned Massachusetts for compensation. He had never borne arms, he said, nor entered into any association, combination or subscription against the Whigs. When he quitted Boston, he stated, too, that he had in his possession a valuable stock of drugs, medicines, paints, groceries and dye stuffs, which having a vessel fully equipped and entirely under his control, he could easily have carried off, but which he left,

* Sabine's Loyalists, Vol. I, p. 459.

of choice, for the benefit of the country, which he knew was in need. The claim was acknowledged to the extent of giving his heirs tickets in the State Land Lottery, by which they obtained nearly six thousand acres in the county of Washington, Maine."*

Washington, on taking possession of Boston, ordered the medicines, etc., in Doctor Gardiner's store, to be transferred to the hospital department for the use of the Continental Army; but the State authorities interfered and required delivery to the Sheriff of Suffolk county. The result, however, was a vote of the council complying with the requisition of the commander-in-chief.

After the peace Doctor Gardiner resided in Newport, Rhode Island, where he still practiced medicine and surgery. There he died suddenly of a malignant fever on August 8, 1786, in his eightieth year. His body was interred under Trinity church and his funeral was attended by most of the citizens. The shipping displayed its colors at half-mast, and much respect was shown by the people. Dr. Gardiner had always been philanthropic and a benefit to mankind. He seems to have been identified in church work wherever he lived and from the following extract appears to have been a member of King's chapel, while residing in Boston: "April 3, 1740.—Rec'd of Mr. Sylvester Gardiner Sixteen Pounds Two Shills, in full for wine for the Chapple for the year past. John Hancock."**

Dr. Gardiner acted conscientiously in his course in remaining loyal and his "Christian fortitude and piety were exemplary as his honesty was inflexible and his friendship sincere."*** In the Episcopal church in Gardiner, Maine, near the pulpit, a beautiful cenotaph of black marble about eight feet high enclosed in a fine oaken frame, is erected to the memory of Dr. Gardiner, by Robert Hallowell Gardiner, his grandson and heir.

JOHN GARDINER, the eldest son of Dr. Sylvester Gardiner, was born in Boston in 1731, and was sent to England, to complete his education. He studied law at Inner Temple and practiced in the courts of Westminster Hall. He received the appointment of Attorney-General in the West Indies at St. Christopher's. He was denied promotion by the British Government because of his sympathy for the Whigs, and in 1783 he returned to Boston. On February 13, 1784, John Gardiner, his wife, Margaret, and their children were naturalized. John Gardiner was an ardent reformer and an active Unitarian. He was the principal agent in transforming the King's Chapel into a Unitarian church. He wrote an able treatise in defence of the theatre. Removing to Pownalborough, Maine, he represented that town in the General Court from 1789 until his death in 1793-94. He was drowned by the loss of a packet in which he was sailing to Boston to attend the session of the Legislature.

* Sabine's Loyalists, Vol. I, p. 460.
** "Dealings with the Dead," by a Sexton of the Old School.
*** Newport Mercury, Aug. 14, 1786.

JOHN SYLVESTER JOHN, son of John Gardiner, was born in Wales in 1765. His father had left America in 1748 before he was of age and resided in England and South Wales until 1768, when he went to St. Christopher's, remaining in the West Indies until 1783. John Sylvester John, became an able theological and political writer. He was rector of Trinity church, Boston, from 1805 until his death, which occurred at Harrowgate Springs, England, in 1830, while traveling for his health.

A tablet was erected in Trinity church to the memory of John Sylvester John Gardiner, who had first been an assistant and later the rector of the church. At the time of the great Boston fire, November 9, 1872, when old Trinity church on Summer street was destroyed, this tablet was the only relic saved from the interior of the church. It was rescued from the flames by a great-grandson of John Sylvester John Gardiner, and is now in Trinity church, Copley square, Boston.

WILLIAM GARDINER, son of the rector, was an eminent Boston lawyer. He had two daughters, Louisa, who married John Cushing of Watertown, and Elizabeth.

WILLIAM GARDINER, the second son of Sylvester Gardiner, removed to Gardinerston, Maine, soon after the settlement commenced. He employed a housekeeper and entertained his friends and was famous for his fun-making. He gave offence to the Whigs because he "would drink tea"; because he refused to swear allegiance to their cause; and because he called them "Rebels." "Arrangements were made to take him from his bed at night, and tar and feather him, but a Whig, friendly to him, carried him to a place of safety. He was, however, made prisoner, tried and sent to jail in Boston."* In March, 1778, he petitioned for release and was soon after allowed to return home where "he was regarded as a harmless man and was allowed for the most part to remain unmolested, except by petty annoyances." William Gardiner died unmarried at Gardiner, Maine, and was buried "beneath the Episcopal vestry."

ANNE GARDINER, third child of Sylvester Gardiner, married the second son of the Earl of Altamont. HANNAH, a fourth child, was the wife of Robert Hallowell. REBECCA, the fifth child, married Philip Dumarisque. Last, ABIGAIL, married Oliver Whipple, counsellor-at-law, Cumberland, Rhode Island, and subsequently of Portsmouth, New Hampshire.

Nearly the whole of the estate in Maine passed under the provisions of Doctor Gardiner's will, to Hannah's only son, Robert Hallowell, who, as one of the conditions of that instrument, added the name of Gardiner. John on account of his political and religious opinions failed to become the principal heir, and William "was not an efficient man."

Sylvanus Gardiner's second wife was the widow of William Eppes of Virginia, daughter of Col. Benj. Pickman of Salem. She died at Poole, England, leaving a son, Wm. Eppes, who married Miss Randolph of Bristol, whose son was a commissary general in the British

* Sabine's Loyalists, Vol. I, p. 462.

Army. A daughter, Love Eppes, married Sir John Lester of Poole, and Abigal Eppes married Richard Routh, a loyalist.

LIST OF CONFISCATED ESTATES BELONGING TO SYLVESTER GARDINER IN SUFFOLK COUNTY AND TO WHOM SOLD.

To William Coleman, Benjamin Coleman, Dec. 12, 1782; Lib. 136 fol. 146; Land and buildings in Boston, Marlborough St. W.; John Sprague and Samuel Partridge S.; alley between said land and land of John Erving E.; Samuel Partridge N.

To Joseph Gardner, Nov. 21, 1783; Lib. 140 fol. 113; Land in Boston, Marlborough St. E.; alley S. and E.; Samuel Dashwood S. and E.; Martin Gay E.; Winter St. S.; heirs of William Fisher W.; S.; W. and S.; heirs of Henderson Inches S.; John Williams and land of the State W.; Jonathan Cole N.; John Lucas E. and N.

To John Boies, March 2, 1784; Lib. 141, fol. 195; Land in Boston, Winter St. N.; John R. Sigourney W.; Dr. John Sprague S. and E.

To Joseph Henderson, Aug. 7, 1784; Lib. 144, fol. 111; Land and buildings in Boston, Long Lane E.; Dr. John Sprague S. and E.; Andrew Johonnot S.; Charles Paxton and Dr. Sprague W.; said Sprague N.

RICHARD KING.

Of Scarborough, he was a prosperous merchant, "with a leaning towards the Government." Many persons had become indebted to him beyond their ability to pay. In consequence, apparently of this circumstance, his troubles soon began, after the attack and destruction of Mr. Hutchinson's residence, of which the following outrage appears to have been an imitation, and the story has been handed down by no less a person than John Adams: "Taking advantage of the disorders occasioned by the passage of the Stamp Act, a party disguised as Indians, on the night of the 16th of March, 1766, broke into his store, and his dwelling-home also, and destroyed his books and papers, containing evidences of debts. Not content with this, they laid waste his property and threatened his life if he should venture to seek legal mode of redress.

John Adam was counsel for King, and he, who had no pity for Hutchinson, but rather rejoiced in the impunity of his assailants, writes: "The terror and distress, the distraction and horror of his family cannot be described by words or painted on canvas. It is enough to move a statue, to melt a heart of stone to read the story."*

The popular bitterness then engendered did not, however, subside, and in 1774, a slight incident occurred which soon caused it once more to break out. A vessel of Mr. King's was found to have delivered a load of lumber in Boston, by special license, after the port had been closed, and the material had been purchased for the use of the troops. On this occasion forty men from the neighboring town of Gorham came over and compelled Mr. King, in fear of his life, to make a disavowal of his opinion. These repeated shocks seem to have been too much for Mr.

* John Adams' Letters to His Wife, Note to No. 9.

King's constitution. He became insane and died in the following March.

Such were the means adopted by the Sons of Despotism, to make patriots, to convert their fellow countrymen to their ways of thinking. Intimidation and oppression are the accompaniments of all successful revolutions. The same holds true of the methods adopted at the present time by the leaders of a strike. The leaders, like the revolutionary leaders, are unwilling to acknowledge that they are disturbers of the peace, or that acting under them their followers are brutally assailing those who seek employment under other than union conditions.

CHARLES PAXTON.

COMMISSIONER OF CUSTOMS.

The subject of this sketch was born at Boston, February 28, 1707. Wentworth Paxton and Faith, his wife, were his parents. Charles Paxton was a Commissioner of Customs and as such early incurred the ill will of the so-called patriotic party. In 1769 he and his associates were posted in the "Boston Gazette," by James Otis. It was this card of Otis which brought on the altercation with Robinson, another commissioner, in the coffee-house in State street, and which resulted in injuries to the head of the first champion of the revolution, from which he never recovered." Otis subsequently became insane and while confined in an asylum met his death, being struck by a bolt of lightning.

Charles Paxton was a warden of King's Chapel in 1762, and was remarkable for finished politeness and courtesy of manners. His office was unpopular and odious and the wags of the day made merry with qualities, which at any other time would have commanded respect. On Pope-day, as the gun-powder plot anniversary, or the 5th of November was called, there was usually a grand pageant of various figures on a stage mounted on wheels and drawn through the streets with horses. The Pretender suspended on a gibbet between the Devil and the Pope, with appropriate implements and dress, were among the objects devised to make up the show. Sometimes political characters, who in popular estimation should keep company with personages represented, were added; and of these, Commissioner Paxton was one. On one occasion he was exhibited between the figures of the Devil and the Pope in proper figure. As the disputes which preceded the war increased, the visits of Paxton to London became more frequent. He went there as the authorized agent to the crown officers, to complain of the merchants for resisting the Acts of Parliament, and for the interest of the supporters of the Crown. After he entered upon his duties he was efficient and active beyond his associates. John Adams says of him that he appeared at one time to have been Governor, Lieutenant-Governor, Secretary and Chief Justice."

Paxton and his fellow-commissioners seized one of Hancock's vessels for smuggling wine which caused a fearful mob and the flight of the officers of the revenue to Castle William. Then came the hanging of Paxton in effigy on the "Liberty Tree," then at the instance of the Commissioner the first troops came to Boston; then the card of Otis, denouncing the commissioners by name, the assault upon him in answer to it, and later came the destruction of three cargoes of tea; then the shutting of the port of Boston; then the first continental congress; then war,—a war which cost England $500,000,000 and the Anglo-Saxon race 100,000 lives in battle, storm and in prison.

In 1776, with his family of five persons, Mr. Paxton embarked at Boston with the British Army for Halifax, and in July of that year sailed for England in the ship Aston Hall. He came under the Confiscation Act and was proscribed and banished. In 1780 he was a pallbearer at the funeral of Governor Hutchinson. In 1781 he was seen walking with Harrison Gray, the last Colonial treasurer of Massachusetts, near Brompton. This able and determined supporter of the crown died in 1788 at the age of eighty-four at the seat of William Burch (one of his fellow commissioners) at Norfolk, England.

JOSEPH HARRISON.

COLLECTOR OF CUSTOMS.

As previously stated, after the close of the last war with France which ended in the conquest of Canada, the Government decided on enforcing the revenue laws.* The frigate Romney of fifty guns had arrived from Halifax and at the same time the sloop "Liberty," owned by John Hancock, arrived loaded with wine from Madeira; there was a duty of £7 per tun on such wines; several cargoes had been smuggled in without payment of the duty, and it seemed probable that there would either be a connivance by the custom house officer in this case, as in others, or there would be a great disturbance by the mob. Harrison determined that there should be no connivance by the officers and that the laws against smuggling should be enforced, even if the vessel did belong to one of the principal merchants and a representative of Boston and an officer of the corps of cadets. Before the vessel arrived it had been frequently mentioned that the duties would not be paid, and it was expected that an open refusal would be made. When the vessel arrived and was lying at Hancock's wharf on the tenth of June, 1768, the custom house officer, Thomas Kirk, went on board, and was followed by Captain John Marshall,—who commanded Mr. Hancock's ship, the London Packet,—with five or six others. These persons confined Kirk below and kept him some three

* Ibid. 33-4, Hutchinson, Vol. III, p. 189

hours, and in the meantime the wine was taken out and no entry made of it at the Custom House or Naval Office. The cargo was landed in the night and carted through the streets of Boston under a guard of thirty or forty stout fellows armed with bludgeons, and though it was notorious to the greatest part of the town, no officer of the customs thought fit to attempt a seizure, nor is it probable that he could have succeeded if he had attempted it. On the liberation of the custom house officer, an entry was made the next morning by the master, Mr. Nathaniel Barnard, who entered four or five pipes of wine, and made oath that that was all he brought into port. This was as much a submission to the authority of the act as if the whole cargo had been seized.

It was determined to seize the sloop upon a charge of false entry, Accordingly Mr. Joseph Harrison, the collector and Benjamin Hallowell, the comptroller, repaired to Hancock's wharf and made the seizure, and fearing an attempt to rescue the vessel, made a signal to the Romney, which lay at a small distance from the shore, and a boat with armed men came to their aid. To prevent a rescue the vessel was taken from the wharf into the harbor. This removal brought on a riot, a mob was soon gathered together and the officers insulted and beaten, several of whom barely escaped with their lives. Among the numerous missiles thrown at Mr. Harrison was a brick or stone which struck him on the breast, from the effects of which he was confined to his bed. His son, Mr. Richard Acklom Harrison, was thrown down, dragged by the hair of his head and otherwise barbarously treated. Mr. Hallowell and Mr. Erving, inspectors, did not fare much better. The former was confined to his home from the wounds and bruises he received and the latter besides having his sword broken was beaten with clubs and sticks, and considerably wounded. The mob next proceeded to the home of Mr. John Williams, the Inspector-General, broke his windows and also those of the Comptroller, Mr. Hallowell. They then took Mr. Harrison's boat and dragged it to the Common and there burned every fragment of it. Captain Marshall, the captain of the "London Packet," died the same night as the riot, at Hancock wharf, and it is said his death was caused by the over-exertion which he made in removing the wine from the sloop Liberty. The most conspicuous man on the part of the mob was Captain Daniel Malcolm, a trader in Fleet street, who, it is said, was deeply interested in the wines attempted to be smuggled. The revenue officer knew him well and owed him no good will, for the reason that some time before they undertook to search his premises for contraband goods, but were obliged to retreat before deadly weapons, without effecting their object. On the occasion of the seizure of the Liberty he headed a party of men who exerted themselves to prevent her removal to the Romney, they said the sloop should not be taken into custody, and declared they would go on board and throw the people belonging to the Romney overboard.*
When the ministry became advised concerning the riots which followed

* Drake's History of Boston, pp. 735-6-7.

the seizure of the sloop Liberty, they gave orders for two regiments to sail for Boston from Ireland.* They arrived September 30, The 29th regiment camped on the Common and the 14th was quartered in Faneuil Hall. The revenue officers retired after the assaults upon them to the Castle until the arrival of the troops. Joseph Harrison and his wife and family went to England. He was succeeded in the collectorship by Edward Winslow, who held the office till the evacuation of Boston.

CAPTAIN MARTIN GAY.

John Gay emigrated to America about 1630. He settled first at Watertown and was a grantee in the great Dividends and in Beaver Brook plowlands, owning forty acres. He was Freeman May 6, 1635 and a Selectman in 1654. He died March 4, 1688, and his wife Joanna died August 14, 1691. He had eleven children.

Nathaniel, third child of John Gay was born January 11, 1643. Was Freeman May 23, 1677, and Selectman in 1704 and other years. He married Lydia Lusher. He died Feb. 20, 1712. His wife died August 6th, 1774, aged ninety-two. He had ten children.

Rev. Ebenezer Gay, D. D., Minister of Hingham was born in 1696 graduated at Harvard University in 1714, and was ordained in 1718. He was a devoted loyalist, and died 1787, at the age of ninety, and in the sixty-ninth year of his ministry. Rev. Doctor Chauncy "pronounces him to have been one of the greatest and most valuable men in the country." His son, MARTIN GAY, was Captain of the Ancient and Honorable Artillery Company. He was born at Hingham on the 29 December, 1726. He married first, 13 December, 1750, Mary Pinckney, by whom he had seven children. After her death he married Ruth Atkins, by her he had two children. He carried on the business of a brass founder, and copper smith, on Union Street, Boston. He was also deacon in the West Church in Lynde Street. On the thirtieth of April, 1775, shortly after the battle of Lexington, Deacon Gay, with Deacon Jones was requested to take care of the plate, etc., belonging to this church, and Congregation." The church and congregation were at this time dispersed and the meeting house occupied as a barrack by the troops, and the pastor had gone to Nova Scotia. Mr. Gay was true to his trust, at the evacuation he took "the plate and linnen" to Nova Scotia and afterwards returned it, for long years after in 1793 the church voted him their thanks for "having taken care of the plate belonging to the church, while the town was in the hands of the British troops, and when it was evacuated." When the new church was built in 1805 he subscribed three hundred dollars towards it. From 1758 to 1774, he was yearly chosen one of the two Assay Masters, and for many years he was chosen one of the sixteen Firewards of the Town, in which office he

* See chapter on Boston Mobs, p. 40.

had as associates John Hancock, Samuel Adams, and Adino Paddock. He was chosen one of the twelve Wardens of the Town in 1771, and occupied many other offices of importance, which shows the esteem in which he was held by his fellow townsmen. In June, 1774, he signed the Address to Governor Hutchinson, and from that time, he was not elected to any town office, owing to his public avowal of Loyalist sentiments.

Mr. W. Allan Gay of West Hingham, a grandson of Martin Gay, has three letters written by the Captain, they have been published in the Collection of the Colonial Society of Mass., Vol. 3. They are interesting as they bring us almost into personal contact with people who were living in Boston more than a hundred years ago, and one of whom saw the Battle of Bunker Hill. The first was written by Captain Martin Gay to his brother Jotham, seven years his elder. He had been an officer in the French war of 1755, and had taken part in the expedition against Nova Scotia under Gen. John Winslow. He afterwards settled in the province he had helped to conquer from the French and at the date of the letter had been for more than ten years a resident of Cumberland, Nova Scotia. Within but three weeks after the battle, it gives one of the first authentic accounts published. The writer's loyalty to his "King and Country" is very apparent, as well as his detestation of all Rebels, and especially the "famous Doctor Warren." The letter in part is as follows: "The victory obtained by about two thousand regular troops commanded by General Howe, over a large body of the County Rebels, ('tis said about six thousand,) on the heights of Charlestown, on the 17ult, was a remarkable Action. It proves that nothing the enemies to Great Britain can do, will daunt the courage of British troops. The Rebels had entrenched themselves on the top of a high hill, with two cannon mounted in the Redoubt, besides several field pieces, on the hill, which is about a quarter of a mile from Charles River in approaching which, the troops had to break through stone walls, and other difficulties, which gave the enemy every advantage they could wish for. However, after a most violent hot fire, the brave soldiers forced the entrenchments to the joy of all the spectators, (myself being one) and others on this side of the river, who are friends to King and Country. Immediately on the King's troops appearing on the top of the Redoubt, the Rebels ran off in great confusion leaving their cannon, entrenching tools and a large number of their dead and wounded. The loss was great on both sides, the action lasted about an hour and a quarter. We have reason to lament the loss of so many valuable brave officers and men, of the King's Army who were killed on the field of battle, and since dead of the wounds they received. I have not seen any account of the transaction of that day made public by authority, therefore will not pretend to say which suffered most in the loss of men. Will mention one on the Rebel side, the famous Doctor Warren, who has for some years been a stirrer up of Rebellion, was killed in the action. Had some others of his disposition which I could name been there, and meet the same fate with him, it would have made the victory of that day the more glorious, though the Rebels meet with a shameful defeat, they still continue in their opposition, in fortifying hills and others places near this town. I am not apprehensive of their ever being able to take or destroy this town, but 'tis a melancoly consideration to be in this situation, which must in time prove fatal to this town and province, if not soon prevented by that almighty being, whose providence preserves and governs the world in all things."

On the evacuation of Boston in March, 1776, by the British troops, he accompanied them to Halifax. There went with him his son Martin, and his daughter Mary, who afterwards married Rev. William Black of Halifax, and also "his man London." He remained in Novia Scotia during the whole period of the war. Mrs. Ruth Gay, second wife of Martin Gay, whose maiden name as already stated was Atkins, remained in Boston during the war, probably with her father's family. Her father, Thomas Atkins, was a bricklayer by trade, and a well-to-do citizen, his real estate having been appraised at his death in 1785 at £1,696. He, with his eldest son, joined the revolutionists, but his second son, Gibbs Atkins, was a loyalist. So were families divided in those days.

The second letter was from his wife in Boston and was sent to him at Halifax. It is interesting as showing some of the devices resorted to by the loyalists, their families and friends, to save at least a portion of their estates for the original owners. The letter is as follows:

Boston, 24 June, 1786.

My Dear Mr. Gay:

My last of the 8th instant containing the melancholy account of the death of my father, I make no doubt you have received. In that I also informed you that the house was to be sold the 15 of this month which was done accordingly. Mr. Whalley chose to bid it of and Brother Timothy bought it at £380. He paid 129 Dollars Earnest money, the rest is to be paid in 6 weeks. I wish you could settle your affairs so as to come home before the time is up. Mr. Walley has sent you the account of the sale properly authentic, and has directed them to be left at Mr. Pike's at Halifax. Do come home as soon as you can. Our friends unite with me in love to you and children. Father Gay has got quite well. Fanny is with me and desires her duty to you. Love to her Brothers and Sisters. Believe me to be your tender, affectionate Wife,

R. GAY.

The sale mentioned by Mrs. Gay took place under the Confiscation Act of 1777-1780. These estates were treated by the Probate Court as those of deceased persons. As Martin Gay's wife was not an absentee she was entitled to her third or dower right in her husband's estate. The Commissioners appointed by the Probate Court assigned to Mrs. Gay as "her third" "the two middle tenements of the house on Union Street, Boston, with the cellars chambers and upper rooms. Also the shop fronting Union Street and the land under same with the liberty to go through the great entry into the said shop, with the use and improvements of the yard, Well' Pump, and Privy." This division was made at her request as a shrewd means of retaining for herself and eventually for her husband, the *whole* of the property, for it would be difficult to sell or to lease the two ends of the house so divided, with the middle taken out. The result was that the remainder of the house was unsaleable and as stated in the letter was bought in by her brother Timothy Atkins. As Mrs. Gay by her right of dower had only a life estate on the property, it was necessary that she should require what is known as the "remainder" which was still vested in the Commonwealth. This was conveyed to her by Act of the Legislature, Feb. 7th, 1807, for the consideration $1,680. In 1809, the widow, Ruth Gay, and her son Ebenezer Gay, sold this property for fifteen thousand dollars.

The third letter is dated at London, 7 July, 1788. In it he says "I cannot pretend to say when my affairs will admit of my return to America. By a late act of parliament a final settlement will (it is sayed) be made with the Loyalists within a few months. I must wait with patience this important event, then prepare to leave this both wonderful and delightful kingdom, and return to my family and friends in my native country, though an Alien when in it."

He remained two years in England and returned to Boston in 1792, when he resumed his business as a coppersmith at his old stand in Union Street, and soon after entered into business relations with Mr. James Davis, a brass founder, then but twenty-two years of age, who had learned the trade from a Hessian, who like many of his countrymen were obliged to remain in the country when Congress violated the terms of the Saratoga Convention.* Mr. Gay subsequently sold the business to Mr. Davis, who incorporated it in 1828 under the name of the Revere Copper Company, Mr. Joseph Warren Revere being one of the incorporators.

Martin Gay died in 1809, and he was buried in the Granary Burial Ground. SAMUEL GAY was the eldest son of Martin Gay who graduated at Harvard in 1775. Owing to the disturbed state of the times, and the quarterings of the rebel troops in the College buildings, he did not take his degree at the College Commencement, which was not held this year. He became a permanent resident of New Brunswick, and was a member of the first House of Assembly organized in the Colony, and represented the County of Westmoreland several years. He was also a magistrate of that County, and Chief Justice of the Court of Common Pleas. He died at Fort Cumberland (where his father had a grant of land from the Crown) January 21, 1847 in the ninety-third year of his age.

EBENEZER GAY was the youngest son of Martin Gay, and can hardly be classed as a loyalist. He was a child when his father went to Halifax, and he remained in Boston with his mother during the war. He graduated at Harvard College in 1789, practiced law, and was a member of the State Senate, and resided at Hingham. Mr. Wickworth Allen Gay, the

* See page 85 for further account of the Saratoga Convention.

artist, is his son. Martin Gay the younger, was fifteen years of age when he accompanied his father to Halifax. Three years later he was accidentally shot by a friend while hunting near Windsor, Nova Scotia.

LIST OF CONFISCATED ESTATES BELONGING TO MARTIN GAY IN SUFFOLK COUNTY AND TO WHOM SOLD.

To John Davis, Jan. 7, 1783; Lib. 136, fol. 228; Land in Boston, Winter St. S.; Samuel Dashwood E. and N.; Dr. Sylvester Gardner, an absentee, W.
To Timothy Atkins, Dec. 13, 1787; Lib. 161, fol. 240; Land and buildings in Boston, Union St. E.; Philip Freeman S.; E.; E. and S.; heirs of Benjamin Andrews W.; N. and W.; Dorothy Carnes N. and W.; Jeremiah Bumstead N.; reserving that part of the premises set off to Ruth Gay, wife of said Martin Gay.

DANIEL LEONARD.

The Leonard family was established in this country in 1652, by three sons of Thomas Leonard, who remained in England. The three sons were James, Henry, and Philip, all of whom have left many descendants. The Leonards were interested in the first iron works established in this country at Lynn, Braintree, Rowley Village, and Taunton, and at a later date at Canton, so that the observation "where you can find iron works there you will find a Leonard" has been almost literally verified. They were probably interested in most, if not all the iron works established in this country within the first century after its settlement, and it is a remarkable fact that the iron manufacure has continued successively, and generally very successfully, in the hand of the Leonards or their descendants, down to the present day.

James was the progenitor of the Leonards of Taunton, Raynham and Norton. He and his sons often traded with the Indians, and were on such terms of friendship with them, that when war broke out King Philip gave strict orders to his men never to hurt the Leonards. Philip resided in winter at Mount Hope, but his summer residence was at Raynham, about a mile from the forge. The family was noted throughout Plymouth County in Colonial times for its wealth, and the number of able men it produced in successive generations, who were entrusted by the public with offices of honor and importance. To this family belonged Daniel Leonard, the third Taunton lawyer, a man who was no unconspicuous actor in the affairs of his time. He was the only son of Ephraim Leonard, a judge of the Court of Common Pleas, a colonel in the militia, and the possessor of a large property, who resided on a homestead of five hundred acres connected with which were extensive iron works, situated in that part of the town of Norton now known as Mansfield. There, in a house on this estate the subject of this sketch was born May 29, 1740. His boyhood was passed tranquilly amid comforts which usually wait on an only child of wealthy and influential parents. Entering Harvard College at an early age, he graduated in 1760 in the class of John Lowell, the celebrated lawyer. He took up law as a profession, and had not been long at the bar before he was engaged in a fair practice, his generous disposition and affable manners having established his popularity, while his acquirements won for him reputation as an orator and a scholar. In 1776 he received from Yale College the degree of M. A.; in 1769 he was appointed as King's Attorney of Bristol County. Having become possessed of a fortune by a Boston heiress, he adopted what for that age and vicinity was considered great style, and display of dress, and mode of living. He set up a chariot, and pair of horses with which he travelled to Boston several times a week, something no lawyer in the Province had ever ventured to do before. In 1769 he began his political career by entering the Legislature where he represented Taunton during the years of 1770-71-73 and 74. At first he made the most ardent speeches, which had been up to that time delivered in the House against Great Britain in favor of the colonists, but in the latter years of his service as a representative, he, like many more of his countrymen, became alarmed at the mob outrages, and the drifting of the country towards rebellion, he slowly changed his opinions and became a Loyalist and a supporter of the government that represented law, and authority. The revolutionists attributed this change to the influence of Governor Hutchinson and Attorney-General Sewall with whom he was on terms of intimacy, although this friendship formed some cause of distrust; the change in his views was not known publicly, or with certainty until the summer of 1774, as is evidenced by his being a member of the Committee of Nine on the state of the Province in the Legislature of that year, a committee made up of those only who were believed to be against the government. In June of that year he became an "addresser" to Governor Hutchinson. A few weeks later he was appointed Mandamus Councellor by the King. When it became known that he had taken the oath for qualifications for this office a mob of upward of two thousand men gathered on the "green" near his home, uttering oaths and angry threats and menacing him with personal indignities, which they would undoubtedly have proceeded to put into execution if they could have found him, but being informed by his father that he had gone to Boston and that he would use his influence to induce his son to resign his office, they were mollified for the time and refrained from pulling the house down, and gradually dispersed. They, however, assembled again the following evening, and seeing a light in the south chamber where Mrs. Leonard lay sick in bed, and thinking that Leonard was there, they fired through the window into the room; the bullets passed through the upper sash and shutter, and lodged in the partition of the next chamber.* Friends had acquainted Mr. Leonard of

* Mrs. Leonard was confined to bed with childbirth. Charles, their only son, was born an idiot, due no doubt to this outrage. The mother of Curtis Guild, the present governor of Massachusetts, was born in this room, she being a descendant of the Leonard family.

the mob's intention to attack his home. He therefore went to Boston where his family soon joined him, and was protected from further violence by the presence of the troops. This outrage upon his home greatly embittered him against the revolutionists and their cause, and was undoubtedly the cause of his writing his celebrated letters, which so ably championed those principles of civil liberty, for which the loyalists so nobly contended.

Daniel Leonard was the author of the famous letters signed Massachusettensis, mis-attributed by the first President Adams to Jonathan Sewall. These letters that appeared in the Massachusetts Gazette "reviewed with much ingenuity with the purpose of showing that the course of the government was founded in law and reason; that the colonies had no substantial grievance; that they were a part of the British Empire and properly subject to its authority." From the great skill in which they were written they were attributed to Jonathan Sewall, a man of much talent. It was more than a generation before the authorship was assigned to Daniel Leonard. John Adams ansewred these papers as "Novanglus," "Massachusettensis" bears dates between December, 1774, and April, 1775, and was published three times in a single year: first, in the "Massachusetts Gazette and Post Boy," next in a pamphlet form; and last, by Rivington, in New York. Still another edition appeared in Boston in 1776. The replies were numerous. "Novanglus" bears dates between January and April, 1775. Both were printed in 1819, with a preface, by Mr. Adams, who remarks of "Massachusettensis," that "these papers were well written, abounded with wit, discovered good information, and were conducted with a subtlety of art and address wonderfully calculated to keep up the spirits of their party, to depress ours," etc. etc.

The following are a few brief extracts from these letters.

"The press when opened to all parties and influenced by none, is a salutary engine in a free state, to preserve the freedom of that state, but when a party has gained the ascendancy, so far as to become the licensers of the press, either by act of government, or by playing off the resentment of the populace against printers, and authors, the press itself becomes an engine of oppression or licentiousness, and is as pernacious to society as otherwise it would be beneficial. It is too true that ever since the origin of our controversy with Great Britain, the press of this town have been indulged in publishing what they pleased, while little has been published on the part of the government. The effect this must have had upon the minds of the people in general is obvious. In short, the changes have been so often rung upon oppression, tyranny, and slavery, that, whether sleeping or waking, they are continually vibrating in our ears, and it is now high time to ask ourselves whether we have not been deluded by sound only. Should you be told that acts of high treason are flagrant through the country, that a great part of the province is in actual rebellion, would you believe it true? Nay, you would spurn it with indignation. Be calm, my friends, it is necessary to know the worst of a disease, to enable us to provide an effectual remedy. Are not the bands of society cut asunder and the sanctions that hold man to man trampled upon? Can any of us recover a debt, or obtain compensation for an injury by law? Are not many persons, whom once we respected, and revered, driven from their homes, and families, and forced to fly to the army for protection, for no other reason but their having accepted commissions under our king? Is not civil government dissolved?

Reader, apply to an honest lawyer (if such a one can be found) and inquire what kind of an offence it is for a number of armed men to assemble, and forcibly to obstruct the courts of justice, to pass governmental acts, to take the militia out of the hands of the king's representatives to form a new militia, to raise men and appoint officers for public purposes, without order or permission of the king or his representatives, or for a number of men to take to their arms, and march with a professed design of opposing the king's troops. Ask, reader, of such a lawyer, what is the crime, and what the punishment, and if, perchance, thou art one that has been active in these things, and art not insensibility itself, his answer will harrow up thy soul.

The shaft is already sped, and the utmost exertion is necessary to prevent the blow. We already feel the effects of anarchy, mutual confidence, affection, and tranquility, those sweetners of human life are succeeded by distrust, hatred, and wild uproar; the useful arts of agriculture and commerce are neglected for caballing, mobbing this or the other man, because he acts, speaks or is suspected of thinking different from the prevailing sentiment of the times, in purchasing arms, and forming a militia. O height of madness! Can you indulge the thought one moment that Great Britain will consent to this? For what has she protected and defended the colonies against the maritime powers of Europe, from their first British settlement to this day? For what did she purchase New York of the Dutch? For what was she so lavish of her best blood and treasure in the conquest of Canada, and other territories in America? Was it to raise up a rival state, or to enlarge her own empire? I mention these things, my friends, that you may know how people reason upon this subject in England, and to convince you that you are deceived, if you imagine, that Great Britain will accede to the claims of the colonies. And now, in God's name, what is it that has brought us to this brink of destruction? Has not the government of Great Britain been as mild and equitable in the colonies, as in any part of her extensive domains? Has she not been a nursing mother to us from the days of our infancy to this time. Has she not been indulgent almost to a fault?

I have as yet said nothing of the difference in sentiment among ourselves. Upon a superficial view we might imagine that this province was nearly unanimous; but the case is far different. A very considerable body of men of property in this province are at this day firmly attached to the cause of government, bodies of men compelling persons to disavow their sentiments, to resign commissions or to subscribe leagues, and covenants, has wrought no change in their sentiments. It has only attached them more closely to government and pray more devoutly for its restoration.

A new, and until lately unheard of mode of opposition, has been devised, said to be the invention of the fertile brain of one of our party agents, called a committee of correspondence. This is the foulest, subtlest, and most venomous serpent that ever issued from the eggs of sedition. These committees when once established, think themselves amenable to none, they assume a dictatorial style, and have an opportunity under the apparent sanction of their several towns, of clandestinely wreaking private revenge on individuals by traducing their characters, and holding them up as enemies of their country, wherever they go, also of misrepresenting facts and propagating sedition through the country. Thus a man of principle and property in travelling through the country would be insulted by persons whose faces he had never seen before. He would feel the smart without suspecting the hand that administered the blow. These committees, as they are not known in law, and can derive no authority from thence. They frequently erect themselves into a tribunal where the same persons are at once legislators, accusers, witnesses, judges, and jurors and the mob the executioners. The accused has no day in court, and the execution of the sentence is the first notice he receives. It is chiefly owning to these committees, that so many respectable persons have been abused and forced to sign recantations and resignation though so many persons, to avoid such reiterated insults, as are more to be deprecated by a man of sentiment than death itself, have been obliged to quit their houses, families and business, and fly to the army for protection. That husband has been separated from wife, father from son, brother from brother, and the unfortunate refugee forced to abandon all the comforts of domestic life. Have not these people that are thus insulted, as good a right to think and act for themselves in matters of the last importance. Why then, do you suffer them to be cruelly treated for differing in sentiment from you? Perhaps by this time some of you may inquire who it is, that suffers his pen to run so freely. I will tell you; it is a native of this province that knew it before many that are now basking in the rays of political sunshine, had a being. He was favored not by whigs, or tories, but the people. He is now repaying your favors, if he knows his own heart, from the purest gratitude. I saw the small seed of sedition when it was implanted; it was as a grain of mustard. I have watched the plant until it has become a great tree; the vilest reptiles that crawl upon the earth are concealed at the root, the foulest birds of the air rest upon its branches.

At the conclusion of the late war Great Britain found that the national debt amounted to almost one hundred and fifty million, and heavy taxes and duties were laid. She knew that the colonies were as much benefited as any part of the empire, and indeed more so, she thought it reasonable that the colonies should bear a part of the national burden, as that they should share in the national benefit. For this purpose the stamp act was passed. At first we did not dream of denying the authority of parliament to tax us, much less legislate for us. We had paid for establishing a post office, duties imposed for regulating trade, and even for raising a revenue to the crown without questioning the right. Some resolves in Virginia denying the right of parliament made their appearance. We read them with wonder, they savoured of independence. It now became unpopular to suggest the contrary, his life would be in danger that asserted it. The newspapers were open to but one side of the question and the inflamatory pieces that issued weekly from the press, worked up the populace to a fit temper to commit the outrages that ensued. It has been said that several thousands were expended in England, to ferment the disturbance there. However that may be, opposition to the ministry was then gaining ground, from circumstances foreign to this. The ministry was changed and the stamp act repealed. When the statute was made imposing duties upon glass, paper, India teas, etc. imported into the colonies, it was said this was another instance of taxation. We obtained a partial repeal of this statute which took off the duties from all articles except teas. We could not complain of the threepenny duty on tea as burdensome, for a shilling which had been laid upon it for the purpose of regulating trade, and therefore was allowed to be constitutional, was taken off; so that we were, in fact, gainers nine pence on the pound by the new regulation. The people were told weekly that the ministry had formed a plan to enslave them that the duty upon tea was only a prelude to a window tax, hearth tax, land tax and poll tax, etc. What was it natural to expect from a people bred under a free constitution, jealous of their liberty, credulous, even to a proverb when told their privileges were in danger. I answer outrages, disgraceful to humanity itself. What mischief was not an artful man, who had obtained the confidence and guidance of such an enraged multitude, capable of doing? He had only to point out this or that man, as an enemy of his country, and no character or station, age or merit could protect the proscribed from their fury. Happy was it for him, if he could secrete his person, and subject his property only to their lawless rage. By such means acts of public violence has been committed as will blacken many a page in the history of our country. They have engrossed all the power of the province into their own hands. A democracy or republic it has been called, but it does not deserve the name of either. It was, however, a despotism cruelly carried into execution by mobs, and riots, and more incompatible with the rights of mankind than the enormous monarchies of the East. The government under the British Constitution consisting of kings, lords, and commons, is allowed both by Englishmen and foreigners to be the most perfect system that the wisdom of ages has produced. The distributions of power are so just, and the proportions so exact, as at once to support and control each other. An Englishman glories in being subject to and protected by such a government.

Let us now suppose the colonies united and moulded into some form of government, in order to render government operative and salutary, subordination is necessary. This our patriots need not be told of, and when once they had mounted the steed and found themselves so well seated as to run no risk of being thrown from the saddle, the severity of their discipline to restore subordination would be in proportion to their former treachery in destroying it. We have already seen specimens of their tyranny, in the inhuman treatment of persons guilty of no crime except that of differing in sentiment. What then must we expect from such scourges of mankind when supported by imperial powers?

I do not address myself to whigs or tories, but to the whole people. I know you well, you are loyal at heart, friends to good order, and do violence to yourselves in harboring one moment, disrespectful sentiments towards Great Britain, the land of our forefathers' nativity, and sacred repository of their bones, but you have been most insidiously induced to believe that Britain is rapacious, cruel and vindictive, and envies us the inheritance purchased by the sweat and blood of our ancestors. Could that thick mist be but once dispelled that you might see our Sovereign, the provident father of all his people, and Great Britain a nursing mother to the colonies, as they really are. Long live our gracious king, and happiness to Britain would resound from one end of the province to the other."*

In February, 1775, Daniel Leonard was appointed Solicitor General of the Commission of Customs with a salary of £200 sterling, a body exercising powers similar to those of a court of admiralty. Thirteen months after this time, March, 1776, he accompanied the British Army to Halifax with his family of eight persons and thence to London, where he practiced as a barrister in the Courts of Westminster.

In 1780, William Knox, Under Secretary of State for the American Department suggested the division of Maine, and a province of the territory between the Penobscot and St. Croix rivers, with Thomas Oliver for Governor, and Daniel Leonard for Chief Justice. The plan was approved by the King and Ministry, but was abandoned because Wederburne, the Attorney-General, gave the opinion that the whole of Maine was included in the charter of Massachusetts.

Mr. Leonard was in Massachusetts in 1799 and again in 1808. He was included in the Banishment Act of 1778 and the Conspiracy Act of 1779. He received the appointment of Chief Justice to Bermuda. After filling this office for many years, he again in his last days took up his residence in London, where he died June 27, 1829, aged 89. His death was the result of an accident while withdrawing the charge from a pistol, he accidentally discharging it so as to cause almost instant death.

The generous temper and affable manners of Mr. Leonard seemed to have fascinated those who were in his household. The nurse who was entrusted with the care of the infant daughter of his first wife, would

* Extracts from Massachusettensis. Letter addressed to the Inhabitants of the Province of Massachusetts Bay, Dec. 12th, 1774.

never leave him. She went with his family in all their wanderings, first to Boston, then to Halifax, London, and Bermuda, then to the United States, back again to the West Indies, then to London, and died in their service. His Deputy Sheriff, who had been a Captain in the Provincial service, a person of great address, wit, and accomplishments, followed his fortunes and was killed in the battle of Germantown, then a Major in the British Army. A young gentleman educated at Harvard College, and in his office, went with him to London where he died.

Daniel Leonard married twice. His first wife was Anna, daughter of Hon. Samuel White of Taunton, his second Sarah Hammock of Boston, who died on the passage from Bermuda to Providence, R. I., aged 78. He left a daughter Anna, who married a Mr. Smith of Antigua, Harriet who died in London in 1849, Sarah who married John Stewart, a captain in British army and afterwards Collector of the Port of Bermuda. Sarah had four children. The eldest Duncan Stewart, on the death of an uncle who died childless, succeeded to an ancient Lairdship in Scotland. His brother, Leonard Stewart, was an eminent physician in London. His sister Emily married a Captain in the service of the East India Company, the other sister, Sarah, married a Mr. Winslow, descended from the ancient governor of Plymouth, and a relative of Lord Lyndhurst. (Copley) whose private Secretary he was during his Chancellorship.* Mr. Leonard had an only son Charles, who was born when the mob attacked his house, and was feeble-minded. He entered Harvard College in 1791, but did not graduate. He was subsequently under the guardianship of Judge Wheaton, and was found dead in the road in Barrowsville, near Taunton in 1831. Col. Ephraim Leonard, who lived till the close of the Revolution devised his large estate to his grandson Charles. It was understood, however, that the father and sisters of Charles were to partici- in the enjoyment of the property. Had Daniel Leonard returned from banishment and taken the oath of naturalization and allegiance to the new government, he would have inherited this large estate, but this he would not do, nothing could swerve him from his loyalty to the old flag.

JUDGE GEORGE LEONARD.

Major George Leonard was the third in descent from James, the immigrant. He removed in 1690 to Norton, then a part of Taunton, where he became the proprietor of very large tracts of land, and was in fact the founder of that town. Here this family, as possessors of great wealth and of the largest landed estate probably of any in New England, have lived for over two hundred years. Major George was Judge of the Court of Common Pleas. His eldest son George, the subject of this sketch, was born March 4, 1698. He was in office from early

* Genealogical Memoir of the Leonard Family, by William R. Deane.

manhood until old age. He served his town in nearly every capacity and was appointed a judge of the Court of Common Pleas, in 1725; a member of the Council in 1741; and Judge of Probate in 1747; while in the Militia he rose to rank of Colonel. In 1740 he was dismissed from the bench, in consequence of his connection with the famous Land Bank scheme, but was restored six years afterwards, and became Chief Justice. He was called a "neutral" by Clark the historian of Norton, and he remarks that though the most influential man in town he took no active part in public affairs during the war. A *neutral* in the Revolution was a Loyalist, the Revolutionists did not allow such a thing as a "neutral" to exist. The fact was that he was an old man, whom all classes respected, and on that account they did not molest him, and drive him out.

He died in 1778, in his eighty-first year. "Tradition," says Clark, "has universally given him a character above reproach, and of sterling worth." He married Rachel Clap, of Scituate, who bore him four children and who died in 1783, in her eighty-second year.

George Leonard, son of the former, was born in 1729, and graduated at Harvard University in 1748. He held several important offices under the Colonial government, and after the adoption of the Federal Constitution, was a member of Congress. It is said "he was a genuine specimen of an American country gentleman," that "he was a kind and considerate landlord, who never raised his rents, and who regarded his old tenants as his friends," that "he was tenaciously attached to old customs, and wore the short breeches and long stockings to the day of his death."

COLONEL GEORGE LEONARD.

Was the son of Rev. Nathaniel Leonard the brother of Judge Leonard and fifth in descent from James the immigrant. He was driven forth from his native land and settled in New Brunswick in 1783, and was much employed in public affairs. The year after his arrival, he was appointed one of the agents of government to locate lands granted to Loyalists, and was soon after made a member of the Council, and commissioned as a Colonel in the militia. He died at Sussex Vale in 1826, at an old age. His wife Sarah, died a year before aged eighty-one. He had several children. His daughter Caroline married R. M. Jarvis, Esq., in 1805, and his daughter Maria married Lieutenant Gustavus Rochfort of the Royal Navy in 1814. His son, Colonel Richard Leonard of the 104th Regiment of the British army and Sheriff of the District of Niagara, died at Lundy's Lane in 1833.

George Leonard, Jr., son of George Leonard, accompanied his father to New Brunswick in 1783. He was a grantee of the city of St. John. He was bred to the law, and devoted himself to his profession. He died at Sussex Vale in 1818.

HARRISON GRAY.

Receiver General of Massachusetts.

HARRISON GRAY, was the son of Edward Gray and his wife Susanna. He was born in Boston, 24 February, 1711.

Edward Gray was from Lancashire, England, was an apprentice in Boston in 1686, and married Susanna Harrison in 1699, by whom he had several children.

Harrison Gray was bred a merchant. His patrimonial inheritance, aided by industry, enabled him to acquire a handsome fortune. In June 1753, he was chosen Treasurer of the province by the General Court and continued in that office till October, 1774. He was an ardent loyalist, and adhered to government from the beginning of the controversy, but the modification of his conduct, his superior fitness for the office and the confidence in his integrity secured him public favor through the stormy period which commenced soon after his first election, and continued until his appointment to, and acceptance of, the office of mandamus counsellor in 1774. But this was an unpardonable offence in the eyes of the "sons of despotism." It was however unsolicited, unexpected, and accepted with great reluctance, being strongly pressed upon him by the leaders of the loyalist party; and as most of those who had been appointed his colleagues living in the country were compelled by the mobs to decline the office, he was led to believe that residing in Boston then garrisoned by the troops, he had no such apology for shrinking from the service, and accordingly sacrificed inclination to a conscientious sense of duty. This brought upon him the ill will and malice of his political opponents, among these was John Adams, who said, "I went in to take a pipe with brother Cranch and there I found Zab Adams. He told me he heard that I had made two very powerful enemies in this town, and lost two very valuable clients—Treasurer Gray, and Ezekel Goldthwaite; and that he had heard that Gray had been to me for my account, and paid it off, and determined to have nothing more to do with me. O the wretched, impotent malice! they show their teeth—they are eager to bite—but they have not strength. I despise their anger, their resentment, and their threats; but I can tell Mr. Treasurer that I have it in my power to tell the world a tale which will infallibly unhorse him, whether I am in the house or out. If this province knew that the public money had never been counted these twenty years, and that no bonds were given last year, nor for several years before, there would be so much uneasiness about it that Mr. Treasurer would lose his election another year." This was one of the meanest and most contemptible statements John Adams ever made. It was a reckless accusation, and insinuation, and was ably answered by his grandson, Harrison Gray Otis, who prepared a clear refutation of the unjust accusation in Russell's Centinel, June, 1830. It was also refuted by subsequent events. In October, 1774, the royal government was superseded by the revolutionary congress who resolved *"that no more taxes be paid to him,"* and made choice of Henry Gardner for his successor. This authority he could not be expected to recognize. He therefore retained the books and files at his office till the evacuation of Boston, and then left them in exemplary order. They are still in the public archives of Massachusetts and show the model of a faithful state treasurer. He might have been justified in retaining a lien upon these as a security against loss and damage to his very valuable real, and personal estate, which he left, and which was soon confiscated, but his high sense of official duty forbade his recourse to any such precaution, and he withdrew from a country which he loved, not less than those who stayed at home, taking nothing which belonged to the public, but surrendered all his property into the keeping of the public that treated him so basely. He was also a creditor to many of the "sons of despotism," at the head of whom was John Hancock, who owed him a large sum for borrowed money, no part of which would he pay in his lifetime, and of which a small part was received from his executors.*

In the House of Representatives, August 8, 1775, "Ordered, that Mr. Hopkins be directed to inquire how the Committee of Supplies have disposed of the horse and chaise formerly Harrison Gray's which was used by the late Dr. Warren, and came to the hands of the said Committee after Dr. Warren's death." The next day, "Ordered, that Dr. William Eustis be, and hereby is directed, immediately to deliver to the Committee of Supplies the horse and chaise which were in the possession of the late Doctor Warren, and which formerly belonged to Harrison Gray."

When Boston was evacuated, Mr. Gray, urged by a sense of duty, with the male members of his family, tore himself away from his adored and only daughter, Mrs. S. A. Otis, which so preyed upon her peace of mind that it finally caused her death.

He went to Halifax with his family of four persons where he stayed a short time. "He was passenger in one of the six vessels that arrived at London from Halifax, prior to June 10, 1776, laden with Loyalists and their families."

In Mr. Gray's house in London about the year 1789, Arthur Savage gave the Rev. Mr. Montague a bullet taken from the body of General Warren the day after his death. Mr. Montague after his return to Boston, became rector of Christ Church. Harrison Gray, in a letter to him, dated London, August 1st, 1791, remarks to him in a spirit of loyalty to the crown of Britain as follows: "The melancholy state in which you represent religion to be in Boston and New England is confirmed by all who come from thence. Is this one of the blessings of your independence to obtain which you sacrificed so many lives? I am glad your federal constitution 'has had a very great and good effect', but very much ques-

---

* This was the same as he did towards Harvard college, when treasurer of same. History of Harvard College by Josiah Quincy.

tion whether you will ever be so happy as you were under the mild and gentle government and protection of Great Britain; for, notwithstanding the freedom my countrymen boast of, if in order to obtain it they have sacrificed their religion, they have made a poor bargain. They cannot, in a religious sense, be a free people till the Son of God has made them free. It is very surprising, considering the establishment of the Roman Catholic religion at Quebec was one of the heavy grievances the American Congress complained of* that your governor and other great men in your town should attend the worship of God in a Roman Catholic church, to hear a Romish bishop on a Sunday; and that he should be one of the chaplains who officiated at a public dinner. I cannot at present account for their inconsistency any otherwise than by supposing the part they took in the late unhappy contests, lays so heavy upon their consciences that they imagine no one can absolve them but a Romish priest."

Mr. Gray lived in England upon a pension granted by the British government. In 1794 at the advanced age of eighty-four, this excellent and virtuous man sunk to rest. Perhaps no man among the many excellent persons who went into exile at this time was more beloved and regretted by his political enemies, for a more genuine model of nature's nobleman never lived.

JOHN GRAY, son of Harrison Gray and his wife Elizabeth, born in Boston, 18th of May, 1755. He went to Ireland soon after the battle of Lexington. Hearing that the difficulties would probably be adjusted, he embarked for Massachusetts, the vessel was taken off Newburyport. He was in Newbury Jail, February, 1776, when at the solicitation of his sister, the mother of Harrison Gray Otis, an order was passed to allow his removal to the Otis homestead in Barnstable on condition of his giving a bond with security in £1,000 not to pass without the limits of that town, or deal or correspond with the enemy. Mr. Gray was in London, January, 1781.

JOSEPH GRAY was descended from an old Boston family, his grandfather Joseph Gray, was married by Rev. Samuel Williard to Rebecca Sears, June 27, 1706. Their son Joseph Gray was born April 9, 1707, and married Rebecca, daughter of John West of Bradford, or Haverhill of Massachusetts. The old people were displeased with the match and cut Rebecca off with "one pine tree shilling." Their son Joseph, the subject of this sketch, was born July 19, 1729. He was a loyalist and settled at Halifax, Nova Scotia, and was a member of the firm of Proctor & Gray, merchants. His wife was Mary, daughter of Hon. Joseph Gerrish. His son, the Rev. Benjamin Gerrish Gray, D. D., was born in 1768, married Mary, daughter of Nathaniel Roy Thomas a Loyalist, and was many years rector of St. George's parish, Halifax, and afterwards of an Episcopal church in St. John, N. B. Died at the latter city in 1854. Another son of Joseph Gray was William, born in 1777. Was British Consul for Virginia for a long time and died in England in 1845

* See Chapter III. in relation to this matter.

Joseph Gray died at Windsor, N. S., in 1803 at the age of seventy-four, leaving a large number of descendants.

John Gray of Boston, another brother of Joseph Gray. He was bred to business in that town by Caleb Blanchard. About the year 1768 he went to England, but returned previous to hostilities, and was appointed Deputy Collector of Customs, in which office he was popular. In 1776 he embarked for Halifax with the Royal Army, and before the close of that year was at Charleston, S. C., and in prison. He was still in that city as late as 1780, when he was an Addresser of Sir Henry Clinton. Before the last mentioned date, however, he had engaged in business as a commission merchant, and had purchased a plantation on account of himself and of John Simpson, a fellow Loyalist of Boston. But involved politically beyond the hope of extrication he sold his interest in the plantation, and invested the proceeds in indigo and in a ship with the intention of sailing for London. The Revolutionists not only defeated this plan, but seized his vessel and his cargo, and the result was that of both he barely saved one hundred guineas. With this sum he fled to his brother Joseph at Halifax, who provided him a passage to England in a ship of war. Without any accession to his fortune yet, with letters to the agents of the East India Company, he soon embarked for India, and, on his arrival there, was well received. The family account is that he wrote a treattise on the Cultivation of Indigo, which the Governor and Council considered so valuable as to grant him £4,000 sterling, and jointly with a Mr. Powell, an extensive tract of land. These two grantees, assisted by the Company, established a factory, and began the culture of indigo, which was said to be the first attempt to cultivate this beautiful dye in India. Both died suddenly in 1782 on the same day. Gray was at the plantation, and Powell was two hundred miles away at the factory, and the supposition was that they had incurred the jealousy of the natives, who had caused their death by poison. Powell's brother told Joseph Gray, prior to 1799 that the estate of our Loyalist and his associate had become "the greatest indigo plantation in the known world."*

Samuel Gray was also a brother of Joseph Gray. He died at Boston in 1776 leaving issue, male and female. His wife was a daughter of Captain Henry Atkins of Boston.

Thomas Gray of Boston was a merchant, a Protester against the Revolutionists, and one of the Addressers of Hutchinson. He died at Boston in 1783.

LIST OF CONFISCATED ESTATES BELONGING TO HARRISON GRAY IN SUFFOLK COUNTY AND TO WHOM SOLD.

To John Stanton, David Devens, Jonathan Harris, Feb. 11, 1780; Lib. 131, fol. 51; Land and two brick dwelling-houses in Boston, Cornhill W.; land purchased by Samuel Allen Otis N.; E. and N.; Wilson's Lane E.; Nathaniel Appleton S.

To Samuel Allen Otis, April 4, 1780; Lib. 131, fol. 93; Land and brick dwelling-house in Boston, Cornhill W.; land purchased by John Stanton and others S.; W. and S.; Wilson's Lane E.; Samuel Vallentine N.

* Sabine, Vol. I., Pp. 490-1.

REV. WILLIAM WALTER.

Rector of Trinity Church, Boston.

Thomas Walter, an Attorney at Law, came to America from Youghall, Ireland, about 1679, bringing a recommendatory letter to the churches in New England from a Congregational church in Youghall,—and by virtue thereof was admitted a member of the Second church, Boston, November 2, 1680. His family were originally of Lancashire, England, and were of gentle blood. He died before the year 1698.

Rev. Nehemiah Walter, son of the former, was born in Ireland, December, 1663, and came to America with his father. He early distinguished himself by proficiency in his studies at school, and by the age of thirteen was a master of the Latin tongue. It soon became evident that his genius pointed to a professional life, and he was sent to Harvard University where he graduated with honors in 1684. Shortly thereafter he removed to Novia Scotia where he resided some months for the purpose of acquiring the French language. He became a distinguished scholar and became noted among the literati of the day. After a careful and impartial examination and great deliberation, "he fell in the way of the Churches of New England, as thinking their constitution practice in general, with respect to worship, discipline and order, most comfortable to gospel institution and primitive practice." He was ordained a colleague of the Rev. John Eliot October 17, 1688 at the age of twenty-five. The first church at Roxbury had, at the earnest request of the venerable Apostle Eliot, been seeking a colleague to share the duties which increasing infirmity rendered irksome to him; and Nehemiah Walter was chosen. Mr. Eliot died soon after this after a life crowned with glory, honors, and labor, and it was a great consolation to him in his latter days to see his people so happily settled under Mr. Walter. For more than sixty years his successor faithfully discharged the duties of his office always to the acceptance of his people. He married Sarah, the daughter of Rev. Increase Mather by Maria, daughter of the distinguished Rev. John Cotton. Nehemiah Walter died September 17, 1750, and he was buried in the ministerial vault in the old burial ground, corner of Washington and Eustis Streets, Roxbury.

Rev. Thomas Walter, second son of Nehemiah Walter, was born in Roxbury, December 13, 1696, and early gave evidence of most extraordinary genius. He graduated from Harvard University in 1713 and was ordained October 29th, 1718, and December 25th of the same year was married to Rebeckah, daughter of Rev. Joseph Belcher. He was a man who combined great wit and humor with infinite learning and excelled in the science of harmony. He published works on music, and one of his sermons upon the 2nd Samuel XXIII 1 "The Sweet psalmist of Israel" which was delivered at the Boston Lecture, has been pronounced "the most beautiful composition among the sermons which have been handed down to us by our fathers." Others of his sermons were also published. Thomas Walter was one of the most distinguished scholars and disputants of the day. "He had all his father's vivacity and richness of imagination with more vigor of intellect." For his genius and powers he was reckoned to be one of the ablest clergymen that New England up to that time had produced. His death occurred on Sunday, January 10, 1724-5, and he expressed his hope that he might die on that day, when lying prostrate with consumption. His tomb is in the old burying ground, Roxbury. His daughter Rebeckah, who was born in 1722, died unmarried January 11, 1780.

Rev. William Walter, the subject of this sketch, was a nephew of Thomas Walter. He was born in 1739, and graduated at Harvard College in 1756. Up to the time of the Revolution the preachers in the Episcopal church occupied the position of missionaries in the American colonies. They were sent here and were in the pay of the "Society for the Propagation of the Gospel in Foreign Parts." The following extracts are from letters written to the Secretary of the Society, and they explain themselves.

"Copy of a letter written to the Reverend Mr. Hooper of Trinity church in Boston, by Mr. Barnard, an eminent dissenting clergyman, in answer to one from the former desiring the latter would be so good as to send him a just and honest character of Mr. William Walter, who was talked of as a fit person to be assistant Minister at said church."

"He came out of our College with the reputation of one of the best classical scholars of his class. He lived first in this town in the business of a Grammar Schoolmaster, which trust he executed for several years to universal acceptance, faithful, and careful. I have reason to believe, in forming the tender minds of his pupils to virtue and religion, as well as forwarding them in their scholastic exercise. When to the sorrow of the town, he quitted that employ, he became connected with the Custom House. This business naturally raised complaints against him among trading people. But all I have heard were of his not being so flexible in some matters as they wished, none of oppression, much less of mean fraudulent ways of filling his own pockets.

"His temper is innocently cheerful, open, and friendly. He has a tender and delicate sense of honor, a just idea of the truest honor. He is kind and compassionate, etc." This letter had the desired effect. It was written Oct. 15th, 1763. He was ordained by the Bishop of London the following year and became an assistant to the Rev. Mr. Hooper, whom he succeeded as rector of Trinity church, the third Episcopal church in Boston, being opened in 1735. It stood on the corner of Summer and Hawley Streets. It was a plain wooden structure without steeple or tower.

In 1767 he joined with the Clergy of Massachusetts and Rhode Island in sending a letter to England requesting that a Bishop be sent to

America. The letter says, "We are too remote and inconsiderable to approach the Throne, yet could His Majesty hear the voice of so distant a people the request for American Bishops would appear to be the crye of many of his most faithful subjects."

"We do, however, think ourselves happy in this, that the Society will omit no favorable opportunity of representing the advantage that may accrue to these Colonies, to religion and to the British Interests, by condescending to this one request."* The Episcopal form of worship was always disagreeable to the Congregationalists, and when they discovered that the ministry entertained the design of sending over a bishop to the colonies, a controversy for years ran high on the subject. So resolute was the opposition to this project that it was abandoned. This controversy John Adams says contributed as much as any other cause to arouse attention to the claims of Parliament. The spirit of the times is well represented in a cartoon in the Political Register of 1769 which is here reproduced.

The Rev. William Walter was a firm Loyalist. At the evacuation of Boston he was obliged to leave his house and accompanied by his family he went to Halifax. In 1776 he went to England, then returned and went to New York, and acted for some time as Chaplain of a British regiment. While in New York he sent a letter to the Secretary of the S. P. G. F. P., dated Dec. 8, 1781. It is interesting as it shows the trials and diffiulties of the ministers of the Church of England during the Revolution. It is in part as follows: "I disbelieve that Mr. Bass ever preached a sermon for cloathing a rebel battalion, or ever read the Declarative Act for independence in his church, or has altered his sentiments since his dismission, but that he opens his church on the days appointed by Congress as Public days, is most certain, and if this is to be criminal, then every clergyman within the rebel lines is criminal, and among others, Dr. Inglis, of this city, who did the same when Mr. Washington's army was here, yet no clergyman stands higher in the esteem of the Society for his loyalty. The occasion of this letter was the stopping of Mr. Bass's salary by the Society, as it had been reported to it that Mr. Bass had gone over to the rebels.

At the peace, accompanied by his family of six persons and by three servants, he went from New York to Shelburne, N. S., where the Crown granted him one town and one water lot. His losses in consequence of his loyalty were estimated at £7,000. In 1791 he returned to Boston and the next year was chosen Rector of Christ church.

William Walter was a zealous supporter of the church and crown, and vindicated his sincerity by the sacrifices he made for them. His discourses are described as rational and judicious, "recommended by an eloquence, graceful and majestical." He was no knight errant, but while adhering to his own convictions with quiet persistency, he exercised a large charity towards all forms of faith and Christian worship. The de-

* Papers relating to the church in Massachusetts, Pp. 506-7, 531-2.

LANDING A BISHOP.

gree of D. D. was conferred on him by Kings College, Aberdeen, in 1784. In 1796 he was invited to deliver the Dudleian lecture at Harvard College and in 1798 he pronounced the anniversary discourse before the Massachusetts Humane Society, which was published. Dr. Walter was a remarkably handsome man; tall and well proportioned. When in the street, he wore a long blue coat over his cassock and gown, wig dressed and powdered, a three-cornered hat, knee breeches of fine black cloth, and with silk hose, and square quartered sleeves with silver buckles. His countenance was always serene, his temper always cheerful; happy himself, he communicated happiness to all around him. In the desk he read the glorious service like one inspired; his voice was clear, musical and well modulated. In his family he was loved, reverenced and admired. His heart, his house, his purse, were ever open to the needy. He married Lydia, daughter of Benjamin Lynde, the younger, of Salem, and by her had seven children. Her death occurred in 1798.

Dr. Walter continued his rectorship at Christ church until his death in 1800, at the age of sixty-one. The Rev. Dr. Parker, who preached his funeral sermon, delineated his character as ornamental to religion and to the church, to literature and humanity. Dr. Walter's grandson, Lynde Minshall Walter, born in 1799, graduated at Harvard University in 1817. He established the Boston Evening Transcript in 1830, and was the first editor of the paper. His death occurred in 1842. Another grandson, William Bicker was born in Boston, April 19, 1796, and graduated at Bowdoin College in 1818. He studied divinity at Cambridge but did not preach. He became best known as an author, possessing an active fancy and a great faculty of versification. He contributed odes and sonnets and translations to the newspapers and in 1821 in Boston, he published "Poems", and "Sukey" a poem. In 1822 he went to the southern states to give lectures on poetry, but he died shortly after his arrival in Charleston, South Carolina, April 23, 1822.

This family so distinguished in ecclesiastical history of New England is believed now to be extinct. There were others of the name in Boston at an early period, who have perhaps left descendants, but they are not known to have any connection with this family.

LIST OF CONFISCATED ESTATES BELONGING TO REV. WILLIAM WALTER IN SUFFOLK COUNTY AND TO WHOM SOLD.

To Leonard Jarvis, Sept. 27, 1784; Lib. 145, fol. 32; Land and buildings in Boston, South St. W.; Samuel Quincy, an absentee, S.; Robert Robbins and heirs of Benjamin Clark, deceased, E.; Samuel Connant N. and E.; Nathaniel Taylor, an absentee, N.

THOMAS AMORY.

Hugh Amory was living in the year 1605 at Wrington in Somersetshire, under the northern side of Mendip Hills, this town and Shepton Mallett was noted at this time for its broad cloth manufactures which, within fifty years had transformed England's industry and commerce in Somerset and Devon. Hugh and one of his sons was a merchant the other was a woolen-draper, the latter, Thomas Amory, was the ancestor of the American branch of the family, his career was the troubled one of a Bristol merchant in the middle of the seventeenth century, when the city was besieged and taken by both the Parliamentary and the King's army. His son Jonathan was born in the county of Somerset in the year 1654, his father owned the estate of St. Anne and other lands in the county which in the next century went to his descendants in this country, but too heavily encumbered to be of any value. Jonathan was brought up under the care of his elder brother Thomas, who married Elizabeth Fitzmaurice a daughter of the 19th Lord of Kerry, ancestor of the present Marquis of Landsdowne. In consequence of this connection he removed to Ireland, taking his younger brother Jonathan with him, who in time became a merchant at Dublin, where he is recorded in 1675 as the purchaser from the city of the north bank of the Liffy. Dublin, hitherto, had lain wholly on the south side of the river. As late as 1816, £2, 10s. annual rent for it from "Jonathan Armory" still formed an item of the city's income. It is now as other crowded city districts, which have wharves at one end and a railway station at the other, with streets of age-blackened tenements and workshops between.

Jonathan Amory married Rebecca Houston in 1677, he went to the West Indies with his brother Robert in 1682, and his wife died at Barbados in 1685. Jonathan Amory then went to South Carolina taking with him his infant son Thomas. He married again, and invested largely in lands and houses. He was elected speaker of the Colonial Legislature, and subsequently treasurer of the Province. He died in the fall of 1699 of yellow fever.

THOMAS AMORY, son of the former, was born in Limerick, Ireland, in 1682 and accompanied his father to South Carolina. In the year 1696 he was sent with his sister Anne to their relatives in England to be educated. He was placed under the care of his cousin, Counsellor Amory, and was sent to the Westminster school. After his father's death he entered the counting-house of Mr. Ozell, a French merchant in London who in the year 1709 sent him to the Azores as supercargo. Here he established himself as a merchant and was appointed Dutch and English consul, and making only an occasional visit to Europe. Here he remained many years. About 1719 he embarked for Boston, and spent the following winter with his sister in Carolina. Returning to Boston he met Rebecca Holmes, daughter of Frances Holmes, and married her in May, 1721.

Thomas Amory bought lands at the South end of Boston, built a house and wharves, hired a counting-house of his friend, Governor Belcher, on the Long wharf and engaged in commerce with England, the Azores and Carolinas. He died in 1728, but his widow long survived him, dying in Boston in 1770 at the age of seventy. He left three sons and two daughters.

THOMAS AMORY, son of the former, was born in Boston April 23, 1722, and entered the Latin school in 1735, and graduated at Harvard College in 1741. He studied Divinity, but never took orders. As eldest son he inherited a double share of his father's estate. He married Elizabeth, the daughter of William Coffin and by her had Rebecca, afterwards the wife of Dr. Aron Dexter. He purchased the house built by Governor Belcher at the corner of Harvard and Washington streets, the gardens of which extended to the water, and this was his principal residence for the rest of his life. Thomas Amory was one of the Addressers of Gage but he did not take an active part in controversies preceding the revolution. He is described in a deed in 1769 as "Thomas Amory gentleman" in 1772 as "Distiller" and at other times as merchant. It was said that as the Revolution drew near he and his brother John planned to withdraw to England, leaving in the care of their brother Jonathan, who was childless, their combined families, to the number of twenty-three. He was on terms of friendship with the British officers and when the troops garrisoned the town, his house was attacked by the mob. He was entertaining some of the officers at his home, when bricks were thrown at his windows. One of these missiles waked his little daughter, by smashing the pane and falling on her bed. He spoke to the mob from the porch and it dispersed, but he had first hastily sent his guests by the garden way, to his boat, by which they were enabled to get to their quarters. His wife's family, the Coffins, were all Loyalists, and Thomas Amory therefore was regarded with some suspicion, especially as he was an "Addresser" of Gen. Gage.

When General Washington entrenched Dorchester Heights, March 1776, in order to command Boston with his guns, the inhabitants saw danger from both sides, Washington's assault would do great damage and the British troops as they withdrew might fire the town. On March 8th Deacon Newhall, chairman of the selectmen, requested Thomas and Jonathan Amory, and their friend, Peter Johonnot, to carry to General Washington a paper prepared by four Selectmen, proposing that the British troops should be allowed to retire unmolested, on condition of doing no harm. The offer was really authorized by General Robertson, acting for General Howe, but this could not be put in writing, nor was the person named to whom the paper was addressed. The messengers, however, delivered it to General Washington, whereupon Colonel Learned on his behalf wrote them an answer to the effect that no notice could be taken of a letter neither addressed to himself, nor authenticated by General Howe. Nevertheless the agreement was kept, as if it had been formally made. Ministers were therefore able to deny to an angry opposition in Parliament that there had been any compromise, or stipulation between General Howe and the rebels, although the Duke of Manchester affirmed that he had private information of it.*

On the evacuation Thomas Amory withdrew to Watertown, where he lived some years. He died shortly after the peace in 1784. His widow survived until 1823. He left nine children, seven of whom were married and resided in Boston. It is interesting to consider how the blood of the loyal and the disloyal afterwards became mixed. At the battle of Bunker Hill June 17, 1776, Captain Linzee of the Kings ship-of-war Falcon cannonaded the works which Prescott the "rebel" defended, but the granddaughter of Linzee was the wife of Prescott the historian who was a grandson of the rebel, and this lady is a daughter of Thomas C. Amory, the eldest son of this notice. Jonathan, the second son of our Loyalist, married Hettie, daughter of James Sullivan, governor of Massachusetts, while the wife of John Amory, another son, was near of kin to Henry Gardner, the "rebel" who succeeded Harrison Gray, the last royal treasurer of the same state. Again Nathaniel, another son, married a niece of Commodore Preble, and her sister was the wife of Admiral Wormley of the Royal Navy. Once more, William, a fifth son, born in 1774, was an officer in the British navy and after the war entered the U. S. navy and distinguished himself in the war with Tripoli, being one of the party that burnt the Philadelphia. He also distinguished himself in an attack under Hull on a fort in South America during the French war. But "loyalty" as understood in olden times, is still represented in the family by the union of Mr. Amory's grandson Charles with Martha Greene and of his grandson, James Sullivan, with Mary Greene, nieces of the late Lord Lyndhurst. Mr. Amory's grandson, Thomas C., married Esther Sargent, and William of the same degree of consanguinity married Anna, daughter of David Sears of Boston. Of the sons here mentioned, Thomas C. Amory, was a successful merchant and died in 1812. Thomas C., Jr., also a descendant, is the author of the Life of Governor Sullivan, his grandfather on his mother's side.*

Jonathan Amory, brother to Thomas, was born in Boston December 19, 1726. He married Abigail Taylor, and resided on what is now the opening of Temple Place into Washington street. His garden is said to have extended two or three hundred feet in either direction, joining his brother John's home which formerly had been Rufus Greene's in Newbury street, at the corner of West street.

Jonathan Amory died in 1797, leaving a large estate to his brother John and John's children.

JOHN AMORY, another brother of Thomas, was born in Boston in 1728. He married Catherine, daughter of Rufus Greene. He was the father of nine children who grew up and settled in his native town. He

* The descendants of Hugh Amory, London, 1901. The Amory Family, Boston, 1856.
* Sabin's Loyalists of the American Revolution.

built a house at the corner of Beacon and Tremont streets, opposite King's chapel, and lived there, and in Washington street on the site where Amory hall afterwards stood. He engaged in commerce with his younger brother. The letters of this business house from 1760 during the Stamp Act excitement and the Tea troubles give many interesting particulars of that period. Parts of this correspondence were published in English papers and to one letter a member of Parliament ascribed influence in the repeal of the Stamp act. In 1757 the store of Jonathan and John Amory was "the sign of the Horse at the head of Dock Square," they afterwards (before 1762) removed into King street "just below the town house." Their store was probably the last of the "old stores" in State street. The house, distill-house stores and wharf were Thomas Amory's share of his father's property. Amory's wharf was at the east end of Castle street, on which in 1777 he had a still-house.

In 1774 John Amory left with his family for England. It was necessary that one of the partners should go on business. At the beginning of hostilities his house owed their English creditors £23,000 sterling which they remitted without delay, while their countrymen who owed them, from inability, or taking advantage of the times paid, if at all, in a depreciated currency.

The illness of his wife, which terminated in her death in 1778, prevented his return to Boston. Shortly before the peace he embarked for America and landing at New York he took the oath of allegiance to the Crown. He was not permitted to live in Boston in consequence of the "Banishment Act." His name had been placed upon the list of the proscribed, and preliminary measures were taken to confiscate his property. His brother wrote him should this be done he would always share what he had with him. He resided in Providence till 1783, some of his family being with him then through the influence of his friends in Boston, and upon his petition to the Legislature, declaring his allegiance to the new government, he was allowed to return to Boston. He died in 1805, leaving six sons and four daughters. One of his daughters married John Lovell, widely known as a political writer, and another was the wife of John McLean, who liberally endowed the Massachusetts General hospital.

REV. HENRY CANER.

RECTOR OF KING'S CHAPEL.

HENRY CANER, D. D., was graduated at Yale College in 1724, and was the "son of Mr. Caner who built the first college and rector's house" at New Haven, Connecticut. For three years after leaving college he lived under the theological teaching of Mr. Johnson of Stratford, who had the general supervision of the Episcopal students of divinity, and who had been his college tutor. Though too young to be ordained, he assisted Mr. Johnson as a catechist and schoolmaster at Fairfield. In 1727 he went to England for ordination. For some years, subsequently, his ministry was confined to Norwalk and Fairfield, Connecticut, and he became a great worker among the missions. His health became impaired by his severe labors and in 1736 he sought relief by a voyage to England, where on the recommendation of Archbishop Potter he had been created M. A. by a diploma at Oxford March 8, 1735. His father died in 1731 at the age of sixty. The name was long preserved in New Haven by "Caner's Pond." The name is also written sometimes Canner, or Conner.

In 1747 the successful missionary was inducted into office as rector of the First Episcopal church (King's Chapel) Boston. On being invited to King's Chapel he received a deserved promotion to the most conspicuous Episcopal pulpit in America; after a laborious ministry of twenty-two years in the mission at Fairfield, Connecticut. On his removal to Boston he left behind him two hundred and three communicants, a large number of those days, in a mission where he had found but twelve. Also a handsome church and a large convenient parsonage nearby.

The old chapel in Boston was built between 1687-1689. In 1710 it was rebuilt to twice its original size under Governor Shirley. After the lapse of nearly half a century King's Chapel was found to be in a ruinous condition and measures were taken to rebuild, which resulted in the well known King's Chapel now standing upon the spot. The erection of this building in 1749 is largely due to the efforts of Dr. Caner, who was then rector.

There is no trace of his printed discourses later than 1765, but the traditions of his preaching give him a high rank as a man of learning and fine intellectual endowments. The first Episcopal church in New England was, prior to the revolution, in a flourishing state. Later, while the British ships were in the harbor and the British troops in the town, many of their officers regularly worshipped at the chapel. When becoming quite infirm in his seventy-seventh year, his age and position placed Dr. Caner at the head of the Church of England clergy in this part of the country. Records show abundantly the pastoral labor which devolved upon him, especially in his military congregation. The last burial records by his trembling hand are those of three soldiers of his Majesty's 65th Regiment of Foot. The Register of burials also notes the funeral, on March 18, 1752, of Ann, "the Pious and Virtuous Consort of Rev. Henry Caner, aged forty-six."

He was a devoted Loyalist, and when it was evident he could no longer be useful in Boston, he went with the British troops to Halifax. In one of the record books of King's Chapel, Dr. Caner made the following entry: "An unnatural rebellion of the colonies against his Majesty's government obliged the loyal part of his subjects to evacuate their dwellings and substance and take refuge in Halifax, London and elsewhere; by which means the public worship at King's Chapel became suspended, and it is likely to remain so until it shall please God, in the course of his providence, to change the hearts of the rebels, or give success to his Majesty's arms for suppressing the rebellion. Two boxes of church plate and a silver christening basin were left in the hands of the Rev. Dr. Breynton at Halifax, to be delivered to me or my order, agreeable to his note receipt in my hands." After being a rector in Boston for twenty-eight years this aged clergyman was driven from his home and native land. Dr. Caner's escape from Boston is thus described by himself in a letter dated Halifax, May 10, 1776: "As to the clergy of Boston, indeed they have for eleven months past been exposed to difficulty and distress in every shape; and as to myself, having determined to maintain my post as long as possible, I continued to officiate to the small remains of my parishioners, though without support, till the 10th of March, when I suddenly and unexpectedly received notice that the King's troops would immediately evacuate the town. It is not easy to paint the distress and confusion of the inhabitants on the occasion. I had but six or seven hours allowed to prepare for this measure, being obliged to embark the same day for Halifax, where we arrived the first of April. This sudden movement prevented me from saving my books, furniture, or any part of my interest, except bedding, wearing apparel, and a little provision for my small family during the passage.

"I am now at Halifax with my daughter and servant, but with no means of support, except what I receive from the benevolence of the worthy Dr. Breynton."

No less than eighteen Episcopal clergymen from Boston and its neighborhood sailed away with the fleet that bore Dr. Caner, and the town of Boston would have been left without any Episcopal clergymen at all, only for Dr. Andrew Eliot, the pastor of the New North church, who called upon Rev. Samuel Parker, assistant to Rev. William Walter of Trinity church. Mr. Parker was packing up his library preparing to depart when called upon by Dr. Eliot, who with true Christian candor, represented to him the destitute situation in which the Episcopalians would be left who should remain in the country, with all their ministers gone, that although it might be prudent for the elder gentlemen to go, who had made known their sentiments, that he, a young man, who had done nothing to render himself obnoxious to the rebels, would be perfectly safe, that it was a duty he owed to that part of the community to stand by them, finally he prevailed upon him to stay, a circumstance that Bishop Parker always acknowledged with gratitude.

From Halifax Dr. Caner went to England. An extract from the diary of Thomas Hutchinson in 1776 says, "I went with Dr. Caner to Lambeth, to introduce him to the Archbishop who was very gracious to him, and gave him an order for One Hundred Pounds on the Treasurer of the moneys received for the clergy of America." He was proscribed and banished, under the statute of Massachusetts, in 1778, and his estate

REV. HENRY CANER.

Born in New Haven, Conn. 1700. Rector of King's Chapel, Boston, 1747-76. Died in England Feb. 11, 1793.

confiscated. A fellow Loyalist wrote in 1785: "By letters from London, I am informed that Dr. Caner had retired with his young wife to Cardiff, in Wales."

Dr. Caner died in England at the close of the year 1792 in his ninety-third year. One of his daughters married a Mr. Gove of Boston. The Boston Gazette (No. 2002) of February 11, 1793, contains the following: "At Long-Ashton, Somersetshire, England, aged ninety-three, the Rev. Dr. Henry Caner, a very respectable character, many years minister of the Chapel church in this town." Foote in his "Annals of King's Chapel" says, "I am informed by Mr. Henry O. B. O'Donoghue of Long-Ashton, near Bristol, that there is no tombstone in the churchyard with Dr. Caner's name, nor any trace to be found of such a person ever having lived in the Parish." It has been said, also, that Dr. Caner died in London in 1792.

Dr. Caner's house stood close to King's chapel on the north side of the old burying-ground, and was a rough wooden structure. This spot was afterwards occupied by the Boston Athenaeum, and later by a Savings Bank. It next was occupied by the Massachusetts Historical Society, who sold it to the city of Boston, and it is now used as an annex to City Hall.

On the evacuation of Boston the church vestments, plate, registers and records were taken from the church, a part of which last was recovered from Dr. Caner's heirs in 1805. King's Chapel and Christ church are now without doubt the only historical buildings remaining unchanged from before the revolution of all those in which Boston was once so rich.

The vestry of the chapel in 1784 applied to Rev. Dr. Caner to have restored to them the "Church Plate and Linnen which he carried away." This he refused to do as his estate was taken from him by the public. He however turned it over to the "Society for Propagation of the Gospel in Foreign Parts, who afterwards disposed of it in the Provinces that remained loyal. In 1787 a silver flagon and covered cup which was presented to the chapel by Governor Hutchinson, having the name of King William and Queen Mary engraved on it, was claimed by Dr. Thomas Bulfinch, Warden, as the property of the King's Chapel, it then being in the hands of Rev. Dr. Parker of Trinity church for safekeeping. It is now the property of the chapel.

LIST OF CONFISCATED ESTATES BELONGING TO REV. HENRY CANER IN SUFFOLK COUNTY AND TO WHOM SOLD.

To Samuel Henly, Sept. 30, 1793; Lib. 177, fol. 82; Land and dwelling-house in Boston, Tremont St. W.; Chapel Burying Ground and heirs of Middlecott Cook deceased S.; John Rowe E.; William Brattle, an absentee, N.

FREDERICK WILLIAM GEYER.

The Gayers or Geyers as it was variously spelled, first settled at Nantucket. Some of the family came very early to Boston. The name is first mentioned in Boston Town Records 1690, when William Gayer married Maria Guard. In her will recorded with Suffolk Probate Records, Vol. 17, p. 80, 1710, she described herself as the wife of William Gayer, Mariner of Nantucket. In 1692 Damaris Gayer, the daughter of William Gayer, married Nathaniel Coffin. Their son William Coffin removed to Boston and was the ancestor of the Boston family of Coffins.

The Geyers were prominent merchants in Boston. They did not interest themselves in political matters or held office. The records mention that in 1765 Mr. Henry Christian Geyer was paid £173. 4. 1. for repairs done on Faneuil Hall.

At the outbreak of the Revolution, Frederick William Geyer was one of the principal merchants of Boston. He was proscribed and banished in 1778, but not being an Addresser, or having taken any active part in politics, he was allowed to come back in 1789 and was restored to citizenship by Act of the Legislature. He was in business with his son at No. 13 Union street, Boston, in 1794. Died at Walpole, N. H., in 1803. A daughter who died near London in 1855 at the age of 81, married Mr. Joseph Maryatt, a West Indian merchant. She was the mother of Captain Maryatt of the British Navy, the well known author of sea tales.

Mr. Geyer's estate was on Summer street, formerly Seven Star Lane, and was one of the finest in Boston. In the inventory of his estate made by the commissioner after his departure, the mansion house is valued at £6,000. It was confiscated and sold to Nathan Frazer, whose daughter afterwards married Frederick W. Geyer, Jr., and the property was once more restored to the family.

The estate once belonged to Leonard Vassall, and contained one of the best gardens in Boston. It was planted as early or before 1642 by Gamaliel Wayte, for we find by the *Book of Possessions* that this land is described as Wayte's Garden. Judge Sewall in his diary states that he lived to the age of 87, and not long before his death was blessed with several new teeth, which shows that he not only had the ability to plant, but to eat his fruits. Mrs. Maryatt, whose gardens at Wimbleton were at one time the finest in England, and we may reasonably conjecture that the taste and skill that produced such marvels, were nurtured and fostered in her younger days among the flower beds of Summer street. This garden occupied the site of the store of C. F. Hovey & Co., and as late as 1870 there was an old pear tree in the yard in a thrifty condition.

Nancy Geyer married Rufus Amory, February 13th, 1794. He was the second son of John Amory the Loyalist, and a very successful lawyer. The wedding is described as "a very gay and brilliant affair." It gained an unexpected distinction in consequence of a heavy snowstorm by which

LEONARD VASSALL AND FREDERICK W. GEYER MANSION, SUMMER STREET.
Site now occupied by C. F. Hovey & Co. The mother of Captain Maryatt was born in this house.

Prince Edward, afterward Duke of Kent and father of Queen Victoria, travelling from Canada to take command of the troops at Halifax, was just then detained at Boston. He accepted Mr. Geyer's invitation to the wedding, and came with his aides. "His Royal Highness" it is recorded, was complaisant and affable in his deportment, and claimed the customery privilege of kissing the bride, and bridesmaids. His host's son who was married the year before to Rebecca Frazer, the daughter of Nathan Frazer, who bought the Geyer mansion when it was confiscated, was an ardent sympathizer with revolutionary France, who disapproved of titles. He put their marriage notice in this form in the Boston Gazette of Jan. 21, 1793. "By Citizen Thatcher, Citizen Frederick W. Geyer, Jr., to Citess Rebecca, daughter to Citizen Nathan Frazer."*

LIST OF CONFISCATED ESTATES BELONGING TO FREDERICK WILLIAM GEYER IN SUFFOLK COUNTY AND TO WHOM SOLD.

To Nathan Frazier, May 12, 1780; Lib. 131, fol. 143; Land and house in Boston, Summer St., formerly Seven Star Lane, in front; land of First Church S. W.; John Rowe S. W.; Benjamin Church, Thomas Thayerweather and heirs of Samuel Sewall N.W.———Green Lane S.W.; John Welsh S.W. and S.W.; John Gooch and others S.E.; James Gooch N.E. and N.W.; John Gooch S.W. and N.W.; James Gooch and others S.W.———Green Lane S.; John Welsh W.; John Gerrish N.; lane from Green Lane to the Mill Pond E.

THE APTHORP FAMILY OF BOSTON.

CHARLES APTHORP was born in England in 1698 and was educated at Eton. He was the son of John Apthorp and Susan his wife, whose maiden name was Ward, of the family of Lord Ward of Bexley.

After the death of his father Charles Apthorp came to New England, and became one of the most distinguished merchants of Boston. He was paymaster and commissary under the British Government of the land and naval forces quartered in Boston. On the 13th January, 1726, he married Grizzel, daughter of John Eastwicke. She was born August, 1708, at Jamaica and came to Boston in 1716. Her mother was Griselda Lloyd, daughter of Sir John Lloyd of Somersetshire, England, who assisted in conveying King Charles II to France after the battle of Worcester.

Charles Apthorp was one of the first Wardens of Trinity church, and one of the committee that waited on Peter Faneuil, and in the name of the town to render him their most hearty thanks for so beautiful a gift." To King's Chapel he was a bountiful benefactor, having given £1,000 towards its rebuilding.

Charles Apthorp had eighteen children, of whom fifteen survived him and eleven married. He died in Boston suddenly in 1758 at the age of sixty. His funeral took place at King's Chapel twelve days later and

*The Descendants of Hugh Amory. Pp. 259, 260

his remains were therein deposited. He was reputed as the "greatest and most noble merchant on the continent." He was also characterized as "a truly valuable member of society," and that "he left few equals behind him." A marble monument with a Latin inscription was placed in King's Chapel to his memory by his sons, "which monument covers the tomb of the truly-noble-minded race of Apthorp."

He was very proficient in and a great admirer of the Fine Arts, especially in painting and architecture; talents which have been transmitted to his descendants as Charles Bulfinch, Esq., the architect of the State House and other edifices. The original mansion in Brighton, Massachusetts, formerly the Charles Apthorp place, still remains and is of great antiquity.

On the death of Charles Apthorp he possessed the whole of Long Island, the largest island in Boston Harbor. Calf island also was formerly known as Apthorp's Island. The Apthorp heirs subsequently sold their interest in Long Island to their sister Grizzell's husband, Barlow Trecothick, Lord Mayor of London. After the death of Trecothick the island passed on the 11th June, 1790, into the possession of his brother-in-law Charles Ward Apthorp of New York.

CHARLES WARD APTHORP, the eldest son of Charles Apthorp, married in New York Mary McEvers. He had three sons and three daughters. Of his daughters, Charlotte Augusta was the only one who left descendants. Her husband was John Cornelius Vanden Heuvel, a Dutch gentleman of fortune, who had been Governor of Demerara and afterwards settled in New York. Maria Eliza, their eldest daughter, married John C. Hamilton, a son of the celebrated Alexander Hamilton.

Charles Ward Apthorp was a member of the Council of New York in 1763 and served until 1783. He had lands in Maine and a large amount of property in Boston, Brookline, and Roxbury, all of which was confiscated. He died at his seat, Bloomingdale, in 1797.

JOHN APTHORP, the second son, went to England, and became connected in business with the house of Tomlinson & Trecothick. He married Alicia Mann of Windsor, sister of Sir Horace Mann, many years resident British minister at Florence. Mr. Apthorp embarked for Italy with his wife who was in a very hazardous state of health, and who died at Gibraltar, leaving two daughters under the care of their grandmother at Windsor. He pursued his travels in Italy, and afterwards returned to Boston, where he married Hannah Greenleaf, daughter of Stephen Greenleaf, the last Royal high sheriff of Suffolk County. He lived about four years at Brighton, when he embarked, with his wife, from New York for Charleston, S. C., to enjoy a warmer winter climate, and they were lost at sea. The children, one son and two daughters, were left under the care of their grandfather who attended most faithfully to their interests and education. One daughter married Charles Bulfinch his cousin, and the other Charles Vaughn, son of Samuel Vaughn, Esq.,

"BISHOP'S PALACE." RESIDENCE OF REV. EAST APTHORP.

John Adams says, "It was thought to be a splendid palace and intended for the residence of the first royal bishop."

of London. The son, Col. John T. Apthorp, married Grace Foster, who lived only one year, leaving an infant. In another year he married her twin sister Mary by whom he had a numerous family.

REV. EAST APTHORP, D. D., was born in Boston in 1733 and was educated at Cambridge, England. He took orders and returned, and became the founder and rector of Christ church in Cambridge, Massachusetts. Here he published a pamphlet in defence of the conduct of the society for "Propagating the gospel" which was attacked by Dr. Mayhew, who was answered by the Archbishop of Canterbury. This controversy rendered his situation irksome and after only six years ministry in this country, he left for England. It was thought by many that the establishment of the Episcopal church at Cambridge was for the purpose of converting the students who were generally dissenters and with ulterior views, which excited the most acrimonious jealousy.

While General Burgoyne's army was detained at Cambridge, Lieutenant Brown, who was out on parole according to the terms of the Convention, was riding with two ladies in a chaise when he was killed in cold blood by a sentinel, a boy scarcely fourteen years old, who levelled his gun at him and shot him through the head. "His remains were interred in Christ's church. The people, during the time the service was being performed, seized the opportunity of the church being open, which had been shut since the commencement of hostilities, to plunder, ransack, and deface everything they could lay their hands on, destroying the pulpit, reading desk, and communion table, and ascending the organ loft they destroyed the bellows and broke all the pipes of a very handsome instrument."* Rev. East Apthorp was afterwards successively vicar of Croydon where Governor Hutchinson resided, and rector of Bow church, London, which he exchanged for the prebendary of Finsbury; he had many friends among the dignitaries of the church and was greatly beloved and respected. By his wife, the daughter of Foster Hutchinson, and niece of Thomas Hutchinson, he had several children. His only son became a clergyman, and his daughters married Dr. Cary and Dr. Butler, heads of colleges, and a third daughter married a son of Dr. Paley.

He published two volumes of Discoveries on the Prophecies, delivered at Warburton lecture, Lincoln's Inn, and a volume in answer to Gibbon. The last twenty-six years of his life were passed at Cambridge, England, with almost total loss of sight, and he died in April, 1816, at the age of eighty-three, closing a life of great usefulness.

THOMAS APTHORP, born 19 October, 1741, continued paymaster of the British forces after his father's death from 1758 to 1776, when he was proscribed, and banished. He went to England and lived several years at Ludlow, Wales. He visited Lisbon for health, where he married. He returned to Ludlow, where he died, leaving a widow and one son.

*Travels through the interior parts of America by Thomas Aubury. Vol. II, pp. 232, 234.

WILLIAM APTHORP, born Feb. 26, 1748, married Mary Thompson. He was a merchant, and was proscribed and banished in 1778. The year after, he came from New York to Boston. He was arrested, and occupied for awhile a private room in the deputy jailer's house, but letters were received to his disadvantage, and he was committed to a close prison by order of the Council, his countrymen would show him no mercy.

SUSAN APTHORP the second daughter of Charles Apthorp, married Thomas the son of Dr. Bulfinch. She had several children, three only that arived at a marriageable age. Charles Bulfinch, the only son was born in August, 1763, and graduated at Harvard College in 1781, and after living abroad for some time returned to Boston in 1786. He inherited talents from his grandfather and became a great architect. He was chairman of the board of Selectmen for twenty-one years during which official service many of the great improvements in the town were executed, including the State House, City Hall, the General Hospital and the building of Franklin Street. After the capitol of the United States was burnt, in 1814, Mr. Bulfinch was appointed by President Munroe to superintend its re-erection. His wife died in 1841, and his death followed three years later on April 15, 1844.

LIST OF CONFISCATED ESTATES BELONGING TO CHARLES WARD APTHORP, IN SUFFOLK COUNTY AND TO WHOM SOLD.

To Joseph Hall, April 27, 1782; Lib. 134, fol. 187; Land and moiety of dwelling-house in Boston, Cole Lane S.W.; Joseph Hall E.; Samuel Barrett N.; Jonathan Williams W.

To Edward Smith, June 10, 1782; Lib. 135 fol. 12; Land and buildings in Boston, Wings Lane N.; Brattle St. E.; land of Elizabeth Clark deceased, [formerly] Lillie W.; John Roulstone S.

To Ephraim Murdock, June 22, 1782; Lib. 135. fol. 47; Lands and part of house in Roxbury; 11 A. opposite dwelling-house of the late Rev. Mr. Walter, road S.; said Murdock W.; heirs of Gov. Dudley N.; said Murdock E. —— 8 A. near where the old meeting-house stood, road N.; John Davis E.; heirs of John Scott S.; Ezra Davis W. —— 2 A., said Murdock N.; John Morrey E., town way S.; William Dudley W.

To Daniel Dennison Rogers, July 4, 1782; Lib. 135 fol. 68; Land and buildings in Boston, Beacon St. in front; highway to Beacon Hill N.W.; John Spooner N. and E.

To John Wheelwright, July 19, 1782; Lib. 135 fol. 114; Land, flats, warehouses and wharf near the South Battery in Boston, Purchase St. N.W.; heirs of Alexander Hunt S.; the sea E.; the highway N.

To John Wheelwright, July 19, 1782; Lib. 135 fol. 116; Land and dwelling-house in Boston, Atkinson St. E.; Burry St. S.; Proprietors of the Irish Meeting House W.; Onesephorus Tileston N.

To Grizzell Apthorp, widow, and Perez Morton, Sept. 24, 1782; Lib. 136 fol. 8; One moiety of land and two brick tenements in Boston, Fleet St. N.; Edward Langdon E.; William and Mercy Stoddard S.; W.; S.; W.; S. and W.

To Andrew Symmes, July 30, 1783; Lib. 139 fol. 117; Assignment of mortgage Lib. 100 fol. 97.

To Francis Johonnot, agent for creditors of Nathaniel Wheelwright, deceased, March 7, 1786; Lib. 155 fol. 225; Assignment of mortgage Lib. 97 fol. 200.

To Samuel Pitts, June 10, 1786; Lib. 157, fol. 222; Assignment of mortgage Lib. 103 fol. 89.

To Nathaniel Greene, April 5, 1787; Lib. 160 fol. 25; One half part of four parcels of land in Roxbury. 2½ A.; 17 A. near the tide-mill; 13½ A. woodland; and piece of salt marsh.

THE GOLDTHWAITE FAMILY OF BOSTON.

Thomas Goldthwaite, ancestor of all of this name in America, was born in England about 1610. The original home is supposed to be what is now Gowthwaite manor, three miles from Pateley Bridge, Yorkshire, West Riding.
He probably came with Governor Winthrop's fleet to America. His first appearance in the Boston records appeared June 14, 1631. Thomas Goldthwaite settled in Roxbury where his name appears as "Thomas Gouldthwaight" in Rev. John Eliot's list of his church members, Eliot having begun his pastorate there in 1632. Thomas was made a freeman in Massachusetts, May 14, 1634. In 1636 he appears in Salem where, as an inhabitant he was granted ten acres of land. His first house lot has been located by some of the best antiquarian authority, as on the southwest corner of Essex and Flint Streets in Salem. In 1636 he married his first wife. Her death occurred some time before 1671 and he then married Rachel Leach, of Salem. He was called "Constable Gouldthwaight" at a meeting of the selectmen, December 14, 1659. Thomas died in March, 1683, at about the age of seventy-three, his wife Rachel surviving him. He left three children, Samuel, Mehitable, and Elizabeth.

SAMUEL GOLDTHWAITE, (of the second generation) like his father, was a cooper, and lived in Salem. For many years during his lifetime and that of his immediate descendants, four family homesteads lay side by side on the original Goldthwaite farm, opposite the site where the Peabody church afterwards was built. He died about the year 1718, leaving ten children and perhaps more.

CAPTAIN JOHN GOLDTHWAITE (of the third generation), son of the former, was born in Salem in 1677. By trade he was a mason and early settled in Boston where he married, March 13, 1701, Sarah Hopkins. They were married by the Rev. Cotton Mather of whose church John Goldthwaite was a member. After the death of Cotton Mather he was one of three who took inventory July 22, 1728. His home was in Boston until 1725, and the birthplace of all his children was on the north side of Charter Street, near Copp's Hill burying-ground, on the property given to his wife and her sisters by their uncle, Major Thomas Henchman. He sold this place May 17, 1725, and removed to another estate he had purchased on the southeast side of Mill pond. Here he passed the remainder of his life. His son Ezekiel inherited the estate after his father's death, and sold it to Thomas Sherburn, his brother-in-law.

Sarah Goldthwaite died Oct. 31, 1715, at the age of thirty-five and is buried in Copp's Hill. John Goldthwaite married Mrs. Jane Halsey of Boston as his second wife. From 1708 to 1758 his name is often mentioned in Boston records. He is one of seventeen named as the founders of the New North church in 1714. His name appears in records of the Ancient and Honorable Artillery Company, and in the town records with the title of captain, in 1741. In his old age he had a barbecue for descendants on North Square. It was held under a tent because they were too numerous to assemble in a house. He died June 25, 1766, and is probably buried in the tomb of his son Ezekiel on Copp's Hill. He had nine children by his first wife and five by his second.

CAPTAIN JOSEPH GOLDTHWAITE (fourth generation) fourth child of John, was born November 11, 1706, in Boston. He married February 8, 1727, Martha Lewis, who was born in Boston and baptized in the second church, Feb. 29, 1707, the daughter of Martha (Burrell) and Philip Lewis. Joseph joined the Artillery Company in 1730 and in 1738 was First Sergeant. In 1745 he joined the Colonial army for the siege of Louisburg and according to records in the British war office, being commissioned adjutant in the first Massachusetts regiment, Honorable William Pepperell, colonel, March 12, 1744-(5) and captain (brevet) March 20, 1744-(5). After his return from the war he became a private citizen, and is seldom spoken of in records by his military title, being rather called esquire, or gentleman. In 1728 he appears as a goldsmith, and later as a merchant, licensed as a retailer at his store on Marlboro Street (part of Washington) in 1737 and again in 1742. He held several appointments and later became constable. His home in 1744 was on Fish, afterwards North Street. In 1773 he and his family retired to a farm purchased by him in western Massachusetts, July 10, 1773, ten acres and mansion house. Here Joseph Goldthwaite died March 1, 1780, aged seventy-two. His widow died October 26, 1783, aged seventy-five, and a double stone marks their graves in Weston. He had ten children.

EZEKIEL GOLDTHWAITE (fourth generation) son of John, born at Boston, July 9, 1710. Married Nov. 2, 1732, Elizabeth Lewis of Boston. For the greater part of his life he was Registrar of Deeds for the County of Suffolk. His first signature as registrar was Nov. 6, 1740. He was an Addressser of Hutchinson in 1774, and a protester against the Revolutionist the same year, although like many other loyalists he was one of the 58 Boston memorilists in 1760 who arrayed themselves against the Crown officials, and having sowed the seeds of sedition, afterwards became alarmed at its results, mob rule.

His last signature as registrar is said to have been written Jan. 17, 1776, two months before the evacuation of Boston. He died seven years later, Dec. 4th, 1782, in his 73rd year. His widow died Feb. 6, 1794, aged 80.

COLONEL THOMAS GOLDTHWAITE (fourth generation) son of John, born in Boston Jan. 15, 1717, married August 26, 1742, Esther Sargent. He became an influential citizen of Chelsea, acting as selectman, moderator of town meetings, and from May, 1757, till his removal from the town, seven years in succession, was its deputy to the House of Representatives, where he was active in introducing important legislation.

He was given many important positions under the Colonial government. In 1763 he was appointed to the command of Fort Pownal, removing his family there from Chelsea. This was an important frontier post, commanding the entrance to the Penobscot River, and offered the advantage, also of a rich trade with Indians, then numerous in those parts. Not long after succeeding to this command in company with Francis Bernard, son of the Governor he purchased a large tract of land, 2,700 acres in the neighborhood of the fort, on condition of their settling thereon thirty families, of building an Episcopal church, and employing a minister. The enterprise was interrupted by the Revolution, in which each side endeavored to get control of all the arms and ammunition possible, and to take into its possession, or render defenceless, such posts as could be held by the enemy. With such an object in view, in April, 1775, Capt. Mowatt, who afterwards burned Falmouth, now Portland, anchored before Fort Pownal, and a letter containing Governor Gage's orders having been delivered to Col. Goldthwaite he carried away the cannon belonging to the fort. The attitude taken by its commander in allowing the fort to be thus disarmed, was never forgiven by the Revolutionists, and he ever after was regarded as a Loyalist. His explanation of his conduct on that occasion is as follows:

"On the 27th of last month about 20 armed men arrived here from St. George's who came in the name, and as a committee from the people of St. George's, and others, who they say had assembled there to the amount of 250; and this party in their name demanded of me the reason of my delivering the cannon belonging to this fort to the King's forces. I went into the fort and got the Governor's letter to me, and it was read to them. I then informed them that this was the King's fort, and built at his expense, that the Governor was commander-in-chief of it; that I could not refuse to obey his orders."

Little is known of Col. Goldthwaite between the surrender of Fort Pownal in the spring of 1775 and his arrival in England early in 1780. Gov. Hutchinson mentions in his diary that, "T. Goldthwaite arrived at Portsmouth Feb. 15, 1780." In an entry of the previous Dec. 4, the Governor mentions a call from "young Goldthwaite, son of J. Goldthwaite now at New York." It must have been quite soon after his arrival that Colonel Goldthwaite settled at Walthamstow, Essex, a few miles north of London. Samuel Curwen in his journal speaks of dining with him there July 29, 1782. His son Thomas married Mrs. Primatt, a lady of fortune, in the summer of 1780, and also lived in the town. The houses of both father and son are still there and easily identified, and are in excelent preservation. The Colonel's residence is of brick or stone covered with stucco, the main portion three stories high, and an entrance with Ionic pillars. The grounds are ample and handsomely laid out with well kept walks and planted with trees and shrubbery.

After a life of nearly twenty years spent in retirement in England, Col. Goldthwaite died Aug. 31, 1799, in his 82 year. Mrs. Catharine, his wife, died Dec. 16, 1796, aged 81. They lie buried in Walthamstow church yard.

MAJOR JOSEPH GOLDTHWAITE, (fifth generation), the eldest of Joseph's children, was born in Boston, October 5, 1730. He entered the Boston Latin school in 1738, and probably commenced his military career, which he afterwards followed near the commencement of the French and Indian war, when about twenty-five years old. He married October 5, 1730, Hannah Bridgham, said to have been of Barre, Massachusetts.

In 1759 he appears as Major in the regiment from Boston under the command of Col. John Phillips, January 1, 1760 to January 10, 1761, on the roll of field and staff officers in Colonel Bagley's regiment in service at Louisburg, in which he acted also as paymaster. He served during the campaign of 1762 as Lieut. Colonel of the regiment commanded by Colonel Richard Saltonstall, roll dated Boston, Feb. 19, 1763, in which he is called "of Roxbury." He was addressed at that time as colonel.

October 5, 1768, Joseph Goldthwaite was appointed as Commissary to the British troops who had been quartered in Boston on account of the resistance the inhabitants had shown to the custom officials. In Massachusetts Historical Society's collections, Vol. X, p. 121, is printed a list of the different nations of Indians that met Sir William Johnson at Niagara, July, 1764, to make peace in behalf of their tribes which was "inclosed in a letter from Colonel Joseph Goldthwaite of Boston, to Dr. Stiles, A. D. 1766."*

Among the Goldthwaites who remained loyal to the crown, Major Joseph was one of the strongest. He was an Addresser of Hutchinson in 1775, and during the siege he passed the winter in Boston. At the evacuation he accompanied the British army to Halifax, and thence to Quebec. Nine days before his departure from Boston he wrote a letter to his uncle Ezekiel Goldthwaite, Esq., of Boston, acquainting him with his property and the household goods he had left behind. "In short, I leave behind me at least three thousand pounds sterling. You give the enclosed to my wife, if you can meet her. When I shall see her God only knows. Don't let her want for anything."**

Some experiences of Major Joseph's wife, Mrs. Hannah, while her husband was shut up in Boston with the British army, appear in the Journal of the Massachusetts House of Representatives.***

August 4, 1775, Mrs. Goldthwaite with her sister-in-law and a Mrs. Chamberlain, left Boston with a horse and chaise and crossed the Winnisimmet Ferry. She was arrested and taken under guard to the general court at Watertown. It appeared on her examination that her health was impaired, and an order was passed to allow her to visit Stafford for the benefit of the waters there, but under the care of the Selectmen, and afterwards to retire to the house of her brother Joseph Bridgham at Rehoboth, and to be under the committee of correspondence. It was Colonel Loammi Baldwin who had them arrested and taken to Watertown and

*Dr. Ezra Stiles, afterwards President of Yale College, and at this time a settled minister at Newport.
**Goldthwaite Genealogy compiled and published by Charlotte Goldthwaite.
***See Forces American Achives. Vol. III, pp. 312, 314, 355.

according to his account, it was an act on their part which must have required considerable courage "no such instance having happened before," the city being then closely besieged.

Mrs. Goldthwaite petitioned the court to allow her to use the waters in Newton instead of at Stafford, her health being very delicate, and the petition was accompanied by her physician's certificate. This was granted to her and she probably remained through the siege at Newton where the family of Mr. Benjamin Goldthwaite had also taken refuge. After the siege she returned to Boston where she died, probably never seeing her husband again.

Major Goldthwaite from Quebec, went to New York, and his death occurred there October 3, 1779. He had been proscribed and banished in 1778. It was at this time he drew up his will, which is at Somerset House, London, dated Feb. 11, 1778. As he died childless, he bequeathed his property to his brother's and sister's children "provided that nome of them are Rebels, and have borne arms against their King, otherwise to go to the next eldest son of the same family who is loyal, and true to his King, and country." Of the several Goldthwaite Loyalists, Major Joseph was one of the most uncompromising in his devotion to his King and country.

CAPTAIN PHILIP GOLDTHWAITE, (fifth generation), brother to Major Joseph Goldthwaite, was born in Boston, March 27th, 1733. He was a member of the Boston Latin School in 1741. He married June 7, 1756, Mary Jordan of Biddeford. His title of captain seems to have come from his command of vessels, and it is interesting to note that in every generation of his descendants to the present day there have been more or less who have chosen the same occupation.

Captain Philip was an officer of the Customs at Winter Harbor, and remained loyal when the war broke out. Sabin says he was one of the two persons of Saco and Biddeford dealt with by the Revolutionists of that section for their loyal principles and that as soon as the war commenced he placed himself under British protection at Boston. An earlier record in regard to him says: "Captain Philip Goldthwaite was brought before the New Hampshire Committee of Safety at Portsmouth, Nov. 23, 1775, on suspicion of being unfriendly to the liberties of America. Upon examination nothing appearing against him, ordered that he be dismissed."

There can be no doubt however, as to Captain Philip's real sentiments. The atmosphere in which he was living must soon have become unendurable to one holding his opinions, and therefore we soon find him in England, where he appears as early as 1780, at that date taking out his brother's administration papers. He bought an annuity in the king's household and became one of the Gentlemen of the bed chamber. In October, 1786, it appears from the probate records at Boston, that he had died probably at sea, for Edward Daws of Boston, trader, is administrator of the estate of Philip Goldthwait, late of Boston, mariner. His inventory contained clothes, a quadrant, books and chest, and amounted to £7, 10 s. He left several sons and daughters, whose descendants are now quite numerous.

SAMUEL GOLDTHWAITE, (fifth generation), brother of the aforesaid Philip, was born in Boston, March 20th, 1735, and married Amy Borden of Newport, R. I., where he became a prominent merchant. He very early came under suspicion as having loyalist sentiments. After the death of his brother, Major Joseph, in New York, October, 1779, he petitioned the Rhode Island General Assembly representing that his brother had lately died in New York, leaving a large estate there in the hands of persons who were wasting it, also that he had been authorized to settle it if he could obtain permission to go to New York, asking to be allowed to do so, and to return with the effects when obtained, which petition the Council, after consideration, granted.

He did not, however, return, and in July 1780, an act was passed by the Rhode Island Assembly, proscribing persons that had left the state and joined the enemy, ordered if they returned they should be apprehended, and imprisoned or transported. "Samuel Goldthwaite, merchant, late of Newport," was included in the list. Orders were also given under the same date that such property as he left in Newport should be inventoried and taken into possession of the Sheriff. About this time Samuel had gone to England on business connected with the settlement of his father's and brother's estates, for in the same year he was administrator on them in London. One year later he had returned to his wife Amy, at that time preferring a petition to the Rhode Island Assembly, stating that her husband was then in New York, and had requested her, with her family, to come to him, and praying the Assembly to permit her with her family, furniture, and effects, to go to him there by the first opportunity. The petiton was granted and she went in a cartel vessel under the direction of William Taggart. The family settled in Baltimore after the Revolution, and have left many descendants there.

DR. MICHAEL B. GOLDTHWAITE, (fifth generation), son of Joseph, of Boston, born there Jan. 5th, 1740, married Sarah Formon, March 8th, 1759. He was an eminent surgeon and attended the army at the taking of Louisburg. Like most physicians of that day, he kept an apothecary shop, which was in 1774 on Hanover Street. He was an Addresser of both Hutchinson and Gage. He died in 1776. He was an ardent sympathizer with the loyalists.

LIEUTENANT HENRY GOLDTHWAITE, (fifth generation) son of Colonel Thomas, of Walthamstow, England, born at Chelsea, March 29, 1759, married in England, Sarah Winch of Brampton, Oxon. Henry's name is found as one of the garrison of Fort Pownal Oct. 23, 1775. He afterwards entered the British Army remaining in America, in that service, for some years after most of his family had taken up their abode in England. The records of the British War Office show that he was ensign, Independent Co. Invalids, Nov. 13, 1793. Lieutenant Royal Garrison Bat-

BENJAMIN FRANKLIN BEFORE THE PRIVY COUNCIL.

He stood there, conspicuous and erect, and without moving a muscle, was compelled to hear himself denounced as a thief, or the accomplice of thieves.

talion, Sept. 9, 1795, and lieutenant half pay Oct. 31, 1796. He died at sea, in the Mediterranean early in 1800. He left two sons, Charles, born 1796, and Henry Barnes, born 1797, whose descendants are living in England.

LIST OF CONFISCATED ESTATES BELONGING TO JOSEPH GOLDTHWAIT IN SUFFOLK COUNTY AND TO WHOM SOLD.

To Perez Morton, Sept. 24, 1782; Lib. 136, fol. 9; One undivided half of land, distill house and other buildings in Boston, Pecks Lane W.; John Osbourn N.; N.W.; N.E. and N.; Francis Johonnot E.; the sea S.

JOHN HOWE.

Abraham Howe came to Dorchester in 1636; was admitted Freeman May 2, 1637, he came from Broad Oak, Essex County, England, and died at Dorchester, Nov. 20th, 1683. His son Isaac Howe, was baptized in Roxbury in 1655. Isaac had a son Isaac, born in Dorchester, July 7, 1675. He had a son Joseph, born in Dorchester, March 27, 1716, who was the father of John Howe, born in Boston, October 14, 1754. Joseph Howe was a reputable tradesman in Marshall's Lane. He apprenticed his son to learn the printing business.

Richard Draper, the publisher of the *Massachusetts Gazette*, and *Boston News Letter* died June 5, 1774. He left no children. His wife conducted the business for several months, and then formed a business connection with John Howe.

Howe had recently become of age, and was a sober, discreet young man. Mrs. Draper, therefore, was induced, a short time before the commencement of the war, to take him into partnership, but his name did not appear in the imprint of the Massachusetts Gazette till Boston was besieged by the Continental Army.

Howe remained with his partner until they were obliged to leave Boston in consequence of the evacuation of the town by the British troops, March 17, 1776, when they went to Halifax, from there he went to Newport, R. I., when the British took possession of the town December 8th.

John Howe was married at Newport by Rev. George Bisset, Rector of Trinity Church, to Miss Martha Minns. Mr. William Minns accompanied his daughter from Boston, and was present at the ceremony. William Minns was born at Great Yarmouth, England, December 16, 1728. In 1737 he accompanied his uncle, Robert Ball, and his widowed mother, and came to Boston. Miss Martha Minns was sixteen years of age when she married John Howe. She was noted for her beauty and her portraite is still in possession of her family. The issue of this marriage was three sons and three daughters.

Mr. Howe commenced the publication of a newspaper for the British at Newport; it was called The Newport Gazette, and the first paper was issued January 16, 1777.

The last number of a bound volume of this paper in possession of the Redwood Library at Newport, is dated January 15, 1778, but the publication of the paper probably continued till the evacuation of Newport by the British, October 25, 1779.

The paper was published in a house on the opposite side of the Parade, the Vaughn estate, now a market. A recent writer says:

"During the time the British were in possession of Newport, it was the office of the Newport "Gazette," the paper printed by the British on the press and type of the Newport "Mercury." Before that the "Mercury" was printed by Solomon Southwick, in Queen Street, but when the island fell into the hands of the enemy, Southwick, as is well-known, buried his type in the rear of what was the old Kilburn House on Broad Street (now Broadway) and left the town. The loyalists recovered the type, and a printer named Howe began the printing of the "Gazette."

A bound file of the newspaper published by Mr. Howe is in the possession of the Redwood Library. It runs, with a few numbers missing, from No. 1, to No. 52, January 15, 1778.

The first number was issued Jan. 16, 1777, with the following introduction.

"The Favours which the Subscriber has received from the Gentlemen of the *Army and Navy*, in Boston and elsewhere, joined with the Importunities of many of the Inhabitants of this Town, has induced him, as speedily as possible, to gratify them with a *Newspaper*. He can only say, that his best endeavors shall not be wanting to render it as entertaining as possible: And he has nothing to wish for, but the Exercise of that Candour he hath so often before been indebted to. Its *size* is at present contracted, owing to the Impossibility of procuring larger printing Paper; but if more Intelligence should at any Time arrive, than this can contain, the Deficiency will be supplied with a *Supplement*. No Subscriptions are received; but if any Gentlemen choose to have the Paper weekly the Boy shall leave it at their houses. Articles of intelligence will be thankfully received and every favor gratefully acknowledged, by their

Obedient humble servant,

JOHN HOWE."

The British evacuated Newport, October 25, 1779, and Mr. and Mrs. Howe accompanied them to New York, and thence removed to Halifax and took up their permanent abode there, on the corner of Sackville and Barrington Streets. Here on Friday, January 5th, 1781, he published the first issue of the Halifax Journal, a paper that continued to be published regularly until 1870. It is said that Mr. Howe brought with him the printing press that had once belonged to Benjamin Franklin, and the first that the philosopher had ever possessed. It did the printing for the Howe family for years. Mr. Howe was for many years King's printer for the Province, which sceured to him all the government printing, including the publishing of the official gazette. For some years previous to his death, he held the office of postmaster-general and justice of the peace, and was living at the time of his death, December 29, 1835, at his beautiful residence on the Northwestarm, in good circumstances, and had the respect of the whole community.

Mr. Howe was a Sandemanian, that is, a follower of Robert Sandeman, who came to Boston from Glasgow in 1764; they held their first meetings at the Green Dragon Tavern, and afterwards had a meetinghouse in the rear of Middle or Hanover street. This society rejected the belief in the necessity of spiritual conversion, representing faith as an operation of the intellect, and speculative belief as quite sufficient to insure final justification. This sect continued till 1823, when the last light was extinguished in Boston. Many of the Sandemanians were Loyalists, and went to Halifax. They may have built on a sandy foundation, but judging from their fruits, we may charitably conclude that in the main they were correct. Probably they did not like a church and state religion; and that may have been all. The few who were in Halifax met every Lord's day in an upper room, in the building lately used by Baxter as a furniture warehouse on Prince Street. The members, male and female, sat together around a table and took the Lord's Supper. This was weekly. There was singing and prayers, and Mr. Howe would afterward stand up, read a chapter of the Bible, and give an address. No doubt it was very good and simple and delivered with a calm, quiet sort of eloquence. When the meeting was over the brothers and sisters in fellowship, (only the more elderly members) rose and kissed one another, and seemed to be remarkably happy. It is said that in the afternoon of every Sunday the old gentlemen members went down to the room below and dined together, and probably edified one another with religious conversation. Those now living who have ever been with these Sandemanians in that upper room will never forget the calm godly faces of such men as old Mr. Howe, Mr. Greenwood and Mr. Mansfield. Strange to say, none of the Howes, and very few, if any, of the other families have followed in the track of these good men and women as to creed. It is to be hoped that many have been influenced for good by what they may have recalled of such worthy ancestors. Old Mr. Greenwood fell dead in the room while reading, and Mr. Mansfield died the same day from some accidental cause.

In a speech delivered by his son JOSEPH HOWE, in Boston, July 4, 1858, he spoke of his father as follows: "The loyalists who left these States were not, it must be confessed, as good republicans as you are, but they loved liberty under their old forms, and their descendants love it too. My father, though a true Briton to the day of his death, loved New England, and old Boston especially, with filial regard. He never lost an opportunity of serving a Boston man, if in his power. At the close of your railway banquet, one gentleman told me that my father had, during the last war, taken his father from the military prison at Melville Island, and sent him back to Boston. Another, on the same evening, showed me a gold watch, sent by an uncle, who died in the West Indies, to his family. It was pawned by a sailor in Halifax, but redeemed by my father, and sent to the dead man's relatives. And so it was all his life. He loved his sovereign, but he loved Boston too, and whenever he got sick in his latter days, we used to send him up here to recruit. A sight of the old scenes and a walk on Boston Common were sure to do him good, and he generally came back uncommonly well." Elsewhere the same son remarked: "For thirty years he was my instructor, my playfellow, almost my daily companion. To him I owe my fondness for reading, my familiarity with the Bible, my knowledge of old colonial and American incidents and characteristics. He left me nothing but his example, and the memory of his many virtues, for all that he ever earned was given to the poor. He was too good for this world. But the remembrance of his high principle, his cheerfulness, his childlike simplicity, and truly Christian character, is never absent from my mind."

Mrs. Martha Howe died Nov. 25, 1790, aged 30 years, and was buried in St. Paul's churchyard, Halifax.

A few years after the death of his first wife, Mr. Howe married Mrs. Austin, a widow with several children, wife of Captain Austin. By her he had two children, Sarah and Joseph. Mrs. Howe died in 1837. He had eight children, and at the present time there are eighty-five of his descendants, out of all these the survivors who bear the name of Howe only number sixteen. Many of his descendants were men of great prominence. His son William Howe, Assistant Commissary-General, who died at Halifax, January, 1843, aged fifty-seven. John Howe, Queen's Printer, and Deputy Postmaster-General, who died at the same place the same year, and David Howe, who published a paper at St. Andrew, N. B., Joseph, born December 13, 1804, became Hon. Joseph Howe, Governor of Nova Scotia in May, 1873.

SAMUEL QUINCY.
Solicitor-General.

Edmund Quincy, the first of the name in New England, landed at Boston on the 4th of September, 1633. He came from Achurch in Northamptonshire, where he owned some landed estate. That he was a man of substance may be inferred from his bringing six servants with him, and that he was a man of weight among the founders of the new commonwealth appears from his election as a representative of the town of Boston in the first General Court ever held in Massachusetts Bay. He was also the first named on the committee appointed by the town to assess and raise the sum necessary to extinguish the title of Mr. Blackstone to the peninsula on which the city stands. He bought of Chickatabut, Sachem of the Massachusetts tribe of Indians, a tract of land at Mount Wollaston, confirmed to him by the Town of Boston, 1636, a portion of which is yet in the family.

Edmund Quincy died the year after making this purchase, in 1637, at the age of 33. He left a son Edmund and a daughter Judith. The son lived, in the main, a private life on the estate in Braintree. He was a magistrate and a representative of his town in the General Court, and Lieutenant-Colonel of the Suffolk Regiment.

Point Judith was named after his daughter. She married John Hull, who, when Massachusetts Bay assumed the prerogative of coining money, was her mint-master, and made a large fortune in the office, before Charles II. put a stop to that infringement of the charter. There is a tradition that, when he married his daughter to Samuel Sewall, afterwards Chief Justice, he gave her for her dowry, her weight in pine-tree shillings. From this marriage has sprung the eminent family of the Sewalls, which has given three Chief Justices to Massachusetts and one to Canada, and has been distinguished in every generation by the talents and virtues of its members.

Lieutenant-Colonel Quincy, who was a child when brought to New England, died in 1698, aged seventy years, having had two sons, Daniel and Edmund.

Daniel died during his father's lifetime, leaving an only son John, who graduated at Cambridge in 1708, and was a prominent public man in the Colony for nearly half a century. He was a Councillor, and for many years Speaker of the Lower House.

He died in 1767, at the time of the birth of his great-grandson, John Quincy Adams, who therefore received the name which he has made illustrious. Edmund, the second son, graduated in 1699, and was also in the public service almost all his life, as a magistrate, a Councillor, and one of the Justices of the Supreme Court. He was also colonel of the Suffolk Regiment, at that time a very important command, since the county of Suffolk then, and long after, included what is now County of Norfolk, as well as the town of Boston. In 1737, the General Court selected him as their agent to lay the claims of the Colony before the home government, in the matter of the disputed boundary between Massachusetts Bay and New Hampshire.

He died, however, very soon after his arrival in London, February 23, 1737, of the smallpox, which he had taken by inoculation. He was buried in Bunhill Fields, where a monument was erected to him by the General Court, which also made a grant of land of a thousand acres in the town of Lennox to his family, in further recognition of his public services.

Judge Edmund Quincy had two sons, Edmund and Josiah.

The first named, who graduated at Cambridge in 1722, lived a private life at Braintree and in Boston.

One of his daughters married John Hancock, the first signer of the Declaration of Independence, and afterwards Governor of Massachusetts. Josiah was born in 1709, and took his first degree in 1728. He accompanied his father to London in 1737, and afterwards visited England and the Continent more than once.

For some years he was engaged in commerce and ship-building in Boston, and when about forty years of age he retired from business and removed to Braintree, where he lived for thirty years the life of a country gentleman, occupying himself with the duties of a county magistrate, and amusing himself with field sports. Game of all sorts abounded in those days in the woods and along the shore, and marvellous stories have come down, by tradition, of his feats with gun and rod. He was Colonel of the Suffolk Regiment, as his father had been before him; he was also Commissioner to Pennsylvania during the old French war to ask the help of that Colony in an attack which Massachusetts Bay had planned upon Crown Point. He succeeded in his mission by the help of Doctor Franklin.

Colonel Josiah Quincy, by his first marriage, had three sons, Edmund, Samuel, Josiah, and one daughter, Hannah. His first wife was Hannah Sturgis, daughter of John Sturgis, one of his Majesty's Council, of Yarmouth. His eldest son, Edmund, graduated in 1752, after which he became a merchant in Boston. He was in England in 1760 for the purpose of establishing mercantile correspondences. He died at sea in 1768, on his return from a voyage for his health to the West Indies.

The youngest son of Colonel Josiah Quincy bore his name, and was therefore known to his contemporaries, and takes his place in history, as Josiah Quincy, Junior, he having died before his father, he was born February 23, 1744, and graduated at Harvard College, 1763. He studied law with Oxenbridge Thacher, one of the principal lawyers of that day, and succeeded to his practice at his death, which took place about the time he himself was called to the bar. He took a high rank at once in his profession, although his attention to its demands was continually interrupted by the stormy agitation in men's minds and passions, which preceded and announced the Revolution, and which he actively promoted by his writings and public speeches. On the 5th of March, the day of the so called "Boston Massacre" he was selected, together with John Adams, by Captain Preston, who was accused of having given the word of command to the soldiers that fired on the mob, to conduct his defence and that of his men, they having been committed for trial for murder. At that moment of fierce excitement, it demanded personal and moral courage to perform this duty. His own father wrote him a letter of stern and strong remonstrance against his undertaking the defence of "those criminals charged with the murder of their fellow citizens," exclaiming, with passionate emphasis, "Good God! Is it possible? I will not believe it!"

Mr. Quincy in his reply, reminded his father of the obligations his professional oath laid him under, to give legal counsel and assistance to those accused of a crime, but not proved to be guilty of it; adding: "I dare affirm that you and this whole people will one day rejoice that I became an advocate for the aforesaid criminals, *charged* with the murder of our fellow citizens. *To inquire my duty and to do it, is my aim."* He did his duty and his prophecy soon came to pass.

There is no more honorable passage in the history of New Engand than the one which records the trial and acquittal of Captain Preston and his men, in the midst of the passionate excitements of that time, by a jury of the town maddened to a rage but a few months before by the blood of her citizens shed in her streets.

In 1774 he went to England, partly for his health, which had suffered much from his intense professional and political activities, and also as a confidential agent of the Revolutionary party to consult and advise with the friends of America there. His presence in London coming as he did at a most critical moment excited the notice of the ministerial party, as well as of the opposition. The Earl of Hillsborough denounced him, together with Dr. Franklin, in the House of Lords, "as men walking the streets of London who ought to be in Newgate or Tyburn." The precise results of his communications with the English Whigs can never be known. They were important enough, however, to make his English friends urgent for his immediate return to America, because he could give information which could not safely be committed to writing. His health had failed seriously during the latter months of his residence in England, and his physicians strongly advised against his taking a winter voyage.

His sense of public duty, however, overbore all personal considerations, and he set sail on the 16th of March, 1775, and died off Gloucester, Massachusetts, on the 26th of April.

The citizens of Gloucester buried him with all honor in their graveyard; after the siege of Boston, he was removed and placed in a vault in the burying ground in Braintree. Josiah Quincy was barely thirty-one years of age when he thus died.

His father, Colonel Quincy lived on at Braintree during the whole of the war. He died on March 3rd, 1784.

His passion for field sports remained in full force till the end, for his death was occasioned by exposure to the winter's cold, sitting upon a cake of ice, watching for wild ducks, when he was in his seventy-fifth year.

SAMUEL QUINCY, the subject of this memoir, was the second son of Colonel Josiah Quincy, and the brother of Josiah, Junior, and Edmund. He was born in that part of Braintree now Quincy, April 23, 1735. He graduated at Harvard College in 1754, and studied law with Benjamin Pratt.

Endowed with fine talents, Mr. Quincy became eminent in the profession of the law, and succeeded Jonathan Sewall as Solicitor-General of Massachusetts. He was the intimate friend of many of the most distinguished men of that period, among whom was John Adams. They were admitted to the bar on the same day, Nov. 6, 1758.

As Solicitor for the Crown, he was engaged with Robert Treat Paine in the memorable trial of Capt. Preston, and the soldiers in 1770; his brother was opposed to him on that occasion, and both reversed their party sympathies in their professional position. It was plain to all sagacious observers of the signs of the times, that the storm of civil war was gathering fast; and it was sure first to burst over Boston. It was a time of stern agitation, and profound anxieties. In their emotion Mr. Quincy and his wife shared deeply, and passionately. The shadows of public and private calamity were already beginning to steal over that once happy home. The evils of the present and the uncertainties of the future bore heavily on their prosperity. The fierce passions which were soon to break out into revolutionary violence and mob rule, had already begun to separate families, to divide friends, and to break up society. Samuel Quincy was a Loyalist and remained true to his oath of office, wherein he swore to support the government. His father and brother were revolutionists; as previously stated his brother died on shipboard off Gloucester, seven days after the hostilities had commenced at Lexington, and when his father saw from his house on Quincy Bay, the fleet drop down the harbor, after the evacuation of Boston on March 17, 1776, it must have been with feelings of sorrow that the stout-hearted old man saw the vessels bear away his only surviving son, never to return again. Such partings were common griefs then, as ever in civil wars, the bitterest perhaps that wait upon that cruelest of calamities.

Samuel Quincy was an addresser of Governor Hutchinson, and a staunch Loyalist. His wife, the sister of Henry Hill, Esq., of Boston, was not pleased with her husband's course in the politics of the times, and he became a Loyalist against her advice, and when he left Boston, a refugee, she preferred to remain with her brother, and never met her husband again. The following letter written to his brother by Mr. Quincy, during the siege of Boston, will explain his position at that time.*

To Henry Hill, Esq., Cambridge.

Boston, May 13, 1775.

Dear Brother:

There never was a time when sincerity and affectionate unity of heart could be more necessary than at present. But in the midst of the confusions that darken our native land, we may still, by a rectitude of conduct, entertain a rational hope that the Almighty Governor of the universe will in his own time remember mercy.

I am going, my dear friend, to quit the habitation where I have been so long encircled with the dearest connections.

* This letter and the following ones are extracts from original papers, copies of which were communicated by Miss Eliza S. Quincy, and published in Curwen's Journal and Letters.

SAMUEL QUINCY.

Born at Braintree, now Quincy, April 23, 1735. Solicitor-General of Massachusetts. Died at sea in 1789. His remains were interred on Bristol Hill, England. From a painting by Copley.

I am going to hazard the unstable element, and for a while to change the scene—whether it will be prosperous or adverse, is not for me to determine. I pray God to sustain my integrity and preserve me from temptation.

My political character with you may be suspicious; but be assured, if I cannot *serve* my country, which I shall endeavor to the utmost of my power, I will never *betray it*.

The kind care of my family you have so generously offered penetrates me with the deepest gratitude. If it should not be within my power to reward you, you will have the recompense greater than I can give you, the approbation of your own heart. Would to God we may again enjoy the harmonious intercourse I have been favored with since my union with your family. I will not despair of this great blessing in some future and not very distant period. God preserve you in health and every earthly enjoyment, until you again receive the salutation of

Your friend and brother,
SAMUEL QUINCY.

Again on August 18th he writes to Mr. Hill and said, You conjure me by the love of my country to use my best endeavors to bring about a reconciliation, suggesting that the Americans are still as determined as ever to die free, rather than live slaves; I have no reason to doubt the zeal of my fellow-countrymen in the cause of freedom, and their firmness in its defence, and were it in my power, my faithful endeavors should not be wanting (nay, I have a right to say they are not) to effect an accommodation. But, my good friend, I am unhappy to find that the opinion I formed in America, and which in a great measure governed my conduct, was but too justly founded. Every proposal of those who are friendly to the colonies, to alter the measures of government and redress the grievances of which they complain, is spurned at, unless attended with previous concessions on their part. This there is less reason every day to expect, and thus the prospect of an accommodation is thrown at a distance; nor is there yet the least reason to suppose that a formidable, if any opposition will be framed against administration in favor of America.

These are facts, not of conjecture only, but visible and operative. Your reflection will perhaps be, we must then work out our own salvation by the strength of our own arm, trusting in the Lord. Really, my friend, if the colonies, according to their late declaration, have made a resistance by force their choice, the contest is in short reduced to that narrow compass. I view the dangerous and doubtful struggle with fear and trembling; I lament it with the most cordial affection for my native country, and feel sensibly for my friends. But I am aware it is my duty patiently to submit the event as it may be governed by the all-wise counsels of that Being "who ruleth in the heavens, and is the God of armies."

In a letter to his wife, London, Jan. 1, 1777, he said: The continuance of our unhappy separation has something in it so unexpected, so unprecedented, so complicated with evil, and misfortune, it has become almost too burdensome for my spirits, nor have I words that can reach its description. I long much to see my father. It is now more than eighteen months since I parted with him in a manner I regret. Neither of you say anything of the family at Braintree. They ought not to think me regardless of them though I am silent; for, however lightly they may look upon me, I yet remember them with pleasure.

Again, on March 12, 1777, he said: You inquire whether I cannot bear contempt and reproach, rather than remain any longer separated from my family? As I always wished, and I think always endeavored, not to deserve the one, so will I ever be careful to avoid the other. You urge as an inducement to my return, that my countrymen will not deprive me of life. I have never once harbored such an idea. Sure I am I have never merited from them such a punishment. Difference of opinion I have never known to be a capital offence, and were the truth and motives of my conduct justly scrutinized, I am persuaded they would not regard me as an enemy plotting their ruin. That I might yet be able to recover in some respect the esteem of my friends, I will not doubt while I am conscious of the purity of my intentions. When I determined on a voyage to England, I resolved upon deliberation, and I still think, with judgment. I did not, indeed, expect so hurried a succession of events, though you must remember, I long had them in contemplation.

I am sorry you say nothing of my father, or the family at Braintree; I have not received a line nor heard from them since I left America. * * God bless you all; live happy, and think I am as much so as my long absence from you will permit.

March 20, 1777.

I am not surprised much that, to the loss of property, I have already sustained, I am to suffer further depredations, and that those to whom I am under contract should avail themselves of this opportunity and endeavor to make what is left their own. All I ask is that my brother and my other friends (if I have any) would think of me as they ought, and to be assured, that as far as they interpose their assistance to save me from suffering, they will not hereafter find me deficient in return.

October 15, 1777.

If things should not wear a more promising aspect at the opening of the next year, by all means summon resolution to cross the ocean. But if there is an appearance of accommodating this truly unnatural contest, it would be advisable for you to bear farther promise; as I mean to return to my native country whenever I may be permitted, and there is a chance for my procuring a livelihood. But I do not say that I will not accept of an opening here, if any one should offer that I may think eligible.

London, April 18, 1778.

If there is an accommodation, I shall certainly turn my views to some part of the continent, unless something very promising should offer elsewhere. It would grieve me very much to think of never again seeing my father; God bless him, and many other worthy friends and relations in New England; but a return to my native country I cannot be reconciled to until I am convinced that I am as well thought of as I know I deserve to be. I shall ever rejoice in its prosperity, but am too proud to live despised where I was once respected—an object of insult instead of the child of favor.

You suggest, that had I remained, I might still have been with you in honor and employment. It may be so, but when I left America I had no expectation of being absent more than a few months, little thinking operations of such magnitude would have followed in so quick a succession; I left it from principle, and with a view of emolument. If I have been mistaken, it is my misfortune, not my fault. My first letters from my friends congratulated me on being out of the way; and I was pleased to find my undertaking met with their approbation as well as my own. The hearts of men were not within my reach, nor the fortuitous event of things within my control. "I am indeed a poor man;" but even a poor man has resources of comfort that cannot be torn from him, nor are any so miserable as to be always under the influence of inauspicious stars. I will therefore still endeavor to bear my calamities with firmness, and to feel for others.

Those who have befriended my family are entitled to my warmest gratitude, and I hope you will never fail to express it for me. Whether it ever will be in my power to recompense them I know not, but no endeavor of mine shall be wanting to effect it. * * * I conjecture, though you do not mention from what quarter, you have received unkindness. There are in this world many things we are obliged and enabled to encounter, which at a distance appear insupportable. You must have experienced this as well as I; and it ought to teach us that best doctrine of philosophy and religion—resignation. Bear up, therefore, with fortitude, and wait patiently in expectation of a calmer and brighter day.

London, May 31, 1778.

By the public prints we are made acquainted with an act of the state of Massachusetts Bay, that precludes those among others from returning, who left it since the 19th of April, 1775, and "joined the enemy." You do not mention this act, nor have I any information by which I am to construe what is meant by "joining the enemy." The love of one's country, and solicitude for its welfare, are natural and laudable affections; to lose its good opinion is at once unhappy, and attended with many ill consequences; how much more unfortunate to be forever excluded from it without offence! It is said also that there is a resolve of congress, "that no absentee shall be permitted to take up his residence in any other colony without having been first received and admitted as a citizen of his own." This may have some effect on a movement I had in contemplation of going southward, where I have a very advantageous offer of countenance and favor.

London, March 15, 1779.

You may remember in some of my former letters I hinted my wish to establish a residence in some other part of the continent, or in the West Indies, and particularly mentioned to you Antigua—where my kinsman, Mr. Wendell, my friend, Mr. David Greene, Dr. Russell and his family, Mr. Lavicourt, Mr. Vassall, and others of my acquaintance, will give the island less of the appearance of a strange place. By the passing of the act of proscription the door was shut against me in my own country, where I own it would have been my wish to have ended my days. This confirmed my resolution. I have since unremittedly pursued various objects, endeavoring to drive the nail that would go.

My first intention was that of transplanting myself somewhere to the southward. On this subject I thought long, and consulted others. I considered climate, friends, business, prospects in every view, and at last formed my opinion. The provinces in the south part of America in point of health were not more favorable than the island—in point of friends they might be preferable, but with respect to business or the means of acquiring it, uncertain; public commotion yet continued, violent prejudices are not easily removed. I had neither property nor natural connections in either of them. I could have no official influence to sustain me. What kind of government or laws would finally prevail it was difficult to tell. These and other reasons determined me against the attempt. But to stay longer in England, absent from my friends and family, with a bare subsistence, inactive, without prospects, and useless to myself and the world, was death to me! What was the alternative? As I saw no chance of procuring either appointment or employ here, the old object of the West Indies recurred, where in my younger days I wished to have remained; and by the influence of some particular gentlemen I have at last obtained the place of "Comptroller of the Customs at the Port of Parham in Antigua;" for which island I mean to embark with the next convoy. My view is to join the profits of business in the line of my profession to the emoluments of office. This I flatter myself will afford me a handsome maintenance. I grow old too fast to think of waiting longer for the moving of the waters, and have therefore cast my bread upon them, thus in hopes that at last, after many days, I may find it.

Transmit to my father every expression of duty and affection. If he retains the same friendship and parental fondness for me I have always experienced from him, he will patronize my children, and in doing this will do it unto me. It was my intention to have written to him, but the subjects on which I want to treat are too personally interesting for the casualties of the present day. He may rest assured it is my greatest unhappiness to be thus denied the pleasing task of lightening his misfortunes and soothing the evening of his days. Whatever may be the future events of his life. I shall always retain for him the warmest filial respect, and if it is my lot to survive him, shall ever think it a pleasure as well as my duty to promote to my utmost the welfare of his posterity. My mother will also accept of my duty and good wishes; the prosperity of the whole household lies near my heart, and they will do me an injustice if they think me otherwise than their affectionate friend. * * *

With respect to my property in America, my wish and desire is, if I have any control over it, that my friends there collectively, or some one singly under your direction, would take it into their hands, and consolidating the debts I owe into one sum, apply it to their discharge. I can think of no better way than this. If eventually I am deprived of it, I will endeavor to bear it with that fortitude which becomes a Christian and philosopher.

P. S. I could wish above all things to preserve my law books.

TO HENRY HILL, ESQ.

London, May 25, 1779.

I have obtained an appointment at Parham, in Antigua, as comptroller of the customs, and am to embark soon for St. Kitts. * * It is this day four years since I left Boston, and though I have been racked by my own misfortunes and my feelings for the distresses of my family and friends, I have still by a good Providence been blessed with health and comforted by the kindness of many friends. If I have not been in affluence, I have been above want, and happy in the esteem of numbers in this kingdom to whom I was altogether a stranger. * * The education of my children is uppermost in my heart. The giving my son the benefit of classical learning by a course of college studies, is a step I much approve. The sequestration of my books is more mortifying to me than any other stroke. If they are not yet out of your power save them for me at all events.

In a copy of a letter to a friend, apparently in the West Indies, but whose name does not appear, Mr. Quincy thus expresses himself:

Antigua, Feb. 1, 1782.

You ask of me an account of my coming to the West Indies, the manner of my existence and destination, &c. The story is long, and would require many anecdotes to give the true history, but you will excuse me if at present I say only, that in the year 1775, just after the battle of Lexington, I quitted America for London on motives of business, intending to return in a few months; but my absence was construed by our good patriots as the effect of my political principles, and improved first to my proscription, afterwards to the very flattering title of traitorous conspirator, and the confiscation of my estate. I remained in England several years, but, tired of waiting for the moving of the waters, and unwilling to waste the flower of my age in a state of indolence, neither profitable to myself nor my family, I resolved to seek my fortune in this part of the world, where I had been in my younger days,—obtained a berth in the customs, which, together with the emoluments of my profession, afford me a comfortable subsistence, and the prospect of something beyond.

Your friend, &c.,
SAMUEL QUINCY.

Mr. Quincy's wife died November, 1782 in Massachusetts. He married again while at Antigua, Mrs. M. A. Chadwell, widow of Hon. Abraham Chadwell.

TO HIS SON, SAMUEL QUINCY, JR., CAMBRIDGE.

June 10, 1785.

How anxious soever I may feel to see my friends and relations once more, I cannot think of doing it at the expense of my liberty; nor will I ever visit that country where I first drew my breath, but upon such terms as I have always lived in it; and such as I have still a right to claim from those who possess it,—the character of a gentleman. * * * The proposal Judge Sumner has hinted to me of keeping his old berth for you at Roxbury, is a good one, at least better than Boston. Cultivate his good opinion, and deserve his patronage; he will bestow the latter for my sake, I trust, as well as his personal esteem for you. It will also stand you in stead at court, where I hope you will one day figure as a legislator as well as an advocate. All depends upon setting out right. You are at the edge of a precipice, or ought to consider yourself so; from whence, if you fall, the *"revocare gradum,"* is a task indeed. Resolve, then, to think right, and act well; keeping up to that resolution will procure you daily the attention of all ranks, and command for you their respect. Keep alive the cause of truth, of reason, of virtue, and of liberty, if I may be permitted to use that name, who have by some injuriously been thought in a conspiracy against it. This is the path of duty, and will be the source of blessing.

July 24, 1789.

I am exceedingly sorry to hear of the distracted political situation of Massachusetts. * * * A constitution founded on mere republican principles has always appeared to me a many-headed monster, and, however applauded by a Franklin, a Price, and a Priestley, that in the end it must become a suicide. Mankind do not in experience appear formed for that finer system, which, in theory, by the nice adjustment of its parts promises permanency and repose. The passions, prejudice, and interests of some will always be in opposition to others, especially if they are in place.

This, it may be said, is the case in all governments, but I think less so in a monarchy than under a republican code. The people at large feel an overbalance of power in their own favor; they will naturally endeavor to ease themselves of all expenses which are not lucrative to them, and retrench the gains of others, whether the reward of merit or genius, or the wages of a hireling.

Tortola, June 1, 1789.

My Dear Son:

Your short letter of the 14th February gave me pleasure, as it informed me of your health and that of your family, and other friends in the neighborhood of Roxbury.

It would be my wish to make you a visit once more in my life, could it be ascertained I might walk free of insult, and unmolested in person. Two things must concur to satisfy me of this,—the repeal of the act passed 1779, against certain crown officers, as traitors, conspirators, &c.; and accommodation with those who have against me pecuniary demands. The first I have never yet learned to be repealed, either in whole or in part, and therefore I consider it as a stumbling-block at the threshold; the second, no steps I suppose have been taken to effect, although I think it might be done by inquiry and proposition—with some by a total release from demand, and with others by a reasonable compromise. If you ever wish your father to repose under your roof, you will take some pains to examine the list, and make the trial. I shall shortly, I hope, be in a situation to leave this country, if I choose it; but whether Europe, of the two objects I have in view, will take the preference, may depend on the answer I may receive from you, upon the hints I have now thrown out for your consideration and filial exertions. * * *

I have been, as I informed you in my last, a good deal indisposed for some time past. I find myself, however, better on the whole at present, though I feel the want of a bracing air. Adieu.

Your affectionate parent,
Samuel Quincy.

Soon after the date of this last letter, Mr. Quincy embarked for England, accompanied by his wife. The restoration of his health was the object of the voyage, but the effort was unsuccessful; he died at sea, within sight of the English coast. His remains were carried to England, and interred on Bristol hill. His widow immediately re-embarked for the West Indies, but her voyage was tempestuous. Grief for the loss of her husband, to whom she was strongly attached, and suffering from the storm her vessel encountered, terminated her life on her homeward passage.

It was a singular coincidence that two of Mr. Quincy's brothers died at sea, as he did on shipboard, Edmund, the eldest and Josiah, the youngest brother.

Samuel Quincy had two sons: Samuel, a graduate of Harvard College in 1782, who was an attorney-at-law in Lenox, Mass., where he died in January, 1816, leaving a son Samuel. His second son, Josiah, became an eminent counselor-at-law of Romney, N. H., and President of the Senate of that State.

Mr. Samuel Quincy was proscribed and banished and his property confiscated.

COLONEL JOHN MURRAY.

About 1750 there appeared in Boston society a very handsome man by the name of Murray, whose antecendents people seemed to be ignorant, when he came to this country he settled at Rutland, and was very poor, and at first "peddled about the country" and then became a merchant. He was a man of great influence in his vicinity, and in the town of Rutland, which he represented many years in the General Court. On election days his home was open to his friends and good cheer dispensed free to all from his store. His wealth, social position, and political influence, made him one of the Colonial noblemen who lived in a style that has passed away in New England. He was a Colonel in the militia, for many years a member of the General Court, and in 1774 was appointed a Mandamus Councillor, but was not sworn into office, because a mob of about five hundred, with the "Worcester Committee of Correspondence," repaired to Rutland, to compel Colonel Murray to resign his seat in the Council. On the way, they were joined by nearly one thousand persons, among whom were a portion of the company who had compelled Judge Timothy Paine to take the same course, marching directly to Rutland the same day.

A delegation went to his house, and reported that he was absent. A letter was accordingly sent to him, to the effect that; unless his resignation appeared in the Boston papers, he would be waited upon again. He abandoned his home on the night of the 25th of August of that year, and fled to Boston.

As previously stated, there was always a mystery surrounding John Murray, regarding who he was and where he came from, but his descendants had some reason for supposing that he was one of the "Athol Family" of Scotland, the surname of the Duke being Murray. Some years since one of Col. Murray's descendants went to "Blair Athol," the family seat of the Dukes of Athol, hoping to hear something about him, and there found an old retainer of the family who recalled the fact that many years ago a younger member of the family had disappeared, nothing being heard of him again, though it was supposed he had run away to America.

Miss Murray, after her father's death, went from St. John to Lancaster, Mass., to be with her relatives, the Chandler Family. She had with her some amount of silver plate, and on each piece was the arms of the "Ducal House of Athol." She had small means, and when in need of money used to sell this silver, one piece at a time. In the grant of the town of Athol by the General Court the first name is that of John Murray, who probably gave the name of his ancestral home to the new town.

In 1776, with a family of six persons, he accompanied the Royal Army to Halifax. Col. Murray left a very large estate when he fled from Boston, and in 1778 he was prosecuted and banished, and in 1779 lost his extensive property under the Confiscation Act.

After the Revolution, Colonel Murray became a resident of St. John, N. B. He built a house in Prince William street, with a large lot of land attached to it, which became very valuable.

A portrait by Copley is owned by his grandson, the Hon. R. L. Hazen of St. John, a member of the Executive Council of New Brunswick. He is represented as sitting in the full dress of a gentleman of the day, and his person is shown to the knees. There is a hole in the wig, which is said to have been done by one of the mob who sought the Colonel at his house after his flight, vexed because he had eluded them, vowed they would leave their mark behind them, accordingly pierced the canvas with a bayonet.

Colonel Murray married several times, his first wife was Elizabeth McLanathan, who was the mother of ten children. His second wife was Lucretia Chandler, the daughter of John and Hannah Gardner, of Worcester. His third wife was Deborah Brinley, the daughter of Francis Brinley, of Roxbury.

Colonel Murray was allowed a pension of £200 per annum by the British Government. His estate valued at £23,367, was confiscated except one farm for his son Alexander, who joined the Revolutionists. He died at St. John, 1794.

DANIEL MURRAY, of Brookfield, Mass., Son of Colonel John. He graduated at Harvard College in 1771. Mr. Murray entered the military service of the Crown, and was Major of the King's American Dragoons. In 1778 he was proscribed and banished. At the peace he retired, on half pay. In 1792 he was a member of the House of Assembly of N. B. In 1803 he left the Colony. In 1832 he died at Portland, Maine.

SAMUEL MURRAY, Son of Colonel John, graduated at Harvard College in 1772. He was with the British troops at Lexington in 1775, and was taken prisoner. In a General Order, dated at Cambridge, June 15, 1775, it was directed "That Samuel Murray be removed from the jail in Worcester to his father's homestead in Rutland, the limits of which he is not to pass until further orders." In 1778 he was proscribed and banished. He died previous to 1785.

Robert Murray, Son of Colonel John. In 1782 he was a Lieutenant of the King's American Dragoons. He settled in N. B., and died there of consumption in 1786.

John Murray, Son of Colonel John. In 1782 he was a Captain in the King's American Dragoons. After the Revolution he was an officer of the Fifty-fourth Regiment, British Army.

JUDGE JAMES PUTNAM.
ATTORNEY-GENERAL OF MASSACHUSETTS BAY.

JOHN PUTNAM, the founder of the Salem family, was born in 1579, at Wingrave, Buckinghamshire, England. He is described in the records an husbandman. His farm was at Burstone in Wingrave. He emigrated to Salem with his three sons in 1640, where grants of land were made by the town of Salem to him and to his sons on their own account, in what was then known as Salem Village, now the town of Danvers.

His sons were Thomas, born 1614, died at Salem Village 1686; Nathaniel, born 1619, died at Salem Village 1700; John, born 1627, died at Salem Village, 1710.

In deeds, John Putnam is described as both husbandman and yeoman. He was a man of substance and of as much education as his contemporaries, but neither seeking or desiring public office. In 1653 he divided his lands between Thomas and Nathaniel, having evidently already granted his homestead to his younger son John. He died in 1662.

The subject of this memoir was a descendent of John Putnam, in the fifth generation, through his youngest son John, known as Captain John. It was in the military affairs and in the witchcraft delusion that his character is best shown. In 1672 he is styled Corporal, in 1678 he was commissioned Lieutenant of the troope of horse at the Village, and after 1687 he is styled "Captain." He served in the Naragansett fight, and retained his military manners throughout his life. In 1679 and later he was frequently chosen to present Salem at the General Court, to settle the various disputed town bounds. He was selectman in 1681. He was deputy to the General Court for many years previous to the new charter.

His residence was on the farm originally occupied by his father, now better known as Oak Knoll, the home of the poet Whittier.

The will of John Putnam is not on record. He seems to have disposed of his property by deed to his children. Rev. Joseph Green makes the following note in his diary: "April 7, 1710, Captain Putnam buried by ye soldiers."

LIEUTENANT JAMES, son of CAPTAIN JOHN, was born in Salem Village, 1661, and died there in 1727. He was a farmer, inheriting from his father the homestead at Oak Knoll. In 1720 he is styled on the records Lieut., which title was always scrupulously given him. Although never caring to hold office, he was evidently esteemed by the townspeople. He had been taught a trade, and he in his turn taught his son the same trade, that of bricklayer. This was a custom among many of the early Puritan families. It is to the credit of all concerned, that farsighted and wealthy men of that day brought up their sons to know a useful trade, in case adversity should overtake them.

JAMES PUTNAM, of the fourth generation, son of the aforesaid Lieut. James, was born in Salem Village in 1689, and died there in 1763. He lived in the house just to the south-east of Oak Knoll on the same road; the house is still standing, in a fine state of preservation.

During his long life, James Putnam took considerable interest in town affairs. He was one of those who succeeded in obtaining the establishment of the district of Danvers. In 1730 he paid the largest tax in the village.

HONORABLE JAMES PUTNAM, of the fifth generation, son of the aforesaid James Putnam, was born in Salem Village, 1726, and died at St. John, N. B., 1789. He graduated from Harvard College in 1746. In his class was Dr. Edward H. Holyoke, whose father, Edward Holyoke, was then president of the College. He studied law, under Judge Trowbridge, who according to John Adams, controlled the whole practice of Worcester and Middlesex Counties, and settled in Worcester in 1749, taking up the practice of the law.

In 1750 he married Eleanor Sprague, by whom he had one daughter, Eleanor, who married Rufus Chandler, of Worcester.

James Putnam, in 1757, held the commission of Major, under Gen. Louden, and saw service. Between the years of 1755 and 1758, John Adams, afterwards President of the United States, taught school in Worcester, and studied law with Mr. Putnam. He also boarded in his family. Mr. Adams remarks that Mr. Putnam possessed great acuteness of mind, had a very extensive and successful practice, and was eminent in his profession. James Putnam was one of the twenty signers to the address from the barristers and attorneys of Massachusetts to Gov. Hutchinson, May 30, 1774. His brothers, Dr. Ebenezer and Archelaus, both addressed Gov. Gage on his arrival, June 11, 1774. In February, 1775, he, with others, was forced by the threatening attitude of the mob to leave Worcester and seek refuge in Boston, he having had his cattle stolen and a valuable grist mill burned, and threatened with bodily harm.

On Oct. 14, 1775, eighteen of those gentlemen who were driven from their habitations in the country to the town of Boston, addressed Gov. Gage on his departure. Among the signers were James Putnam and James Putnam, Jr.

In 1778 the Massachusetts Legislature passed an act confiscating the estate of 308 Loyalists and banishing them; if they returned a second time, to suffer death without the benefit of clergy. Among these was the Hon. James Putnam, who had in 1777 succeeded Jonathan Sewell as attorney general of Massachusetts, the last under the Crown.

During the siege of Boston on the 17th Nov. 1775, the following order was issued by the British Commander: "Many of his Majesty's Loyal American subjects having offered their services for the defence of the place" are to be formed into three companies under command of Hon. Brigadier-General Ruggles, to be called the Loyal American Associates, to be designated by a white sash around the left arm. James Putnam was commissioned captain of the second company, and James Putnam, Jr. was commissioned second lieutenant of the second company. At the evacuation of Boston, both James Putnam and his sons, James and Ebenezer, accompanied the army to Halifax, and New York, where his sons engaged in business. He sailed for Plymouth, England, December, 1779, with Mrs. Putnam and his daughter Elizabeth.

While in England he wrote numerous letters to his brothers, from which we make the following quotations. Under date of Nov. 13th, 1783, he writes from London: "My countrymen have got their independence (as they call it) and with it in my opinion, have lost the true Substantial Civil liberty. They doubtless exult as much at the acquisition they have gained as they do at the loss the Tories, as they call them, have sustained."

"America, the thirteen states, at last separated from this country, never more to be connected. For you may believe me when I say I firmly believe, and on good grounds, that even the present administration would not now accept of the connection, if America would offer it on the old footing."

"You may be assured there is nothing I wish for more than to see my dear brother and other dear friends in America again."

"At the same time, I can tell you with truth, unpleasing as you may think the situation of the Loyalists to be, I would not change with my independent countrymen with all imaginary liberty, but real heavy taxes and burdens, destitute in a great measure, as I know they are, of order and good government."

"Having this view of things, you can't expect to see me in Massachusetts soon, even if I was permitted or invited to return with perhaps the offer of the restoration of my estate. For what would it be worth but to pay all away in taxes in a short time."

"I'm not yet determined whether to remain in this country or go abroad to Nova Scotia or elsewhere."

Again, under date of July 20, 1784, he writes: "Your country is so changed since I left it, and in my opinion for the worst, that the great pleasure I should have in seeing my dear friends, would be lost in a great measure in the unhappy change of government."

His next letter was from Parr, on the river St. John, N. B., Nov. 18, 1784. He says: "Dear Brother. I have been at this place about ten days, am surprised to find a large flourishing town, regularly laid out, well built, consisting of about two thousand houses, many of them handsome and well finished—And at the opposite side of the river at Carlton, about five hundred more houses on a pleasant situation. A good harbor lies between the two towns, which never freezes, and where there are large ships and many vessels of all sizes. The country appears to me to be very good, and am satisfied will make a most flourishing Province."

He writes again the next year: "You may wonder perhaps at my saying I hope I'm settled in this Province for life, and that I can be contented or happy in the place formerly called Nova Scotia."

"I want to see you and my friends, if I have any, but I don't wish to live in your country or under your government, I think I have found a better. No thanks to the Devils who have robbed me of my propeity. I do not wish to live with or see such infernals."

"God bless you, your wife, your son, your daughter, my brother, etc., who I shall be glad to see again, but not in the American States."

In another letter, dated St. John, N. B., May 13, 1785, to his brother, he says: "As to seeing you any more, you have no reason to expect it in your State.

"You may be assured, I should be exceeding happy in seeing you both here. I can give you a comfortable lodging, and wholesome good fresh provisions, excellent fish and good spruce beer, 'the growth and manufacture of our own Province.

"Tho' we should be glad to see the few friends we have remaining there among you, we don't wish to give them the pain of seeing us in your State, which is evidently overflowing with *freedom and liberty** without restraint.

The people of the States must needs now be very happy, when they can all and every one do just what they like best. No taxes to pay, no *stamp act, more money* than they know what to do with, *trade and navigation as free as air.*"

Under date of Nov. 4, 1786, he writes: "The people of your State seem to be stirring up another revolution. What do they want now? Do they find at last, to be freed from the British Government, and becoming an independent State does not free them from the debts they owe one another, or exempt them from the charge of taxation. I wish they would pay me what they justly owe, they may then have what government they please, or none, if they like that best."

He was appointed in 1784 Judge of the Supreme Court of New Brunswick, and a member of the Council. It was said that he was the ablest lawyer in all America. Judge Putnam was the first of the council and bench of New Brunswick, who died from failing health; he had not attended council meetings for over a year. He died 23 Oct., 1789, in his 65th year. In character he was upright and generous; his health was never robust; and loss of country, friends and wealth must have been a severe blow. Sabine says: "I have often stood at his grave and mused upon the strange vicissitudes of human condition, by which the Master,

---

* During 1785 Shay's rebellion occurred in Massachsetts and was put down by General Lincoln.

one of the giants of the American Colonial Bar, became an outlaw, and an exile, broken in fortune and spirit, while his struggling and almost friendless pupil, elevated step by step by the very same course of events, was finally known the world over as the Chief Magistrate of a Nation." It is thus in all successful Revolutions, those that were at the head of affairs are hurled from power, and their fortunes wrecked, whilst young men like John Adams, of great abilities but poor, and little prospects for advancement, are elevated to the highest offices. Who would have ever heard of the "Little Corporal" had it not been for the French Revolution, then there would not have been any "Napoleon the maker of Kings."

Judge Putnam had two relatives who became famous in the Colonial wars, and the Revolution. Major-General Israel Putnam was of the fourth generation from John. He was born in Salem Village. 1717. He distinguished himself at Crown Point, Montreal and Cuba, and later at Bunker Hill. General Rufus Putnam was of the fifth generation. After serving in the Colonial wars under his cousin Israel Putnam, he took part in the siege of Boston, and constructed the works on Dorchester Heights, on the 4th of March, 1776, that forced the evacuation of Boston.

At no time during the youth of these two men would one have predicted that they would be two great soldiers. Their early education was very defective, partly because school advantages were then very meagre in the rural districts, in which they passed their youth, and partly no doubt, because their strong inclinations were for farming and active outdoor life, rather than for books and sedentary occupation. Robust and full of energy, they were as boys, given to feats of strength and daring.

In 1780 General Rufus Putnam "bought on easy terms" the confiscated property of Colonel Murray, who married Lucretia Chandler. This property was situated in Rutland, and consisted of a large farm and spacious mansion.

JAMES PUTNAM, JR., son Judge Putnam, graduated at Harvard College in 1774. He was one of the eighteen country gentlemen who addressed Gen. Gage, and were driven into Boston. He went to England and died there in 1838, having been a barrack master, a member of the household, and an executor of the Duke of Kent, the father of Queen Victoria.

JUDGE TIMOTHY PAINE.

STEPHEN PAINE, from whom so many of the family in America are descended, came from Great Ellingham, near Hingham, Norfolk County, England. He was a miller, and came with a large party of immigrants from Hingham and vicinity, in the ship Diligent, of Ipswich, John Martin master, in the year 1638, bringing with him his wife Rose, two sons and four servants.

Mr. Paine first settled at Hingham, Mass., where he had land granted to him, was made a freeman in 1639 and elected Deputy in 1641. In 1642 he, with four others, settled at Seekonk, and became prominent in the affairs of the new settlement at Rehoboth.

Mr. Paine survived the eventful period of King Philip's war and died in 1679, outliving his two sons, Stephen having died at Rehoboth in 1677, and Nathaniel in 1678.

NATHANIEL PAINE, son of the aforesaid Nathaniel, of the third generation, was born at Rehoboth 1661, married Dorothy, daughter of Jonathan Rainsford, of Boston. He removed in early life to Bristol, Mass., now R. I., and was one of the original proprietors of that place. In 1710 he was appointed Judge of the Court of Common Pleas, and Judge of Probate. He was one of the Council of Mass. Bay from 1703 till his death in 1723, with the exception of the year 1708. Nathaniel Paine died at Bristol, R. I., in 1723, and his wife Dorothy Rainsford, in 1755.

NATHANIEL PAINE, of the fourth generation and fourth son of the preceding Nathaniel, was born at Bristol 1688. He was an active and influential citizen of Bristol, was for five years elected Representative. In 1723 he was a member of a Court of Admiralty for the trial of pirates. In 1724 was a Judge of the Court of Common Pleas.

Mr. Paine married Sarah, daughter of Timothy Clark of Boston. After his death in 1729, his widow married John Chandler and removed to Worcester.

TIMOTHY PAINE, son of the aforesaid Nathaniel and Sarah Clark, his wife. He was born in Boston in 1730 and married Sarah Chandler in 1749, the daughter of John Chandler, so these young people had probably been brought up under the same roof from early childhood. He graduated at Harvard College in 1748, and was a stout government man in the controversies which preceded the Revolution.

Soon after leaving college, Mr. Paine was engaged in public affairs, and the number and variety of offices which he held exhibit the estimation in which he stood. He was at different times Clerk of the Courts, Register of Deeds, Register of Probate, member of the executive council of the Province, in 1774 he was appointed one of his Majesty's Mandamus Councillors, Selectman and Town Clerk, and Representative many years in the General Court. In 1771 he was also Special Justice of the Supreme Court. Solid talents, practical sense, candor, sincerity, ability, and mildness, were the characteristics of his life.

When the appeal to arms approached, many of the inhabitants of Worcester, most distinguished for talents, influence, and honors, adhered with constancy to the Government. Educated with veneration for the sovereign to whom they had sworn fealty; indebted to the government for the bounty, honor and wealth which they possessed—loyalty and gratitude alike influenced them to resent acts that were treasonable, and rebellious. The sincerity of their motives were attested by the sacrifice of life, property, loss of power, and all the miseries of banishment, confiscation and exile.

The struggle between the revolutionist, and the loyalty of a minority of the people, powerful in numbers, as well as talents, wealth, and influence, arrived at its crisis in Worcester early in 1774, and terminated in the total defeat of the loyalists.

Among the many grievances of the revolutionists, was the vesting of the government in the dependents of the King, it aggravated the irritation, and urged the mobs to acts of violence.

Timothy Paine, Esq., had received a commission as one of the Mandamus Councillors. High as was the personal regard, and respect for the purity of private character of this gentleman, it was controlled by the political feelings of a period of excitement; and measures were taken to compel his resignation of a post which was unwelcome to himself, but which he dared not refuse, when declining would have been construed as contempt for the authority of the King, by whom it was conferred.

August 22, 1774, a mob of nearly 3000 persons collected from the surrounding towns, visited Worcester and entered the town before 7 o'clock in the morning. They chose a committee to wait upon Mr. Paine and demand his resignation as Councillor. They went to his house, and he agreed to resign from that office, and drew up an acknowledgement, mentioning his obligations to the country for favors done him, his sorrow for having taken the oath, and a promise that he never would act in that office contrary to the charter, and after that he came with the committee to the common, where the mob made a lane between them, through which he and the committee passed and read divers times as they passed along, the said acknowledgment. At first one of the committee read the resignation of Mr. Paine in his behalf. It was then insisted that he should read it with his hat off. He hesitated and demanded protection from the committee, which they were incapable of giving him. Finally, with threats of tar and feathers, and personal violence, in which his wig was knocked off, he complied, and was allowed to retire to his dwelling unharmed.

At the commencement of the Revolution some American soldiers quartered at his house repaid his perhaps too unwilling hospitality, and signified the intensity of their feelings towards him by cutting the throat of his full length portrait.

Madam Paine, in passing the guard house, which stood nearly where the old Nashua Hotel stood in Lincoln square, heard the soldiers say "Let us shoot the old Tory." She turned around facing them and said: "Shoot if you dare," and then she reported to General Knox the insult she had received, which was not repeated.

Mrs. Timothy Paine or Madam Paine, as she was styled from respect to her dignity and position, was a woman of uncommon energy and acuteness. She was noted in her day for her zeal in aiding as far as was in her power the followers of the crown, and in defeating the plans of the rebellious colonists. In her the King possessed a faithful ally. In her hands his dignity was safe, and no insult offered to it, in her presence, could go unavenged.

Her wit and loyalty never shone more conspicuously than on the following occasion: When President Adams was a young man, he was invited to dine with the court, and bar, at the home of Judge Paine, an eminent loyalist of Worcester. When the wine was circulating around the table, Judge Paine gave as a toast "The King." Some of the Whigs were about to refuse to drink it, but Mr. Adams whispered to them to comply, saying "we shall have an opportunity to return the compliment." At length, when he was desired to give a toast, he gave "The Devil." As the host was about to resent the indignity, his wife calmed him, and turned the laugh upon Mr. Adams, by immediately exclaiming "My dear! As the gentleman has been so kind as to drink to our King, let us by no means refuse in our turn to drink to his."

Timothy Paine and Sarah Chandler, his wife, not only feared God, but honored the King, so the old record goes. They belonged to families, often associated together in the remembrance of the present generation, as having adhered through the wavering fortunes and final success of the Revolution, devoted and consistent to the British Crown. Solid talents, practical sense, candor, sincerity, affability, and mildness, were the characteristics of his life. He died July 17, 1793, at the age of sixty-three. His widow died at Worcester, in 1811.

DR. WILLIAM PAINE.

William Paine, son of the aforesaid Timothy Paine, was born in Worcester, Mass., June 5, 1750. He graduated at Harvard College in 1768, his name standing second in a class of more than forty, when they were arranged in the catalogue according to the dignity of families.

He then began the study of medicine with a very distinguished physician, Dr. Edward A. Holyoke, of Salem, while here he made the acquaintance of the lady whom he married a few years later.

One of his earliest instructors was John Adams, who was then reading law in the office of Hon. James Putnam, at Worcester. He began the practice of medicine in Worcester in 1771. That year Mr. Adams revisited Worcester, after an absence of sixteen years, and notes the impression of his former pupils as follows: "Here I saw many young gentlemen who were my scholars and pupils, John Chandler, Esq., of Petersham, Rufus Chandler, the lawyer, and Dr. William Paine, who now studies physics with Dr. Holyoke of Salem, and others, most of whom began to learn Latin with me."

In 1771, after about three years of study, he returned to Worcester, with every prospect of becoming a leader in the medical profession. In

1773 he entered into partnership with two other physicians or "Traders in the Art, Mystery and Business of an Apothecary and the practice of Physick." This interest was confiscated in 1779.

In 1773 Dr. Paine was married to Miss Lois Orne of Salem, with a fortune of 3,000 pounds sterling. Six children were born from this union.

For the purpose of facilitating his business abroad and of perfecting his medical education, Dr. Paine in Sept. 1774, sailed for England, and the following winter was passed in the study of medicine. During his visit there he was presented to the King, and Queen Charlotte, wearing the court dress prescribed for medical men, which was a gray cloth coat with silver buttons, a white satin waistcoat, satin small clothes, silk hose and wearing a sword, and a fall of lace from cravat or collar, and lace in the sleeves. It is interesting to read some of his letters written as he was about leaving England. In one of them he writes "The Colonists had better lay down their arms at once, for we are coming over with an overwhelming force to destroy them." His wife and children seemed to have remained with his father and mother while he was in England, but finding their position in Worcester unpleasant on account of their unpopular political opinions, she left and went to Rhode Island.

Dr. Paine returned to America in 1775, shortly after hostilities commenced, and while there was apparently no legal impediment to his return to Worcester, it was doubtless a very prudent decision of Dr. Paine not to make the attempt. His feeling of personal loyalty to the government was too strong to allow him even to appear to yield to the Revolutionists, then dominating his native town, and he wisely returned to England. His study of medicine there must have been pursued with unusual zeal and success, for Nov. 1775, he received from Marischal College, Aberdeen, the degree of M. D.

Soon after obtaining this distinction, he received an appointment as Apothecary to the British forces in America, and served in Rhode Island and New York till 1781, when he returned to England, in company with his patient, Lord Winchelsea. While, in England, in 1782, he is said to have been made Licentiate of the Royal College of Physicians of London.

October 23, 1782, he was commissioned Physician to His Majesty's Hospitals within the district of North America, commanded by Sir Guy Carleton, and he reported for duty at Halifax, N. S. Letters which have been preserved show that during this year at Halifax he had won the respect, friendship and confidence, not only of his immediate medical superior, Dr. Nooth, but also of Lord Wentworth, Governor of the Province.

In the summer of 1784, Dr. Paine took possession of La Tete, an island in Passamaquoddy Bay, granted him by the British Government, for his services in the war. He remained there less than one year, and then made his residence in St. John, N. B., where he took up the practice of his profession. The cause of the removal from the island was the protest of his wife that the children could not receive a proper education in that isolated spot.

He was elected member of the Assembly of New Brunswick from the county of Charlotte, and was appointed Clerk of the House. He was commissioned as a justice for the county of Sunbury. There is abundant evidence of the high estimate placed on his character and ability in the numerous offices which he held during his residence here.

July 29, 1786, he wrote to a friend: "I do a great deal of Business in my Profession, but I get very little for it. The truth is we are all very poor, and the most industrious and economical gets only a bare subsistence. However, it will soon be better as the Province is daily filling with stock of all kinds."

In 1787 Dr. Paine made application for leave to visit and reside in New England while remaining on half pay, and a permit to that effect was issued by the War Office.

In Salem he devoted himself to the practice of medicine in the town where he had been known as a student of the famous Dr. Holyoke, and where his wife had spent her early life.

In 1793 his father died, and he removed to Worcester, and for the remaining forty years of his life he resided in the paternal mansion. His father's property was large, and as he was not an absentee, it was not confiscated. By his will it was equally divided between his children, the farm and homestead covered 1230 acres. Dr. Paine bought the shares of his brothers, and sisters in same for 2,000 pounds sterling, but the deeds were given to Nathaniel Paine in trust for William, for the doctor was as yet, but an alien in his native state. The year 1812 was a critical one, bringing a most important question for him to decide, for war arose between Great Britain and the United States, and he was still a half-pay officer in His Majesty's service. He therefore resigned from the British service, and in 1812 petitioned the Legislature for its consent to his being a naturalized citizen of the United States.

William Paine was one of the founders of the American Antiquarian Society of Worcester. His name was omitted from the act of incorporation because he was an alien. The next year, 1813, he was elected Vice President of same.

He occupied the old paternal mansion on Lincoln street in a quiet, very dignified and almost luxurious manner as befitted a country gentleman. Here he died at the ripe age of 83, March 19, 1833.

SAMUEL PAINE, son of Timothy, was born at Worcester, Mass. Graduated at Harvard College in 1771. The Worcester County Convention, Sept. 7, 1774, voted to take notice of Mr. Samuel Paine, assistant clerk, for sending out *venires*. Voted, that Mr. Samuel Dennison go to Mr. Samuel Paine forewith, and desire his immediate attendance before this body, to answer for sending *venires* to constables commanding their compliance with the late Act of Parliament.

Mr. Paine appeared and stated that he felt bound by the duty of his office to comply with the Act, "Voted that Mr. Paine has not given satisfaction, and that he be allowed to consider till the adjournment of this meeting."

On September 21, he transmitted a paper to the Convention explanatory of his conduct; but that body voted that it "was not satisfactory, and that 'his letter be dismissed' and Mr. Paine himself "be treated with all neglect."

In 1775 he was sent to the Committee of Worcester under guard, "to Watertown or Cambridge, to be dealt with as the honorable Congress or Commander-in-Chief shall, upon examination, think proper." His direct offenses consisted, apparently, in saying that the Hampshire troops had robbed the home of Mr. Bradish; that he had heard the Whig soldiers were deserting in great numbers, and that he was told "the men were so close stowed in the Colleges that they were lousy." This is the substance of the testimony of a neighbor, the only witness who appeared against him.

In 1776 Mr. Paine accompanied the British Army to Halifax when they evacuated Boston. During the war he wandered from place to place without regular employment. He returned to Worcester where he died in 1807. The British government allowed him an annual pension of £84.

JOHN CHANDLER.

The founder of this family, so large and so influential before the Revolution, came to these shores from England in 1637, when William Chandler and Annice, his wife, settled in Roxbury. Mr. Chandler died in 1641, "having lived a very religious and godly life," and "leaving a sweet memory and savor behind him." Annice Chandler must have been an attractive woman, for she was not only soon married to a second husband, but to a third, and her last one evidently expected her to enter into matrimony a fourth time, for in his will he provided that she shall have the use of his warming pan only so long as she remained his widow. Goodwife Parmenter, however, died in 1683, in full possession of the warming pan, the widow of the third husband.

JOHN CHANDLER, a son of William, emigrated to Woodstock, Conn., and became a farmer. He was selectman and deacon of the church, and died there in 1703, leaving a family and property valued at £512.

The second John Chandler, son of the first of that name, had before his father's death, moved to New London, Conn., where he married, and in 1698 had opened a "house of entertainment" there. He at a later date moved back to South Woodstock, and in 1711 was chosen representative to the General Court at Boston for several years. After the erection of Worcester County by Act of the Legislature of Massachusetts, April 2,

1731, the first Probate Court in Worcester was held by Col. Chandler as Judge in the meeting house, 13th of July, 1731, and the first Court of Common Pleas and General Sessions on August 10 following, by the Hon. John Chandler, commissioned June 30, 1731, Chief Justice. These offices he held until his death, as well as Colonel of Militia to which stations of civil, judicial and military honors, he rose by force of his strong mental powers, with but slight advantages of education. Judge John Chandler died August 10, 1743, in his 79th year, leaving in his will £8,699.

JOHN CHANDLER, the third of that name, son of the Hon. John Chandler, held nearly all the offices in the town of Worcester, Selectman, Sheriff, Probate Judge, Town Treasurer, Register of Probate, Register of Deeds, Chief Judge of County Courts, Judge of Common Pleas, Representative to the General Court, Colonel of Militia and a member of the Governor's Council. He died in 1762, wealthy and full of honors.

JUDGE CHANDLER, was married to Hannah Gardner, daughter of John Gardner of the Isle of Wight (known afterwards as Gardner's Island), in 1716. She died in Worcester in 1738, aged 39 years, leaving nine children, the first members of the Chandler family who were born and bred in Worcester.

JOHN CHANDLER, son of the aforesaid, the fourth to bear that name was born in New London, Connecticut, in 1720, was married twice and had sixteen children. His father removed to Worcester when he was eleven years of age. At his father's death he succeeded him to the principal county offices. He was Colonel in the militia, and was in service in the French war, and he was Sheriff, Judge of Probate and County Treasurer. Up to 1774 John Chandler's life had been one of almost unbroken prosperity, but when the rebellion broke out, his loyalist sentiments brought upon him the wrath of the mob, and he was compelled to leave home, and family and retire to Boston. When Boston was evacuated, he went to Halifax, and thence to London, and two years after he was proscribed and banished. He sacrificed his large possessions, £36,190 as appraised in this country by commissioners here, to a chivalrous sense of loyalty. In the schedule exhibited to the British Commissioners, appointed to adjust the compensation to the Americans who adhered to the government; the amount of real and personal property which was confiscated, is estimated at £11,067, and the losses from office, from destruction of business, and other causes, at nearly £6,000 more. So just and moderate was this compensation ascertained to be, at a time when extravagant claims were presented by others, that his claim was allowed in full; he was denominated in England "The Honest Refugee." Sabine says "I am assured that, while he was in Boston he was supported for a considerable time by the sale of silver plate sent him by his family; and that when he left home he had no idea of quitting the country. I am assured also, that when the Revolutionary Commissioners took an inventory of his household furniture, the females were plundered of their very clothing." His adherence to the government, and his departure for England, seems to have been his only offences, yet he was treated as harshly as though he had borne arms in the field.

He is spoken of as having a cheerful temperament, engaging in manner, hospitable as a citizen, friendly and kind as a neighbor, industrious and enterprising as a merchant, and successful as a man of business. He died in London in 1800, and was buried in Islington churchyard. In 1741 he married Dorothy, daughter of Colonel Nathaniel Paine. She died in 1745. His second wife was Mary, daughter of Colonel Church, of Bristol, R. I., a descendant of the warrior who fought King Philip. She died at Worcester in 1783. His portrait in oil is preserved in the rooms of the American Antiquarian Society, Worcester. George Bancroft, the distinguished historian, and the widow of Governor Davis of Massachusetts, are Colonel Chandler's grandchildren.

CLARK CHANDLER, son of Colonel John, was born at Worcester in 1743. At first a clerk in the office of the Register of Probate, he became joint Register with Hon. Timothy Paine, and held the appointment from 1766 to 1774. He was also Town Clerk of Worcester from 1768 to 1774. In 1774 he entered upon the town Records a remonstrance of the Loyalists to the great anger of the Revolutionists, who voted in town meeting that he should then and there "obliterate, erase, or otherwise deface, the said recorded protest, and the names thereto subscribed, so that it may become illegible and unintelligible." This he was obliged to do, in presence of the revolutionists, to blot out the obnoxious record by dipping his fingers in ink, and drawing them over the protest.

He left home in June, 1775, and went to Halifax, and thence to Canada. He returned in September of the same year, and was imprisoned in the common jail. Confinement impaired his health, and he was removed to his mother's home. Finally he was allowed to go to Lancaster, on giving security that he would not depart from that town. He returned to Worcester and kept store at the corner of Main and Front streets. His person was small, and he wore bright red small clothes; was odd and singular in appearance, which often provoked jeers and jokes of those around him, but apt at reply "he paid the jokers in their own coin." He was never married, and died in Worcester in 1804.

RUFUS CHANDLER, fifth child of Colonel John by Mary Church, his second wife. He was born in 1747, and graduated at Harvard College in 1776 in a class of forty, with the rank of the fourth in "dignity of family." He read law in the office of his uncle, Hon. James Putnam, in Worcester, where he afterwards practised his profession until the courts were closed by the mobs in 1774. He was one of the barristers and attornies who addressed Hutchinson in the last mentioned year. He inherited the loyalty of his family and left the country at the commencement of hostilities. He went to Halifax in 1776 and in 1778 was proscribed and banished. His mother used a part of his estate for the support of his daughter; but the remainder appraised at £820, was confiscated. He resided in England as a private gentleman, and died in London in 1823, at the age of 76, and his remains were laid with those of his fathers in Islington churchyard. His wife was Elizabeth Putnam, his only child, who bore her mother's name, married Solomon Vose, of Augusta, Maine.

GARDNER CHANDLER, son of Colonel John, of Hardwick, Mass., was born in 1749, and was a merchant in that town. His property was confiscated, and the proceeds paid into the treasury of the state. He left the colony and returned some time after to Hardwick. He made acknowledgments satisfactory to his townsmen, it was voted by the town "that as Gardner Chandler has now made acknowledgment, and says he is sorry for his past conduct, that they will treat him as a friend and neighbor, so long as he shall behave himself well." He removed to Brattleboro, Vermont, and again to Hinsdale, N. H. He died in the last named town. His wife was Elizabeth, daughter of Brigadier Timothy Ruggles.

NATHANIEL CHANDLER, son of Colonel John, was born in Worcester, 1750, graduated at Harvard College in 1768. He was a pupil of John Adams, and commenced the practice of law in Petersham. His brother-in-law, the Rev. Dr. Bancroft, wrote "that he possessed personal manliness and beauty," that "he was endowed with a good mind and a lively imagination" that "in disposition he was cheerful." He was one of the eighteen county gentlemen who addressed General Gage on his departure in 1775. In 1776 he went to Halifax. In 1778 he was proscribed and banished, and his estate confiscated. Entering the British service he commanded a corps of Volunteers and did good service. He returned to Petersham in in 1784, and engaged in trade, but relinquished business on account of ill health, and returned to Worcester. Citizenship was restored in 1789, by Act of the Legislature of Mass. He was a very pleasant companion, and a favorite singer of songs in social parties. He never married. He died at Worcester in 1801.

WILLIAM CHANDLER, eighth child of Colonel John, was born at Worcester in 1752, and graduated at Harvard College in 1772. At that time students in that institution were ranked according to "dignity of family" and William was placed in the highest class. He was one of the eighteen county gentlemen who were driven from their homes to Boston, and who addressed General Gage on his departure in 1775. In 1776 he went to Halifax. He was proscribed and banished under the Act of 1778, but returned to Mass., after the close of the Revolution. Among the articles in the inventory of his estate when it was confiscated was seven pairs of silk hose, at fourteen shillings; plated shoe buckles, six shillings; and pair of velvet breeches.

Gardiner Chandler, brother of Colonel John. He was born in Woodstock in 1723. In the French war he was a major and was in service at the surrender of Fort William Henry. He was Treasurer of Worcester County eight years and succeeded his brother John, as sheriff, in 1762. He presented General Gage an Address in behalf of the Judges of the Court of Common Pleas in 1774; and was compelled by a Convention of the Committee of Correspondence to sign a "Recantation." In time, he regained the confidence of the community, and was suffered to live undisturbed. He died in Worcester, in 1782. His first wife was Hannah Greene, of Providence, R. I., his second, Ann Leonard, of Norton, Mass.

The Chandlers were in every respect the most eminent family in Worcester County, and furnished many men of distinction in its ante-revolutionary history. They were closely allied by blood, marriage or friendship with the aristocracy of the county and province, in which they had unbounded sway. They had large possessions, and shared with the Paine family (with whom they were allied), the entire local influence at Worcester, but did not, like that family, survive the shock of the Revolution, and retain a local habitation and a name. Their property was confiscated and they were declared traitors.

The family was broken up; some members of it went abroad and died there, others were scattered in this country, yet not a few of their descendants eminent in the most honorable pursuits, and in the highest positions in life under different names and in various localities, represent that ancient, honorable and once numerous race, wrecked by the Revolution.

John Adams says in his diary, "The Chandlers exercised great influence in the County of Worcester until they took the side of the government in the Revolution, and lost their position. They were well bred, agreeable people, and I visited them as often as my school, and my studies in the lawyer's office would admit."

JOHN GORE.

John Gore, of Roxbury, and his wife Rhoda, were both church members in 1635. He died June 2, 1657, and his widow married Lieut. John Remington. He had ten children, of whom John, Samuel, Abigail, Mary, Mylam, and Hannah, were mentioned in his will.

Samuel Gore, son of the former, lived in Roxbury, and was a carpenter. He married August 28, 1672, Elizabeth, daughter of John Weld. He died July, 1692. They had seven children.

Obadiah Gore, son of Samuel, was also a carpenter, and lived in Boston. He married, October 26, 1710, Sarah Kilby. He died October 8, 1721, and was survived by five children, all of whom were baptized at the Brattle Street church.

John Gore, son of the former, lived in Boston, and was a painter and merchant. He married, May 5, 1743, Frances, daughter of John Pinkney. She was born September 20, 1726. They had fourteen or fifteen children, nine of whom lived to be married. The baptisms of nine of his children are given in the records of the Brattle Street Church. John Gore was an Addresser of Gage, and in 1776 went to Halifax and thence to England. He was proscribed and banished in 1778, and pardoned by the Legislature in 1787. He died in Boston in 1796, aged seventy-seven. His will is in the Suffolk Register, Lib. 94, F. 182. His son, CHRISTOPHER GORE, was born in Boston, Sept. 21st, 1758. He was educated in the public schools of Boston, and was prepared at the South Latin school under the tuition of Mr. Lovell, the most noted educator of his day. At the age of 13, Christopher entered Harvard College, and was among the youngest of his class. But he commenced his collegeate course in troubleous times, for in his junior year the Revolution broke out, which created confusion and disorder through society, and deranged the plans, and changed the pursuits of many in every grade and profession. The College at Cambridge was considered by the Revolutionists as "nest of tories" and during the siege of Boston the college buildings were taken possession of by the continental army stationed at Cambridge, and the students were dispersed for several months. Young Gore was determined to follow out his course of college training, however, and to this end went to Bradford, in Essex County, and studied under the direction and in the family of Rev. Mr. Williams, afterwards professor of mathematics and natural philosophy in Harvard College. When the college removed to Concord he, with most of the students, repaired thither, and resumed his studies. He graduated in 1776, the year that his father was driven from the land of his birth.

Christopher Gore soon commenced the study of law in the office and under the direction of Judge John Lowell, in whose family he resided while a student. He commenced the practice of law in Boston with every prospect of success. He had to depend on himself alone, for not only had he his own fortune to make, but after he left college, he had to contribute to the support of his mother and three unmarried sisters, who were left in Boston without means when his father went to Halifax.

By his own exertion and industry, he paid his college bills after he entered on his profession, in addition to his other responsible duties, devolving upon him with honor to himself. During 1809-10 Mr. Gore was Governor of Massachusetts. While Governor, he occupied the home corner of Park and Beacon streets, and it is said he drove through the streets of Boston in a carriage drawn by four horses. This was more than the plain republican people of Boston could stand, and they did not want him for Governor again, besides it is undeniable that Mr. Gore was a good deal of an aristocrat at heart, and consequently more or less a loyalist. But he made a fine administrator, and at the end of the term retired to private life, and did not resume the practice of his profession.

In 1791 Christopher Gore purchased in Waltham about 1000 acres of land which formerly belonged to an ancestor of President Garfield. Here Governor Gore erected a stately mansion upon a knoll or rise of the land not far distant from Gore street, where one of the drives, leading to it, runs under rows of stately trees, and through a finely kept lawn. In the rear of the house are the flower gardens, and conservatory, and behind that the kitchen garden; to the west of this is the deer park.

After the death of Governor Gore this stately structure was sold to General Theodore Lyman, who after living there seven years sold it to Singleton Copley Greene, the son of Gardner Green, who married a daughter of Copley the artist, the sister of Lord Lyndhurst: (see p. 216.) Christopher Gore married Rebecca Payne, 11 Nov. 1783. They had no children. Gov. Gore died 1 March 1827, his widow 22 Jan. 1833.

JOHN JEFFRIES.

David Jeffries was born at Rhoad, in Wiltshire, England, 1658, and arrived at Boston, May 9, 1677. He married Sept. 15, 1686, Elizabeth, daughter of John and Elizabeth Usher, by whom he had several children. Of his two sons, John, born Feb. 5, 1688, and David, born June 15, 1690, John became Town Treasurer, was a very prominent citizen. He married Sept. 24, 1713, Anne Clarke, and had issue, an only child Anne, who died young. He went to London in 1710, and returned in 1713. He resided in Tremont Street opposite the King's Chapel.

David Jeffries, Jr., who continued the name, married in 1713, Katherine, daughter of John and Katherine Eyre, by whom he had an only child David, born 23 Oct. 1714. He was a merchant, and in 1715 he sailed for England, and was lost in the Amity, Sept. 13, 1716, on the sands near Dungeness. His son,

DAVID JEFFRIES, married his cousin, Sarah Jaffrey, 1741, by whom he had eight children, all of whom died young except John, born Feb. 4, 1744, alone preserved the name.

JOHN JEFFRIES, the only son of the former, graduated from Harvard College in 1763, having pursued his medical studies with Doctor Lloyd. He continued his study of medicine in London, and was honored with the degree of M. D. at Aberdeen in 1769. In 1771 he was appointed surgeon to the "Captain" a British Ship-of-the-line in Boston Harbor, by his friend, Admiral Montague. He held that position until 1774.

Dr. Jeffries practised in Boston until the Revolution. He landed with the forces at the battle of Bunker Hill, and assisted in dressing the wounded of the Royal Army, and, it is said, identified the body of Warren, in the presence of Sir William Howe. He accompanied the British troops at the evacuation in 1776 to Halifax, and was appointed Chief of the Surgical Staff of Nova Scotia. In 1779 he went to England; and on his return to America, held a high professional employment to the British forces at Charleston and New York. He resigned in 1780, and going to England again, commenced practice in London.

On the 17th of January, 1785, Dr. Jeffries crossed the English channel with Blanchard in a baloon, landing in the forest of Guines in France. This feat procured for him the attention of the most distinguished person-

DR. JOHN JEFFRIES.

Born in Boston Feb. 4, 1774. In his balloon costume. Dr. Jeffries and Blanchard were the first to cross from England to France in a balloon. Died in Boston Sept. 16, 1819.

ages of the day and an introduction to all the learned and scientific societies of Paris.*

Dr. Jeffries' first wife was Sarah Rhoads, whom he married in 1770. By her he had three children, who died unmarried. He married again, Sept. 8, 1787, Hannah, the daughter of William and Hannah Hunt. In 1790 Dr. Jeffries returned to Boston in the ship Lucretia.

He resumed his practice, and delivered the first public lecture on anatomy, a branch of his profession of which he was very fond.** He was eminent as a surgeon, midwife and physician. He attended the poor as faithfully and cheerfully as the rich, and was never known to refuse a professional call. His death occurred in Boston, September 16th, 1819, aged 76 years, after a successful practice of fifty-three years.

Dr. Jeffries had by his second wife eleven children, all of whom died unmarried excepting John, Katherine who married G. C. Haven, Julia Ann, who married Thomas E. Eckley, and George J., who took the name of Jaffrey.***

John Jeffries, son of the doctor, was born March 23, 1796, and became the only representative of the name in the city. He was a distinguished physician in Boston. He married, November 8, 1820, Anne Geyer, daughter of Rufus Greene and Ann (McLean) Amory. His children were Catherine, Anne, Sarah, Augustus, Edward P. and Henry N. Jeffries.

George Jaffrey, an elder son of Dr. John Jeffries, the loyalist, was born December 21, 1789. George Jaffrey, his grand-uncle, who graduated from Harvard College in 1736, became a Counsellor and held various important positions in Portsmouth, N. H. He married Lucy, the daughter of Adam Winthrop, but had no issue. His loyalty to the crown involved him in trouble several times, but he died in 1802 leaving property, then a large amount to George Jaffrey Jeffries, on condition that "he should drop the name of Jeffries; become a permanent resident of Portsmouth, and never follow any profession except that of being a gentleman."

George Jaffrey made his home in Portsmouth and for many years was librarian of the Portsmouth Athenaeum. He died May 4, 1856, and a merited tribute was paid to his character and his labors by Mr. Brewster in the Portsmouth Journal of the 10th.****

The Jeffries family have always ranked among the gentry of Boston, and have maintained that position from the date of the earliest settlement, to the present time.

THOMAS BRINLEY.

Thomas Brinley, Auditor general to Charles First and Second, had

* A narrative of his two aerial voyages was published in London in 1786, exact and entertaining, with a portrait of the adventurer and a view of the monument erected by the French government, on the spot where he landed.
** Curwen's Journal, P. 537.
*** New Eng. Hist. & General Reg., Vol. 15, P. 16.
**** New Eng. Hist. & General Reg., Vol. 15, P. 17.

a son Francis who settled at Barbados, but the climate not being suited to his habits and constitution, came to New England and settled at Newport, R. I., in 1652. This was about fourteen years after the settlement of that place, and Francis Brinley held various offices; among them that of Judge. He occasionally resided in Boston, owning a large estate at the corner of Hanover and Elm streets. He died there in 1719, aged eighty-seven, and was buried in a grave in the King's Chapel burial-ground in Boston, on the spot where the family tomb now stands.

Thomas, son of the latter, was one of the founders of King's Chapel, and resided in Boston. He married Mary Apthorp, and in 1684 went to England, where he died in 1693. His daughter Elizabeth married William Hutchinson, Esq., a graduate of Harvard College, in 1702. Mrs. Brinley, Francis and Elizabeth, returned to Newport, R. I.

Francis Brinley, the son of Thomas, was born in London in 1690, and was educated at Eton. He became a colonel and resided in Roxbury. His mansion was named Datchet from the house of that place in England. Colonel Brinley returned to London, where he died November 27, 1765. Francis Brinley's wife was Deborah, daughter of Edward and Catherine Lyde, and his marriage took place April 18, 1718. They had five sons and two daughters; one of whom married Colonel John Murray, and the other Godfrey Malbone.

Of the sons, THOMAS BRINLEY was a Mandamus Councillor, and lived on Harvard Street. He married his cousin Elizabeth, the daughter of George Cradock, but they left no children. He was a graduate of Harvard College in 1744, and became a Merchant in Boston.

His name appears among the one hundred and twenty-four merchants and others, who addressed Hutchinson in Boston in 1774; and among the ninety-seven gentlemen and principal inhabitants of that town, who addressed Gage in October of the following year. In 1776 he went to Halifax, and thence to England in the same year. In 1778 he was proscribed and banished. His death occurred in 1784, and Elizabeth, his widow, died in England in 1793.

EDWARD BRINLEY, brother of Thomas, married Sarah, daughter of Thomas Tyler and left many descendants.

NATHANIEL BRINLEY, another brother, also married his cousin, Catharine Cradock, was a resident in South Street and at one time lived in Framingham. About 1760 he leased the "Brinley Farm" of Oliver DeLancey, agent of the owner, Admiral Sir Peter Warren, of the Royal Navy, and as is said, employed fifteen or twenty negroes, in its cultivation. It is related that Daniel Shays, the leader of the insurrection in 1786, was in the service of Mr. Brinley on this farm. In 1775 he was an Addresser of Gage, and was ordered, in consequence, to confine himself to his own leasehold. He fled to the Royal Army in Boston, and after the evacuation of that town, he was sent to Framingham by sentence of a Court of Inquiry, ordered to give bond in £600, with two sureties, to remain there four months and to be of good behavior.

"In September 1776, Ebenezer Marshall, in behalf of the Committee of Correspondence, Inspection and Safety, represented that the 'people take him for a very villain,' as he had declared that 'Parliament had an undoubted right to make void the charter in part or in whole'; 'that ten thousand troops, with an artillery, would go through the continent, and subdue it at pleasure'; that he had conveyed 'his best furniture to Roxbury, and moved his family and goods into Boston,' and had himself remained there, 'as long as he could have the protection of the British troops;' that he approved of General Gage's conduct in the highest terms;' that 'his most intimate connections were some of our worst enemies and traitors;' and that, while he had been under their inspection, they had seen nothing 'either in his conduct or disposition, that discovers the least contrition, but otherwise.' "*

To some of these allegations, Mrs. Brinley replied in two memorials to the General Court. She averred that, by the conditions of the recognizance, her husband was entitled to the freedom of the whole of the town of Framingham; that he was in custody on the sole charge of addressing Gage; and that instead of being a refuge in Boston, he was shut up in that town while accidently there, etc. She stated that he at one time had been compelled to work on John Fisk's farm, without liberty to go more than twenty rods from the house unless in Fiske's presence; and that he was denied the free use of pen, ink and paper. She said that after Mr. Brinley had been transferred to the care of Benjamin Eaton, he was not allowed to go from the house, and was fearful that his departure from it would occasion the loss of his life; also that she or any other person was not allowed to converse with him, unless in the hearing of some member of Eaton's family. She urged that he might be removed to some other inland town, and be treated in accordance with his sentence. Mr. Brinley's defence of himself seems to have been the simple remark: "I am a gentleman and have done nothing to forfeit that character." He merely had a rational opinion, but that was enough.

On the 17th September, 1776, the General Court, by resolve, committed him to the care of his father, on security in £600 for his appearance; and, in October of the same year, the committee of Framingham reported to the council that they had disposed of his farm, stock, farm-utensils and household furniture. Nathaniel Brinley removed to Tyngsborough, where his son Robert, married Elizabeth, daughter of John Pitts. This staunch loyalist died at that place in 1814, at the age of eighty-one.

LIST OF CONFISCATED ESTATES BELONGING TO THOMAS BRINLEY IN SUFFOLK COUNTY AND TO WHOM SOLD.

To Gustavus Fellows, Sept. 28, 1782; Lib. 136 fol. 11; Land, dwelling-house, distill house and wharf in Boston, Hollis St. S.; heirs of Joshua Henshaw deceased W.; low water mark..

* Sabine's Loyalists, Vol. 1, P. 256.

REV. JOHN WISWELL.

John and Thomas Wiswell were early residents of Dorchester. John's name is found in the records as early as 1634. His brother Thomas came to Dorchester about 1635. Noah, son of Thomas, born in 1640, was a military man, and was in command in the desperate battle with the Indians near Wheelwright's Pond, N. H., where he and his son John were killed, July 6th, 1690. Another son of Thomas, Inchabod, born in 1637, was minister of Duxbury. He had a son Peleg, born in 1683, who was schoolmaster at Charlestown in 1704. John Wiswell, son of Peleg, married Elizabeth, daughter of Dr. Samuel Rogers, graduated from Harvard College in 1705, was a master of a Boston Grammar School in 1719. He died in 1767, aged 84 and is buried in Copps Hill burying ground.

JOHN WISWELL, son of the aforesaid, was born in 1731, and graduated from Harvard College in 1749. In 1753 he was teaching school in Maine, but he pursued the study of divinity as a Congregationalist. Occasionally he preached, and in 1756 he was invited to become the pastor of the New Casco parish in Falmouth, now Portland, and was ordained November third of that year. In 1761 he married Mercy, the daughter of Judge John Minot, of Brunswick.

In 1764 John Wiswell suddenly changed his religious views and left his people. He embraced the Episcopal form of worship, and preached for several Sundays in the town-house. On September 4, 1764, the Parish of St. Paul's Church, Falmouth, was organized and Mr. Wiswell was invited to become their rector. For want of a bishop in the colonies, he was obliged to go to England to receive ordination. A writer at this time says, "There was a sad uproar about Wiswell, who has declared for the church and accepted of the call our churchmen have given him to be their minister." They voted him £100 a year and later he received £20 as a Missionary from the Missionary Society. After a years elapse, he was able to report to the Society in London for the propagation of the Gospel in Foreign Parts, that his Congregation had increased to seventy families, and the admittance of twenty-one persons to the communion. In 1765 the parish addressed a letter to the Rev. Mr. Hooper of Boston, asking his good offices in enlisting the sympathy of the churchmen there, in behalf of their oppressed fellow-worshippers in Falmouth. John Wiswell was an ardent Loyalist, as were about twenty of the leading men of his church. He continued to preach until the revolution broke out. After the trouble came in the colonies, he was siezed while out walking one day with Captain Mowatt, by Colonel Samuel Thompson of Brunswick, who had arrived with about fifty men unknown to the inhabitants. Colonel Thompson refused to release Mr. Wiswell, and Captain Mowatt, but finally seeing that the town was against him, he consented to release them if they would give their parole to deliver themselves up next day. After his capture, the clergyman was obliged to declare his abhorrence of the doctrine of passive obedience and non-resistance, and was then released. Mr. Wiswell now joined the British Forces, and after going on board a man-of-war addressed a letter to the wardens of his church, resigning his charge. After Captain Mowatt burned Falmouth, he sailed to Boston, and then to England. After leaving his parish he was for three years a chaplain on the British Naval Ship Boyne, and later for a short time was a curate in Suffolk. He and fifteen others from Falmouth had their estates confiscated, and were banished.

At the close of the war, Mr. Wiswell accepted the call of some of his former parishioners, and settled in Cornwallis, Nova Scotia, over a parish they had formed there, and in 1782 he was appointed a missionary of that place. Having lost his first wife, he married a widow Hutchinson from the Jerseys, as the Rev. Jacob Bailey, the frontier missionary writes, who married them. John Wiswell was afterwards a missionary at Aylesford, and after a very full and worthy life, died at Nova Scotia in 1812, at the age of eighty-one. He left two sons, born in Falmouth, who were Lieutenants in the Navy. Peleg, one of his sons, was appointed Judge of the Supreme Court, of Nova Scotia, in 1816 and died at Annapolis in 1836, at the age of seventy-three. When the Rev. John Wiswall lived in Falmouth, Maine, he occupied a house painted red, which stood on the corner of Middle and Exchange Streets, afterwards owned and occupied by James Deering, and which gave place to the brick block built by that gentleman.

HENRY BARNES.

John Barnes, and his wife Elizabeth (Perrie) came to Boston about 1710. He was a prominent merchant, and was in partnership with John Arbuthnot, who married Abigall Little, of Pembroke, in 1719, and whose daughter Christian married Henry, the son of John Barnes, Sept. 26, 1746. John Barnes was a prominent Episcopalian, was vestryman of King's Chapel from 1715 to 1724, warden from 1724 to 1728, was the first mentioned of the trustees concerned in the purchase of land for Christ Church, and afterwards of those who bought of Leonard Vassal, Esq., his estate on Summer street (see p. 286) for the building of Trinity Church. His home in Boston was on the north side of Beacon street, extending from Freeman Place to Bowdoin street, a portion of which is now occupied by the Hotel Bellevue, he purchased this property in 1721, and died, seized of it. In 1756 it was conveyed by John Erving (see p. 298) to James Bowdoin.

John Barnes died early in 1739 at Clemente Bar, St. Mary Co., Maryland. His wife died in 1742 in Boston.

Among their children was Elizabeth, who married Nathaniel Coffin the Cashire (see p. 234). Among their distinguished children were

General John Coffin and Admiral Sir Isaac Coffin, of the British Navy.

Catherine, another daughter, born in 1715, married Colonel Thomas Goldthwaite (see p. 356). She was his second wife, and died at Walthamston, England, 1796, aged 81.

HENRY BARNES. The subject of this memoir was baptized Nov. 20, 1723. He was brought up in his father's business, and established himself as a merchant in Marlborough, Mass., in 1753, and was appointed magistrate. He was possessed of considerable property, and was one of the largest tax payers in the town, and was the owner of several slaves, one of whom "Daphne," he left in Marlborough, and she was supported out of his estate.

Henry Barnes was thoroughly loyal, and for that reason he was probably the best hated man in Marlborough. A late town history says Marlborough was cursed by a Loyalist named Henry Barnes.

Towards the close of February, 1775, General Gage ordered Captain Brown and Ensign D'Bernicre to go through the Counties of Suffolk and Worcester, and to sketch the roads as they went, for his information, as he expected to march troops through that country the ensuing spring. Their adventures after their departure for Marlborough, are related by one of them as follows:

"At two o'clock it ceased snowing a little, and we resolved to set off for Marlborough, which was about sixteen miles off. We found the roads very bad, every step up to our ancles; we passed through Sudbury, a large village near a mile long; the causeway lies over a great swamp, or overflowing of Sudbury river, and is commanded by a high ground on the opposite side. Nobody took the least notice of us, till we arrived within three miles of Marlborough, (it was snowing very hard all the while,) when a horseman overtook us, and asked us from whence we came—we said from Weston; he asked us if we lived there—we said no; he then asked where we resided, and, as we found there was no evading his questions, we told him we lived in Boston. He then asked us where we were going; we told him to Marlborough, to see a friend; (as we intended to go to Mr. Barnes's, a gentleman to whom we were recommended, and a friend to the Government;) he then asked us, if we were of the army; we said no, but were a good deal alarmed at his asking us that question; he asked several rather impertinent questions, and then rode on for Marlborough, as we suppose, to give them intelligence of our coming—for on our arrival the people came out of their houses (though it snowed and blew very hard) to look at us; in particular, a baker asked Capt. Brown, 'Where are you going, Master?' He answered, to see Mr. Barnes.*

"We proceeded to Barnes's, and on our beginning to make an apology for taking the liberty to make use of his house, and discovering to him that we were officers in disguise, he told us that we need not be at

---

* The horseman that met them was Col. Timothy Bigelow, of the Committee of Safety.

the pains of telling him, that he knew our situation, that we were very well known, he was afraid, by the town's people. We begged he would recommend some tavern where we should be safe; he told us we would be safe no where but in his house; that the town was very violent, and that we had been expected at Col. Williams's tavern, the night before, where there had gone a party of liberty people to meet us. While we were talking, the people were gathering in little groups in every part of the town (village).

"Mr. Barnes asked us who had spoken to us on our coming into town; we told him a baker; he seemed a little startled at that, told us that he was a very mischievous fellow, and that there was a deserter at his house. Capt. Brown asked the man's name; he said it was Sawin, and that he had been a drummer. Brown knew him too well, as he was a man of his own Company, and had not been gone above a month; so we found we were discovered. We asked Mr. Barnes, if they did get us into their hands what they would do with us; he did not seem to like to answer; we asked him again; he then said, he knew the people very well, that we might expect the worst treatment from them.

"Immediately after this, Mr. Barnes was called out; he returned a little after, and told us the Doctor of the town had come to tell him, he was come to sup with him, (now this fellow had not been within Mr. Barnes's doors for two years before, and came now for no other business than to see and betray us). Barnes told him he had company, and could not have the pleasure of attending him that night; at this the fellow staid about the house, and asked one of Mr. Barnes's children, who her father had got with him; the child innocently answered, that she had asked her papa, but he told her it was not her business; he then went, I suppose, to tell the rest of his crew.

"When we found we were in that situation, we resolved to lie down for two or three hours, and set off at twelve o'clock at night; so we got some supper on the table, and were just beginning to eat, when Mr. Barnes, who had been making inquiries of his servant, found the people intended to attack us; he then told us plainly, that he was very uneasy for us, that we could be no longer in safety in the town; upon which we resolved to set off immediately, and asked Mr. Barnes if there was no road round the town, so that we might not be seen. He took us out of his house by the stable, and directed us by a by-road which was to lead us a quarter of a mile from the town; it snowed and blew as much as I ever saw in my life. However, we walked pretty fast, fearing we should be pursued; at first we felt much fatigued, having not been more than twenty minutes at Barnes's to refresh ourselves, and the roads were worse, if possible, than when we came; but in a little time it wore off, and we got on without being pursued, as far as the hills which command the causeway at Sudbury, and went into a little wood, where we eat a bit of bread that we took from Barnes's, and eat a little snow to wash it down.

"A few days after our return, Mr. Barnes came to town from Marlborough, and told us that immediately after our quitting town, the Committee of Correspondence came to his house, and demanded us; he told them we were gone; they then searched his house from top to bottom, looking under the beds and in the cellar, and when they found we were gone, they told him, if they had caught us in his house, they would have pulled it down about his ears. They sent horsemen after us on every road, but we had the start of them, and the weather being so very bad, they did not overtake us, or missed us. Barnes told them we were not officers, but relatives of his wife's from Penobscot, and were going to Lancaster; that perhaps deceived them."

In the House of Representatives, November, 1775, the "Petition of Henry Knox * humbly showeth. That your petitioner having been obliged to leave all his goods and home furniture in Boston, which he has no prospect of ever getting possession of again, nor any equivalent for the same, therefore begs the Honorable Court, if in their wisdom see fit, to permit him to exchange house furniture, with Henry Barnes, late of Marlborough, which he now has in his power to do." The prayer was refused, but he was allowed to *use* the Loyalist's goods, on giving receipt to account for them to the proper authorities.

In December, 1775, Catherine Goldthwaite prayed the interposition of the General Court, stating in a petition that she was the neice and adopted heir of Barnes; that she had resided with him about seventeen years, that at his departure from town, she was left with a part of his family in possession, and that the committee of Marlborough had entered upon his estate, sold a part, and proposed to dispossess her entirely. No redress could be obtained.

Through the violence of the mob Henry Barnes was forced to seek shelter in Boston early in 1775. From there he went to England. In 1777 he was at Bristol with his wife and neice, and in September thirteen of his fellow Loyalists were his guests, and later still in the same year he dined with several of the Massachusetts exiles at Mr. Lechmere's, when the conversation was much about the political condition of their native land.

Mr. Barnes was proscribed and banished, and his estate confiscated. He died at London in 1808, at the age of eighty-four.

THOMAS FLUCKER.

Secretary of Massachusetts Bay.

The Fluckers were descended from a French Huguenot family who settled in England. Captain James Flucker, mariner, came to America and married Elizabeth Luist at Charlestown, Mass., May 30, 1717. He

* Subsequently Chief of Artillery in the Revolutionary Army, and Secretary at War under Washington.

was taxed there from 1727 to 1756 and died 3 Nov. 1756. She died Sept. 1770. They had eight children.*

THOMAS FLUCKER, son of the aforesaid, was born at Charlestown, 9 Oct. 1719. He was a merchant in Boston and owned an estate on Summer street. He was commissioned a Justice of the Peace 14 Sept. 1756, was a member of the Council in 1761-68. A Selectman of Boston in 1766, succeeded Andrew Oliver as Secretary, 12 Nov. 1770, was made a Mandamus Councillor 9 Aug. 1774. He married 1st, 12 June 1744, Judith, daughter of Hon. James Bowdoin, a Boston Huguenot family, and as a testimony to the public spirit of this famous family, Bowdoin College remains. 2nd, 14 Jan. 1751, he married Hannah, daughter of General Samuel Waldo, proprietor of the Waldo Patent Main, to whose heirs the great domain descended. The portion belonging to Mrs. Flucker and her brother, were confiscated.

Thomas Flucker was a staunch Loyalist. He was banished and his estates confiscated. He left Boston at the evacuation, March 17, 1776, for Halifax. He afterwards went to London, where he was a member of the Brompton Row Association of Loyalists, who met weekly for conversation and a dinner. An extract from Hutchinson's Diary, July 13, 1776, says:

"Flucker dined with us; depends on the truth of the report of his family's being arrived in Ireland; has 300£ allowed by treasury; last (?) of the Council 200£." Thomas Flucker died in England suddenly on Feb. 16, 1783. His wife remained in England, but survived him only three years.

THOMAS FLUCKER, of Massachusetts, son of the former, graduated at Harvard University in 1773. During the Revolution he was a Lieutenant in the 60th British regiment at St. Augustine, Fla., in 1777. By the University catalogue, it appears that he and his father died the same year, 1783.

LUCY FLUCKER, another child, born 2 August 1756, married General Henry Knox of the revolutionary army, and afterwards Secretary at War. The young rebel had at the time a flourishing bookstore opposite Williams Court in Cornhill, a fashionable morning resort at that time for the British officers and their ladies. Harrison Gray Otis says that Miss Lucy "was distinguished as a young lady of high intellectual endowments, very fond of books, especially of the books sold by Knox, at whose premises was kindled as the story went, 'the guiltless flame' which was destined to burn on the hymeneal altar." Henry Knox became Chief of Artillery in the Revolution, and in Washington's Administration, Secretary of War. He acquired on easy terms, a very large share of Mrs. Flucker's property, which had been confiscated, and settled on it at Thomaston, Maine, building a fine mansion in which he himself died in 1806, and his wife in 1824.

Sally Flucker, another daughter of Thomas Flucker, Jr., who per-

* See Life of Henry Knox by F. G. Drake, P. 125.

formed in Burgoyne's "Maid of the Oaks" in private theatricals given by British officers in Boston, accompanied the family to England and married Mr. Jephson, a member of the Irish Parliament. Copley painted her portrait.

Hannah Flucker, daughter of Thomas, married 2 Nov. 1774, James Urquhart, captain in the 14th regiment, which was engaged in the battle of Bunker Hill.

MARGARET DRAPER.

Richard Draper and his brother William emigrated to the Colonies and settled at Boston about 1680. He was a merchant in that city. The Boston Records state that Richard Draper and John Wentworth furnished the lumber from which Faneuil Hall was built. In his will he says that he is the son of Edward and Ann Draper, of Branbury, in the County of Oxford, Great Britain, deceased, and only brother to William Draper Senr. of Boston. This will was probated Jan. 25th, 1728.

About the year 1700 the Postmaster of Boston was one John Campbell, a Scotchman, and son of Duncan Campbell, the organizer of the postal system of America. He was also a bookseller. In those early days the dissemination of news was in the hands of the postmasters of each town, and John Campbell on Monday, April 24, 1704, improved the present system by *printing the news.* He issued the first number of the Boston "News Letter," the first newspaper issued in America. The first sheet of the first number was taken damp from the press by Chief Justice Sewell, to show to President Willard, of Harvard College, as a wonderful curiosity. Bartholomew Green, eldest son of Thomas Green, printer to Cambridge University, was the printer. He obtained possession of the newspaper in 1721, shortly after Campbell was removed from the post-office in Boston. On his death in 1733, it passed into the hands of his son-in-law, John Draper, son of Richard Draper, who continued to publish it until his death in 1762, when he was succeeded by his son Richard Draper, who changed the title to the "Massachusetts Gazette and Boston News Letter." He was brought up a printer by his father, and continued with him after he became of age, and was for some years before his father's death a silent partner with him. He was early appointed printer to the Council and Government, which he retained during life. Under his successful editorship, the paper was devoted to the Government, and in the controversy with Great Britain, he strongly supported the Loyalists cause, and illustrated the head of his paper with the King's Arms. Many able advocates of the Government filled the columns of the "News-Letter" but the opposition papers were supported by writers at least equally powerful and numerous.

The Drapers were considered the most eminent and successful printers in America. A list of works containing their imprints would fill pages.

Richard Draper was a man of feeble health, and was remarkable for the delicacy of his mind and gentleness of his manner. No stain rests on his character. He was attentive to his affairs, and was esteemed as the best compiler of news of his day. Having been successful in his business and acquired a competency, he erected a handsome brick home on a convenient spot in front of the old printing home in Newbury, now Washington street, where he resided, and which was afterwards confiscated. He died June 6th, 1774, aged 47, without children, and was succeeded by his widow, Margaret, who was a granddaughter of Bartholomew Green.

A month before his death, he had taken John Boyle into partnership, but at the outbreak of hostilities, his sympathies being strong for the Revolutionary cause, he was not agreeable to Widow Margaret, and was succeeded in the partnership by John Howe, who was a devoted loyalist, and continued with her until the final suspension of the paper, which occurred on the evacuation of Boston, by the British troops, when Margaret departed with the soldiers, going first to Halifax and thence to England, where she enjoyed a pension from the British Government for the remainder of her life, in return for her loyalty and devotion to the Government.

Margaret Draper's paper was the only one published in Boston during the siege. It had been published without intermission for 72 years. She died in London in 1807, and was included in the confiscation and banishment Act.

LIST OF CONFISCATED ESTATES BELONGING TO MARGRATE DRAPER IN SUFFOLK COUNTY AND TO WHOM SOLD.

To Richard Devens, Feb. 7, 1783; Lib. 137, fol. 48; Land and buildings in Boston, Newbury St. W.; heirs of Benjamin Church S. and E.; Josiah Waters, Jr. N.

RICHARD CLARKE.

RICHARD CLARKE was the son of Francis Clarke, merchant, a descendant of an old Boston family. Richard graduated at Harvard College in 1729. He and his sons were the consignees of a part of the tea destroyed in Boston by the celebrated "Tea Party" December 1773. In a letter from Messrs. Clarke & Sons to Mr. Abram Dupuis they say: "On the morning of the 2nd inst. about one o'clock, we were roused out of our sleep by a violent knocking at the door of our house, and on looking out of the window we saw (for the moon shone very bright) two men in the courtyard. One of them said he brought us a letter from the country. A servant took the letter from him at the door, the contents of which was as follows:

Boston, 1st Nov., 1773.

Richard Clarke & Son:

The Freemen of this Province understand from good authority, that there is a quantity of tea consigned to your house by the East India Company, which is destructive to the happiness of every well wisher to the country. It is therefore expected that you personally appear at Liberty Tree, on Wednesday next, at twelve o'clock at noon day, to make a public resignation of your commission, agreeable to a notification of this day for that purpose.

Fail not upon your peril. O. C.

In this you may observe a design to create a public belief that the factors had consented to resign their trust on Wednesday, the 3d inst., on which day we were summoned by the above-mentioned letter, to appear at Liberty Tree at 12 o'clock noon. All the bells of the meeting houses for public worship were set a-ringing at 11 o'clock, and continued ringing till twelve; the town cryer went thro' the town summoning the people to assemble at "Liberty Tree." By these methods, and some more secret ones, made use of by the authors of this design, a number of people supposed by some to be about 500, and by others more, were collected by the time and place mentioned in the printed notification.

They consisted mostly of people of the lowest rank, very few reputable tradesmen, as we are informed, appeared amongst them. The gentlemen who are supposed the designed factors for the East India Company, viz: Mr. Thos. Hutchinson, Mr. Faneuil, Mr. Winslow and Messrs. Clarke, met in the forenoon of the 3rd inst., at the latter's warehouse, the lower end of King street. You may well judge that none of us entertained the least thought of obeying the summons sent us to attend at Liberty Tree. After a consultation amongst ourselves and friends, we judged it best to continue together, and to endeavour, with the assistance of a few friends, to oppose the designs of the mob, if they should come to offer us any insult or injury. And on this occasion we were so happy as to be supported by a number of gentlemen of the first rank. About one o'clock, a large body of people appeared at the head of King Street, and came down to the end, and halted opposite to our warehouse. Nine persons came from them up into our counting room, viz., Mr. Molineux, Mr. Wm. Dennie, Doctor Warren, Dr. Church, Major Barber, Mr. Henderson, Mr. Gabriel Johonnot, Mr. Proctor and Mr. Ezekiel Cheever. Mr. Molineux as speaker of the above Committee, addressed himself to us, and the other gentlemen present, and told us that we had committed an high insult on the people, in refusing to give them that most reasonable satisfaction which had been demanded in the summons which had been sent us, then read a paper proposed by him, to be subscribed by the factors importing, that they solemnly promise that they would not land or pay duty on any tea that should be sent by the East India Company, but they would send back the tea to England in the same bottom, which extravagent demand being firmly refused, and treated with proper contempt by all of us. Mr. Molineux then said that since we had refused their most reasonable demands, we must expect to feel, on our first appearance, the utmost weight of the people's resentment, upon which he and the rest of the committee left our counting room and warehouse, and went to, and mixed, with the multitude that continued before our warehouse. Soon after this the mob having made one or two reverse motions to some distance, we perceived them hastening their pace towards the store, on which we ordered our servant to shut the outward door; but this he could not effect, although assisted by some other persons amongst whom were Nathaniel Hatch, Esq., one of the Justices of the inferior Court for this country, and a Justice of the Peace for the county. This gentleman made all possible exertions to stem the current of the mob, not only by declaring repeatedly, and with a loud voice, that he was a magistrate, and commanded the people, by virtue of his office, and in his Majesty's name, to desist from all riotous proceedings, and to disperse, but also by assisting in person; but the people not only made him a return, of insulting and reproachful words, but prevented his endeavors by force and blows, to get our doors shut, upon which Mr. Hatch, with some other of our friends, retreated to our counting room. Soon after this, the outward doors of the store were taken off their hinges by the mob, and carried to some distance; immediately a number of the mob rushed into the warehouse, and endeavoured to force into the counting room, but as this was in another story, and the staircase leading to it narrow, we, with our friends,—about twenty in number—by some vigorous efforts, prevented their accomplishing their design. The mob appeared in a short time to be dispersed, and after a few more faint attacks, they contented themselves with blocking us up in the store for the space of about an hour and a half, at which time, perceiving that much the greatest part of them were drawn off, and those that remained not formidable, we, with our friends, left the warehouse, walked up the length of King Street together, and then went to our respective homes without any molestation, saving some insulting behavior from a few dispicable persons.

The night following, a menacing letter was thrust under Mr. Faneuil's door, to be communicated to the other consignees, with a design to intimidate them from executing their trust, and other methods have since been made use of in the public papers and otherwise, for the same purpose."*

On the morning of November 17, 1773, a little party of family friends had assembled at the home of Richard Clarke, Esq., near the King's Chapel on School Street, to welcome young Jonathan Clarke, who had just arrived from London. All at once the inmates of the dwelling were startled by a violent beating at the door, accompanied with shouts and the blowing of horns, creating considerable alarm. The ladies were hastily bestowed in places of safety, while the gentlemen secured the avenues of the lower story, as well as they were able. The yard and vicinity

* "Tea Leaves." pp. 282, 3, 4, 5, 6.

were soon filled with people. One of the inmates warned them from an upper window, to disperse, but getting no other reply, than a shower of stones, he discharged a pistol. Then came a shower of misseles, which broke in the lower windows and damaged some of the furniture. Some influential Revolutionists had by this time arrived, and put a stop to the proceedings of the mob, which then dispersed. The consignees then called upon the governor and council for protection.

The eventful Thursday, December 16, 1773, a day ever memorable in the annals of Boston, witnessed the largest mob yet assembled in Boston. Nearly seven thousand persons collected at the Old South Meeting House. The tea ships had not taken out clearance papers, the twenty days allowed by law terminated that night. Then the revenue officers could take possession, and under cover of the naval force, land the tea, and opposition to this would have caused bloody work. The Revolutionists desired to avoid this issue, so it was decided to destroy the tea. Rotch, the owner of the "Dartmouth," applied to Governor Hutchinson, at his residence in Milton, for a pass to proceed with his vessel to London, for the governor had ordered Colonel Leslie, commander of the castle, and Admiral Montagu, to guard the passages to the sea, and permit no unauthorized vessels to pass. The governor offered Rotch a letter to Admiral Montagu, commending ship and goods to his protection, if Rotch would agree to have his ship haul out into the stream, but he replied that none were willing to assist him in doing this, and the attempt would subject him to the ill will of the people. The governor then sternly refused a pass, as it would have been "a direct countenancing and encouraging the violation of the acts of trade."

Between six and seven o'clock in the evening three different mobs disguised as Indians proceeded from different parts of the town, arrived with axes and hatchets, and hurried to Griffin's (now Liverpool wharf), boarded the three tea ships, and, warning their crews and the custom house officers, to keep out of the way, in less than three hours time had broken and emptied into the dock three hundred and forty-two chests of tea, valued at £18,000. A Loyalist writer of the time says: "Now this crime of the Bostonians, was a compound of the grossest injury and insult. It was an act of the highest insolence towards government, such a mildness itself cannot overlook or forgive. The injustice of the deed was also most atrocious, as it was the destruction of property to a vast amount, when it was known that the nation was obliged in honor to protect it." This memorable occurrence was undoubtedly in the immediate sequence of the events which it produced, the proximate cause of the American Revolution.*

Richard Clarke was treated with much severity by the Revolutionists. His name is found with the Addressers of General Gage. He arrived in London December 24, 1775, after a passage of "only" twenty-one days from Boston. He was one of the original members of the Loyalist Club,

* See Page 48 for further particulars concerning the Tea Pary Mob.

for a weekly dinner, and discourses. He lived with his son-in-law, Copley the painter, Leicester Square. Lord Lyndhurst was his grandson. He died in England in 1795.

JONATHAN CLARKE, son of Richard Clarke, accompanied his father to England. He was his father's partner in business. He was a member in 1776 of the Loyalists Club, in London, and had lodgings in Brompton Row the next year. In 1778 he was proscribed and banished. After the Revolution he went to Canada.

ISAAC WINSLOW CLARKE, son of Richard Clarke, was born in Boston, 27 October, 1746. He was sent by his father to Plymouth to collect debts, but in the night was assaulted by a mob and obliged to flee from the town, to escape from personal injuries. He became Commissary-General of Lower Canada, and died in that Colony in 1822, after he had embarked for England. His daughter Susan married Charles Richard Ogden, Esq., Solicitor-General of Lower Canada, in 1829.

PETER JOHONNOT.

The Johonnots in America are of French Huguenot origin. Daniel Johonnot, who was born in France about 1668, was one of the first parties of thirty families that arrived in Boston in 1686. He was in company with his uncle Andrae Sigournie, Distiller, from Rochelle, and went with him to Oxford in New England, remaining there until the settlement was broken up by the incursion of Indians August 25, 1696. Jean Jeanson (John Johnson) and his three children were killed during the massacre. Mrs. Johnson was Andrew Sigourney's daughter, and tradition in the Johonnot family relates that she was rescued at that time from the Indians by her cousin, Daniel Johonnot, to whom she was subsequently married.*

The first record we have of Daniel Johonnot in Boston was at the time of his marriage "on the 18th of April, by the Rev. Samuel Willard of the Old South Church, to Susan Johnson." This was in the year 1700. In 1714 it appears by the Suffolk Records he purchased for £300 "current money," of John Borland and Sarah his wife, an estate near the Mill Creek and bounded by Mill Pond, and the street leading to said pond (Union Street) etc. His last purchase of real estate was near the Old South Church and this land was afterwards occupied by one of the descendants of his daughter Mary, Mary Anne (Boyer), number 156 Washington street, opposite the Province House. At the time of Daniel Johonnot's death it was occupied by his grandson, and must have been Mr. Johonnot's last residence, as in an inventory it is described as being in the possession of Mr. Daniel Boyer. In Mr. Johonnot's French Bible, Amsterdam Edition of 1700, are recorded the births of his six

*New England Hist. and Geneological Register. Vol. 6. P. 357.

children in French, all children of Daniel and Serzane Johonnot. This Bible later came into the possession of one of his descendants. Daniel Johonnot died in Boston in June, 1748 at the age of eighty years. His wife died some time after 1731, and before the death of her husband. He was remembered as being a friend to the poor, always industrious and frugal.

Zacherie (Zachariah) Johonnot, the eldest son of the preceding was born in Boston January 20, 1700-1. His first wife was Elizabeth Quincy, who died during the revolution, and he married again, April 24, 1777, Margaret Le Mercier. daughter of Andrew Le Mercier, Minister of the French Protestant church in Boston.

Like his father he was a Distiller and engaged in mercantile pursuits. His dwelling house and store was on Orange street at the South part of the town, and his distillery was on Harvard street directly opposite his dwelling. At the end of the same street was his wharf, and wooden distil-house, storehouses, etc. His house and store were burnt at the time of the great fire, April 20, 1787. The spacious gardens filled with rare fruit trees, beautiful flowers and shrubs from his father's land were mostly destroyed.

Mr. Johonnot died in Boston in 1784 at the age of eighty-three. To his son Peter (then in England) he bequeathed "his mansion house, store adjoining, yard and garden, as the same is now fenced in, etc." He had ten children, all by his first wife.

PETER JOHONNOT, the fourth child of the preceding, was born in Boston September 23, 1729. He was married January 10, 1750 to Katherine Dudley by the Rev. Mather Byles. She was the daughter of the Honorable William Dudley (son of Governor Joseph Dudley). Peter Johonnot was a Distiller, and lived in Boston. In 1775 he was an Addresser of Gage. The next year he was one of the committee with Thomas and Jonathan Amory, chosen by the citizens of Boston March 8, 1776, to communicate with General Howe and take measures to avert the impending destruction, threatened by him, in case his army should be molested while evacuating the town.

In 1776 Peter Johonnot went to Halifax and thence to England. In 1778 he was proscribed and banished, and in 1779 he was a loyal Addresser to the King. Mrs. Johonnot's death occurred in Boston in 1769. Mr. Johonnot died in London August 8, 1809, at the age of eighty, and left no issue.* The following occurs in the Diary of Dr. P. Oliver:—"1809, Aug.—Peter Johonnot died this month in London, aged 79."

FRANCIS JOHONNOT, son of Daniel, was born November 30, 1709. He married Mary Johnson of Boston, widow, 1752. He was a distiller and engaged in mercantile pursuits. His distillery was near Essex street on the margin of the South Cove. His "Mansion house" was on Newbury, now Washington street, the same was owned and occupied

*New England Hist. and Gen. Reg. Vol. 7. P. 142.

for many years by his son-in-law Eben Oliver, Esq. He was a loyalist, and at the beginning of the revolution went to England. He died March 8, 1775. Mary, his widow, who died in Boston March 17, 1797, in her seventy-third year, administered upon his estate in Massachusetts. They had seven children.

MARY JOHONNOT, daughter of Andrew Johonnot, and cousin to Peter the Loyalist, was born in 1730. She married Thomas Edwards of Boston, June 13, 1758, the ceremony being performed by the Rev. Henry Caner of King's Chapel. Mr. Edwards for a while was engaged in mercantile business in Middletown, Connecticut, but later returned to Boston, and was employed by the government. He was a loyalist and went to Halifax in 1776 and thence to England. He died in London at an advanced age. Mary Johonnot, his wife, died in Boston, February 14, 1792. They had five children.

LIST OF CONFISCATED ESTATES BELONGING TO PETER JOHONNOT IN SUFFOLK COUNTY AND TO WHOM SOLD.

To Ebenezer Seaver, Sept. 4, 1782; Lib. 135, fol. 190; Land and buildings in Boston, Orange St. E.; Samuel Pope and Hopestill Foster S.; Joseph Lovell and heirs of William Ettridge W.; Zachariah Johonnot N.

JOHN JOY.

The name of Joy was probably derived from Jouy in Normandy and may have reached England in the form of "de Jouy." William Joy was a Vicar in England in 1395. The name was borne with distinction in England and Ireland for at least five centuries.

Thomas Joy, of Boston, Massachusetts, was born about 1610 in the county of Norfolk, England. The first time he appears in Boston records is "on the 20th of 12th Month, called February, 1636." By trade he was a builder and probably continued that occupation in Massachusetts. He married in 1637 Joan Gallop, the daughter of a well-known townsman, and she became mother of the American Joys. Her father's land included several of the harbor islands, one of which still bears his name.

Thomas Joy built in 1657-8, the house in the Market Place, which was at once the armory, court house, and town hall of Boston, and the first seat of government in Massachusetts. On account of political troubles, Thomas Joy exchanged part of his possessions in Boston for property in Hingham. In 1648 he removed to that town, but his Boston connections were still maintained. He had interests in mills at Hingham, and died in that town, October 21, 1678. His widow survived him more than twelve years, dying in Hingham, March 20, 1690-1.

Both are buried in the hill, back of most ancient Protestant church in the United States, where they worshipped. They had ten children.

Joseph, the fourth child, was born in Boston, April 1, 1645. He lived on Bacheler (Main Street,) Hingham, nearly opposite the meeting house, of which he is thought to have been the builder. He married August 29, 1667, Mary, daughter of John and Margaret Prince, of Hingham, and by her had fifteen children. He died in that town, May 31, 1697.

Joseph Joy, his eldest son was born in Hingham July 30, 1688. He was constable in 1697-1711. He married May 22, 1690 Elizabeth, daughter of Captain Thomas Andrews. He died in Hingham, April 29, 1716. His gravestone with inscription still legible in the Hingham churchyard is the most ancient Joy grave mark in America.* He had nine children.

John, the fourth child, was born in Hingham February 7, 1695-6. He lived on Main street at Hingham Centre. December 7, 1724, he married Lydia, daughter of Samuel Lincoln, and by her had seven children. His death is not recorded.

JOHN JOY, the second child of the preceding, was born in Hingham June 4, 1727. He lived in Boston, and by trade was merchant and housewright. He married Sarah, daughter of Michael and Sarah (Kneeland) Homer, of Boston. In 1767 and 1773 he was one of the "principal citizens" to visit the schools with the Governor. In 1774 Mr. Joy was an addresser of Hutchinson, and in 1775 of Gage. In 1776 he went to Halifax with his familly and in 1778 he was proscribed and banished. In 1779 he was in England, where he remained, though several of his sons afterwards returned to America. Hutchinson in his diary, June 7, 1776, speaks of a number of Loyalists who had recently arrived at Dover. Mr. Joy's name was among those mentioned. The Loyalist died in London, December, 1804. His portrait by Copley, is an heirloom in the family of the late Charles Joy of Boston. Mrs. Joy died in England in 1805.

A letter of John Wendell (1806) mentions among his early friends in Boston, "Mr. John Joy, who served his time with our respected neighbor, Captain Benjamin Russell, and who afterwards married Mr. Homer's daughter." Mr. Joy had seven children.

DR. JOHN JOY, the eldest son, was an apothecary, and returned to America in 1783, and lived in Boston. His estate on Beacon Hill, once the "elm pasture" of Judge Samuel Sewell, the diarist, was bounded by Beacon, Walnut, Mt. Vernon and Joy street, and included about 100,000 sq. ft. of land. Bowditch says Dr. Joy was desirous of getting a house *in the country*, and selected this locality as "being country enough for him," "the barberry bushes were flourishing over this whole area." His land cost about $2000, and in 1833 his heirs sold this lot for $98,000. On the southeastern part of this estate he built a modest and graceful wood-

*Thomas Joy and His Descendants by James R. Joy.

en building, which was eventually moved to South Boston Point. He married Abigal Green of Boston, and died in 1813.

MICHAEL JOY, another son, was born at Boston in 1754, went to England with his father and died at Hartham Park, England July 10, 1825. Graduated B. A., Harvard College, 1771, and admitted to the same degree at Princeton College, N. J., 1771. He married a lady named Hall in England. His son Henry Hall Joy, of Hartham Park, was a lawyer and Queen's Counsel, was buried in the Temple Church, London.

BENJAMIN JOY, the third son of the Loyalist, was born in Boston, Dec. 27th, 1757, and died at Boston, April 14, 1829. He returned to Boston, was a merchant and was the first Consul General of the United States at Calcutta, holding his commission from President Washington. In 1808 he bought of the trustees of the First Church their property on Cornhill Square, on which he erected Joy's Building, which for three-fourths of a century was a landmark of Boston, people came from miles around to view the stately edifice, and were greatly astonished at its magnificence. The Rogers Building, in front of Young's Hotel, now occupies its site. He was one of the Mt. Vernon proprietors that acquired the valuable lands of John Singleton Copley on Beacon Hill, and a spring in one of his houses on the east side of Charles street, is the famous spring of water which William Blackstone, the first white settler of Boston, mentioned as one of the chief attractions of the Shawmut peninsula.

RICHARD LECHMERE.

Hon. Thomas Lechmere was for many years Surveyor General of His Majesty's Customs for the Northern District of America. His brother was Lord Lechmere of Evesham, who married the daughter of the Earl of Carlisle.

Thomas Lechmere married Ann Winthrop, a descendant of Governor Winthrop, the ceremony was performed by Rev. Eben Pemberton, Nov. 17, 1709. He died at an advanced age, June 4th, 1765, having been born in June, 1683. His wife died in 1746.

RICHARD LECHMERE, son of the above, married Mary Phips, of Cambridge in 1753. She was the daughter of Spencer Phips, who was Lieut. Governor for many years; his farm was what is now known as East Cambridge, and the house stood near where the modern Court House, afterwards was built; General Gage landed his detachment here, which marched to Lexington. About one hundred yards from the West Boston Bridge, a fort was erected on December 11th, 1775, during its erection several soldiers of the revolutionary army were killed at this redoubt. It was considered the strongest battery erected during the siege of Boston, and was known as "Lechmere Point Redoubt," Leachmere having acquired this property from his wife. It was known for many years as Lechmere's Point. The farm was confiscated, and during the siege of Boston was occupied by Washington's army.

Richard Lechmere was an Addresser of Hutchinson in 1774; was appointed Mandamus Councillor, but did not accept. In 1776 he went to Halifax, with his family of eleven persons, and thence to England. In 1778 he was proscribed and banished, and his estate confiscated; the next year he was included in the Conspiracy Act. His home was at Bristol in 1780. He died in England in 1814, aged eighty-seven.

Richard Lechmere left no male representatives, his daughters, are represented by Coores of Scrunten Hall, Yorkshire. Sir Edward Russell of Ashford Hall, Ludlow and Worralls, whose representatives now are Sir H. Lechmere Stuart, Bart., and Eyre Coote of West Park Eyre. In Colonel Lechmere Russell's possession is Ann Winthrop's bible, with, in her son Richard Lechmere's writing, the statement it was his mother's bible. A piece of land at Hanley, in Worcestershire, the residence of the Lechmere's, is called New England, and is planted with oaks, the seed of which were sent from America by Thomas Lechmere, the settler here.

Nicholas Lechmere, son of Thomas Lechmere, and brother of Richard, was born at Boston, July 29, 1772. He was appointed an Officer of the Customs of Newport, Rhode Island. In 1765, fearing the loss of life in the tumult of that year, he fled to the Cygnet, sloop-of-war, and refused to return to his duties without assurance of protection. From 1767 to the commencement of the Revolution, the disagreements between him and the revolutionists were frequent. In December, 1775, he refused to take the oath tendered by General Lee, and was conveyed under guard to Providence. He went to England, and in 1770, was with his brother at Bristol in 1780. He was banished and his estate confiscated.

LIST OF CONFISCATED ESTATES BELONGING TO RICHARD LECHMORE IN SUFFOLK COUNTY AND TO WHOM SOLD.

To Mungo Mackey, June 11, 1783; Lib. 139, fol. 14; Land and dwelling-house in Boston, Cambridge St. S.; Staniford St. W.; passageway N.; Timothy Newell E. and N.; Jeremiah Allen E.———One undivided half of land, brick distill house and other buildings, Cambridge St. N.; George St. E.; heirs of John Guttridge deceased S.; Belknap St. W.

EZEKIEL LEWIS.

William Lewis belonged to the Braintree Company, which in 1632 removed from Braintree to Cambridge, thence about 1636 to Hartford, about 1659 to Hadley, which town he represented in the General Court 1662, from thence to Farmington, where he died Aug., 1683. Captain William Lewis, son of the above, married May Cheever, daughter of the famous schoolmaster. He died 18 Aug., 1690. Ezekiel Lewis, son of Captain William, was born at Farmington, Conn., Nov. 7, 1674. Graduated at Harvard College in 1695. In 1699 it was decided that the town of Boston required an assistant in the Latin School for Mr. Ezekiel Cheever. It being committed to the Selectmen, Mr. Ezekiel Lewis, his grandson, was selected to fill the position, and to have a salary of not exceeding forty pounds a year. He entered upon his duties the following August. He afterwards became a great merchant in Boston, was Representative 1723 to 1727.

A document dated March 8th, 1707-8 contains the signatures of the Overseers of the Poor for the town of Boston at that period. Ezekiel Lewis' name appears among the seven mentioned. The men who held the position of Overseers were of high standing in the community, and were usually distinguished for their business talents, wealth and charities.*

In 1742, when Faneuil Hall was opened, Ezekiel Lewis was among the Selectmen and representatives of the town of those who were "to wait upon Peter Faneuil, Esq., and in the name of the town to render him their most hearty thanks for so beautiful a gift," etc.

EZEKIEL LEWIS, the Loyalist, was born at Boston, 15 April, 1717, and graduated at Harvard College, 1735. Under the Act of 1777-8, by which the Judge of Probate was authorized to appoint agents for the estates of absentees in each county, the name of Ezekiel Lewis appears in Suffolk County Probate Records, 1779. Docket 16800.

BENJAMIN CLARK.

Dr. John Clark was the first of a prominent Boston family of that name. He was a gentleman of college education, and a leading physician of that day. He died in 1680, aged 85. Their only son, Hon. Dr. John Clark, of Boston, died in 1690, leaving three sons, John, born 1667, William 1670, Samuel 1677.

HON. WILLIAM CLARK, ESQ. became a wealthy merchant and member of the Governor's Council. His residence was situated in North Square, on the corner of Garden Court and Prince street. This mansion was a monument of human pride, in all colonial Boston there was not its peer, and it was without doubt built to outvie that of Hutchinson's, Clark's wealthy next-door neighbor, whose home was demolished by the mob. The principal feature which distinguished this house, was the rich, elaborate and peculiar decoration of the north parlor, on the right of the entrance hall, which was a rich example of the prevalent style, found in the mansions of wealthy citizens of the colonial period, in and around Boston.

*Memorial Hist. of Boston. Vol. IV. P. 646-647.

The peculiar decoration consisted of a series of raised panels filling these compartments, reaching from the surbase to the frieze, eleven in all, each embellished with a romantic landscape painted in oil colors, the four panels opposite the windows being further enriched by the emblazoned escutcheons of the Clarks, the Saltonstalls, and other allied families. Beneath the surbase, the panels, as also those of the door, were covered with arabesques. The twelfth painting was a view of the house upon a horizontal panel over the mantel, from which this engraving was made, and beneath this panel inscribed in an oval, was the monogram of the builder, W. C. At the base of the gilded and fluted vault of the buffet was a painted dove. The floor was inlaid with divers woods in multiform patterns. In the center, surrounded by a border, emblazoned in proper colors, was the escutcheon of the Clarks, with its three white swans.

The mere enumeration of the details fails to give an idea of the impression made by this painted and gilded parlor, not an inch of whose surface but had been elaborated by painter, gilder, carver or artist, to which the blazoner had added heraldic emblems; so that, as you looked round these walls, the romantic ruins and castles seemed placed there to suggest, if not to portray, the old homes of a long line of ancestors, and the escutcheons above to confirm the suggestion, thereby enhancing the splendor of the present by the feudal dignity of an august past.

The house is supposed to have been built about 1712-1715, for the land was purchased of Ann Hobby, widow, and several other heirs, December 10, 1711, for £725 current money. If so, Councillor Clark lived many years to enjoy the sumptuousness of his new house and the envy of his neighbors. His death, in 1742, was attributed by some to the loss of forty sail of vessels in the French war. After his death the estate was conveyed to his son-in-law, Deacon Thomas Greenough, for £1.400, old tenor, and was by him sold to Sir Charles Henry Frankland, Bart., for £1,200 sterling. The mansion, afterwards was known as the Frankland House.

There were numerous places in Boston named after Clark. There was Clark's Wharf, afterwards changed to Hancock's, and now known as Lewis; Clark street from Hanover to Commercial, still named, in 1788; Clark Square, now North Square, where the Clark mansion was built, was named in 1708, "The Square living on ye Southly side of the North Meeting House including ye wayes on each side of ye watchhouse"; Clark's Corner, 1708, corner of Middle, now Hanover street and Bennet street, Dr. Clark's Corner, 1732; corner of Fish, now North street, and Gallops alley, now Board alley and Clark's Shipyard.

CLARK-FRANKLAND HOUSE.

LADY AGNES FRANKLAND.

Sir Harry Frankland, as he was familiarly called here, was heir to an ample fortune, and what added to his interest in this puritanical colony was that he was a descendant in the fourth generation from Oliver Cromwell, he came here in 1741 as Collector of the Port of Boston, preferring that office to the Governorship of Massachusetts, the alternative offered him by George II. The story of his marriage is romantic enough. Upon an official visit to Marblehead, he was struck by the radiant beauty of a young girl of sixteen, maid-of-all-work at the village inn, bare-legged, scrubbing the floor; inquired her name, and, upon a subsequent visit, with the consent of her parents, conveyed her to Boston and placed her at the best school. The attachment he conceived for her appears to have been returned, though Sir Charles did not offer her marriage. The connection between this high official and his fair protege causing scandal, Frankland purchased some 500 acres of land in Hopkinton, which he laid out and cultivated with taste, built a stately country-house and extensive farm buildings, and there entertained all the gay companions he could collect with deer and fox hunts without, with music and feasting within doors, duly attending the church of his neighbor, the Rev. Roger Price, late of King's Chapel, Boston, of which Frankland had been, from his arrival, a member. Called to England by the death of his uncle, whose title he inherited as fourth baronet, he journeyed to Lisbon, and there, upon All Saints Day, 1755, on his way to high mass, he was engulfed by the earthquake, his horses killed, and he would have perished miserably but for his discovery and rescue by the devoted Agnes. Grateful and penitent, he led her to the altar, and poor Agnes Surriage, the barefooted maid-of-all-work of the inn at Marblehead, was translated into Lady Agnes Frankland.

It was upon Sir Harry Frankland's return from Europe in 1756 that he became the owner of the Clark House, lived in it one short year, entertaining continually, with the assistance of his French cook, Thomas, as appears by frequent entries in his journal; was then transferred to Lisbon as Consul General, and so, with the exception of brief visits to this country in 1759 and 1763, disappearing from our horizon.

After his death at Bath, England, in 1768, his widow returned here with her son, but not until she had recorded her husband's virtues upon a monument "erected by his affectionate widow, Agnes, Lady Frankland,"—dividing her year between Boston and Hopkinton, exchanging civilities with those who had once rejected her, till the contest with England rendered all loyalists and officials unpopular.

At Hopkinton, May, 1775, she was alarmed at the movement of the revolutionists, her Ladyship asked leave to remove to Boston. The Committee of Safety gave her liberty to pass to the capital with her personal effects, and gave her a written permit, signed by Benjamin Church,

Jr., chairman. Thus protected, she set out on her journey with her attendants; but was arrested by a party of armed men, who detained her person, and effects, until an order for the release of both was obtained. To prevent further annoyance, the Provincial Congress furnished her with an escort, and required all persons who had any of her property in their possession to place the same at her disposal. Defended by a guard of six soldiers, Lady Frankland entered Boston about the first of June, 1775; witnessed from her window in Garden Court street the battle of Bunker Hill, took her part in relieving the sufferings of the wounded officers, and then in her turn disappeared, leaving her estates in the hands of members of her family, thereby saving them from confiscation, which was the fate of her neighbor Hutchinson. Upon her death in England in 1782 the town mansion passed by her will to her family, and was sold by Isaac Surriage in 1811 for $8000 to Mr. Joshua Ellis, a retired North End merchant, who resided there till his death. Upon the widening of Bell Alley, in 1832, these two proud mansions, the Frankland and Hutchinson houses long since deserted by the families whose importance they were erected to illustrate and perpetuate, objects of interest to the poet, the artist, and the historian, alike for their associations with a seemingly remote past, their antique splendor, and for the series of strange romantic incidents in the lives of their successive occupants, were ruthlessly swept away.

COLONEL DAVID PHIPS.

The most picturesque and remarkable in character and personal fortune of all the royal governors, was the first of them, Sir William Phips. He was a characteristic product of the New England soil, times and ways. Hutchinson thus briefly and fitly designates him: "He was an honest man, but by a series of fortunate incidents, rather than by any uncommon talents, he rose from the lowest condition in life to be the first man in the country."

Cotton Mather informs us that William Phips was one of twenty-one *sons* and of *twenty-six* children, of the same mother, born to James Phips of Bristol, England, a blacksmith, and gunsmith, who was an early settler in the woods of Maine, at the mouth of the Kennebec River. But records and history are dumb as to facts about the most of these scions of a fruitful parentage, other than that of their having been born. William was born Feb. 2, 1651; was left in early childhood without a father. What the mother's task was, in poverty, with hard wilderness surroundings, of bears, wolves, and savages, we may well imagine. Her famous son, untaught and ignorant, tended sheep, till he was eighteen years of age. Then he helped to build coasters, and sailed in them. This was at that time, and afterwards a most thriving business, the foundation of fortunes to rugged and enterprising men, born in indigence.

He went to Boston in 1673, at the age of twenty-two, worked at his trade, he had early visions of success and greatness, for the first time he learned to read, and also to do something that passed for writing. He married the widow of John Hull, the mint master, they suffered straits together, but he used to comfort her with the assurance that they would yet have "a fair brick house in the Green Lane of North Boston." And so they did. That "Greene Lane" became Charter street, when in 1692, he came back as Sir William Phips, from the Court of London, bringing the Province Charter as the first Governor under it. The "fair brick house" long served as an Asylum for boys, at the corner of Salem and Charles streets.

But a strange wild daring, and romantic interval of adventure preceded his honors, and wealth. He wrought at intervals in Maine, and here, as a ship carpenter, sailed coasters, and engaged in expeditions against the Indians. In 1684 he went in a search in the waters of the Spanish Main for a treasure ship known to be sunk there. Going to London, the Admiralty, and James II. gave him the command of an eighteen-gun ship and ninety-five men. A two years' cruise in the West Indies, in which he showed a most signal intrepidity, heroism and ingenuity of resource, in suppressing a mutinous crew, was unsuccessful, except in acquainting him, through an old Spaniard, of the precise spot where a treasure-laden galleon had foundered fifty years before. He returned to England for a new outfit. The king favored him, but not with another war ship. The Duke of Albemarle and others, as associates, provided him with a vessel on shares. The hero had heroic success. Cotton Mather informs us that "Captain Phips arrived at *Port de la Plata*, made a stout *canoo* of a stately cotton-tree, employing his own *hands* and *adse* in constructing it, lying abroad in the woods many nights together. The piriaga, as they called it, discovered a reef of rising shoals called *"The Boilers"*, here an Indian diver dove down and perceived a number of *great-guns*, and upon further diving the Indian fetched up a *sow*, or lump of silver, worth two or three hundred pounds. In all, thirty-two tons of silver, gold, pearls and jewels were recovered from the wreck. Besides which, one Adderly of Providence, one of the Bahama Islands, took up about six tons of silver, which he took to the Bermudas. Captain Phips returned to London in 1687 with more than a million and a half of dollars, in gold and silver, diamonds, precious stones, and other treasures. His own share in the proceeds was about a hundred thousand dollars. To this was added the honors of knighthood, and a gold cup for Lady Phips, of the value of five thousand dollars.

He returned home in the capacity of high-sheriff, under Andros, who did not want him, for he was utterly ignorant of law, and could not write legibly. He soon made another voyage to England, and returned to Boston, built the "fair brick house," of his vision, engaged in a successful military expedition against Acadia, in which he took and plundered Port Royal, and other French settlements. He then instigated and conducted as commander, a naval expedition against Quebec, which proved a failure. He again went to England, and returned as the first Governor under the new Charter, May 14, 1692. The appointment was made to conciliate the people of the province, and it was supposed would be gratifying to them, it was however a risky experiment, this attempt to initiate a new order of things, under the lead of an illiterate mechanic, utterly unskilled, in legal, and administrative affairs, a rough seaman, and a man of hot temper. Yet after he arose to these high offices, he showed no false pride, and often alluded to his lowly origin. He gave his fellow ship carpenters a dinner in Boston, and when borne down with public distraction, would wish himself back to his broad-axe again. He was pure in morals, upright in his dealings, and owed his success in life to his own energy and prowess. All incompetent as he was for the stern exigency, he had to meet the appalling outburst of the Witchcraft delusion with its spell of horrors. During the greater part of the proceedings of the courts, he was absent at the eastward, in an expedition against the Indians, and engaged in building a fort at Pemaquid. When he returned to Boston he found that even his own wife had been "cried out upon" as a witch, and he at once put a stay upon the fatuous proceedings. His weak and troubled administration lasted two and one-half years. He then went to England to answer to complaints made against his administration, when he died suddenly Feb. 18, 1695, aged forty-five years. He was buried in the church of St. Mary Woolnoth, London, where his widow caused a monument to be erected to his memory. He died childless.

Governor Phips' widow married the rich merchant, Peter Sergent, who built and occupied the stately mansion, afterwards purchased by the Province, as a residence for the Governor, and known as the Province House.

SPENCER PHIPS was a nephew of Governor Phips' wife. The governor having no children, adopted as his heir, Spencer Bennett, he was Lieu. Governor between 1733 and 1757, and married Elizabeth Hutchinson. He resided mainly at Cambridge. His farm consisted of that part of Cambridge afterwards known as Lechmere Point, now East Cambridge, his daughters married Andrew Boardman, John Vassall, Richard Lechmere and Joseph Lee. Lieu. Governor Phips died in March, 1757.

DAVID PHIPS, only son of Lieutenant Governor Spencer Phips, graduated at Harvard College in 1741. He was Colonel of a troop of guards in Boston, and Sheriff of Middlesex County. He was an Addresser on three occasions, as his name is found among the one hundred and twenty-four merchants, and others, of Boston, who addressed Governor Hutchinson in 1774, among the ninety-seven gentlemen and principal inhabitants of that town, and among the eighteen country gentlemen who were driven from their homes, and who addressed General Gage in October, 1775. He went to Halifax at the evacuation of Boston in 1776, and was proscribed and banished under the Act of 1778. His home at Cambridge was confiscated. He died at Bath, England in 1811, aged eighty-seven.

THE DUNBAR FAMILY OF HINGHAM.

Robert Dunbar, a Scotchman, became a resident of Hingham shortly after 1650, and probably was the ancestor of all the families who have borne this surname in Plymouth county. The Christian name of his wife was Rose. She survived him and died 10 Nov. 1700. Robert died, 19 Sept., 1693. He had eight sons and three daughters, and died possessed of considerable property. His grandson Joseph removed to Halifax, Plymouth County, in 1736.*

DANIEL DUNBAR, son of the aforesaid Joseph was born in Hingham, March 8, 1733. He was an ensign of Militia at Halifax, Mass., and in 1774 had his colors demanded of him by the mob, some of the selectmen being the chief actors. He refused and they broke into his house, took him out, forced him upon a rail, where for three hours, he was held, and tossed, up and down, until he was exhausted. He was then dragged and beaten, and gave up the standard to save his life. In 1776 he went to Halifax, Nova Scotia, with the Royal Army. In 1778 he was proscribed and banished.

JESSIE DUNBAR, of the fourth generation, was born in Hingham, June 26, 1744. He removed to Bridgewater, Plymouth County.**

He bought some fat cattle of Nathaniel Ray Thomas, a Mandamus Councillor, in 1774, and drove them to Plymouth for sale; one of the oxen being skinned and hung up, the "Sons of Liberty" came to him and finding where he bought it, commenced punishing him for the offence. His tormentors put the ox in a cart, and fixing Dunbar in his belly, carted him four miles and required him to pay one dollar for the ride. They then delivered him to a Kingston mob, which carted him four miles further, and forced from him another dollar, then delivered him to a Duxbury mob, who abused him by beating him in the face with the creature's tripe, and endeavored to cover his person with it, to the endangering his life. They then threw dirt at him, and after other abuses, carried him to Councillor Thomas's house, and made him pay another sum of money, and he, not taking the beef, they flung it in the road and quitted him. Jesse Dunbar died at Nobleboro, Maine, in 1806, leaving many descendants.

The outrageous and brutal treatment he received from the "Sons of Despotism" are among the worst on record.

*Hist. of Hingham. Vol. II. P. 195-7-9.
**Dunbar Genealogy. P. 19.

EBENEZER RICHARDSON.

The Richardson family were the earliest settlers of Woburn, Massachusetts. Ezekiel, Samuel and Thomas Richardson, three brothers, with four other persons, laid the foundations of the town, in 1641. In 1642 it was incorporated under the name of Woburn, the name of a town in Herefordshire.

Samuel Richardson, the ancestor of Ebenezer Richardson, came to Charlestown, about 1636, as his name appears on the records of July 1 of that date as one of a committee to "lay out lots of land for hay." When the three brothers settled at Woburn, they lived near each other on the same street, which was laid out in 1647, as Richardson's Row, by which name it has ever since been known. It runs almost due north and south, in the N. E. part of the present town of Winchester.

Lieut. John Richardson, eldest son of Samuel, was born Nov. 12, 1639, was a yeoman, and soldier in King Philip's war, and passed his life in Woburn, and died there in 1696. John Richardson, son of Lieut. John was a carpenter, and lived in Woburn. He died March 18, 1715.

Timothy Richardson, son of John, was born in Woburn, 1687, was badly wounded in Lovewell's Indian fight at Pigwacket. The colony having offered one hundred pounds for Indian scalps, Captain Lovewell went with forty-six men on a scalp hunt into Maine. Captain Lovewell was the first one killed. The fight lasted ten hours, those who left the fatal battle ground, were twenty in number, of whom eleven were badly wounded, among whom was Timothy Richardson, who lived for ten years afterwards, but in great suffering he died in Woburn in 1735.

EBENEZER RICHARDSON, eldest son of Timothy, and Abigail Johnson, was born in Woburn, March 31, 1718, and married Rebecca (Fowle) Richardson, daughter of Captain John and Elizabeth (Prescott) Fowle, of Woburn, and widow of Phineas Richardson. His father's farm was bounded easterly by the Woburn and Stoneham line, it was here probably that Ebenezer was born.*

Ebenezer Richardson was an officer of the Customs in Boston. On the 22 Feb., 1770, he was assailed by a mob who chased him to his home, bricks and stones were thrown at the windows. Richardson, provoked, fired at random into the mob, dangerously wounding one of them, Samuel Gore, and mortally wounding another, Christopher Snider, a poor German boy, who died the next morning.

The excitement was intense, the funeral of the boy was attended by the revolutionists, and the event taken advantage of to fire the passions of the people. On the 20th of April, Richardson was tried for his life and brought in guilty of murder. Chief Justice Hutchinson viewed the guilt of Richardson, as everybody would now, a clear case of justifiable homicide, and consequently refused to sign a warrant for his execution,

*Richardson Memorial by Vinton. P. 34, 199, 242.

and after lying in prison two years, was, on application to the King, pardoned and set at liberty.* To reward Richardson for what he had suffered, he was appointed in 1773 as an officer of the Customs of Philadelphia.

Historians have treated Richardson very unfairly, and caused his memory to be execrated. He was a Custom House officer, and the duties of his office caused him to seize smuggled goods, as any custom house officer would at the present time, previous to that he belonged to the secret service division for the detection of illicit traders, on this account he has always been contemptuously called an "informer". He was not any worse than hundreds of secret service agents employed at the present time by the United States Government, to detect law-breakers. They are of course detested by the criminal classes, and the mountaineer moonshiners of Kentucky consider it no crime to kill them, when the opportunity offers. After Richardson's release, he went to Philadelphia to reside, so as to escape mob violence; the malignity of the revolutionists, however, followed him, and a scurrilous effusion was published there entitled "The Life and Humble Confession of Richardson the Informer."

The broadside was embellished with a rude wood cut of Richardson firing into the mob, and the killing of the boy Snider. The same has been recently republished, and the author states "Whatever facts it may contain, are doubtless expanded beyond the limits of the actual truth.**

COMMODORE JOSHUA LORING.

Thomas Loring came from Axminster in Devonshire, England, to Dorchester with his wife, Jane, whose maiden name was Newton, in the year 1634, they removed to Hingham, and finally settled and died at Hull in 1661, leaving many descendants, who still reside in Hull, and Hingham.

COMMODORE JOSHUA LORING was descended from Thomas Loring. He was born at Boston, Aug. 3, 1716. He was apprenticed to Mr. Mears, a tanner of Roxbury. When he was of age he went to sea. About 1740 he married Mary, daughter of Samuel Curtice, of Roxbury. In 1744 he was master of a Brigantine Privateer of Boston, and while cruising near Louisburg, was taken by two French Men of War.

He purchased an estate in 1752, on Jamaica Plain, Roxbury, of Joshua Cheever, on which he erected what has since been known as the Greenough mansion. It is said to have been framed in England and was one of the finest residences in Roxbury. It was situated opposite the intersection of Center and South streets, opposite the soldiers' monument.

*For further particulars see pages 310, 311.
**William R. Cutter, Librarian of the Woburn Public Library.

On December 19, 1757, he was commissioned captain in the British Navy, was Commodore of the naval forces on Lakes Champlain and Ontario, and participated in the capture of Quebec under Wolfe, and in the conquest of Canada in the succeeding campaign of Amherst. He was severely wounded in the leg while in command on Lake Ontario, and at the close of the war he retired on half pay, at which time he settled down at Jamaica Plain, Roxbury. He was one of the five Commissioners of the revenue, and General Gage by writ of mandamus appointed him a member of his Council, and he was sworn in Aug. 17, 1774. This immediately subjected him to the strictest surveillance by the revolutionists, and the greatest pressure was brought to bear upon him to throw up the obnoxious office. A diarist, under date of Aug. 29, speaking of a Roxbury town meeting recently held says, "Late in the evening a member visited Commodore Loring, and in a friendly way advised him to follow the example of his townman Isaac Winslow, (who had already resigned). He desired time to consider it. They granted it, but acquainted him if he did not comply he must expect to be waited on by a large number, actuated by a different spirit. (Tarred and feathered and rode on a rail). On the morning of the Lexington battle, after passing most of the previous night in consultation with Deacon Joseph Brewer, his neighbor and intimate friend, upon the step he was about to take, he mounted his horse, left his home and everything belonging to it, never to return again, and pistol in hand, rode at full speed to Boston, stopping on the way only to answer an old friend, who asked "Are you going, commodore?" "Yes," he replied. "I have always eaten the king's bread, and always intend to." The sacrifice must have been especially painful to him, for he was held in high esteem by his friends and neighbors, but he could not spurn the hand that had fed him, and rather than do a dishonorable act, he would sacrifice all he possessed, even the land of his birth. At the evacuation he went to England. He received a pension from the crown until his decease at Highgate, in October, 1781, at the age of sixty-five. Joshua Loring was proscribed, banished and his large estate confiscated. His mansion house was in May, 1775, headquarters of General Nathaniel Greene, and afterwards for a brief period, a hospital for American soldiers, many of whom were buried on the adjacent grounds. Later Captain Isaac Sears bought the property of the State, and lived there for several years.

Mary, his widow, was, through the influence of Lord North, pensioned for life; she settled at Englesfield, Berkshire County, England, where she died in 1789 at the age of eighty.

JOSHUA LORING, JR. was a twin brother of Benjamin Loring, sons of Commodore Loring. He was born Nov., 1744. He was an Addresser of Governor Hutchinson in 1774, and of Gen. Gage in 1775. One of the last official acts of the latter in Boston was his proclamation of June 7, 1775, appointing Mr. Loring "sole vendue-master and auctioneer." He was High Sheriff and a member of the Ancient and Honorable Artillery Company in 1769. In 1776 he went to Halifax with the Royal Army, and, early the next year, he was appointed Commissary of Prisoners by Sir William Howe. He was severely criticized at the time by the Revolutionists, for cruelties to his unfortunate countrymen who were prisoners, but as Sabine truly says, "it is not easy to ascertain the truth or to determine his personal responsibility in the treatment of prisoners."* He was proscribed and banished, and died in England in 1789, aged forty-five. His wife was a Miss Lloyd, to whom he was married at the house of Colonel Hatch in Dorchester in 1769. His son,

SIR JOHN WENTWORTH LORING was born in Roxbury, Oct.; 1773; was baptized in Trinity church by Rev. D. Walters, Nov. 29; was a midshipman in the British navy, and from 1819 to 1837 was Lieut. Governor of the Royal Naval College. In 1841 was advanced to the rank of Rear Admiral of the Red and in 1847 was promoted Vice Admiral of the White. His son, William, was Captain of the "Scout" in the Royal Navy.

DR. BENJAMIN LORING, twin brother of Joshua Loring, Jr., born in 1744, graduated at Harvard College in 1772. He was a Surgeon in a Regiment in the King's service in South Carolina. At the peace, accompanied by his family of five persons, and by one servant, he went from New York to Shelburne, Nova Scotia. His losses in consequences of his loyalty were estimated at $15,000. He was an absentee but not proscribed. He returned to Boston and died there in 1798, aged sixty-five.

COMMODORE JOHN LORING, son of Commodore Joshua, was a midshipman in the Royal Navy, at fourteen years of age. In 1776 he was one of four prisoners taken in the schooner Valent, and sent into Boston, as there was no place provided for prisoners he was sent to Concord Jail by the Council, who ordered "that Edward Marsh, and John Loring should not use pen or paper, nor any one allowed to speak to them, but in the presence of the jailor. His uncle Obediah Curtis being a very influential man, interceded for him so strenuously, he being but quite a youth, that he was released and sent to the care of Col. Buckminster of Framingham, his wife's father. His kind host was in danger of having his home demolished for harboring a "young Tory", on account of the young man calling his neighbors "rascally rebels." In 1776 he was exchanged and returned to England. He was early a Post Captain. In 1793 he had command of the British Squadron in the Camatic. In 1803 he had command of the Frigate Bellerophon (which in 1813 conveyed Napoleon to St. Helena) and captured the French Frigate Duquesne, 74 guns, and a national schooner. In the same year he was Commodore of

*A similar case occurred during the Civil War, there was probably no man whose memory was more execrated, and who was regarded as a monster than Wirz, the Commander at Andersonville, who was hanged by the U. S. Government, and yet forty-five years afterwards the Daughters of the Confederacy have erected a beautiful monument to his memory at Andersonville.

**Ancestral Records of the Loring family. Type Written Copy in the New England Historic Genealogical Society. Pp. 129 to 182.

the British Fleet off Cape Francoix, which blockaded and defeated the French squadron, and the troops under Rochambeau, Nov. 30, 1803. Commodore John Loring died at his seat in Farehan, Nov. 9, 1808, leaving a widow and children. The Naval service lost in him "one of its most brave, zealous and humane officers. He married Miss Macneal of Campleton Argyleshire, a lady of great beauty. His son Hector, became captain of the Howe, 120 guns, of the Royal Navy. He married Miss Charlotte Jessy, daughter of James Jamison of the Royal Bengal Medical Service. His eldest son John, a midshipman on board of the Eurylas, in 1820, died of the yellow fever at Bermuda.

JOSEPH ROYAL LORING, son of Commodore Joshua, probably never married. He was captain of the Brigantine "William," owned by Richard Clarke and Sons, of Boston, engaged in bringing tea from London to Boston. It was the fourth and last vessel on the East India Company's account to sail there. She was cast ashore at Provincetown on Cape Cod. The tea was saved and conveyed to the Castle in Boston Harbor. Very little is known afterwards of Captain Royal Loring.

LIST OF CONFISCATED ESTATES BELONGING TO JOSHUA LORING IN SUFFOLK COUNTY AND TO WHOM SOLD.

To John Keyes, Aug. 31, 1779; Lib. 130, fol. 191; Land 19 A., mansion house and barn in Roxbury, Joshua Loring N. and N.E.; Lemuel May E.; Ebenezer Weld S.; road leading to Dedham W.; then running S.; E. and N. on land of John Keyes.

To Isaac Sears, Oct. 28, 1779; Lib. 130, fol. 237; Farm, 54 A. 3 qr. 9 r., and mansion house in Roxbury, road leading by Jamaica meeting-house to Boston W.; heirs of Mr. Burroughs deceased N. and N.W.; lane N.E.; lane and Capt. May E.; land of Joshua Loring, absentee, now of John Keyes S.———6 1-2 A. salt marsh, creek W.; Mr. Bowdoin S.; heirs of Joseph Weld deceased E.; heirs of John Williams deceased N.

To James Swan, Feb. 1, 1782; Lib. 134, fol. 6; Wood or pasture land, 8 A. 31 r., in Brookline, road W.; Mr. Crafts N.W. and N.E.; Capt. Baker S.E.

To John Tufts, Apr. 28, 1783; Lib. 138, fol. 101; Land and dwelling-house in Boston, common or training-field N.W.; West St. N.E.; David Colson S.E.; heirs or assigns of Dr. George Stewart S.W.

To Ellis Gray, Nov 23, 1795; Lib. 181, fol. 275; Wood and pasture land, 24 1-2 A. 7 r., in Roxbury, near Henry Williams; Caleb Williams and Mr. Morries S.E.; Ebenezer Chanies S.W.; Mr. Bourn N.W. and N.E.

ROBERT WINTHROP.

The most prominent name in Massachusetts History is that of Winthrop. Governor John Winthrop has been called the "Father of Boston." From the date of the first settlement of Massachusetts to the present time, the name of Winthrop has been prominent in each generation.

The family of Winthrops of Groton Manor, Suffolk County, England, took its name by tradition, from the village of Winthrope, near Newark, in Nottinghamshire. The earliest ancestor of whom anything is known with certainty is

I. Adam Winthrop, known to have been living at Lavenham, in Suffolk in 1498, who had, by his wife Jane Burton, a son—

II. Adam Winthrop second of that name, born in Lavenham, Oct. 9, 1498, died in Groton, Nov. 9, 1562, who became a wealthy London merchant, acquired the manor of Groton, near Lavenham, in 1544; was inscribed Armiger by Edward VI. in 1548, and in 1551 was Master of the influential Company of Clothworkers. He had thirteen children, several of whom became distinguished. His third son was—

III. Adam Winthrop, third of that name, who came into possession of Groton Manor. He was born in London, Aug. 10th, 1548, died at Groton March 28, 1623. He was a lawyer and county magistrate, and married Alice, sister of Dr. John Still, Bishop of Bath and Wells. His only son was—

IV. John Winthrop, born Jan. 12, and died in Boston, March 26, 1649. He was a lawyer and magistrate, and became a great Puritan leader, and led the greatest emigration that had ever gone forth from England up to this time. In February, 1630, preparations began to be made with vigor for the embarkation of a great colony, by the end of the month a fleet of fourteen vessels was ready with men, women and children, and all necessary men of handicrafts, and others of good condition, wealth, and quality, to make a firm plantation. In this fleet were congregated the forefathers of Massachusetts, with their wives and little ones, about to quit forever their native country, kindred, friends and asquaintances. They were to leave the land of their fathers, perhaps forever, to break assunder those chords of affection, which so powerfully bind a good man to his native soil, and to dissolve those tender associations which constitute the bliss of civil society, and to seek in an unknown wilderness, a new home, which in time would become a great nation. On the 8th of June, 1630, the fleet sighted land, Mt. Desert, and regaled themselves with fish of their own catching. "So pleasant a scene here they had, as did much refresh them, and there came a smell off the shore, like the smell of a garden." On the 12th, they came to anchor in Salem harbor, and by 14th of July, thirteen out of the fourteen ships had arrived safely, the other vessel, the Mary & John, was the first to arrive, and had landed their passengers at Dorchester. Governor Winthrop, after his arrival at Salem, determined to remove to a point of land between two rivers flowing into Boston Harbor, and named the town Charlestown, in honor of Charles I. The next year the Governor caused the settlement to remove across the Charles river to another point of land called by the Indians "Shawmut," signifying the place of living waters, which caused the removal there. The Governor settled alongside of the "Great Spring" on the present site of the Old South church, next to Spring Lane, which runs into Water street, hence the name. The place was called Boston, named after Boston, Lincolnshire, England, from which place some of the settlers came, and the County was named Suffolk.

Thus Boston was settled by the English Puritans under the leadership of Governor Winthrop.*

Governor Winthrop had five daughters and two sons, the elder resided chiefly in Connecticut and the younger in Massachusetts, generally known as, VI, Wait Still Winthrop or Wait Winthrop, born in Boston, Feb. 27, 1642, died Nov. 7, 1717. A soldier of the Indian wars, for more than thirty years Major General commanding the Provincial Forces of Mass., Judge of the Superior Court, Judge of Admiralty and some time Chief Justice of Mass. He married Mary, daughter of Hon. William Brown, of Salem, by whom he had one daughter, Ann, wife of Thomas Lechmere, brother of Lord Lechmere, and an only son, VII, John Winthrop, born in Boston, Aug. 26, 1681, died at Sydenham Aug. 1, 1747, graduated at Harvard College in 1700. Failing to receive the political preferment to which claim he conceived a sort of hereditary claim, he went to England to reside in 1727. He became an active member of Royal Society, of whose transactions one volume is dedicated to him, he resided there until his death. He had five daughters and two sons, the eldest, VIII, John Still Winthrop, born in Boston, Jan. 15, 1720, died June 6, 1776. Graduated at Yale College in 1737. In early life he resided with his father in England, and occasionally in Boston, but after his marriage, chiefly in New London, Conn., where he built a large house, still standing at the head of Winthrop's Cove, described in 1787 as the best house in the Province. He had fourteen children, five daughters and nine sons. Of his sons, two died in childhood. John and William died unmarried. Francis Bayard Winthrop went to New York, also Benjamin Winthrop. Joseph Winthrop went to Charleston, S. C.

THOMAS LINDALL WINTHROP. Born March 6, 1760, died in Boston, Feb. 21, 1841. Graduated at Harvard College 1780, was Lieutenant Governor of Massachusetts from 1826 to 1833. He married in 1786, Elizabeth, daughter of Sir John Temple, Bart., and granddaughter of James Bowdoin of Boston, Governor of Massachusetts. Their son, the Hon. Robert C. Winthrop, was the most conspicuous member of the family in America for a long period. In his memoir of the Winthrop family he says "From the above five brothers descend the numerous branches of the Winthrop family, now widely scattered in different parts of the United States and Europe."** It does not appear that either of them joined the revolutionists or took any part in the war, except the youngest son, who was a staunch loyalist, and was of great service to his country.

The youngest son of John Still Winthrop, was, IX, Robert Winthrop, the subject of this sketch, born in New London, Dec. 7, 1764, died at Dover, England, May 10, 1832. During the Revolution he was appointed a Midshipman in the Royal Navy. In 1790 he was a Lieutenant; and

*For a detailed account of the career and writings of this illustrious man, see two volumes of his "Life and Letters," by his descendant, Hon. Robert C. Winthrop.

**A Short Account of the Winthrop family by Robert C. Winthrop.

six years later a Post Captain. He attained the rank of Rear Admiral in 1809, and of Vice Admiral in 1830. He served on board of the flagship of Sir George B. Rodney in the memorable victory over the French April 12, 1782. The French Admiral, Count de Grasse, fresh from his victory at Yorktown, had refitted at Martinique's dock yards, and with the assistance of the Spaniards, who had fitted out a fleet at Havana, intended to capture Jamaica, and drive the English out of the West Indies. All the Lesser Antilles were his own, except St. Lucia. There alone the English flag still flew as Rodney lay in the harbor of Castries, and saw the French fleet becalmed under the high lands of Dominica. All day long the cannon roared, and one by one the French ships struck their flags or fought on till they sank. Rodney's flagship came alongside of the Ville de Paris, the pride of France and the largest ship in the world, on which De Grasse commanded in person. He fought after all hope had gone, with her masts shattered, her decks littered with mangled limbs and bodies. He gave up his sword to Rodney. The French fleet was destroyed, fourteen thousand were killed, besides the prisoners. On that memorable day the British Empire was saved and Yorktown was avenged. He was at the conquest of Martinique and St. Lucia in 1794, also captured a French corvette. He was wrecked in the frigate Undaunted. He was on duty in the North Sea. He superintended the landing of troops in the expedition against Ostend. Entrusted with a small squadron to cruise off Holland, his boats burned a store-ship, made prize of fifteen merchant vessels, a sloop-of-war, and an armed schooner. He assisted in the capture of the Helder. Stranded in the frigate Stag, he was compelled, after saving her stores, to burn her. Stationed on the coast of Spain, in the Ardent of sixty-four guns, he drove on shore a French frigate, which was set on fire and burned by her own crew. Such is the bare outline of the great services he rendered on the ocean.

In 1807 the Sea Fencibles of the Dover district was placed under his orders. He married Miss Farbrace. He died at Dover in 1832. Two sons and four daughters survived him.

NATHANIEL HATCH.

Colonel Estes Hatch was one of the most prominent and wealthy men of Dorchester. He owned many negro slaves who worked on his extensive estate, comprising sixty acres of land on the southerly side of Dudley street, lying part in Roxbury and a part in Dorchester. It included Little Woods, afterward known as Swan's woods.

Col. Hatch commanded the Troop of Horse, in Boston, led a company at the capture of Louisberg and died in 1759. He was prominent in town affairs, and held the principal military offices, and at the time of his death was Brigadier General of Horse. His wife was Mary, daughter of Rev. Benjamin Rolfe, her father and mother and their youngest child were killed by the Indians in their home at Haverhill in 1708. Col. Hatch and Mary Rolfe were married Nov. 9th, 1716.

NATHANIEL HATCH, son of Col. Hatch, graduated at Harvard College in 1742, and subsequently held the office of Clerk of the Courts. He was a firm loyalist, and at the evacuation of Boston in 1776, he went to Halifax with the British troops. In 1778 he was proscribed and banished, and in 1779 was included in the Conspiracy Act, by which his large and valuable estate was confiscated, it was bought afterwards by Captain James Swan, who paid £18,000 for it, and who soon afterwards offered it to Gov. Hancock for £45,000. Writing to Hancock, Swan says: "The mansion house can be refitted in as elegant a manner as it once was for about £4,000." During Swan's residence here he made the house a seat of hospitality, entertaining among others persons of distinction. The Marquis de Viomel, second in command of Rochambeau's army, Admiral d'Estaing, the Marquis de Lafayette and General Knox.*

Nathaniel Hatch married July 7, 1755, Elizabeth Lloyd. They had several children, Paxton, born Oct. 9, 1758; Mary, born Jan. 14, 1760; Addington, born Sept. 22, 1761; Jane, born March 10, 1767; Susannah Paxton, born March 13, 1770. Nathaniel Hatch died in 1780.

LIST OF CONFISCATED ESTATES BELONGING TO NATHANIEL HATCH IN SUFFOLK COUNTY AND TO WHOM SOLD.

To Samuel Dunn, Jr., July 11, 1781; Lib. 132, fol. 263; Land, 60 A.; and mansion house in Dorchester, road to Dorchester meeting house N.; Jonas Humphrey, Thomas Wiswall and James Bird E. and S.; John Holbrook S.; John Williams, Samuel Humphrey and brook between Dorchester and Roxbury W. and N.

CHRISTOPHER HATCH.

Of Boston. When the Royal Army evacuated that town, March 17, 1776, cannon, shot, and shells were left on his wharf, and in the dock. In 1778 he was proscribed and banished. He accepted a commission under the crown, and was a Captain in the Loyal American regiment. He was wounded and commended for his gallantry. At the peace he retired on half pay, about £80 per annum. He was a grantee of the city of St. John, N. B., soon after going there established himself as a merchant near the frontier, and finally at St. Andrews. He was a magistrate, and colonel, in the militia. He died at St. Andrews, 1819, aged seventy. Elizabeth, his widow, died at the same place, 1830, at the age of seventy-five.

HARRIS HATCH, son of Christopher, was a gentleman of consideration in New Brunswick, where he held the office of Member of her Maj-

*Town of Roxbury by F. S. Drake. P. 134, 135.

esty's Council Commission of Bankruptcies, Surrogate, Registrar of Deeds, member of the Board of Education, Lieut. Colonel in the Militia, and Judge of the Court of Common Pleas.

HAWES HATCH, of Boston, brother of Christopher Hatch. He went to Halifax with the Royal Army in 1776. In 1778 he was proscribed and banished. He entered the service, and in 1782 was a captain in De Lancey's Second Battalion. He retired on half pay at the close of the war, and was a grantee of the city of St. John. For some years after the Revolution, he lived at and near Eastport, Maine, on the frontier. He died at Lebanon, N. H., in 1807.*

WARD CHIPMAN.

John Chipman was born in Whitechurch, near Dorchester, England, about 1614, and died April 7, 1708. He sailed from Barnstable, Devon County in May, 1631, in the ship Friendship, arriving in Boston July 14th, 1631. John Chipman was the first and only one of the name to seek a home in America, and up to 1850 there was no Chipman in this country who was not descended from him. He was for many years a selectman, then in Plymouth County invested with the authority of a magistrate, and was often a "Deputy to Court" and he, with three assistants, was designated to frequent the early Quaker meetings and "endeavor to reduce them from the errors of their wayes". In 1646 he married Hope, second daughter of John and Elizabeth Howland, born in Plymouth, Mass., 1629, died 1683.

John Chipman had eleven children, and except a son and daughter who died in infancy, all survived him. His eldest son Samuel Chipman, was born in Barnstable, Mass., 1661, and died in 1723. He built on the paternal homestead near the Custom House the "Chipman Tavern," which continued in the line of his posterity until 1830. He was by record a yeoman, and an inn-holder. He too had eleven children.

Rev. John Chipman, of the third generation, was the third son of Samuel aforesaid, was born in Barnstable 1691, died March 23, 1775. He graduated from Harvard College in 1711, and was ordained 1715 as pastor of the first church in the precinct of Salem and Beverly, now North Beverly. He married, first, Rebecca Hale, and, second, Hannah, daughter of Joseph Warren, of Roxbury. He had fifteen children, all by the first marriage.

John Chipman of the fourth generation, eldest son of Rev. John Chipman, was born in Beverly 1722, died 1768. Graduated from Harvard College in 1738, admitted to the practice of law, which at the time of his death embraced only twenty-five barristers in Massachusetts, which also included then the district of Maine. He had abilities of a rare order,

*Sabine's Loyalists.

his services were appreciated and sought in distant localities. While arguing a case before the Superior Court at Falmouth (Portland), Maine, he was suddenly seized with apoplexy, from which he died. He had twelve children.

WARD CHIPMAN, the subject of this biography, was of the fifth generation, and the fourth son of the aforesaid John Chipman. He was born in Marblehead, Mass., July 30, 1754, and died at Fredericton, N. B., Feb. 9, 1824. He graduated from Harvard College in 1770. His graduation oration being the first delivered there in the vernacular language. He studied law in Boston under the direction of Hon. Daniel Leonard, and Hon. Jonathan Sewell, Chief Justice of the Supreme Court of Massachusetts. Ward Chipman and Daniel Leonard, with fifteen other names, appear upon "The Loyal Address" to Gov. Gage on his departure from Boston in 1775 as "of those gentlemen who were driven from their Habitations in the country to Boston."* He left Boston at the evacuation and went with the army to Halifax, "being obliged to abandon his native land." He then went to England, where he was allowed a pension in common with a long list of his suffering fellow-countrymen, but a state of inaction being ill-suited to his ardent mind, in less than a year he relinquished his pension and rejoined the King's troops at New York, where he was employed in the Military Department and in the practice of the Court of Admiralty. In 1782 he held the office of Deputy Mustermaster-General, of the Loyalist forces.

In 1783 he was one of the fifty-five who petitioned for extensive grants of lands in Nova Scotia, out of which was erected the province of New Brunswick, of which province he was appointed Solicitor-General and continually afterwards bore a conspicuous part, and attained the highest honors. He was a member of the House of Assembly and Advocate at the Bar, a Member of his Majesty's Council, a Judge of the Supreme Court, Agent for the settling of disputed points of boundary with the United States until he closed his mortal career while administering the Government of the Colony as President, and Commander in Chief, during a vacancy in the office of Lieut. Governor. His remains were conveyed from Fredericton to St. John where a tablet, adds to above quoted statement, the following: "Distinguished during the whole of his varied and active life, for his superior abilities and unweariable zeal, for genuine integrity and singular humanity and benevolence, his loss was universally deplored; and this frail tribute from his nearest connection affords but a feeble expression of the affectionate respect with which they cherished the memory of his virtues."

Hon. Ward Chipman married Elizabeth, daughter of Hon. William Hazen of Haverhill, Mass., and his wife, the only daughter of Dr. Joseph LeBaron of Plymouth, Mass. She died at St. John in 1852 in her eighty-sixth year. The wife of Hon. William Gray of Boston was his sister. Ward, his only child, was born July 21, 1787, graduated at Harvard Col-

*Chipmans of America.

lege in 1805, where so many of his ancestors had before him. He held many places of honor and trust; was finally chief justice of New Brunswick, and died at St. John in 1851 in his sixty-fifth year. While the Prince of Wales, now King Edward VII., was in that city in August, 1860, he occupied the Chipman mansion.

GOVERNOR EDWARD WINSLOW.

EDWARD WINSLOW was born at Droitwich, Worcestershire, England, 19 October, 1595. He appears to have been a well educated and accomplished man. In the course of his travels on the continent of Europe he went to Leyden and there became acquainted with Mr. John Robinson, and the church under his pastoral charge, which he joined in 1617. He married the 16th of May, 1618, and settled in that city till the church removed to America in 1620. In his "Brief Narration" he says: And when the ship was ready to carry us away the bretheren that stayed feasted us that were to go at our pastor's home. After tears and singing of psalms they accompanied us to Delph's Haven, where we were to embark, and there feasted us again. But we, going aboard ship lying at the quay ready to sail, the wind fair, we gave them a volley of small shot and three pieces of ordnance, and so lifting up our hands to each other and our hearts to the Lord we departed, etc.

Winslow's name is third on the list of those who subscribed to the Covenant, or compact, before the disembarkation at Cape Cod. He was one of the first who came on shore to seek out the most eligible place for founding a settlement in this wild and unknown land. He was a gentleman of the best family of any of the Pilgrims, his father, Edward Winslow, Esq., being a person of importance in Droitwich. In all the initiatory labor for establishing this little colony, the nucleus of a great nation, he was ever active and influential in promoting the welfare of the Pilgrims, who on account of the respectability of his family, and the excellent qualities of his mind and heart appear to have regarded him with more than ordinary respect and confidence, which was never misplaced.

At the annual election in 1624 Mr. Winslow was elected Assistant and in 1644 Governor of Plymouth Colony.

In 1655 Oliver Cromwell appointed three commissioners, of which number Winslow was the chief, to go with an expedition against the Spaniards in the West Indies under Admiral Penn and General Venables. The three commissioners to direct their operations. After an unsuccessful attack on St. Domingo, the fleet sailed for Jamaica, which surrendered without any resistance. But Mr. Winslow, who partook of the chagrin of defeat, did not live to enjoy the pleasure of victory. In the passage between Hispaniola and Jamaica the heat of the climate threw him into a fever, which put an end to his life on May 8, 1655, in the sixty-first year of his age. His body was committed to the deep, with the honors of war, forty-two guns being fired by the fleet on that occasion.

After Bradford, Plymouth Colony owed to no man so much as to Edward Winslow. Always intelligent, generous, confident, and indefatigable, he was undoubtingly trusted for any service at home or abroad which the infant settlement required.

JOSIAH WINSLOW, the only surviving son of Governor Edward Winslow, was born at Plymouth in 1629 and died on the family estate, Careswell, Marshfield, Dec. 18, 1680, in the 52nd year of his age. He was buried at the expense of the colony "in testimony of the colony's endeared love and affection for him." He married Penelope, daughter of Herbert Pelham, Esq., who came to Boston in 1645.

He stood upon the uppermost heights of society, he reached every elevation that could be obtained, and there was nothing left for ambition to covet, because all had been gained. He was the first native-born general and the first native-born governor. The governor acquired the highest military rank and had engaged in active and successful warfare with the highest command in New England. He presided over the legislative, executive and judicial departments of the government. In addition to his military and civil distinction he acquired that of being the most delightful companion in the colony. He lived on his ample paternal domain and his hospitality was magnificent and the attractions of the festive board at Careswell were heightened by the charm of his beautiful wife. He was elected governor in 1673, which office he held until his death. He was succeeded by his only surviving son.

ISAAC WINSLOW, born in 1670 and died Dec. 6, 1738. This eminently distinguished man sustained the chief places of power and honor in the colony, and was a worthy successor to his father in being its chief military commander, a member of the Council for more than 20 years and for some time its president, and for several years Chief Justice of the Court of Common Pleas, and Judge of Probate; the last office he held at his death. His eldest son, Josiah, graduated at Harvard College in 1721, was killed in battle with the French and Indians at Georges Island, May 1st, 1724. His second son, great grandson of the first governor of Plymouth, was the celebrated

JOHN WINSLOW, born in Marshfield, May 27, 1702, and died in Hingham, 1774, in his 73rd year. No native of New England, probably, except Sir William Pepperell, was more distinguished as a military leader. In 1740-1 he was a captain in the unfortunate expedition to Cartagena under the command of Admiral Vernon, and subsequently endured much hard service in the several enterprises against Crown Point and Nova Scotia. He will be remembered in our annals principally in removing the Arcadians from Nova Scotia. The forces employed by the Colony at this period was composed almost entirely of Massachusetts troops, specially enlisted for the service to act as a distinct body. They formed into a regiment of two battilions, of which Governor Shirley was the Colonel, and of which Winslow, then a half-pay Captain in the British army and a Major-General in the Militia, was Lieutenant-Colonel. As Shirley could not leave his government to take command in person, Monckton, a Lieutenant-Colonel in the Army, was appointed to conduct the first battilion and Winslow the second. The plan for abducting the Arcadians was kept a profound secret, both by those who formed it and by those who were sent to execute, the home government knew nothing about it and it appears to have been done solely by the Colonial government; Colonel Winslow was but the instrument and acted under the Governor's written and positive instructions.

In 1756 Major-General Winslow took the field with eight thousand men raised in New England and New York to repel the French invasion and marched against Montcalm, who to save Crown Point and Ticonderoga made a movement from Oswego by the St. Lawrence River. As soon as the French General returned to Canada, Winslow and his army returned to Massachusetts.

In 1762 he was appointed with William Brattle and James Otis to act as Commissioner "to repair to the river St. Croix, determine where the easterly line of Maine is to begin and extend the said line as far as should be thought necessary." In compliment to General Winslow, "the fourth of a family more eminent for their talents, learning and honors than any other in New England," one of the towns on the Kennebec River in 1771 was called by his name. Of this town he was one of the original grantees. He died at Hingham in 1774, aged seventy-one, leaving two sons and a widow, who embarked with the Royal Army from Boston in 1776. She was in England in 1783, and enjoyed a pension from the government.

Pelham Winslow, eldest son of General John, was born June 8th, 1737, graduated at Harvard College in 1753, and entered the office of James Otis to fit himself for the bar, was a staunch loyalist. In 1774 he abandoned his home to escape mob violence and took refuge in Boston. At the evacuation in 1776 he accompanied the Royal Army to Halifax, and thence went to New York, where he entered the military service of the Crown, and was Major. In 1778 he was proscribed and banished. He died at Brooklyn, New York, in 1783, leaving a wife and an infant daughter.

Dr. Isaac Winslow, second son of General John, born April 7, 1739, graduated at Harvard College in 1762, died in 1819. He commenced the practice of physic, and though of the same principles as other members of his family, remained upon his estate during the war, and his life, thereby saving it from confiscation, for although he was a strong loyalist his medical services were of such great value to the revolutionists that they did not drive him forth and deprive him of his property. Sabine says: I find it said, and the authority good, that in 1778 he treated about three hundred patients inoculated with smallpox, and such was his remarkable success not one of them died. His son John, an eminent lawyer, deceased at Natchez in 1820. His widow, Frances, died at Hingham in 1846, aged eighty-four. The family tomb of the Winslows is at Marshfield, on the Careswell estate, of which Governor Winslow was the first owner. It was afterwards purchased by Daniel Webster, on which he resided until his death.

EDWARD WINSLOW, only brother of General John, born June 7, 1714, died at Halifax in 1784, aged seventy-two years. He graduated at Harvard College in 1765, resided at Plymouth, was Clerk of the Courts, Register of Probate, Collector of the Port. He was obliged to seek shelter in Boston from mob violence, at the evacuation in 1776 went with the Army to Halifax, Nova Scotia, where he died. The ceremonies at his funeral were of a style to confer the highest honors to himself, and his illustrious family. His estates in Massachusetts were confiscated, but every branch of his family was amply provided for by the generosity of the British Government.

EDWARD WINSLOW, JR., only son of the aforesaid Edward. He was born in 1745, died at Fredericton, N. B., 1815, aged seventy years, graduated at Harvard College in 1765. In 1774, the Plymouth County Convention "Resolved, That Edward Winslow, Jr., one of the two clerks of the Court of General Sessions of the Peace and Court of Common Pleas for this County, has, by refusing this body a copy of an Address made at the last term in this County, to Thomas Hutchinson, Esq., betrayed the trust reposed in him, by refusing his attendance when requested, treated the body of this county with insult and contempt, and by that means rendered himself unworthy to serve the county in said office."

In 1775 he joined the Royal Army at Boston, and entering the service became a Colonel. In 1778 he was proscribed and banished. In 1782 he was Muster-Master-General of the Loyalist forces employed under the Crown. After the war he settled in New Brunswick, and was a member of the first Council formed in that Colony, Surrogate-General, Judge of the Supreme Court, and finally Administrator of the Government. The Royal Arms which for many years were displayed in the Council Chamber in the Old State House in Boston, still exist, and are carefully preserved in Trinity church, St. John, N. B. The story of their exit from Boston, and by what means they came to find a permanent home at St. John, were not known till recently, when documents were found, which leave no question or room for doubt.

In the winter of 1785 Edward Winslow was at Halifax and Ward Chipman, a fellow refugee from Boston, had taken up his residence at St. John. In a letter of Mr. Winslow to Mr. Chipman on the 16th January, 1785, he says, "Give my old Custom House seal to Mr. Leonard, and tell him I'll forward *the famous carv'd Coat of Arms* by the first conveyance from Halifax." A subsequent letter to Mr. Chipman, refers more fully to the subject which is in part as follows:

Halifax, 25 March, 1785.

My Dear Fellow:

By the schooner Halifax I send a small assortment of stationery as per invoice. . . . In the box with your stationery is a venerable Coat of Arms, which I authorize you to present to the Council Chamber, or any other respectable public Room, which you shall think best entitled to it. They (Lyon & Unicorn) were constant members of the Council at Boston (by mandamus) ran away when the others did—have suffered —are of course Refugees and have a claim for residence at New Brunswick. Cordially yours

ED. WINSLOW.*

Ward Chipman, Esq.

Judge Winslow was one of the founders of the Old Colony Club, at Plymouth, and was one of its most active members. He delivered the first anniversary address of that association on the 22 of December or Forefathers' Day, in 1770.

ISAAC WINSLOW was a Boston merchant, son of Col. Edward Winslow, born May 2, 1709. He was the third in descent from John Winslow who came from Droitwich to Boston in 1655, and died in 1674. He was a brother of Governor Edward of the Plymouth Colony. He was a gentleman highly esteemed for his benevolence and other virtues. He graduated at Harvard College in 1727, then entered the counting room of James Bowdoin, and subsequently with his brother Joshua carried on an extensive and profitable business in Boston. They also became considerable ship owners, and had one ship constantly in the London trade. Joshua was one of the consignees of the tea destroyed by the mob. Isaac retired from business in 1753, and became a resident of Roxbury. He was the last occupant of the Dudley mansion, which was razed to the ground a few days after the battle of Bunker Hill, to make way for the works erected here by the Americans. The Universalist church was built upon its site. In making the necessary excavation for the church, the wine cellar of the mansion was unearthed and strange to say, as it may seem, the liquors were, after a lapse of forty-five years, found intact.**

In June 1760 he received the thanks of the town for a gift of land near Meeting House Hill. His first wife, Lucy, daughter of Gen. Samuel Waldo, died in Roxbury in 1763, at the age of forty-three.

In 1774 he was an Addresser of Gov. Hutchinson, and 1775 of Gen. Gage. He was appointed Mandamus Councillor, and was qualified. This was an offence that could not be forgiven by the disunionists.

Though a loyalist, his moderation and his character made him less obnoxious to the revolutionists than his neighbors, Auchmuty, Hallowell, and Loring. His virtues, however, could not save him from the fury of

*See Royal Memorials by Rev. Edmund F. Shafter. Also cut of Coat of Arms on outside cover of this work.
**The Town of Roxbury. Francis S. Drake. pp. 355-6.

the mob. Immediately after the Lexington affair, he took refuge in Boston.

In 1776, with his family of ten persons, he accompanied the Royal Army to Halifax, and in 1778 was proscribed and banished, and his estates confiscated. In his religious belief he was a Sandemanian. Jemima, his widow, died at London in 1790.

REV. EDWARD WINSLOW was an Episcopal minister of Braintree, now Quincy, Mass. He was born in Boston in 1722. Graduated at Harvard College in 1741. His father Joshua was a brother of the aforesaid Isaac Winslow, and son of Colonel Edward Winslow.

The North Precinct of Braintree, now Quincy, had the reputation of being a "nest of Tories," owing to the presence of the Church of England people, connected with Christ Church. The mother English society was most liberal in dealing with its offshoot and until the Revolution, it annually sent over sixty pounds sterling for the support of the minister. In all, it is said to have spent over thirteen thousand dollars in building up this church. Naturally the society was inclined to a friendly feeling toward the hand which fed it. To it the Apthorpe's, the Vassall's, the Borland's, the Cleverly's and the Millers, indeed all the gentry of the neighborhood with the exception of the Quincy's, belonged, the Adam's not being in this class at that time. It was here the same as elsewhere throughout the colonies, the ministers of the Established Church of England stood condemned in the eyes of revolutionists, neither seclusion, insignificance nor high character was able to save the clergy from the fury of the mobs.

In June, 1777, a town meeting was called for the purpose of agreeing upon a list of those persons who were "esteemed inimical" to the popular cause. This was in the nature of a formal indictment of the whole society, for among the names of those recorded as "inimical" were its rector, its wardens, and all its leading members.

The Rev. Edward Winslow, the rector of Christ Church, found his situation uncomfortable in the extreme, nor was it any longer safe for him to read the prayer for the King. Yet he seems to have struggled on vainly hoping for better days, until his salary was stopped, and many of his people had moved away. Then in 1777, taking very properly the ground that his ordination oath compelled him to conform literally to the Prayer Book he "with sad and silent musings" resigned his charge. Going to New York, which was then in British occupation, Mr. Winslow died there in 1780 before the close of the war. He lies buried under the alter of St. George's Church in that city. Jane Isabella, his widow, died at Fayetteville, North Carolina, in 1793, aged sixty-six.

Joseph Winslow of Boston was a merchant, he was born in 1724, and died in 1777, was the son of Kenelm, the great grandson of Kenelm of Droitwich, the brother of Governor Winslow, who died at Salem in 1672.

He was possibly the Joseph Winslow who took part at the Siege of

SIR ROGER HALE SHEAFFE, BARONET.

Born in Boston in 1763. Though reluctant to serve against his countrymen, yet at Queenstown's Heights he drove the American army over the heights into the Niagara river, for which he received the title of Baronet. Died at Edinburgh in 1851.

Louisberg, and was amongst the number to volunteer under the command of Bacon to attack the island Battery, and was the Joseph Winslow referred to by the Committee of Newport, R. I., of which Jonathan Otis was chairman, who wrote to the Committee of Easthampton, New York, in June, 1775, that he was "an inveterate enemy of our country" and that "it was generally thought" he had gone to a hospital to take the small pox for the purpose of spreading the disease in the Whig Camp at Cambridge." Sabine says the truth of this averment may be doubted.

LIST OF CONFISCATED ESTATES BELONGING TO ISAAC WINSLOW IN SUFFOLK COUNTY AND TO WHOM SOLD.

To Ebenezer Crosbey, June 15, 1782; Lib. 135, fol. 20; Assignment of mortgage Joseph Crosby to Isaac Winslow, dated Aug. 5, 1768.

SIR ROGER HALE SHEAFFE, BARONET.

WILLIAM S. SHEAFFE, of Charlestown, was born in 1649, and married in 1672 Ruth Woods. He was a mariner, and they had three sons and three daughters. His son William, born 1683, married Mary Longfellow, a widow, in 1704. He died in 1718, and his widow in 1720. They had five sons and two daughters. His eldest son William Sheaffe, Jr., was born 13 Jan., 1705. He graduated at Harvard College in 1723, and married Susanna Child, Oct. 1st, 1752.*

WILLIAM SHEAFFE was Deputy Collector of Customs of Boston. He frequently acted as Collector in the absence of Sir Henry Frankland, who held that office in 1759, and when the Baronet was removed for inattention to his duties, he was appointed to fill the vacant place, and issued the celebrated "Writs of Assistance," giving the Revenue officers the right to search for smuggled goods. Roger Hale succeeded as Collector in 1672, when Sheaffe was again Deputy. He continued in that office under Joseph Harrison, who was the last Royal Collector of the port. Mr. Sheaffe died in 1771, leaving a large family in poverty. There is ample evidence that Mrs. Sheaffe was an intelligent, excellent woman, and bore many trials with pious resignation, and that the Sheaffe's were a loving and happy family. Mrs. Sheaffe died in 1811.

SUSANNA, Mr. Sheaffe's eldest daughter, who died in 1834, married Captain Ponsonby Molesworth, a nephew of Lord Ponsonby. The family account is that on the day of the landing of the British troops in Boston, a regiment halted in Queen (Court) street, opposite Mr. Sheaffe's

*There was a family of Sheaffe's in Boston much earlier than 1672, when William Sheaffe's name first appears on the records, but I do not find any connection between the two families, except that James Sheaffe of Portsmouth, N. H., of the Boston family, was a loyalist. He was allowed to remain, although much persecuted. (See Heraldic Journal, Vol. IX. p. 85, also Wyman's Genealogies and Estates of Charlestown, and History of Portsmouth, N. H.)

house, that, Susanna attracted by the music, accompanied by her younger sisters, went upon the balcony, that Captain Molesworth saw her, was struck with her great beauty, gazed upon her intently, and at last, said to a brother officer, who like himself was leaning against a fence, "That girl seals my fate." An introduction, and a visit followed, and the maiden's heart rapidly won, but then came sorrow, for Susanna was barely fifteen, and parental consent to her marriage was refused. Her governess, to whom she entrusted her grief, espoused her cause, and favored immediate union, and the result accordingly was, the flight of the three to Rhode Island, where the loving pair were married. Molesworth sold his commission in 1776, and in December of that year was in England with his wife. Their married life proved uncommonly happy; and they lived to see their children's children.

Another daughter, Helen, of remarkable beauty, married a revolutionist, James Lovell, who became Naval Officer of Boston. Their grandson, Mansfield Lovell, was a General in the Confederate service, and was in command at New Orleans, when it was captured by the Union forces. The General was true to the disunion instincts of his grandfather.

SIR ROGER HALE SHEAFFE, BARONET, the subject of this sketch, was son of William Sheaffe. Born in Boston in 1763. His mother, after the death of his father, removed to a wooden house which was standing till recently on the corner of Essex and Columbia (formerly Auchmuty street) which was owned by her father. Lord Percy, afterward, Duke of Northumberland hired quarters there, soon became attached to Roger, and assumed the care of him. It would seem that the original intention of his Lordship was to provide for the boy in the Navy, for Mrs. Sheaffe wrote, in December 1776, she was told "Earl Percy had taken my son Roger from the Admiral's ship, given him a commission in the Army (which I must not say that I am sorry for), and sent him to England to an academy for education under his patronage." In 1778 Roger was dangerously ill, and on becoming convalescent, passed two months in Devonshire, with his sister, Mrs. Molesworth. In a letter dated at the Academy, Little Chelsea, early in 1779, he said, Lord Percy is as good as ever. He has given me a commission in his own regiment, the Fifth, now in the West Indies. I shall not join it for a year.

My love to my dear sister and brother. Remember me kindly to all my friends in Boston. You may be sure that I shall follow your advice strictly, that I may be all that you wish, shall be the endeavor of your most dutiful and affectionate son.

In 1786 Captain Molesworth said in a letter to his mother-in-law, Mrs. Sheaffe, The Duke of Northumberland has lodged money to buy Roger a Company, which, when he is in possession of, he will have it in his power more fully to manifest his affection for so good a mother. Roger's sister, Mrs. Molesworth, at the same period wrote her mother, "He is as good a young man as ever lived. Lord Percy continues his kindness to him. He improves very much, and is a great favorite with all his masters." Again, "Roger behaves remarkably well, is much liked in the Regiment; he is tall, well made, and reckoned handsome, very lively, yet prudent and steady in matters of consequence. He wishes, as much as we do, to go to Boston."

In 1791 Lieutenant Sheaffe was at Detroit, which post was still held by England, on account of the non-fulfillment of some of the terms of the treaty of peace. In 1794, before the surrender of the "Western Posts" as they were called, Lieutenant Sheaffe delivered a letter to Capt. Williamson, which was unequivocally of a military and hostile nature.

"I am commanded to declare that during the inexecution of the treaty of peace between Great Britain and the United States, and until the existing differences respecting it, shall be mutually and finally adjusted, the taking possession of any part of the Indian territory, either for purposes of war or sovereignty, is held to be a direct violation of his Britannic Majesty's rights, as they unquestionably existed before the treaty, and has an immediate tendency to interrupt, and in its progress destroy, that good understanding which has hitherto subsisted between his Britannic Majesty and the United States of America. I, therefore require you to desist from any such aggression. R. H. Sheaffe, Lieut. 5th Reg't. and Qr. M'r. Gen. Dept. of his Britannic Majesty's service.'

In 1801 he was in service in the attack on Copenhagen under Lord Nelson; and though poor, just one-half of his prize money was sent to his mother in Boston.

At the battle of Queenstown Heights, he was a Colonel in General Brocks army; that gallant officer was slain at 7 o'clock in the morning. At noon, Colonel Sheaffe moved up from Niagara, took command of the forces and drove the Americans over the rocky heights into the river. For this victory he was made a Major General, and created a Baronet. At this period General Scott (who was the conqueror of Mexico, and Commander in Chief of the United States forces at the outbreak of the Civil War,) was a Colonel, and was taken prisoner by General Sheaffe, who related to him some of the circumstances of his military career, in substance, that in 1775, he was living in Boston with his widowed mother with whom Earl Percy had his quarters, that his Lordship was very fond of him, and took him away with him in view of providing for him, which he did, by giving him a military education, and by purchasing a commission and promotion to as high rank as is allowed by the rules of the service, and that the war then existing found him stationed in Canada. He stated moreover, that, reluctant to serve gainst his own countrymen, he solicited to be employed elsewhere, but at that time his request had not been granted."

Major General Sheaffe, commanded the British Army in person, and after the battle of Queenstown Heights, he moved upon Little York, now Toronto, and captured it. During these operations he lost his baggage and papers, which General Dearborn informed the Secretary of War "were a valuable acquisition."

In April, 1813, within a week of the fall of Little York, in a letter from his wife's mother to her niece, Miss Child, dated at Quebec, she says, "It is possible that you may not have heard that your cousin, Sir Roger Sheaffe has had the title of Baronet of Great Britain conferred on him, by our Prince Regent, a handsome compliment, which I trust will be followed by something substantial to support it. Sir Roger is so pressed with public business as to allow him scarcely time to attend to his private concerns. My dear Margaret is still in Quebec, with her lovely little Julia, as Upper Canada is still the seat of war. Her elevation to rank, has not in the least deprived her of her native humility and meekness. The manner it was announced to her was rather singular. She was met by a gentleman in the street, as she was going to church, who accosted her by the title of 'Lady Sheaffe', and put a letter in her hand from the Duke of Northumberland, addressed to 'Lady Sheaffe' which she received with her usual equanimity."

In 1841 he writes to his cousin, Miss Susan Child of Boston, "The year 1834 was indeed a sad one, in it we lost the last of our children, and in the same year died my sister Molesworth, a brother of Lady Sheaffe, my late brother William's eldest son, named after me, a Captain in the Army, and also Lord Cragie, the brother of your cousin. Mrs. Cragie's husband I retain a good share of activity, as well as of erect military carriage, my sight is good, my teeth in a state to create envy in a majority of American misses, my appetite never fails and I sleep well. In January, 1842, he spoke of William, eldest surviving son of his brother William thus: He is my natural heir, and having adopted him when he was ten years of age; and it having pleased God to take all my children from me. I regard him as a son.

Sir Roger H. Sheaffe died at Edinburgh in 1851, aged eighty-eight. He visited Boston, his native town, four times, namely, in 1788, in 1792-3, in 1803 and in 1806. He was respected and loved by his kinsmen to a remarkable degree. He was of medium stature, his person was well formed, his face was fine, his eyes of the deepest blue, full and prominent; and his teeth were of the purest white, regular and even, and were retained to the close of his life. Lady Sheaffe was Margrate, daughter of John Coffin and a cousin of Lieutenant-General John and of Admiral Sir Isaac Coffin. She was the mother of four children, who, as we have seen, died before her husband. The remains of Sir Roger's father and mother, of his brother Thomas Child, of his sisters Helen, Salley, Nancy, and Margaret, and of others of his lineage, were deposited in the Child Tomb, Trinity Church, Summer street, Boston.*

Nathaniel Sheaffe, oldest brother of Sir Roger, was a clerk in the Custom House, but at the death of his father in 1771, he left, in order to better provide for his mother and sisters, of whom he had the care. At

*Most of the information contained in this article was obtained by L. Sabine, from Miss Isabella Child, Thomas Hale Child and Miss Mary P. Hale, relatives of Sir Roger H. Sheaffe.

the outbreak of the Revolution, he went to Jamaica, "where he intended to stay till the times will permit him to come home." He died January 29, 1777, and was buried in the churchyard at Morant Bay, Jamaica.

THOMAS CHILD SHEAFFE, brother of Sir Roger, went to New York after the evacuation of Boston. He was engaged in trade with the West Indies and Souther Ports. He died in Boston previous to 1793.

JONATHAN SAYWARD.

The name Saward or Sayward is an ancient Teutonic personal name, sae, the sea and weard, a keeper—the Guardian of the Sea, and was applied to the high admiral in Saxon times.

Henry Sayward came over to this country from England in 1637. He resided a few years at Hampton and Portsmouth, and then came to York. He was by occupation a millwright and carpenter, a man much needed, as mills were the principal sources of income to the new settlers. The town of York granted him three hundred acres of upland on the west side of the York river, and the selectmen laid the same out to him June 20th, 1667. Here he settled, and built a saw mill, and carried on a large business. He also at this time built the meeting house at York. He was constable of York in 1664, Selectman in 1667, Grand Juryman in 1668-9. His wife's name was Mary, and it has been claimed she was the daughter of John Cousins, of Casco Bay. He died in 1679. There is no record of the birth of their children, as the records of the Town of York were destroyed by the Indians on Feb. 5, 1692, but there is a deposition and deeds, which prove they had three sons and three daughters.

JONATHAN SAYWARD, the second son of Henry and Mary Sayward, resided in York. Very little is known concerning him. In 1687 there was a grant of land made to him by the town, on Little River, near Wells. He died previous to 1699.

JOSEPH SAYWARD, son of the aforesaid, was born at York, March 17, 1702. He was constable in 1716. Moderator and Selectman in 1721, At this date the meeting voted "that Mr. Joseph Sayward shall have the full management to build a sufficient fortification about our Parsonage home, of ten foot high, and fifty foot square, with two good buskins, or flancers, of ten foot square, all to be built of square hard timber, of ten inches thick, to be built forthwith, and said Sayward to keep a just and full account of ye cost and charge thereof." In 1723 the Indians were troublesome. A company under Captain Bragdon was sent in pursuit of them, a journal of their proceedings was kept by Joseph Sayward, which is in the Mass. Archives.

He married Mary, daughter of Samuel and Deborah Webber, of York, and had five sons and four daughters.

JONATHAN SAYWARD, eldest son of the aforesaid Joseph, and of the fourth generation in this country, and the subject of this sketch, was born at York, November 9, 1713. He began to take an interest in public affairs early in life. He was chosen town clerk in 1736, and constable in 1741. He was commissioned by Governor Shirley to command the sloop "Sea Flower" in the expedition against Louisburg in 1744, in which he took an important part.

He was chosen Representative to the General Court of Massachusetts for the years 1766, 7, 8.

In 1772 he was appointed by Governor Hutchinson as Special Justice of the Court of Common Pleas, and Judge of Probate for York County.

He was for many years extensively engaged in shipping, and at one time owned about twenty vessels, which were employed in the Southern and West India trade. He was one of the most extensive land owners in York, and was one of the proprietors of the town of Shapleigh.

When the Revolution broke out he was living in affluence in the beautiful mansion which he had built on the York river, near the mill site granted to his ancestors. At this time he had several vessels with valuable cargoes in the West Indies, and large sums of money invested in personal securities, on the income of which he enjoyed a satisfactory and honorable independence, but all was swept away in the Revolution.

Judge Sayward was one of the seventeen "Rescinders." He was not only decided in his attachment to the Crown, but was of the opinion that the Revolution would cause the decline of national virtue and prosperity in America. He fared hard at the hands of the "Sons of Liberty," and by remaining was obliged to bear contempt and insult, and by his own account never went out without £100 in his pocket, so as to be ever ready to escape from his persecutors. But, however bad he was treated in the early days of the great struggle, he seems to have regained the confidence of his townsmen, for in 1780 he was elected Moderator of the town meeting, and auditor of selectmen accounts in 1782.

His mansion home previously referred to is among the most interesting of the many historic homes in the ancient town of York, and what makes it doubly so is the fact that it contains all the original furniture, books, painting, silver plate, and the "loote" he obtained at the capture of Louisburg and brought home with him, consisting of rare chinaware, two very large candlesticks, a pair of andirons, a warming pan and brass tongs, all of which are now in a good state of preservation. There is also a full length portrait of Judge Sayward and another of his wife, with costumes of their times, and one of his daughter Sarah, at the age of twenty-three, painted by Blackburn at Charleston in 1761, a pupil of Copley. As works of art these paintings are pronounced by connoisseurs as exceedingly fine. The family coat of arms of the Saywards, in color, occupies a conspicuous place over the mantel piece, on the back of which is the following memorandum, which proves conclusively that it was legally granted:

London, July 1st, 1762.

The arms of Jonathan Sayward, Esqr., of Old York, in the Province of the Massachusetts Bay, in New England, Merchant, Recd this 1st of July, 1762, from the College of Arms, Herald's Office. The painting, Vellum, Frame and Glass as it now stands cost 32-6 Sterling Rec'd by his most dutifull Humble Servt.

Nath. Barrell.

There is also a commission from Governor Shirley to Jonathan Sayward, to command the sloop "Sea Flower" in the Louisburg expedition. The mansion is full of articles worth the attention of those of historical, antiquarian taste. Judge Sayward died May 8, 1797, and is buried in the old burying ground in York Village.

He married in 1736 Sarah Mitchell, who died in 1775. They had only one child, Sarah, born 1738, who married Nathaniel Barrell of Portsmouth, merchant. They were married at the judge's mansion in 1758. She was a great belle in her time, and was the general favorite of the village. She died in 1808, and her husband in 1831, aged 99 years. They had eleven children.

The mansion was for many years owned and occupied by Elizabeth and Mary Barrell, daughters of Jonathan Sayward Barrell, granddaughters of the Judge. They took great pleasure in exhibiting the house and the many interesting relics and hierlooms of their grandfather, and it is largely due to them that the same was kept intact, and not distributed at their death, as many members of the family desired. Elizabeth died in the old mansion November 12, 1883, aged 84 years, and her sister Mary died at the same place, June 6, 1889, aged 85 years.*

DEBLOIS FAMILY.

ETIENNE DEBLOIS was born in France, and for a time lived in Belgium. He was a French Hugenot, and the family name was DeChatillon. He was descended from the last counts of Blois and was banished from France at the revocation of the Edict of Nantes. After living in the Low Countries, he removed to England and was present at the battle of the Boyne. His sister was burnt at the stake in Ireland by the Papists, and he died in England.

Stephen Deblois, son of Etienne, was born in Oxford, England, in 1699. He came to New York in the Frigate Sea Horse, commanded by Captain Dumaresq. In 1720 he removed to Boston. He married February 6, 1721, Ann Farley, of English parentage. His death occurred in Boston in 1785, and his large estate was settled in 1790. In his will he says: "My two sons has been obliged to leave and I do not expect to see them again."

*The Sayward Family, 1890.

GILBERT DEBLOIS, son of the latter was born in New York city, March 17, 1725. He became a prosperous Merchant in Boston. In 1749 he married Ann, daughter of William and Ann Holmes Coffin, and granddaughter of Nathaniel Coffin. In 1774 Gilbert Deblois was an Addresser of Hutchinson, and in 1775 an Addresser of Gage. In 1776 he went to Halifax with his younger brother Lewis, and then must have returned to New York before his departure for England, according to an account in Hutchinson's Diary.

Dec. 23, 1776—Gilbert Deblois arrived in one of the transports from New York.

While residing in Boston, Mr. Deblois planted some elms in front of the Granary, just opposite his house on Tremont Street. These famous trees afterwards became known as the Paddock elms. Mr. Deblois had asked Paddock to keep an eye to their safety, and Adino Paddock performed this duty faithfully.

In a letter written by James Murray to a friend in New York, dated September 30, 1769, he speaks of Mr. Deblois' assistance to him when he was attacked by a mob. "Mr. Deblois threw himself in my rear, and suffered not a little in my defence."

In 1778 Gilbert Deblois was proscribed and banished, and his estate confiscated. The year following he was in London and addressed the king. His death occurred in that city in 1792, aged sixty-seven.

LEWIS DEBLOIS, brother to Gilbert, married Elizabeth Jenkins of Boston, in 1748. He was a prominent merchant in Boston, was an Addresser of General Gage in 1775. He went to Halifax on the evacuation of Boston in 1776.

He was proscribed and banished.. He died very suddenly in England, (after being out all day) in 1779, aged seventy-one.

George Deblois, son of the aforesaid was born in Boston in 1753. He was a merchant in Salem. He was an Addresser of General Gage in 1774. He went to England. In 1784, there was a George Deblois, a merchant at Halifax, N. S., probably his son. The widow of a George Deblois died in the same city in 1827, aged seventy-four.

LEWIS DEBLOIS, brother of the aforesaid, was born in Boston in 1762. He went to New Brunswick and was a prominent merchant in St. John, and in 1795 a member of the company of Loyal Artillery. He died in that city in 1802. His daughter Elizabeth Cranston married James White, Esq., Sheriff of the County of St. John.

LIST OF CONFISCATED ESTATES BELONGING TO GILBERT DEBLOIS IN SUFFOLK COUNTY AND TO WHOM SOLD.

To Gilbert Deblois, Jr., Feb. 3, 1783; Lib. 137 fol. 28; Two thirds of land and brick warehouse in Boston, Cornhill W.; Spring Lane N.; Stephen Minot E.; land of Old South Church S.

To Ann Deblois, wife of Gilbert Deblois, Oct. 17, 1785; Lib. 151 fol. 217; Two thirds of land and house in Boston, Common St. W.; Martha Symmes N.; E.; N. and E.; Moses Gill N.; William Dana E.; Rawsons Lane S.

LYDE FAMILY.

Edward Lyde married in 1660 Mary, daughter of Rev. John Wheelwright, and died before 1663. He had an only son Edward, who married Susanna Curwin, daughter of Captain George Curwin. His second wife was Deborah, daughter of Hon. Nathaniel Byfield, 1696. In 1685 Edward Lyde and William Williams witnessed a deed that the Indian Chief Wamatuck and his Counsellors signed by making their marks. It was concerning land in Boston Harbor. In 1702-3 he was a warden of Kings Chapel.

Byfield Lyde, eldest son of the preceding, was born in Boston in 1704. Graduated at Harvard College in 1723. He was an Addresser of Governor Hutchinson in 1774, and a Protester against the disunionists the same year, and in 1775 he was an Addresser of General Gage. His wife, Sarah, the only daughter of Governor Belcher, died in Boston, October 10, 1768, aged sixty-one. In 1776 he accompanied the Royal Army to Halifax and died there the same year.

EDWARD LYDE, second son of Edward Lyde, was born in Boston in 1725. He was a merchant, and was proscribed, banished, and his property confiscated. It was bought in by his brother Nathaniel (born in 1735) who was allowed to remain.

Hutchinson, in his diary May 3rd, 1776, says: "Landed at Halifax. Edward Lyde, Esq., invited me to his house, where I tarried till I embarqued for England. I was very happy in being at Mr. Lyde's as there was so great an addition to the inhabitants from the navy and army and Refugees from Boston which made the lodgings for them very scarce to be had, and many of them when procured, quite intolerable." Again in his diary June 7, 1776, Hutchinson says: "Ned Lyde had arrived with others at Dover."

Edward Lyde died in New York in 1812, aged eighty-seven.

GEORGE LYDE, of Boston, in 1770, was appointed Collector of the Port of Falmouth, (Portland) Maine, and continued there until the beginning of the Revolution. He was an Addresser of Governor Hutchinson in 1774, and in 1778 was proscribed and banished. He was in England in 1780.

LIST OF CONFISCATED ESTATES BELONGING TO EDWARD LYDE IN SUFFOLK COUNTY AND TO WHOM SOLD.

To Nathaniel Byfield Lyde, Feb. 21, 1785; Land and buildings in Boston, Summer St. S.; Bishop's Alley W.; heirs of Andrew Cunningham deceased N.; land formerly of John Simpson deceased E.

JAMES BOUTINEAU.

STEPHEN BOUTINEAU was one of the French Protestants, or Huguenots who came to Falmouth (Portland), Maine, in 1687, in company with Peter Bowdoin, Philip LeBretton, Philip Barger and others. He married Mary, daughter of Peter and Elizabeth Bowdoin in 1708. He was in 1748 the only surviving elder of the French Church on School street, Boston, of which Andrew Le Mercier was minister.* His son James Boutineau was born 27 January, 1710, he was an Attorney-at-law. In 1774 he was appointed Mandamus-Counsellor, and was one of the ten who took the oath of office. His daughter Nancy was married on Oct. 5, 1769, to John Robinson, a commissioner of the customs, but previous to this marriage Robinson was accused of assault upon James Otis, the latter, one of the most formidable of the "Patriots" met Commissioner Robinson at the Coffee-house and trouble ensued. As usual in all such cases, the friends of each party made out a good case for their respective sides, the matter was carried into court, where it was kept for about four years and the jury finally brought in damages in favor of Otis. In the meantime Robinson and his wife had gone to England, and as Mr. Boutineau was a lawyer, he managed the case for his son-in-law, who apologized for injuring Otis. Mr. Otis refused the fine of 2,000 pounds sterling, and nothing was demanded of Robinson but the costs of court and the amount of Mr. Otis' surgeon's bill, altogether amounting to about 112 pounds, lawful money. The affair ended in the Courts about 1772.

James Boutineau was included in the Conspiracy Act of 1779, and his estate was confiscated under its provisions. He went to England, and his death occurred in that country. Mrs. Boutineau was a sister of Peter Faneuil, and another sister married Edward Jones, a merchant in Boston. Mrs. Jones went to Halifax, Nova Scotia, and while there received a letter from the Boutineaus in England, in which she was informed that, "Mr. and Mrs. Faneuil, who lodge in the same house with us, make it agreeable;" and that "there are one or two other genteel gentlemen and ladies, so that during the winter we drank tea with each other four days in the week." Of other fellow Loyalists, Mrs. Boutineau writes, that "Lodgings have been taken for Mr. Sewell, of Cambridge, and family,—they are expected here this day. Colonel Murray's family are gone to Wales, as well as Judge Browne and Apthorp's. All the New England people here, are Barnes and family, Captain Fenton and daughter, besides those in the house." In a postcript, she adds: "I desire you to inform me (if you can) who lives in my house in Boston." In a letter to her sister, dated April 1, 1785, Mrs. Boutineau tells Mrs. Mary Ann Jones who was residing in Boston at that time that her health

*New Eng. His. Gen. Vol. 8, p. 247.

is "very indifferent," and that "Mr. Faneuil had a letter lately from Mr. Jones, who is going soon to be very well married," etc.

LIST OF CONFISCATED ESTATES BELONGING TO JAMES BOUTINEAU, ET AL., IN SUFFOLK COUNTY AND TO WHOM SOLD.

To Samuel Clark, Feb. 26, 1780; Lib. 131 fol. 58; Land and dwelling-house in Boston, School St. S.; the town's land W.; John Rowe N.; Joseph Green E. —— Garden land near the above, Cook's Alley W.; Leverett Saltonstall N.; William Powell E.; S. and E.; Leverett Saltonstall S. [Description corrected in margin of record.]
To Samuel Broome, July 24, 1780; Lib. 131 fol. 327; Land and dwelling-house in Boston, Milk St. S.; land of Old South Church W.; Stephen Minot N.; widow Jones E.; N. and E. —— Pasture land, 1 A. 10 r. opposite said dwelling-house, Milk St. N.; Cole, —— Decoster et al. E.; heirs of Barnabas Binney et al. S.; heirs of John Greenleaf deceased W.

COLONEL WILLIAM BROWNE.

The Brownes of Salem, Mass., are descended from an old respected family of "Browne Hall," Lancashire, England. Simon Browne, Barrister, resided there in 1540, and removed to Brundish, Suffolk. His son Thomas died there in 1608, and his son Francis died there in 1626. His son Hon. William, born 1608, came to Salem in 1635, became a merchant in Salem, and was eminent for his exemplary life, and public charities. He died in 1687. Major William Browne, son of the preceding, was born in 1639. He was a Councillor and Judge of the Court of Common Pleas for Essex County. He was a successful merchant, and a man of great influence in the Colony. He married Hannah, daughter of Captain George Curwin. He died in 1716, at the age of seventy-eight.

COLONEL SAMUEL BROWNE, son of the aforesaid, was born in 1669. He was the first town Treasurer of Salem, was many years a Representative, Judge of the Court of Common Pleas for Essex County, was also Chief Justice of said Court, also Colonel and Councillor. He was said to be by far the greatest merchant in his day, in the County of Essex. He emulated the beneficence of his father, uncle, and grandfather, in bequeathing large sums to Harvard College, and to schools in Salem. He died in 1731, aged 62. His son Samuel graduated at Harvard College, 1727. He married a daughter of John Winthrop, F. R. S., of New London, Conn., and died in 1742, aged 34. He was concerned in mercantile affairs.

COLONEL WILLIAM BROWNE, son of the aforesaid Samuel, was born at Salem in 1737, was a grandson of Governor Burnet. He graduated at Harvard College in 1755, the third in his class. He married his cousin, a daughter of Governor Wanton of Rhode Island, and was doubly connected with the Winthrop family, the wives of the elder Browne and Governor Wanton being daughters of John Winthrop, F. R. S., great-grandson of the first governor of Massachusetts. William Browne was Colonel of the Essex regiment, a member of the General Court in 1768, was one of the seventeen Rescinders, Judge of the Supreme Court, one of the ten Mandamus Counsellors who was sworn in. Colonel Browne was esteemed among the most opulent and benevolent individuals of the province before the Revolution, and so great was his popularity that the gubernatorial chair was offered him by the "Committee of Safety" as an inducement for him to remain and join the "Sons of Liberty." But he felt it his duty to remain on the side of the government, which represented law and authority, even at the expense of his great landed estates, both in Massachusetts and Connecticut, in the latter there were fourteen valuable farms, all of which were afterwards confiscated. After the passage of the Boston Port Bill, he was waited upon by a committee of the Essex delegates, which consisted of Jeremiah Lee, Samuel Holton, and Elbridge Gerry. They informed him that "It was with grief that the country had viewed his exertions for carrying into execution certain acts of parliament, calculated to enslave, and ruin his native land, that while the country would continue the respect for several years paid him, it resolved to detach every future connection all such, as shall persist in supporting or in any countenancing the late arbitrary acts of Parliament; that the delegates in the name of the country, request him to excuse them from the painful necessity of considering, and treating him as an enemy to his country, unless he resigned his office as counsellor and judge, Colonel Browne replied as follows: "As a Judge, and in every other capacity, I intend to act with honor, and integrity, and to exert my best abilities, and be assured, that neither persuasion can allure me, nor menaces compel me, to do anything derogatory to the character of a Counsellor of his majesty's province of Massachusetts. I cannot consent to defeat his Majesty's intentions, and disappoint his expectations by abandoning a post to which he has been graciously pleased to appoint me."

He was an Addresser of General Gage, was included in the Banishment Act of 1778, and in the Conspiracy Act of the year following. He was in London as early as May 4, 1776, and gave his fellow exiles some particulars relative to the evacuation of Boston. His wife, who complained of her treatment at Salem, and Boston, after his departure, does not appear to have joined him in England until the spring of 1778. In 1781 he was appointed Governor of the Bermudas, and administered the affairs of these islands in a manner to secure the confidence of the people. Under his judicious management the colony flourished. He found the financial affairs of the islands in a confused and ruinous state, and left them flourishing. In 1788 he left for England, deeply and sincerely regretted by the people. He died in England, February, 1802, aged sixty-five.

William Browne, son of the aforesaid, born at Salem, was an officer in the British Army, and was at the siege of Gibraltar. He was in England in 1784.

Colonel Benjamin Pickman, writing in 1793, said of the Brownes: "I would observe that the family of the Brownes has been the most remarkable family that has ever lived in the Town of Salem, holding places of the highest trust in the Town, County, and State, and possessing great riches. Their donations to the schools have been considerable, and their mercantile engagements have very much contributed to the growth of the Town."

The Browne mansion, erected by William Browne in 1740, upon the summit of Browne's Hill. He named "Browne Hall" after a place in Lancashire, England, that belonged to his ancestors.

The building consisted of two wings, two stories high, connected by a spacious hall, the whole presenting 80 feet front. The dwelling was one of the most magnificent in the Colony, it was finished in a most thorough and costly manner, corresponding with the wealth of the owner. The house was confiscated and later came into the possession of Hon. William Gray, who resided there till 1800. Subsequently it was known as "Sun Tavern," and then taken down.*

ARCHIBALD CUNNINGHAM.

ARCHIBALD CUNNINGHAM, of Boston, Massachusetts, was a prosperous merchant and a member of the North church in that city. He was high in office among the Free Masons. In 1776 he went to New York and on account of his loyalty was proscribed and banished in 1778.

At the peace he went from New York to Shelburne, Nova Scotia, accompanied by his family of six persons and one servant. In Nova Scotia he was Clerk of the Peace, and Register of Probate. On account of adhering to the royal cause his losses were estimated at £1100. As he was a man of learning, a reader, and of an observant nature, he left many valuable papers. His death occurred in 1820.

CAPTAIN JOHN MALCOMB.

There is not much known of this person. I find that he lived at Brunswick, Maine, and that in 1760 he married Abigail Trundy, of Falmouth (Portland). He was commissioned Ensign by Governor Shirley, and served under Colonel Waldo, in the 2nd Massachusetts Regiment against Louisburg in 1745. He was also Captain of a vessel that took despatches from there to Boston in the same year.

It was not often that the same man was tarred and feathered more

*Essex Inst. His. Coll. Vol. xxxii., pp. 201-238. Curwen's Journal, pp. 500-1, Sabine's Loyalists, pp. 255-6.

than once, but this unhappy experience twice befell John Malcom. His offence appears to have been in the exercise of his duty as custom house officer, of seizing a vessel at Falmouth, now Portland, for want of a register, and freely speaking of the actions of the "Sons of Liberty." We are informed by the papers of that period* "That John Malcom was genteely Tarr'd and Feathered at Pownalborough" (now Dresden, Maine) "on November first, 1773, and on January 25th, 1774, a mob in Boston "tore his cloaths off, and tarr'd his Head and Body, and feathered him, then they set him on a chair in a cart, and carried him through the main Street into King Street, from thence they proceeded to "Liberty Tree," and then to the Neck, as far as the Gallows, where they whipped, beat him with Sticks, and threatened to hang him."

The "Sons of Despotism" detained him under the gallows for an hour. He was then conveyed to the north end of the town, and thence back to his house. He was kept stripped four hours, and was so bruised and benumbed by the cold that his life was despaired of. It was by such means that the disunionists made converts to their cause. His offence for this Boston outrage, was that he struck one of his tormentors, a tradesman who had frequently insulted him, when a warrant was issued against him, but as the constable had not been able to find him, a mob gathered about his house and broke his windows. Malcomb was in the house, and pushing his sword through a broken window, wounded one of his assailants. The mob then made a rush, broke in, and finding him in a chamber, lowered him by a rope into the cart, and treated him as before mentioned in the newspapers.

THE RUSSELL FAMILY OF CHARLESTOWN.

The Russell family was eminent in social station and distinguished in the many public offices held by them in Boston and Charlestown for nearly two centuries. The first of this family to come to this country was the Hon. Richard Russell, son of Paul, of Hereford, England, born 1611, was an apprentice at Bristol, 1628, arrived here in 1640 with his wife, both admitted to the church in 1641, was a prominent merchant, Representative, Councillor, Speaker, Treasurer, Assistant. He died in 1676, aged 65. His son James, born 1640, died 1709. He also was Judge, Councillor and Treasurer, etc. He had an only son Daniel, born 1685, died 1763. He married Rebecca Chambers, and was also Councillor, Commissioner, Treasurer, etc.

CHAMBERS RUSSELL, son of the preceding, was born 1713. He was Judge, Councillor and a prominent lawyer, in whose office John Adams and Judge Sewall studied law. He graduated at Harvard College 1731,

*Boston Gazette, Nov. 15, 1773. Boston, News Letter, Jan. 27, 1774. Feb. 3, 1774. Massachusetts Spy, Jan. 27, 1774.

married Mary Wainwright, resided at Lincoln, which was incorporated in 1754, and named by him, after Lincoln in England, where some of his ancestors resided. His wife died in 1762, and he went to England, and died Nov. 24, 1767, at Guilford County, Surrey.

JAMES RUSSELL, brother of Chambers, married Catherine Greaves, 1738. He was Judge, Representative, and in 1774 was appointed Mandamus Councillor, but did not take the official oath. This saved him from the wrath of the revolutionists. He was not solicitious to shine, but was anxious to do good, and to be on friendly terms with his neighbors. He was incessant in his endeavors to promote the happiness and advance the prosperity of the community in which he lived. A bridge from Charlestown to Boston was among the enterprises which he projected. By his persevering efforts, the work was accomplished, and the Charlestown Bridge was the first structure of the kind ever build across a broad river in the United States. Through his great benevolence, and public spirit, he was not driven from his home as his sons were, the revolutionists allowed him to remain, and he died at Charlestown, Sept. 17th, 1798, aged 83 years.

JAMES RUSSELL, JR., son of the preceding, was obliged to leave and go to England. Was in London, February 1776, and at Exeter in 1779. A year later the fortunate captures made by a privateer gave him a fortune, and he was "bound in the matrimonial chain to Mary, second daughter of Richard Lechmere, a Boston Loyalist. They were married in 1780 at St. Peter's Church, Bristol, where he resided as a merchant. Among their children was Lechmere-Coor-Graves, Charles James, who died in service of Royal Navy, Katherine-Sarah, who married Major Miller of Bombay Artillery, Lucy Margaret, married Rev. Robert Cope Wolf.

DR. CHARLES RUSSELL, brother of James, was also a staunch loyalist. Graduated at Harvard College 1757. Married Feb. 15, 1768, Elizabeth, only daughter of Colonel Henry Vassell of Cambridge. He succeeded to his uncle, Judge Chambers Russell's estate at Lincoln, was proscribed and banished, and his estate confiscatd. He was a physician at Antigua, where his wife owned considerable property. He died there in 1780, and his wife died at Plymouth in 1802.*

EZEKIEL RUSSELL

Was a Printer and born in Boston, he served an apprenticeship with his brother Joseph. This family had no connection with the Charlestown Russells. In November, 1771, he commenced a political publication called "The Censor." It was printed in Marlboro Street, was a weekly publication, designed to defend the action of the government, and was supported by the loyalists. The articles were written with great ability

*Wyman Genealogies and Estates in Charlestown.

by Lieut. Gov. Oliver, Dr. Benjamin Church, and other loyalists. The first number reprinted from the Massachusetts Spy, the then famous letter of Joseph Greenleaf attacking Governor Hutchinson, and answered it with vehemence and spirit. In succeeding numbers the controversy was prolonged with increasing bitterness, and at last became intensely personal. The issue of Feb. 8, 1772, contained a recipe to make a modern patriot for the Colonies, especially for Massachusetts, as follows:

"Take of impudence, virulence and groundless abuse quantum sufficit, atheism, deism and libitinism ad libitum; false reports, well adapted and plausible lies, with groundless alarms, one hundred wt. avoirdupois; a malignant abuse of magistracy, a pusilanimous and diabolical contempt of divine revelation and all its abbettors, an equal quantity; honor and integrity not quite an atom; fraud, imposition, and hypocrisy, any proportion that may seem expedient; infuse therein the credulity of the people one thousand gallons, as a menstrum stir in the phrenzy of the times, and at the end of a year or two this judicious composition will probably bring forth a 'A *** and Y *** an O *** and a M *****."

Probatum est I. N."

The Censor not proving a success, Mr. Russell attempted to establish a newspaper at Salem, but that also failed. He returned to Boston, where he obtained support principally by printing and selling ballads, and small pamphlets. His wife was an active and industrious woman, who not only assisted him in printing, but sometimes wrote ballads on recent tragical events, which were published, and had frequently a considerable run. Ezekiel Russell died September 1796, aged fifty-two years. Joseph Russell, brother of Ezekiel, son of Benjamin and Elizabeth Russell, was born at Boston, 8 September, 1734, and died at St. John, New Brunswick, in 1808, aged 74 years.

JONATHAN SEWALL.

ATTORNEY GENERAL OF MASSACHUSETTS.

The family of Sewall is traced to two brothers, Henry, and William Sewall, both Mayors of Coventry, England, Henry Sewall born about 1544, was a Linen Draper, Alderman of Coventry, Mayor in 1589 and 1606. Died 1628, aged 84. Buried in St. Michael's Church, Coventry. Married Margaret, eldest daughter of Avery Grazebrook.

Their son Henry Sewall, emigrated to New England in 1634. He came over "out of dislike to the English Hierarchy" and settled at Newbury. He died at Rowley in 1657, aged 81 years. Married Anne Hunt. They brought with them their son, Henry Sewall, born in Coventry, in 1614, died in 1700, aged 86. Married Jane Dummer in Newbury, 1646. He went back to England and resided for some years at Warwick. In 1659 he returned to New England, "his rents at Newbury coming to very little when remitted to England." His son Stephen was born at Badesly, England, in 1657. He came to New England in 1661, settled at Salem and was a Major in the Indian wars. He died in 1725. Married Margaret, daughter of Rev. Jonathan Mitchell of Cambridge in 1682. They had an only son Jonathan, who was a merchant at Boston. He married Mary, sister of Edward Payne, of Boston. They had a son,

JUDGE JONATHAN SEWALL, the subject of this notice. He was born at Boston in 1728. Graduated at Harvard College in 1748, and was a teacher at Salem till 1756. He married Esther, daughter of Edmund Quincy, Esq., of Braintree, afterwards of Boston, and sister of Dorothy Quincy, wife of Governor Hancock, and of Elizabeth Quincy, wife of Samuel Sewall, of Boston, the father of Samuel Sewall, Chief Justice of Massachusetts. Jonathan Sewall studied law with Judge Chambers Russell, of Lincoln, commenced practice in his profession at Charlestown. He was an able and successful lawyer. He was Solicitor General, and his eloquence is represented as having been soft, smooth and insinuating, which gave him as much power over a jury as a lawyer ought ever to possess. At the death of Jeremy Gridley, he was appointed Attorney-General of Massachusetts, September, 1767. In 1768 he was appointed Judge of Admiralty for Nova Scotia. He went there twice in that capacity, and remained but a short period.

He was a gentleman and a scholar. He possessed a lively wit, a brilliant imagination, great subtlety of reasoning and an insinuating eloquence.

He was an intimate friend of John Adams, they studied together in Judge Russell's office, and afterwards, while attending court, they lived together, frequently slept in the same chamber, and often in the same bed, and besides the two young men were in constant correspondence.

He attempted to dissuade John Adams from attending the first Continental Congress, and it was in reply to his arguments, and as they walked on the Great Hill at Portland, that Adams used the memorable words, used so often afterwards in 1861 when the ordinance of secession was passed: "The die is now cast, I have now passed the Rubicon; sink or swim, live or die, survive or perish with my country, is my unalterable determination." They parted, and met no more until 1788. Adams, the Minister of the new republic at the Court of St. James, and the eloquent and gifted Sewall, true to the Empire, met in London, Adams laying aside all etiquette made a visit to his old friend and countryman, he said, "I ordered my servant to announce John Adams, I was instantly admitted, and both of us forgetting that we had ever been enemies, embraced each other as cordially as ever. I had two hours conversation with him in a most delightful freedom, upon a multitude of subjects." In the course of the interview, Mr. Sewall remarked that he had existed for the sake of his two children, that he had spared no pains or expense in their education and that he was going to Nova Scotia in hope of making some provision for them.

In 1774, he was an Addresser of Governor Hutchinson, and in September of that year his elegant home in Cambridge (which he rented from John Vassal, afterwards Washington's head-quarters, since occupied by the poet Longfellow) was attacked by the mob and much injured. He fled to Boston to escape from the fury of the disunionists. He had ably vindicated the characters of Governors Bernard, Hutchinson and Oliver, he was esteemed an able writer, and a staunch loyalist. He was proscribed in the Conspirators Act of 1779. He resided chiefly in Bristol till 1788, for the education of his children, then he removed to St. John's, N. B., having been appointed Judge of Admiralty for Nova Scotia and New Brunswick. He immediately entered upon the duties of his office, which he held till his death, which occurred September 26, 1796, at the age of sixty-eight. His widow survived him, and removed to Montreal, where she died January 21, 1810.

JONATHAN SEWALL, son of the aforesaid, was born at Cambridge, 1766, was educated at Bristol, England, and afterwards resided at Quebec, where he occupied the offices of Solicitor and Attorney General and Judge of the Vice Admiralty Court, until 1808, when he was appointed Chief Justice of Lower Canada, which he resigned in 1838. For many years he was President of the Executive Council, and Speaker of the Legislative Council.

In 1832 he received the degree of Doctor of Law from Harvard College. He died at Quebec in 1840, aged seventy-three. His son Stephen was Solicitor General of the same Province in 1810 and resided in Montreal. He died there of Asiatic cholera in the summer of 1832.

SAMUEL SEWALL, son of Henry Sewall and brother of Major Stephen Sewall, was the first chief justice of Massachusetts. This was the famous Sewall that sat in judgment upon the witches and afterwards repented it, who refused to sell an inch of his broad acres to the hated Episcopalians to build a church upon, who was one of the richest, most astute, sagacious, scholarly, bigoted and influential men of his day, who has left us in his Diary a transcript almost vivid in its conscientious faithfulness of that old time life, where he tells us of the courts he held, the drams he drank, the sermons he heard, the petty affairs of his own household and neighborhood, and where he advised with the governor touching matters of life and death. He married Hannah, the only child of John Hull, the mintmaster, who it is said gave her, on her marriage, a settlement in pine tree shillings equal to her weight. Hull owned a large farm of 350 acres in Longwood, Brookline, which descended to his son-in-law, and was known afterwards as Sewall's Farm.*

Samuel Sewall, son of the aforesaid, married Rebecca Dudley, a daughter of the governor. His son, Henry Sewall, born in 1719, died in 1771, was a gentleman much respected, and a lawyer of prominence. His son,

SAMUEL SEWALL, the subject of this article, was born at Brookline, December 31, 1745. Graduated at Harvard College in 1761. He studied law and settled in Boston. His name occurs among the barristers and attorneys who addressed Governor Hutchinson in 1774, and in the Ban-

* Curwen Journal, pp. 463-5, 506. Sabine's Loyalists, pp. 265-8.

ishment and Proscription Act in 1778, when his large estate which he had inherited from his ancestors, was confiscated. He went to England, and in 1776 was a member of the Loyalist Club, London. Two years later he was at Sidmouth, a "bathing town of mud walls and thatched roofs." In 1780 he was living in Bristol, and on the 19th of June amused himself loyally celebrating Clinton's success at Charleston in the discharge of a two-pounder in a private garden, and three days later was shot at by a highwayman and narrowly escaped with his life. Early in 1782 he was at Taunton, and at Sidmouth. He died at London, after one day's confinement to his room, May 6th, 1811, aged fifty-six years. He was unmarried.

LIST OF CONFISCATED ESTATES BELONGING TO SAMUEL SEWALL IN SUFFOLK COUNTY AND TO WHOM SOLD.

To Edward Kitchen, Wolcott, July 19, 1782; Lib. 135, fol. 113; Land 263 A. 1 qr., in Brookline, Thomas Aspinwall E.; marsh road to Charles River N.E.; Charles River N.; Thomas Gardner and Moses Griggs S. and S.W.; Solomon Hill S. and S.E. ——Land, 16 A. 3 qr. and half of house in Brookline on Sherburn Road and the marsh lane, bounded by Capt. Cook, Samuel Craft and Elisha Gardner.

To John Heath, Nov. 12, 1782; Lib. 136, fol. 102; Land and buildings in Brookline. 9 A. 33 r., Sherburn Road S.E.; a town way N.E.; Mr. Aker N.W.; a town way S.W.——32 A. 3 r., Daniel White and the pound S.W.; road and Joseph Williams S.E.; Joshua Boylston and William Hyslop N.E.; Sherburn Road N.W.——18 A. 2 qr. 5 r., Samuel White N.W.; John Dean S.W. and S.; a town way S.E.; said Dean N.E.; S. E. and S.; said town way E.; road N.E.——59 A. 3 qr. 4 r., Benjamin White and Dr. Winchester N.E.; Sarah Sharp S.W.; Samuel White and heirs of Justice White S.E.; Benjamin White N.E.; S.E. and N.E.; Sherburn Road N.E.——23 A. 3 qr. 33 r., Ebenezer Crafts and Caleb Gardner N.W.; said Gardner and Benjamin White S.W.; Moses White S.E.; Benjamin White and Moses White N.E.; Moses White S.E.; a town way N.E.——3 A. 28 r., Ebenezer Craft S.W.; S.E. and N.E.; the County line N.W.——8 A. 1 qr., 31 r., Daniel White N.W.; the County line S.W.; David Cook S.E.; heirs of Ebenezer Davis N.E.——5 A. 2 qr. 38 r., said Craft N.W.; saw mill meadow W.; William Heath S. and S.E.; Benjamin White and William Hammon N.E.——7 A. 2 qr. 32 r., Edward K. Walcott S. and W.; Benjamin White S.; William Acker S.E.; John Child E.; Charles River N.; Joseph Adams and Daniel White W.——4 A. 26 r., Moses White W., Esquire White, Ebenezer Craft and a creek S.; Nehemiah Davis and heirs of Caleb Denny S.E.; the marsh road N.

To John Molineux, William Molineux, Aug. 11, 1783; Lib. 139, fol. 153; Land and buildings in Boston, Newbury St. W.; Daniel Crosby, John Solely and heirs of Benjamin Church deceased S.; land late of Frederick William Geyer E.; Thomas Fairweather, Sampson Reed, John Homands and Edward Hollowday N.; said Sewall W.; N.; W. and N.

To John McLane, Dec. 18, 1783; Lib. 140, fol. 207; Land and buildings in Boston, Newbury St. W.; said Sewall S.; E.; S. and E.; Edward Hollowday N.

THOMAS ROBIE.

William and Elizabeth Robie were inhabitants of Boston as early as 1689, when their son Thomas was born on March 20th of that year. He graduated at Harvard College in 1708, and died in 1729. He was tutor, librarian, and Fellow of the college. He published an account of a remarkble eclipse of the sun on Nov. 27, 1772, also in the *Philosophical Transactions* of the Royal Society, papers on the Alkaline Salts, and the Venom of Spiders (1720-24). The following extract from the diary of

President Leverett shows the estimation in which he was held. "It ought to be remembered that Mr. Robie was no small honor to Harvard College by his mathematical performances, and by his correspondence thereupon with Mr. Durham and other learned persons in those studies abroad." In mathematics and natural philosophy he was said to have no equal in New England.

His mother was Elizabeth Taylor, daughter of James Taylor, long treasurer of the Province.* He went to Salem and established himself in the practice of physic, and married a daughter of Major Stephen Sewall.

THOMAS ROBIE, of Marblehead, was a son of the preceding Dr. Robie. He was a merchant, and married a daughter of the Rev. Simon Bradstreet, who was the great grandson of Gov. Bradstreet, called the Nestor of New England. Mr. Robie was a staunch loyalist, was an Addresser of Gov. Hutchinson, and thus brought upon himself and family the ire of the Revolutionists. They were obliged to leave the town and take refuge in Nova Scotia. Crowds of people collected on the wharf to witness their departure, and many irritating and insulting remarks were addressed to them concerning their Tory principles, and their conduct towards the Whigs. Provoked beyond endurance by these insulting taunts, Mrs. Robie retorted, as she seated herself in the boat that was to convey her to the ship: "I hope that I shall live to return, find this wicked rebellion crushed and see the streets of Marblehead run with rebel blood." The effect of this remark was electrical among the Revolutionists and only her sex prevented them from doing her person injury. But there were other loyalists in Marblehead who, if not so demonstrative, were not less sincere in this opinion. With fortitude and silence they bore the taunts and insults to which they were subjected, honestly believing that their friends and neighbors were engaged in a treasonable rebellion against their lawful sovereign.

Mr. Robie first went to Halifax, but afterwards to London, Feb. 5, 1776. He passed his time of exile mostly in Halifax, where one of his daughters married Jonathan Stearns, Esq., another refugee; another was married to Joseph Sewall, Esq., late treasurer of Massachusetts.

After the war was over some of the refugees attempted to return to their former homes. During the month of April, 1783, the town was thrown into a state of the greatest excitement by the return of Stephen Blaney, one of the loyalists. Rumors were prevalent that other refugees were also about to return, and on April 24 a town meeting was held, when it was voted that "All refugees who made their appearance in town were to be given six hours notice to leave, and any who remained beyond that time were to be taken into custody and shipped to the nearest port of Great Britain." Late one afternoon after this action of the town a vessel from the provinces arrived in the harbor. It was soon ascertained that the detested Robie family were on board, and, as the news spread through the town, the wharves were crowded with angry people, threatening

*Memorial His. of Boston. Vol. Iv. p. 492, Vol. II. p. 549.

vengeance upon them if they attempted to land. The dreadful wish uttered by Mrs. Robie at her departure still rankled in the minds of the people and they determined to give the Robies a significant reception. So great was the excitement that it was feared by many of the influential citizens that the unfortunate exiles might be injured and perhaps lose their lives at the hands of the infuriated populace. During the night, however, a party of gentlemen went on board of the schooner and removed them to a place of safety. They were landed in a distant part of the town and secreted for several days in a house belonging to one of the gentlemen. In the meantime urgent appeals were made to the magnaminity of the turbulent populace, and the excitement subsided.

Mr. Robie went into business again in a limited extent, and died at Salem about 1812, well esteemed and respected. The large brick mansion house of Thomas Robie is situated on Washington street, near the head of Darling street, Marblehead.

SAMUEL BRADSTREET ROBIE, son of the above, of Halifax, was appointed solicitor-general of Nova Scotia in 1815, speaker of the house of of assembly in 1817, 1819-20, member of the council in 1824, and master of the rolls in 1825, and died at that city January, 1858, in his eighty-eighth year.

BENJAMIN MARSTON.

The origin of the name Marston, is the English of Marsius (Lat.) Marson (Ger.) and signifies warrior, being derived from Mars, the god of war.

John Marston, the first of this name to come to America came from Ormsby, Norfolk, England, to Salem, in 1637, when he was 22 years of age. He married Alice, surname unknown, on Aug. 4, 1640, and on June 2, 1641 was admitted freeman. He had ten children between 1641 and 1661. His occupation was that of carpenter. He was diligent and prosperous in his business, and at his death bequeathed to his children "his house and land, and some money." His sons were influential in town matters, and three were chosen representatives to the general court.

He died Dec. 19, 1681, and was buried in the Old Salem Burying Ground.

BENJAMIN MARSTON, the first of this name and lineage, was the fourth son of the preceding John Marston, and was born in Salem, Jan. 9, 1651. He was an active and enterprising merchant and carried on for many years an extensive and profitable business with the West Indies, Spain, Nova Scotia, and Southern Colonies. He owned two warehouses, and the wharves on which they stood, several vessels, Brigantines, Ketches, Shallops and Sloops. In the year 1700 he built a large and handsome brick dwelling house, the first brick house in Salem. It was built by George Cabot, a mason from Boston. Its location was afterwards occupied by the Lee house on the corner of Essex and Crombie streets. Towards the close of his life, his estate suffered great losses, some of his vessels were lost at sea, some taken by the French and pirates, and others having lost all their crew by disease, or otherwise, "ye voiages were spiled." In June, 1719, he sailed with his son Benjamin, Jr., in "The good Briganteen Essex" from Salem to Ireland. His son wrote from Dublin, Nov. 6, 1719, to his mother announcing "the death of his father there, from the Small Pox, and that he was taken ill of the same distemper, the night he died, and that he had recovered and was not much marked."

BENJAMIN MARSTON, the second of this name, son of the preceding Benjamin Marston, was born in Salem, Feb. 24, 1697. He graduated from Harvard College in 1715. It appears after the death of his father he remained in Ireland, conducting all the business matters connected with the Essex, with a degree of energy and capacity not often found in a young man of 22 years of age. The voyage turned out to be much more profitable than was expected, and much of the property that had been sold or mortgaged by his father was redeemed.

He engaged in business at Salem as a merchant and gained a reputation among his fellow townsmen as a "man of honorable motives and strict integrity of character." He was chosen representative to the general court in 1727-28-29. Was High Sheriff of Essex till 1737, was Justice of General Session and Common Pleas Courts. In 1729 he married Elizabeth Winslow, daughter of Hon. Isaac Winslow of Marshfield. In 1740 he retired from business, and bought a large and valuable property at Manchester, known for many years as the Marston farm. Here he passed the remainder of his days, and died May 22, 1754, aged 57 years, leaving a large estate including the Great and Little Misery Islands, for which he had paid £516. 13.9. A part of the income of the island he left for the purpose of "Propagating the Gospel among the Indians."

BENJAMIN MARSTON, the third of this name, and family, and son of the preceding, was born in Salem, Sept. 30, 1730. He graduated at Harvard College in 1749. After leaving college he travelled in Europe and visited some other of the British colonies. He married Sarah Sweet, whose sister, Martha, married Col. Jeremiah Lee of Marblehead. After his marriage he "settled down" in Marblehead, where for many years he carried on a large and successful business as a merchant. He owned a store in King street, and other stores, and warehouses, and jointly with his partners, Jeremiah Lee and Robert Hooper, several large ships. He also owned a pleasant and commodious dwelling house, and much real estate, and other property in Marblehead and elsewhere. He was considered by his friends and neighbors as a man of pure life, and great integrity of character, active in business, energetic in public matters, hospitable and benevolent in private, a great reader and scholar, and fond of literary pursuits, always occupying one of the most respectable positions in society, and greatly esteemed by all who knew him." Here he continued to live for twenty years, actively engaged in business, and doing his duty towards his town. He was chosen selectman, and overseer of the poor, thirteen times in fifteen years, fireward twelve times in fourteen years, assessor in 1760, moderator of town meetings, fourteen times in eight years, and occupied many other important offices of trust. After 1768, however, when the troubles which preceded the Revolution began to increase the confidence of the people, that were influenced by the Revolutionists, appear to have been withheld. They still chose him moderator of all town meetings, but he was not again appointed on any important committees. He was known to be "an uncompromising adherant to the lawful government of the British Colonies," but as he had violated no agreements, and never attempted to counteract the plans of the conspirators, though frequently and openly expressing his disapprobation of their violent proceedings, he was for some time unmolested. At an early period, however, he discovered the storm brewing, and as if apprehensive of future difficulties he began "to sell off some of his property."

Benjamin Marston was one of the Addressers of Governor Hutchinson, and thus incurred the displeasure of the Revolutionists. After this he was harshly and brutally treated by the "Sons of Liberty." In the year 1775, his home was mobbed by a Marblehead *Committee*, who without any legal authority, entered his doors, broke open his desk, embezzled his money, and notes, and carried off his books and accounts. He made his escape from the town with difficulty, the turbulent "Sons of Despotism" would have probably tarred and feathered him if he had come within their reach. He remained concealed among his friends for some time, till he could reach Boston and place himself under the protection of the British. A letter from Hon. Wm. Brown, who also had sought shelter in Boston, to his friend Judge Curwen, a fellow Loyalist, said "About 2 months ago, Mr. Marston came here by night from Col. Fowle's farm. He knows nothing about Salem. His wife died last summer."

After the evacuation of Boston he went to St. John, N. B., and then to Windsor, N. S., finally settling down at Halifax, and there engaging in trade and venturing to sea, he was taken prisoner and carried into Plymouth, and remained "in duress in Boston until he was exchanged, and then went to Halifax. He returned to Boston after the peace in 1787, in the spring of which year he visited his friends in Plymouth, for the last time, and soon after embarked for London. His after life is best described in a letter to his sister, Mrs. Elizabeth Watson, of Plymouth, wife of William Watson, Esq., under date of London, March 19, 1792. He says: "I now sit down and write to you with satisfaction, for I have at length fairly waded thro the *Slough of Despond*. I am now landed on the opposite side and shall go on my way rejoicing, having once more emerged into active life. In fact, I am engaged to go with a large Company, who are going to make a Settlement on the Iland Bulama, on the coast of Africa, as their Land Surveyor General on a pretty good lay. No expedition could have hit my taste and humor more exactly than this one promises to do. It is so of the *Robinson Crusoe* kind, that I prefer it, vastly to any employment of equal emolument and of a more regular kind, that might have been offered to me in this country.

"You say you have mourned me as *dead and buried*. In truth, my dear Sister, I have been much worse off. I have for more than four years been *buryed alive*. As to gratifying your wish in making my native country the residence of the remainder of my days, it is not at present in my power to do, for want of means. There is not remaining in my mind the least resentment to the Country because the party whose side I took in the late great Revolution, did not succeed, for I am now fully convinced. It is better for the world that they have not. I don't mean by this to pay any complements to the first instigators of our American Revolution, although it has been of such advantage to mankind, I should as soon think of erecting monuments to Judas Iscariot, Pontius Pilate and the Jewish Sanhedrim for betraying and crucifying the Lord of Life, because that event was so importantly and universally beneficial."

The expedition to Africa resulted disastrously, and Benjamin Marston died on the Island of Bulama of the African fever, on the 10th of August, 1792.

From the scanty materials which have been here brought together, will be sufficient to convince the reader that it was no personal consideration, no expectation of honors and rewards, or desire of rank and distinction, but simply from a deep conviction of duty, a clear sense of loyalty to the British crown, that he gave up everything that was dear to him, his "pleasant and spacious dwelling" house, with its "fine old garden for morning exercise," his cherished library, his "much property," his well-earned reputation as a merchant, a magistrate and a citizen, his relatives, friends, and native country, and become a refugee and a wanderer on the face of the earth, "without a place that he could command to lay his head," and those that bore his name, were more proud of it than if he left rank and honor and large possessions to his representatives. There were very few of those who embraced the cause of the Mother Country, in those trying times, that were led by more honorable, or disinterested motives, or are more deserving of remembrance than Benjamin Marston of Marblehead.

HON. BENJAMIN LYNDE CHIEF JUSTICE OF MASSACHUSETTS.

It appears from the registry in the Church of St. John, the parish church of Hackney, near London, that Enoch Lynde was married on the 25th of October, 1614, to Elizabeth Digbie, a descendant of Sir John Digby. Enoch Lynde resided in London, was a merchant engaged in foreign trade, and was for some years connected with the postal service between England and Holland. He died the 23rd of April, 1636, aged fifty years.

SIMON LYNDE, the third son of Enoch Lynde, was born in London in 1624. He engaged in mercantile pursuits, and went to Holland. In 1650 he came to New England, and in the following year married Hannah, a daughter of Mr. John Newgate. During the thirty years of his life in the colony, he was a person of prominence, and acquired large landed possessions, in Massachusetts, Connecticut and Rhode Island. In 1687 he was appointed one of the Justices of the Superior Court. He died 22nd Nov. 1687, possessed of a large estate, and many children, who survived him.

BENJAMIN LYNDE, the sixth son of Simon, was born 22nd September, 1666. He records of himself that he was admitted to Harvard College on the 6th of September, 1682, by the Rev. Increase Mather, after having received his preparatory education under the famous grammar Master, Ezekiel Cheever, and received his first Degree in 1686. His father desired that he should complete his education in England. On 27th June, 1692, he sailed for England, and was admitted he says "for the study of Law, into the honorable Society of the Middle Temple, Oct. 18, 1692." "I was called to the Bar as Counsellor at Law in 1697, and received a commission under the great Seal, for King's Advocate, in the New Court of Admiralty, in New England, in the same year." He returned to America Dec. 24, 1697. On the 27 of April, 1699, he married Mary, daughter of Hon. William Browne of Salem. In 1712 he was appointed a Judge of the Superior Court, and in the following year a Councillor. On the resignation of Judge Sewall in 1728, he was made Chief Justice of the Province, which office he held at the time of his death, Jan. 28, 1745, in the 79th year of his age. The Boston Evening Post said of him, "Inflexible justice, unspotted integrity, affability, and humanity were ever conspicuous in him. He was a sincere friend, most affectionate in his relations, and the delight of all that were honored with his friendship and acquaintance." He left two sons, the younger, William, died unmarried, in 1752. His eldest son,

BENJAMIN LYNDE, JR. was born on the 5th of October, 1700. He graduated from Harvard College in 1718, and in 1721 he took his master's degree at Cambridge. He soon after received the appointment of Naval Officer for Salem. In 1734 he was appointed a special judge of the Court of Common Pleas, for Suffolk. In 1737 he was one of the agents in the settlement of the boundary line between New Hampshire and Massachusetts. Two years later he was made one of the Standing Judges of Common Pleas for Essex, and in 1745, the year of his father's death, he was raised to the Superior Bench of the Province. He was a member of the Council for many years, but declined a re-election in 1766, in consequence of the controversy that arose in that year between the House and Government as to the right of Judges to sit as Councillors. On the promotion of Chief Justice Hutchinson to the executive chair, in 1771, Judge Lynde was appointed to the place now vacant, and became Chief Justice of the Province. He resigned not many months after, pending the contoversy respecting the payment of judges' salaries by the town. He had now reached the age of 72, and "not being inclined to ride the Circuit longer" he accepted the more humble and less laborious position of Judge of Probate for Essex, which office he held until the breaking out of the Revolution, not many years before his death, which was occasioned by the kick from a horse, from the effects of which he did not recover, and he died Oct. 5th, 1781, aged 81 years. It was a remarkable coincidence that both father and son should have been Chief Justices of the Supreme Court, and occupied a seat on that bench, between them for nearly sixty years. The most important trial that took place during his judicial term was that of the so-called "Boston Massacre," where the soldiers fired on the mob in King street. At this trial Judge Lynde presided. It was a time of great political excitement, and the occasion was one that required the utmost firmness, and skill on the part of the judge, to ensure a just and impartial decision. These trials lasted several days, and, as has been said, "proceeded with care and patience, on the part of the Bench, and counsel, and both judges and jury seemed to have acted with all the impartiality that is exhibited in the most enlightened tribunals." "The result," says Judge Washburn, "is a proud memorial of the purity of the administration of justice in Massachusetts." Judge Lynde was noted for his learning, his liberality, and his public spirit. He was a diligent student of our Colonial history, and his diary, published by one of his descendants, Dr. F. E. Oliver, recalls names and events, that belong to the earlier years of the province, and records the daily life of persons holding official positions during a period with which many are not now familiar. He left three daughters, of whom Mary, the eldest, married Hon. Andrew Oliver, Jr., one of the Judges of the Court of Common Pleas for Essex; Hannah, who died unmarried and Lydia who married Rev. William Walter, the rector of Trinity Church of Boston.* Both of his sons-in-law being staunch loyalists.

PAGAN FAMILY.

ROBERT PAGAN was a native of Glasgow, Scotland, was born in 1750 and came to Falmouth in 1769. From that time to the commencement of the war he carried on a large lumber business and ship building. The ships which were built were not generally employed in our trade, but with their cargoes sent to Europe and sold. Robert Pagan & Co. kept on the corner of King and Fore Streets, the largest stock of goods which was employed here before the war. He was a man of popular manners, and much beloved by the people. He early became involved in the controversies of the times, and abandoned his business and country soon after the burning of Falmouth by Mowatt. In his testimony before the

*Diaries of Benjamin Lynde and of Benjamin Lynde, Jr.

Claim Commission he testified* "That he uniformly declared his sentiments in favor of Great Britain. Never submitted to join the rebels or to take no part with them." He early applied for leave to quit Casco Bay with the property belonging to himself and copartnery. This was refused him. In the month of February, 1776, he privately embarked his family on board a Brig he had in the harbor of Falmouth and sailed for Barbados. From that he went home. He afterwards carried on trade at New York and Penobscot, at the latter place he remained until the end of the war, when he removed to St. Andrews." Mr. Pagan was proscribed and banished. He settled at St. Andrews, N. B., in 1784, and became one of the principal men of Charlotte County. After serving the Crown as agent for lands in New Brunswick, and in superintending affairs connected with grants to Loyalists, he was in commission as a magistrate, as a Judge of a Court, and as Colonel in the militia, and, being a favorite among the freeholders of the county, was elected to the House of Assembly, and for several years was a leading member of that body. Judge Pagan died at St. Andrews, November 23, 1821 and Miriam, his widow, a daughter of Jeremiah Pote) deceased at the same place January, 1828, aged 81. They were childless.

THOMAS PAGAN, brother to Robert Pagan. He was with his brother during the war, and at the peace went to St. John, New Brunswick; was one of the grantees of that city, and established himself there as a merchant. He removed to Halifax, and while absent in Scotland for the benefit of his health, died in 1804.

WILLIAM PAGAN, brother of Robert and Thomas, was with his brothers during the war, and at the peace settled in New Brunswick, and was a member of the House of Assembly and of the Council. His death occurred at Fredericton, March 12, 1819.

THE WYER FAMILY OF CHARLESTOWN.

Edward Wyer came from Scotland. He was a tailor, and in 1658 married Elizabeth Johnson. He died May 3rd, 1693, aged 71 years. His son William was a sea captain, and married Eleanor Jennes, Oct. 26, 1701. He died Feb., 1749, aged 69 years.

DAVID WYER, son of William, was born at Charlestown, Feb. 24th, 1711. He also was a sea captain. Married Rebecca Russell, Feb. 2, 1738. He removed to Falmouth (Portland) and was an officer of the Customs there. All the officers of the revenue of that port were loyal except one, Thomas Child, who joined the Revolutionists. They all became refugees, and abandoned their country. During the military possession of the town by Thompson (before the burning of it by Captain Mowatt) he was required to give his presence before the Board of War as being a Tory.

*Bureau of Archives, Ontario, 2nd Report, Vol. I, p. 340.

DAVID WYER, JR., son of the aforesaid David was born at Charlestown in 1741, and graduated at Harvard College in 1758. In 1762 he was admitted to the bar, and commenced the practice of law at Falmouth. On the testimony of other lawyers who practiced in Maine prior to the Revolution, it was said of Wyer, that "he was a high-minded stirling fellow of strong talents, an able and eloquent advocate, and extremely independent in his opinions and character." Without the regular appointment and commission of Attorney of the Crown, Mr. Wyer acted in that capacity when occasion required the services of such an officer in the Courts of Maine. He died in 1776 at Stroudwater, to which place he removed after the burning of Falmouth, at the age of thirty-five, of an epidemic which prevailed at that time, and which carried off many persons old and young. Mrs. Wyer, a niece of Hon. Thomas Russell and two children survived him. One of the latter married Captain Samuel Waite of Portland.

THOMAS WYER, brother of David Wyer, Jr., was born at Charlestown, June 15, 1744. Married Sarah Francis, March 8th, 1766 in Medford. He removed to Falmouth with his father, was also employed as an officer of the Customs. He lost £325 in real and personal estate by the burning of the town in 1775. He did all he could to support the government; he refused to serve in the rebel army, on which he was taken up and abused by the mob, and obliged to pay a fine. Was taken before the Provincial Congress at Watertown, and obliged to quit Falmouth in 1777. in an open boat with his father-in-law, Jeremiah Pote, in which they went to Nova Scotia. In 1778 he was proscribed and banished. In 1779 he was in New York and was commissioned as captain of an armed vessel, the brigantine "British Tar," 65 men. He was in command of this vessel for nine months, during which time he had two engagements with two rebel privateers at different times. He had a house and lot in Falmouth, which was confiscated, and a half interest in a cargo burned at Falmouth. In 1784, he went to St. Andrew, N. B., with other Loyalists, and continued there until his decease. He was an Agent of the British Government for settling and allotting lands to adherents of the Crown in the Revolution. The first Sheriff of Charlotte County, was a Judge of the Court of Common Pleas and Deputy Colonial Treasurer. In 1790 he went on a year's tour to Europe, and on his return became a merchant, and had extensive lumber interests. He died February 24th, 1824. He had a numerous family, was married three times, his first wife Sarah Francis of Medford, second Joanna Pote of Falmouth, third Mary Hunt, who died 25 October, 1801, aged 37. An only son survived him.

THOMAS WYER, JR., a member of her Majesty's Council, Justice of the Common Pleas, member of the Board of Education, Commissioner of Wrecks, and Lieutenant-Colonel in the militia. He married Sarah, daughter of Thomas Tompkins, of St. Andrews, 24 March, 1808, and died at St. Andrews, December, 1848, aged sixty-nine.

JEREMIAH POTE.

WILLIAM POTE was in Marblehead as early as 1688. He married Hannah Greenfield. His second wife was Ann Hooper, whom he married in 1689. His son William was born at Marblehead, 1690, who married, June 2, 1718, Dorothy Getchell.

JEREMIAH POTE, son of the aforesaid, was born at Marblehead, Jan. 18, 1724. His father removed to Falmouth, now Portland, and died there. Jeremiah Pote became one of the principal merchants of the town, he owned and occupied one of the two principal wharves in that town previous to the Revolution. He transacted a large business and filled offices of trust and honor. In his testimony before the Claim Commission* "Claimt says He is a native of America. Lived at Falmouth. Casco Bay, when trouble broke out. He did everything in his power against the measure of the Rebels. He happened to be one of the selectmen at Falmouth, whose business it was to give notice of Town Meetings. Claimt refused to notify the meetings desired by the Rebels. In consequence of this he was persecuted. Was imprisoned several times. Had his things taken from him by force, so that he was forced to quit home, got to Nova Scotia, went in open boat. Went from Halifax to New York in 1778. Was employed by Admiral Gambin to pilot a vessel to New Hampshire, which was going with Sir Henry Clinton, Manisfestoes. The vessel was seized and the whole crew made prisoners and kept in prison during the winter. Went to Penobscot in 1780 to St. Andrews in the beginning of 1784."

In 1774 a public meeting was called to consider the state of public affairs, which he attended, but he desired that his dissent might be entered against a resolution relative to the Ministry and East India Company, which was introduced and passed.

In 1775, during the trouble with Captain Mowatt, which resulted in the burning of the town, in which he lost £1,000, he brought upon himself the vengeance of the Revolutionists, who under Thompson, assumed the government, and organized themselves into a board of war, and required him to contribute money and provisions, and to give a bond of £2,000 to appear at the Provincial Congress of Massachusetts, and give an account of his conduct. In 1778 he was proscribed and banished. After the peace he settled at St. Andrews at the mouth of the St. Croix river, the boundary line between Maine and New Brunswick, where he died November 23, 1796, aged seventy-one years. His son Robert, deceased at the same place November 8, 1794, at the age of twenty-five, and his daughter, Joanna, married Thomas Wyer, Jr., his widow Elizabeth Berry of Kittery, died December 24, 1809, aged seventy-nine.

*Bureau of Archives, Ontario, 2nd Report, Vol. II, p. 904.

EBENEZER CUTLER.

JOHN 1 CUTLER came from Spranston, two miles from north of Norwich, and about eight miles south of Hingham, in the County of Norfolk, England. His name first appears among the persecuted adherents of Rev. Robert Peck, A. M., of Hingham, who "sold their possessions for half their value, and named the place of their settlement after their natal town." He embarked, it is believed, in the Rose of Yarmouth, William Andrews, Jr., Master, which sailed on or about April 18, 1637. He was at Hingham by or a little after June 10th following, when land was assigned him. He came attended by his wife Mary, seven children, and one servant. He died the following year, which must have subjected his widow and children to great hardships. His third son,

SAMUEL 2 CUTLER, was born in England in 1629, was of Marblehead in 1654, of Salem in 1655, of Topsfield and Hingham in 1671, and of Gloucester, March 17, 1693. In 1671 he as heir and attorney for his brothers and sisters, united with his mother in the sale of their patrimonial estate in Hingham. He was often called to settle and appraise estates. He died in 1700, 71 years of age. He had two sons and three daughters. His second eldest son,

EBENEZER 3 CUTLER, was born at Salem in 1664, where he married Mary, daughter of Zacheray and Mary March. Mr. Cutler died about 1729 at Salem and the widow in 1734, the sale of the homestead being effected soon after, and the family removed from Salem. He had six children, four sons and two daughters. The eldest son,

EBENEZER 4 CUTLER, was born in Salem, October 1, 1695. He was a farmer and brickmaker. He married May, daughter of William Stockwell, Oct. 16, 1732. He inherited the farm in Sutton, Mass., purchased of William Stockwell by his father, and on which he settled previous to 1728. It is said that three of his sons resided on this farm at one time, each occupying separate houses. He died in 1779, and had two daughters and five sons.

EBENEZER 5 CUTLER, son of the aforesaid,* settled in the town of Oxford, Mass., as an inn keeper and trader. He married Miriam Eager, sister of his brother Zackeus' wife, and daughter of James Eager of Westboro, Mass., Nov. 24, 1764. Mrs. Cutler was a sister of Colonel Eager, who was a Loyalist and settled in Victory, Nova Scotia.

Before the commencement of hostilities he tried to be neutral, but when the tea troubles arose, he went quietly at night, and purchased a quantity of it, on the return with his supply a masked band interrupted him, took the tea from him and burnt it. That decided him, which side to take, and he became a staunch loyalist.

Ebenezer Cutler was a trader which caused him to travel considerably about the country, and being very independant and outspoken he soon

*See Cutler Genealogy for descent of Ebenezer 4.

had many enemies among the Revolutionists, and a price was set on his capture. He had many narrow escapes before they got him. Once he was hidden in a farmhouse between the chimney and outer wall, most suffocated by smoke.

The Committee on Correspondence made charges against him, and sent him with the evidence of his misconduct to General Ward at Cambridge, the charges were as follows:

Northboro, May 17th, 1775.

Sir:

We the Committee of Correspondence of the Town of Northboro having taken into our custody Mr. Ebenezer Cutler, late of Groton, but now of this town, which from his conduct appears to us to be an avowed enemy of his Country, he has set at naught and despises all the Resolutions of the Continental and Provincial Congress, and also utterly refuses to act in any defence of his now perishing country whatever, and as he has from his past conduct, ever since we have been struggling for the Liberties of our Country appeared in the eyes of the Public to be aiding and abetting, in defeating the plans of the good people of this Province, and has been riding from one part of this province to the other, and in our opinion for no good design, we think it highly necessary to send him to the Council of war, to know whether he may (as he desires) have a pass to go into Boston: we also inclose the substance of two evidences concerning said Cutler.

By order of the Committee of Correspondence,

GILMAN BASS, Clerk.

N. B. General Ward, we apprehend is well acquainted with the character and conduct of said Cutler.*

His case was submitted to Congress, when it appeared that he had spoken "many things disrespectful of the Continental and Provincial Congress" that he had "acted against their resolves," had said that "he would assist Gage," had called such as signed the town-covenant or non-consumption agreement "dammed fools" etc., etc. A resolve to commit him to prison was refused a passage, and a resolve that he be allowed to join the British troops at Boston was also lost. But subsequently he was allowed to go into that town "without his effects." On the evacuation of Boston he accompanied the British Army to Halifax. He settled at Annapolis Royal, and with the money which the British government paid him in compensation for his losses, he established himself in business there. After his home in Oxford was broken up, his wife Miriam, and children, went to her mother, Mrs. Eager, in Worcester. His wife died there. Mrs. Eager was a strong Loyalist, one day a party of Rebels vis-

*"Royalists" in Mass. Archives, Vol. I, p. 6.

ited her, and she sent them off by some ready quotations of scripture. She and her sons brought the family to Annapolis and then settled on a farm in Nisteaux.

After a few years Ebenezer Cutler went to England on a visit and there married Mary, daughter of Colonel Hicks, of the 70th Regiment. Two children were born in England and four in N. S. He was protonotary of the County of Annapolis, and was a zealous Episcopalian. He died there in 1831, quite aged. Mary, his widow, died at the same place in 1839. He was proscribed and banished in 1778, and his property was confiscated and inventoried April 5th, 1779. Aug. 3rd the judge appointed a commission to settle his estate. His first wife, Miriam, died at Northboro, Mass., and her estate was inventoried Sept. 10, 1784, amounting to £100. He had by her eight children.

EBENEZER 6 CUTLER, son of the aforesaid, was born at Oxford, Mass., Aug. 27th, 1765. He was a student at Harvard at the commencement of hostilities, when he was obliged to leave. Opposite his name in the College archives, is the name "Traitor," which means just the opposite, that he was a Loyalist. He went to Nova Scotia with his father. He was an expert accountant, and crown land surveyor. Here he resided several years, but settled finally at Moncton. One day in going up the street, passing Mr. Wilmot's, he saw a very beautiful girl leaning over the gate, a visitor of Mrs. Wilmot, Olivia Dickson. It was a case of love at first sight. He met a friend a few minutes after and told him that he had just seen his wife that was to be. In due time they were married. On one of his voyages as supercargo, the vessel was taken by a Spanish privateer, off Jamaica. The captain recognized him as a Free Mason, gave him liberty, set him ashore at Port Antonio, where he obtained a mule, and crossed the mountains to Kingston where he took a vessel for Nova Scotia. He died in 1839. He had ten children, six daughters and four sons, the tenth child born was

REBECCA 7 CUTLER, who married John Whitman of Annapolis, whose ancestor came from Plymouth County, Mass., and settled in Nova Scotia previous to the Revolution. William Whitman of Boston and Clarence Whitman of New York are children of John Whitman and Rebecca Cutler.

Robert J. Dysart and Hugh Dysart, accountants of Boston, are descendants in the third generation from Ebenezer Cutler and Olivia Dickson.

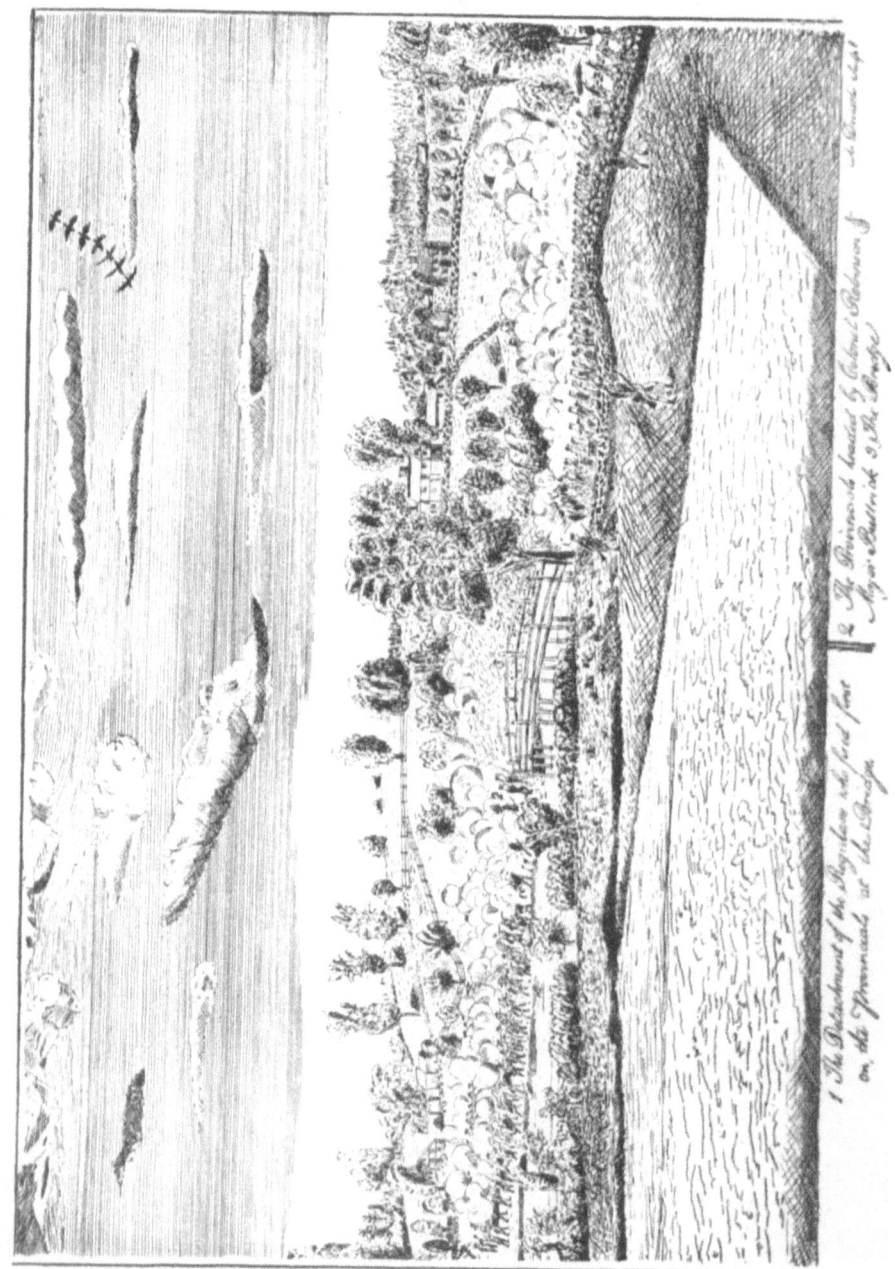

The Engagement at the North Bridge in Concord.

APPENDIX.

THE TRUE STORY CONCERNING THE KILLING OF THE TWO SOLDIERS AT CONCORD BRIDGE, APRIL 19TH, 1775. THE FIRST BRITISH SOLDIER KILLED IN THE REVOLUTIONARY WAR.

See page 53.

After the skirmish at Lexington, the king's troops marched into Concord in two columns, the infantry coming over the hill from which the Americans had retreated, and the grenadiers and marines followed the high road. On reaching the Court house Colonel Smith ordered six companies (about two hundred men) under Captain Parsons, to hold the bridge and destroy certain stores on the other side. With the balance of his command he remained in the center of the town destroying such warlike stores as could be found, this being the object of the expedition.

Captain Parsons in the meantime, posted three companies under Captain Laurie at the bridge, while he proceeded to Colonel Barrett's home in search of stores. The Americans had gathered on the high ground, west of the bridge, and now numbered about four hundred and fifty men, representing many of the neighboring towns. The Acton company in front, led by Capt. Isaac Davis, marched in double file and with trailed arms for the bridge. The British guard, numbering about one hundred men, drew up in line of battle on the opposite side of the bridge, and opened fire upon them. Capt. Davis, and Abner Hosmer, of the same company, both fell dead. Seeing this, Major Buttrick shouted "Fire, fellow soldiers! for God's sake fire!" The order was instantly obeyed. One of the British was killed, and several wounded, one severely, who was left on the ground, when the British retreated to the center of the village. The Americans turned aside to occupy favorable positions on the adjacent hills.* A young man named Ammi White was chopping wood for Rev. William Emerson at the "Old Manse" at the east end of the bridge, while the firing was going on he hid under cover of the wood-pile, when it was over he went to the bridge, saw one British soldier dead, another badly wounded,

---

*This description of the affair at Concord Bridge, was written by Rev. E. G. Porter, President of the New England Historic Genealogical Society for a work entitled "Antique Views of Boston." Pp. 234-8 compiled by me in 1882. J. H. Stark.

grasping his axe he struck the wounded soldier on the head crushing in his skull, then taking the soldier's gun, he went off home. The gun is now in the rooms of the Antiquarian Society of Concord. In the meantime, the detachment under Capt. Parsons returned from the Barrett house, crossed the bridge, passed the dead bodies of the soldiers and joined the main body unmolested. They reported when they arrived at Boston, that the wounded soldier at the bridge had been scalped and his ears cut off.

Very little was said during the past hundred years concerning the inhuman act of Ammi White, in fact this is the first time the name of the perpetrator of the outrage has been published. It was not a popular subject to be discussed in the Council of the "Sons and Daughters of the American Revolution" when assembled to recount the "brave deeds of their patriotic forefathers." Hawthorne mentions it in the "Old Manse" pp. 12, 13.

The writer's attention was first drawn to it by an article in the Boston papers concerning the observances of "Patriots Day," April 19th, 1903. It was as follows:

"A story of the Concord fight not told by guides who take tourists to the graves of the soldiers by the Concord bridge was told by the Rev. Franklin Hamilton, preaching on "Patriots' Day and Its Lessons" last evening at the First Methodist Episcopal Church.

"It shows," said he, "that the British soldiers were men like you and me. It shows that the story of that fateful battle hour found many weeping hearts across the sea. Your histories tell you how two British soldiers, a sergeant and a private, were killed, and are buried under the pines by the wall. One was killed and the other wounded. As the wounded soldier was crawling away he was met by a boy who had been chopping wood, and who, inflamed with the spirit of the hour, struck him dead with his axe. Mr. Bartlett of Concord tells me that not so long ago a young woman came to Concord and asked to be shown where the British soldiers lay. She came from Nottinghamshire, and was a relative of one of them. She went to the graves and placed upon them a wreath, singing as she did so 'God Save the King.'"

This led me to examine into the case. I found that there was considerable rivalry of feeling between the towns of Concord and Acton as to the part each took in the fight. There was a saying that "Acton furnished the men, and Concord the ground." And that there was not a Concord man killed, wounded or missing in the "Concord Fight." In the Centennial observances at Acton in 1835, the Address was delivered by Josiah Adams. He said:

"That two were killed at the bridge is certainly true, and it is true too that historians have published to the world that they were killed in the engagement. It is true also, that a monument is about to be placed over them on the spot to perpetuate American valor. The manner in which one of them met his death as disclosed in the depositions of Mr. Thorp, Mr. Smith and Mr. Handley, namely by a hatchet after he was wounded and left behind, was well known at the time. It was the action of an excited and thoughtless youth who was afterwards sufficiently penitent and miserable and whose name therefore will not be given. But the attempt to conceal the act from the world which was made at the time, and has since continued, cannot be approved. It would surely have been better to have given it to the world accompanied by the detestation and horror which it merited and received. Thorp in his deposition said: "Two of the enemy were killed—one with a hatchet after being wounded and helpless. This act was a matter of horror to all of us. I saw him sitting up and wounded as we passed the bridge."

Smith said: "One of them was left on the ground wounded and in that situation was killed by an American with a hatchet." Handley said: "The young man who killed him told me in 1807 that it worried him very much."

This inhuman act was of course reported by the British and a Boston paper represented that one killed at the bridge at Concord was scalped and the ears cut off from his head. This led to a deposition from Brown and Davis that the truth may be known. They testified that they buried the bodies at the bridge, that neither of those persons were scalped, nor their ears cut off.

If there be any one left to advocate such a proceeding, he will say that the deposition was true to the letter. But alas! it was in the letter only. It had the most essential characteristic of falsehood—the intention to make a false impression in regard to what was known to be the subject of inquiry to have it believed that both men were killed in the engagement."

"If a monument is to be erected by the authority of a town, one of the most respectable in the County of Middlesex, let it be seen that its inscription contains the truth, the whole truth, and nothing but the truth, relative to the subject matters thereof." *

My attention was next attracted to the soldiers' graves at Concord Bridge by the following letters that appeared in the Boston Transcript:

BRITISH GRAVES AT CONCORD.

To the Editor of the Transcript:

I want to say in your columns something which has been on my mind frequently since I went to Concord Bridge on my recent visit to America. It has mingled some sadness with an otherwise most delightful visit.

By the side of the road there are the graves of the British soldiers who fell there, unnamed and unhonored by us, yet they died doing what they conceived to be their duty just as your men did. The loneliness and unrecognized character of these graves struck me sadly, and I have often since wished that they, too, might have some tribute to their stanch, if misplaced bravery. Now in looking (as I constantly do) through the writings of my most dear friend and counsellor, James Russell Lowell, I find he has exactly struck the note I want in his poem, "Lines suggested by the graves of the two English soldiers on Concord Battleground." The third verse would make a fitting tribute to the character of these men. It runs as follows:

> "These men were brave enough and true
> To the hired soldiers' bull-dog creed;
> What brought them here they never knew,
> They fought as suits the English breed:
> They came three thousand miles and died
> To keep the past upon its throne—
> Unheard, beyond the ocean tide,
> Their English mother made her moan."

Do you think there might be found, among the splendidly patrotic Daughters of the Revolution, some sufficiently generous-minded to put this American poet's recognition of the worth of these poor fellows on a small tablet near the graves? I would at least ask whether the last two lines of this verse do not move the heart of any woman.

I do not know how public sentiment toward the sacred ground of Concord battlefield might regard such an intrusion, and if the words were those of any but such a man as Lowell, so associated with the locality and imbued with all that that fight meant to your nation, I would not be so bold as to suggest it. I know that this is really a national, not an individual, matter and that a stran-

*Centennial Address delivered at Acton, July 21, 1835, by Josiah Adams, pp. 44-5-6.

ger ought not to intermeddle with it. I am only making my little moan in sympathy with the English mother whose heart Lowell so beautifully understands.

ALBERT WEBB.

Elderslie, London Road, Worcester, Eng., March 31, 1909."

The editor's comments on the letters was in part as follows:

"The letter in another column pleading for a memorial tablet, bearing suggested and suggestive lines from Lowell, at the grave of the two British soldiers slain at the North Bridge, Concord, should challenge attention and it is difficult to see why it should challenge antagonism. The grave is now marked by two stones half sunken in the mold with which kindly nature everywhere seeks to efface the evidences of human strife. It is protected by chains which were provided some thirty years ago by a British resident of Boston. On a stone of the wall sheltering the grave is an inscription setting forth who sleep below. Neither the inscription nor the defence was strictly necessary, for all Concord knows where the grave is, and tradition has preserved the names of the two men who buried the slain, giving them hasty but not irreverent interment. Nor has there ever been danger of vandalism. The old New England reverence for the last resting place of the dead protected the sleepers for one hundred years, and the chain fence is more the tribute of a countryman to these friendless and nameless victims of George III.'s policy than a precaution. The same spirit which protected these two soldiers' resting place would doubtless not see anything objectionable in a bronze tablet carrying Lowell's lines. Certainly the people of Concord, the descendants of the Minutemen, would be the last to feel incensed at this tribute, if tribute it be, or this reminder of permanent material, of the historic dust that must in these one hundred and thirty-four years have turned into earth.

These two soldiers are none the less historical characters because their identity is unknown. What their names or grades neither history nor research tells. They were just common men in the ranks, in the era when the private soldier was simply so much food for powder.

But apart from the influence of local sentiment, there is a broad public opinion that guards a soldier's sepulchre, even if he was an enemy in life. This opinion is expressed in the general custom in this country to allow both sides memorials on the great battlefields of our Civil War.

If the suggested tablet should be erected at Concord, if "patriotism" should at first think too much honor were done these "hireling soldiers," would not reflection remind that when the "embattled farmers"—who, by the way, were led by a veteran and accomplished officer—and the regulars faced one another across the narrow stream both were proud of the name of Englishmen? Concord was then a microcosm of English America, which up to the very verge of hostilities had drunk the king's health and had clung desperately to the foolish fond belief that he was a good sovereign misled by designing ministers."

This led me to further investigate this matter, for I had been informed that the graves had been desecrated some years ago under authority of the town officials. I therefore caused to be published in the Boston Transcript under the heading of "Notes and Queries" the following query:

(7891.) 1. Can anyone give the names of the two British soldiers killed at Concord Bridge, or inform me if there were any papers taken from their bodies that would identify them? I have been informed that there were.

2. One of the soldiers was left wounded on the bridge; what was the name of the "young American that killed him with a hatchet"?

3. When did the selectmen of Concord give Professor Fowler permission to dig up the two bodies of the British soldiers and remove the skulls to be used for exhibition purposes?   J. H. S.

April 6, 1906.

MONUMENT TO COMMEMORATE THE SKIRMISH AT CONCORD BRIDGE.

The only answer received was the following:

7891. 3. The indirect intimations of J. H. S. are shrewd, but before the alleged action of the selectmen excites the Concord people, they should insist upon his producing adequate evidence." ROCKINGHAM.

The adequate evidence was produced and is as follows:

"The Worcester Society of Antiquity,
Worcester, Massachusetts, April 12, 1909.

Mr. James H. Stark,
Dear Sir:

Mr. Barton has handed your letter to me and I write to say that the skulls of those two British Soldiers killed at the bridge in Concord were once the property of this Society, we having purchased them of the Widow of Prof. Fowler, the phrenologist, who some years ago went about the country giving lectures and illustrating his subjects. Prof. Fowler got permission to dig up those skulls from the Selectmen of Concord, and he carried them about with him and used them in his lecturing. After his death one of the members learned of them and we purchased the skulls and they were in our museum some time. The late Senator Hoar learning that we had them, came to know if we would be willing to return them to Concord that they might be put back in the ground from whence they were taken. As he seemed quite anxious about it, consent was given, and they were sent to Concord to be placed in their original resting place. Presume they are there at the present time.

Yours,
ELLERY B. CRANE.
Librarian."

The only excuse offered for the inhuman act of Ammi White was found over one hundred years after the crime was committed. It is now said that he was only a boy, and that the wounded soldier cried out for water, and that while giving it to him he tried to kill him with his bayonet. This is all false, there is no evidence whatever to prove it, in fact Thorp, one of the deponents said "he was killed with a hatchet after being wounded and helpless, and the act was a matter of horror to all of us." Handley said 'The young man who killed him told me in 1807 that it worried him very much." Here is not the slightest evidence that White killed him in self defence, neither was he the boy as represented, for I find that he enlisted five days after killing the soldier, in Capt. Abishai Brown's Co. Col. John Nixon's (5) Regiment. He enlisted April 24, 1775, June 10, 1775 signed advance pay order at Cambridge, Aug. 1, 1775, Private on muster roll at that date. Service 3 months 15 days. Company return dated Sept. 30, 1775.*

I am pleased to state that a few weeks after the aforesaid letters appeared in the Transcript, that the town authorities at Concord gave permission to the "British Army and Navy Veterans" of Boston, to march on Memorial Day, May 30, 1909, to the graves of the two soldiers and to decorate same, which was accordingly done. The graves of the soldiers are referred to in the Transcript article as being "protected by chains, which were provided some thirty years ago by a British resident of Boston." The party referred to was Mr. Herbert Radcliffe, a member of the British Charitable Society. The

*Rev. Soldiers and Sailors. Vol. 17, p. 42.

facts which I have stated here, concerning what occurred, "Where once the embattled farmers stood and fired the shot heard round the world" is not done with a view of reviving old grievances, or re-opening old sores, but that the historic truth may be known concerning "the shot heard round the world." for history should know no concealment, and as Josiah Adams truly said, "the truth, the whole truth and nothing but the truth, should be told relative to this matter."

If it be said that these are old stories of the past, we reply that these misrepresentations are being quoted as having actually occurred and are made living issues for to-day by numerous societies formed for that; and kindred purposes. Even those societies designed to keep in remembrance their honored ancestors' part in the Revolution, make it a point to perpetuate their historic fables and falsehoods in the belief that anything is good enough to be said of their historic opponent.

THE ENGAGEMENT AT THE NORTH BRIDGE IN CONCORD, WHERE THE TWO SOLDIERS WERE KILLED.

In the American army which was formed at Cambridge immediately after the affair at Lexington and Concord, there were two young artists from Connecticut, Amos Doolittle, afterwards a well known engraver, and a portrait painter by the name of Earl, both members of the New Haven company. During their stay at Cambridge, these young men improved the opportunity by visiting Lexington and Concord, for the purpose of studying the battle field and making drawings of the several localities, the buildings, and the forces in action. The drawings were mostly made by Earl, and afterwards engraved by Doolittle, on his return to New Haven the same year. The four plates were each twelve by eighteen inches in size, and have been claimed to be the first series of historical prints ever published in this country. "Plate III., the battle of the North Bridge in Concord" shown here in reduced size from the reproduction of the original in "Stark's Antique Views of Boston." In this engraving, one soldier is seen falling, near the spot where the two soldiers are buried.

THE BIRTHPLACE OF THE AMERICAN REVOLUTION.

Boss or ring rule is not a modern invention, for at the time of the Revolution, Sam Adams was the political boss of Boston, Gordon in his "History of the American Revolution" under date of 1775, traces this practice to a much earlier date. "More than 50 years ago Mr. Samuel Adams' father and 20 others, one or two, from the north end of the town, where all the ship business is carried on used to meet, make a caucus, and lay their plans for introducing certain persons into places of trust and power. By acting in concert, together with a careful and extensive distribution of ballots, they generally carried the elections to their own mind." In this manner Sam Adams first became a representative for Boston, and then its Boss. At this period ship building was one of the leading industries of Boston. Originally the "Caucus Club" was a mechanics club called from the leading trade in it the "Calkers' Club," which name, with a variation it still retained after it had passed in the hands of politicians.

It is impossible to exaggerate the influence such secret societies as the Caucuses, and Sons of Liberty, had upon the events which helped to bring on the conflict with the mother country. The "Sons of Liberty" met in a distillery, and also the Green Dragon Tavern, and arose out of the excitement attending the passage of the Stamp Act. John Adams in his diary gives some interesting glimpses of their clubs, where the Revolution was born, he says "Feb. 1, 1763. This day learned that the Caucus Club meets at certain times in the garret of Tom Dawes, the adjutant of the Boston regiment. He has a large house, and he has a movable partition in his garret, which he takes down and the whole club meets in one room. There they smoke tobacco till you cannot see from one end of the garret to the other. Then they drink flip I suppose, and there they choose a moderator, who puts questions to the vote regularly, and selectmen, assessors, collectors, wardens, and representatives, are regularly chosen before they are chosen in the town. Fairfield, Story, Ruddock, Adams, Cooper, and a rudis indigestaque moles of others are members."

"January 15, 1766. Spent the evening with the Sons of Liberty at their own apartments in Hanover Square near the Tree of Liberty. It is a counting-room in Chase & Speakman's distillery; a very small room it is. There were present John Avery, a distiller of liberal education; John Smith, the brazier; Thomas Chase, distiller; Joseph Fields, master of a vessel; Henry Bass, George Trott, jeweler; and Henry Wells. I was very cordially and respectfully treated by all present. We had punch, wine, pipes and tobacco, biscuit and cheese, etc."

Chas. J. Gettemy in commenting on same, says:*

"From which it appears that politicians are much the same in all times. Public officials were chosen by a ring in Boston in the year of our Lord 1763 before they were "chosen by the town" and the Revolution was hatched in a rum-shop, while those upon whom history has placed the seal of greatness and statesmanship filled themselves with "flip" in an atmosphere dense with tobacco smoke as they plotted and planned the momentous events of the time!"

PAUL REVERE THE SCOUT.

Paul Revere was born in Boston, Dec. 21, 1734, his father was a Huguenot named Rivoire, which in time became Revere. When Revere left school he went into his father's shop to learn the art of gold and silver smith.

His first military experience was when he was twenty-one years old, in the expedition against Crown Point, in which he held the king's commission from Gov. Wm. Shirley as second lieutenant of artillery. The service proved uneventful, it continued for six months and then the enterprise was abandoned.

On his return he took an increasing and prominent part in the political

*The True Story of Paul Revere. p. 45, by Charles J. Gettemy, Chief of the Bureau of Statistics and Labor of the Commonwealth of Massachusetts.

life of the time, and on one occasion his pugnacious disposition got him into the police court, in 1761, where he had to pay a fine and be bound over to keep the peace.

Revere became quite skilled in drawing and engraving on copper, and the exciting political events of the time readily lent themselves to pictorial treatment. Probably the best known of Revere's copper-plate engraving, was that of the so-called "State Street Massacre." It has since, however, been discovered that in this instance he appropriated the work of Henry Pelham, the half brother of Copley the artist* as the following letter will show:

Boston, March 29th, 1770.

Sir:

When I heard that you was cutting a plate of the late Murder, I thought it impossible as I knew you was not capable of doing it unless you copied it from mine and as I thought I had intrusted it in the hands of a person who had more regard to the dictates of Honor and Justice than to take the undue advantage you have done of the confidence and trust I reposed in you. But I find that I was mistaken and after being at great Trouble and Expense of making a design, paying for paper, printing, etc., find myself in the most ungenerous Manner deprived not only of any proposed Advantage, but even of the expense I have been at as truly as if you had plundered me on the highway. If you are insensible of the Dishonour you have brought on yourself by this Act, the World will not be so. However, I leave you to reflect and consider of one of the most dishonorable Actions you could well be guilty of.

H. PELHAM.

This is a serious charge against Revere's honor and integrity, for it seems that Pelham loaned Revere a drawing of the "Massacre" from which Revere made an engraving and sold copies without giving the real artist credit for his sketch, since the Revere plate bears the inscription Engraved, Printed and Sold by Paul Revere.

Revere was one of the chief actors in the tea mobs that destroyed the tea which precipitated the Revolution. The North End Caucus had, on Oct. 23, 1773, declared that its members would "oppose at peril of life and fortune the vending of any tea that might be imported by the East Indian Company." A song was composed which became very popular. One of them commenced with

"Our Warren's there and bold Revere
With hands to do and words to cheer."

Revere took a prominent part in this tumultuous affair, and the next day he was selected as the man to take the news to New York and Philadelphia. From this time on he was the chief scout of the Boston Revolutionists. He was one of a band of thirty formed to watch the movements of the British that had been sent to Boston after the destruction of the tea. Finally the vigilance of these scouts was rewarded. It became apparent that something unusual was occurring in the British camp on the evening of April 18th, 1775, for Revere says "On Tuesday evening, the 18th, it was observed that a number

*See Atlantic Monthly, April 1893, "Some Pelham Copley Letters."

PURSUIT AND CAPTURE OF PAUL REVERE.
He and another scout, named Dawes, was captured on the road to Lexington, April 19, 1775.

of soldiers were marching towards the bottom of the Common," which meant that they were going in boats across the river to Charlestown or Cambridge, instead of making a long march around by land. About ten o'clock Dr. Warren sent in great haste for me and begged that I would immediately set off for Lexington. I found he had sent an express by land, a Mr. William Dawes." I then went home, took my boots and surtout, went to the north part of the town, where I kept a boat; two friends rowed me across Charles River. When I got into town, I met Colonel Conant and several others. They said they had seen our signals. I told them what was acting, and went to get a horse." Mounted on Deacon Larkin's horse, he said "I alarmed nearly every home till I got to Lexington. After I had been there about half an hour, Mr. Dawes arrived, who came from Boston over the Neck. We set off for Concord." They had gone but a short distance when they were taken prisoners. Revere said "I saw four of them, who rode up to me with their pistols in their hands, said G—d d—n you, stop, if you go an inch further you are a dead Man." The result was that neither Revere nor Dawes reached Concord.

On the day following these events Revere was permanently engaged by Dr. Warren, as a scout to do outside business for the Committee of Safety. This patriotic service had a commercial value, and the Committee in auditing the bill thought he was disposed to value his labors too highly, for they reduced his charges from five shillings to four shillings a day.* In his financial dealings with the government he hardly ever failed to send in bills for work done which the authorities deemed extravagant charges and pruned down accordingly.

Most men like Revere, somewhat above the masses, but not possessing the elements of enduring fame, are remembered by a circle of admiring and respecting friends until they pass away, and are ultimately forgotten, finding no place upon the pages of written history. Paul Revere was rescued from this fate by an accident, a poet's imagination of things that never occurred. His famous ride remained unsung, if not unhonored for eighty-eight years, or until Longfellow, in 1863 made it the text for his Landlord's Tale in the Wayside Inn. It is to the "poetic license" of Longfellow, that most persons owe their knowledge of the fact that such a person as Revere ever existed. The poet did not mention the name of Dawes, yet he was entitled to as much credit, for what he did on the eve of the historic skirmish at Lexington, as Revere.

Poetry and history sometimes become sadly mixed, the poet and romancist, in so far as they deal with matters of verifiable records should keep closer to the truth, and make use of poetic license as little as possible. To be sure the poet's statement concerning the lantern, and that Revere reached Concord was long ago shown to have been incorrect, but its persistent virility only goes to prove that truth is not the only thing which crushed to earth, will rise again. Very little is said by historians, concerning the Penobscot Expedition despatched in the summer of 1779 by the Massachusetts Council against the British on the coast of Maine. It was an episode of the Revolution that

*Paul Revere's Bills can be seen in the Archives at the State House, Boston.

resulted in disaster so complete, so utterly without excuse, and so thoroughly discreditable to American arms as to make its contemplation without feelings of shame and humiliation impossible. An overwhelming force of Colonial troops, through the clear cowardice of an admiral bearing the proud name of Saltonstall, allowed itself to be frightened into an ignominious and panic-stricken desertion of its post of duty by a ridiculously ill equipped enemy. The ensuing scandal besmirched reputations hitherto untarnished, and the State of Massachusetts was plunged, on account of the expedition, into a debt of eight million dollars sterling. "To attempt to give a description of this terrible Day," wrote General Lovell, "is out of my Power. It would be a fit subject for some masterly hand to describe it in its true colors, to see four ships pursuing seventeen Sail of Armed Vessels, nine of which were stout Ships, Transports on fire. Men of War blowing up every kind of Stores on Shore, throwing about, and as much confusion as can possibly be conceived."*

Thus did this little Garrison with three Sloops of War, by the unwearied exertions of soldiers and seamen, writes John Calef in his Journal under date of August 14, 1779, whose bravery cannot be too much extolled, succeed in an enterprise of great importance, against difficulties apparently unsurmountable, and in a manner strongly expressive of their faithful and spirited attachment to the interests of their King and Country. Calef gives the total number of American ships of war, brigs and transports as 37, of which 26 were burnt and 11 captured.** "The soldiers and crew took to the woods, and singly or in squads, made their way to the Kennebec, where most of them arrived after a week's suffering from hunger and exposure."***

Lieutenant-Colonel Paul Revere was in command of the artillery train, and this episode was a serious event in his life, and came near stripping him of the laurels he had won by his earlier exploits, he was arrested on charges of cowardice, censured after an investigation, court martialled, and was grudgingly acquitted, after three years persistent effort.

Paul Revere's Masonic Record also has its blemishes. He received his degrees in St. Andrews Lodge in 1760-1. He afterwards became Grand Master. There being too many Loyalists or "Gentry" in St. Andrews Lodge to suit the taste of Revere, the leader of the mechanics, he and his friends therefore withdrew from same, and started "Rising States Lodge," but it did not succeed. The members soon fell to quarrelling among themselves. Some twenty members came together and voted the lodge out of existence, and divided the funds of the lodge, amounting to $1,577.50 among twenty-five members of the lodge, among whom was Paul Revere and his son. This was contrary to all Masonic precedents. The funds and paraphernalia of the Lodge should have been returned to the Grand Lodge. A committee was appointed to investigate the matter. They made a very scathing report in which it said "To divide it among members of a Lodge whenever they think proper to dissolve this union, is making the funds an object of speculation, it is treating

*Lovell's Journal, p. 105.
**The Siege of the Penobscot, etc., pp. 23, 25.
***Mass. Archives, Vol. 145, pp. 230-237. (Todd's report).

the noble example of departed donors with contempt and devoting their sacred deposit to individual emoluments, it is taking bread from the hungry, it is multiplying the tears of the widow and fatherless."

The Grand Lodge ordered that the funds of the lodge should be devoted to charity and a report of same printed and sent to each member of Rising States Lodge.*

WILLIAM FRANKLIN, SON OF BENJAMIN FRANKLIN.

William Franklin, Last Royal Governor of New Jersey, was a natural son of Dr. Benjamin Franklin. He was born about 1731. His father said of him: "He imagined his father had got enough for him; but I have assured him that I intend to spend what little I have myself, if it pleases God that I live long enough; and, as he by no means wants acuteness, he can see by my going on that I mean to be as good as my word." He served as Postmaster of Philadelphia, and as clerk of the House of Assembly of Pennsylvania. In the French war he was a captain and gained praise for his conduct at Ticonderoga. Before the peace, he went to England with his father. While there, Mr. Strahan wrote Mrs. Franklin, "Your son I really think one of the prettiest young gentlemen I ever knew from America. He seems to me to have a solidity of judgment, not very often to be met with in one of his years." While abroad young Franklin visited Scotland and became acquainted with the celebrated Earl of Bute, who recommended him to Lord Fairfax, who secured for him, as is said, the appointment of Governor of New Jersey, in 1763, without the solicitation of himself or his father. All intercourse between him and his father was suspended for more than a year before the actual commencement of hostilities. He was involved in a helpless quarrel with the delegates, and the people of New Jersey. In May, 1775, in a message he sent to the Assembly he said, "No office of honor in the power of the Crown to bestow would ever influence him to forget or neglect the duty he owed his country, nor the most furious rage of the most intemperate zealots induce him to swerve from the duty he owed his Majesty." On the 20th of May, the day this message was transmitted, the Assembly was prorogued, and Governor Franklin never communicated with that body again. Three days after the first Provincial Congress commenced their session at Trenton, and the Royal Government ceased, and William Livingston became Franklin's successor.

Congress ordered the arrest of Governor Franklin as an enemy to his country. He was accordingly placed in the custody of a guard commanded by a captain who had orders to deliver him to Governor Trumball in Connecticut. He was conveyed to East Windsor, and quartered in the house of Captain Ebenezer Grant. In 1777 he requested liberty to visit his wife who was a few miles distant, and sick. This Washington refused, saying, "It is by no means in my power to supersede a positive Resolution of Congress under which your present confinement took place." His wife was born in the West Indies and it is said that she was much affected by the severity of Doctor Franklin to her husband while he was a prisoner. She died in 1778 in her

*See copy of report on "Rising States Lodge," in Library of Mass. Grand Lodge.

49th year, and is buried in St. Paul's Church, New York. It is inscribed upon the monumental tablet erected to her memory that "Compelled to part from the husband she loved, and at length despairing of the soothing hope of his speedy return, she sunk under accumulated distresses, etc.

In 1778, after the arrival in America of Sir Henry Clinton, an exchange was effected and Governor Franklin was released, and went to England. In West's picture of the Reception of the American Loyalists, by Great Britain in 1783, Governor Franklin and Sir William Pepperell are the prominent personages represented. (See page 214.)

In 1784, the father and son, after an estrangement of ten years, became reconciled to one another, for Doctor Franklin writes, "It will be very agreeable to me, indeed nothing has ever hurt me so much, and affected me with such keen sensation, as to find myself deserted in my old age by my only son, and not only deserted, but to find him taking up arms against me in a cause wherein my good fame, fortune and life were all at stake. You conceived, you say, that your duty to your king and regard for your country required this. I ought not to blame you for differing in sentiment with me in public affairs. We are all men, subject to errors, etc. In his will, dated June 23, 1789, a few months before his decease, he showed his shrewdness and craftiness for which he was always noted, in leaving his Nova Scotia lands to his son, the title to which was doubtful on account of the part he took in the Revolution. He says "I give and devise all the lands I hold or have a right to in the Province of Nova Scotia, to hold to him, his heirs and assigns forever. I also give to him all my books and papers which he has in his possession, and all debts standing against him on my account-books, willing that no payment for, nor restitution of the same be required of him by my executors. The part he acted against me in the late war, which is of public notoriety, will account for my leaving him no more of an estate he endeavored to deprive me of."

Governor Franklin continued in England during the remainder of his life. He received a pension from the British Government of £800 per annum. His personal estate valued at £1800, which was confiscated, the government allowed him full compensation for. He had several shares in back lands and grants and real estate in New York and New Jersey, all of which he conveyed to his father, as he was indebted to him. He died in Nov., 1813. His son, William Temple Franklin, was Secretary to Dr. Franklin, and edited his works. He died at Paris in May, 1823.

ROYAL COAT OF ARMS.

The Royal Coat of Arms embossed on the outside cover of this work is an exact reproduction of the Coat of Arms that was formerly above the Governor's seat in the Council Chamber in the Old State House in Boston. It was made from a photograph taken from the original in Trinity Church, St. John, N. B., for a fuller description of same, see p. 436. The seal embossed on the outside back cover, is a reproduction of the seal of "The Colony of the Massachusetts Bay in New England" from which the present seal of the State of Massachusetts is derived. It was the seal that was used on all official documents down to the time of the Revolution.

APPENDIX   483

PELHAM'S MAP OF BOSTON.

This plan was made by Henry Pelham, the half brother of Copley the painter. It was made under permission of J. Urquhart, Town Major, August 28, 1775. It shows the lines about the Town and the Harbor, and is the most important of the early maps of Boston and the one upon which all subsequent revolutionary maps are based. It was printed in two sheets published in London, June 2, 1777, done in aquatinta by Francis Jukes. This copy is reproduced from the original in the Massachusetts Historical Society's Library and is drawn on a photographic print from which this engraving is made.

JUDGE CHAMBERLAIN'S OPINION OF COL. THOS. GOLDTHWAITE.

Col. Goldthwaite was a man of ability, unbounded enterprise, and considerable influence. Chamberlain in his History of Chelsea says of him: "Some very unfavorable accounts of Col. Goldthwaite have been published, which I do not feel at liberty to withhold, but in referring to them suggest, first, that they were mainly written after he had become obnoxious as a loyalist; secondly: that his position on the Penobscot was one in which it would have been impossible to protect the just rights of the Indians against turbulent frontiersmen outside any efficient government without incurring their hostility, since their only sense of justice was their desire for exclusive possessions of lands which rightfully belonged to the original occupants."

GOV. JOHN WINTHROP—See Page 426.

John Winthrop, born Jan. 12, 1587, died at Boston March 26, 1649, by his first wife Mary Forth, had

    John, born Sept. 12, 1606   Forth, born Dec. 30, 1609
    Henry, born Jan. 19, 1608   Mary, born probably 1612
    Ann, baptised Aug. 8, 1614 and died soon after
    Ann (again) baptised June 26, 1615

By his second wife, Thomasine Clopton, had a child who died at the same time as its mother.

By his third wife, Margaret Tyndal, he had

    Stephen, Mar. 31, 1619   Nathaniel, Feb. 20, 1625, died young
    Adam, April 7, 1620   Samuel, August 26, 1627
    Deane, March 23, 1623
    Ann, April 29, 1630, who died on the voyage over
    William, Aug. 14, 1632, probably died early
    Sarah, baptized Jan. 29, 1634, probably died early

By his fourth wife, Martha, a widow of Thomas Coytmore, sister of Increase Nowell of Charlestown, he had Joshua, baptised December 17, 1648

His eldest son, John Winthrop, born Sept. 12, 1606, at Groton, who afterwards became Governor of Connecticut, died and was buried in Boston; it is his line of descendants that is given on page 426; the other branches of the family became extinct in the male line.

INDEX.

Abercrombie, 226.
Achmuty (see Auchmuty).
    Robert, 126.
Adams, Charles Francis, 37.
    Frances, 286.
    James, 286.
    John, 5, 24, 25, 29, 32, 35, 37, 45, 46, 48, 54, 68, 69, 77, 83, 89, 93, 95, 105, 153, 163, 181, 226, 317, 318, 327, 334, 340, 366, 368, 379, 385, 391, 392, 452, 455, 477.
    John, Mrs., 282.
    John Quincy, 180, 365.
    Joseph, 138.
    Josiah, 472, 473, 476.
    Samuel, 37, 38, 39, 44, 46, 48, 51, 59, 83, 152, 153, 157, 160, 161, 162, 163, 165, 166, 189, 219, 310, 322, 476.
    Zab, 334.
Albemarle, Duke of, 419.
Allen, Ebenezer, 134.
    James, 295.
    Martha, 295.
    William, 204.
Almon, W. J., 279.
Altamont, Earl of, 316.
Ambrose, Robert, 128.
Ames, Fisher, 98.
    Gov., 47.
Amherst, 20, 198, 227.
Amory, Abigail Taylor, 345.
    Ann Geyer, 395.
    Ann McLean, 395.
    Anne, 343.
    Catherine Green, 345.
    Charles, 221, 345.
    Elizabeth Fitzmaurice, 343.
    Esther Sargent, 345.
    Hattie Sullivan, 345.
    Hugh, 343.
    John, 137, 249, 344, 345, 346, 350.
    Jonathan, 343, 344, 345, 346, 410.
    Martha Greene, 345.
    Mrs., 234.
    Nancy Geyer, 350.
    Nathaniel, 345.
    Rebecca, 343, 344.
    Robert, 128, 343.
    Rufus, 350.
    Rufus Greene, 395.
    Thomas, 132, 343, 344, 345, 410.
    Thomas C., 233, 242, 243, 345.
    Thomas Coffin, 51.
    William, 345.
Ancient and Honorable Artillery Co., 118, 181, 356, 424.
Anderson, James, 125, 132, 137.
Andrews, Elizabeth, 412.

    Thomas, 412.
    William, Jr., 468.
Andros, 419.
    Barrett, 133.
    Edmond, Sir, 16.
Appleton, John, 262.
Apthorp, 60, 438, 448.
    Alicia Mann, 352.
    Charles, 351, 352, 354.
    Charles Ward, 352.
    Charlotte Augusta, 352.
    East (Rev.), 353.
    Grace Foster, 353.
    Grizzell, 352, 354.
    Grizzell Eastwicke, 351.
    Hannah, Greenleaf, 352.
    John, 351, 352.
    John T. (Col.), 353.
    Mary, 352, 353, 396.
    Mary McEvers, 352.
    Mary Thompson, 354.
    Susan, 353.
    Susan, Ward, 351.
    Thomas, 125, 137, 354.
    William, 137, 354.
Arbuthnot, Abigail Little, 399.
    Christian, 399.
    John, 399.
    Miss, 251.
Archer, Mary, 287.
Argenson, 23.
Arnold, 90.
    Benedict, 180.
Asby, James, 125.
Ashburton, Lord, 114, 115.
Ashley, Joseph, 133, 138.
Ashton, Jacob, 131.
Astor, John Jacob, 209.
Atkins, David, 139.
    Gibbs, 134, 137, 323.
    Ruth, 321.
    Thomas, 323.
Atkinson, John, 125, 132, 133, 137.
Attucks, Crispus, 44, 83.
Auchmuty, 163, 437.
    James, 302.
    Maria M., 304.
    Richard, Harrison, 304.
    Robert, 138, 142, 249, 300, 302.
    Robert Nicholls, 304.
    Samuel, Sir, 304.
    Samuel, Rev., 303, 304.
Austin, Capt., 364.
    Mrs., 364.
Avery, John, 477.
Alywin, Thomas, 125.
Ayres, Eleanor, 134.

INDEX 485

Bache, Benjamin F., 75, 76.
Bacon, 439.
Badger, Moses, Rev., 134, 138, 275.
Bagley, Col., 358.
Bailey, Jacob, Rev., 399.
Baird, D. Sir, 304.
Baker, John, 134, 139.
    Walter, 183.
Baldwin, Henry, 361.
    Loammi, Col., 262, 266, 271, 358.
Ball, Robert, 361.
Bancroft, George, 390.
    Rev. Dr., 391.
Bangs, Seth, 139.
Barber, Major, 406.
Barger, Philip, 448.
Barker, Ann, 310.
Barnard, John, 134.
    Thomas, 127.
Barnes, Catherine, 400.
    Christian Arbuthnot, 399.
    Elizabeth, 255, 399.
    Henry, 132, 138, 235, 399, 400, 401, 402.
    Mr., 251.
    Surgeon-General, 112.
Barnett, John, 239.
Barnsfare, 244.
Barre, 28, 31.
Barrell, Elizabeth, 445.
    Jonathan Sayward, 445.
    Mary, 445.
    Nathaniel, 445.
    Samuel B., 136.
    Sarah Sayward, 445.
    Theodore, 136.
    Walter, 133.
Barrett, Col., 471.
Barrick, James, 133, 137.
Barron, Jonathan, 286.
    Lucy, 286.
Barry, 218.
Barton, David, 132.
    M., 475.
Bass, Gilman, 469.
    Henry, 477.
    Mr., 340.
Bath, Lord, 23.
Beaman, Thomas, 139.
Beath, Mary, 134.
Beaumarchais, 84, 85.
Beecher, Henry Ward, 111.
Belcher, Andrew, 181.
    Eliza, 181.
    Governor, see Jonathan.
    Jonathan (Gov.), 181, 233, 275, 276, 344, 447.
    Joseph (Rev.), 338.
    Rebeccah, 338.
    Sarah, 447.
Bennett, Barbara, 255.
    Spencer (see Phips, Spencer), 420.
Bentham, Jeremy, 164.
Benton, Senator, (Thos. H.), 115.
Bernard, 292, 301.
    Amelia, 201.
    Francis, Rev., 191.
    Francis, Sir, 35, 41, 42, 50, 137, 142, 149, 157, 176, 191, 192, 193, 194, 196, 197, 199, 200, 203, 204, 207.
    Godfrey, 191.
    Governor, see Sir Francis.
    John, 201.
    John, Sir, 203.
    Julia, 193, 201, 202.
    Scrope, 201, 202.
    Thomas, 191, 196, 197, 200, 202, 203, 204.
Berry, Edward, 137.
    Elizabeth, 467.
    John, 125.
Bethel, Robert, 133.
Bethune, George, 125, 239.
    George A., 229.
Bicker, William, 342.
Bigelow, Timothy, Col., 400.
Bissett, George, 361.
Black, David, 137.
    John, 134.
Blackburn, 444.
    Mr. Justice, 151.
Blackstone, Mr., 364.
    William, 217, 413.
Blackwell, John, Jr., 139.
Blair, John, 134.
    Robert, 137.
    William, 124.
Blanchard, 394.
Bland, 80.
Blaney, Joseph, 131.
Bligh, Thomas, 13.
Bliss, Daniel, 126, 138.
    Jonathan, 249.
    Samuel, 138.
Blodgett, Susannah, 261.
    Thomas, 261.
Blowers, Sampson S., 126, 137, 249.
    Sampson Salter, 137.
Bloye, Henry, 125.
Boardman, Andrew, 420.
Bollan, Mr., 301.
Bolton, Col., 234.
    Mrs., 234.
Borland, 438.
    John, 125, 409.
    Mrs., 251.
    Sarah, 409.
Boucher, 202.
Bourn, Edward, 139.
    Elisha, 139.
    Lemuel, 139.
    William, 139.
Boutineau, James, 125, 136, 142, 448.
    Mary Bowdoin, 448.
    Mrs., 448.
    Nancy, 448.
Bowen, John, 134, 139.
    Nathan, 128.
Bowes, Ann Whitney, 224.
    Arthur, 224.
    Dorcas Champney, 224.
    Edmund Elford, 224.
    Emily, 224.
    Harriet Troutbeck, 224.
    Lucy Hancock, 224.
    Martha Remington, 224.
    Martin (Sir), 224.
    Mary Stoddard, 224.
    Nicholas, 224.
    Sarah, 224.
    Sarah Hubbard, 224.
    William, 125, 132, 134, 137, 224, 225.
Bowditch, 412.
    Joseph, 131.
Bowdoin, 163, 165.
    Elizabeth, 448.
    James, 29, 399, 402, 428, 437.
    Judith, 403.
    Mary, 448.
    Peter, 448.
Bowman, Archibald, 132, 134.
Boyd, Gen., 104.

486 INDEX

Boydell, Alderman, 218.
Boyer, Daniel, 409.
Boyle, John, 405.
Boyleston, Mr., 250.
Boylston, Ward Nicholas, 249.
Braddock, Gen., 19, 51, 179.
Bradford, Gov., 434.
Bradish, Ebenezer, 126.
    Mr., 388.
Bradshaw, Sarah Thompson, 297.
Bradstreet, 11, 17.
    Simon, 458.
Bragdon, Capt., 443.
Brandon, 134.
Brattle, Katherine, 295.
    Katherine Saltonstall, 296, 297.
    Thomas, 137, 294, 296.
    William, 132, 134, 161, 294, 295, 296, 435.
Braxton, 80.
Bray, John, 205, 208.
    Margery, 205.
Breck, Abigail, 313.
    John, 313.
    Margaret, 313.
Brewer, Daniel, 140.
    Joseph, 424.
Breynton, Rev. Dr., 348.
Bridgewater, Chief Justice, 279.
    Mary, 279.
Bridgham, Ebenezer, 125, 133, 137.
    Hannah, 358.
    Joseph, 358.
Briggs, Mathyas, 285.
Brigham, Ebenezer, 132.
Bright, John, 110.
Brimmer, Martin, 196.
Brindley, see Brinley.
Brinley, also Brindley.
    Catherine Craddock, 396.
    Deborah, 377, 396.
    Edward, 396.
    Elizabeth, 396.
    Elizabeth Pitts, 397.
    Francis, 377, 396.
    George, 125, 132, 137.
    Mary Apthorp, 396.
    Mrs. (Nathaniel), 397.
    Nathaniel, 132, 396.
    Robert, 397.
    Sylvester Oliver, 190.
    Thomas, 125, 132, 134, 137, 249, 395, 396, 397.
Britton, David, 131.
Brock, Gen., 103, 441.
Broderick, John, 134.
Brooks, Susanna, 298.
Broomer, Joshua, 139.
Brown, Abishai (Capt.), 475.
    Capt., 400, 401.
    Gawler, 280.
    Gen., 104.
    Lieut., 353.
    Mary, 428.
    Mather, 280.
    Shearjashub, 126.
    Thomas, 134.
    William, 138, 428.
Browne, 250.
    Elizabeth, 242.
    Hannah Curwin, 449.
    Judge, 448.
    Mary, 463.
    Samuel, 449.
    Simon, 449.
    William, 131, 136, 142, 189, 449, 450, 451, 461, 463.

Bruce, James, 137.
Brunsden, Charles, 220.
Bryant, Seth, 139.
Brymer, Alexander, 137.
Bubier, Joseph, 128.
Buckminster, Col., 425.
Bulfinch, Charles, 352, 354.
    Susan Apthorp, 353.
    Thomas, 349, 354.
Bumpus, Thomas, 139.
Bumstead, Thomas, 307.
Burch, William, 137, 142, 319.
Burden, William, 139.
Bureau, Ann, 229.
Burgoyne, Gen., 84, 85, 250.
Burke, 28, 31, 164.
Burnett, Gov., 449.
Burr, Aaron, 180.
Burrell, Colbourn, 125.
    Martha, 356.
Burton, Jane, 427.
    Mary, 134.
    William, 125, 137.
Bush, David, 139.
Bute, Lord, 40, 153, 481.
Butler, Benjamin F., 109.
    Dr., 353.
    Gen., 111.
    Gilliam, 134.
Buttrick, Maj., 471.
Byfield, Deborah, 447.
    Nathaniel, 447.
Byles, Anna, 280.
    Belcher, 280.
    Elizabeth, 275, 280.
    Josiah, 275.
    Mather, Rev., 134, 275, 276, 277, 278, 279, 280, 410.
    Mather, Jr., 137, 279.
    Mather (3), 279, 280.
    Rebecca, 279.
    Sarah, 275.
Bymer, Alexander, 132.

Cabot, 251.
    Francis, 127, 131.
    George, 459.
    William, 131, 249.
Calef, John, 480.
Calhoun, John C., 102, 116, 180.
Callahan, Charles, 140.
Callendar, Edward B., 5.
Callender, James Thompson, 76.
Camden, 28.
Campbell, Alexander, 312.
    Duncan, 404.
    Elizabeth, 256.
    John, 404.
    Thomas, 255.
    William, 134.
Caner, Ann, 347.
    Henry (Rev. Dr.), 134, 202, 346, 347, 348, 349, 411.
Canner, Henry, 137.
Canning, 77.
Capen, Hopestil, 125.
Carew, Charles Hallowell, 284.
    Robert Hallowell, 284.
Carleton, Guy (Sir), 234, 237, 241, 242, 244, 396.
Carlisle, Earl of, 413.
    Mr., 55.
Carpenter, 251.
Carr, Mr., 134.
    Patrick, 46.
    Robert (Sir), 13, 14.

INDEX 487

Carroll, Charles, 31, 80.
    John (Rev.), 31, 32.
Carter (Lieut), 89.
Cartwright, Geo. (Col.), 13, 14.
Carver, Caleb, 139.
    Melzor, 134, 139.
Cary (Dr.), 353.
    Nathaniel, 125, 132.
Cazneau, Andrew, 126, 132, 134, 137.
    William, 125, 132.
Cednor, William, 134.
Chambers, Rebecca, 452.
Chace (see also Chase).
    Ami, 139.
    Levi, 139.
    Shadrach, 139.
Chadwell, Abraham, 374.
    M. A., 374.
    Samuel, 133.
Chalmers (Richard-?-), 212.
Chamberlain, Joseph, 8.
    Mrs., 358.
Champney, Dorcas, 224.
Chandler, Ann, Leonard, 392.
    Annice, 388.
    Clark, 390.
    Dorothy, Paine, 390.
    Dr., 212.
    Eleanor Putnam, 391.
    Elizabeth Ruggles, 379.
    Gardner, 139, 391.
    Hannah Gardner, 389.
    John, 35, 132, 134, 139, 383, 385, 388, 389, 390, 391.
    John (Col.), 389.
    Lucretia, 382.
    Nathaniel, 133, 134, 139, 391.
    Rufus, 126, 139, 379, 385, 390.
    Sarah, 383.
    William, 133, 134, 139, 388, 399.
Channing, Dr., 114.
Charles I., 10, 427.
Charles II., 11, 12, 16.
Chase (see also Chace and Speakman, 477).
    Samuel, 31.
    Thomas, 477.
Chatham, 25, 28, 31.
Chauncy (Rev. Dr.), 321.
Checkley, Anthony, 308.
Cheever, Ezekiel, 406, 463.
    Joshua, 423.
    Mary, 414.
Chickatabut, 365.
Child, Isabella, 442.
    Susan, 442.
    Susannah, 439.
    Thomas, 442, 465.
    Thomas Hale, 442.
Chipman, Hannah Warren, 431.
    Hope Howland, 431.
    John, 431, 432.
    John (Rev.), 431.
    Rebecca Hale, 431.
    Samuel, 431.
    Ward 133, 431, 432, 436.
Church, Benjamin, 137, 166, 286, 406, 454.
    Benjamin, Jr., 417.
    Colonel, 390.
    Mary, 390.
Ciely, John, 133.
Clap, Rachel, 333.
Clarence, Duke of, 243.
Clark (see also Clarke).
    Benjamin, 124, 415.
    Isaac, 137.

    John, 137, 415.
    Jonathan, 137, 249.
Clark, Mary, 188.
    Richard, 132, 137, 249.
    Samuel, 415.
    Sarah, 383.
    Thomas, 260.
    Timothy, 383.
    William, 188, 415.
Clarke (see also Clark), 60.
    Anne, 394.
    Francis, 405.
    Isaac Winslow, 245, 409.
    Jonathan, 407, 409.
    Margaret Winslow, 245.
    Richard, 165, 216, 217, 245, 405, 406, 407, 408, 409.
    Susan, 409.
    and Sons, 405.
Clay, Henry, 102, 180.
Cleveland, President, 117.
Cleverly, 438.
Clinton, Henry (Sir), 467, 482.
Cobb, Nicholas, 139.
Cochrane, Alexander (Sir), 240.
    Capt. 51.
Codner, William, 124, 132, 137.
Coffin, Ann, 243, 446.
    Ann Holmes, 446.
    Aston (Sir), 283.
    Caroline, 239.
    Ebenezer, 234.
    Elizabeth, 233.
    Elizabeth Amory, 344.
    Elizabeth Barnes, 399.
    Francis Holmes, 245.
    Froman H. (Admiral), 233.
    Guy Carleton (Gen.), 238.
    Hector (Capt.), 243.
    Henry Edward, 238.
    Isaac, Sir (Admiral), 233, 238, 239, 240, 241, 242, 243, 283, 400, 442.
    Isaac Sir (Gen.), 245.
    Isabella, 244.
    James, 233, 245.
    John, 125, 137, 234, 243, 244, 245, 442.
    John (Gen.), 233, 235, 236, 237, 238, 242, 243, 283, 400.
    John T. (Admiral), 242.
    John Townsend, 238.
    Jonathan Perry, 243.
    Lieut. Col., 244.
    Margaret, 244.
    Margrate, 442.
    Mary, 239.
    Nathaniel, 125, 132, 133, 137, 233, 234, 235, 239, 243, 245, 249, 251, 350, 399, 446.
    Nathaniel, Jr., 125.
    T. (Admiral), 238.
    Thomas, 245.
    Thomas Aston, 234.
    Thomas Aston (Sir), 233, 243.
    Tristram, 233, 243.
    William, 125, 134, 137, 233, 234, 235, 243, 245, 309, 344, 350, 446.
    William, Jr., 132, 134, 234.
    William Foster, 245.
Collins, Stephen, 248.
Colonial Club, 193.
Conant, Col., 479.
Congreve, Mary, 215.
    William (Sir), 215.
Conkey, Israel, 139.
Connors, Mrs., 134.
Converse, Hannah, 261.

488 INDEX

Cook, Robert, 134.
Cookson, 133.
Cooley, John, 134.
Coombs, Mr., 252.
Cooper, Jacob, 312.
    Samuel, 163.
    William, 314.
Coote, Eye, 414.
Coores, 414.
Copley, Elizabeth Clark, 221.
    Georgiana, Susan, 221.
Copley, John Singleton, 125, 165, 216, 217, 218, 219, 249, 280, 394, 404, 409, 412, 413, 444.
    John Singleton (2) (See also Lyndhurst, Lord), 219, 220, 221, 283.
Copley, Richard, 216.
    Sarah Elizabeth, 221.
    Sophia, Clarence, 221.
    Susan Penelope, 221.
Cornwallis, 236, 251.
Corwell, Anna, 223.
    Jemima, 223.
    Richard, 223.
Cotton, John, 145, 338.
    Maria, 338.
    Mr., 272.
Courtney, Thomas, 132, 134, 137.
Cousins, John, 443.
Cox, Edward, 125, 137.
Cradock, Catherine, 396.
    Elizabeth, 396.
    George, 396.
Crage, James, 139.
Cragie, Lord, 442.
    Mrs., 442.
Craigie, Admiral, 244.
    John, 244.
    Lord, 244.
Cranch, 334.
Crane, Ellery B., 475.
    Major, 194.
Crehore, Zeedah, 129.
Cromwell, Oliver, 11, 71, 122, 417, 433, 439.
Crowne, William (Col.), 12.
Cummins, A., 134.
    E., 134.
Cunningham, Archibald, 132, 137, 451.
Curtice (See also Curtis).
    Mary, 423.
    Samuel, 423.
Curtis (See also Curtice).
    Charles, 132, 138.
    Obediah, 425.
Curwen, George, 246, 254, 447, 449, 461.
    Hannah, 449.
    Jonathan, 246.
    Samuel, 64, 131, 246, 247, 254.
    Susannah, 447.
Cushen, John, 285.
Cushing, William, 189.
Cushman, Elkanah, 133.
Cutler, Ebenezer, 134, 139, 468, 469, 470.
    John, 230, 468.
    Mary, 230, 468.
    Mary Hicks, 470.
    Mary March, 468.
    May Stockwell, 468.
    Miriam, 469, 470.
    Miriam Eager, 468.
    Olivia Dickson, 470.
    Rebecca, 470.
    Samuel, 468.
    Zackeus, 468.
Cutts, Joseph (Capt.), 209.
    Sally, 209.
    Thomas, 208.

Dabney, Nathaniel, 127.
Dalglish, Andrew, 127, 131.
Danforth, Judge, 187.
    Samuel, 136.
    Thomas, 126, 134, 138.
Daphne (a slave), 400.
Dartmouth, Lord, 162, 291, 292.
Daubney (See also Dabney).
    Nathaniel, 131.
Davenport, Addington, 232.
    Jane, 232.
    Samuel, 129, 130.
Davie, 86.
Davis, Ann, 288.
    Benjamin, 125, 132, 137.
    Governor, 390.
    Isaac (Capt.), 471.
    James, 324.
    Jefferson, 110, 111, 112.
    Miss, 251.
Dawes, William, 479.
Daws, Edward, 359.
D'Bernicre (Ensign), 400.
D'Estaing (Admiral), 240, 430.
De Brisay (see Des' Brisay).
De Chatillon, 445.
De Grasse, 240, 252, 283, 428.
De la Bere, David, 235.
De Lancy, 431.
    Oliver, 396.
De Viomel, 430.
Deane, Silas, 84, 102.
Dearborn (Gen.), 104, 441.
Debarrett, Mrs., 248.
Deblois (including De Blois).
    Ann, 446.
    Ann Coffin, 446.
    Ann Farley, 445.
    Elizabeth Cranton, 446.
    Elizabeth Jenkins, 446.
    Etienne, 445.
    George, 131, 446.
    Gilbert, 125, 132, 134, 137, 306, 307, 446.
    James Smith, 306.
    Lewis, 125, 132, 134, 137, 223, 446.
    Mrs., 234.
    Ruth, 223.
    Stephen, 445.
Dechezzar, Adam, 134.
Decrow, Thomas, 139.
Deering, James, 399.
Dennie, William, 406.
Dennison, Samuel, 387.
Derby, Richard, Jr., 127.
Des' Brisay, Thomas (Gen.), 280.
Devens, Richard, 405.
Devereaux, Anna, 222.
    Hannah, 222.
    John, 222.
Dewey, George (Admiral), 118.
Dexter, Aaron, 344.
Dexter, Mrs., 234.
    Rebecca Amory, 344.
Dickenson, Nathaniel, 134, 138.
Dickerson, William, 132.
Dickson, Olivia, 470.
    William, 124.
Dieskau, Baron, 19, 226.
Digby, Admiral, 268, 269.
    John (Sir), 462.
Dillon, 110.
Doolittle, Amos, 476.
Dorchester Historical Society, 184.
Dorchester, Lord (see also Sir Guy Carleton), 234.
Dougherty, Edward, 134.

INDEX 489

Dowse, Joseph, 131.
Doyle, Major, 268.
Doyley, Francis, 134.
    John, 134.
Drake, Samuel G., 43.
Draper, Ann, 404.
    Edward, 404.
    John, 404.
    Margaret, 134, 404, 405.
    Richard, 361, 404, 405.
    William, 404.
Driver, Richard, 225.
Duane, 102.
    William, 76.
Duche, Jacob (Rev.), 78, 83.
Duddington (Lieut.), 52.
Dudley, Charles, 133.
    Joseph (Gov.), 410.
    Katherine, 410.
    Rebecca, 456.
    William, 410.
Duelly, William, 134.
Dulaney (Daniel ?), 212.
Dumaresq, Capt., 445.
    Philip, 125, 132, 133, 137, 316.
    Rebecca, Gardiner, 316.
Dummer, Jane, 454.
Dunbar Daniel, 138, 421.
    Jessie, 421.
    Joseph, 421.
    Robert, 421.
    Rose, 421.
    William, 254.
Duncan, Alexander, 134.
    James (Major), 273.
Dunlap, Daniel, 134.
Dunn, Samuel, 430.
Dunning, Mr., 164.
Du Portail, 25.
Dupuis, Abram, 405.
Durham, 458.
Du Vassall (see also Vassall), 285.
Duyer, Edward, 133.
Dysart, Hugh, 470.
    Robert J., 470.

Eager, James, 468.
    John, 139.
    Miriam, 468.
    Mrs., 469, 470.
Earl, James, 468.
East India Company, 124.
Eastwicke, Guzzel, 351.
    John, 351.
Eaton, Benjamin, 397.
Eckley, Thomas E., 395.
    Julia Ann Jeffries, 395.
Edgar, James, 139.
Edward IV., 427.
    VII., 433.
Edwards, Thomas, 411.
    Mary Johonnot, 411.
Edson, Josiah, 133, 136, 138, 142.
Eldridge, Joshua, 139.
Eliot, Andrew, 160.
    Andrew (Rev.), 348.
    Asaph, 290.
    Elizabeth, 290.
    Jacob, 309.
    John, 309.
    John (Rev.), 338, 355.
    William, 272.
Ellis, Ephriam, Jr., 139.
    Joshua, 418.
Ellsworth, 86, 108.

Emerson, John, 134.
    William (Rev.), 471.
Emsley, Chief Justice, 282.
    Mrs., 282.
Endicott, John (Gov.), 10.
Eppes, Abigail, 314, 317.
    Love, 215, 317.
    William, 316.
Erving, Abigail, 298.
    Col. 250.
    George, 125, 133, 137, 142, 292, 293, 299.
    John, 132, 133, 298, 306, 399.
    John, Jr., 125, 136, 137, 142.
    Maria Catherine, 299.
    Mr., 320.
    Shirley (Dr.), 299.
Etter, Peter, 134.
Eustis (Gov.), 179.
    William (Dr.), 335.
Evans, 133.
Everett, Edward, 184.
    Oliver, 184.
Eyre, John, 394.
    Katherine, 394.

Fairfax, Lord, 179, 481.
Fales, 228.
Faneuil, 60, 250, 251, 406.
    Andrew, 230.
    Benjamin, 134, 137, 165, 229.
    Benjamin, Jr., 132.
    Jane, 232.
    Mary, 232.
    Mary Ann, 232.
    Peter, 165, 229, 230, 231, 232, 351, 415, 448.
Farbrace, Miss, 428.
Farley, Ann, 445.
Farnum, Susannah, 216.
Fellows, Gustavus, 397.
Fenton, Capt., 448.
Ferguson, Major, 90.
Fields, Joseph, 477.
Finney, Francis, 139.
    John, 131.
    Wilfret, 134, 137.
Fisk, John, 397.
Fitch, 212.
    Martha, 295.
    Samuel, 126, 132, 134, 137, 142.
Fitzclarence, Mary, 289.
Fitzmaurice, Elizabeth.
Flagg, Samuel, 131.
Fleming, John, 138.
Fletcher, Robert, 293.
Flucker, Elizabeth Luist, 402.
Flucker, Hannah, 404.
    Hannah Waldo, 403.
    James, 402.
    Judith Bowdoin, 403.
    Lucy, 403.
    Mrs., 134.
    Sally, 404.
    Thomas, 136, 137, 142, 159, 249, 402, 403, 404.
    Thomas, Jr., 403.
Foote, 349.
Forbes, John (Rev.), 257, 260.
    Dorothy, 258.
Forest, James, 134.
Formon, Sarah, 360.
Forrest, James, 125, 137.
    James (Capt.), 228.

Foster, Comfort, 183.
    Edward, 125, 134.
    Edward, Jr., 134, 137.
    Grace, 353.
    Jonathan, 298.
    Mary, 353.
    Thomas, 133, 134.
Fowle, Col., 461.
    Elizabeth Prescott, 422.
    Jacob, 128.
    John, 128, 422.
    Rebecca, 422.
Fowler, Professor, 474, 475.
Fox (Charles James), 28, 31, 165, 289.
Francis, Sarah, 466.
Frankland, Agnes (Lady), 417, 418.
Frankland, Charles Henry Sir, (alias Sir Henry and Sir Harry), 416, 417, 418, 439.
Franklin, Benjamin, 5, 22, 24, 25, 26, 31, 37, 38, 75, 91, 102, 115, 152, 163, 164, 181, 214, 280, 362, 367, 481, 482.
    William (Sir), 214, 481, 482.
    William Temple, 482.
Frary, Mehitable, 308, 309.
    Theophilus, 309.
Frazer, Nathan, 350, 351.
    Rebecca, 351.
Freeman, 76.
    James, 288.
Freneau, Philip, 75.
Frye, P., 131.
Full, Thomas, 134.

Gage, Thomas (General and Governor), 50, 52, 58, 127, 131, 132, 144, 168, 187, 189, 200, 295, 306, 344, 397, 400, 408, 413, 446.
Gale, Anna, 275.
    Ruth 286.
Gallison, John, 128.
Gallop, Antill, 411.
Gallop, Joan, 411.
Galloway (Richard), 212.
Golway, William, 138.
Gambin, Admiral, 467.
G. A. R., 120.
Gardiner, Abigail, 316.
    Ann, 316.
    Ann Gibbons 314.
    Benoni, 313.
    Catherine Goldthwait, 314.
    Hannah, 281, 316, 377, 389.
    Henry, 131, 335, 345.
    John, 102, 315, 316, 377, 389.
    John Sylvester John, 316.
    Jonathan, 251.
    Joseph, 313.
    Lucretia Chandler, 377.
    Mrs., 250.
    Rebecca, 316.
    Robert Hallowell, 315, 316.
    Sylvanus, 316.
    Sylvester (also Silvester), 125, 132, 137.
    (Dr.), 134, 281, 313, 314, 315, 316.
    Weld, 131.
    William, 313, 316.
Garrick, Mr. (David), 249.
Garrison, 48.
Gates, General, 85.
Gay, Ebenezer (Rev.) 321.
    Ebenezer, 324.
    Joanna, 321.
    John, 321.
    Jotham, 322.
    Lydia Lusher, 321.
    Martin, 125, 132, 134, 137.
    Martin, Capt., 321, 322, 323, 324, 325.
Gay, Mary, 323.
    Mary Pinckney, 321.
    Nathaniel, 321.
    Ruth, 323, 324.
    Ruth Atkins, 321.
    Samuel, 324.
    W. Allen, 322.
    Wickworth Allen, 324.
Gayer (see also Geyer).
    John (Sir), 233.
    William, 233, 350.
George (Capt.), 17.
George III., 83, 97.
Geray, Sarah, 220.
    Thomas (Lt. Col.), 221.
Germain, Lord George, 213, 267, 280.
Gerrish, Cabot, 131.
    Joseph, 336.
    Mary, 336.
    William, 131.
Gerry, Elbridge (Gov.), 188, 450.
Getchell, Dorothy, 467.
Gettemy, Charles J., 477.
Geyer, Damaris, 350.
    Frederick William, 137, 350, 351.
    Henry Christian, 350.
    Maria Guard, 350.
    Nancy, 350.
    William, 350.
Gibbons, Ann, 314.
    John, 314.
Gibbs, Henry (Sir) 246.
Gilbert, Bradford, 139.
    Perez, 139.
    Samuel, 134, 139.
Gilbert, Thomas, 134, 139.
    Thomas, Jr., 139.
Glover, Jonathan, 128.
Gladstone (William E.), 110.
Goffe, 12.
Goldsbury, Samuel, 134, 138.
Goldsmith, Georgiana, 221.
    Lewis, 221.
Goldthwait, Benjamin, 359.
    Catherine, 314, 357, 402.
    Catherine Barnes, 400.
    Charles, 361.
    Elizabeth, 355.
    Ezekiel, 125, 334, 356, 358.
    Hannah, 358, 359.
    Hannah Bridgham, 358.
    Henry (Lieut.), 360.
    Henry Barnes, 361.
    Jane Halsey, 355.
    John, 355, 356.
    Joseph, 125, 137, 356, 358, 359, 360.
    Martha Lewis, 356.
    Mary Jordan, 350.
    Mehitable, 355.
    Michael B., 125, 132, 360.
    Philip (Capt.), 359.
    Rachel, 355.
    Samuel, 355, 360.
    Sarah, 355.
    Sarah Formen, 360.
    Sarah Hopkins, 355.
    Sarah Winch, 360.
    Thomas, 355, 356, 357, 360, 400.
Goodale, Nathan, 127, 131.
Goodhue, Jonathan, 131.
Gordon, Hugh Mackay, 283.
Gore, Abigail, 392.
    Christopher (Gov.), 394.

Elizabeth Weld, 392.
Frances Pinckney, 392.
Hannah, 392.
John, 125, 132, 134, 137, 392.
Mary, 392.
Mylain, 392.
Obadiah, 392.
Rebecca Payne, 394.
Rhoda, 392.
Samuel, 392, 422.
Sarah Kilby, 392.
Gorham, David, 126.
  Nathaniel, 253.
Goss, Phebe, 286.
Gould, Anne, 281.
  General, 281.
Gouldthwaight, Thos. (see Goldthwaite), 355.
Grant, Charles, 239.
  Ebenezer (Capt.), 181.
  Gen., 111, 120.
  James, 131, 134.
  Major, 237.
Grattan, Thomas Colley, 114.
Graves (Admiral), 240, 314.
  John, 140.
Gray, 60.
  Andrew, 134.
  Benjamin Gerrish, 336.
  Edward, 334.
  Elizabeth, 336.
  Ellis, 426.
  Harrison 125, 133, 136, 137, 142, 249, 280, 319, 334, 336, 345.
  Harrison, Jr., 125, 137.
  Gray, Horace, 29n, 151.
  John, 134, 336.
  Joseph, 336.
  Lewis, 132, 137.
  Mary, 134.
  Mary Gerrish, 336.
  Rebecca, 336.
  Susannah, 334.
  Thomas, 125.
  William, 336, 432, 451.
Grazebrook, Avery, 454.
  Margaret, 454.
Grazier, Col., 237.
Greathouse, 90.
Greecart, John, 132.
Green (see also Greene).
  Abigail, 413.
  Bartholomew, 404, 405.
  Benjamin, 125.
  Benjamin, Jr., 125.
  David, 125, 137, 249.
  Francis, 125, 132, 134, 137.
  Gen., 267.
  Jeremiah, 124.
  Joseph, 125, 136, 137, 249.
  Joseph, Rev., 378.
  Mr., 249.
  Phoebe, 290.
  Richard, 132.
  Rufus, 125.
  Thomas, 404.
Greene, Catherine, 345.
  David, 249, 372.
  Gardiner, 218, 221, 230, 394.
  Hannah, 392.
  Martha, 345.
  Martha B., 221.
  Mary, 345.
  Nathaniel, 354, 424.
  Rufus, 345.
  Singleton Copley, 394.
Greenfield, Ann, 222.

Hannah, 222, 467.
  Peter, 222.
Greenlaw, John, 124, 137.
Greenleaf, Hannah, 352.
  Joseph, 454.
  Stephen, 132, 352.
Greenough, Thomas, 416.
  William, 275.
Greenwood, Mr., 363.
  Nathaniel, 125.
  Samuel, 134.
Grenville, George (Lord Chancellor of Exchequer), 22, 34, 37, 38, 151, 198.
Gridley, Benjamin, 125, 126, 132, 134, 137.
  Jeremy, 193, 455.
Griffin, Edmund, 134.
Griffith, Mrs., 134.
Grison, Edward, 134.
Grozart, John, 134.
Guard, Maria, 350.
Guild, Curtis, Jr., 326.

Hale, Mary P., 442.
  Rebecca, 431.
  Roger, 439.
  Samuel, 135.
Hall, Adam, (3rd), 139.
  Ebenezer (Jr.), 298.
  James, 124, 137, 354.
  Luke, 134, 139.
Hallowell, 35, 154, 302, 437.
  Ann, 281.
  Benjamin, 133, 320.
  Benjamin (Capt.), 281, 282.
  Benjamin (Admiral), 284.
  Benjamin (Sir), 283 (see Carew).
  Hannah, 281.
  Hannah Gardiner, 316.
  Henry, 142.
  Robert, 132, 133, 137, 251, 281, 316.
  Rebecca, 134.
  Sarah, 281.
  Ward Nicholas (see Boylston), 282.
Halsey, Jane, 355.
Halson, Henry, 137.
Hamilton, Alexander, 66, 75, 77, 352.
  Franklin (Rev.), 472.
  John C., 352.
  Mary Eliza Heuval, 352.
Hammock, Sarah, 332.
Hammond, Green, 133.
Hancock, John, 5, 35, 42, 48, 49, 50, 59, 79, 153, 160, 161, 165, 166, 224, 281, 288, 298, 315, 319, 320, 322, 335, 366, 430, 455.
Hancock, Lucy, 224.
  Thomas, 224.
Handley, 472, 473, 475.
Harcourt, Vernon (Sir), 29.
Hardwicke, Lord, 24.
Harris, Benjamin, 223.
  Lucy Devereaux, 223.
  Mary, 223.
Harrison, Joseph, 319, 320, 321, 439.
  Richard Acklom, 320.
  Susannah, 334.
Hassam, John T., 174.
Hatch, Addington, 430.
  Christopher, 137, 430.
  Col., 425.
  Elizabeth Lloyd, 430.
  Estes (Col.), 429.
  Harris, 430.
  Hawes, 134, 137, 431.
  Jane, 430.
  Mary, 430.

Nathaniel, 125, 133, 138, 142, 407, 429, 430.
Paxton, 430.
Susannah, 430.
Hathaway, Calvin, 139.
Ebenezer, Jr., 139.
Luther, 139.
Shadrach, 139.
Haven, G. C., 395.
Katherine Jeffries, 395.
Haward, John, 197.
Hawley, Joseph, 161.
Hawthorn (Justice), 246.
Hawthorne, Nathaniel, 194.
Hay, Dr., 262.
Hazen, Elizabeth, 432.
R. L., 377.
William, 432.
Heard, Isaac (Sir), 300.
Heath, William, 135.
Hefferson, Jane, 135.
Henly, Samuel, 349.
Henchman, Thomas (Major), 355.
Henderson, James, 134, 137.
Mr., 406.
Henry, Patrick, 36, 37, 40, 83.
Hester, John, 135.
Heuvel, Charlotte Augusta Apthorp, 352.
John Cornelius Vanden, 352.
Mary Eliza, 352.
Hichborn, Benjamin (Col.), 183.
Samuel, 183.
Hicks, Colonel, 470.
John, 134, 138.
Mary, 470.
Higginson, Henry, 131.
Stephen, 131.
Hill, Henry, 368, 373.
William, 134.
Hillsborough (Earl of), 159, 200, 367.
Hinkly, Richard, 128.
Hinston, John, 137.
Hirons, Richard, 125.
Hirst, Grove, 207.
Mary, 207.
Hitchcock, E. A., 112.
Gen., 111.
Hoar, George F. (Senator), 5, 475.
Hobby, Ann, 416.
Hodges, Samuel, 137.
Holland, Georgianna Anne, 289.
Henry, 289.
Lady (see Webster, Elizabeth), 289.
Lord, 289.
Mary Elizabeth (see Lilford), 289.
Richard, 139.
Holmes, Benjamin M(ulberry), 125, 132, 134, 137.
Francis, 343.
Rebecca, 343.
Holton, Samuel, 450.
Holyoke, E. A., 127, 131.
Edward, 379.
Edward A. (Dr.), 385.
Edward H., 379.
Hombersley, Ruth, 177.
Homer, Michael, 412.
Sarah, 412.
Sarah Kneeland, 412.
Honourable Artillery Company, 118.
Hood, Admiral, 240, 284.
Hooper, Ann, 467.
Anna Corwell, 223.
Alice Tucker, 222.
Elizabeth Whittaker, 224.
Greenfield, 222.

Henry, 222.
Jacob, 134.
John, 222.
Joseph, 128, 223.
"King," 221, 222, 223.
Mary Harris, 223.
Mary McNeil, 223.
Rev. M., 339, 342, 398.
Robert, 128, 136, 222, 223, 224, 460.
Robert, Jr., 128.
Robert, 3d, 128.
Sweet, 128, 223.
Hopkins, Mr., 335.
Sarah, 355.
Horn, Henry, 135.
Horrey, Col., 267.
Horsemauden, Samuel, 302.
Horton, Benjamin, 129.
Hosmer, Abner, 471.
Joseph, 271.
Hotham, 283.
House, Joseph, 134, 139.
Houston, Rebecca, 343.
Hovey, C. F. & Co., 350.
How, Josiah, 129, 130.
Howe, Abraham, 361.
Gen., 250, 266, 344, 345, 410.
Isaac, 361.
James Murray, 260.
John, 138, 361, 362, 363, 364, 405.
Joseph, 361, 363, 364.
Lord, 20, 79, 81, 192.
Martha (Mrs.), 364.
Murray, 257.
Sarah, 364.
William, 364.
William (Sir), 304, 394, 425.
Howland, Elizabeth, 431.
Hope, 431.
John, 431.
Hubbard, Daniel, 125.
Joshua, 285, 286.
Margaret, 286, 288.
Sarah, 224.
Hubbel, Lewis, 140.
Hughes, Peter, 125.
Samuel, 125, 132, 134.
Hull, 103, 345.
Hannah, 456.
John, 365, 419, 456.
Judith Quincy, 365.
Hulton, Henry, 133, 142.
Hunt, Anne, 454.
John (3rd), 132.
Hannah, 395.
Mary, 466.
William, 395.
Hunter, William, 132.
William (Lieut.), 240.
Hurlston, Richard, 134.
Hutchinson, Abigail, 177.
Anne, 178.
Edward, 132.
Edward H., 145.
Eliakim, 178, 179, 180, 308.
Elisha, 137, 165, 177, 249, 308, 309.
Elizabeth Brinley, 396.
Foster, 133, 136, 137 142, 177, 189, 312, 313, 353.
Hannah, 309.
John Rogers, 117.
Mary, 177.
Mary Oliver, 176, 177, 190.
Mrs., 135.
Peter Orlando, 175.
Richard, 178.

INDEX   493

Sarah, 172, 188.
Thomas (Governor), 29, 34, 35, 38, 39,
    40, 41, 44, 48, 50, 60, 84, 123, 125,
    126, 127, 128, 129, 130, 137, 142, 145,
    147, 148, 149, 150, 151, 153 to 173,
    177, 178, 188, 189, 192, 193, 199,
    200, 247, 249, 283, 292, 298, 299,
    302, 309, 311, 317, 322, 326, 348,
    349, 353, 406, 408, 422, 436, 444,
    447, 454, 463.
Thomas, Jr., 132, 136, 137, 165, 175,
    176, 177, 191.
Widow, 309.
William, 177, 178, 180, 249, 396.
Hutton, Elizabeth, 215.
Henry, 215.

Ingersoll, David, 126, 140.
Inglefield (Commissioner), 284.
Inglis, 59.
Dr., 340.
Ingraham, 212.
Inman, John, 125, 132, 135.
Mrs., 259.
Ralph, 132, 258.
Ireland, John, 135.

Jackson, Richard, 154.
William, 125, 132, 137.
Jaffrey, George, 395.
George J., 395 (see also Jeffries,
    George J.).
Lucy Winthrop, 395.
Sarah, 394.
James, II., 16, 419.
Jamison, Charlotte Jessy, 426.
James, 426.
Jarvis, Caroline Leonard, 333.
Charles (Dr.), 215.
John (Admiral, Sir), 283.
Leonard, 342.
R. M., 333.
Robert, 124, 132, 135, 137.
Jay, John, 25, 64, 75, 105.
Jeanson, Jean, 409 (see also Johnson,
    John).
Jefferson, Thomas, 25, 36, 75, 77, 87, 102,
    103, 104, 183.
Jeffries, Ann, 394, 395.
Ann Geyer Amory, 395.
Anne Clarke, 394.
Augustus, 395.
Catherine, 395.
David, 394.
Edward P., 395.
Elizabeth Usher, 394.
George J., 395 (see Jaffrey, George
    J.).
Hannah Hunt, 395.
Herry W., 395.
John, 46, 137, 394, 395.
John (Dr.), 135, 395.
John, Jr., 132.
Julia Ann, 395.
Katherine, 395.
Katherine Eyre, 394.
Sarah, 395.
Sarah Jaffrey, 394.
Sarah Rhoads, 395.
Jenkins, Elizabeth, 446.
Robert, 225.
Jernes, Eleanor, 465.
Jephson Mr., 404.
Sally Flucker, 404.
Johnson, Capt., 248.

Elizabeth, 465.
Gabriel, 255.
Gov., 255.
Holton (Capt.), 252.
John, 409.
Mary, 410.
Mr., 346, 347.
Susan, 409.
William (Sir), 226, 358.
Johonnet, Andrew, 411.
Daniel, 409, 410.
Elizabeth Quincy, 410.
Francis, 354, 410.
Gabriel, 406.
Katherine Dudley, 410.
Mary, 411.
Margaret Le Mercier, 410.
Peter, 125, 132, 135, 137, 344, 409, 410,
    411.
Serzane, 410.
Susan Johnson, 409.
Zachariah (also Zasherie), 410.
Joice, Isaac, 139.
Jones Deacon, 321.
Edward, 232, 448.
Elisha, 140.
Ephraim, 140.
John, 232.
Jonas, 140.
Mary, 135.
Mary Ann, 232, 448.
Miss, 230.
Paul, 250.
Jordan, Mary, 359.
Jouy, 411 (see Joy).
Joy, Abigail Green, 413.
Benjamin, 413.
Charles, 412.
Elizabeth Andrews, 412.
Henry Hall, 413.
James R., 412.
Joan Gallop, 411.
John, 125, 132, 135, 137, 411, 412.
Joseph, 413.
Lydia Lincoln, 412.
Michael, 413.
Mary Prince, 412.
Sarah Homer, 412.
Thomas, 411.
Junius Americanus (see Arthur Lee), 182.

Kalm, 23.
Kast, P. G., 131.
Kent (Duke of) 238, 245, 351, 382.
Keyes, John, 426.
Kerry (Lord), 343.
Kidd, Capt., 145.
Kidder, Samuel, 298.
Kilby, Sarah, 392.
King, Edward, 125, 135, 317, 318.
Rufus, 270.
Samuel, 135.
Kirk, Thomas, 319.
Kirkwood, Col., 239.
Knight, John (Sir), 190.
Thomas, 125, 137.
Knox, Henry (Gen.), 277, 384, 402, 403, 430.
430.
William, 331.
Knutton, John, 137.
Knutter, Margaret, 135.

Lafayette, 89, 183, 430.
Lansdowne (Marquis of), 343.
Laughton, Henry, 125, 135, 137.

Laurens, Henry, 240.
Laurie, Capt., 471.
Lavicourt, Mr., 372.
Lavosier, Anthony Lawrence (General), 270.
Lawton, Henry, 132.
Lazarus, Samuel, 135.
Leach, Rachel, 355.
Learned (Col.), 344.
Leavitt, Mr., 251.
Le Baron, Joseph (Dr.), 432.
Le Bretton, Philip, 448.
Lechmere, Ann Winthrop, 413, 428.
   Lord, 413, 428.
   Mary, 453.
   Mary Phips, 413.
   Mrs., 402.
   Nicholas, 251, 414.
   Richard, 125, 133, 136, 137, 142, 184, 251, 413, 414, 420, 453.
   Thomas, 413, 414, 428.
Lecky (W. E. H.), 35, 70.
Leddel, Henry, 135, 137.
Lee, Arthur (Junius Americanus), 182.
   Charles (Gen.), 230, 293, 414.
   Jeremiah, 450, 460.
   John, 128.
   Joseph, 128, 136, 420.
   Judge, 187.
   Martha Sweet, 460.
   Richard Henry, 248.
Leffingwell, E. H., 39.
Leigh, Egerton (Sir), 212.
Lemaistre, Elizabeth, 287.
Le Mercier, Andrew, 410, 448.
   Margaret, 410.
Leonard, 60, 212.
   Ann, 392.
   Anna, 332.
   Anna White, 332.
   Caroline, 333.
   Charles, 326, 332.
   Daniel, 126, 133, 136, 139, 142, 325, 327, 331, 332, 432.
   Ephraim, 332.
   George, 125, 132, 135, 137, 332, 333.
   George, Col., 333.
   George, Judge, 333.
   Henry, 325.
   James, 325, 332.
   Maria, 333.
   Nathaniel, 333.
   Philip, 325.
   Rachel Clap, 333.
   Richard, Col., 333.
   Sarah, 332, 333.
   Sarah Hammock, 332.
   Thomas, 325.
Leslie, Col., 408.
Lester, John (Sir), 317.
   Love Eppes, 317.
Leverett, President, 458.
Lewis, Ann, 286.
   Ezekiel, 414, 415.
   John, 133, 286.
   Martha, 356.
   Martha Burrell, 356.
   Mary Cheever, 414.
   Philip, 356.
   Thomas, 128.
   William, 414, 415.
Lilford, Lord, 289.
Lillie, Ann, 313.
   Edward, 308.
   Elizabeth 308.
   John, 309, 313.
   Mehitable, 309, 313.
   Samuel, 308, 309.
   Samuel (Mrs.), 309.
   Theophilus, 124, 132, 135, 308, 309, 310, 311, 312, 313.
Lilly, William, 131.
Lincoln, Abraham, 112.
   Lydia, 412.
   Samuel, 412.
Lindall, Henry, 132.
Linkleter, Alexander, 135.
Linzee (Capt.), 345.
Liste, Mrs., 135.
Little, Abigail, 399.
Livingston, R. R., 161.
   William, 481.
Lloyd, 212.
   Dr., 394.
   Elizabeth, 430.
   Griselda, 351.
   Henry, 132, 135, 137.
   James, 132.
   John (Sir), 351.
   Miss, 425.
   Samuel, 133.
Logan (Cayuga, chief), 90.
Longfellow, Henry W., 287, 479.
   Mary, 439.
   Samuel, 139.
Longueuil, Baron de (see Grant, Charles), 239.
Loring, 437.
   Benjamin, 424, 425.
   Charlotte Jessy Jamison, 426.
   Hector, 426.
   Jane, Newton, 423.
   John, 425, 426.
   John, Commodore, 425.
   John Wentworth (Sir), 425.
   Joseph, Royal, 426.
   Joshua, 138, 142, 423.
   Joshua (Commodore), 136, 423.
   Joshua, Jr., 125, 132, 135, 138, 424.
   Mary, 424.
   Thomas, 423.
   William (Capt.), 425.
Loudon (Gen.), 379.
Louis XVI., 115.
Love, John, 132.
Lovel, John, Sir, 135.
Lovell, General, 480.
   James, 440.
   John, 346.
   Mansfield (Gen.), 440.
   Master, 231.
Lovewell (Capt.), 422.
Lowe, Charles, 135.
Lowell, James Russell, 184, 188, 473.
   John, 126, 326, 414.
Luist, Elizabeth, 402.
Lusher, Lydia, 321.
Lutwiche, Edward Goldston, 135.
Lyddell, Henry, 125.
Lyde, Byfield, 132, 135, 447.
   Catherine, 396.
   Deborah, 396, 447.
   Edward, 137, 396, 447.
   George, 139, 447.
   Mary Wheelwright, 447.
   Nathaniel, 447.
   Sarah Belcher, 447.
   Susanna, Curwin, 447.
Lyman, Theodore (Gen.), 394.
Lynch, 80.
Lynde, Benjamin, 131, 342, 462, 463, 464.
   Byfield, 125.

INDEX

Chief Justice, 46, 190, 193.
Elizabeth Dizbie, 462.
Enoch, 462, 463.
George, 125.
Hannah, 464.
Hannah Newgate, 463.
Lydia, 342, 464.
Mary, 190, 464.
Mary Browne, 463.
Simon, 308, 463.
William, 463.
Lyndhurst, Lord (see also John Singleton Copley, 2nd.), 216, 332, 345, 394, 409.

Macauley, Thomas Babington, 289.
Macdonald, Dennis, 135.
Mackay, 239, 256.
   Mrs., 135.
Mackey, Mungo, 225, 414.
MacKinstrey, Mrs., 135.
Mackintosh, 157.
   ("Capt."), 166, 167, 234.
Macknight, 212.
Maclean (Col.), 244.
Macneal, Miss, 426.
Madison, James (President), 25, 102.
Magdalen, Earl of (see Sir Isaac Coffin), 243.
Malbone, Godfrey, 396.
Malcolm, Daniel, 320.
Malcomb, Abigail Trundy, 451.
   John (Capt.), 451, 452.
Manchester, Duke of, 345.
Mann, Alicia, 352.
   Horace (Sir), 352.
Mansfield, Isaac, 128.
   Lord, 29, 83, 151, 173.
Mansfield, Mr., 363.
March, Mary, 468.
   Zacheray, 468.
Marion, 90.
Marsh, Edward, 425.
Marshall, Ebenezer, 397.
   John, 77.
   John (Capt.), 319.
Marston, Alice, 459.
   Benjamin, 128, 135, 138, 459, 460, 461, 462.
   Benjamin, Jr., 460.
   Elizabeth Winslow, 460.
   John, 459.
   Sarah Sweet, 460
Martin, Capt., 244.
   John, 382.
   Michael, 139.
   William, 137.
Maryatt, Captain, 350.
   Joseph, 350.
   Mrs., 350.
Mascarene, John, 131.
Mason, Jonathan, 218.
   Mr., 187.
   and Slidell, 110.
Masters, John, 312.
Mather, Cotton, 309, 355.
   Elizabeth, 275.
   Increase, 275, 338.
   Samuel, 133.
   Sarah, 338.
Matthews, Ann, 237.
   William, 237.
Mandult, Mr., 249.
Maverick, Moses, 222.
   Samuel, 13, 14.

Maxwell, Mary, 284.
   Murray (Sir), 284.
May, Dr., 353.
McAlpine, William, 124, 132, 135, 137.
McArthur (Gen.), 104.
McCall, George, 128|
McClintock, 135.
McCobb, Samuel, 297.
McClure (Gen.), 104
McEwen, James, 124.
McEvers, Mary, 352.
McIntosh, Elizabeth, 291.
McKeron, John, 135.
McLanathan, Elizabeth, 377.
McLean, John, 346.
McLellan, Arthur, 308.
McMasters, Daniel, 132, 135.
   James, 125.
   Patrick, 125, 135.
McMullen, Alexander, 135.
McMurdo (Col.), 244.
   Isabella, 244.
   Susannah, 244.
McNiel, Archibald, 125, 132, 135, 137.
   Hector, 223.
   Mary, 223.
McSparran, James (Rev.), 313.
Mears, Mr., 423.
Meserve, George, 133.
Messengham, Isaac, 133.
Middleton, 80.
Mifflin (Col.), 89.
Miller, 438.
   Katherine Sarah Russell, 453.
   Col., 194.
   Major, 453.
   Stephen, 128, 129, 130.
Mills, Nathaniel, 135, 138.
Minns, Martha, 361.
   William, 361.
Minot, Christopher, 133, 137.
   John, 398.
   Mercy, 398.
   Samuel, 125.
Mitchell, Jonathan, 455.
   Margaret, 455.
   Sarah, 445.
   Thomas, 135, 137.
Mitchelson, David, 125, 135.
Molesworth, Ponsonby (Capt.), 439, 440, 442.
Molineaux, Mr., 406, 407.
Montague (Admiral), 240, 394, 408.
   Rev. Mr., 335.
Montgomery, 89.
   (General), 244.
Moody, John, 135.
   John J., 135.
Moore, John, 135.
Moreland, 239.
Morgan, 250.
Morris, Gouverneur, 75.
   Henry Gage, 209.
   Roger, 209.
Morrison, John, 135.
Morton, Perez, 354, 361.
Mowatt (Capt.), 357, 398, 399, 465, 467.
Mulcainy, Patrick, 135.
Mulhall, Edward, 133.
Mullins, Thomas, 139.
Munroe, 77, 183, 354.
Murdock, Ephraim, 354.
Murray, Alexander, 377.
   Col., 382, 448.
   Daniel, 139, 377.

Dorothy, 257, 260.
Elizabeth, 255, 257, 260.
Elizabeth McLanathan, 377.
James, 128, 129, 130, 132, 133, 137, 254, 255, 256, 257, 258, 259, 446.
John, 133, 139, 142.
John (Col.), 136, 376, 377, 378, 396.
John (Sir), 254.
Lucreia Chandler Gardner, 377.
Miss, 377.
Robert, 377.
Samuel, 139, 377.
William, 135.

Nagers, John, 225.
Nassawano, Lawrence, 225.
Nelson, Lord, 283, 284.
Nevin, Lazarus, 135.
Newcastle (Duke of), 26.
Newgate, Hannah, 463.
John, 463
Newhall (Deacon), 344.
Newton, Jane, 423.
Nicholls, Richard, 131, 303.
Richard (Col.), 13, 14.
William, 161.
Nixon, John (Col.), 475.
Noble, Benjamin, 140.
Francis, 140.
Nooth (Dr.), 386.
North, Lord, 250, 424.
Northumberland (Duke of), 440.
Norton, 12.
Nutting, John, 127, 131, 138.

O'Brien, 110.
O. C., 406.
Ochterlony, 239.
Alexander, 300.
Catherine, 300.
Charles Metcalf, 300.
David (Sir, Maj. Gen.), 283, 299, 300.
David Ferguson (Sir), 300.
Gilbert, 300.
Katherine Tyler, 300.
O'Donoghue, Henry O. B., 349.
Offley, Amelia, 191.
Stephen, 191.
Ogden, Charles R., 239.
Charles Richard, 409.
Mary, 239.
Susan Clarke, 409.
Oliver, Andrew (Lt. Gov. etc.), 40, 136, 153, 159, 175, 181, 183, 184, 190, 454, 464.
Andrew (of Salem), 190.
Ann, 183.
Daniel, 126, 133, 139, 181, 188, 189.
Eben, 411.
Elizabeth, 183, 287.
F. E. (Dr.), 464.
Isaac, 183.
James, 138.
Lt. Gov., 133, 164, 251.
Mary Lynde, 464.
Peter, 132, 133, 136, 138, 142, 150, 181, 188, 189, 190, 302, 410.
Peter (Dr.), 135, 175, 189.
Richard, 183.
Robert, 183, 184.
Thomas (Lt. Gov., etc.), 125, 136, 137, 142, 181, 183, 184, 187, 188, 287, 331.
W. S. (Cap. R. N.), 176.
William Sanford, 135, 190.

William Sanford (Jr.), 190.
O'Neil, Joseph, 135.
Orange, Prince of (William III.), 16.
O'Reilly, John Boyle, 47.
Orne, Lois, 386.
Timothy, 131.
Otis, Harrison Gray, 218, 219, 334, 336, 403.
James, 5, 21, 35, 37, 149, 150, 153, 157, 160, 318, 319, 435, 448.
James (Col.), 192, 193.
Jonathan, 439.
S. A. (Mrs.), 335.
Overing, Henrietta, 304.
Henry John, 304.
Oxford, Earl of, 289.
Oxnard, Edward, 139, 249.
Thomas, 139.
Ozell, Mr., 343.

Paddock, Adnio, 125, 132, 135, 137, 305, 306, 307, 322, 446.
Adino (the younger), 307.
John, 305, 307.
Lydia Snelling, 307.
Mary McLellan, 307.
Rebecca Thacher, 305.
Robert, 305.
Thomas, 307.
Zachariah, 305.
Pagan, Miriam Pote, 465.
Robert, 139, 464, 465.
Thomas, 465.
William, 465.
Page, Abiel, 310.
George 135.
Paine, Dorothy, 390.
Dorothy Rainsford, 383.
Lois Orne, 386.
Nathaniel, 383, 387, 390.
Samuel, 135, 387, 388.
Sarah Chandler, 383.
Sarah Clark, 383.
Stephen, 382, 383.
Robert Treat, 368.
Rose, 382.
Thomas, 76.
Timothy, 136, 382, 383, 384, 385, 387 390.
William, 139, 385, 386.
William (Dr.), 385, 386, 387.
Paley (Dr.), 353.
Palmer, Charles Thomas (Sir), 215.
Harriet, 215.
Thomas, 136.
Parker, Rev. Dr., 342.
Samuel (Rev.), 348, 349.
William, 48.
Parmenter (Goodwife), 388.
Parnell, 110, 111.
Parr, 380.
Parsons, Capt., 471, 472.
Patten, George, 135.
Thomas, 298.
Patterson, 133, 212.
William, 135.
Paxton, 154, 200, 302.
Charles, 133, 138, 142, 318, 319.
Paxton, Faith, 318.
Wentworth, 318.
Payne, Edward, 455.
Mary, 455.
Rebecca, 394.
Pearson, Thomas (Sir), 239.
Peck, Robert (Rev.), 468.

INDEX

Peddock, Leonard (Capt.), 305.
Pedrick, John, 128.
Pelham, Henry, 135, 216, 478.
   Herbert, 434.
   Penelope, 434.
   Peter, 216.
Pemberton, Eben (Rev.), 413.
   Rev. Mr., 310.
Penn, Admiral, 433.
Pepperell, Andrew, 206.
   Elizabeth, 207, 208, 214.
   Harriet, 214, 215.
   Margery Bray, 205.
   Mary, 215.
   Mary Hirst (Lady), 207, 208.
   William, 205.
   William, Sir (1st), 206, 209.
   William, Sir (2nd), 136, 138, 142, 176, 194, 201, 205, 207, 208, 209, 212, 213, 214, 215, 292, 293, 294, 356, 434, 482.
Percy, Earl, 314, 440, 441.
Perkins, James, 124, 132.
Perkins, Nathaniel, 132, 135, 138.
   William, Lee, 132, 135, 138.
Perrie, Elizabeth, 399.
Perry, Samuel, 139.
   Seth, 139.
   Silas, 139.
   Stephen, 139.
   Thomas, 139.
   William, 125, 132.
Peters, Parson, 249.
Petit, John Samuel, 133.
Phillips, Ebenezer, 135, 139.
   Frederick, 209.
   John (Col.), 358.
   Joseph, 131.
   Martha, 135.
   Mary, 20.
   Richard, 128.
Phips (also Phipps).
   A. F., 125.
   David, 125, 132, 135, 138, 418, 420.
   Elizabeth, 184, 286.
   James, 418.
   Lady, 419.
   Mary, 413.
   May, 184.
   Sheriff, 187.
   Spencer, Lt. Gov., 184.
   Spencer, 286, 413, 420.
   William Sir, 17, 418, 419.
Pickering, Benjamin, 249.
   Timothy (Col.), 108.
Pickman, Benjamin, 131, 138, 249.
   Benjamin (Col.), 316, 451.
   C. Gayton, 127, 131.
   William, 126, 131.
Pierce, Edward Lillie, 313.
   George, 313.
   Josiah, 262.
   President, 87.
Pine, Samuel, 132.
Pinckney, Mary, 321.
Pinkney, Frances, 392.
   John, 392.
Pitcairn, 314.
Pitt, 19, 33, 98, 193.
Pitts, Elizabeth, 397.
   John, 397.
   Samuel, 354.
Pollard, Benjamin, 135.
Pond, Eliphalet, 125.
Ponsonby, Lord, 439.
Porter, Alexander S., 307.

E. G. (Rev.), 471.
   James, 133.
   Samuel, 126, 131, 138, 249.
Pote, Ann Hooper, 467.
   Dorothy Getchell, 467.
   Elizabeth Berry, 467.
   Hannah Greenfield, 467.
   Jeremiah, 465, 466, 467.
   Joanna, 466, 467.
   Miriam, 465.
   Robert, 467.
   William, 467.
Powell, Jeremiah, 136.
   John, 125, 132, 135, 138.
Pownall, Thomas (Gov.), 191, 292.
Poynton, Thomas, 131.
Pratt, Benjamin, 367.
   Judge, 301.
Preble (Commodore), 345.
Prentice, John, 128.
Prescott, 240.
James, 297.
   William H., 343.
Preston, Captin, 43, 44, 45, 46, 158, 366, 368.
Price, Benjamin, 135.
Priestly, 164.
Primatt, Mrs., 357.
Prince, John, 128, 131, 412.
   John, Capt., 196.
   Margaret, 412.
   Mary, 412.
   Samuel, 125, 137.
   Thomas, Rev., 275.
Prindall, Jonathan, 140.
Proctor, Mr., 406.
   Thomas, 128.
Proctor & Gray, 336.
Punderson, Mr., 249.
Purchis, Oliver, 13.
Putnam, Archelaus, 131, 379.
   Ebenezer, 127, 131, 379, 380.
   Eleanor Sprague, 379.
   Elizabeth, 380, 391.
   General, 94.
   Israel, 382.
   James, 126, 132, 135, 139, 378, 379, 380, 387, 382, 385, 390.
   James, Jr. 133.
   John 378, 382.
   Nathaniel, 378.
   Rufus, 382.
   Thomas, 378.
Pynchon, 251.
   William, 126, 127, 131.
Quincy, 59, 277, 438.
Quincy, Daniel, 365.
   Dorothy, 455.
   Edmund, 105, 365, 366, 376, 455.
   Elizabeth, 410, 455.
   Esther, 455.
   Hannah, 366.
   John, 365.
   Josiah, 45, 50, 98, 100, 102, 108, 155, 166, 365, 366, 367, 376.
   Judith, 365.
   Samuel, 126, 138, 142, 249, 364, 366, 367, 368, 369, 374, 375.
Radcliffe, Herbert 475.
Rainsford, Dorothy, 383.
   Jonathan, 383.
Ramage, John, 135.
Randolph, 80, 212.
   Edward, 15.
   Miss, 316.
Read, Charles, 135.

498   INDEX

John, 179.
Reed, Joseph, 72, 248.
  Richard, 128.
  Samuel, 138.
Remington, John, 392.
  Martha A., 224.
  Rhoda Gore, 392.
Revere Copper Co., 324.
  Joseph Warren, 324.
  Paul, 5, 260, 477, 478, 479, 480.
Reynolds, Fleetwood B. (Sir), 289.
  Joshua, Sir, 218.
Rhoads, Sarah, 395.
  Henry, 135.
Richards, Owen, 133, 138.
Richardson, Ebenezer, 310, 311, 421, 422..
  Ezekiel, 421.
  John, 422.
  Miss, 135.
  Mrs., 135.
  Phineas, 422.
  Samuel, 422.
  Timothy, 422.
  Thomas, 422.
Rives, Mr., 115.
Roath, Richard, 135.
Robbins, Edward Hutchinson, 260.
  Mary, 260.
Roberts & Co., 124.
  Mr., 55.
Robertson, William (Gen.), 212, 213, 344.
Robie, Elizabeth, 457.
  Elizabeth Taylor, 459.
  Samuel Bradstreet, 459.
  Thomas, 128, 138, 457, 458, 459.
  William, 459.
Robinson, John, 433, 448.
Rochambeau, 426, 430.
Rochfort, Gustavus, 333.
  Maria Leonard, 333.
Rodney, Lord, 240, 241, 252, 283, 428.
Rogers, 163.
  Daniel Dennison, 354.
  Elizabeth, 398.
  Jeremiah Dummer, 126, 135, 138.
  Samuel, 135, 138, 398.
Ruck, Hannah, 309.
  John, 309.
Ruggles, Elizabeth, 391.
  Hannah, 229.
  John, 135, 139, 229.
  Joseph, 139.
  Nathaniel, 139.
  Richard, 135, 139, 229.
  Samuel, 225.
  Sarah, 229.
  Timothy, 133, 136, 137, 142, 225, 226, 227, 228, 229, 380, 391.
  Timothy (2nd), 229.
  Timothy, Rev., 225.
Ruggles, Timothy, Amherst, 229.
Rolfe, Col., 263.
  Benj., 265.
  Benj. (Rev.), 430.
  Mary, 429, 430.
  Sarah, 263.
Rome, 212.
Root, Elihu, 116.
Rose, Peter, 135.
Ross, Margaret, 307.
  Thomas, 139.
Rotch, 408.
Routh, Richard, 131, 317.
Royall, 60.
  Elizabeth, 208, 294.
  Isaac, 136, 138, 291, 292, 293, 299, 309.

  Isaac (of Antigua), 286.
  Isaac (Gen.), 192, 290.
  Mrs. 309.
  Penelope, 286, 291.
  William, 290.
Roycroft, Ann, 284.
Rumford, Count (see also Sir Benjamin Thompson), 261, 262, 263, 264, 266, 270, 271, 272.
  Countess (Sarah), 272.
Rummer, Richard, 135.
Rush, Mr., 77.
Russell, Benjamin, 412, 454.
  Catherine Greaves, 453.
  Chambers, 301, 302, 452, 453, 455.
  Charles, 138.
  Charles James, 453.
  Daniel, 452.
  Dr., 372, 453.
  Edward (Sir), 414.
  Elizabeth, 454.
  Elizabeth Vassall, 453.
  Ezekiel, 453, 454.
  James, 136, 253, 452, 453.
  James, Jr., 453.
  John (Lord), 289.
  Joseph, 453, 454.
  Katherine, 453.
  Lechmere (Col.), 414.
  Lechmere-Coor-Graves, 453.
  Lucy Margaret, 453.
  Mary Lechmere, 453.
  Mary Wainwright, 453.
  Nathaniel, 135.
  Paul, 452.
  Rebecca, 465.
  Rebecca Chambers, 452.
  Richard, 452.
  Thomas, 466.
Sabine, 71.
Sackett, Hannah, 229.
  Thomas (Dr.), 229.
Salisbury, Lord, 117.
Saltonstall, 59.
  Gurdon, 295.
  Katherine, 295, 296.
  Leverett, 136, 274.
  Mr., 250.
  Nathaniel, 273, 274, 275.
  Richard, 132, 138, 273, 274.
  Richard, Col., 358.
  Richard (Sir), 272.
  Thomas, 272.
Sampson, John, 132.
Sanford, Margaret, 146.
Sargent, Esther, 345, 356.
  John, 131, 138.
Saumerez, Thomas L. Marchant, 288.
Saunders, Henry, 128.
Savage, Abraham, 125, 136, 138.
  Arthur, 133, 139, 335.
  Rowland, 131.
  Thomas, 308.
Saward, see Sayward.
Sayward, Henry, 443.
  Jonathan, 443, 444, 445.
  Joseph, 443.
  Mary, 443.
  Mary Webber, 439.
  Sarah, 444, 445.
  Sarah Mitchell, 445.
Scammel, Thomas, 136.
Scheaffe (see also Sheaffe), 239.
Schuyler, Gen., 89.
Scott, Joseph, 135.
Scollay, John, 166.

Scott, Duncan C., 61.
   Governor, 299.
   Joseph, 125, 132, 138.
   Winfield (Gen.), 245, 441.
Scoville, William, 280.
Sears, Anna, 345.
   David, 345.
   Ebenezer, 411.
   Isaac, 424, 426.
   Rebecca, 336.
Selby, John, 133.
Seikrig, James, 124, 132, 136, 138.
   Thomas, 138.
Semple, John, 125, 132, 138.
   Robert, 132, 135, 138.
Sergeant, Peter, 420.
Serjeant, John, 135.
Service, Robert, 136, 138.
Sewall, 59, 60.
Sewall, Ann Hunt, 454.
   Chief Justice, 149, 192, 404, 452, 463.
   Esther Quincy, 455.
   Hannah Hull, 456.
   Henry, 454, 456.
   Jane Drummond, 454.
   Jonathan, 125, 138, 142, 207, 249, 327, 367, 379, 432, 454, 455, 456.
   Joseph, 458.
   Joseph (Rev.), 275.
   Judge, 250, 251, 254, 327, 350.
   Margaret Grazebrook, 454.
   Margaret Mitchell, 455.
   Mary Payne, 455.
   Mr., 448.
   Rebecca Dudley, 456.
   Samuel, 126, 138, 249, 251, 412, 455, 456, 458.
   Stephen, 454, 456.
   William, 454.
Shattock, Samuel, 12.
Shays, Daniel, 336.
Sheaffe, Col., 245.
   Helen, 440, 442.
   Lady, 442.
   Margaret, 442.
   Margaret Coffin, 442.
   Mary Longfellow, 439.
   Mrs. 439, 440.
   Nancy, 442.
   Nathaniel, 442.
   Roger Hale (Sir), 244, 245, 283, 439, 440, 441, 442, 443.
   Ruth Woods, 439.
   Sally, 442.
   Susannah, 439, 440.
   Susannah Child, 439.
   Thomas Child, 443.
   William, 439, 440, 442.
   William, Jr., 439.
   William S., 439.
Shepard, Joseph, 136.
Sherburn, Thomas, 355.
Sherman, Gen., 111.
Sherwin, Richard, 138.
Shippen, Dr., 248.
Shirley, Elizabeth, 178.
   Maria Catherina, 299.
   William, Gov., 178, 179, 180, 273, 301, 347, 435, 444, 445, 451, 477.
Sigourney, Andrew, 409.
Sigourney, Andrae, 409.
Silsby, Daniel, 125, 249.
   David, 138.
Simcoe, Gov., 59, 90.
Singleton, Mary, 216.
Simonds, Ruth, 262.

William, 135.
Simpson, John, 135.
   Jonathan, 125, 132, 136, 138.
   Jonathan, Jr., 135.
   Mr., 251.
   William, 138.
Skinner, 133.
   Francis, 138.
Slidell, 110.
Small, Major, 314.
Smith, Abigail, 37.
Smith, 472, 473.
   Adam, 33, 34, 38.
   Anna Leonard, 332.
   Col., 471, 472.
   Edward, 136, 354.
   Elizabeth, 258.
   Goldwin, 58.
   Henry, 135, 138.
   Isaac, 249.
   James, 255, 256, 257, 305, 306.
   John, 477.
   Joseph (Rev.), 202.
   Joshua, 138.
   Richard, 125, 138.
   Solomon, 139.
   Sydney, 276.
   Thomas, 248.
   William, 161.
Symthe, Frederic, 302.
Smythers, Walter Tyson, 284.
Snelling, Jonathan, 124, 132, 136, 138.
   Lydia, 305.
   Lydia Dexter, 305.
   Robert, 305.
Snider, Christopher, 310, 422.
Southwick, Solomon, 362.
Sparhawk, Andrew, 215.
   Andrew Pepperell, 207.
   Harriet Hirst, 215.
   Mary Pepperrell, 207, 215.
   Nathaniel, 127, 131, 207, 215.
   Samuel, 133.
   Samuel Hirst, 124, 132, 207, 215.
   William Pepperrell, 207.
Speakman, William, 286.
Spooner, Ebenezer, 136.
   George 125, 138.
   John J., 183.
Sprague, Eleanor, 379.
   John, 126.
Spry, Commodore, 209.
Square, Richard, 140.
Stacy, Richard, 128.
Stanton, E. M., 112.
Stark, Caleb (Major), 84.
   James H., 250, 471, 474, 475, 476.
   John, 71, 293.
   John (Gen.), 84.
   William, 293.
Stayner, Abigail, 136.
Stearns, Jonathan, 133, 136, 458.
Sterling, Benjamin Ferdinand, 135.
   Elizabeth, 135.
   Lord, 303.
Stevens, 212.
Stewart (Col.), 72.
   Duncan, 332.
   Emily, 332.
   John (Capt.), 332.
   Leonard, 332.
   Sarah, 332.
   Sarah Leonard, 332.
Stiles, Ezra (Dr.), 358.
Still, Alice, 427.
   John (Dr.), 427.

Stimson, John, 128.
Stockwell, May, 468.
    William, 468.
Stoddard, Mary, 224.
    Simeon, 125, 286.
Story, Josep, 114.
Stow, Edward, 135, 138.
Strachan, John (Dr.), 103, 104.
Strahan, Mr., 481.
Strange, Lot (3rd), 139.
Stromach, 228.
Stuart, H. Lechmere (Sir), 414.
Sturgis, Hannah, 366.
    John, 366.
Sullivan, Bartholemew, 136.
    Gen., 51, 90.
    George, 135.
    Hettie, 345.
    James (Gov.), 296, 345.
Sumner, Increase, 302, 374.
    Prof. (W. G.), 77, 78.
Sumpter, 90.
Surriage, Agnes (see also Lady Frankland), 417.
    Isaac, 418.
Swain, 401.
Swan, James, 426.
    James (Capt.), 430.
Swasey, Joseph, 128.
Sweet, Martha, 460.
    Sarah, 460.
Swift, Jonathan, 276.
Sylvester, John (Rev.), 102.
Symmes, Francis, 354.
Symonds, Mr., 237.
Tailor, Rebecca, 275.
    William, 125.
    William (Lt. Gov.), 275.
Tarbett, Hugh, 132.
Taylor, Abigail, 345.
    Elizabeth, 458.
    James, 458.
    John, 125, 132.
    Joseph, 138, 249.
    Mrs., 136.
    Nathaniel, 132, 133, 138.
    William, 132, 136, 138.
Temple, 163.
    Elizabeth, 428.
    John, Sir, 428.
Terree, Zebedco, 139.
Terry, William, 136.
    Zebedee, 136.
Thatcher, "Citizen," 351.
    Oxenbridge, 366.
    Samuel, 297.
Thayer, Arodi, 138.
    Ziphion, 125.
Thomas, Mary, 336.
    Nathaniel, Ray, 133, 136, 139, 142, 336, 421.
Thompson, 465, 467.
Thompson, Benj. (Sir), Count Rumford, 261, 262, 263, 264, 266, 267, 268, 269, 270, 271, 272, 297.
    Ebenezer, 261, 262.
    Elizabeth, 261.
    James, 136, 261.
    Joseph, 297, 298.
    Mary, 354.
    Miss, 256.
    Rebecca, 297.
    Samuel (Col.), 398.
    Sarah, 270.
    Sarah Bradshaw, 297.
Thorp, 472, 475.

Tiernay, 240.
Tilden, Israel, 139.
Tilghman, 80.
Timmins, John, 125, 132.
Tisdel, 139.
Tomlinson & Trecothick, 352.
Tompkins, Sarah, 466.
    Thomas, 466.
Tonancour, 245.
Townsend, Gregory, 125, 138.
Tropmane, Lewis, 239.
Trecothick, Barlow, 352.
Trott, George, 477.
Troutbeck, John, 132, 138, 224.
    Harriet, 224.
    Mr., 249.
Trowbridge, Edmund, 189, 379.
Trumbull, Gov., 481.
Trundy, Abigail, 451.
Tucker, Alice, 222.
    Andrew, 222.
Tufts, John, 426.
    Simon, 138.
Tupper, Eldad, 139.
Turbett, Hugh, 125.
Turner, John, 131.
    Miss, 215.
Turill, Joseph, 124, 132.
Tylden, John Maxwell (Sir), 304.
    Richard, 304.
    William Burton, 304.
Tyler, Andrew, 300.
    Thomas, 396.
    Katherine, 300.
    Miriam Pepperell, 300.
    Sarah Brinley, 396.
Tyng, Elizabeth, 294.
    William, 139, 294.
Tyron, Gov., 90, 161.
Upham, Joshua, 138.
Upshall, Nicholas, 11.
Urquhart, Hannah Flucker, 404.
    James (Capt.), 404.
    Major, 249.
Usher, Elizabeth, 394.
    John, 394.
    Lt. Gov., 291.
Van, Murray, 86.
Vane, Harry (Sir), 145.
Vans, William, 131.
Vassaile (see also Vassall).
    Anna, 285.
    Anne, 285, 286.
    Frances, 285, 286.
    John, 285.
    Judith, 285.
    Margaret, 285, 286.
    Mary, 286.
    William, 285.
Vassall, 60, 372, 438.
    Ann, 288.
    Anne Davis, 288.
    Catherine, 288.
    Charlotte, 288.
    Elizabeth, 184, 289, 453.
    Elizabeth, Lemaestre, 287.
    Fanny, 288.
    Florentinus, 288.
    Francis, 288.
    Henry, 286, -288.
    Henry (Col.), 291, 453.
    John, 125, 138, 251, 285, 286, 287, 420, 455.
    John, Col., 184.
    John (Jr.), 183.
    John (Maj.), 287, 288.

INDEX 501

Leonard, 286, 287, 288, 350.
Lucretia, 288.
Margaret, 288.
Margaret Hubbard, 288.
Mary, 287.
Mary Archer, 287.
Nathaniel, 288.
Rawdon, John Popham (Col.), 288.
Richard, 289.
Robert Oliver, 287.
Ruth Gale, 286.
Samuel, 285, 286.
Sarah, 288.
Spencer Lambert Hunter, 287.
Spencer Thomas, 287.
Thomas Oliver, 287, 288.
William, 136, 138, 285, 286, 287, 288.
Vaughn, Charles, 352.
  Samuel, 281, 352.
  Sarah, 281.
Venables, Gen., 433.
Vergennes, 23, 115.
Vernon, Admiral, 434.
Victoria, Queen, 118, 238.
Vose, Elizabeth, 313.
  Elizabeth Putnam, 391.
  Solomon, 391.
Wainwright, E. D. (Col.), 304.
  Maria M., 304.
  Mary, 453.
Wait, Richard, 13.
Waite, Samuel, 466.
Waldo, Col., 451.
  Frances, 139, 251.
  Hannah, 403.
  Joseph, 249.
  Lucy, 437.
  Samuel, 437.
  Samuel (Gen.), 403.
Walker, Adam, 139.
  Benjamin, 139.
  Col., 265.
  Gideon, 139.
  John, 139.
  Timothy (Rev.), 263.
  Zera, 139.
Walpole, 26.
Walter, Lydia Lynde, 342, 464.
  Lynde, Minshall, 342.
  N. (Rev.), 279.
  Nehemiah (Rev.), 338.
  Rebecca, 279, 339.
  Rebeckah Belcher, 338.
  Rev. Dr., 282, 425.
  Sarah Mather, 338.
  Thomas, 338.
  Thomas (Rev.), 338, 339.
  William, 132, 138.
  William, Rev., 338, 339, 340, 464.
Wamatuck (Indian Chief), 447.
Wanton, Gov., 302, 449.
Ward, Elizabeth, 273.
  Gen., 469.
  John, Rev., 273.
  Lord, 351.
  Samuel Curwen, 254.
  Susan, 351.
Warden, James, 125.
  Joseph, 136.
  William, 136, 138.
Ware, Nicholas, 285, 286.
Warren, Abraham, 136.
  Hannah, 431.
  Joseph (Dr.), 165, 322, 335, 394, 406, 431, 479.
  Peter (Sir), 209, 396.

Washington, George, 5, 24, 25, 36, 37, 45, 51, 70, 71, 72, 73, 75, 76, 77, 78, 83, 87, 89, 103, 108, 153, 179, 216, 230, 248, 315, 344, 481.
  John Augustine, 74.
Waterhouse, Samuel, 133, 138.
Watson, Elizabeth, 461.
  George, 136.
  George, Col., 177.
  William, 461.
Watts, 278.
  John, 161.
Wayte, Gamaliel, 350.
Webb, Albert, 474.
  John, 128.
  Nehemiah, 139.
Webber, Deborah, 443.
  Mary, 443.
  Samuel, 443.
Webster, Daniel, 114, 115, 180, 436.
  Elizabeth (Lady Holland), 289.
  Godfrey (Sir), 289.
  Godfrey Vassall (Sir), 289.
  Harriet, 289.
  P——, 249.
Wedderburn (Solicitor Gen.), 164, 165.
Weld, Elizabeth, 392.
  John, 392.
Wells, Henry, 477.
  William V., 39.
Welsh, James, 136.
  Peter, 136.
Wendell, John, 412.
  John Mico, 295, 297.
  Madame, 295.
  Mr., 372.
Wentworth, Gov., 263.
  John, 404.
  John (Sir), 51.
  Lord, 386.
West, Benjamin, 213, 214, 216, 249, 280, 336, 482.
  Nathaniel (Capt.), 253.
  Rebecca, 336.
Wetmore, William, 131.
Whalley, 12, 323.
Whatley, Thomas, 162.
  Thomas William, 162.
Wheaton, Caleb, 131.
  Judge, 332.
Wheelwright, John, 354.
  John, Rev., 447.
  Joseph, 136.
  Mary, 447.
Whipple, Abigail Gardiner, 316.
  Ebenezer, 139.
  Oliver, 316.
Whiston, Obadiah, 136, 138.
White, Ammi, 471, 472, 475.
  Anna, 332.
  Benjamin, 225.
  Charles, 202.
  Cornelius, 138, 139.
White, Daniel, Jr., 139.
  Elizabeth Cranston Deblois, 446.
  Gideon, 136.
  Gideon (Jr.), 139.
  James, 446.
  John, 124.
  John, 138.
  Mary, 225.
  Mr., 237.
  Peregrine, 286.
  R. H. & Co., 308.
  Resolved, 285.
  Samuel, 128, 332.

Susannah, 225.
Whitman, Clarence, 470.
   John, 470.
   William, 470.
Whitney, Ann, 224.
Whittaker, Elizabeth, 224.
   Nathaniel (Rev.), 224.
Whitworth, Miles, 124, 132.
Wilbore, Joshua, 139.
Wildridge, James, 139.
Wilkes, 28, 83, 84.
Wilkinson, Gen., 104.
Willard, Abel, 126, 136, 139.
   Abijah, 133, 136, 139, 142.
   President, 404.
   Samuel (Rev.), 336, 409.
William III., 45.
Williams (Indian Sachem), 89.
   Col., 159, 401.
   Elijah, 138.
   Henry H., 125.
   Israel, 136.
   Job, 136.
   John, 184, 320.
   Seth, 136.
   Seth, Jr., 132, 139.
   William, 447.
Williamson, Capt., 441.
Willis, David, 136, 138.
Wilmot, George, 310, 311, 470.
Wilson, Archibald, 124, 136, 138.
   Mr., 272.
Winch, Sarah, 360.
Winchelsea, Lord, 386.
Winnet, John, Jr., 136.
Winslow, 59, 406.
   Edward, 132, 133, 136, 321, 433, 434, 436, 437, 438.
   Edward, Jr., 133, 138.
   Edward, Rev., 438.
   Elizabeth, 460.
   Frances, 436.
   Hannah, 136.
   Isaac, 125, 132, 136, 138, 424, 434, 437, 438, 439, 460.
   Isaac (Dr.), 435.
   Isaac, Jr., 125, 132.
   Jane Isabella, 438.
   John, 124, 125, 136, 434, 435, 436, 437.
   John, Gen., 322.
   John, Jr., 138.
   Joseph, 438, 439.
   Joshua, 125, 165, 434, 437, 438.
   Kenelm, 438.
   Lucy Waldo, 437.
   Pelham, 133, 136, 138, 435.

Winthrop, 59.
   Adam, 308, 395, 427.
   Alice Still, 427.
   Ann, 413, 414, 428.
   Benjamin, 428.
   Elizabeth Temple, 428.
   Francis Bayard, 428.
   Jane Burton, 427.
   John, 9, 69, 261, 426, 427, 428, 449.
   John Still, 428.
   Joseph, 428.
   Lucy, 395.
   Mary Brown, 428.
   Robert, 426.
   Robert, Admiral, 428.
   Robert C., 298, 428.
   Thomas L., 428.
   Wait Still, 427.
   William, 428.
Wiswell, 11, 249.
   Elizabeth Rogers, 398.
   Inchabod, 398.
   John, 139, 398.
   John (Rev.), 39.
   Mercy Minot, 398.
   Noah, 398.
   Peleg, 398, 399.
   Thomas, 398.
Wittington, William, 136.
Wolf, General, 19, 293.
   Lucy Margaret Russell, 453.
   Robert Cope (Rev.), 453.
Woods, Ruth, 439.
Woodbridge, Timothy, 136.
Woolen, 133.
Wormley, Admiral, 345.
Worrall, 414.
   Thomas Grooby, 136.
Worthington, John, 136.
Wright, Daniel, 136.
   James (Sir), 213.
   John, 139.
Wyer, David, 465.
   David (Jr.), 466.
   Edward, 465.
   Eleanor James, 465.
   Elizabeth Johnson, 465.
   Joanna Pote, 466, 467.
   Mary Hunt, 466.
   Rebecca Russell, 465.
   Sarah Francis, 466.
   Sarah Tompkins, 466.
   Thomas, 139, 466.
   Thomas (Jr.), 466, 467.
   William, 465.
Young, Thomas (Dr.), 165.

Space in this volume would not permit of the giving of the biographies of all of the Loyalists of Massachusetts, while the names of all the Loyalists obtainable are given, yet there is material enough to fill another volume with their biographies which it is the intention of the author to publish if he receives sufficient encouragement in the sale of this volume.

List of Loyalists of Massachusetts whose names or Biographies are not found in this work.

Acre, Thomas
Allen, Jeremiah
Allen, Jolley
Auchard, Benjamin
Barclay, Andrew
Barrell, Colburn
Beath, Mary
Black, William
Borland, John Lindall
Bowman, Archibald
Bowles, William
Boylston, John
Boylston, Thomas
Bradstreet, Samuel
Brown, David
Bryant, John
Bulfinch, Samuel
Burroughs, John
Butler, James
Butter, James
Calef, Robert
Capen, Hopestill
Carr, Mrs.
Case, James
Caste, Dennis
    Thomas (Dr.)
Cazneau, Edward
Ceely, John
Cheever, William Down
Clark, Joseph
Clemmens, Thomas
Clement, Joseph, Capt.
Clementson, Samuel
Colepepper, James
Courtney, James
    Richard
Cox, Lemuel
Crane, Timothy
Crowe, Charles
Davies, William
Davis, Edward
Demsey, Roger
Dickinson, Francis
Elton, Peter
Emerson, John
Fall, Thomas
Fillis, John
Fisher, Turner
    Wilfred
Fullerton, Stephen
Gamage, James
Gemmill, Matthews
Goddard, Lemuel
Goldthwait, M. B.
Gookin, Edmund
Gorman, Edward
Gray, Samuel
Green, Hammond
Greenwood, Isaac
Harper, Isaac

Haskins, John
Hewes, Shubal
Hodgson, John
Hodson, Thomas
Homans, John
Jeffrey, Patrick
Jennex, Thomas
Kerland, Patrick
Knutton, William
Laughton, Joseph
Lawler, Ellis
Lear, Christopher
Leslie, James
Linning, Andrew
Lovell, Benjamin
Lush, George
Lynch, Peter
McKean, Andrew
McNeil, William
Madden, Richard
Magner, John
Massingham, Isaac
Mein, John
Mewse, Thomas
Moore, Augustus
Morrow, Col.
Mossman, William
Norwood, Ebenezer
Orcutt, Joseph
Pashley, George
Pecker, Dr. James
Phillips, Benjamin
Pitcher, Moses
Powell, William D.
Prout, Timothy
Ramage, John
Rand, Dr. Isaac
Randall, Robert
Reeve, Richard
Rice, John
Roberts, Frederic
Rogers, Nathan
Simpson, Jeremiah
Spillard, Timothy
Stevens, John
Stewart, Adam
Story, William
Taylor, Charles
Thomas, Jonathan
Thompson, George
Townsend, Shippy
Tull, Thomas
Turill, Thomas
Vincent, Ambrose
Wendell, Jacob
Wentworth, Edward
Wheaton, Obediah
Wheelwright, Job
Whitworth, Nathaniel
Wilson, Joseph

INDEX OF SUBJECTS.

Absentees Act, 143.
Acadia, operations against, 18, 19.
Acadians, removal of, 434, 435.
Acton, centennial of, 472.
Adams, John, on restoration, 24; on mobs, 49; on the loyalists, 49; quotes tory opinion of disunionists, 68; on jealousies in Congress, 68; on his conduct during the revolution, 69.
    Josiah, Centennial address at Acton, 472.
    Samuel, defaulting tax collector of Boston, 5, 38, his character and career, 38.
Aeronaut, Dr. John Jeffries, an early, 394.
American Military Academy, proposed, 270.
Amnesty for Loyalists, 94, 95.
Amory, Thomas, biog., 343; mobbed, 344.
Andros, Edmund, Sir, administration of, 16.
Annapolis, N. S., 229.
Apthorp, East, biog., 353.
Antigua, 183.
    Family, 351.
Aroostook War, 113.
Ashburton Treaty, 113, 114; American duplicity in, 114, 115.
Ashted, Warwickshire, 190.
Association of Loyalists in London, 211; proposed American, 227, 228.
Attucks monument, 47.
"Aurora," The, 76 (see also Bache, Benj. F.).
Aylesbury, 203.
Bache, Benjamin F., attacks Washington in the "Aurora," 76.
Bahamas, 180.
Banishment Act of Massachusets, 137.
Barbadoes, 204.
Barnes, Henry, biography, 399.
    Barristers and Attorneys address to Gov. Hutchinson, 125.
Barre, 172.
Bastra, Siege of, 283.
Bath, 203.
Bavaria, Benjamin Thompson, in the service of, 269.
Beaumarchais, furnishes arms and powder, 85.
Berkley, 139.
Bernard, Francis (Sir), biog., 191.
Berwick, 208.
Blackstone's title to early Boston, 364.
Black List of Pennsylvania, 55.
Blanchard, with Dr. Jeffries, crosses the English channel in a balloon, 394.

Blurton, 177.
Boston, Founding of, 427.
Boston Massacre, 43, 366; Captain Preston and his men tried for, 45; Revere's engraving of, stolen from Pelham, 478. Mobs: Attack on Hutchinson, 40; Hutchinson's account of, 151, 154, 155, 156; destruction of guard house at the Neck, 43; attack on Andrew Oliver and destruction of his house, 40; attack on Amory, 344; on Col. Erving, 298; on Hallowell, 281; on Theophilus Lillie, 310; Stamp Act Mob, 181; Sloop "Liberty" affair, 321; the "Tea Party" Mob, 48, 231, 405, 406, 407, 408, 478.
Boston Latin School, 300.
Boston News Letter, 361.
Boston, Pelham's Map of, 483.
Boston People who went to Halifax at the Evacuation, 133.
Boston Port Bill, 168.
Boston, Streets and places in:
    Auchmuty Lane, 302.
    Beacon Hill, 217.
    Bunch of Grapes Tavern, 233.
    Copp's Hill, 172.
    Elm Street, 396.
    Essex Street, 234.
    Fleet Street, 174.
    Fort Hill, 182.
    Freeman Place, 399.
    Griffin's Wharf, 182.
    Hancock's Wharf, 182.
    Hanover Street, 174, 396.
    Harrison Avenue, 234.
    Hollis Street, 233.
    Hutchinson Street, 172.
    Kilby Street, 233.
    King Street, 233.
    Long Wharf, 182, 254.
    Mackerel Lane, 233.
    Marlboro Street, 453.
    Middle Street, 310.
    Murray's Barracks, 258.
    North Square, 151.
    Old Corner Book Store, 178.
    Olivers Dock, 182.
    Pearl Street, 172.
    Pemberton Hill, 287.
    Queen Street, 255.
    Rainsford Lane, 234.
    Short Street, 302.
    Smith's Barracks, 258.
    State Street, 233.
    Summer Street, 207.
    Swing Bridge, 117.

INDEX OF SUBJECTS

Union Street, 182, 350.
Bounties paid to Continental Soldiers, 72.
Bowes, William, biog., 224.
Boylston, Nicholas Ward, biog., 282.
Braddock's Defeat, 179.
Brattle House, 295, 296.
  William, Gen., biog., 295.
Breynton, Rev. Dr., possession of King's Chapel Plate, 348.
Bridgewater, 138.
Bright, John, opposed to Southern Confederacy, 110; Congress refuses to pass resolutions on his death, 110.
Brightwell, 110.
Brinley, Thomas, biog., 396.
Bristol, England, 181, 188.
British graves at Concord, 473; skulls taken from, 474; Prof. Fowler exhibits them, 474, 475.
  Soldier, murdered at Concord, 53, 472.
British troops, removed to the Castle, 44; arrival of in Boston, 199; quartered by James Murray, 258.
Brookfield, 139.
Brown, Capt. and Ensign D'Bernicre make a reconnaissance of Suffolk, Middlesex and Worcester County, 400.
  Lieut. murdered at Cambridge, 353.
  Mather, Artist, biog., and account of his work, 280.
Browne, William, Col., biog., 449.
Brush Hill, Milton, 257.
Bulfinch, Charles, Architect, his work, 354.
Bungay, England, 223.
Bunker Hill, battle of, 235; Gay's description of, 322; John Coffin at, 235.
Burgoyne Convention at Saratoga, violation of, 67.
Byles, Mather, Rev., biog., 275; Anecdotes of, 276, 277, 278.
Calker's Club, (see Caucus Club), 476.
Callender, James Thompson, professional lampooner, 76.
Cambridge, Gage captures powder at, 52; Mob threaten Danforth, Lee and Oliver, 281.
Canada, Rev. John Carroll sent to by Congress, 31; failure of his mission, 32; Loyalist settlement of, 93 to 97; attempted invasion of in 1812, 98; Jefferson on the acquisition of, 102; Gen. McArthur invades, 104; boundary line, 113; Ashburton treaty, 113.
Canadian Confederation regarded as a menace to the United States, 116.
Caner, Henry, Rev., biog., 346.
Caner's Pond, 347.
Cape Breton (see Louisbourg), Auchmuty advocates expedition against, 301.
Cape Fear, N. C., 255.
Cape St. Vincent, Battle of, 283.
Carlisle, execution of, 55.
Carlton, N. B., 380.
Carr, Patrick, Account of Boston Massacre, 46.
Carroll, Rev. John, sent to Canada by Congress to induce Canadians to join the Americans, 31.
Cartagena, 239.
Castle William, 44, 198.
Caucus Club, origin of, 476.
Caughnawaga Indians confer with Col. Mifflin about joining revolutionists, 89.
"Censor," The Newspaper, 453.
Chamberlain, Mellen. Estimate of Col.

Thos. Goldthwaite, 483.
Chandler, John, biog., 308.
Charles II. Accession of observed with sorrow in Boston, 12.
Charlestown, Destruction of Convent at, 48.
Charleston, S. C., Investment of, 267, 268.
Charter, The first, 7; limitations of, 11; arrival of Royal Commissioners under, 12, 13; annulment of, 15.
  The second, 16.
Chippewa, devastated, 104.
Christ Church, 342.
Church of England, 18; Puritan belief in, 8. (See Established church).
Citizenship, restored to Loyalists, 391.
Civil War, Great Britain's attitude during, 107.
Clark, Richard (biog.), 405.
Confiscation Act, 94, 141; of doubtful legality, 208, 209; legal aspect of, 288; Congress to recommend repeal of, 66.
Confiscation, Commissioners of, Judge Curwen on, 64.
Coffin Family, The, 233.
  Isaac, Admiral Sir (biog.), 239.
  John, General, biog., 235.
  Thomas Aston, Sir, biog., 234.
Coinage in Massachusetts Bay, Illegal, 13.
Colonization of New England, Character of, 8.
Committees of Correspondence organized, 54.
Concord, skirmish at, 53, 471; no Concord men killed or wounded, 472; Ammi White kills wounded British soldier at, 472; town of gives permission to Prof. Fowler to open graves of soldiers and remove skulls, 474; skulls returned, 475; correspondence concerning same, 475.
Constitutional Aspect of the relations between Colonies and Great Britain, 27.
Continental Army, Desertions, mutiny in, 73; complaints against officers, violations of parole, rascally surgeons, 73; Adams on quarrels of officers, 74; stealing of stores, 74; Washington on the character and inefficiency of officers, 74; plundering and incendiarism. 74.
Continental Congress, second, Adams on jealousies in, 68; Jay and Morris on rascality in, 75; Rev. Jacob Duche, chaplain, of letter to Washington on the personnel of, 80, 90.
Conway, 138.
Copley, John Singleton, biog., 216; litigation over estate of, 218, 220; paintings by at Harvard and Public Boston Library, 218, 221.
Crime of adhering to Great Britain made capital, 55.
Crown Point Expedition, 226, 477.
Croydon, England, 172.
Culloden, 50.
Cumberland, N. S., 322.
Currency, Continental, Resolve relating to, 75.
  New England, 146; Mass., 148; Adams on Hutchinson's knowledge of, 148.
Curwin, Samuel, biog., 246.
Custom House, Mob, 42.
Danvers, 227, 378, 379.
Dartmouth, 139.
Davis, Jefferson, Complains of English Government favoring northern cause, 111.

INDEX OF SUBJECTS

D'Bernicre, Ensign, reconnaissance of Suffolk, Middlesex and Worcester Counties, 400.
Deblois Family, Account of, 445.
D'Estaing, Admiral, 240, 430.
Demerara, 352.
Democracy, John Winthrop, on, 69.
Democratic Party, fosters feeling against England, 99.
Derbyshire, 191.
Detroit, Fort, 197.
Dominica, Engagement at, 241.
Dorchester, 182.
Draper, Richard, Founds Massachusetts Gazette, 361.
Draper, Margaret, biog., publishes Massachusetts Gazette, 404.
Duane, William, assists Bache in the "Aurora" attacks on Washington, 76.
Duche, Jacob, Rev. Chaplain of Congress, letters to Washington on Second Continental Congress, 78 to 83.
Dudleian Lecture, 342.
East Granby, Conn., Loyalists confined in prison at, 56. See "Newgate."
East Hoosuck, 146.
Eastport, 203.
East Tergnmouth, Eng., 176.
Elective franchise, 8, 12.
Episcopal Church, Puritan alleged belief in, 8, 9; Endicott's view of, 8; reference to, 8, 18, 339, 340, 438; clergy of Support the Government, 54; Eighteen of the clergy leave Boston at the Evacuation and go to Halifax, 348; Services conducted in Boston after evacuation by Rev. Samuel Parker, 348.
Fairfax County Resolves, 25.
Fairfield, Conn., 347.
Falmouth (Now Portland), 140, 357; burned by Capt. Mowatt, 390.
Faneuil Family, 229.
Hall, gift of, 230; dedication of, 231.
Federalists, on the results of the war of 1812, 105.
Fenian Raid of 1866, 113.
Fisheries, Loss of, 105.
Flucker, Thomas, Sec'y of Mass. Bay, biog., 402.
Fontenoy, 50.
Forbes of Milton, 257.
Fort Pownal, 356, 357.
Fort William Henry, Surrender of, 273.
Fort William and Mary (Newcastle, N. H.) attack on, 51.
France, Maj. Caleb Stark on Aid from, 84.
Frankland, Lady Agnes, biog., 417.
Franklin Treaty, 86.
Franklin, Benj., his false scalp story, 91; denounced for his part in the theft of the Hutchinson letters, 163.
Franklin, William, Gov., biog., 481.
Frenau, Philip, in the National Gazette attacks Washington and his cabinet, 75.
French Spoliation Claims, 85, 86, 87.
Freetown, 139.
Gage, Addresses and Addressers, 131, 132.
Gardiner, Sylvester, Dr., biog., 313; his medicines seized for use of revolutionists, 315.
Maine, 281.
Gaspee, Destruction of, 52; Inquiry into the destruction of, 302.
Gay, Martin, biog., 321; letters of, 322, 324.
Geyer, Frederick, William, biog., 350.

Gladstone, William E., favors Southern Confederacy, 110.
Goldthwaite Family, Account of, 355.
Thomas, Col., biog., 356. (See also Chamberlain, Mellen.)
Gore, John, biog., 393.
Granby, Conn., Escape of Loyalist prisoners at, 57.
Grand Manan, 105.
Grattan, Thomas Colley, on the Ashburton Treaty, 114.
Gray, Harrison, Treas. of Mass. Bay, biog. of, 334; John Hancock heavily indebted to, 335.
Great Barrington, 140.
Green Dragon Tavern, 363.
Green Field, 139.
Grenada, 279.
Grenville's Scheme of American taxation, 22.
Guadaloupe, 23.
Gunpowder Plot, anniversary of observed in Boston, 239.
Halifax, 138, 177, 190, 362.
Halifax Journal, original publication of, 362.
Hallowell, Maine, named, 281.
Hallowell, Benjamin, mobbed at Cambridge, 281.
Family, account of, 281.
Robert, mobbed, 281.
Hamilton, Alexander, biog. of, 77.
Hampstead, 201.
Hampton, 208.
Hancock, John, Suits against, 5; engaged in smuggling, owner of the sloop "Liberty," 42; leader in Tea Party mob, 48; his sloop Liberty seized, 49; as treasurer of Harvard college, defaulter, 50; inclined to Toryism, papers suppressed, 160; heavily indebted to Harrison Gray, 335.
Hardwick, 139, 225.
Harper's Ferry Raid, 107, 139.
Harvard College, John Hancock as treasurer of defaults in his accounts, 50; Many graduates of among those who departed with Gage, 58; reference to, 146, 177; Harvard Hall burned, Gov. Bernard assists in rebuilding, 197; buildings of converted into barracks, 271; a nest of Tories, 393.
Harwich, 139.
Hatfield, 138.
Haverhill, 138, 274; Mob at, Attacks Saltonstall, 273.
Henry, Patrick, character and training, 36; Jefferson on, 36.
Hiers Islands, Naval Engagement off, 283.
Hooper, King, biog., 221.
Howe, John, biog., 361.
Joseph, speech at Boston, July 4, 1858, 363.
Howe, Lord, Mass. erects a monument to at Westminster Abbey, 20.
Hubbard, History of Mass., reason for its want of completeness, 208.
Hubbardston, 208.
Hull, John, Colonial Mint Master, 365.
Huntington, Long Island, 268.
Hutchinson, Eliakim, biog., 178.
Elisha, biog., 177.
Foster, biog., 177.
Hutchinson Letters, Franklin complicity in theft of, 162, 163.
Thomas, biog., 146; his home destroyed

INDEX OF SUBJECTS

by mob, 40; addresses to, 123, 125, 126, 127, 128, 129.
Indians, in the Revolution, 88, 89; troubles with in 1763, 197, 198; Lovewell's fight at Pigwacket, 422.
Inhabitants of Boston who removed Halifax at the evacuation, 133.
Intolerance of Puritans, 13, 14.
Ipswich, 273.
Irish volunteers (Loyal) formed at Boston, 228.
Isle of Shoals, 205.
Jamaica, 240.
Pond, 207.
Jay, John, opinion of second Continental Congress, 75; burned in effigy, 105.
Jefferson, Thomas, suggests burning of London, 102.
Jeffries, John, biog., 394; crosses English Channel in balloon, 394.
Journalism. Scurrilous American, 75.
Judith, Point, named in honor of Judith Quincy, 365.
Kalm, on the dependency of the Colonists, 23.
King's American Dragoons, 268, 378.
American Regiment, 237.
King, Richard, biog., 317.
King's Chapel, 179, 209, 230, 255, 346, 347; change in liturgy of, 288; erection and rebuilding of, 347; worship suspended in, 347, 348; church plate taken to Halifax, 348; final disposition of plate and records, 349; Charles Apthorp contributor to, 351.
King's College, N. Y., saved by British troops, 303.
Kirk, Ireton, Derbyshire, 177.
Kittery, 205, 208, 215.
Lafayette, raises troop of Indians, 89.
Lancaster, 139.
Land Bank, The, 38, 147, 333.
Lanesborough, 140.
Lecky, W. E. H., on the Revolutionary movement, 70.
Leominster, 139.
Leonard, Daniel, biog., 325; home fired on by mob, 326; author of "Massachusettenses Letters," 327, 328, 329, 330, 331.
Leonard, Geo., Col., biog., 333.
Lexington, engagement at, 53, (see Concord).
"Liberty" Sloop, a smuggler, (see also John Hancock), 42, 48, 49; account of seizure, 319.
"Liberty Tree," Site of, 234, 235.
Lillie, Theophilus, biog., 308.
Limerick Academy, 224.
Lincoln, 138
Litchfield, Eng., 177.
Littleton, 138.
Liverpool, N. S., 105.
Logan. Indian Chief, family murdered by Greathouse, 90.
London (Eng.), Jefferson suggests burning of, 102.
Loring, Joshua, Commodore, biog., 423.
Louisbourg, Cape Breton, 246, 451, 429; Cost of expedition to reimbursed, 18; surrender of, 19; description of, 206.
Lovewell's Fight at Pigwacket, 422.
Loyal American Regiment, 430.
Loyal American Association formed in Boston, 228.
Loyalists of Massachusetts, 54; denied legal rights, 55; character of, 58, 65;

expulsion of, 93, Associations formed in London, 211; Club, 218.
Lyndeborough, N. H., 222.
Lyndhurst, Lord, biog., 216.
Machias, 203.
Magdalen Islands, 238.
Mandamus Councillors, 137, 167, 184.
Marblehead, 222; address of inhabitants of to Hutchinson, 127.
Marshfield, 139.
Martinique, 23.
Maryatt, Captain, Sea writer, mother of a native of Boston, 350.
Massachusetts Gazette, founded by Richard Draper, 361; continued publication by Margaret Draper, 404.
Massachusetts General Hospital, endowment of, 346.
Medford, 138, 291.
Medicines of Dr. Sylvester Gardiner seized for the use of Continental Army, 315.
Merry Meeting Bay, Vassal holdings near 289.
Middleborough, 138, 189.
Middleton, N. S., 229.
Mifflin, Col., confers with Caughnawaga Indians, 89.
Militia, John Adams on the cowardice of, 75.
Milton, Inhabitants of Address to Hutchinson, 128, 171.
Minorca, 242.
Mobs, see Boston, Cambridge, Haverhill, Salem, N. H., Scarborough.
Molasses Act, Gov. Bernard request reduction of duties under, 197.
Monroe Doctrine, 77, 110, 118.
Moose Island, 105, 203.
Moravian Indians, Massacre of, 92.
Mount Desert, 192, 196, 203.
Mowatt, Capt., at Fort Pownall, 357; burns Falmouth, 399.
Mowhawk Indians, Congress addresses, 88.
Murray, James, biog., 254.
John, Col., 376.
Nantucket Settlement, 233.
"National Gazette," The, see Frenan Philip.
Naval Officers, British of American birth usually remained loyal, 239.
Nazing, Eng., 225.
Nepaulese War, Gen. Octherloney's services in, 300.
Neutrality of England in Civil War, 109.
New Castle, New Hampshire, Attack on and powder from, used at Bunker Hill, 51.
New England Coffee House, London, 249.
New Englanders in London and Bristol, 249, 250, 251, 252, 253, 254.
"Newgate Prison," at East Granby, Conn. desc. of, 56.
New Hampshire, boundry line dispute settled by Hutchinson, 146.
New Plymouth Company, 156.
Newport, Evacuation of 240, 362.
"Gazette," 362.
"Mercury," 362.
New York, burning of attributed to New England troops, 74; saved from destruction by British troops, 303.
Nile, Battle of, 190.
Non-importation agreement, 310.
Norridgewock, 289.
Norton, 325.
Norwalk, Conn., 347,

INDEX OF SUBJECTS

Nottinghamshire, 472.
"Novaughes," letters by John Adams, 327.
Oakham, 139.
Octherlony, David, Maj. Gen., Sir, biog., 299.
Old Colony Club at Plymouth, 437.
Oliver, mob, 153.
Oliver, Andrew, biog., 180; mob destroys his house, 40.
Oliver, Thomas, biog., 183; mobbed at Cambridge, 185.
Orange, Rangers, 236.
Oregon Boundry, 116.
Ossawatomie Engagement, 107.
Otis, James, on taxation of the Colonies, 35; Hutchinson's opinion of, 35; assault on, by Robinson, 448.
Oxford, Mass., 312.
Paddock, Adino, Col., biog., 305; Paddock building named for, 307; Paddock Elms, 306, 307.
Paine, Thomas, attacks Washington, 76.
Timothy, Judge, biog., 382.
Parker, Rev. Samuel, conducts services for Episcopalians in Boston after Evacuation, 348.
Parr, Town, 190, 380.
Patriot, recipe for making one, 454.
Paxton, Charles, biog., 318.
Pennsylvania Line, Mutiny in, 69.
Penobscot Expedition, 479.
Pepperrell, William Sir, biog., 205.
Petersham, 139.
Phips, Sir William, career of, 418.
Pickering, Timothy, of Salem, an early secessionist, 108.
Pigwacket, Lovewell's Indian fight at, 422.
Pine Tree Shillings, The tradition of, 365.
Pittsfield, 140.
Pleasant Point, 203.
Plymouth, 138.
Purchase, 314.
Point Judith, named for Judith Quincy, 365.
Pontiac Conspiracy, 90.
Poole, Eng., 314.
Port Mahon, 242.
Port Talbot, devastated, 104.
Portsmouth, Eng., 13.
Portsmouth, N. H., 208, 215.
Athenaeum, 395.
Pownalborough, 140, 315.
Preston, Capt., Trial of, in connection with Boston Massacre, 45; defence of, 366.
Princeton, 139.
Prisoners of War, Northern and Southern, comparative losses, 111, 112.
Providence, 52.
Provincial Congress, address Mowhawk Indians, 88.
Province House, description of, 194.
Puritans, Intolerance of, 8, 9, 13, 14.
Putnam, James, Judge, biog., 378; letters of, 380, 381.
Quakers, Puritan maltreatment of, 11, 13.
Quebec Act., 29, 336; effect of, 29, 30; denounced by Colonists as a "Popish Measure," 31.
Address to the Inhabitants of, by Congress, 31; see Carroll, Rev. John.
Capture of, 20; Montgomery's Attack on, and the Defence of, 244.
Queenstown Heights, battle of, 245, 441.
Quincy, 438.

Josiah, defends Capt. Preston et al, "Boston Massacre," 366, 367, 368.
Josiah, on the War of 1812, 98.
Josiah, on John Hancock as defaulting Treasurer of Harvard College, 50.
Judith, her name given to Point Judith, 365.
Samuel, biog., Solicitor General of Mass., biog., 364, 368, 369, 370, 371, 372, 373; letters of, 374, 375, 376.
Ramillies, 45.
Randolph, Edward, arrival at Boston, 14; reception and treatment of, by Colonial authorities, 15.
Recanters, 126.
Repudiation, Congress makes, of financial obligations, 75.
Restoration, Desires for, by Adams, Jefferson, Jay, Washington, Madison, 25.
Revere, Paul, Scout of the Revolution; his ride, financial dealings with state authorities, Penobscot Expedition, 479; Masonic record, 480.
Revolution, Causes of, 27 to 29.
Revolutionists, A Tory opinion of, 68.
Richardson, Ebenezer, biog., 422; mobbed, 422; treatment of, by historians, 423; trial of with Wilmot, 311.
Riots, see Boston Mobs.
Rivingston's Gazette, 267.
Roberts, Execution of, at Philadelphia, 55.
Rochester, Mass., 225, 229.
Roman Catholicism, 336; see Quebec Act, and Carroll.
Roxbury, 138, 178.
First church at, 338.
Royal Arms of the Old State House, 436, 437, 482.
Royal Society, Benjamin Thompson, a member of, 267.
Royall, Isaac, Gen., biog., 290.
Mansion, description of, 291, 292.
Professorship of Law at Harvard, 293.
Ruggles, Timothy, biog., 225.
Rumford, Count, see Thompson, Benj., 263.
Rutland, 139.
Russian friendship for United States, 118.
Sabine, on the rascality of the Whigs, 72.
Saco, 208.
Salaries to Supreme Court Judges, Royal Grant of, 188, 189.
Salem, 138, 168, 246.
Salem Village, 378, 379. See also Danvers.
Saltonstall, Col. Richard, biog., 272.
Sandemanianism, founder of in Boston, 363; description of their services at Halifax, 363.
Sandwich, 139.
Saratoga Convention, Violation of, 85.
Savannah, D'Estaing repulsed at, 240.
Scarborough, 208; mob at destroys property of Richard King, 317.
Scituate, 138, 285.
Scott, General, captured by Gen. Sheaffe, 411.
Search Warrants, 149; see also "Writs of Assistance."
Secession in early period, 108.
Sewall, Jonathan, Atty. Gen., biog., 454.
Shay's Rebellion, 69, 381.
Sheaffe, Sir Roger Hale, biog., 439.
Shelburne, N. S., 340.
Shepton, Mallet (Eng.), 250, 283.

INDEX OF SUBJECTS 509

Ships,
Arabella, 9, 272.
Aston Hall, 235, 282.
Barfleur, 240.
Bellerophon, 425.
Culloden, 190.
Diligent, 240, 382.
Duquesne, 425.
Fowey, 240.
Gaspee, 240.
Glorieux, 241.
Kingfisher, 240.
King George, 281.
Liberty, 298.
Le Pincon, 240.
London Facket, 319.
Mary and John, 427.
Melampus, 242.
Minerva, 170.
Neptune, 244.
Philadelphia, 345.
Pocahontas, 210.
Prince George, 269.
Rose, 17.
Royal Oak, 240.
Scarborough, 266.
Shrewsbury, 241.
Swiftsure, 283.
Sybil, 240.
Thisbe, 241, 242.
Undaunted, 429.
Ville de Paris, 241, 429.
William, 426.
Shirley Hall, Roxbury, 178.
Shrewsbury, Eng., 139.
Mass., 189.
Sidmouth, Eng., 175.
Simcoe's Queen's Rangers, 90.
Simsbury, Conn., 57.
Smith, Adam, On taxation of the Colonies, 34.
James, biog., 255.
Smuggling, Extent of, 33, 35, 193; Gov. Bernard orders seizure of vessels for, 197; Hancock's sloop "Liberty" seized, 319; see Hancock.
Snider, Christopher, killing and burial of, 310.
Society for the Propagation of the Gospel in Foreign Parts, 339.
Sons of Despotism, 54, 179, 264, 318, 335, 453.
Liberty, 54, 158, 273, 477.
South Kingston, R. I., 313.
Spanish War, 117, 118.
Springfield, 138.
Spring, Garden Coffee House, London, meeting place of Loyalists, 249, 250.
St. Croix, 203.
David, village of, burned, 104.
Eustacia, 49.
John's Island, 237.
John, N. B., 190.
Kitts, 240.
Lucia, 23; reduction of, 284.
Paul's Parish, Portland, 398.
Vincent, 204.
Stamp Act, Passed, its enforcement, 37; repeal of, 47; incidents of, 152, 156, 157, 181, 198. Bernard advocated its repeal, 199; congress, 226, 346.
Stockbridge, Indians, Company of enlisted in Revolutionary army, 88.
Strachan, Dr. John, on the burning of York, Can., 103; to Jefferson on American atrocities in Canada, 104.

Sumner, Prof. (W. G.) on Colonial distinctions in taxation, 78.
Sunderland, 138.
Supreme Court Judges, Royal Grant of Salaries to, 188, 189.
Surriage, Agnes, see Lady Frankland.
Taunton, 139.
Tavistock, 205.
Taxation, colonial notions of, 34, 35, 78; see Stamp Act, Tea Tax, Molasses Act, Grenville.
Tea Mob alias Tea Party, 47, 165, 166, 167; account of, 407.
Tea Tax, 47.
Thompson, Benj. Sir, Count Rumford, biog., 261.
Joseph, biog., 297.
Sarah, Countess Rumford, biog., 272.
Townsend, Mass., 138.
Transcript, Boston Evening, founded, 342.
Trinity Church, Boston, 338.
N. Y., invaded by Lord Stirling; closed by Dr. Auchnuty, destroyed by fire, 303.
Troops, British, Arrival and treatment of at Boston, 42, 157, 158.
United Empire Loyalists, 245.
Unthank (Scot), 254.
Vassal Family, 285.
Venezuelian, Episode, 117.
Walter, Lynde Minshall, founds Boston Evening Transcript, 342.
Nehemiah, Rev., biog., 338.
William, Rev., biog., 338.
War of 1812, Sketch of. 98.
Warren, Joseph, Dr., death of, 335.
Washington, Burning of, 103.
Washington, Geo. Gen., on the inefficiency and want of patriotism in the Continental Army, 72; on people supplying British in Philadelphia with provisions, 72; places guard over grave of foreign officer to preventing robbing of body, 73.
Waterloo, 45, 221.
Wedderburn, Sol., Gen., denounces Franklin for theft of Hutchinson letters, 164, 165.
West, Benj., Picture, reception of the Loyalists, desc. of 213.
West, Church, plate of preserved by Martin Gay, 321.
White, Ammi, kills wounded British Soldier at Concord. See Concord.
Whiskey Insurrection, 69.
Wilkes Riots, 83, 84.
Wilmington, N. C., 255.
Wilmot, N. S., 229.
Winslow, John, biog., 434.
Winthrop, John, on Puritan loyalty to Church of England, 9; his children, 483; on democracy, 69.
Robert, biog., 426.
Wiswell, John, Rev., biog., 398.
Witchcraft delusion, 17.
Woburn, 261, 263, 264, 265, 272.
Wolfe, Gen., captures Quebec, 19, 20.
Wollaston, Mount, 365.
Wooden Figure, affair at Lillie's Mob, 311.
Worcester, 139, 474.
Worcester Resolutions against Absentees and Refugees, 141.
Wrentham, 138.
Writs of Assistance, 29, 149, 150, 151, 193.
York, Canada, burning of, 104.
Yorktown, Surrender of, 237.

www.ingramcontent.com/pod-product-compliance
Lightning Source LLC
Chambersburg PA
CBHW021111300426
44113CB00006B/118